EDM

The Educator's Diagnostic Manual of Disabilities and Disorders

Roger Pierangelo, Ph.D. • George Giuliani, J.D., Psy.D.

John Wiley & Sons, Inc.

Published by Jossey-Bass
A Wiley Imprint
989 Market Street, San Francisco, CA 94103-1741 www.josseybass.com

The Educator's Diagnostic Manual of Disabilities and Disorders (EDM) provides specified diagnostic criteria for each of the disabilities defined under the Individuals with Disabilities Education Improvement Act of 2004 (IDEA 2004). They are offered as structured guidelines for professionals and parents, since the use of consistent agreement can only benefit children with disabilities as they move through the special education process. Although the EDM is both extensive and comprehensive in its coverage, the disabilities and disorders explained in it may not encompass every diagnosis that students in special education receive.

Jossey-Bass books and products are available through most bookstores. To contact Jossey-Bass directly call our Customer Care Department within the U.S. at 800-956-7739, outside the U.S. at 317-572-3986, or fax 317-572-4002.

Jossey-Bass also publishes its books in a variety of electronic formats. Some content that appears in print may not be available in electronic books.

Credits appear on page 525

Library of Congress Cataloging-in-Publication Data

Pierangelo, Roger.
The educator's diagnostic manual of disabilities and disorders / Roger Pierangelo, George Giuliani. — 1st ed.
p. cm.
Includes bibliographical references.
ISBN: 978-0-7879-7812-9 (pbk.)
1. Children with disabilities—Identification. 2. Children with disabilities—Education—Ability testing.
3. Children with disabilities—Medical care. I. Giuliani, George A., 1938– II. Title.
LC4019.P524 2007
371.9'04—dc22

2006032161

Printed in the United States of America
FIRST EDITION
PB Printing 10 9 8 7 6 5 4 3 2 1

About the Authors

Roger Pierangelo, Ph.D., is an executive director of the American Academy of Special Education Professionals, an executive director of the National Association of Special Education Teachers, and vice president of the National Association of Parents with Children in Special Education. He is a full-time associate professor in the Department of Special Education and Literacy at Long Island University. He has been an administrator of special education programs, served for eighteen years as a permanent member of committees on special education, has over thirty years of experience in the public school system as a general education classroom teacher and school psychologist, and is a consultant to numerous private and public schools, Parent-Teacher Association, and Special Education Parent-Teacher Association groups. He has also been an evaluator for the New York State Office of Vocational and Rehabilitative Services and a director of a private clinic. He is a New York State licensed clinical psychologist, certified school psychologist, Diplomate Fellow in Forensic Psychology, and a Diplomate Fellow in Child and Adolescent Psychology.

Dr. Pierangelo earned his B.S. from St. John's University, M.S. and Professional Diploma from Queens College, Ph.D. from Yeshiva University, and earned Diplomate Fellow status in both Forensic Psychology and Child and Adolescent Psychology from the International College of Professional Psychology. He is a member of the American Psychological Association, New York State Psychological Association, Nassau County Psychological Association, New York State Union of Teachers, and Phi Delta Kappa.

George Giuliani, J.D., Psy.D., is an executive director of the American Academy of Special Education Professionals, an executive director of the National Association of Special Education Teachers, and the president of the National Association of Parents with Children in Special Education. He is the director of the Special Education program at Hofstra University, as well as a tenured full-time associate professor in the University's School of Education and Allied Health and Human Services in the

Marjorie Butler, Eve Byrne, and Andy Consilio. I also thank my brother and sister, Roger and Claudia; my mother-in-law, Ursula Jenkeleit; my sisters-in-law, Karen and Cindy; and my brothers-in-law, Robert and Bob. They have provided me with encouragement and reinforcement in all of my personal and professional endeavors.

This book is dedicated to my loving wife, Jackie, and my two children, Jacqueline and Scott, of whom I am so proud, who provide me with the love and purpose for undertaking projects that I hope will enhance the lives of others. My life has been blessed by their loving presence.

I also dedicate this book to my parents, who provided me with the secure and loving foundation from which to grow; my sister, Carol, who makes me smile and laugh; and my brother-in-law, George, who has always been a positive guiding light in my professional journey.

—R.P.

This book is dedicated to my incredibly supportive, caring, and loving wife, Anita, and two children, Collin and Brittany, who give me the greatest life imaginable. The long hours and many years it took to finish this book would never have been possible without the encouragement of my loving wife. Her constant reinforcement, understanding, and love provided me with the strength I needed to accomplish the goal of completing EDM. I thank her with all my heart. I also dedicate this book to my parents, who have given me support and guidance throughout my life. Their words of encouragement and guidance have made my professional journey a rewarding and successful experience.

—G.G.

Contents

An Overview of *The Educator's Diagnostic Manual of Disabilities and Disorders*

The purpose of *The Educator's Diagnostic Manual of Disabilities and Disorders* (EDM) is to provide all professionals working in the field of special education, college students preparing to work with children with special needs, administrators, college professors, parents, and students with disabilities the information necessary to determine the most comprehensive, detailed, and precise diagnoses of disabilities or disorders seen in infants, toddlers, children, and adolescents, particularly in the educational environment.

Rationale for the Publication of the EDM

The sole responsibility for interpreting the specific disabilities associated with the classifications under the Individuals with Disabilities Education Improvement Act of 2004 (IDEA) has been at the discretion of the district committee responsible for classification and placement. However, simple word definitions are open to interpretation and potentially significant subjectivity. Since many of the specific disorders contained under an IDEA 2004 category are not provided, there was a strong need to objectify this process. The EDM provides specific descriptions of the areas of concern, as well as the levels to which the disability (or disabilities) adversely affects the educational performance of the child (an important concern often addressed but never defined in IDEA classifications).

Individualized Education Programs and the EDM

Under IDEA 2004, every child who is classified as child with a disability in special education receives an Individualized Education Program (IEP). An IEP is a written statement for a child with a disability that is developed, reviewed, and revised in a meeting in accordance with certain requirements of law and regulations. The purpose of the IEP is to provide an individualized document that will guide the programming for the student with a disability and allow the team to determine if the student is making progress (Stephens, 2006). The IEP meeting serves as a communication vehicle between parents and school personnel and enables them, as equal participants, to make joint, informed decisions regarding the child's needs and appropriate goals; the extent to which the child will be involved in the general curriculum and participate in the general education environment and state and districtwide assessments; and the services needed to support that involvement and participation and achieve agreed-on goals (National Dissemination Center for Children with Disabilities, 2002).

The IEP is developed by a team whose members meet, review the assessment information available about a child, and design an educational program to address the child's educational needs that result from his or her disability (Disability Exchange, 2005). According to IDEA 2004, a child's IEP must be reviewed at least once a year and thereafter at an annual review meeting to determine whether the annual goals are being achieved and must be revised as appropriate (IDEA, Section 300.343(c)).

The child's IEP notes the IDEA classification of the child. For example, a child's IEP could state that the classification is: Specific Learning Disability, or Emotional Disturbance, or Speech and Language Impairment. Unfortunately, all too often, teachers, parents, professionals, and students have little or no idea of what specific type or types of disability the child has with respect to his or her classification on the IEP.

For example, a child with a reading disability (Dyslexia), math learning disability (Dyscalculia), and writing disability (Dysgraphia) and another child with a visual processing disorder might all be classified as students with Specific Learning Disabilities. In these students' IEPs, the diagnoses would be Specific Learning Disabilities, not the specific types. So nowhere on the IEP would it state, "The child has a specific learning disability in reading (dyslexia)" or "The child has a specific learning disability in mathematics (dyscalculia)." It would just be a general classification of "Specific Learning Disability." Furthermore, for numerous types of disabilities, there are subtypes. For example, there are over ten different types of dyslexia. Which one(s) does this child have? On the IEP, there would be no statement of that whatsoever. A teacher reading these students' IEPs would have no clear idea of an exact diagnosis, let alone the specific subtypes that would facilitate the educational direction best suited for these children.

IDEA is the frame of reference for the categories chosen for the EDM; all are defined under this federal law (Section 300.7(a)(1)). The disorders discussed in this book represent the types and subtypes under each of these disability categories that may apply to children with disabilities from birth through twenty-one years of age. Now, with the EDM coding system, students will have five levels of diagnoses stated on their IEPs. Ultimately this aids professionals in establishing appropriate remediation, accommodations, educational placement, and teaching techniques for each child with a disability.

Importance of the EDM

In schools today, after a comprehensive assessment is completed for a child with a suspected disability, there is no common and agreed-on diagnostic book that all professionals turn to when making a determination of whether the child meets the criteria for a specific disability as defined by IDEA. This goes against all common sense; there should be some standard and guide by which educators make decisions regarding the specific diagnoses of disabilities and disorders, as well as educational decisions for a child.

All mental health professionals are provided with the *Diagnostic and Statistical Manual* (DSM-IV-TR) (American Psychiatric Association, 2000), medical professionals have a variety of manuals that provide specific information on all types of medical conditions that they can use as reference sources, and lawyers have reference guides as well.

The EDM is the first diagnostic manual created specifically for the field of special education that provides definitions, symptoms, characteristics, types, and subtypes for all IDEA 2004 disabilities and the numerous disorders that professionals and parents need to understand within educational settings.

Using the EDM

The EDM provides guidelines, information, and examples for a variety of situations that commonly occur in education. Consider these situations:

- A child in a classroom has been diagnosed with a disability that a teacher, special educator, and school administrators know very little or nothing about in terms of symptoms and other characteristics. The EDM provides a quick reference to that disability and its important features.
- A special education professional who is speaking with the parent of a child who has a disorder listed on the IEP needs some immediate reference material. The EDM provides the specific type and possible subtype of the disorder, which will make it easier for the professional to gather detailed information.
- A parent of a child diagnosed with a disorder is in need of further information or a list of organizations by disability category. The EDM provides lists of organizations for every IDEA category.
- A special education professional is attending a child study team meeting for a child with a specific disability or disorder and needs to present information specific to it. The EDM provides the information for the disability and disorder.
- A child study team determines that a student meets the criteria for a disability as defined by IDEA. Although the team knows that the student has a disability, it is unsure of the specific type of disability. For example, they know the student has a speech and language impairment but not whether it is a phonological

A child who shows the characteristics of autism after age three could be diagnosed as having autism if the criteria above are satisfied.

Deaf-Blindness

Deaf-blindness means concomitant (simultaneous) hearing and visual impairments, the combination of which causes such severe communication and other developmental and educational needs that they cannot be accommodated in special education programs solely for children with deafness or children with blindness.

Developmental Delay

This refers to children aged three through nine who experiencing developmental delays. The term *child with a disability* for children aged three through nine may, at the discretion of the state and LEA and in accordance with Section 300.313, include a child:

- Who is experiencing developmental delays, as defined by the state and as measured by appropriate diagnostic instruments and procedures, in one or more of the following areas: physical development, cognitive development, communication development, social or emotional development, or adaptive development.
- Who therefore needs special education and related services.

Emotional Disturbance

Emotional disturbance means a condition exhibiting one or more of the following characteristics over a long period of time and to a marked degree that adversely affects a child's educational performance:

- An inability to learn that cannot be explained by intellectual, sensory, or health factors
- An inability to build or maintain satisfactory interpersonal relationships with peers and teachers
- Inappropriate types of behavior or feelings under normal circumstances
- A general pervasive mood of unhappiness or depression
- A tendency to develop physical symptoms or fears associated with personal or school problems

The term includes schizophrenia. It does not apply to children who are socially maladjusted unless it is determined that they have an emotional disturbance.

Hearing Impairments (Including Deafness)

Hearing impairment means an impairment in hearing, whether permanent or fluctuating, that adversely affects a child's educational performance but is not included under the definition of deafness. *Deafness* means a hearing impairment so severe that a child is impaired in processing linguistic information through hearing, with or without amplification, that adversely affects a child's educational performance.

Mental Retardation

Mental retardation means significantly subaverage general intellectual functioning, existing concurrently (at the same time) with deficits in adaptive behavior and manifested during the developmental period, that adversely affects a child's educational performance.

Multiple Disabilities

Multiple disabilities means concomitant (simultaneous) impairments, such as mental retardation–blindness and mental retardation–orthopedic impairment, the combination of which causes such severe educational needs that they cannot be accommodated in a special education program solely for one of the impairments. The term does not include deaf-blindness.

Orthopedic Impairments

Orthopedic impairments means a severe orthopedic impairment that adversely affects a child's educational performance. The term includes impairments caused by a congenital anomaly (such as clubfoot of the absence of some member), impairments caused by disease (such as poliomyelitis or bone tuberculosis), and impairments from other causes (such as cerebral palsy, amputations, and fractures or burns that cause contractures).

Other Health Impairments

Other health impairments means having limited strength, vitality, or alertness, including a heightened alertness to environmental stimuli, that results in limited alertness with respect to the educational environment. It (1) is due to chronic or acute health problems such as asthma, attention deficit disorder or attention deficit hyperactivity disorder, diabetes, epilepsy, a heart condition, hemophilia, lead poisoning, leukemia, nephritis, rheumatic fever, and sickle cell anemia; and (2) adversely affects a child's educational performance.

Specific Learning Disabilities

Specific learning disabilities means a disorder in one or more of the basic psychological processes involved in understanding or in using language, spoken or written, that may manifest itself in an imperfect ability to listen, think, speak, read, write, spell, or do mathematical calculations. The term includes such conditions as perceptual disabilities, brain injury, minimal brain dysfunction, dyslexia, and developmental aphasia. The term does not include learning problems that are primarily the result of visual, hearing, or motor disabilities; mental retardation; emotional disturbance; or environmental, cultural, or economic disadvantage.

Under IDEA, the definition of "a specific learning disability" is unchanged. However, Section 1414(b)(6) OF IDEA 2004 states that schools "shall not be

The classification system used in IEP development was considered the most problematic issue when trying to establish specific academic, social, management, and physical goals for a child with a disability. The single broad disability category (stating only that the child has "specific learning disability) significantly limits the ability to find the correct remediation, modifications, accommodations, assistive technology, and management solutions for any child receiving special education services.

In response to this concern, the EDM was developed to provide all professionals in the field of special education with a very clear five-level disability coding system. This multilevel coding system provides professionals with the ability to:

- Identify the specific IDEA 2004 classification (Level I)
- Identify the specific disorders for this classification (Level II)
- Identify the specific types of disorders (Level III)
- Identify the specific subtypes of the disorder (Level IV)
- Determine the degree to which the disability adversely affects the child's educational performance (Level V)

The EDM multilevel coding system and the practical ways in which it can be applied to diagnosis of disabilities, disorders, and future IEP development are provided in the next section, "EDM Multilevel Coding System.".

References

American Psychiatric Association. (2000). *Diagnostic and statistical manual of mental disorders (DSM)* (4th ed.). Washington DC: Author.

Disability Exchange. (2005). *The individualized educational program.* Retrieved January 4, 2006, from http://www.disabilityexchange.org/taxonomy/detail.php?fid=4&path=4_1189&c=2&tid=1505.

National Dissemination Center for Children with Disabilities. (2002). *Developing your child's IEP.* Retrieved April 12, 2006, from http://nichcy.org/pubs/parent/pa12txt.htm.

Stephens, T. J. (2006). *Writing a good IEP.* Retrieved March 10, 2006, from http://www.usd.edu/cd/autism/topicpages/printer/Good%20IEP.pd.

U.S. Department of Education. (2004). *Individuals with Disabilities Education Act (IDEA) data.* Washington, DC: Author. Retrieved February 1, 2005, from http://wwwIDEAdata.org/PartBdata.asp.

EDM Multilevel Coding System

The multilevel coding system used in EDM is designed to ensure the most descriptive identification of a child with a disability. In order to accomplish this, EDM provides a five-level diagnostic coding system. The five levels, when applicable, will:

- Identify the specific IDEA 2004 classification (Level I)
- Identify the specific disorders for this classification (Level II)
- Identify the specific types of disorders (Level III)
- Identify the specific subtypes of the disorder (Level IV)
- Determine the degree to which the disability adversely affects the child's educational performance (Level V)

Each level of the EDM coding system will now be explained in detail by providing examples of five students with different disabilities. For each student, you will see how the coding system develops and results in the most descriptive identification of the student's disability.

Level I: IDEA 2004 Disability Classifications

Level I categories represent each of the thirteen IDEA 2004 disabilities. They can be identified by the uppercase two-letter or three-letter abbreviation for the IDEA 2004 disability, as indicated in Table 1. (For a detailed definition of IDEA's 2004 definition of a child with a disability, refer to page 2 of "EDM Multilevel Coding System.")

Table 1. Level I EDM Identification Codes

Level I Disability Category	Level I EDM Code
Autism	AU
Deaf-Blindness	DB
Developmental Delay (Ages Three to Nine)	DD
Early Intervention	EI[1]
Emotional Disturbance	ED
Hearing Impairment	HI
Specific Learning Disabilities	LD
Mental Retardation	MR
Multiple Disabilities	MD
Orthopedic Impairment	OI
Other Health Impaired	OHI
Speech and Language Impairment	SL
Traumatic Brain Injury	TBI
Visual Impairment	VI

1. Although Early Intervention (EI) is not a specific IDEA disability category, it is included in EDM to represent an infant or toddler from birth to thirty-six months of age

In most cases, only one disability category will be listed under Level I—for example:

Student 1:

Level I: Specific Learning Disability LD

Student 2:

Level I: Traumatic Brain Injury TBI

Student 3:

Level I: Speech and Language Impairment SL

Student 4:

Level I: Other Health Impairment OHI

For a child with a classification of Multiple Disabilities, two or more individual IDEA 2004 disability categories would be listed:

Student 5:

Level I: Multiple Disabilities MD

Level IA: Mental Retardation MR

Level IB: Hearing Impairment HI

Level II: Specific Disorders

Once you have identified the Level I IDEA 2004 disability for a student, you need to identify whether there is a specific disorder associated with this Level I IDEA 2004 disability. A disorder can be defined as a general disturbance in mental, physical, or psychological functioning (Hardman, Drew, & Egan, 2006).

Level II coding represents specific disorders of a Level I IDEA 2004 disability. A Level II disorder is normally diagnosed through a comprehensive multidisciplinary assessment or by outside medical, psychological, or other professionals.

Level II disorders can be identified as a whole number (for example, 1, 2, 3) followed by .00 after that whole number: 1.00, 2.00, 3.00, and so on.

Student 1 was classified with a specific learning disability (LD). Suppose the specific areas of difficulties were associated with reading. This is known as dyslexia. Dyslexia in EDM is coded as follows (see Chapter One, page 24):

Level I: Specific Learning Disabilities	LD
Level II: Dyslexia	LD 4.00

Student 2 was classified with a traumatic brain injury (TBI). Suppose it was due to a penetrating skull fracture (such as a gunshot wound). A penetrating skull fracture in EDM is coded as follows (see Chapter Eleven, page 387):

Level I: Traumatic Brain Injury	TBI
Level II: Penetrating Skull Fracture	TBI 7.00

Student 3 was classified with a speech and language impairment. Suppose the specific speech deficits were in articulation. An articulation disorder in EDM is coded as follows (see Chapter Two, page 73):

Level I: Speech and Language Impairment	SL
Level II: Articulation Disorder	SL 2.00

Student 4 was classified with another health impairment (OHI). Suppose this was because the child was diagnosed with cancer by an outside medical specialist. In EDM, the category cancers of childhood is coded as follows (see Chapter Five, page 207):

Level I: Other Health Impairment	OHI
Level II: Cancers of Childhood	OHI 11.00

In the case of multiple disabilities, each category must be coded separately. Student 5 was classified with multiple disabilities as having two documented IDEA 2004 disabilities: mental retardation and a hearing impairment. Suppose the mental retardation was due to a chromosomal abnormality, and the hearing impairment is a conductive hearing loss. In this situation, the student would have the following EDM coding:

Level I: Multiple Disabilities	MD
Level I(A): Mental Retardation	MR
Level II: Mental Retardation due to Chromosomal Abnormalities	MR 1.00
Level I(B): Hearing Impairment	HI
Level II: Conductive Hearing Loss	HI 2.00

In some cases, more than one Level II disorder may be present, so each needs to be identified—for example:

Level I: Emotional Disturbance	ED
Level II: Inappropriate Behavior or Feelings Disorder	ED 3.00
Level II: Pervasive Mood Disorder	ED 4.00

Level I: Speech and Language Impairment	SL
Level II: Speech Fluency Problems	SL 4.00
Level II: Expressive Language Disorders	SL 9.00
Level II: Receptive Language Disorders	SL 10.00

Level I: Specific Learning Disabilities	LD
Level II: Dyscalculia	LD 2.00
Level II: Dysgraphia	LD 3.00
Level II: Organizational Disorder	LD 9.00
Level II: Visual Processing Disorder	LD 12.00

Level III: Specific Types of Disorders

Once you have identified the Level I IDEA 2004 disability for a student and then the Level II disorder, you will need to identify whether there is a specific type of disorder.

Level III coding represents specific types of disorders. A Level III disorder is normally diagnosed through a comprehensive multidisciplinary assessment or by outside medical, psychological or other professionals.

Level III disorders can be identified as a whole number (for example, 1, 2, 3), followed by anything other than .00 after that whole number (for example, 1.01, 2.12, 3.04, 7.03).

Student 1 was classified with a specific learning disability (LD). The specific areas of difficulties were associated with reading. This is known as dyslexia. Suppose the student has been identified with a specific type of dyslexia, known as dysphonetic dyslexia. Dysphonetic dyslexia in EDM is coded as follows (see Chapter One, page 29):

Level I: Specific Learning Disabilities	LD
Level II: Dyslexia	LD 4.00
Level III: Dysphonetic Dyslexia	LD 4.07

Student 2 was classified with a traumatic brain injury (TBI). The TBI was due to a penetrating skull fracture (for example, a gunshot wound). Suppose the penetrating skull fracture has significantly affected the child's communication skills. A penetrating skull fracture with communication impairments in EDM is coded as follows (see Chapter Eleven, page 388):

Level I: Traumatic Brain Injury	TBI
Level II: Penetrating Skull Fracture	TBI 7.00
Level III: Penetrating Skull Fracture with Communication Impairments	TBI 7.04

Student 3 was classified with a speech and language impairment. The specific speech deficits were in articulation. Suppose the specific articulation problems are that the student consistently substitutes incorrect letters for the correct ones. In EDM, this is known as a substitution articulation disorder. Substitution articulation disorder in EDM is coded as follows (see Chapter Two, page 74):

Level I: Speech and Language Impairment	SL
Level II: Articulation Disorder	SL 2.00
Level II: Substitution Articulation Disorder	SL 2.03

Student 4 was classified with an other health impairment (OHI). This resulted from the child being diagnosed with cancer by an outside medical specialist (an oncologist). Suppose the specific type of cancer was leukemia. In EDM, leukemia is coded as follows (see Chapter Five, page 209):

Level I: Other Health Impairment	OHI
Level II: Cancers of Childhood	OHI 11.00
Level III: Leukemia	OHI 11.02

Student 5 was classified with multiple disabilities. In the case of multiple disabilities, each category must be coded separately. This resulted from the child having two documented IDEA 2004 disabilities at the same time: mental retardation and a hearing impairment. Suppose the mental retardation was due to a specific type of chromosomal abnormality known as Down syndrome and the specific type of conductive hearing loss for this child is otosclerosis.

In this situation, the student would have the following EDM coding:

Level I: Multiple Disabilities	MD
Level I(A): Mental Retardation	MR
Level II: Mental Retardation due to Chromosomal Abnormalities	MR 1.00
Level III: Down Syndrome	MR 1.03
Level I(B): Hearing Impairment	HI
Level II: Conductive Hearing Loss	HI 2.00
Level III: Otosclerosis	HI 2.03

Various disorders in EDM may not have a Level III classification. In that case this should be coded using the words *Not Applicable,* for example:

Level I: Autism	AU
Level II: Asperger's Syndrome	AU 1.00
Level III:	Not Applicable
Level I: Hearing Impairment	HI
Level II: HI 9.00 Acoustic Neuroma	HI 9.00
Level III:	Not Applicable
Level I: Specific Learning Disabilities	LD
Level II: Gerstmann's Syndrome	LD 6.00
Level III:	Not Applicable

In some cases, more than one Level III type of disorder may be present, so each will need to be identified separately.

For example, suppose a student was diagnosed with various types of speech and language disorders: stuttering, expressive language phonological disorder, and receptive language syntactical disorder. Under the EDM coding system, this would be written as follows:

Level I: Speech and Language Impairment	SL
Level II: Speech Fluency Problems	SL 4.00
Level III: Stuttering	SL 4.02
Level II: Expressive Language Disorders	SL 9.00
Level III: Expressive Language Phonological Disorder	SL 9.02

Level II: Receptive Language Disorders	SL 10.00
Level III: Receptive Language Syntatical Disorder	SL 10.04

Suppose a student was diagnosed with various types of learning disabilities: significant specific types of difficulties in math, writing, organization, and visual processing. Under the EDM coding system, this would be written as follows:

Level I: Specific Learning Disabilities	LD
Level II: Dyscalculia	LD 2.00
Level III: Navigation Dyscalculia	LD 2.09
Level III: Language Dysclaculia	LD 2.06
Level II: Dysgraphia	LD 3.00
Level III: Spatial Dysgraphia	LD 3.03
Level II: Organizational Disorder	LD 9.00
Level III: External Disorganization Disorder	LD 9.04
Level II: Visual Processing Disorder	LD 12.00
Level III: Visual Depth Perception Processing Disorder	LD 12.03

Level IV: Specific Subtypes of Disorders

Once you have identified the Level I IDEA 2004 disability for a student, then the Level II disorder, and then Level III type of disorder, you will need to identify whether there is a specific subtype of the disorder.

Level IV coding represents specific subtypes of disorders. A Level IV subtype of disorder is normally diagnosed through a comprehensive multidisciplinary assessment or by outside medical, psychological or other professionals.

Level IV subtypes of disorders can be identified as an EDM code followed by a lowercase letter (for example, a, b, c). Examples of Level IV codes are 2.12a, 3.04e, 7.03b, 8.04c. The lowercase letter at the end signifies that it is a Level IV subtype of a disorder.

Level IV subtypes do not occur frequently in the EDM coding system. When there is no Level IV code, write the words *Not Applicable.*

Student 1 was classified with a specific learning disability (LD). The specific areas of difficulties were associated with reading. This is known as dyslexia. The student has a specific type of dyslexia, known as dysphonetic dyslexia. Because there is no specific subtype of dysphonetic dyslexia, it is coded as follows:

Level I: Specific Learning Disabilities	LD
Level II: Dyslexia	LD 4.00

Level III: Dysphonetic Dyslexia	LD 4.07
Level IV:	Not Applicable

Student 2 was classified with a traumatic brain injury (TBI). The TBI was due to a penetrating skull fracture (for example, a gunshot wound). The penetrating skull fracture has significantly affected the child's communication skills. Since there is no specific subtype for a penetrating skull fracture with communication impairments, it is coded as follows:

Level I: Traumatic Brain Injury	TBI
Level II: Penetrating Skull Fracture	TBI 7.00
Level III: Penetrating Skull Fracture with Communication Impairments	TBI 7.04
Level IV:	Not Applicable

Student 3 was classified with a speech and language impairment. The specific speech deficits were in articulation. The specific articulation problems are that the child consistently substitutes incorrect letters for the correct ones. In EDM, this is known as a substitution articulation disorder. Since there is no specific subtype of substitution articulation disorder, it is coded as follows:

Level I: Speech and Language Impairment	SL
Level II: Articulation Disorder	SL 2.00
Level II: Substitution Articulation Disorder	SL 2.03
Level IV:	Not Applicable

Student 4 was classified with an other health impairment (OHI). This resulted from the child being diagnosed with cancer by an outside medical specialist (an oncologist). The specific type of cancer was leukemia. Suppose the specific type of leukemia is acute lymphocytic leukemia. In EDM, acute lymphocytic leukemia is coded as follows (see Chapter Five, page 209):

Level I: Other Health Impairment	OHI
Level II: Cancers of Childhood	OHI 11.00
Level III: Leukemia	OHI 11.02
Level IV: Acute Lymphocytic Leukemia	OHI 11.02c

Student 5 was classified with multiple disabilities. This resulted from the child having two documented IDEA disabilities at the same time. This particular student has both mental retardation and a hearing impairment.

The mental retardation was due to a specific type of chromosomal abnormality known as Down syndrome. The Level IV specific subtype of Down syndrome is known as Down syndrome due to trisomy 21. The specific type of conductive hearing loss for this child is otosclerosis. The specific Level IV subtype of otosclerosis is known as classic otosclerosis. In this situation, the student would have the following EDM coding because each category must be coded separately:

Level I: Multiple Disabilities	MD
Level I(A): Mental Retardation	MR
Level II: Mental Retardation due to Chromosomal Abnormalities	MR 1.00
Level III: Down Syndrome	MR 1.03
Level IV: Down Syndrome due to Trisomy 21	MR 1.03c

Level I(B): Hearing Impairment	HI
Level II: Conductive Hearing Loss	HI 2.00
Level III: Otosclerosis	HI 2.03
Level IV: Classic Otosclerosis	HI 2.03a

Level V: Degree to Which the Disability Adversely Affects the Child's Educational Performance

Level V is the degree to which the child's disability adversely affects his or her educational performance. This decision should be made by the IEP team (also referred to as an eligibility committee or committee on special education).

The determination of Level V by the IEP team should be the result of several factors. The team's decision should be based on the results of the multidisciplinary assessment, teacher interviews, professional input, parent interviews, informal assessments, observations, and all other appropriate information.

In order to determine the appropriate EDM Level V coding for a student, the team should determine the extent to which the child needs the following:

- modifications
- related services, particularly examining the frequency, intensity and duration
- assistive technology
- classroom accommodations
- a restrictive educational program outside of the general education classroom (e.g., resource room, self-contained classroom, special education day school, residential placement, etc.)

Ultimately the IEP team's decision regarding Level V for a specific student should answer this question based on the above needs: "To what degree does the child's disability adversely affect his or her educational performance?"

The terms used for Level V coding are as follows:

- Mild adverse effect: Mild adverse effect implies a minimal difference between the needs of the student with a disability when compared to the reasonable expectations of nondisabled peers of the same age and or grade level.
- Moderate adverse effect: Moderate adverse effect implies a significant difference between the needs of the student with a disability when compared to the reasonable expectations of nondisabled peers of the same age and or grade level.
- Severe adverse effect: Severe adverse effect implies a pervasive difference between the needs of the student with a disability when compared to the reasonable expectations of nondisabled peers of the same age and or grade level.

Student 1 was classified with a specific learning disability (LD). The specific areas of difficulties were associated with reading. This is known as dyslexia. The student has a specific type of dyslexia, known as dysphonetic dyslexia. In EDM, there is no specific subtype of dysphonetic dyslexia. Suppose the IEP team has determined that the disability has a moderate adverse effect on educational performance. Therefore, it is coded as follows:

Level I: Specific Learning Disabilities	LD
Level II: Dyslexia	LD 4.00
Level III: Dysphonetic Dyslexia	LD 4.07
Level IV:	Not Applicable
Level V:	Moderate

Student 2 was classified with a traumatic brain injury (TBI). The TBI was due to a penetrating skull fracture (for example, a gunshot wound). The penetrating skull fracture has significantly affected the child's communication skills. In EDM, there is no specific subtype for a penetrating skull fracture with communication impairments. Suppose the IEP team has determined that the disability has a severe adverse effect on educational performance. Therefore, it is coded as follows:

Level I: Traumatic Brain Injury	TBI
Level II: Penetrating Skull Fracture	TBI 7.00
Level III: Penetrating Skull Fracture with Communication Impairments	TBI 7.04
Level IV:	Not Applicable
Level V:	Severe

Student 3 was classified with a speech and language impairment. The specific speech deficits were in articulation. The specific articulation problems are that the child consistently substitutes incorrect letters for the correct ones. In EDM, this is known as a substitution articulation disorder. In EDM, there is no specific subtype of substitution articulation disorder. Suppose the IEP team has determined that the disability has a mild adverse effect on educational performance. Therefore, it is coded as follows:

Level I: Speech and Language Impairment	SL
Level II: Articulation Disorder	SL 2.00
Level II: Substitution Articulation Disorder	SL 2.03
Level IV:	Not Applicable
Level V:	Mild

Student 4 was classified with an other health impairment (OHI). This resulted from the child being diagnosed with cancer by an outside medical specialist (an oncologist). The specific type of cancer was leukemia. The specific type of leukemia is known as acute lymphocytic leukemia. Suppose the IEP team has determined that the disability has a severe adverse effect on educational performance. Therefore, it is coded as follows:

Level I: Other Health Impairment	OHI
Level II: Cancers of Childhood	OHI 11.00
Level III: Leukemia	OHI 11.02
Level IV: Acute Lymphocytic Leukemia	OHI 11.02c
Level V:	Severe

Student 5 was classified with multiple disabilities. This resulted from the child having two documented IDEA disabilities at the same time. This particular student has both mental retardation and a hearing impairment.

The mental retardation was due to a specific type of chromosomal abnormality, known as Down syndrome. The Level IV specific subtype of Down syndrome is known as Down syndrome due to trisomy 21. The IEP team has determined that the mental retardation has a severe adverse effect on educational performance.

The specific type of conductive hearing loss for this child is otosclerosis. The specific Level IV subtype of otosclerosis is known as classic otosclerosis. The IEP team has determined that the classic otosclerosis has a moderate adverse effect on educational performance.

In the case of multiple disabilities, each category must be coded separately as follows. In this situation, the student would have the following EDM coding:

Level I: Multiple Disabilities	MD
Level I(A): Mental Retardation	MR
Level II: Mental Retardation due to Chromosomal Abnormalities	MR 1.00

Level III: Down Syndrome	MR 1.03
Level IV: Down Syndrome due to Trisomy 21	MR 1.03c
Level V:	Severe
Level I(B): Hearing Impairment	HI
Level II: Conductive Hearing Loss	HI 2.00
Level III: Otosclerosis	HI 2.03
Level IV: Classic Otosclerosis	HI 2.03a
Level V:	Moderate

Reference

Hardman, M., Drew, C., & Egan, W. (2006). *Human exceptionality: School, community, and family* (8th ed.). Boston: Allyn & Bacon.

EDM

The Educator's Diagnostic Manual of Disabilities and Disorders

CHAPTER 1

SPECIFIC LEARNING DISABILITY

EDM CODE: LD

- LD 1.00 Auditory Processing Disorders
  - LD 1.01 Auditory Association Processing Disorder
  - LD 1.02 Auditory Blending Processing Disorder
  - LD 1.03 Auditory Closure Processing Disorder
  - LD 1.04 Auditory Discrimination Processing Disorder
  - LD 1.05 Auditory Figure Ground Processing Disorder
  - LD 1.06 Auditory Language Classification Processing Disorder
  - LD 1.07 Auditory Long Term-Memory Processing Disorder
  - LD 1.08 Auditory-to-Written Expression Processing Disorder
  - LD 1.09 Auditory Sequential Memory Processing Disorder
  - LD 1.10 Auditory Short-Term Memory Processing Disorder
  - LD 1.11 Auditory Visual Integration Processing Disorder
  - LD 1.12 Auditory Verbal Reproduction Processing Disorder
  - LD 1.13 Other Types of Auditory Processing Disorders
- LD 2.00 Dyscalculia
  - LD 2.01 Abstract Concepts Dyscalculia
  - LD 2.02 Attention-to-Sequence Dyscalculia
  - LD 2.03 Basic Number Fact Dyscalculia
  - LD 2.04 Developmental Anarithmetria
  - LD 2.05 Estimation Dyscalculia
  - LD 2.06 Language Dyscalculia
  - LD 2.07 Measurement Dyscalculia
  - LD 2.08 Monetary Dyscalculia
  - LD 2.09 Navigation Dyscalculia
  - LD 2.10 Number-Word Translation Dyscalculia
  - LD 2.11 Spatial Dyscalculia
  - LD 2.12 Temporal Dyscalculia
  - LD 2.13 Other Types of Dyscalculia
- LD 3.00 Dysgraphia
  - LD 3.01 Dyslexic Dysgraphia
  - LD 3.02 Motor Dysgraphia
  - LD 3.03 Spatial Dysgraphia
  - LD 3.04 Other Types of Dysgraphia
- LD 4.00 Dyslexia
  - LD 4.01 Auditory Linguistic Dyslexia
  - LD 4.02 Direct Dyslexia
  - LD 4.03 Dysnomia
  - LD 4.04 Dyseidetic Dyslexia
  - LD 4.05 Dysnemkinesia Dyslexia
  - LD 4.06 Alexic Dyslexia
  - LD 4.07 Dysphonetic Dyslexia
  - LD 4.08 Neglect Dyslexia
  - LD 4.09 Phonological Dyslexia
  - LD 4.10 Other Types of Dyslexia
- LD 5.00 Dysorthographia
- LD 6.00 Gerstmann Syndrome
- LD 7.00 Gifted with Learning Disabilities
- LD 8.00 Nonverbal Learning Disabilities
  - LD 8.01 Motoric Nonverbal Learning Disability
  - LD 8.02 Social Nonverbal Learning Disability
  - LD 8.03 Visual-Spatial-Organizational Nonverbal Learning Disability
  - LD 8.04 Other Types of Nonverbal Learning Disabilities
- LD 9.00 Organizational Learning Disorders
  - LD 9.01 Catastrophic Response Organizational Disorder
  - LD 9.02 Cognitive Disorganization Disorder
  - LD 9.03 Directionality Organizational Disorder
  - LD 9.04 External Disorganization Disorder
  - LD 9.05 Temporal Disorganization Disorder

IDEA 2004 Definition of a Specific Learning Disability

Under IDEA 2004, *specific learning disability* is defined in this way:

(i) General. The term means a disorder in one or more of the basic psychological processes involved in understanding or in using language, spoken or written, that may manifest itself in an imperfect ability to listen, think, speak, read, write, spell, or to do mathematical calculations, including conditions such as perceptual disabilities, brain injury, minimal brain dysfunction, dyslexia, and developmental aphasia.

(ii) Disorders not included. The term does not include learning problems that are primarily the result of visual, hearing, or motor disabilities, of mental retardation, of emotional disturbance, or of environmental, cultural, or economic disadvantage [34 C.F.R. 300.7(c)(10)].

The definition of *specific learning disability* under IDEA 2004 remains unchanged from IDEA of 1997. However, under the new provisions under IDEA 2004,

> a local educational agency is not required to take into consideration whether a child has a severe discrepancy between achievement and intellectual ability in oral expression, listening comprehension, written expression, basic reading skill, reading comprehension, mathematical calculation or mathematical reasoning. In determining whether a child has a specific learning disability, a local educational agency may use a process that determines if a child responds to scientific, research-based intervention as a part of the evaluation procedures [USC sec. 614(b)(2)(3)].

Overview of Specific Learning Disabilities

On April 6, 1963, the term *learning disabilities* was coined by Sam Kirk and others at a meeting of parents and professionals in Chicago (Pierangelo & Giuliani, 2006b). In 1975, the disability category "specific learning disability" was first included in the federal Education for All Handicapped Children Act, PL 94–142 (Hunt & Marshall, 2005).

In general, *learning disabilities* refers to a neurobiological disorder related to differences in how an individual's brain works and is structured. Furthermore, *learning disability* is a general term that describes specific kinds of learning problems. A learning disability can cause a person to have trouble learning and using certain skills (Lerner, 2005). The skills most often affected are reading, writing, listening, speaking, reasoning, and doing math (Pierangelo & Giuliani, 2006b; Heward, 2006; National Dissemination Center for Children with Disabilities, 2004).

Learning disabilities (LD) vary from person to person and encompass a heterogeneous group of disorders. One person with LD may not have the same kind of learning problems as another person with LD. Another person with LD may have problems with understanding math. Still another may have trouble in several areas, as well as with understanding what people are saying. Therefore, no single profile of an individual with LD can be accurate because of the individual differences in the disorder (Friend, 2005*).

Children with learning disabilities are not "dumb" or "lazy." In fact, they usually have average or above-average intelligence. Their brains just process information differently (Gargiulo, 2004). The general belief among researchers is that learning disabilities exist because of some type of dysfunction in the brain, not because of external factors such as limited experience or poor teaching (Hallahan & Kauffman, 2006**; Friend, 2005).

Causes-Etiology of Specific Learning Disabilities

Despite intense research activity over the years, pinpointing the precise cause or causes of learning disabilities has remained an elusive goal (Turnbull, Turnbull, Shank, & Smith, 2004; Deutsch Smith, 2004).

Once scientists thought that all learning disabilities were due to the effects of a single neurological problem (Hallahan & Kauffman, 2006). Research now indicates that the causes are diverse and complex (Pierangelo & Giuliani, 2006b). New evidence seems to show that most learning disabilities do not stem from a single,

---

* From Marilyn Friend, *Special Education: Contemporary Perspectives For School Professionals.* Published by Allyn and Bacon, Boston, MA. © 2005 by Pearson Education. By permission of the publisher.

** From Daniel P. Hallahan and James M. Kauffman, *Exceptional Learners: An Introduction to Special Education,* 10/e, Published by Allyn and Bacon, Boston, MA. © 2005 by Pearson Education. By permission from the publisher.

specific area of the brain, but from difficulties in bringing together information from various brain regions (Lerner, 2005; University of Maryland Medicine, 2004).

Research has suggested various possible causes for specific learning disabilities, which we explore in the following sections.

Genetics

Over the years, evidence has accumulated that learning disabilities can be inherited (Hallahan & Kauffman, 2006). The fact that learning disabilities tend to run in families indicates that there may be a genetic link (Winkler, 2003). Researchers have found that about 35 to 45 percent of first-degree relatives of persons with reading disabilities—that is, the immediate birth family (parents and siblings)—have reading disabilities. Twin studies have shown that if one twin has a reading disability, the probability of the other twin also having a reading disability is 68 percent for identical twins (monozygotic) and 40 percent for fraternal twins (dizygotic). The research evidence generally supports the hypothesis that certain types of learning problems, including reading disabilities, are more common among identical twins than fraternal twins. Some experts are beginning to suggest that an interactive relationship among several genes establishes the risk factors for reading disabilities (Wood & Grigorenko, 2001). Similar findings are also observed in twins with speech and language disorders (Wood & Grigorenko, 2001).

Tobacco, Alcohol, and Other Drug Use During Pregnancy

Research shows that a mother's use of cigarettes, alcohol, or other drugs during pregnancy may have damaging effects on the unborn child (Surgeon General's Report on Women and Smoking, 2001; Wakschlag, Lahey, & Loeber, 1997; Roy, 1994).

Scientists have found that mothers who smoke during pregnancy may be more likely to bear smaller babies. This is a concern because small newborns, usually those weighing less than five pounds, tend to be at risk for a variety of problems, including learning disorders (Surgeon General's Report on Women and Smoking, 2001; Wakschlag, Lahey, & Loeber, 1997; Roy, 1994).

Alcohol also may be dangerous to the fetus's developing brain (Mayo Clinic, 2005; Wegmann, 2000; Mattson et al., 1994; Dumas, 1994; Hanson, 1992; Coles, 1991; Kennedy & Mukerji, 1986; Streissguth, Barr, & Sampson, 1986; Lucchi & Covelli, 1984; Gusella & Fried, 1984; Sulik, Johnston, & Webb, 1981; Shaywitz & Cohen, 1980; Rawat et al., 1977). It appears that alcohol may distort the developing neurons. Any alcohol use during pregnancy may influence the child's development and lead to problems with learning, attention, memory, or problem solving.

The extensive use of drugs like marijuana and cocaine has been associated with increases in symptoms associated with learning disabilities (Fried & Smith, 2001; Fried & Watkinson, 1992; Abel, 1985). Because children with certain learning disabilities have difficulty understanding speech sounds or letters, some researchers believe that learning disabilities, as well as attention deficit–hyperactivity disorder, may be related to faulty receptors. Current research points to drug abuse as a possible cause of receptor damage.

Complications During Pregnancy

Other possible causes of learning disabilities involve complications during pregnancy (University of Maryland Medicine, 2004). In some cases, the mother's immune system reacts to the fetus and attacks it as if it were an infection. This type of disruption seems to cause newly formed brain cells to settle in the wrong part of the brain. Or during delivery, the umbilical cord may become twisted and temporarily cut off oxygen to the fetus. This too can impair brain functions and lead to LD.

Low-birth-weight babies are at risk for learning disabilities. According to some studies, children whose birth weight was less than two pounds (eight hundred grams) lagged behind their peers academically and displayed other subtle behavioral characteristics that undermined their efforts at school. Poor motor skills and neurological immaturity were found in many of these preschool-age children (Learning Disabilities Association of British Columbia, 2005).

Environmental Toxins

New brain cells and neural networks continue to be produced for a year or so after birth, and these cells are also vulnerable to certain disruptions. Researchers are looking into environmental toxins that may lead to learning disabilities, possibly by disrupting childhood brain development or brain processes (Continuing Medical Education, 1999):

- Mercury poisoning: Mercury, prevalent in the environment, is becoming a leading focus of neurological research (Leong, Syed, & Lorscheider, 2001; Archibold, Bayorh, & Sung, 1999; Echeverria, Heyer, Martin, & Naleway, 1995). Mercury, like lead, is particularly harmful to children. Mercury exposure can occur by breathing vapors, by direct skin contact, or by eating food or drinking water contaminated with mercury. It can result in lowered intelligence, learning problems, birth defects, and brain damage.
- Cadmium exposure: Cadmium is a natural element in the earth's crust, usually found as a mineral combined with other elements such as oxygen (cadmium oxide), chlorine (cadmium chloride), or sulfur (cadmium sulfate, cadmium sulfide) (U.S. Department of Labor, 2004). Some researchers suggest that cadmium exposure is related to learning disabilities in children. Much of the cadmium that enters the body by ingestion comes from plants grown in soil or meat from animals that have ingested plants grown in soil.
- Lead poisoning: Approximately 434,000 U.S. children aged one to five years have blood lead levels greater than the Centers for Disease Control's (2004) recommended level of ten micrograms of lead per deciliter of blood. Lead was once common in paint and gasoline and is still present in some water pipes. Young children

under the age of six are especially vulnerable to lead's harmful health effects because their brains and central nervous system are being formed. For them, even very low levels of exposure can result in reduced IQ, learning disabilities, attention deficit disorders, behavioral problems, stunted growth, impaired hearing, and kidney damage (National Safety Council, 2005).

Poor Nutrition

There seems to be a link between nutritional deprivation and poor biochemical functioning in the brain. A poor diet and severe malnutrition can reduce the child's ability to learn by damaging intersensory abilities and delaying development. Studies over the past ten years and clinical trials, conducted at Purdue University in the United States and Surrey and Oxford universities in the United Kingdom, indicate that some learning disabilities may have a nutritional basis. Other studies indicate that some learning disabilities might be caused by allergies to certain foods, food additives and dyes, or environmental allergies (Pierangelo & Giuliani, 2006b).

Maturational Delay

Another theory to explain learning disabilities suggests that they occur because there is maturational delay, rather than a permanent dysfunction, within the neurological system. Some typical symptoms of maturational delay are (Nalanda Institute, 2002):

- Slow maturation of language skills, especially those of reading
- Delayed development of motor skills
- Uneven performance patterns on measures of intellectual development
- Visual-motor problems
- Incomplete or mixed dominance
- Right-left confusion
- Immaturity

Prevalence of Specific Learning Disabilities

According to the *Twenty-Sixth Annual Report* of the U.S. Department of Education (2004), 2,816,361 students between six and twenty-one years of age were identified as having specific learning disabilities. This represents approximately 47 percent of all students having a classification in special education, or about 5.0 percent of all school-age students.

There are many conflicting reports on the actual number of individuals with specific learning disabilities. Since 1976–1977, when the federal government started keeping prevalence figures, the size of the specific learning disability category has more than doubled (Hallahan & Kauffman, 2006), and the number of students identified as having a specific learning disability has grown by over 250 percent, from approximately 800,000 students to almost 3 million (U.S. Department of Education, 2004).

Learning disabilities has also been the fastest-growing category of special education since the federal law was passed in 1975. Furthermore, the number of students with learning disabilities increased almost 30 percent from 1995 to 2004, a rate of growth much greater than the overall rate of growth for the number of students in school (Friend, 2005).

Age of Onset of Specific Learning Disabilities

Some forms of learning disabilities become apparent in preschool, while others might not be apparent until later in elementary school or even middle school. The number of students with learning disabilities increases steadily between the ages of six and nine, which is not too surprising considering the increasing academic demands of the elementary school curriculum. The bulk of students served (42 percent), however, are between the ages of ten and thirteen, with a sharp decrease observed for individuals between sixteen and twenty-one years of age (U.S. Department of Education, 2000, cited in Gargiulo, 2004).

Gender Features of Specific Learning Disabilities

The matter of gender and LD is one of controversy among researchers in the field. Although some studies have indicated that the prevalence of learning disabilities is equally distributed between males and females (Alexander, Gray, & Lyon, 1993), a number of researchers have found that the ratio of boys to girls identified as having learning disabilities is three to one (Hallahan and Kauffman, 2006), four to one (Lerner, 2005; Gargiulo, 2004), or even higher (Lyon, 1997; McLeskey, 1992).

Cultural Features of Specific Learning Disabilities

The 1997 IDEA Amendments mandated that states collect special education "child count" data by race/ethnicity, beginning with the 1998–1999 school year. The U.S. Department of Education (2000) reported special education identification rates by race/ethnicity and disability for children ages six through twenty-one. According to this report, 4.27 percent of white children were identified as having LD. Corresponding figures for other race/ethnicity groups were as follows: American Indian/Alaska native, 6.29 percent; black, 5.67 percent; Hispanic, 4.97 percent; and Asian/Pacific Islander, 1.7 percent.

Familial Pattern of Specific Learning Disabilities

The fact that learning disabilities tend to run in families indicates that there may be a genetic link (Bishop, Cherny, Corley, DeFries, & Hewitt, 2003; Wadsworth, Corley, Hewitt, Plomin, & DeFries, 2002; Knopik et al., 2002; Kaplan et al., 2002;

Davis, Knopik, Olson, Wadsworth, & DeFries, 2001). For example, children who lack some of the skills needed for reading, such as hearing the separate sounds of words, are likely to have a parent with a related problem. However, a parent's learning disability may take a slightly different form in the child. A parent who has a writing disorder may have a child with an expressive language disorder. For this reason, it seems unlikely that specific learning disorders are inherited directly. Possibly what is inherited is a subtle brain dysfunction that can lead to a learning disability.

Comorbidity of Specific Learning Disabilities

According to Chandler (2004), *comorbidity* means that certain diseases and disorders tend to occur together. For example, heart disease and stroke often occur in the same person. There are many neuropsychiatric disorders that tend to occur together. About 50 percent of children with learning disabilities have another neuropsychiatric disorder (Jongmans, Smits-Engelsman, & Schoemaker, 2003). Assessing children for only learning disabilities and learning disorders without looking for other comorbid conditions is problematic. The most important advances in pediatric psychiatry have been the result of researchers' carefully checking children for all possible conditions.

Of particular importance to note is the comorbid occurrence of attention deficit–hyperactivity disorder (ADHD) and learning disorders. Learning disabilities and ADHD often occur in combination (Deutsch Smith, 2004). If a student has a learning disorder, he or she has a 20 to 40 percent chance of having ADHD. That is about a five times increase over the general population. Some studies have shown that 70 percent of children with ADHD also have a learning disability (Mayes, Calhoun, & Cromwell, 2000).

Characteristics of Specific Learning Disabilities

No one sign shows a person has a learning disability. However, "unexpected underachievement" is the defining characteristic of learning disabilities (Hallahan & Kauffman, 2006; Friend, 2005; Deutsch Smith, 2004; Gargiulo, 2004; Vaughn, Elbaum, & Boardman, 2001). Experts look for a noticeable difference between how well a child does in school and how well he or she could do, given his or her intelligence or ability.

A child with a learning disability may exhibit the following characteristics:

Cognitive Difficulties

- Poor selective attention (Zera & Lucian, 2001)
- Inattention or difficulty focusing on the task
- Problems with memory—either short term or long term or both (Swanson, 2000)
- Perceptual problems (Lerner, 2005; Smith, 1998)

Academic Difficulties

- Difficulty with oral fluency (Mercer, Campbell, Miller, Mercer, & Lane, 2000)
- Many mistakes made when reading aloud, and repeating and pausing often
- Very messy handwriting or holding a pencil awkwardly
- Difficulty processing information
- Learning language late and having a limited vocabulary
- Trouble remembering the sounds that letters make or hearing slight differences between words
- Difficulties in written language (Roth, 2000; Wong, 2000)
- Mispronouncing words or using a wrong word that sounds similar
- Trouble organizing what he or she wants to say or unable to think of the word he or she needs for writing or conversation
- Difficulties in reading (Bell, McCallum, & Cox, 2003)
- Difficulties in mathematics (Witzel, Smith, & Brownell, 2001; Mazzocco, 2001)
- Trouble learning the alphabet, rhyming words, or connecting letters to their sounds
- Confusing math symbols and misreading numbers
- Unable to retell a story in order (what happened first, second, third)
- Not knowing where to begin a task or how to go on from there

Social and Emotional Difficulties

- Deficits in social skills (Kavale & Forness, 1996)
- Rejection by peers and classmates (Pavri & Luftig, 2000)
- Difficulties making and keeping friends (Pavri & Monda-Amaya, 2001)
- Feeling lonely and isolated in adolescence (Tur-Kaspa, Weisel, & Segev, 1998)
- Poor social skills (Gresham, Sugai, & Horner, 2001)
- Not following the social rules of conversation, such as taking turns, and may stand too close to the listener

In addition, difficulties in communicating with others can lead to inappropriate behavior (Vallance, Cummings, & Humphries, 1998). For example, the child may have trouble understanding jokes, comic strips, and sarcasm or; trouble following directions.

Educational Implications of Specific Learning Disabilities

Learning disabilities tend to be diagnosed when children reach school age (National Dissemination Center for Children with Disabilities, 2004). This is because school focuses on the very things that may be difficult for the child: reading, writing, math, listening, speaking, and reasoning. Teachers and parents notice that the child is not learning as expected. These students' low achievement separates them more each school year from their classmates without disabilities (Deshler et al., 2001).

Effective instruction can help children with LD learn more easily and successfully. For school-aged children (including preschoolers), special education and related services are important sources of help. Over thirty years of research findings about learning disabilities and those students affected have shown that intervention using validated and best practices (Hallahan & Kauffman, 2006) makes a positive difference in these students' performance (Swanson & Sachse-Lee, 2000).

Permissions and Authorization to Use Proprietary and Nonproprietary Sources

Due to the scientific and detailed nature of certain Level II and Level III disorders described in this chapter, we thought that some were best explained by national institutes and centers that conduct comprehensive scientific research in respective fields of study. The sources obtained were all written with explicit permission that the scientific and diagnostic information they prepared is in the public domain and can be used without restriction.

We thank the following national research offices for the opportunity to freely disseminate their scientific research and writing in this chapter:

- National Dissemination Center for Children with Disabilities
- National Institutes of Health
- National Institute of Neurological Disorders and Strokes
- National Institute on Deafness and Other Communication Disorders

Permission to include materials from proprietary sources was granted by the following professionals and organizations for this chapter:

- Learning Disabilities Association of America
- Robert Toler
- Bonnie Terry, M.Ed., BCET
- National Center for Learning Disabilities
- LDOnlinc

We thank all of these sources for permission to use their research and writing in this chapter.

EDM Codes, Definitions, and Explanations of Specific Learning Disabilities

LD 1.00 Auditory Processing Disorders

Definition Auditory processing disorders (APD) interfere with an individual's ability to analyze or make sense of information taken in aurally (through the ears). This is different from problems involving hearing, such as deafness or being hard of hearing. Difficulties with auditory processing do not affect what is heard by the ear. The "disorder" part of auditory processing disorder means that something is adversely affecting the processing or interpretation of the information (National Institute on Deafness and Other Communication Disorders, 2004).

Diagnostic Symptoms Diagnostic symptoms of individuals with auditory processing disorders include (Gertner, 2003; Ciocci, 2002):

- Difficulty with some or all listening activities
- Problems when the activities occur in less-than-ideal listening environments
- Problems with sound discrimination
- Errors when speaking on a one-to-one basis, especially when there is competing background noise or speech
- Difficulty understanding information when speakers talk rapidly
- Difficulty understanding information when they are not devoting their complete attention to the listening task
- Difficulty with the discussion topic when it is unfamiliar to them
- Difficulty performing or remembering several verbal tasks in a row
- Weak phonemic systems (speech sound memories used in phonics, reading, and spelling)
- Often appear as though they do not hear well
- Frequently say, "what?" or "huh?" in response to questions.
- Not always in touch with the sounds in the environment and do not always grasp exactly what has been said
- A history of middle ear infection
- Lower academic performance
- Need for extra time to process information
- Difficulties with reading comprehension, vocabulary, and spelling
- Behavior problems

Further Key Points Auditory processing disorder is sometimes misunderstood because many of the behaviors also appear in other conditions, such as attention deficit–hyperactivity disorder and even depression. Symptoms can range from mild to severe and can take many forms (Gray, 2003).

An auditory processing disorder does not interfere solely with speech and language; it can affect all areas of learning, especially reading and spelling. When instruction in school relies primarily on spoken language, the individual with an auditory processing disorder may have serious difficulty understanding the lesson or the directions (National Center for Learning Disabilities, 2004).

Types of Auditory Processing Disorders

LD 1.01 Auditory Association Processing Disorder

Definition This auditory processing disorder is specifically associated with difficulties in relating to orally presented material (words and concepts) in a meaningful way (Florida Department of Education, 2001).

Explanation A student with auditory association processing disorder often has great difficulty organizing and associating aurally presented material in a meaningful way. For example, this child does not appear to understand what someone else is saying, needs that person to repeat information, and frequently asks, "What did you say?" or, "Could you repeat that?"

Any medical problems associated with this child's hearing have been ruled out as a primary cause of the child's difficulties. The difficulties are in the internal processing of information, not due to a hearing impairment.

LD 1.02 Auditory Blending Processing Disorder

Definition This auditory processing disorder is specifically associated with difficulties in processing or putting together phonemes (the smallest phonetic unit in a language that is capable of conveying a distinction in meaning) to form words (National Center for Learning Disabilities, 2004).

Explanation A child with auditory blending type processing disorder has difficulties tying letters together in order to form a complete word. As a result, although the child knows the "b" sound, the "a" sound, and the "t" sound, he or she struggles with putting them together as a whole to form the word *bat.* It should be noted that any medical problems associated with this child's hearing have been ruled out as a primary cause of the child's difficulties. The difficulties are in the internal processing of information, not due to a hearing impairment.

LD 1.03 Auditory Closure Processing Disorder

Definition This auditory proccssing disorder is specifically associated with difficulties in combining sounds that are presented orally to make words (Terry, 2001).

Auditory closure is the term used to describe the ability to understand the whole word or message when a part is missing (American Speech-Language-Hearing Association, 2005).

Explanation In everyday life, when pieces of a word are deleted, we automatically fill in the missing sounds to decode the word. For example, if we hear "elephan," we can close off the word, knowing that it is *elephant.* However, if a child with auditory closure processing disorder hears "auto–o-bile," he or she may not be able to identify it as *automobile;* "ase-ball" as *baseball,* "acoroni" as *macaroni,* "tele-ision" as *television,* and "air-pla" as *airplane.*

Because students with auditory closure processing disorder have difficulties closing off words, sentences, or phrases, they may lack total comprehension of what is being discussed both in and outside the classroom.

It should be noted that any medical problems associated with this child's hearing have been ruled out as a primary cause of the child's difficulties. The difficulties are in the internal processing of information, not due to a hearing impairment.

LD 1.04 Auditory Discrimination Processing Disorder

Definition This auditory processing disorder is specifically associated with difficulties in recognizing differences in phonemes (sounds). This includes the ability to identify words and sounds that are similar and those that are different (National Center for Learning Disabilities, 2004; Terry, 2001).

Explanation A student with auditory discrimination processing disorder often experiences difficulties acquiring, understanding, or using spoken language. Auditory discrimination processing problems can lead to problems in telling the difference between similar sounds. For example, this student may hear what he thinks is the word *mall,* when it was actually *wall; seventeen* instead of *seventy; finger* instead of *ringer, boat* instead of *bat;* or discerning an angry rather than a joking tone of voice. The student's difficulty lies in processing the words, not the ability to hear the words themselves.

It should be noted that any medical problems associated with this child's hearing have been ruled out as a primary cause of the child's difficulties. The difficulties are in the internal processing of information, not due to a hearing impairment.

LD 1.05 Auditory Figure Ground Processing Disorder

Definition This auditory processing disorder is specifically associated with difficulties attending to one sound against a background of sounds (for example, hearing the teacher's voice against classroom noise) (Terry, 2001).

Explanation A student with auditory figure ground processing disorder often experiences difficulties with following oral instructions because he or she may not be able to separate the instruction from background conversations. For example, a teacher may tell her students to take out their pens and open their book to page 152. The student with this disorder may not process this information, not because he is not paying attention but rather because he is focused on the background noise of a fan in the room or the ticking of a clock. This child may be unable to process that the telephone is ringing when listening to the radio or have difficulty hearing someone talking at a party when music is playing (Terry, 2001).

It should be noted that any medical problems associated with this child's hearing have been ruled out as a primary cause of the child's difficulties. The difficulties are in the internal processing of information, not due to a hearing impairment.

LD 1.06 Auditory Language Classification Processing Disorder

Definition This auditory processing disorder is specifically associated with difficulties in classifying objects by category when presented aurally to an individual (Terry, 2001).

Explanation Auditory language association and classification difficulties can lead to difficulties with holding two or more concepts in relationship to one another, being able to identify and verbalize concepts, or learning to classify or categorize concepts. For example, a student with this disorder may have difficulties answering the following questions:

- Would "bat" go with "ball" or "mitten"?
- Would "bird" go with "airplane" or "car"?
- How are a dog and a cat alike?

It should be noted that any medical problems associated with this child's hearing have been ruled out as a primary cause of the child's difficulties. The difficulties are in the internal processing of information, not due to a hearing impairment.

LD 1.07 Auditory Long-Term-Memory Processing Disorder

Definition This auditory processing disorder is specifically associated with difficulties in retaining and recalling general and specific long-term auditory information (Rabiner, 1999).

Explanation Long-term auditory memory is the ability to remember something heard some time ago (National Center for Learning Disabilities, 2005a). A child with this disorder may not be able to retain orally presented information learned on Monday for a test on Friday or may have difficulties remembering homework assigned on Wednesday morning for Wednesday night. When asked about an event from the previous year, the child may appear confused and have no recollection of the event.

It should be noted that any medical problems associated with this child's hearing have been ruled out as a primary cause of the child's difficulties. The difficulties are in the internal processing of information, not due to a hearing impairment.

LD 1.08 Auditory-to-Written Expression Processing Disorder

Definition This auditory processing disorder is specifically associated with difficulties in reproducing orally presented material or experiences in writing.

Explanation An example of auditory-to-written expression processing disorder can be seen when a child is asked to spell the word *cat.* He or she will have no problem saying that the letters are c-a-t. However, when asked to spell *cat* by writing the word on paper, the student has tremendous difficulty. Here, repeating it verbally is not the issue. The difficulties are in processing what he or she heard into a written form of expression.

It should be noted that medical problems associated with this child's hearing have been ruled out as a primary cause of the child's difficulties. The difficulties are in the internal processing of information, not due to a hearing impairment.

LD 1.09 Auditory Sequential Memory Processing Disorder

Definition This auditory processing disorder is specifically associated with difficulties in recalling prior auditory information in the correct order or sequence.

Explanation Individuals with auditory sequential memory processing disorder often experience difficulties remembering or reconstructing the order of items in a list or sounds in a word or syllable (National Center for Learning Disabilities, 2004). Their problems lie in putting together the sequence of events or items presented to them orally.

Examples of this disorder include:

- Confusing multidigit numbers, such as 74 and 47
- Confusing lists and other types of sequences; for example, when given the numbers 3–4–7–9 and asked to repeat them, the student may either not remember the numbers or give them in an incorrect order, such as 7–3–9–4.
- Remembering the correct order of a series of instructions

It should be noted that any medical problems associated with this child's hearing have been ruled out as a primary cause of the child's difficulties. The difficulties are in the internal processing of information, not due to a hearing impairment.

LD 1.10 Auditory Short-Term Memory Processing Disorder

Definition This auditory processing disorder is specifically associated with difficulties in retaining and recalling general and specific short-term auditory information (Rabiner, 1999).

Explanation Short–term memory is the part of the memory system where information is stored for roughly thirty seconds. When you are trying to recall a telephone number that you heard a few seconds earlier, the name of a person who has just been introduced, or the substance of the remarks just made by a teacher in class, you are calling on short-term memory, or working memory (LDOnline, 2005a).

Individuals with this disorder may have difficulties following verbal instructions or recalling information from a story read aloud. Auditory short-term memory difficulties can lead to difficulties retaining or recalling auditory experiences or directions. Some people with this disorder find it hard to recognize auditory stimuli they have heard before; others remember hearing the stimuli but cannot reproduce it accurately.

It should be noted that any medical problems associated with this child's hearing have been ruled out as a primary cause of the child's difficulties. The difficulties are in the internal processing of information, not due to a hearing impairment.

LD 1.11 Auditory Visual Integration Processing Disorder

Definition This auditory processing disorder is specifically associated with difficulties in accurately relating an auditory sound with a visual symbol (Terry, 2001).

Explanation Individuals with this disorder often experience difficulties relating what they hear to the corresponding item that makes the specific sound associated with it.

For example, suppose you were to show a child a picture card with four items on it: a car, a window, a bell, and a horn. Then you play the sound of a bell and ask the child to point to the picture associated with the sound. The child with auditory visual integration processing disorder may have serious problems performing this task or even be unable to do so. He or she has tremendous difficulties relating what he or she hears (the sound of the bell) to the corresponding item that makes the specific sound associated with it (the picture of the bell).

Auditory visual integration difficulties can potentially present difficulties with spelling tests, since students are required to use the correct letters with the corresponding sounds.

It should be noted that any medical problems associated with this child's hearing have been ruled out as a primary cause of the child's difficulties. The difficulties are in the internal processing of information, not due to a hearing impairment.

LD 1.12 Auditory Verbal Reproduction Processing Disorder

Definition An auditory processing disorder specifically associated with difficulties in verbally reproducing orally presented material or experiences.

Explanation A student with this disorder may have serious difficulties orally repeating a series of words, sentences, instructions, or learned information when asked to do so. However, the same student will have no problem reproducing this same information when asked to do so in writing.

For example, if given a series of five numbers, 2–6–7–8–4, and told to write down what he or she hears, the student should have no problems with this task. However, if given the same series of numbers but told to orally repeat back to me what he or she hears, the student will have significant difficulties in performing this task.

Students with this disorder have significant difficulties establishing a connection between what is heard and repeating that information (North Bay Guide for Disability Services, 1998).

It should be noted that any medical problems associated with this child's hearing have been ruled out as a primary cause of the child's difficulties. The difficulties are in the internal processing of information, not due to a hearing impairment.

LD 1.13 Other Types of Auditory Processing Disorders

LD 2.00 Dyscalculia (Arithmetic Disorder)

Definition *Dyscalculia* is a term referring to a wide range of life-long learning disabilities involving math (National Center for Learning Disabilities, 2005b). It affects a person's ability to understand and manipulate numbers, perform mathematical operations, or conceptualize numbers themselves as an abstract concept of comparative quantities.

Diagnostic Symptoms Diagnostic symptoms of dyscalculia include these difficulties (Learning Disabilities Association, 2005; Newman, 1998):

- Organizing problems on the page, keeping numbers lined up, following through on long division problems
- Putting language to math processes
- Understanding and doing word problems
- Keeping score during games or difficulty remembering how to keep score in games like bowling
- Remembering dance step sequences and rules for playing sports.
- Sight-reading music, learning fingering to play an instrument
- Understanding the abstract concepts of time and direction
- Grasping and remembering math concepts, rules, formulas, sequence (order of operations), and basic addition, subtraction, multiplication, and division facts
- Recalling schedules and sequences of past or future events.
- Strategic planning ability for games like chess
- Being on time

- Mentally figuring change due back and the amounts to pay for tips and taxes
- Sense of direction
- Grasping concepts of formal music education
- Understanding money and cash transactions
- Athletic coordination (for example, keeping up with rapidly changing physical directions as in aerobic, dance, and exercise classes)
- Recalling dates or addresses
- Visualizing or picturing the location of the numbers on the face of a clock or the geographical locations of states, countries, oceans, and streets, for example
- Long term-memory (retention and retrieval) of concept mastery; may be able to perform math operations one day, but draw a blank the next
- Memory for the layout of things (for example, gets lost or disoriented easily)

Further Key Points Difficulties in mathematics are often major obstacles in the academic paths of students with learning disabilities, as they frequently continue to cause problems throughout high school. Mastery of fundamental quantitative concepts is vital to learning more abstract and complex mathematics, a requirement of youth with learning disabilities who are seeking to complete high school and attend colleges or universities (Cirino, Morris, & Morris, 2002). Further research on difficulties with mathematics and on effective instruction for students encountering such problems grows more important as young people with learning difficulties seek to achieve more challenging educational goals.

Given these difficulties, it is not surprising that 50 percent of students with learning disabilities have Individualized Education Program goals in math. As with reading and writing, explicit, systematic instruction that provides guided meaningful practice with feedback usually improves the math performance of students with learning disabilities (Fuchs & Fuchs, 2001).

Types of Dyscalculia

LD 2.01 Abstract Concepts Dyscalculia

Definition A type of dyscalculia specifically associated with difficulties in understanding abstract math concepts and higher forms of mathematical concepts. Normally diagnosed in only older students such as high school students.

Explanation Students with abstract concepts dyscalculia have a tendency of reaching a limited ceiling in their ability to comprehend abstract math concepts. As a result, as they enter into and move through high school, they are able to function on only a concrete level of understanding in math.

For example, these students may have great difficulty understanding theorems in geometry, trigonometry formulas, principles of calculus, and other higher forms of mathematics. They may also reach a ceiling in their ability to do math at a lower level than expected for other students.

LD 2.02 Attention-to-Sequence Dyscalculia

Definition A type of dyscalculia associated with difficulties in following the specific and necessary sequence of rules and procedures when performing mathematical tasks or operations.

Explanation Students with attention-to-sequence dyscalculia often omit key steps when performing mathematical operations (Yisrael, 2000). For example, they will add 25 + 16 and get an answer of 31, because they forgot to "carry the 1" after adding the 5 + 6.

Or a student who multiplies 10.5 × 2 gets an answer of 210. The correct answer is 21.0, but the student got an answer of 210 because he or she did not follow the last step in the process, which is to move the decimal point over to the right (as the sequence requires in this operation).

Successful students in math understand that it is essential that they follow a step-by-step sequence of rules and procedures. If any step of the steps is omitted, it will almost assuredly result in an incorrect answer. These types of problems are often evident in students with attention-to-sequence dyscalculia.

LD 2.03 Basic Number Fact Dyscalculia

Definition A type of dyscalculia specifically associated with difficulties in memorizing and retaining basic arithmetic facts (for example, the answers to 8 – 2, 7 + 1, or 12 × 2).

Explanation Individuals with basic number fact dyscalculia may have the ability to remember certain arithmetic facts but have great difficulty memorizing and remembering as many of these facts as other children compared to their age and grade level.

They also appear to forget facts rather easily. For them, they may struggle for years, will count their fingers to add and subtract, and seem unable to develop or have severe difficulties developing efficient memory strategies on their own (Garnett, 1998).

LD 2.04 Developmental Anarithmetria (Incorrect Operation Dyscalculia)

Definition A type of dyscalculia specifically associated with difficulties and confusion in performing the correct arithmetic operations; for example, although addition of numbers was required for a problem, a student subtracted the numbers instead or multiplied two numbers when division was required (Yisrael, 2000).

Explanation Students with developmental anarithmetria use the incorrect operations when performing math problems. For example, the student states that 5 + 2 = 3. Here, the student performed the operation of subtraction instead of addition. Another example is a student who states that 30 × 5 = 6. Again, an incorrect operation is performed (the student divided 30 by 5 instead of multiplying the numbers).

LD 2.05 Estimation Dyscalculia

Definition A type of dyscalculia specifically associated with difficulties in understanding and estimating number size.

Explanation Students with estimation dyscalculia seem to have an impaired sense of number size, which may affect tasks involving estimating numbers in a collection, as well as comparing numbers. For example, When asked to estimate the number of marbles in a jar of twelve, a student says, "about 100." And when looking at a picture of a full football stadium of fifty thousand fans and asked, "How many fans do you think are in this stadium?" the child estimates that there are about three hundred.

LD 2.06 Language Dyscalculia

Definition A type of dyscalculia specifically associated with difficulties in understanding or explaining the vocabulary involved in understanding math.

Explanation According to Garnett (1998), some students with learning disabilities are particularly hampered by the language aspects of math. They are confused about terminology, have difficulty following verbal explanations, or have weak verbal skills for monitoring the steps of complex calculations.

They frequently become confused with the language of math, such as understanding or explaining the meaning of terms such as *square root, logarithm, equilateral, greater than* and *less than, numerator,* and *denominator.*

In general, it is not the math itself that presents the problem but the understanding of the vocabulary and language of math that poses the greatest obstacles towards success.

LD 2.07 Measurement Dyscalculia

Definition A type of dyscalculia specifically associated with difficulties in understanding measurement concepts used in math.

Explanation Students with measurement dyscalculia often experience difficulties in comprehending or applying measurement principles associated with math. These include such concepts as speed (miles per hour), temperature (energy per unit of mass), averages, or proportions.

LD 2.08 Monetary Dyscalculia

Definition A type of dyscalculia specifically associated with monetary concepts such as counting, handling, and budgeting money.

Explanation Individuals with monetary dyscalculia have difficulties with monetary concepts and counting money. Older students may exhibit difficulties with money and credit and cannot do financial planning or budgeting, and they may have trouble balancing a checkbook. They may have a fear of money and cash transactions and may be unable to mentally figure change due back or the amounts to pay for tips and taxes, for example.

LD 2.09 Navigation Dyscalculia

Definition A type of dyscalculia specifically associated with difficulties in going forward and backward with number sequences, for example, counting to one hundred by fives or counting backward from sixty by fours.

Explanation Children with mathematical navigation dyscalculia can usually learn the sequence of counting but experience difficulty navigating back and forth, especially in twos, threes, or more.

For example, when asked to count to fifty by twos, the child becomes easily confused and may be unable to complete the task, or when the child is asked to count backward from thirty by threes, he or she has many pauses or incorrect answers, or is unable to perform the task.

LD 2.10 Number-Word Translation Dyscalculia

Definition A type of dyscalculia specifically associated with difficulties in the translation between numbers and their corresponding words.

Explanation Individuals with number-word translation dyscalculia often experience significant problems in translating number words to numerals or translating numerals to words.

For example, the child may have difficulty writing out in number form "one thousand six hundred twenty-two," and the process in reverse: taking the number 1,622 and writing out the words "one thousand six hundred twenty two."

LD 2.11 Spatial Dyscalculia

Definition A type of dyscalculia specifically associated with difficulties in the visual-spatial-motor organization used in math (Yisrael, 2000).

Explanation Students with spatial dyscalculia often experience deficits in visual-spatial-motor organization. This may result in weak, or no, understanding of concepts, poor number sense, specific difficulty with pictorial representations, or poorly controlled handwriting and confused arrangements of numerals and signs on the page (Garnett, 1998). They might have difficulties aligning numbers in proper columns, organizing the size of their print to fit the page, or drawing specific math shapes in their appropriate form or size.

LD 2.12 Temporal Dyscalculia

Definition A type of dyscalculia specifically associated with difficulties in relating to time, telling time, keeping track of time, and estimating time.

Explanation Individuals with temporal dyscalculia have numerous difficulties understanding basic principles of time. They often:

- Over- or underestimate how long a period of time is; for example, tell them, "Ten more minutes," and they will either be back in two minutes or thirty minutes later
- State the incorrect time due to position on the clock (for example, saying, "It's 3:00," instead of the correct time of 9:00 or saying, "It's 12:00," instead of the correct time of 6:00
- Lose track of time
- Incorrectly estimate the amount of time it will take to complete an assignment, homework, or exam

LD 2.13 Other Types of Dyscalculia (Arithmetic Disorders)

LD 3.00 Dysgraphia (Writing Disorders)

Definition Dysgraphia is a neurological disorder characterized by writing disabilities (Pierangelo & Giuliani, 2006b). This writing disorder causes a person's writing to be distorted or incorrect. In children, the disorder generally emerges when they are introduced to writing. They make inappropriately sized and spaced letters or write wrong or misspelled words despite thorough instruction (National Institute of Neurological Disorders and Strokes, 2006).

Diagnostic Symptoms Diagnostic symptoms of dysgraphia include (International Dyslexia Association, 2005):

- Generally illegible writing (despite appropriate time and attention given the task)
- Inconsistencies: mixtures of print and cursive, upper- and lowercase, or irregular sizes, shapes, or slant of letters
- Unfinished words or letters, omitted words
- Inconsistent position on the page with respect to lines and margins
- Inconsistent spaces between words and letters

- Cramped or unusual grip, especially holding the writing instrument very close to the paper or holding the thumb over two fingers and writing from the wrist
- Unusual wrist, body, or paper position
- Talking to self while writing or carefully watching the hand that is writing
- Slow or labored copying or writing, even if the writing is neat and legible
- Content that does not reflect the student's other language skills
- Combination of fine motor difficulty, inability to revisualize letters, and inability to remember the motor patterns

Further Key Points Students' handwriting problems can arise from their lack of fine motor coordination, failure to attend to task, inability to perceive or remember visual images accurately, or inadequate handwriting instruction in the classroom (Friend & Bursuck, 2002).

Many students struggle to produce neat, expressive written work, whether or not they have accompanying physical or cognitive difficulties. They may learn much less from an assignment because they must focus on writing mechanics instead of content. After spending more time on an assignment than their peers, these students understand the material less. Not surprisingly, their belief in their ability to learn suffers. When the writing task is the primary barrier to learning or demonstrating knowledge, accommodations, modifications, and remediation for these problems may be in order (Jones, n.d.; LDOnline, 2005b).

Types of Dysgraphia

LD 3.01 Dyslexic Dysgraphia

Definition A type of dysgraphia specifically associated with difficulties in producing spontaneously written text or spelling; however, drawing or copying or finger-tapping speed (a measure of fine-motor speed) are within the normal range for age and grade levels (International Dyslexia Association, 2006).

Explanation Students with dyslexic dysgraphia often exhibit spontaneously written text (writing a story on request rather than copying something) that is illegible, especially when the text is complex, such as an essay or a book report (Kay, 2005). The student may also have great difficulties spelling.

It should be noted that any medical problems associated with this child's physical abilities to write have been ruled out as a primary cause of the child's difficulties. The difficulties are in the internal processing of information, not due to a physical impairment (International Dyslexia Association, 2006).

LD 3.02 Motor Dysgraphia

Definition A type of dysgraphia specifically associated with difficulties in producing spontaneously written and copied text, drawing, and finger-tapping speed; however, oral spelling is within the normal range when compared to age and grade levels (International Dyslexia Association, 2006).

Explanation Individuals with motor dysgraphia (also referred to as dysgraphia due to motor clumsiness) exhibit spontaneously written and copied text (for example, writing a short story, a book report, copying notes off the board, a written spelling test) that may be illegible. Their drawing and finger-tapping speed are usually problematic as well (Kay, 2005).

It should be noted that any medical problems associated with the child's physical abilities to write have been ruled out as a primary cause of the child's difficulties. The difficulties are in the internal processing of information, not due to a physical impairment (International Dyslexia Association, 2006).

LD 3.03 Spatial Dysgraphia

Definition A type of dysgraphia specifically associated with difficulties in writing and drawing or copying; however, oral spelling and finger-tapping speed are within the normal ranges when compared to age and grade levels (International Dyslexia Association, 2000).

Explanation Individuals with spatial dysgraphia (also referred to as dysgraphia due to a defect in understanding of space) often display illegible writing, whether spontaneously produced or prepared. Drawing or copying designs and other figures are problematic. However, their oral spelling and finger-tapping speed are normal (Kay, 2005).

It should be noted that any medical problems associated with the child's physical abilities to write have been ruled out as a primary cause of the child's difficulties. The difficulties are in the internal processing of information, not due to a physical impairment (International Dyslexia Association, 2006).

LD 3.04 Other Types of Dysgraphia (Writing Disorders)

LD 4.00 Dyslexia (Reading Disorders)

Definition Dyslexia is the learning disability associated with reading (Pierangelo and Giuliani, 2006b). According to the National Center for Learning Disabilities (2005a), "Dyslexia is a specific learning disability that is neurological in origin. It is characterized by difficulties with accurate and/or fluent word recognition and by poor spelling and decoding abilities. These difficulties typically result from a deficit in the phonological component of language that is often unexpected in relation to other cognitive abilities and the provision of effective classroom instruction. Secondary consequences may include problems in reading comprehension and reduced reading experience that can impede growth of vocabulary and background knowledge."

Diagnostic Symptoms According to the International Dyslexia Association (2005), diagnostic symptoms of dyslexia vary based on age and grade level of the child. Listed below are the diagnostic symptoms of dyslexia for preschoolers to adults (Pierangelo & Giuliani, 2006b; International Dyslexia Association, 2005; Spafford & Grosser, 2005; Hallahan & Kauffman, 2006; Lerner, 2005):

- May have trouble learning the alphabet, rhyming words, or connecting letters to their sounds
- May make many mistakes when reading aloud and repeat and pause often
- May not understand what he or she reads
- May have excess trouble with spelling
- May learn language late and have a limited vocabulary
- May have trouble remembering the sounds that letters make or hearing slight differences between words
- May have trouble understanding jokes, comic strips, and sarcasm
- May have trouble following directions
- May mispronounce words or use a wrong word that sounds similar
- May have trouble organizing what he or she wants to say or not be able to think of the word needed for writing or conversation
- May not follow the social rules of conversation, such as taking turns, and may stand too close to the listener
- May confuse math symbols and misread numbers
- May not be able to retell a story in order (what happened first, second, third)
- May not know where to begin a task or how to go on from there

Further Key Points Dyslexia is a brain-based type of learning disability that specifically impairs a person's ability to read (Pierangelo & Giuliani, 2006b). These individuals typically read at levels significantly lower than expected despite having normal intelligence. Although the disorder varies from person to person, common characteristics among people with dyslexia are difficulties with phonological processing (the manipulation of sounds) and rapid visual-verbal responding (National Institute of Neurological Disorders and Strokes, 2005a).

Types of Dyslexia

LD 4.01 Auditory-Linguistic Dyslexia

Definition A type of dyslexia specifically associated with difficulties in the ability to sound out words that the reader does not know. It is characterized by an inability to distinguish phonemic (or smallest) units of speech and a subsequent inability to learn the relationships between the visual appearances and sounds of letters and words (Learning Disabilities Association of Canada, 1996).

Explanation Individuals with auditory linguistic dyslexia often attempt to learn to read by pure memorization without trying to sound out words. They rarely consider the length of words or the number of syllables in them, often confusing small words that could be easily read by someone his or her own age.

They often have unusual spelling and misreading errors that are not phonetic (Yisrael, 2000). Examples may include reading the word *bell* as *beautiful* or the word *girl* as *gulil.*

It should be noted that any medical problems associated with the child's vision have been ruled out as a primary cause of the child's difficulties. The difficulties are in the internal processing of information, not due to a visual impairment.

LD 4.02 Direct Dyslexia

Definition A type of dyslexia specifically associated with difficulties in reading comprehension (Stevenson, 2002). The deficits lie not in the decoding of words but rather in the comprehension of the material being read.

Explanation Direct dyslexia can be thought of as the learning disability associated with reading comprehension. The student has limited or no difficulty reading words (decoding) but has many problems with the comprehension of what was read (comprehension).

A student with direct dyslexia may be able to read every word of the sentence, "The man wore a blue scarf," but when asked "What did the man wear?" is unable to respond correctly because he or she did not understand what he or she had just read (Carlson, 1998).

It should be noted that any medical problems associated with the child's vision have been ruled out as a primary cause of the child's difficulties. The difficulties are in the internal processing of information, not due to a visual impairment.

LD 4.03 Dysnomia

Definition A type of dyslexia specifically associated with difficulties in remembering names or recalling words needed for oral or written language. It is the inability to retrieve the correct word from memory when it is needed.

Explanation Dysnomia is the learning disability associated with "the tip-of-the-tongue" experience. However, those with dysnomia have this experience frequently every day. The person usually has severe difficulty in recalling words or names needed for oral or written language (Nalanda Institute, 2005).

Nominal recall problems are a frequent problem for students with learning disabilities. They have difficulties summoning up naming words. Nominal recall problems are memory problems that cause specific difficulties with nouns. Nominal recall inefficiency often coexists with auditory memory problems. It is often seen where auditory memory and visual memory problems exist too. It is less often seen where visual memory problems exist by themselves (Apodixis Press, 2005). This problem may be particularly prominent if the person is asked to answer a question immediately. However, when the person speaks spontaneously, without prompting, his or her speech appears perfectly normal (Nalanda Institute, 2005).

It should be noted that any medical problems associated with the child's vision have been ruled out as a primary cause of the child's difficulties. The difficulties are in the internal processing of information, not due to a visual impairment.

LD 4.04 Dyseidetic Dyslexia (Visual Dyslexia, Dyseidesia or Surface Dyslexia)

Definition A type of dyslexia specifically associated with difficulties in identifying patterns of letters when grouped together (Dyslexia Institutes of America, 2006; Spafford & Grosser, 2005). It is a deficit in the ability to perceive whole words as visual forms and to make the connection with auditory forms; for example, the student reads *ball* for *bell*, writes *enuf* for *enough*, or spells *bisnis* for *business*.

Explanation Students with the dyseidetic dyslexia are often able to sound out individual letters phonetically with limited or no difficulties. However, they have trouble identifying patterns of letters when they are grouped together. As a result, their spelling tends to be phonetic even when it is incorrect (*laf* for *laugh*).

These students often have problems with memory of letters and word shapes. As such, development of sight vocabulary is often problematic. Other signs and symptoms of dyseidetic dyslexia include these:

- Difficulties in visualizing letters and words; produces spelling errors in simple, frequently encountered words
- Confusion with letters that differ in terms of spatial orientation, including shape (for example, *b d p q s z*)
- Reversal of words (for example, *saw* for *was*)
- When sounding out simple words, an inability to perceive the gestalt configurations of whole words
- Sounding out every word as if newly encountered and thus an inability to recognize words quickly when flashed

- Limited sight word recognition vocabulary; omits letters from words, omits words from reading, and frequently loses his or her place when reading
- A tendency to spell phonetically but inaccurately
- Difficulties in spelling irregular words that cannot be sounded out because of difficulty with the perception and recall of word shapes (Beacon Literacy, 2005)

It should be noted that any medical problems associated with the child's vision have been ruled out as a primary cause of the child's difficulties. The difficulties are in the internal processing of information, not due to a visual impairment.

LD 4.05 Dysnemkinesia Dyslexia

Definition A type of dyslexia specifically associated with symbol orientation. Individuals with dysnemkinesia dyslexia tend to be distinguished by their abnormally high frequency of letter reversals (for example, *d* for *b,* as in *doy* for *boy* or *w* for *m,* as in *wet* for *met*). It is the dysfunction most people think about when they hear the word *dyslexia* (McMains, 2002).

Explanation Individuals with dysnemkinesia dyslexia often have serious difficulties with symbol orientation. For example, *p, b, q,* and *d* are all the same symbol oriented in different ways. These students will not see the symbol as being different letters when oriented differently and subsequently confuse them. They tend to transpose letters and syllables, exhibit faulty eye movements, demonstrate excessive reversals, and have spatial difficulties.

This is a dysfunction that involves memory and motor movement and is a developmental issue. It is thought to occur due to poor development of the visual spatial skills known as laterality and directionality (McMains, 2002).

Individuals with dysnemkinesia dyslexia often have poor sight recognition and tend to have trouble building a sight vocabulary. Reading tends to be slow and difficult for them, since they often read and spell phonetically (McMains, 2002).

It should be noted that no medical problems associated with the child's vision are an issue. The difficulties are in the processing of information, not due to a visual impairment.

LD 4.06 Alexic Dyslexia (Mixed Dyseidetic, Dysphonetic Dyslexia)

Definition A type of dyslexia specifically associated with both dyseidetic dyslexia and dysphonic dyslexia. It is an impairment in the ability to correctly associate the sound of a given letter or letter combination within a word as a whole and to pronounce it correctly. It is the most common form but may favor one type of dyslexia over the other (Dyslexia Centers of Tennessee, 2006).

Explanation Children with alexic dyslexia have both the dyseidetic and dysphonic types of reading disorders. Alexic dyslexia combines the deficit of both groups.

The mixed dyseidetic and dysphonetic reader and speller:

- Has deficits in both the visual and auditory systems
- Spells nonphonetically, and responses are often unrelated to any known words
- Fails to perceive words as visual wholes and is unable to sound them out
- May have disabilities in sight vocabulary, phonetic skills, reading, and spelling (Beacon Literacy, 2005)

It should be noted that no medical problems associated with the child's vision are an issue. The difficulties are in the processing of information, not due to a visual impairment.

LD 4.07 Dysphonetic Dyslexia (Dysphonesia or Auditory Dyslexia)

Definition A type of dyslexia specifically associated with difficulties in linking the auditory equivalent of a word to the visual component. It is the learning disability in relating symbols with sounds (Davis International Dyslexia Association, 2005).

Explanation Individuals with dysphonetic dyslexia have difficulties linking the auditory equivalent of a word to its visual component (Johnson & Myklebust, 1967). It involves difficulty with sounds of letters or groups of letters. The sounds are perceived as jumbled or not heard correctly.

Dysphonetic dyslexia is characterized by problems with integrating and processing what is heard. Individuals with this problem also have difficulties with recalling sounds and being able to put a sound with the letter it represents. The person labeled "dysphonetic" has difficulty connecting sounds to symbols and might have a hard time sounding out words. This is also sometimes called auditory dyslexia because it relates to the way the person processes the sounds of language (Davis International Dyslexia Association, 2005).

A student with dysphonetic dyslexia often:

- Fixates on the visual or orthographic configurations of words rather than the sounds and parts (word shape)
- Performs phonetic analysis that is slow and laborious, reading syllable by syllable
- Has difficulty in discriminating individual sounds within complex words
- Has difficulty in analyzing the sequence of sounds within words
- Has difficulty in blending sounds even when these are provided orally
- Has difficulty in discriminating and matching rhyming sounds
- Spells nonphonetically using visual memory (Wiertelak, 2003)
- Guesses at unknown words (usually from initial letter sound) rather than use phonetic rule (Beacon Literacy, 2005)

Dysphonetic readers have severe difficulties relating letters to sounds. As a result, their spelling abilities tend to be well below the normal limits of age and grade levels. These students are able to recognize words they have memorized but cannot sound out new ones to figure out what they are.

It should be noted that no medical problems associated with the child's vision are an issue. The difficulties are in the processing of information, not due to a visual impairment.

LD 4.08 Neglect Dyslexia

Definition A type of dyslexia specifically associated with problems in the completion of words, such that letters in a particular position in a word or nonword are neglected when they are read (Coltheart, 1998; Sharma, 1996).

Explanation Students with neglect dyslexia neglect either the left or the right side of words, a problem highlighted in reading long words. For example, if asked to read *trout,* the student may read it as *out*, omitting the *tr* of the word. Given the word *slacks* to read, students with neglect dyslexia will miss some of the first few letters. For example, they may read it simply as *acks*, omitting the *sl* in the word. There may also be a problem with compound words. For example, a compound word such as *cowboy* may be read partially as *cow* or *boy* (Sharma, 1996) or *rainbow* may be read as *bow*.

It should be noted that no medical problems associated with the child's vision are an issue. The difficulties are in the processing of information, not due to a visual impairment.

LD 4.09 Phonological Dyslexia

Definition A type of dyslexia specifically associated with difficulties in converting letters to their sounds. Individuals are often able to read words that are already familiar to them but have great difficulty reading unfamiliar or novel words (Sharma, 1996). The greatest percentage of individuals with dyslexia show poor word identification due to an impairment in print-to-sound conversion (Phonological Dyslexia). These individuals have deficits in decoding written words using phonic or sound principles.

Explanation Phonological dyslexia occurs when an individual has difficulty in converting letters to their sounds (Pierangelo & Giuliani, 2006b; Coltheart, 1998). Students diagnosed with this form of dyslexia can read words that are already familiar to them but have trouble reading unfamiliar or new words. They also struggle in reading a nonword such as *slad.* They may misread this nonword as a real word that looks similar (for example, reading *slid* instead of the actual nonword, *slad*). Sometimes these students misread actual words as other ones that also look similar (for example, reading *bat* instead of reading it as the correct word *but*. (The word *shut* may pose this particular problem, much to a listener's dismay.)

It should be noted that no medical problems associated with the child's vision are an issue. The difficulties are in the processing of information, not due to a visual impairment.

LD 4.10 Other Types of Dyslexia (Reading Disorders)

LD 5.00 Dysorthographia (Spelling Disorders)

Definition Dysorthographia is the learning disability associated with spelling (Pierangelo and Giuliani, 2006b; Akron Children's Hospital, 2003): the ability to use letters to construct words in accordance with accepted use. Spelling ability is viewed by some teachers and school administrators equally with other academic skills. Being a poor speller does not necessarily mean that a child has a learning disability. However, when poor spelling occurs with poor reading or arithmetic, there may be reason for concern (Pierangelo & Giuliani, 2006b).

Diagnostic Symptoms Diagnostic symptoms of dysorthographia include (Hallahan & Kauffman, 2006; Turnbull et al., 2004):

- Addition of unneeded letters
- Omission of needed letters
- Reversals of vowels
- Reversals of syllables
- Phonemic spelling of nonphonemic words
- Difficulty in understanding the correspondence between sounds and letters

Further Key Points Spelling problems, like reading problems, originate with language learning weaknesses. Spelling disability does not reflect a general visual memory problem but a more specific problem with awareness of and memory for language structure, including the letters in words (International Dyslexia Association, 2005).

LD 6.00 Gerstmann Syndrome

Definition Gerstmann syndrome is a neurological disorder characterized by four primary symptoms: a writing disability (dysgraphia), a lack of understanding of the rules for calculation or arithmetic (dyscalculia), an inability to distinguish right from left, and an inability to identify fingers (sometimes referred to as finger agnosia) (National Institute of Neurological Disorders and Stroke, 2005b).

Diagnostic Symptoms The diagnostic symptoms of Gerstmann syndrome include (National Institute of Neurological Disorders and Stroke, 2005b):

- Poor handwriting and spelling skills
- Difficulty with math functions, including adding, subtracting, multiplying, and dividing
- An inability to differentiate right from left and to discriminate among individual fingers

In addition, many children suffer from constructional apraxia, an inability to copy simple drawings, and frequently there is impairment in reading.

Further Key Points There are few reports of Gerstmann syndrome in children. The cause is not known. Most cases are identified when children begin school and are challenged with writing and math exercises(National Institute of Neurological Disorders and Stroke, 2005).

LD 7.00 Gifted with Learning Disabilities

Definition Students who are gifted and also have learning disabilities are those who possess an outstanding gift or talent and are capable of high performance, but also have a learning disability that makes some aspect of academic achievement difficult (Brody & Mills, 1997).

Diagnostic Symptoms According to Beckey (2006), there are at least three subgroups of twice-exceptional students whose dual exceptionality remains unacknowledged. The first of these groups comprises students who have been identified as gifted yet are exhibiting difficulties in school and are often considered underachievers. Many of these students are working at grade level and are likely to be overlooked by the screening procedures that are necessary to identify subtle learning disabilities. Their underachievement is often attributed to poor self-concept, lack of motivation, or laziness. It is often not until school becomes more rigorous that their academic difficulties may increase to the point that they fall considerably behind peers. Only then does someone consider that a student has a disability.

In the second group are students who have been identified as having learning disabilities but whose exceptional abilities have never been recognized or addressed. Inadequate assessments or depressed IQ scores often lead to an underestimation of their intellectual abilities. If students' exceptional aptitudes remain unrecognized, their strengths never become the focus of their instructional program. These students are first noticed for what they cannot do instead of the talent that they are demonstrating.

The last and perhaps largest group of unserved students are those who are in general classrooms and are considered unqualified for services provided for students who are gifted or have learning disabilities. The students may appear to possess average abilities due to the fact that their abilities and disabilities mask each other. They typically perform at grade level but are also performing well below their potential (Baum, 1990; Brody & Mills, 1997).

Further Key Points Because these students may be on grade level and are considered gifted, they are likely to be overlooked for screening procedures necessary to identify a subtle learning disability. Identification of a subtle disability would help them understand why they are experiencing academic difficulties. More important, professionals could offer learning strategies and compensation techniques to help them deal with their duality of learning behaviors.

LD 8.00 Nonverbal Learning Disabilities (Nonverbal Learning Disorders)

Definition Nonverbal learning disorder (NLD) is a neurophysiological disorder originating in the right hemisphere of the brain. Reception of nonverbal or performance-based information governed by this hemisphere is impaired in varying degrees, including problems with visual-spatial, intuitive, organizational, evaluative, and holistic processing functions (Nonverbal Learning Disorders Association, 2004).

Diagnostic Symptoms Diagnostic symptoms for nonverbal learning disabilities include:

- Deficits in the areas of nonverbal problem solving, concept formation, and hypothesis testing
- Difficulty dealing with negative feedback in novel or complex situations
- Difficulty in dealing with cause-and-effect relationships
- Difficulty in the appreciation of incongruities
- Well-developed rote verbal capacities and rote verbal memory skills
- Overreliance on prosaic rote and, consequently, inappropriate behaviors in unfamiliar situations
- Relative deficiencies in mechanical arithmetic as compared to proficiencies in reading (word recognition) and spelling
- Rote and repetitive verbosity
- Content disorders of language
- Reliance on language for social relating, information gathering, and relief from anxiety
- Misspelling almost exclusively of the phonetically accurate variety
- Significant deficits in social perception, social judgment, and social interaction skills

- Marked tendency for social withdrawal and isolation as age increases
- High risk for social-emotional disturbance if no appropriate intervention is undertaken
- Sensory integration difficulty (Nonverbal Learning Disorders Association, 2004)

Further Key Points The interpersonal and social aspects of NLD have great significance for a student's life. The individual who does not attend to or accurately interpret the nonverbal communication of others cannot receive a clear message. Our concept of self is shaped in large measure by the reflection of how others view us. The person who has NLD may not receive feedback from others and may suffer from a less clear concept of self. The diminished ability to engage with others greatly limits the possibility of defining self based on such feedback.

Because of their verbal strengths, many individuals with NLD succeed in formal educational situations. However, if their social competence has not developed commensurately, they may not find and keep employment at the level for which their education has prepared them. On a positive note, individuals with NLD make considerable progress in areas of weakness when instruction is appropriate. Accurate diagnosis and appropriate instruction can have great benefit for their lives (Foss, 2001). Finally, according to the Nonverbal Learning Disabilities Association, anxiety disorders may also develop as a result of NLD due to the difficulty that students often have processing their surroundings. Since processing speed is generally slow in students with NLD, the environment can play a critical role, as smaller is better since there is less to process.

Types of Nonverbal Learning Disabilities

Although there are no specific types of nonverbal learning disabilities noted in the research, students with nonverbal learning disabilities will experience specific deficits. Some may be more predominant than others. For EDM, we categorize nonverbal learning disabilities according to the three major types of deficits noted by the Nonverbal Learning Disorders Association that are predominantly observed in students. They are motor deficits, social deficits, and visual-spatial-organizational deficits. For the purposes of coding, these will be represented by LD 8.01, 8.02, and 8.03, respectively. Therefore, a student can have a nonverbal learning disability with one or more types of deficits.

LD 8.01 Nonverbal Learning Disability-Motoric Deficits

Definition A type of nonverbal learning disability specifically associated with difficulties in psychomotor coordination—or example, coordination, balance, or fine motor writing skills (Nonverbal Learning Disorders Association, 2005).

Explanation Students with nonverbal learning disabilities-motoric deficits often exhibit three primary symptoms: lack of coordination, weak trunk muscles, hypotonia, balance problems, and difficulties with graphomotor/fine motor skills (Nonverbal Learning Disorders Association, 2005). These symptoms lead to other everyday struggles for these children, as they often:

- Spill things at mealtime because of problems with motor coordination
- Have trouble dressing themselves
- Struggle with puzzles and other tasks involving spatial relations
- Have difficulty tying their shoes
- Have difficulty riding a bicycle (some)
- Have trouble catching a ball
- Write slowly, with handwriting that may be illegible (Wagner, 2003; Nonverbal Learning Disorders Association, 2001)

An important point to recognize is that there may be a recognizable difference between the dominant and nondominant sides of the body, with more noticeable problems on the left side of the body (Thompson, 1997).

It should be noted that any medical problems associated with the child's physical and motoric abilities have been ruled out as a primary cause of the child's difficulties. The difficulties are in the internal processing of information, not due to a physical or motoric impairment (International Dyslexia Association, 2006).

LD 8.02 Nonverbal Learning Disability-Social Deficits

Definition A type of nonverbal learning disability specifically associated with difficulties in perceiving and interpreting social cues or social situations. The primary deficits are in social judgment and social interaction (Nonverbal Learning Disorders Association, 2001).

Explanation Students with nonverbal learning disabilities-social deficits often have trouble understanding nonverbal communication such as facial expression, body language, and tone of voice. They may not correctly interpret shrugs, winks, grins, or wrinkled foreheads. They may have trouble adjusting to transitions and novel situations or difficulty gauging appropriate personal space. Their deficits in social judgment and social interaction may cause them to seem immature. Other people may consider them annoying (Nonverbal Learning Disorders Association, 2001).

One result of having trouble processing nonverbal and spatial information is missing or misinterpreting subtle social cues like facial expressions, gestures, and tones of voice. For example, a phrase like, "Nice going," means something different to a child who has just dropped a ball or tripped over a skipping rope (again) than to one who has gotten a perfect score on a spelling test.

Unlike students who have difficulties reading but do well with social and sports activities, students with nonverbal LD are affected in all areas. Their form of learning disability can lead to social isolation. Consequently, these children sometimes try to alleviate this by interacting only with adults, who are normally more appreciative of their verbal strengths and less concerned about physical awkwardness or violations of social conventions (Wagner, 2003).

It should be noted that any medical problems associated with the child's physical and motoric abilities have been ruled out as a primary cause of the child's difficulties. The difficulties are in the internal processing of information, not due to a physical or motoric impairment (International Dyslexia Association, 2006).

LD 8.03 Nonverbal Learning Disability—Visual-Spatial-Organizational Deficits

Definition A type of nonverbal learning disability specifically associated with difficulties in visual perception and visual imagery (Nonverbal Learning Disorders Association 2005).

Explanation Students with nonverbal learning disabilities (visual-spatial-organizational deficits) normally have poor visual recall or difficulties with spatial relations. They may get lost easily, have difficulty finding things that are in plain sight, and may not be able to tell left from right (Nonverbal Learning Disorders Association, 2001). They function best in an uncluttered visual space. They do not have the social ability to comprehend nonverbal situations (e.g., "read the room"). They have difficulty with the "theory of mind."

Spatial and coordination problems make printing and writing, learning math, telling time, reading and coloring maps, and keeping their place on the page difficult from early grades (Wagner, 2003). By high school, more complex verbal language is based on nonverbal processes like spatial relationships (in science, for example), logical ordering, and sequencing (both skills necessary for writing essays).

Students with this disability have difficulty forming visual images and therefore cannot revisualize something they have seen previously. They tend to focus on the details of what is seen, often failing to grasp the total picture (Thompson, 1997).

It should be noted that any medical problems associated with the child's physical and motoric abilities have been ruled out as a primary cause of the child's difficulties. The difficulties are in the internal processing of information, not due to a physical or motoric impairment (International Dyslexia Association, 2006).

LD 8.04 Other Types of Nonverbal Learning Disabilities

LD 9.00 Organizational Learning Disorders

Definition An organizational learning disorder is a type of learning disability specifically associated with difficulty in organization. Children with this disorder may require constant support in organizing, arranging, setting priorities, and establishing time management when it comes to school tasks.

Diagnostic Symptoms The diagnostic symptoms of an organizational disorder include difficulties in these areas:

- Temporal-sequential disorganization
- Allocating and estimating time
- Following schedules
- Meeting deadlines
- Solving problems in stages
- Material-spatial organization
- Keeping track of possessions
- Maintaining notebooks
- Arranging desks
- Finding objects like pencils and books
- Settling down and functioning effectively when expectations or settings change
- Remembering what they are required to do (Levine, 1995)

Further Key Points Developing good organizational skills is a key ingredient for success in school and in life. Although some people by nature are more organized than others, anyone can put routines and systems in place to help a child become more organized (LDOnline, 2005b). Chronic disorganization is a handicap that often goes unnamed in schools throughout entire school years. Yet it accompanies other learning disabilities in slightly more than half of the cases surveyed. For most children with chronic disorganization, the causes are neurological. Furthermore, children with chronic disorganization may require daily coaching because less frequent help is not effective (Schwarzbeck, 2006).

Types of Organizational Disorders

LD 9.01 Catastrophic Response Organizational Disorder

Definition A type of organizational disorder specifically associated with difficulties in handling too many stimuli or too much information at one time (Learning Disabilities Association, 2005).

Explanation Individuals with catastrophic response organizational disorder may exhibit an involuntary and overwhelmed reaction to too many sights, sounds, or extreme emotions. They may become dazed or unaware of their surroundings, even freezing for a short time. For example, a student with this disorder may freeze up or be unable to think clearly when presented with a page of twenty math problems. In general, the student is overwhelmed by too much stimuli (Peniston, 1998).

LD 9.02 Cognitive Disorganization Disorder (Internal Disorder)

Definition A type of organizational disorder specifically associated with difficulties in thinking in an orderly, logical way, often leading to incomplete thoughts and statements (Learning Disabilities Association of Ontario, 2005).

Explanation Students with cognitive disorganization disorder struggle with organizing their thoughts and feelings. They frequently exhibit many of the following symptoms:

- Difficulty thinking of words (but for the most part can communicate normally)
- Slow mental process
- Failures in thinking and speech that can be corrected easily
- Loss of train of thought
- Forgetting what they are thinking or talking about
- Leaving statements incomplete
- Sudden unexplained shifts in trend of thought or speech that they can correct with effort if asked
- Thoughts or statements that become incoherent and difficulties clarifying them
- Difficulty thinking in an orderly, logical way
- Jumping to conclusions and difficulty planning tasks
- Missing or forgetting steps in a sequence (Peniston, 1998)

LD 9.03 Directionality Organizational Disorder

Definition A type of organizational disorder specifically associated with difficulties in directionality, for example, distinguishing left from right; learning north, south, east, west; or learning the layout of a large, symmetrical building (Learning Disabilities Association of Ontario, 2005).

Explanation Students with directionality organizational disorder have great difficulty orienting themselves in the right direction. They frequently get lost, roam as if they lack direction or purpose, and seem confused and unable to maneuver around the school or community without getting lost.

These problems become quite apparent during physical education or locating a new classroom at the beginning of the school year. In physical education, this individual has significant problems copying the movements of the teacher, as well as difficulties mirroring responses. Going in the correct direction may require many practice runs before exhibiting adequate skills (Peniston, 1998).

LD 9.04 External Disorganization Disorder

Definition A type of organizational disorder specifically associated with difficulties in being neat, structured, and organized in school, home, and other environments where organization of materials is essential for everyday functioning.

Explanation Students with external disorganization disorder are outwardly disorganized. Almost everything that they work on or have to do appears to lack structure, is messy, and borders on completely unorganized. These children exhibit many of the following symptoms:

- Desks that are always cluttered and disorganized
- Notebooks and loose-leaf binders with papers falling out
- Ripped pages
- Limited or no awareness of order or neatness
- Absentmindedness
- Apparent inability to incorporate suggestions dealing with organizational skills
- Difficulty organizing their room, clothing, and homework assignments
- Frequent forgetfulness
- Misplacing things
- Confusion with the reactions of frustration on the part of those around them

LD 9.05 Temporal Disorganization Disorder

Definition A type of organizational disorder specifically associated with difficulties in time management and the organization of time for the completion of assignments (Learning Disabilities Association of Ontario, 2005).

Explanation Spatial-temporal processing deficits result in disorganization that is apparent in a lack of ability to organize oneself to accomplish a task. The more steps required to accomplish a task, the more apparent the disorganization will be. In school, this can frequently lead to assignments not being completed on time. This deficit is often interpreted as a lack of motivation, inefficiency, or lack of initiative, when in reality it is due to an inability to organize one's time and firmly grasp time management principles (Learning Disabilities Association of Ontario, 2005).

Students with temporal disorganization disorder exhibit many of the following symptoms:

- Confusion about sequences and time
- Are often late for events they need to attend
- Have difficulty remembering when an assignment is due
- Do not know how much time to allow themselves to complete an assignment or job

- Appear never to be quite sure what to do first, what to do second, and what to do third when they write a report or work on a project
- Lack appropriate time management skills

LD 9.06 Other Types of Organizational Disorders

LD 10.00 Sensory Integration Disorders

Definition Although sensory disorders can be present in any child, studies indicate that approximately 70 percent of children with learning disabilities have sensory issues (Childhood Anxiety Network, 2005). Sensory integration disorder or dysfunction (SID) is a neurological disorder that results from the brain's inability to integrate certain information received from the body's five basic sensory systems, which are responsible for detecting sights, sounds, smell, tastes, temperatures, pain, and the position and movements of the body. The brain then forms a combined picture of this information in order for the body to make sense of its surroundings and react to them appropriately (Kapes, 2002).

Diagnostic Symptoms Children with sensory integration disorders may exhibit the following behaviors (Childhood Anxiety Network, 2005):

- Overly sensitive or undersensitive to sound (for example, the child may cover his or her ears and pull away from most noises or crave a lot of multiple sound stimuli)
- Overly sensitive or undersensitive to lights (for example, the child covers his or her eyes and may not be able to tolerate bright or flashing lights)
- Underreactive to sensory stimulation (for example, the child craves spinning, jumping, moving constantly or has difficulty with most movement)
- Unusually high or low activity level; may seem hyperactive or hypoactive
- Coordination problems; may seem clumsy or careless
- Delays in speech, language, and motor skills
- Below-par academic performance
- Poor organization of behavior (for example, impulsive, distractible, frustrated, aggressive)
- May seem lazy, bored, or unmotivated
- Difficulty making transitions; difficulty with routine changes and difficulties with season changes (for example, going from wearing shorts to wearing long pants and vice versa)
- Social or emotional problems (for example, acts out, has frequent temper tantrums)

- Easily distracted
- Physical clumsiness or apparent carelessness
- Inability to unwind or calm self
- Poor self-concept

Further Key Points The ongoing relationship between behavior and brain functioning is called sensory integration (SI), a theory that was pioneered by A. Jean Ayres in the 1960s (Kapes, 2002).

While research indicates that sensory integrative problems are found in up to 70 percent of children who are considered learning disabled by schools, the problems of sensory integration are not confined to children with learning disabilities. SID transfers through all age groups, intellectual levels, and socioeconomic groups. Factors that contribute to SID include premature birth; autism and other developmental disorders; learning disabilities; delinquency and substance abuse due to learning disabilities; stress-related disorders; and brain injury. Two of the biggest contributing conditions are autism and attention deficit–hyperactivity disorder (Kapes, 2002).

Types of Sensory Integration Disorders

LD 10.01 Tactile Defensiveness Sensory Integration Disorder (Immature Tactile Type)

Definition A type of sensory integration disorder specifically associated with difficulties in being touched because of an immature tactile system (Sensory processing disorder.com). Tactile defensiveness refers to a pattern of observable behavioral and emotional responses, which are aversive, negative, and out of proportion to certain types of tactile stimuli that most people would find to be nonpainful (Chu, 2000).

Explanation The tactile system is the sense of touch through different sensory receptors in the skin. We say that a child is tactile defensive when he or she is extremely sensitive to light touch.

One important role of the tactile system is its protective function that alerts us when something is unpleasant or dangerous. For some children, this function of the tactile system is not working normally. They may perceive most touch sensations to be uncomfortable or scary and react with a fight-or-flight response (Chu, 2000).

Theoretically, when the tactile system is immature and working improperly, abnormal neural signals are sent to the cortex in the brain and can interfere with other brain processes. This causes the brain to be overly stimulated and may lead to excessive brain activity, which can be neither turned off nor organized. This type of overstimulation in the brain can make it difficult for an individual to organize his or her behavior and concentrate and may lead to a negative emotional response to touch sensations (Hatch-Rasmussen, 2001).

Often children with tactile defensiveness avoid touching textured materials or items, "messy" things, or vibrating toys (Sensory processing disorder.com). They may also be significantly bothered by and avoid the following:

- A hug
- A kiss
- Certain clothing textures
- Seams on socks
- Tags on shirts
- Light touch
- Their hands being dirty

LD 10.02 Proprioceptive Perceptual Sensory Integration Disorder

Definition A type of sensory integration disorder specifically associated with difficulties knowing where one is in space. It is the sense of the position of our body parts in relation to our own bodies (Learning Disabilities Association, 2005; Hatch-Rasmussen, 2001).

Explanation The proprioceptive sense is the sense of the position of our body parts in relation to our own bodies. This information is essential to coordinate and integrate movement because it allows us to know where we are in space. According to Hatch-Rasmussen (2001), the proprioceptive sense is responsible for providing the body with the necessary signals to allow us to sit properly in a chair or step off a curb smoothly. Some common signs of proprioceptive dysfunction are:

- A lack of awareness of body position in space
- A tendency to fall
- Clumsiness
- Difficulty manipulating small objects
- Eating in a sloppy manner
- Minimal crawling when young
- Odd body posturing
- Resistance to new motor movement activities (Hatch-Rasmussen, 2001)

LD 10.03 Tactile Pressure Sensory Integration Disorder

Definition A type of sensory integration disorder specifically associated with difficulties in judging the appropriate amount of pressure needed to perform motor acts (Learning Disabilities Association, 2005).

Explanation Children with tactile pressure sensory integration disorder have trouble judging the right amount of pressure needed to perform motor acts—for example, holding an egg in two fingers without breaking or dropping it, tapping someone playfully rather than hitting him or her, strumming a guitar softly, or pushing an elevator button with the right amount of pressure.

LD 10.04 Vestibular Dysfunction Sensory Integration Disorder

Definition A type of sensory integration disorder specifically associated with difficulties in processing information coming from the vestibular receptors located inside the ears (Packer, 2004).

Explanation Vestibular processing refers to the information that is provided by the receptors within the inner ear. These receptors are stimulated by movement of the head and input from other senses. This input tells where we are in relation to gravity, whether we are still or moving, how fast we are going, and in which direction. It also influences the development of balance, equilibrium, postural control, and muscle tone.

A child whose vestibular system does not develop or integrate normally may be hypersensitive to ordinary childhood activities such as swinging on swings or going down slides. She or he may also experience difficulty walking on or negotiating unlevel surfaces such as hills or stairs. Children with this kind of hypersensitive vestibular system often appear clumsy. But not all children with vestibular dysfunction are hypersensitive. Some are under- or hyposensitive. Children with hyposensitive vestibular systems often engage in what appears to be sensation-seeking behaviors. They may whirl around, jump, or spin (Packer, 2004).

Hatch-Rassmusen (2001) has identified these symptoms of vestibular dysfunction sensory integration disorder:

- Becoming overly excited while watching other children moving
- Craving or avoiding movement
- Creating self-movement such as rocking or moving or repositioning in chair
- Daredevil behaviors
- Decreased attention to task
- Dislike of upside-down play
- Erratic arousal level
- Fear of going up or down stairs
- Fearful when feet leave the ground
- In constant motion
- Poor or decreased balance skills
- Putting head in an upside-down position or rapid head turning or shaking

- Running or moving about quickly
- Spinning self or objects
- Toe walking
- Moving up and down out of a seat frequently or falling off a chair

LD 10.05 Other Types of Sensory Integration Disorders

LD 11.00 Social Cue Disorder

Definition Individuals with social cue disorder have difficulties in behaving in an automatic way. This is a problem with the self-governing part of the brain that stops people from doing such things as laughing at the wrong time, talking aloud to oneself, or coughing without covering their mouth. They might abruptly interrupt a conversation or talk aloud to themselves in public. Social interactions require a child to interpret what other people communicate. Picking up on spoken and unspoken cues is a complex process. Having read another person's social cues, a child must next process the information, extract meaning, and decide how to respond effectively.

Diagnostic Symptoms Diagnostic symptoms of children with social cue disorder include (Giler, 2000) an inability to read facial expressions or body language (kinesis), misinterpreting the use and meaning of pitch (vocalics), and misunderstanding the use of personal space (proxemics).

According to the Learning Disabilities Association of America (2005), individuals who have learning disabilities may be less observant in their social environment, may misinterpret the social behavior of others at times, and may not learn as easily from experiences or social cues as their friends. Some children may exhibit an immaturity and social ineptness due to their learning disability. While seeking acceptance, their eagerness may cause them to try too hard in inappropriate ways. Consequently, this problem may manifest itself in the following symptoms:

- Inability to interpret environment and social cues
- Poor judgment; little thought about logical consequences
- Poor impulse control
- Need for immediate gratification
- Inability to set realistic priorities and goals
- Inappropriate conclusions due to deficient reasoning ability
- Illogical reasons for actions
- Inability to develop meaningful relationships with others

- Immature and bossy behavior
- Low frustration tolerance, resulting in disruptive behavior

Further Key Points This disorder may best be determined by a trained professional in social behavior after careful observation in several different settings over a period of time, review of social and developmental history, teacher interviews, and interviews with the parents. The school psychologist or a clinical psychologist may be the best individual to determine the presence of this condition.

LD 12.00 Visual Processing Disorders

Definition A visual processing, or perceptual, disorder refers to a hindered ability to make sense of information taken in through the eyes. This is different from problems involving sight or sharpness of vision. Difficulties with visual processing affect how visual information is interpreted or processed by the brain (National Center for Learning Disabilities, 2004).

Diagnostic Symptoms Diagnostic symptoms of individuals with visual processing disorders vary with age and grade level (National Center for Learning Disabilities, 2005a):

Symptoms in Early Childhood

- Misunderstanding or confusing written symbols (for example, a plus or multiplication sign, a slash, or an ampersand)
- Easily distracted, especially by competing visual information
- Writing within margins or on lines or aligning numbers in math problems.
- Judging distances (for example, bumping into things, placing objects too close to an edge)
- Fluidity of movement (for example, getting out of the way of a moving ball, knocking things over)
- Differentiating colors or similarly shaped letters and numbers (for example, *b, d; p, q; 6, 9;* or *2, 5*)

Symptoms in School-Age Children

- Organizing and solving math problems
- Finding and retaining important information in reading assignments or tests
- Writing coherent, well-organized essays
- Copying from the board or books
- Sewing or other types of fine motor activities
- Writing neatly and quickly
- Reading with speed and precision

Symptoms in Adults

- Accurately identifying information from pictures, charts, graphs, and maps
- Organizing information from different sources into one cohesive document
- Finding specific information on a printed page (for example, finding a number in the telephone book)
- Remembering directions to a location

Further Key Points Interventions need to be aimed at the specific needs of the child. No two children share the same set of strengths or areas of weaknesses. An effective intervention is one that uses a child's strengths in order to build on the specific areas in need of development. Therefore, interventions need to be viewed as a dynamic and ever-changing process. Although this may sound overwhelming initially, it is important to remember that the process of finding successful interventions becomes easier with time and as the child's learning approach, style, and abilities become more easily seen (National Center for Learning Disabilities, 2004).

Types of Visual Processing Disorders

LD 12.01 Visual Agnosia (Object Recognition Visual Processing Disorder)

Definition A type of visual processing disorder specifically associated with difficulties in object recognition. Object recognition is the ability to place an object in a category of meaning (PsychNetUK, 2005).

Explanation Visual agnosia is a neurological disorder distinguished by the inability to recognize familiar objects (PsychNetUK, 2005). Many children are unable to visually recognize objects that are familiar to them or even objects they can recognize through their other senses, such as touch or smell. One school of thought about this difficulty is that it is based on an inability to integrate or synthesize visual stimuli into a recognizable whole. Another school of thought attributes this difficulty to a visual memory problem, whereby the person cannot retrieve the mental representation of the object being viewed or make the connection between the mental representation and the object itself (National Center for Learning Disabilities, 2006).

Educationally, this difficulty can interfere with the child's ability to consistently recognize letters, numbers, symbols, words, or pictures. It can obviously frustrate the learning process because what the child learns on one day may not be there, or not be available to the child, the next. In cases of partial agnosia, what is learned on day one and "forgotten" on day two may be remembered again without difficulty on day three.

It should be noted that medical problems associated with the child's vision have been ruled out as a primary cause of the child's difficulties. The difficulties are in the internal processing of information, not due to a visual impairment.

LD 12.02 Visual Closure Processing Disorder

Definition A type of visual processing disorder specifically associated with difficulties in knowing what an object is when only parts of it are visible (Behavioral Neurotherapy Clinic, 2006; National Center for Learning Disabilities, 2006).

Explanation Difficulties in visual closure can be seen in such school activities as when the young child is asked to identify or complete a drawing of a human face (Behavioral Neurotherapy Clinic, 2006). This difficulty can be so extreme that even a single missing facial feature (a nose, eye, mouth) could render the face unrecognizable by the child.

Symptoms of visual closure disorder include difficulties in recognizing a picture of a familiar object from a partial image (for example, a truck without its wheels), identifying a word with a letter missing, or recognizing a face when one feature (such as the nose) is missing (Terry, 2001).

It should be noted that medical problems associated with the child's vision have been ruled out as a primary cause of the child's difficulties. The difficulties are in the internal processing of information, not due to a visual impairment.

LD 12.03 Visual Depth Perception Processing Disorder

Definition A type of visual processing disorder specifically associated with difficulties in depth perception (Thomas, 2005).

Explanation Depth perception is an important advantage for humans and other binocular animals. Not only does it give us an accurate sense of where objects are in relation to one another but also where we stand in relation to those same objects. Although there are monocular clues to depth perception, our binocular vision makes coordination between hand and eye much more accurate (Thomas, 2005).

A student with visual depth perception processing disorder is often unable to perceive the world in three dimensions. This lack of depth perception prevents the student from accurately gauging the distance to an object; for example, he or she may not know how close the pen is to his or her hand or how far to reach to put a glass of water on the table.

It should be noted that medical problems associated with the child's vision have been ruled out as a primary cause of the child's difficulties. The difficulties are in the internal processing of information, not due to a visual impairment.

LD 12.04 Visual Discrimination Processing Disorder

Definition A type of visual processing disorder specifically associated with difficulties in noticing and comparing the features of different items to distinguish one item from another (Behavioral Neurotherapy Clinic, 2006). This is the ability to differentiate objects based on their individual characteristics (National Center for Learning Disabilities, 2006).

Explanation Visual discrimination allows us to tell the difference between similar objects, tell where one object ends and another begins, and recognize objects and symbols when only part of it can be seen (or when it is fuzzy). Individuals who have visual discrimination processing disorder often mix up letters or numbers and have difficulty reading or scanning pictures for information (Behavioral Neurotherapy Clinic, 2006).

Visual discrimination is vital in the recognition of common objects and symbols. Attributes that children use to identify different objects include color, form, shape, pattern, size, and position. Visual discrimination also refers to the ability to recognize an object as distinct from its surrounding environment (Terry, 2001).

For reading and mathematics, visual discrimination difficulties can interfere with the ability to identify symbols; gain information from pictures, charts, or graphs; or be able to use visually presented material in a productive way. The ability to recognize distinct shapes from their background, such as objects in a picture or letters on a chalkboard, is largely a function of visual discrimination.

It should be noted that medical problems associated with this child's vision have been ruled out as a primary cause of the child's difficulties. The difficulties are in the internal processing of information, not due to a visual impairment.

LD 12.05 Visual Figure-Ground Discrimination Processing Disorder

Definition A type of visual processing disorder specifically associated with difficulties in distinguishing a shape or printed character from its background (Terry, 2001).

Explanation An individual with visual figure-ground discrimination processing disorder is unable to find a designated stimulus without being distracted by the background. For example, the student will have trouble seeing a specific image within a competing background, finding a face in a crowd, finding keys on a crowded desk, of picking out one line of print from the other lines in a book. Children with this disorder cannot visually process things that others can see; to them, the keys on the crowded desk are not there (National Center for Learning Disabilities, 2006).

It should be noted that medical problems associated with the child's vision have been ruled out as a primary cause of the child's difficulties. The difficulties are in the internal processing of information, not due to a visual impairment.

LD 12.06 Visual Integration Processing Disorder

Definition A type of visual processing disorder specifically associated with difficulties in integrating the relationship between an object and symbol in its entirety and the component parts which make it up (Behavioral Neurotherapy Clinic, 2006; National Center for Learning Disabilities, 2006).

Explanation Some individuals have difficulty perceiving or integrating the relationship between an object and symbol in its entirety and its component parts. These children may perceive only the pieces, while others are able to see only the whole (Behavioral Neurotherapy Clinic, 2006). Children with a visual integration disorder have difficulty learning to read (dyslexia) and recognizing symbols (Behavioral Neurotherapy Clinic, 2006; National Center for Learning Disabilities, 2006).

In school, children are required to continuously transition from the whole to the parts and back again. A "whole perceiver," for example, might be adept at recognizing complicated words but have difficulty naming the letters within it. "Part perceivers" might be able to name the letters or some of the letters within a word but have great difficulty integrating them to make up a whole, intact word. In creating artwork or looking at pictures, the part perceivers often pay great attention to details but lack the ability to see the relationship between the details. Whole perceivers might be able to describe a piece of artwork only in very general terms or lack the ability to assimilate the pieces to make any sense of it at all (National Center for Learning Disabilities, 2006).

It should be noted that medical problems associated with the child's vision have been ruled out as a primary cause of the child's difficulties. The difficulties are in the internal processing of information, not due to a visual impairment.

LD 12.07 Visual Memory Processing Disorder

Definition A type of visual processing disorder specifically associated with difficulties in recalling and using visual information from the past (Behavioral Neurotherapy Clinic, 2006). This skill helps children remember what they read and see by adequately processing information through their short-term memory, from where it is filtered out into the long-term memory (Toler, 2005).

Explanation There are two kinds of visual memory. Long-term visual memory is the ability to recall something seen some time ago. Short-term visual memory is the ability to remember something seen very recently. Visual memory is a critical part of academic skills. It allows us to recognize objects and to remember letters, numbers, symbols, words, and pictures. In cases of visual memory processing disorder, what is learned on day one and "forgotten" on day two may be remembered again without difficulty on day three.

Among the symptoms of individuals with visual memory processing disorder are these:

- Difficulty remembering the spelling of familiar words with irregular spelling
- Difficulty in reading comprehension
- Difficulty using a calculator or keyboard with speed and accuracy
- Difficulty remembering telephone numbers

It should be noted that medical problems associated with the child's vision have been ruled out as a primary cause of the child's difficulties. The difficulties are in the internal processing of information, not due to a visual impairment.

LD 12.08 Visual Motor Processing Disorder

Definition A type of visual processing disorder specifically associated with difficulties in using feedback from the eyes to coordinate the movement of other parts of the body (National Center for Learning Disabilities, 2006; Terry, 2001).

Explanation An individual with visual motor processing disorder is often unable to relate visual stimuli to motor responses in an appropriate way (Toler, 2005). Symptoms of this disorder include:

- Writing within lines or margins of a piece of paper
- Copying from a board or book
- Moving around without bumping into things
- Participating in sports that require well-timed and precise movements in space

It should be noted that medical problems associated with the child's vision have been ruled out as a primary cause of the child's difficulties. The difficulties are in the internal processing of information, not due to a visual impairment.

LD 12.09 Visual Pursuit and Tracking Disorder

Definition A type of visual processing disorder specifically associated with difficulties in tracking moving objects while seated or standing and the ability to keep a stable visual image when the head or eyes are in motion (Behavioral Neurotherapy Clinic, 2006).

Explanation To function comfortably and safely in the world, our eyes must be able to smoothly follow a moving object, make continuous adjustments in the positions of our eyes as we move about, and shift our gaze quickly and accurately from one object to another. An individual with visual pursuit and tracking disorder is unable to track his or her eyes from left to right in an efficient manner (Behavioral Neurotherapy Clinic, 2006).

For success in school, children must have other equally important visual skills besides their sharpness of sight, or visual acuity. They must also be able to coordinate their eye movements as a team. They must be able to follow a line of print without losing their place, maintain clear focus as they read, or make quick focusing changes when looking up to the board and back to their desks (Terry, 2001). And they must be able to interpret and accurately process what they are seeing. If children have inadequate visual skills in any of these areas, they can experience great difficulty in school, especially in reading (Children's Vision Information Network, 2005).

It should be noted that medical problems associated with the child's vision have been ruled out as a primary cause of the child's difficulties. The difficulties are in the internal processing of information, not due to a visual impairment.

LD 12.10 Visual Sequencing Processing Disorder

Definition A type of visual processing disorder specifically associated with difficulties in remembering the order of symbols, words, or images when presented visually (National Center for Learning Disabilities, 2006).

Explanation An individual with visual sequencing processing disorder has difficulties storing or retrieving items in a specific order that they were given visually. When given a sheet of paper with the numbers 3–7–6–4 to remember, the student might be able to identify the numbers just read but not in the correct order.

It should be noted that medical problems associated with the child's vision have been ruled out as a primary cause of the child's difficulties. The difficulties are in the internal processing of information, not due to a visual impairment.

LD 12.11 Visual Spatial Relationships Processing Disorder

Definition A type of visual processing disorder specifically associated with difficulties in understanding how objects are positioned in space in relation to oneself. It involves the understanding of distance (near or far), as well as the relationship of objects and characters described on paper or in a spoken narrative (Behavioral Neurotherapy Clinic, 2006; National Center for Learning Disabilities, 2006).

Explanation The ability to perceive the location of objects in relationship to other objects is a critical skill in reading, math, and handwriting; a child must be able to recognize the symbols, perceive their direction, tell the difference between similar shapes, and determine where these are located in relationship to each other. Individuals who have difficulty with spatial relationships may seem unusually clumsy or accident prone, may have difficulty reading or may refuse to read, or may have poor handwriting (dysgraphia) (Behavioral Neurotherapy Clinic, 2006; National Center for Learning Disabilities, 2006).

Reading and math are two subjects where accurate perception and understanding of spatial relationships are very important. Both of these subjects rely heavily on the use of symbols (letters, numbers, punctuation, math signs). Examples of how difficulty may interfere with learning are in being able to perceive words and numbers as separate units, directionality problems in reading and math, and confusion of similarly shaped letters, such as *b* and *d* or *p* and *q*. The importance of being able to perceive objects in relation to other objects is often seen in math problems. To be successful, the person must be able to associate that certain digits go together to make a single number, others are single-digit numbers, and the operational signs are distinct from the numbers but demonstrate a relationship between them. The only cues to such math problems are the spacing and order between the symbols. These activities presuppose an ability and understanding of spatial relationships (Behavioral Neurotherapy Clinic, 2006; National Center for Learning Disabilities, 2006).

It should be noted that medical problems associated with the child's vision have been ruled out as a primary cause of the child's difficulties. The difficulties are in the internal processing of information, not due to a visual impairment.

LD 12.12 Other Types of Visual Processing Disorders

LD 13.00 Other Types of Specific Learning Disabilities

References

Abel, E. (1985). Combining alcohol and marijuana increases miscarriage: *Teratology, 31,* 35–40.

Akron Children's Hospital. (2003). *Tips to grow by.* Retrieved September 10, 2005, from http://www.akronchildrens.org/tips/pdfs/KT411.pdf.

Alexander, D., Gray, D. B., & Lyon, G. R. (1993). Conclusions and future directions. In G. R. Lyon, D. B. Gray, J. F. Kavanagh, & N. A. Krasnegor (Eds.), *Better understanding of learning disabilities: New views from research and their implications for education and public policies* (pp. 1–13). Baltimore: Paul H. Brookes.

American Speech-Language-Hearing Association. (2005). *Speech-language disorders and the speech-language pathologist.* Retrieved September 10, 2005, from http://www.asha.org/students/professions/overview/sld.htm.

Apodixis Press. (2005). *Dysonmia.* Retrieved September 10, 2005, from http://www.learning-apodixis.com/dysnomia.asp.

Archibold, E., Bayorh, M., & Sung, F. (1999, July). Neurobehavioral effects of low-level lead exposure in human neonates. *American Journal of Obstetrics and Gynecology, 181*(18), 28–118.

Baum, S. (1990). *Gifted but learning disabled: A puzzling paradox.* Reston VA: Council for Exceptional Children. (ERIC Document Reproduction Service No. ED 321 484)

Beacon Literacy. (2005). *Determining a possible dyslexic condition.* Retrieved September 10, 2005, from http://www.beaconliteracy.com/r_dyslexia.html.

Beckey, D. (2006). *Gifted and learning disabled: Twice exceptional students.* Retrieved April 21, 2006, from http://www.ldonline.org/article.php?max=20&id=967&loc=24.

Behavioral Neurotherapy Clinic. (2006). *Visual processing disorder and dyslexia.* Retrieved April 21, 2006, from http://www.adhd.com.au/Visual_Processing_Disorders.htm.

Bell, S. M., McCallum, R. S., & Cox, E. A. (2003). Toward a research-based assessment of dyslexia: Using cognitive measures to identify reading disabilities. *Journal of Learning Disabilities, 36,* 505–515.

Bishop, E. G., Cherny, S. S., Corley, R., DeFries, J. C., & Hewitt, J. K. (2003). Developmental genetic analysis of general cognitive ability from 1 to 12 years in a sample of adoptees, biological siblings, and twins. *Intelligence, 31,* 31–49.

Brody, L. E., & Mills, C. J. (1997). Gifted children with learning disabilities: A review of the issues. *Journal of Learning Disabilities, 30,* 282–296.

Carlson, N. R. (1998). *Physiology of behavior.* Needham Heights, MA: Allyn & Bacon.

Centers for Disease Control. (2004). *CDC childhood lead poisoning prevention program.* Retrieved September 10, 2005, from http://www.cdc.gov/nceh/lead/about/program.htm.

Chandler, J. (2004). *What is a learning disorder*? Retrieved September 10, 2005, from http://www.klis.com/chandler/.

Childhood Anxiety Network. (2005). *Sensory integration disorder.* Retrieved September 10, 2005, from http://www.dyspraxiafoundation.org.uk/dyspraxia-information/PDFfiles/Tactile percent20Defensiveness.pdf.

Children's Vision Information Network. (2005). *Vision and dyslexia.* Retrieved September 10, 2005, from http://www.childrensvision.com/dyslexia.htm.

Chu, S. (2000). *Tactile defensiveness: Information for parents and professionals.* Retrieved September 4, 2005, from http://www.dyspraxiafoundation.org.uk/dyspraxia-information/PDFfiles/Tactile percent20Defensiveness.pdf.

Ciocci, S. (2002). *Auditory processing disorders: An overview.* ERIC Digest, E364, Washington D.C.

Cirino, P. T., Morris, M. K., & Morris, R. D. (2002). Neuropsychological concomitants of calculation skills in college students referred for learning difficulties. *Developmental Neuropsychology, 21*(2), 201–218.

Coles, C. (1991). Reading test scores lower in children whose mothers drank alcohol. *Neurotoxicology and Teratology, 13,* 357–367.

Coltheart, M. (1998). Seven questions about pure alexia (letter-by-letter reading). *Cognitive Neuropsychology, 15,* 1–6.

Continuing Medical Education. (1999). *Learning disabilities.* Retrieved September, 10, 2005, from http://www.healthieryou.com/learn.html.

Davis International Dyslexia Association. (2005). D*yslexia.* Retrieved September 7, 2005, from http://www.interdys.org/servlet/compose?section_id=0&page_id=184.

Davis, C. J., Knopik, V. S., Olson, R. K., Wadsworth, S. J., & DeFries, J. C. (2001). Genetic and environmental influences on rapid naming and reading ability: A twin study. *Annals of Dyslexia, 51,* 231–247.

Deshler, D. D., Schumaker, J. B., Lenz, B. K., Bulgren, J. A., Hock, M. F., Knight, J., & Ehren, B. J. (2001). Ensuring content-area learning by secondary students with learning disabilities. *Learning Disabilities Research and Practice, 16,* 96–108.

Deutsch Smith, D. (2004). *Introduction to special education: Teaching in an age of opportunity* (5th ed.). Needham Heights, MA: Allyn & Bacon.

Dumas, R. (1994). Early memory loss occurs when offspring's mother exposed to alcohol. *Neurotoxicology and Teratology 16*(6), 605–612.

Dyslexia Centers of Tennessee. (2006). *The dyslexia questionaire.* Retrieved November 3, 2006, from http://www.dyslexiacentershelp.com/index.html.

Dyslexia Institutes of America. (2006). *Types of dyslexia.* Retrieved April 21, 2006, from www.diaread.com/dyslexiatypes.htm.

Echeverria, D., Heyer, M., Martin, C. & Naleway, J. (1995). Neurological problems among dentists—New concerns for mercury. *Neurotoxicology and Teratology, 17*(2), 161–168.

Florida Department of Education. (2001). *Auditory processing disorders.* Division of Public Schools and Community Education-Bureau of Instructional Support and Community Services (Paper No. FY 2001–9). Retrieved September 10, 2005, from http://www.firn.edu/doe/bin00014/pdf/y2001–9.pdf.

Foss, J. M. (2001). *Nonverbal learning disability: How to recognize it and minimize its effects.* ERIC EC Digest #E619. Retrieved September 17, 2005, from http://ericec.org/digests/e619.html.

Fried, P. A., & Smith, A. M. (2001). A literature review of the consequences of prenatal marihuana exposure: An emerging theme of a deficiency in aspects of executive function. *Neurotoxicology and Teratology, 23*(1), 1–11.

Fried, P., & Watkinson, B. (1992). Marijuana use increases symptoms of attention deficit disorder in first grade children. *Neurotoxicology and Teratology, 14,* 299–311.

Friend, M. (2005). *Special education: Contemporary perspectives for school professionals.* Needham Heights, MA: Allyn & Bacon.

Friend, M., & Bursuck, W. D. (2002). *Including students with special needs: A practical guide for classroom teachers* (3rd ed.). Needham Heights, MA: Allyn & Bacon.

Fuchs, L. S., & Fuchs, D. (2001). Principles for sustaining research-based practice in the schools. A case study. *Focus on Exceptional Children, 33*(6), 1–14.

Gargiulo, R. M. (2004). *Special education in contemporary society: An introduction to exceptionality.* Belmont, CA: Thompson-Wadsworth.

Garnett, K. (1998). *Math learning disabilities.* Retrieved September 10, 2005, from http://www.ldonline.org/ld_indepth/math_skills/garnet.html.

Gertner, A. (2003). *Facts about auditory processing disorders.* Retrieved September 10, 2005, from http://www.homestead.com/agertner/HOMEPAGE.html.

Giler, J. Z. (2000). *Socially ADDept: A manual for parents of children with ADHD and/or learning disabilities.* Retrieved September 13, 2005, from http://www.ldonline.org/article.php?max=20&id=770&loc=47.

Gray, A. G. (2003). *Auditory processing disorder.* Retrieved September 10, 2005, from http://www.schoolpsych.info/audiory_processing.htm.

Gresham, F. M., Sugai, G., & Horner, R. H. (2001). Interpreting outcomes of social skills training for students with high-incidence disabilities, *Exceptional Children, 67,* 331–344.

Gusella, J., & Fried, P. (1984). Language skills damage easily from light social drinking. *Neurobehavioral Toxicology and Teratology, 6,* 13–17. Retrieved September 22, 2005, from http://www.stir.ac.uk/postgrads/psychology/pgm1/Dyslexia.htm.

Hallahan, D. P., & Kauffman, J. M. (2006). *Exceptional learners: Introduction to special education* (10th ed.). Needham Heights, MA: Allyn & Bacon.

Hanson, J. (1992). Fetal alcohol syndrome. *Journal of Pediatrics, 92*(3), 457–460.

Hardman, M. L., Drew, C. J., & Egan, M. W. (2005). *Human exceptionality: School, community, and family.* Needham Heights, MA: Allyn & Bacon.

Hatch-Rasmussen, C. (2001). *Sensory integration.* Retrieved September 10, 2005, from http://www.suite101.com/article.cfm/autistic_spectrum_disorder/81055/2.

Heward, W. L. (2006). *Exceptional children: An introduction to special education* (8th ed.). Upper Saddle River, NJ: Pearson Education.

Hunt, N., & Marshall, K. (2005). *Exceptional children and youth* (4th ed.). Boston: Houghton Mifflin.

International Dyslexia Association. (2005). *Common signs of dyslexia.* Retrieved September 10, 2005, from http://www.interdys.org/servlet/compose?section_id=5&page_id=40.

International Dyslexia Association. (2006). *Dysgraphia.* Retrieved April 10, 2006, from http://www.interdys.org/servlet/compose?section_id=5&page_id=49.

Johnson, D., & Myklebust, H. (1967). *Learning disabilities: Educational principles and practices.* New York: Grune & Stratton.

Jones, J. (n.d.). *Accommodations and modifications for students with handwriting problems and/or dysgraphia.* Retrieved September 10, 2005, from http://www.ldonline.org/ld_indepth/writing/dysgraphia.html.

Jongmans, M. J., Smits-Engelsman, B.C.M., & Schoemaker, M. M. (2003). Consequences of comorbidity of developmental coordination disorders and learning disabilities for severity and pattern of perceptual-motor dysfunction. *Journal of Learning Disabilities, 36*(6), 528–537.

Kapes, B. (2002). *Sensory integration disorder: Health A to Z.* Retrieved September 3, 2005, from http://www.healthatoz.com/healthatoz/Atoz/ency/sensory_integration_disorder.jsp.

Kaplan, D. E., Gayán, J., Ahn, J., Won, T.-W., Pauls, D., Olson, R. K., & DeFries, J. C. (2002). Evidence for linkage and association with reading disability. *American Journal of Human Genetics, 70,* 1287–1298.

Kavale, K. A., & Forness, S. R. (1996). Social skill deficits and learning disabilities: A meta-analysis. *Journal of Learning Disabilities, 29,* 226–237.

Kay, P. (2005). *Dysgraphia.* Retrieved September 11, 2005, from http://www.nldontario.org/.

Kennedy, L., & Mukerji, S. (1986). Damage to astrocyte brain cells following "realistic" alcohol exposures. *Neurobehavioral Toxicology and Teratology, 8,* 17–21.

Knopik, V. S., Smith S. D., Cardon, L., Pennington, B., Gayán, J., Olson, R. K., & DeFries, J. C. (2002). Differential genetic etiology of reading component processes as a function of IQ. *Behavior Genetics, 32,* 181–198.

Learning Disabilities Association. (2005). *Types of learning disabilities.* Retrieved September 10, 2005, from http://www.ldanatl.org/aboutld/adults/social_emotional/independence_ch2.asp.

Learning Disabilities Association of British Columbia. (2005). *Brain development and learning disabilities.* Retrieved September 10, 2005, from http://www.ldav.ca/articles/brain_dev.html.

Learning Disabilities Association of Canada. (1996). *Tactics for teaching dyslexic students.* Retrieved September 10, 2005, from http://www.cfc-efc.ca/docs/ldac/00000455.htm.

Learning Disabilities of Ontario. (2005). *Phonological processes.* Retrieved September 10, 2005, from http://learn-ontario.ca/dyslexia.htm#td.

LDOnline. (2005a). *Decade of the brain.* Retrieved September 15, 2005, from http://www.ldonline.org/ld_indepth/general_info/gen-nimh-booklet.html.

LDOnline. (2005b). *Learning disabilities.* Retrieved September 10, 2005, from http://www.LDOnline.org.

Leong, C. C., Syed, N. I., & Lorscheider, F. L. (2001). Retrograde degeneration of neurite membrane structural integrity of nerve growth cones following in vitro exposure to mercury. *Neuroreport, 12*(4), 733–737.

Lerner, J. W. (2005). *Learning disabilities: Theories, diagnosis, and teaching strategies* (10th ed.). Boston: Houghton Mifflin.

Levine, M. (1995). Childhood neurodevelopmental dysfunction and learning disorders. *Harvard Mental Health Letter, 12,* 5–7.

Lucchi, L., & Covelli, V. (1984). Attention deficit disorder (A.D.D.) link brain neurotransmitter dopamine lower after alcohol exposure. *Neurobehavioral Toxicology and Teratology, 6,* 19–24.

Lyon, G. R. (1997). Progress and promise in research in learning disabilities [electronic version]. *Learning Disabilities: A Multidisciplinary Journal, 8*(1), 1–6.

Mattson, S., Riley, P., et al. (1994). Abnormal brain area (in basal ganglia) found in children prenatally exposed to alcohol. *Neurotoxicology and Teratology, 16*(3), 283–289.

Mayes, S. D., Calhoun, S. L., & Cromwell, E. W. (2000). Learning disabilities and ADHD: Overlapping spectrum disorders. *Journal of Learning Disabilities, 33,* 417–424.

Mayo Clinic. (2005). *Dyslexia.* Retrieved September 10, 2005, from http://www.mayoclinic.com/invoke.cfm?objectid=0FF39FE3-C8C5–42F0–941DDA29D38E21D7.

Mazzocco, M. (2001). Advances in research on the fragile X syndrome. *Mental Retardation and Developmental Disabilities Research Reviews, 6*(2), 96–106.

McLesky, J. (1992). Students with learning disabilities at primary, intermediate, and secondary grade levels: Identification and characteristics [electronic version]. *Learning Disability Quarterly, 15,* 13–19.

McMains, M. (2002). *Dyslexia.* Retrieved September 10, 2005, from http://www.visionandlearning.org/dyslexia.htm.

Mercer, C. D., Campbell, K. U., Miller, M. D., Mercer, K. D., & Lane, H. B. (2000). Effects of a reading fluency intervention for middle schoolers with specific learning disabilities. *Learning Disabilities Research and Practice, 15,* 179–189.

Nalanda Institute. (2002). *Learning disabilities: Causes.* Retrieved September 10, 2005, from http://www.nalandainstitute.org/aspfiles/cau.asp.

Nalanda Institute. (2005). *Types of learning disabilities.* Retrieved September 10, 2005, from http://www.nalandainstitute.org/aspfiles/types.asp#dysnomia.

National Center for Learning Disabilities. (2004). *Auditory processing disorders: In detail.* Retrieved November 2, 2006, from http://www.ncld.org/index.php?option=content&task=view&id=473.

National Center for Learning Disabilities. (2005a). *Visual and auditory processing disorders.* Retrieved September 10, 2005, from http://www.ldonline.org/ld_indepth/process_deficit/visual_auditory.html.

National Center for Learning Disabilities. (2005b). Dyslexia. Retrieved September 10, 2005, from http://www.ldonline.org/ld_indepth/dyslexia.html.

National Center for Learning Disabilities. (2006). *Visual processing disorders.* Retrieved November 1, 2006, from http://www.ncld.org/content/view/302/326/.

National Dissemination Center for Children with Disabilities. (2004). *Learning disabilities: A fact sheet.* Retrieved September 10, 2005, from http://www.nichcy.org/pubs/factshe/fs7txt.htm.

National Environmental Trust. (2005). *Mercury contamination.* Retrieved September 7, 2005, from http://www.net.org/air/mercury.vtml.

National Institute of Neurological Disorders and Stroke. (2005a). *Dyslexia.* Retrieved September 10, 2005, from http://www.ninds.nih.gov/disorders/dyslexia.htm.

National Institute of Neurological Disorders and Stroke. (2005b). *Gerstmann's syndrome.* Retrieved September 10, 2005, from http://www.ninds.nih.gov/disorders/gerstmanns/gerstmanns.htm.

National Institute of Neurological Disorders and Stroke. (2006). *What is dysgraphia.* Retrieved November 6, 2006, from http://www.ninds.nih.gov/disorders/dysgraphia/dysgraphia.htm.

National Institute on Deafness and Other Communication Disorders. (2004). *Auditory processing disorder in children.* Washington, DC: Author.

National Safety Council. (2005). *Lead poisoning.* Retrieved September 10, 2005, from http://www.nsc.org/library/facts/lead.htm.

Newman, R. (1998). *Gifted and math learning disabled: The dyscalculia syndrome.* Retrieved September 3, 2004, from http://www.dyscalculia.org/Edu561.html.

Nonverbal Learning Disorders Association. (2001). *The paradox of NLD: Nonverbal learning disorders in adults and children.* Retrieved September 7, 2005, from http://www.nldline.com/paradox.htm.

Nonverbal Learning Disorders Association. (2004). *Nonverbal learning disorders.* Retrieved September 10, 2005, from http://www.nlda.org/.

Nonverbal Learning Disorders Association. (2005). *Nonverbal learning disorders.* Retrieved September 10, 2005, from http://www.nlda.org/.

North Bay Guide for Disability Services. (1998). *Glossary of terms.* Retrieved September 10, 2005, from http://www.matrixparents.org/GuideAppendixGlos.html.

Packer, L. E. (2004). *Overview of sensory integration disorder.* Retrieved September 10, 2005, from http://www.schoolbehavior.com/conditions_sensoryoverview.htm.

Pavri, S., & Luftig, R. (2000). The social face of inclusive education: Are students with learning disabilities really included in the classroom [electronic version]? *Preventing School Failure, 45*(1), 8–14.

Pavri, S., & Monda-Amaya, L. (2001). Social support in inclusive schools: Student and teacher perspectives. *Exceptional Children, 67,* 391–411.

Peniston, L. (1998). *Developing recreation skills in persons with learning disabilities.* Reprinted with permission from LDOnline (1998). Champaign, IL: Sagamore Publishing.

Pierangelo, R., & Giuliani, G. (2006a). *Assessment in special education: A practical approach* (2nd ed.). Needham Heights, MA: Allyn & Bacon.

Pierangelo, R. & Giuliani, G. (2006b). *Learning disabilities: A practical approach to foundations, assessment, diagnosis and teaching.* Needham Heights, MA: Allyn & Bacon.

PsychNetUK. (2005). *Agnosia.* Retrieved September 10, 2005, from http://www.psychnet-uk.com/dsm_iv/agnosia.htm.

Rabiner, D. (1999). *ADHD, central auditory processing disorder, and learning disabilities: Attention research update—cited in understanding auditory difficulties and paying attention.* Retrieved September 26, 2005, from http://www.incrediblehorizons.com/Auditory-Difficulties.htm.

Rawat, A., et al. (1977). Brain neurotransmitter reduced after alcohol exposure. *Journal of Neurochemistry, 28,* 1175–1182.

Roth, F. P. (2000). Narrative writing: Development and teaching with children with writing difficulties [electronic version]. *Topics in Language Disorders, 20*(4), 15–28.

Roy, T. S. (1994). Nicotine damages brain cell quality: Effects of prenatal nicotine exposure on the morphogenesis of somatosensory cortex. *Neurotoxicology and Teratology, 16*(40), 1.

Schwarzbeck, C. (2006). *Chronic disorganization: A bad handicap, unrecognized.* Retrieved April 21, 2006, from http://www.simplyfamily.com/display.cfm?articleID=disorganization.cfm.

Sensoryprocessingdisorder.com. (2006). *Tactile defensiveness.* Retrieved April 21, 2006 from http://www.sensory-processing-disorder.com/tactile-defensiveness.html.

Sharma, V. P. (1996). *There are many types of dyslexia.* Retrieved September 11, 2005, from http://www.mindpub.com/art169.htm.

Shaywitz, S., & Cohen, D. (1980). Hyperactivity—A.D.D. and behavior disorders linked with alcohol exposure. *Journal of Pediatrics, 96,* 978.

Smith, C. R. (1998). History, definitions, and prevalence. In C. R. Smith (Ed.), *Learning disabilities: The interaction of learner, task, and setting* (4th ed.). Needham Heights, MA: Allyn & Bacon.

Spafford, C. A., & Grosser, G. S. (2005). *Dyslexia and reading disabilities: Research and resource guide for working with all struggling readers.* Needham Heights, MA: Allyn & Bacon.

Stevenson, N. (2002). *Dyslexia.* Retrieved September 10, 2005, from http://serendip.brynmawr.edu/bb/neuro/neuro99/web1/Stevenson.html.

Streissguth, A., Barr, H., & Sampson, P. (1986). Attention deficit and distractibility increase when mothers consumed alcohol during pregnancy. *Neurobehavioral Toxicology and Teratology, 8,* 717–725.

Sulik, K., Johnston, M., & Webb, M. (Nov. 20, 1981). *Fetal alcohol syndrome (FAS) occurs after one binge drinking episode.* Retrieved September 10, 2005, from http://www.chem-tox.com/pregnancy/alcohol.htm.

Surgeon General's Report on Smoking and Women. (2001). *Surgeon General's Report on Smoking and Women—Centers for Disease Control and Prevention.* Retrieved September 19, 2005, from http://www.cdc.gov/tobacco/sgr/sgr_2004/Factsheets/11.htm.

Swanson, H. L. (2000). Issues facing the field of learning disabilities [electronic version]. *Learning Disability Quarterly, 23,* 37–51.

Swanson, H. L., & Sachse-Lee, C. (2000). Meta-analysis of single-subject design intervention research for students with LD. *Journal of Learning Disabilities, 33,* 114–136.

Terry, B. (2001). *Areas of perception that affect learning.* Retrieved September 9, 2005, from http://parentpals.com/gossamer/pages/Detailed/890.html.

Thomas, R. (2005). *Vision.* Retrieved September 10, 2005, from http://members.lycos.co.uk/brisray/optill/vision1.htm.

Thompson, S. (1997). *Nonverbal learning disorders.* Retrieved September 10, 2005, from http://www.nldline.com/.

Toler, R. L. (2005). *Visual abilities, vision therapy, and the myths of 20/20 vision.* Retrieved September 1, 2005, from http://www.vision-therapy.com/drtoler/booklet.htm.

Tur-Kaspa, H., Weisel, A., & Segev, L. (1998). Attributions for feelings of loneliness of students with learning disabilities. *Learning Disabilities Research and Practice, 13*(2), 89–94.

Turnbull, R., Turnbull, A., Shank, M., & Smith, S. J. (2004). *Exceptional lives: Special education in today's schools* (4th ed.). Upper Saddle River, NJ: Prentice Hall.

U.S. Department of Education (2000). *Twenty-Second Annual Report to Congress on the Implementation of IDEA.* Washington, DC: U.S. Department of Education.

U.S. Department of Education. (2004). *Twenty-Sixth Annual Report to Congress on the Implementation of IDEA.* Washington DC: U.S. Department of Education

U.S. Department of Labor (2004). *Guidelines for medical surveillance and biological monitoring for miners exposed to arsenic, cadmium, lead and mercury.* Retrieved September 10, 2005, from http://www.msha.gov/S&HINFO/TOOLBOX/METALEXP/METALEXP.PDF.

University of Maryland Medicine. (2004). *Learning disabilities: Causes.* Retrieved September 16, 2005, from http://www.umm.edu/mentalhealth/ldcause.htm.

Vallance, D. D., Cummings, R. L., & Humphries, T. (1998). Mediators of the risk for problem behavior in children with language learning disabilities. *Journal of Learning Disabilities, 31,* 160–171.

Vaughn, S., Elbaum, B., & Boardman, A. G. (2001). The social function of students with learning disabilities: Implications for inclusion. *Exceptionality, 9,* 45–65.

Wadsworth, S. J., Corley, R. P., Hewitt, J. K., Plomin, R., & DeFries, J. C. (2002). Parent offspring resemblance for reading performance at 7, 12 and 16 years of age in the Colorado Adoption Project. *Journal of Child Psychology and Psychiatry, 43*(6), 769–774.

Wagner, D. (2003). *What are nonverbal learning disabilities?* Retrieved September 21, 2005, from http://www.ldrc.ca/contents/view_article/176/.

Wakschlag, L., Lahey, B., & Loeber, J. (1997). Smoking during pregnancy increases conduct disorders. *Archives of General Psychiatry, 54,* 670–676.

Wegmann, J. (2000). *Fetal alcohol syndrome.* Retrieved September 10, 2005, from http://www.cnn.com/HEALTH/library/DS/00184.html.

Wiertelak, R. (2003). *Types of dyslexia.* Retrieved September 13, 2005, from http://www.macalester.edu/~psych/whathap/UBNRP/Dyslexia/types.html.

Winkler, M., (2003). *Causes of learning disabilities and dyslexia: Genetic and biological.* Retrieved September 13, 2005, from http://web4health.info/en/answers/child-learn-biology.htm.

Witzel, B., Smith, S. W., & Brownell, M. T. (2001). How can I help students with learning disabilities in algebra? *Intervention in School and Clinic, 37*(2), 101–104.

Wong, B.Y.L. (2000). Writing strategies instruction for expository essays for adolescents with and without learning disabilities. *Topics in Language Disorders, 20*(4), 29–44.

Wood, F. B., & Grigorenko, E. L. (2001). Emerging issues in the genetics of dyslexia: A methodological preview. *Journal of Learning Disabilities, 34,* 503–511.

Yisrael, L. (2000). *Fast facts on developmental disabilities.* Retrieved September 10, 2005, from http://www.moddrc.com/InformationDisabilities/FastFacts/Learning Disabilities.htm.

Zera, D. A., & Lucian, D. G. (2001). Self organization and learning disabilities: A theoretical perspective for the interpretation and understanding of dysfunction [electronic version]. *Learning Disability Quarterly, 24,* 107–118.

CHAPTER 2

SPEECH AND LANGUAGE IMPAIRMENTS

SL

EDM CODE: SL

- SL 1.00 Apraxia of Speech
  - SL 1.01 Acquired Apraxia of Speech
    - SL 1.01a Acquired Apraxia of Speech with Aphasia
    - SL 1.01b Acquired Apraxia of Speech with Dysarthria
  - SL 1.02 Developmental Apraxia of Speech
  - SL 1.03 Other Types of Apraxia of Speech
- SL 2.00 Articulation Disorders
  - SL 2.01 Distortion Articulation Disorder
  - SL 2.02 Omission Articulation Disorder
  - SL 2.03 Substitution Articulation Disorder
  - SL 2.04 Addition Articulation Disorder
  - SL 2.04 Neurogenic Articulation Disorder
  - SL 2.05 Other Types of Articulation Disorders
- SL 3.00 Phonological Processing Prob lems
  - SL 3.01 Consonant Sequence Reduction Disorder
  - SL 3.02 Final Consonant Deletion Disorder
  - SL 3.03 Velar Deviation Fronting Disorder
  - SL 3.04 Other Types of Phonological Processing Disorders
- SL 4.00 Fluency Disorders
  - SL 4.01 Cluttering
  - SL 4.02 Stuttering
    - SL 4.02a Developmental Stuttering Disorder
    - SL 4.02b Neurogenic Stuttering Disorder
    - SL 4.02c Psychogenic Stuttering Disorder
  - SL 4.03 Other Types of Speech Fluency Disorders
- SL 5.00 Voice Disorders
  - SL 5.01 Muscle Tension Dysphonia
    - SL 5.01a Primary Muscle Tension Dysphonia
    - SL 5.01b Secondary Muscle Tension Dysphonia
  - SL 5.02 Resonance Disorders
    - SL 5.02a Hypernasality Resonance Disorder
    - SL 5.02b Hyponasality Resonance Disorder
  - SL 5.03 Spasmodic Dysphonia (Laryngeal Dystonia)
    - SL 5.03a Adductor Spasmodic Dysphonia
    - SL 5.03b Abductor Spasmodic Dysphonia
    - SL 5.03c Mixed Spasmodic Dysphonia
  - SL 5.04 Other Types of Voice Disorders
- SL 6.00 Dysarthria
  - SL 6.01 Ataxic Dysarthria
  - SL 6.02 Flaccid Dysarthria
  - SL 6.03 Hyperkinetic Dysarthria
  - SL 6.04 Hypokenetic Dysarthria
  - SL 6.05 Mixed Dysarthria
  - SL 6.06 Spastic Dysarthria
- SL 7.00 Aphasia
  - SL 7.01 Anomic Aphasia
  - SL 7.02 Broca's Aphasia
  - SL 7.03 Conduction Aphasia
  - SL 7.04 Global Aphasia
  - SL 7.05 Landau-Kleffner Syndrome
  - SL 7.06 Transcortical Aphasia
    - SL 7.06a Transcortical Motor Aphasia
    - SL 7.06b Transcortical Sensory Aphasia
    - SL 7.06c Mixed Transcortical Mixed Aphasia
  - SL 7.07 Wernicke's Aphasia
  - SL 7.08 Other Types of Aphasia
- SL 8.00 Central Auditory Processing Disorders
  - SL 9.00 Language Delay
  - SL 9.01 Acquired Language Delay
  - SL 9.02 Developmental Language Delay
  - SL 9.03 Other Types of Language Delays
- SL 10.00 Expressive Language Disorders
  - SL 10.01 Expressive Morphological Language Disorder
  - SL 10.02 Expressive Phonological Language Disorder
  - SL 10.03 Expressive Pragmatic Language Disorder

SL

- SL 10.04 Expressive Syntax Language Disorder
- SL 10.05 Expressive Semantics Language Disorder
- SL 10.06 Other Types of Expressive Language Disorders

SL 11.00 Receptive Language Disorders

- SL 11.01 Receptive Morphological Language Disorder
- SL 11.02 Receptive Phonological Language Disorder
- SL 11.03 Receptive Pragmatic Language Disorder
- SL 11.04 Receptive Syntax Language Disorder
- SL 11.05 Receptive Semantics Language Disorder
- SL 11.06 Other Types of Receptive Language Disorders

SL 12.00 Medically Based Language Disorders or Other Types of Speech and Language Disorders-Be Specific

IDEA 2004 Definition of Speech and Language Impairments

Under IDEA 2004, a speech or language impairment is defined as "a communication disorder, such as stuttering, impaired articulation, language impairment, or a voice impairment that adversely affects a child's educational performance" (34 C.F.R. 300.7(c)(11)).

Overview of Speech and Language Impairments

Communication is the process of sharing information between two or among more individuals (Hallahan & Kauffman, 2006). It is the interactive exchange of information, ideas, feelings, needs, and desires (McCormick, Loeb, & Schiefelbusch, 2003; Heward, 2006). Communication requires a message (the information or knowledge), a sender (the person who transmits the message), and a receiver (the person who grasps the message). It also involves a channel, that is, a route through which the message travels (Friend, 2005).

Communication disorders relate to the components of the process affected: speech or language (American Speech-Language-Hearing Association, 2002; Stuart, 2002; Hulit & Howard, 2002; Hallahan & Kauffman, 2006). Communication disorders are generally divided into two major groups: speech impairments and language impairments. Although considered one special education category under IDEA, speech impairments and language impairments are really two separate, though related, disabilities (Deutsch Smith, 2004).

Speech is the most common expression of language (American Speech-Language-Hearing Association, 2005). It requires coordination of the neuromusculature of the breathing and voice-producing mechanisms, as well as integrity of the mouth or oral cavity (Gargiulo, 2004). Speech is the audible, oral output of language (Heward, 2006). It is the use of the oral channel for exchanging information and knowledge (Shames & Anderson, 2002).

Speech disorders are impairments in the production and use of oral language (Turnbull, Turnbull, & Wehmeyer, 2007). They include difficulties in making speech sounds, producing speech with normal flow, and producing voice (Turnbull et al., 2007; Hallahan & Kauffman, 2006). Speech is often considered impaired when "it deviates so far from the speech of other people that it (1) calls attention to itself, (2) interferes with communication, or (3) provokes distress in the speaker or listener (Van Riper & Erickson, 1996). In general, speech is "abnormal" when it is unintelligible, unpleasant, or interferes with communication (Hall, Oyer, & Haas, 2001).

Language is the communication of ideas and the verbal system by which human beings communicate (Hunt & Marshall, 2005). It is a socially shared, rule-governed code used for communication (Friend, 2005). Encoding (or sending messages) is referred to as *expressive language* (Hallahan & Kauffman, 2006). Decoding (or understanding messages) is referred to as *receptive language.*

According to the American Speech-Language-Hearing Association (2005), a language disorder is "impaired comprehension and/or use of spoken, written, and/or other symbol systems. The disorder may involve (1) the form of language, (2) the content of language, and/or (3) the function of language in communication in any combination" (p. 40).

In general, language disorders are classified as primary (the cause is unknown) or secondary (the cause is due to another disorder or disability, such as mental retardation, hearing impairment, or brain injury; Hallahan & Kauffman, 2006). These types of disorders can range from simple sound substitutions to the inability to understand or use language or use the oral-motor mechanism for functional speech and feeding (Morales, 2005a). According to Friend (2005, p. 335), "When students have language disorders that are primary as opposed to secondary, they are referred to as having specific language impairments (SLI)."

Causes-Etiology of Speech and Language Impairments

There are many theories as to the causes of speech or language disorders. The American Speech-Language-Hearing Association (2005) has identified these causes of speech and language disorders:

- *Developmental language disorder*. This is the most common reason for speech/language problems in children. The cause of this disorder has something to do with the nervous system, but the exact cause is unknown.
- *Hearing loss*. A hearing impairment is the most frequently overlooked but the most easily found cause of language problems. It is important that a child's hearing be tested at least every school year. Normal speech and language development depends on good hearing and listening skills. If a child has a hearing problem, his or her speech and language may not develop at a normal rate (Roberts & Ziesel, 2002).
- *Mental retardation*. Children with any level of mental retardation will also have language problems. A child who is intellectually impaired is likely to have problems in all aspects of language.
- *Autism or pervasive development disorder* (PDD). A child with autism or PDD will usually have problems with communication.

- *Learning disabilities.* Children who have learning disabilities have neurologically based learning problems that may be observed as a short attention span, poor memory, or delayed or disordered language development. These learning difficulties can interfere with a child's success in school and social interactions with peers.
- *Not having a good example.* Learning language depends a lot on hearing others speak. There must be enough language models available for the child to develop normal language skills.
- *Developmental delays related to prematurity.* Many premature babies are considered at high risk for delays in their intellectual, motor, and language skills. All areas of their development must be carefully watched.
- *Neurological impairment.* Some motor disorders, such as cerebral palsy, muscular dystrophy, and traumatic brain injury, affect a child's muscles, including those involved in speech production.
- *Structural abnormalities.* Many structural abnormalities affect speech. These can include cleft lip or cleft palate, tracheal deformities, or craniosynostosis (deformity of the skull).
- *Impaired decoding of speech.* A child who cannot decode speech sounds has a disorder known as word deafness. Using visual communication such as sign language or gestures works for these children.

The majority of voice disorders in children usually result from frequent vocal abuse associated with excessive throat clearing, coughing, screaming, or yelling. This abuse can cause inflammation of the larynx (vocal cords) or the formation of nodules and polyps, which are small growths, on the vocal cords (Hallahan & Kauffman, 2006). Allergies, smoking, and the consumption of alcoholic beverages are other factors that may adversely affect the larynx (vocal cords), resulting in varying degrees of voice disorders later in life (Hamaguchi, 2001).

Prevalence of Speech and Language Impairments

According to the *Twenty-Sixth Annual Report* (U.S. Department of Education, 2004), 1,118,543 students between the ages of six and twenty-one years of age were identified as having speech and language impairments. This represents approximately 19 percent of all students having a classification in special education, or about 1.7 percent of all school-age students (Hunt & Marshall, 2005). This estimate does not include children who have speech or language problems secondary to other conditions, such as mental retardation, traumatic brain injury, autism, cerebral palsy, or deafness (Friend, 2005).

Estimating the prevalence of communication disorders is difficult because they are extremely varied, sometimes difficult to identify, and often occur as part of other disabilities (Hallahan & Kauffman, 2006).

During the 2003–2004 school year, approximately 88.2 percent of children with speech or language impairments were served in the regular classroom, 6.8 percent in resource rooms, and 4.6 percent in separate classes (U.S. Department of Education, 2004).

Age of Onset of Speech and Language Impairments

It is probably reasonable to estimate that about 10 to 15 percent of preschool children and about 6 percent of students in elementary and secondary grades have speech disorders, and about 2 to 3 percent of preschoolers and about 1 percent of the school-age population have language disorders (Heward, 2006). Approximately 98 percent of the cases of these disorders are identified before ten years of age.

Gender Features of Speech and Language Impairments

Data from the National Institute on Deafness and Other Communication Disorders (2002f) identify boys as being more likely than girls as having speech disorders in a ratio of approximately 2 to 1. They appear more likely to have language disorders in a ratio of approximately 1.75 to 1 (Friend, 2005).

Cultural Features of Speech and Language Impairments

According to Friend (2005, p. 338), prevalence related to race or ethnicity is difficult to establish because of the many complicating factors that can arise from evaluating students with speech and language disorders (Kim & Kaiser, 2000; Nipold, 2001). However, it is essential to recognize that the fact that a student does not use the speech or language that is expected in school does not necessarily mean that he or she has a speech and language impairment. The most important question for a child whose speech or language is different from what is standard or expected is whether the student is an effective communicator in his or her speech and language community (Goldstein, Fabiano, & Iglesias, 2004).

Familial Pattern of Speech and Language Impairments

There is some indication of a familial pattern in speech and language impairments, with clinicians noting patterns across generations. As of the 1990s, research suggested a possible genetic link, though there are still many problems in identifying such a gene. Sometimes the siblings of an affected child show milder forms of the difficulty, complicating the picture (National Institute on Deafness and Other Communication Disorders, 2002f). One of the major stumbling blocks is the definition of the disorder, because the population of children with language impairments is still much more heterogeneous than required to support a search for a gene (National Dissemination Center for Children with Disabilities, 2004).

Characteristics of Speech and Language Impairments

A child with a communication disorder may present many different symptoms. These may include difficulty following directions, attending to a conversation, pronouncing words, perceiving what was said, expressing oneself, or being understood because of a stutter or a hoarse voice (Brice, 2001).

Speech disorders refer to difficulties producing speech sounds or problems with voice quality (Turnbull, Turnbull, & Wehmeyer, 2006). They might be characterized by an interruption in the flow or rhythm of speech, such as stuttering, which is called dysfluency (Gargiulo, 2004). Stuttering has been long thought to be caused by emotional factors, but researchers who studied adults with persistent stuttering found that these individuals had anatomical irregularities in the areas of the brain that control language and speech (American Academy of Neurology, 2001).

Speech disorders may be problems with the way sounds are formed, called articulation or phonological disorders, or they may be difficulties with the pitch, volume, or quality of the voice (Friend, 2005). There may be a combination of several problems. People with speech disorders have trouble using some speech sounds, which can also be a symptom of a delay (National Institute on Deafness and Other Communication Disorders, 2002e). They may say *see* when they mean *ski,* or they may have trouble using other sounds like *l* or *r.* Listeners may have trouble understanding what someone with a speech disorder is trying to say. People with voice disorders may have trouble with the way their voices sound (Gargiulo, 2004).

Students with language impairments have significant difficulties understanding or using words in context, both verbally and nonverbally (Turnbull et al., 2004). Among the characteristics of language disorders are these:

- Improper use of words and their meanings
- Inability to express ideas
- Inappropriate grammatical patterns
- Reduced vocabulary
- Inability to follow directions

One or a combination of these characteristics may occur in children who are affected by language learning disabilities or developmental language delay (National Institute on Deafness and Other Communication Disorders, 2002d). Children may hear or see a word but not be able to understand its meaning. They may have trouble getting others to understand what they are trying to communicate.

According to the Child Development Institute (2005), a child with a possible hearing problem may appear to strain to hear, ask to have questions repeated before giving the right answer, demonstrate speech inaccuracies (especially dropping the beginnings and endings of words), or exhibit confusion during discussion. Detection and diagnosis of hearing impairment have become very sophisticated. It is possible to detect the presence of hearing loss and evaluate its severity in a newborn child.

Students who speak dialects different from Standard English may have communication problems that represent language differences or, in more severe instances, language disorders.

As a result of the numerous factors that contribute to these disorders, treatment can be complex (Barlow & Gierut, 2002; Forrest, 2002; Forrest, Elbert, & Dinnsen, 2002; Gierut & Champion, 2001; Gierut, 2001; Dodd & Bradford, 2000).

Educational Implications of Speech and Language Impairments

Children who struggle with speech and language impairments frequently suffer pervasive negative effects related to the entire educational process and are therefore at risk for developing social and emotional problems (Gargiulo, 2004).

Because all communication disorders carry the potential to isolate individuals from their social and educational surroundings, it is essential to find appropriate and timely intervention. While many speech and language patterns can be called "baby talk" and are part of a young child's normal development, they can become problems if they are not outgrown as expected. In this way, an initial delay in speech and language or an initial speech pattern can become a disorder that can cause difficulties in learning (National Institute on Deafness and Other Communication Disorders, 2002d). Because of the way the brain develops, it is easier to learn language and communication skills before the age of five. When children have muscular disorders, hearing problems, or developmental delays, their acquisition of speech, language, and related skills is often affected.

Speech-language pathologists assist children who have communication disorders in various ways. They provide individual therapy for the child, consult with the child's teacher about the most effective ways to facilitate the child's communication in the class setting, and work closely with the family to develop goals and techniques for effective therapy in class and at home (Hunt & Marshall, 2005). The pathologist may assist vocational teachers and counselors in establishing communication goals related to the work experiences of students and suggest strategies that are effective for the important transition from school to employment and adult life (Heward, 2006).

Vocabulary and concept growth continue during the years children are in school. Reading and writing are taught, and as students get older, the understanding and use of language becomes more complex. Communication skills are at the heart of the education experience. Speech or language therapy may continue throughout a student's school years in the form of direct therapy or on a consultant basis (National Institute on Deafness and Other Communication Disorders, 2002d).

Many speech problems are developmental rather than physiological, and so they respond to remedial instruction. Language experiences are central to a young child's development. In the past, children with communication disorders were routinely removed from the regular class for individual speech and language therapy. This is still the case in severe instances, but the trend is toward inclusion, keeping the child in the general education classroom as much as possible (Hallahan & Kauffman, 2006).

Helping students overcome speech and language disorders is not the responsibility of any one professional (Deutsch-Smith, 2004). Rather, identification is the joint responsibility of the classroom teacher, speech pathologist, and parents (Hallahan and Kauffman, 2006). In order to accomplish this goal, teamwork among these individuals is essential. Speech and language improvement and correction should be blended into the regular classroom curriculum and the child's natural environment.

Permissions and Authorization to Use Proprietary and Nonproprietary Sources

Due to the scientific and detailed nature of certain Level II, Level III, and Level IV disorders described in this chapter, we thought that some were best explained by national institutes and centers that conduct comprehensive scientific research in respective fields of study. The sources obtained were all written with explicit permission that the scientific and diagnostic information they prepared was in the public domain and can be used without restriction.

We thank the following national research offices for the opportunity to freely disseminate their scientific research and writing in this chapter:

- National Dissemination Center for Children with Disabilities
- National Institutes of Health
- National Institute of Neurological Disorders and Strokes
- National Institute on Deafness and Other Communication Disorders

SL

EDM Codes, Definitions, and Explanations of Speech and Language Impairments

Speech Disorders

SL 1.00 Apraxia of Speech (Verbal Apraxia or Dyspraxia)

Definition Apraxia of speech, also known as verbal apraxia or dyspraxia, is a speech disorder in which a person has trouble saying what he or she wants to say correctly and consistently. It is characterized by a disruption of motor planning and programming so that speech is slow, effortful, and inconsistent (Hallahan & Kauffman, 2006).

Apraxia is a motor disorder in which volitional or voluntary movement is impaired without weakness or paralysis of the speech muscles, such as the muscles of the face, tongue, and lips (National Institute on Deafness and Other Communication Disorders, 2002a). It is a motor speech disorder that affects the way in which a student plans to produce speech (Turnbull et al., 2004) even though he or she has no paralysis or weakness of the muscles used in speech.

Oral apraxia indicates that the child has difficulty with volitional control of nonspeech movement. For instance, perhaps the child has difficulty sticking out and wagging his or her tongue when requested to do so or difficulty sequencing movements for the command, "Show me how you kiss. Now smile. Now blow."

Verbal apraxia indicates that the child has difficulty with volitional movement for the production of speech. This can be at the level of sounds, syllables, words, or even phrases (connected speech). The motor struggle is most typically seen with sounds sequencing (Childhood Apraxia of Speech Association, 2005).

Diagnostic Symptoms Apraxia is a motor planning disorder in the absence of muscle weakness (Hedge & Maul, 2006). People with apraxia of speech may have a number of different speech characteristics or symptoms. One of the most notable symptoms is difficulty putting sounds and syllables together in the correct order to form words. Longer or more complex words are usually harder to say than shorter or simpler words. People with apraxia of speech also tend to make inconsistent mistakes when speaking (National Institute on Deafness and Other Communication Disorders, 2002a). For example, they may say a difficult word correctly but then have trouble repeating it, or they may be able to say a particular sound one day and have trouble with the same sound the next day. They often appear to be groping for the right sound or word and may try saying a word several times before they say it correctly. Another common characteristic of apraxia of speech is the incorrect use of prosody—that is, the varying rhythms, stresses, and inflections of speech that are used to help express meaning (National Institute on Deafness and Other Communication Disorders, 2002a).

Children with apraxia of speech generally can understand language much better than they are able to use it to express themselves. Some children with the disorder may also have other problems, for example, other speech problems such as dysarthria; language problems such as poor vocabulary, incorrect grammar, and difficulty in clearly organizing spoken information; problems with reading, writing, spelling, or math; coordination or motor skill problems; and chewing and swallowing difficulties (Anderson & Shames, 2006).

Apraxia is evident when the child cannot position articulators correctly for speech production even though there is no muscular problem (Hedge & Maul, 2006). The severity of apraxia of speech varies from person to person. Apraxia can be so mild that a person has trouble with very few speech sounds or only occasional problems pronouncing words with many syllables. In the most severe cases, a person may not be able to communicate effectively with speech and may need the help of alternative or additional communication methods (National Institute on Deafness and Other Communication Disorders, 2002a).

Individuals with speech apraxia may have a number of different symptoms, which may include (Golisano Children's Hospital, 2005):

- A tendency to grope for words or sounds
- A tendency to say a word several times before saying it the right way
- Poor language skills, including poor vocabulary and grammar
- Difficulty putting sounds or syllables together in the correct order to form words
- Errors using vowels
- Problems with reading, writing, spelling, or math
- Difficulty organizing spoken information clearly
- Other speech disorders or coordination or motor skill problems
- Inconsistent or improper use of rhythms, stresses, and inflections of speech that are used to convey meaning
- Inconsistent speech errors, even when repeating a word just said
- Incorrect timing of speech movements and their accompanying sounds
- Increased tendency to make errors as the length of words or sentences increases
- Limited ability to make speech sounds automatically
- Chewing and swallowing difficulties
- Understanding language better than using it

Further Key Points Researchers are searching for the causes of apraxia of speech, including the possible role of abnormalities in the brain or other parts of the nervous system. Students with apraxia need frequent therapy that focuses on repetition, sound sequencing, and movement patterns (Caruso & Strand, 1999). Generally, treatment for individuals with apraxia includes physical, speech, or occupational therapy. If apraxia is a symptom of another disorder, the underlying disorder should be treated. The prognosis for individuals with apraxia varies and depends partly on the underlying cause. Some individuals improve significantly, while others may show very little improvement (National Institute on Deafness and Other Communication Disorders, 2002a).

Types of Apraxia of Speech

SL 1.01 Acquired Apraxia of Speech

Definition A type of apraxia of speech specifically associated with damage to the parts of the brain that are involved in speaking or the loss or impairment of existing speech abilities (Hallahan & Kauffman, 2006). Acquired apraxia may occur together with muscle weakness affecting speech production (dysarthria) or language difficulties caused by damage to the nervous system (aphasia).

Explanation Acquired apraxia of speech can affect a person at any age. It is due to the effects of damage to the parts of the brain that are involved in speaking and involves the loss or impairment of existing speech abilities. The disorder may result from a stroke, head injury, tumor, or other illness affecting the brain (National Institute on Deafness and Other Communication Disorders, 2002a).

Acquired apraxia of speech is a condition in which the strength and coordination of the speech muscles are unimpaired, but the individual experiences difficulty saying words correctly in a consistent way (Anderson & Shames, 2006). This type of disorder can create tremendous anxiety and tension for students diagnosed with it. For example, a student may repeatedly stumble on the simple word *tomorrow* when asked to repeat it, but then be able to say it in a statement such as, "I'll try to say it again tomorrow" (National Institute on Deafness and Other Communication Disorders, 2002a).

SL 1.01a **Acquired Apraxia of Speech with Aphasia** Acquired apraxia of speech may occur together with language difficulties due to the effects of damage to the nervous system (aphasia). Aphasia is a total or partial loss of the ability to use or understand language, usually due to the effects of recent insult to the brain such as a stroke, brain disease, or injury (Hedge & Maul, 2006).

SL 1.01b **Acquired Apraxia of Speech with Dysarthria** Acquired apraxia of speech may occur together with muscle weakness affecting speech production (dysarthria). Dysarthria is a complex set of communication problems due to impaired neural control of muscles involved in speech production (Shames & Anderson, 2006; Hedge & Maul, 2006).

SL 1.02 Developmental Apraxia of Speech

Definition A type of apraxia of speech specifically associated with a child's ability to plan and sequence speech sounds for clear and intelligible speech (Hallahan & Kauffman, 2006). Children with developmental apraxia of speech (DAS) have difficulty preparing and coordinating their muscles for speech production (Hearing, Speech & Deafness Center, 2005).

Explanation Developmental Apraxia of Speech is also known as DAS, Developmental Verbal Dyspraxia, Developmental Verbal Apraxia, Articulatory Dyspraxia, and Childhood Apraxia of Speech. It occurs in children and is present from birth (Anderson & Shames, 2006). It is a neurologically based communication disorder that interferes with a child's ability to correctly pronounce sounds, syllables, and words (Hearing, Speech & Deafness Center, 2005). There are no specific lesion sites in the brain in cases of developmental apraxia (whereas acquired apraxia can be linked to specific lesion sites).

DAS is different from what is known as a developmental delay of speech, in which a child follows the typical path of speech development but does so more slowly than normal. It appears to affect more boys than girls (National Institute on Deafness and Other Communication Disorders, 2002a).

Typical speech characteristics of children with DAS include (Anderson & Shames, 2006; Hearing, Speech & Deafness Center, 2005):

- Additions of sounds
- Difficulties with sound sequencing
- Distortions of sounds
- Disturbances in timing of movements and accompanying sounds
- Inconsistent speech errors, even on repetitions of the same word
- Increased errors as word and sentence length increases
- Significantly impaired intelligibility of connected speech
- Limited speech sound repertoire (very few speech sounds that a child can use automatically) and multiple speech sound errors present: omissions of sounds (very common), substitutions of one sound for another, and vowel errors, for example

The cause or causes of DAS are not yet known. Some scientists believe that DAS is a disorder related to a child's overall language development. Others believe it is a neurological disorder that affects the brain's ability to send the proper signals to move the muscles involved in speech. However, brain imaging and other studies have not found evidence of specific brain lesions or differences in brain structure in children with DAS (National Institute on Deafness and Other Communication Disorders, 2002a).

SL 1.03 Other Types of Apraxia of Speech

SL 2.00 Articulation Disorders

Definition Articulation is the process by which sounds, syllables, and words are formed when the tongue, jaw, teeth, lips, and palate alter the airstream coming from the vocal folds. Articulation is a speaker's production of individual or speech sounds (Turnbull et al., 2004).

An articulation disorder occurs when a child cannot correctly pronounce the various sounds and combinations of speech (Friend, 2005; Turnbull et al., 2004; Gargiulo, 2004). Articulation disorders are difficulties with the way sounds are formed and strung together (Hunt & Marshall, 2005; Hallahan & Kauffman, 2006; Heward, 2006; PsychNet-UK, 2005), usually characterized by substituting one sound for another (*wabbit* for *rabbit*), omitting a sound (*han* for *hand*), adding a sound (*elephepetant* for *elephant*) or distorting a sound (*ship* for *sip*).

A person has an articulation problem when he or she produces sounds, syllables, or words incorrectly so that listeners do not understand what is being said or pay more attention to the way the words sound than to what they mean (American Speech-Language-Hearing Association, 2005).

It should be noted that articulation patterns that can be attributed to cultural or ethnic background are not considered articulation disorders.

Diagnostic Symptoms Diagnostic symptoms of articulation disorders include (American Speech-Language-Hearing Association, 2005; Deutsch-Smith, 2004; PsychNet-UK, 2005):

- *Omissions:* Sounds in words and sentences may be completely omitted: "I go o coo o the bu" for "I go to school on the bus."
- *Substitutions:* Children do not pronounce the sounds clearly or they replace one sound for another, for example, they substitute *w* for *l* or *r.*
- *Distortions:* The child tries to make the correct sound but it results in a poor production. For example, a distorted /s/ sound may whistle, or the tongue may be thrusting between the teeth causing a frontal lisp.
- *Additions:* Extra sounds or syllables are added to the word, for example, *animamal.* The most common error sounds are *s, l,* and *r.* The speech is primarily unintelligible and difficult to understand.

Further Key Points Articulation disorders constitute the most numerous of all speech disorders. About three out of five of all speech and language disorders are related to articulation problems (American Speech-Language-Hearing Association 2005).

Children who do not receive speech therapy and do not outgrow their speech difficulties often continue to make speech errors as adults (Speech-Language Pathology Website, 2005). Since articulation disorders can have a serious negative impact on a student's social, emotional, educational, or vocational status, receiving speech language services for remediation of the problems is often essential for a young child (Turnbull et al., 2004).

Types of Articulation Disorders

SL 2.01 Distortion Articulation Disorder

Definition A type of articulation disorder specifically associated with errors in the formation of individual speech sounds whereby incorrect letters are added to a word (Marshall University, 2005; New Jersey Speech and Hearing Association, 2005).

Explanation Distortion articulation errors occur when a sound is not left out or substituted yet does not sound right. There is an attempt to make the sound, but the sound is nevertheless misarticulated. The sound is said inaccurately but sounds something like the intended sound. Common distortions, called lisps, occur when *s, z, sh,* and *ch* are mispronounced (Turnbull et al., 2004). Examples of distortion articulation errors are saying *shlip* for *ship, thand* for *sand, wabbit* for *rabbit,* and *schleep, zleep,* or *thleep* for *sleep* (Heward, 2006).

SL 2.02 Omission Articulation Disorder

Definition A type of articulation disorder specifically associated with errors in the formation of individual speech sounds whereby an incorrect letter is omitted from a word (Marshall University, 2005; New Jersey Speech and Hearing Association, 2005).

Explanation Omission articulation errors occur when a sound that is too hard to say for the person is left out. Children often omit sounds from consonant pairs. Examples include saying *ed* for *red, at* for *hat, ouse* for *house, rabbi* for *rabbit, oo* for *shoe, cool* for *school,* and *ost* for *lost* (Heward, 2006; Turnbull et al., 2004).

SL 2.03 Substitution Articulation Disorder

Definition A type of articulation disorder specifically associated with errors in the formation of individual speech sounds whereby incorrect letters are substituted for the correct one (Marshall University, 2005; New Jersey Speech and Hearing Association, 2005).

Explanation Substitution articulation errors occur when a sound is substituted by the individual for one he or she cannot make yet. For example, many times children substitute *th* for *s,* so that *sun* is pronounced *thun.* Other examples are *fumb* for *thumb, tat* for *cat, meighbo*r for *neighbor, santastic* for *fantastic, train* for *crane,* and *doze* for *those* (Friend, 2005; Turnbull et al., 2004).

Children with this problem are often certain they have said the correct word and may resist correction. This can be very frustrating to the listener, who is often confused by what the child has stated (Heward, 2006).

SL 2.04 Addition Articulation Disorder

Definition A type of articulation disorder specifically associated with errors in the formation of individual speech sounds whereby additional and incorrect letters are added to words (Hallahan & Kauffman, 2006; Marshall University, 2005).

Explanation Addition articulation errors occur when the individual adds a sound to a word. Examples are saying: *galue* for *glue, happity* for *happy, televelephone* for *telephone, buhrown* for *brown*, and *hamber* for *hammer* (Heward, 2006).

SL 2.04 Neurogenic Articulation Disorder

Definition A type of articulation disorder specifically due to the effects of or arising from the nervous system (Downey, 2004).

Explanation The word *neurogenic* means "due to the effects of or arising from the nervous system." A neurogenic articulation disorder may be developmental or acquired and can result in major articulation problems. Developmental disorders occur during maturation and are often the result of insult or lesions to the brain. Acquired injuries occur after the onset of speech development. Either can cause a dysfunction of the musculature associated with speech production and voice quality (Downey, 2004).

SL 2.05 Other Types of Articulation Disorders

SL 3.00 Phonological Processing Disorders

Definition Phonology is the sound system of a language and the rules that govern the sound combinations. It is the study of how sounds are organized and used in natural languages. The phonological system of a language includes an inventory of sounds and their features and rules that specify how sounds interact with each other (LinguaLinks Library, 2005). The term *phonological processing* refers to the use of speech-sound information in processing written and oral language (Learning Disabilities of Ontario, 2005).

Diagnostic Symptoms Individuals with phonological processing disorders may exhibit these typical characteristics (Bowen, 2005; Learning Disabilities Association of Ontario, 2005; Jacobsen, n.d.):

- Problems with speech clarity in the preschool years
- Difficulty learning to read and difficulties with reading comprehension in the early school years

- Problems with speech clarity in the preschool years, with no subsequent reading and spelling problems
- Fatigue toward the end of classes and school or workday from the intense concentration needed for listening
- Inconsistent performances (one of the most common characteristics seen, so individuals may often be perceived as unmotivated, lazy, overdependent, pragmatically awkward, or inattentive)
- Daydreaming or disruptive behaviors in response to the frustrations experienced from communication breakdowns
- Difficulty listening in the presence of background noise, localizing sounds, following directions, and attending, with daydreaming or distractibility often present
- Confusing similar-sounding words as well as having a reduced recognition of stress patterns and word boundaries between words within sentences, especially during rapid speech or listening without visual cues, as with telephone conversation
- Sensitivity to specific sounds.
- Speech and reading problems and difficulty with spelling
- Speech and spelling problems but no reading difficulties
- Speech clarity problems in the preschool years
- Difficulty with written expression in primary school

Further Key Points According to Burgess (2005):

> Recent research suggests that humans possess a phonetic module. This module is a part of our biology and is preprogrammed for speech. When people speak they produce articulatory gestures which are perceived and processed by the phonetic module. The phonetic module is responsible for the phonological processing which is essential for learning to read.
>
> Phonological processing uses phonemes to process verbal and written information in short and long term memory. This process involves coding and retrieving information.
>
> Coding involves translating stimuli from auditory to written form, or vice versa. This translation can be divided into two domains: encoding and recoding. Encoding takes auditory sound and translates it into a phonological code which can then be used for storing and creating information. Recoding translates graphemes to phonemes then stores the information by attaching it to meaning in the brain's lexicon in long term memory. The lexicon is the brain's "dictionary" of known words.
>
> Phonological processing also involves retrieving information. This requires accessing the lexicon and calling up knowledge which is stored in either the

SL

brain's short- or long-term memory. Without phonologic awareness, a person's phonetic module may not be coded correctly. This faulty coding will lead to difficulties learning to read [pp. 1–2].

Types of Phonological Processing Disorders

SL 3.01 Consonant Sequence Reduction Disorder (Cluster Reduction)

Definition A type of phonological processing disorder specifically associated with simplifying a consonant sequence by deleting one or more sounds (Bowen, 2005). Consonant clusters occur when two or three consonants occur in a sequence in a word. In cluster reduction, part of the cluster is omitted.

Explanation Children with cluster reduction omit one or more sounds in a group of consonants—for example: *bead* for *bread, pay* for *play, des* for *desk, pos* for *post, wak* for *walked, back* for *black, pider* for *spider,* and *at* for *ant* (Novita Children's Services, 2005; Bowen, 2005).

SL 3.02 Final Consonant Deletion Disorder

Definition A type of phonological processing disorder specifically associated with the omission of sounds at the end of words (Novita Children's Services, 2005).

Explanation In final consonant deletion disorder, the individual leaves the sounds off the end of words, omitting the final consonant in the word (Bowen, 2005)—for example, *ca* for *cat, do* for *dog, bulle* for *bullet,* and *carniva* for *carnival.*

SL 3.03 Velar Deviation Fronting Disorder (Fronting)

Definition A type of phonological processing disorder specifically associated with the substitution of sounds normally produced in the back of the mouth, for example, *tea* for *key, dame* instead of *game,* or *take* instead of *cake.*

Explanation Children who exhibit fronting use sounds that are produced at the front of the mouth rather than those produced at the back, for example, *do* for *go* (Novita Children's Services, 2005). For these children, /k/ is replaced by /t/, /g/ is replaced by /d/, and *ng* is replaced by /n/. *Kiss* is pronounced as *tiss*, *give* is pronounced as *div*, and *wing* is pronounced as *win* (Bowen, 2005).

SL 3.04 Other Types of Phonological Processing Disorders

SL 4.00 Fluency Disorders

Definition Fluent speech is smooth, flows well, and appears effortless. Fluency disorders are characterized by interruptions in the flow of speaking, such as atypical rate or rhythm as well as repetitions of sounds, syllable, words, and phrases (Hunt & Marshall, 2005; Turnbull et al., 2004).

Fluency can be broken down into three categories:

- Continuity: repetitions and fragmented speech
- Rate: irregular tempo, slow or fast, and jerking
- Effort: obvious muscular or mental effort

It is important to note that all speakers have moments of dysfluency. Fluency disorders are diagnosed when the frequency of dysfluency surpasses the average range. Children suffering from fluency disorders may also exhibit secondary characteristics, such as eyeblinks, gaze aversion, and head nods during moments of dysfluency (Oswego Community Unit, 2005).

Diagnostic Symptoms Fluency disorders occur when a child's speech flow is interrupted by multiple repetitions, prolongations of sounds, or blocks of sound production. Diagnostic symptoms of speech fluency disorders include (Magee, 2003):

- Repeating sounds, parts of words, and sometimes entire words
- Pausing between words or within a word; sometimes the pauses are silent
- Substituting simple words for those that are hard to speak
- Using incomplete phrases
- Making interjections (such as adding "uh" or "um" in the middle of a sentence)
- Showing obvious tension or discomfort while talking
- Making parenthetical remarks

Other physical symptoms may occur, such as eyeblinking or head nodding.

Further Key Points Speech and language pathologists diagnose fluency disorders by determining the percentage of the child's speech that is dysfluent. If a fluency disorder is diagnosed, they teach the child strategies to decrease the frequency and length of dysfluency. In addition, therapy focuses on the child's feelings and emotions associated with dysfluency (Oswego Community Unit, 2005).

One of the most commonly known fluency problems is stuttering (Boston College, 2005). Stuttering associated with normal speech development (normal dysfluency) usually resolves on its own before puberty. More severe forms of stuttering (developmental stuttering) usually do not resolve without treatment (Magee, 2003).

SL 4.01 Cluttering

Definition A type of fluency disorder specifically associated with a speech delivery rate that is either abnormally fast or irregular, or both. In cluttered speech, the person's speech is affected by one or more of the following: (1) failure to maintain normally expected sound, syllable, phrase, and pausing patterns; (2) evidence of greater-than-expected incidents of dysfluency, the majority of which are unlike those typical of people who stutter (St. Louis, Raphael, Myers, & Baker, 2003).

Explanation Cluttering is a speech fluency disorder characterized by a rapid, irregular speech (Anderson & Shames, 2006). It happens when speech becomes cluttered with faulty phrasing and unrelated words to the extent that it is unintelligible. Unlike stuttering, which involves hesitation and repetition over key words, cluttering usually includes effortless repetition of syllables and phrases. Consequently, the affected person is often not aware of any communication difficulties.

Cluttering is a disturbance in the fluency of speech. People who clutter often speak at a more rapid rate than normal, which causes them to stumble and double back in their attempt to impart meaning. It is characterized by poor attention span, perceptual weakness, and poorly organized thinking (National Institute on Deafness and Other Communication Disorders, 2002e).

SL 4.02 Stuttering

Definition A type of fluency disorder specifically associated with a disruption in the normal flow of speech by frequent repetitions or prolongations of speech sounds, syllables, words, or an individual's inability to start a word. The speech disruptions may be accompanied by rapid eyeblinks, tremors of the lips or jaw, or other struggle behaviors of the face or upper body that a person who stutters may use in an attempt to speak (Anderson & Shames, 2006).

Certain situations, such as speaking before a group of people or talking on the telephone, tend to make stuttering more severe, whereas other situations, such as singing or speaking alone, often improve fluency (Hallahan & Kauffman, 2006). Stuttering may also be referred to as stammering, especially in England (National Institute on Deafness and Other Communication Disorders, 2002e).

Explanation It is estimated that approximately 1 percent (2 to 3 million) of Americans stutter (Turnbull et al., 2004). Stuttering affects individuals of all ages but occurs most frequently in children between the ages of two and six who are developing language. Boys are three times more likely to stutter than girls. Most children outgrow their stuttering, and it is estimated that less than 1 percent of adults stutter.

Symptoms of stuttering may include:

- Repeating sounds, parts of words, and sometimes entire words
- Pausing between words or within a word
- Substituting simple words for those that are hard to speak
- Showing obvious tension or discomfort while talking
- Using incomplete phrases

- Making interjections (such as adding "uh" or "um" in the middle of a sentence)
- Making parenthetical remarks (adding explanatory or seemingly unrelated words or phrases)

Stuttering often becomes worse during stressful situations such as public speaking. Interestingly, it often does not occur during other activities, such as singing, whispering, talking while alone or to pets, or during choral reading (Fackler, 2005).

SL 4.02a **Developmental Stuttering Disorder** The most common form of stuttering is thought to be developmental, that is, it is occurring in children who are in the process of developing speech and language. This relaxed type of stuttering is felt to occur when a child's speech and language abilities are unable to meet his or her verbal demands. Stuttering happens when the child searches for the correct word. Developmental stuttering is usually outgrown (National Institute on Deafness and Other Communication Disorders, 2002e).

SL 4.02b **Neurogenic Stuttering Disorder** Another common form of stuttering is neurogenic. Neurogenic disorders arise from signal problems between the brain and nerves or muscles: the brain is unable to coordinate adequately the different components of the speech mechanism. Neurogenic stuttering may also occur following a stroke or other type of brain injury (National Institute on Deafness and Other Communication Disorders, 2002e).

SL 4.02c **Psychogenic Stuttering Disorder** Other forms of stuttering are classified as psychogenic, or originating in the mind or mental activity of the brain such as thought and reasoning. Whereas at one time the major cause of stuttering was thought to be psychogenic, this type of stuttering is now known to account for only a minority of the individuals who stutter. Although individuals who stutter may develop emotional problems, such as fear of meeting new people or speaking on the telephone, these problems often result from stuttering rather than causing the stuttering. Psychogenic stuttering occasionally occurs in individuals who have some types of mental illness or individuals who have experienced severe mental stress or anguish (National Institute on Deafness and Other Communication Disorders, 2002e).

SL 4.03 Other Types of Speech Fluency Disorders

SL 5.00 Voice Disorders (Dysphonia)

Definition Voice (or vocalization) is the audible sound produced by passage of air through the larynx (Melfi & Garrison, 2004). It is not always produced as speech, however. Infants babble and coo; animals bark, moo, whinny, growl, and meow;

and adult humans laugh, sing, and cry. Voice is generated by airflow from the lungs as the vocal folds are brought close together.

When air is pushed past the vocal folds with sufficient pressure, the vocal folds vibrate. If the vocal folds in the larynx did not vibrate normally, speech can be produced only as a whisper. An individual's voice is as unique as his or her fingerprint. It helps define his or her personality, mood, and health (National Institute on Deafness and Other Communication Disorders, 2002f).

Voice disorders are a group of problems involving abnormal pitch, loudness, or quality of the sound produced by the larynx (voice box) (University of Virginia, 2004). Approximately 7.5 million people in the United States have trouble using their voices. Disorders of the voice involve problems with pitch, loudness, and quality. *Pitch* is the highness or lowness of a sound based on the frequency of the sound waves. *Loudness* is the perceived volume (or amplitude) of the sound, and *quality* refers to the character or distinctive attributes of a sound. Many people who have normal speaking skills have great difficulty communicating when their vocal apparatus fails. This can occur if the nerves controlling the larynx are impaired because of an accident, a surgical procedure, a viral infection, or cancer (National Institute on Deafness and Other Communication Disorders, 2002f).

Diagnostic Symptoms Common symptoms of a voice disorder include (Lahey Clinic Foundation, 2005; Psychology Today, 2005):

- Breathy vocal quality
- Chronic cough or excessive throat clearing
- Decreased breath support during speech
- Deviations in the loudness of voice
- Diplophonic (double-toned) quality
- Hoarseness
- Inability to speak loudly
- Loss of voice
- Quality deviations
- Reduced pitch range or sudden change in overall pitch
- Sudden or gradual change in overall vocal quality
- Tremulous quality in the voice
- Vocal strain or fatigue

Further Key Points A voice is termed disordered when the vocal quality of an individual is altered or changed in such a way that it is thought to be abnormal to the listener. The onset and development of these disorders can be sudden or slow. Examples of characteristics of sudden onset are trauma, infection, cardiovascular accident, injurious inhalation, intubation, conversion reaction, or a severe allergic reaction. Degenerative neurological disease, musculoskeletal tension, vocal abuse and misuse, growths of folds, gastro-esophageal reflux, and chronic allergies may characterize slow onset (Murray State University, 2005).

Researchers suggest that there are two specific categories of voice disorders: functional voice disorders and organic voice disorders. Organic voice disorders are disorders with a known cause. Functional disorders encompass all disorders that result in physical change but do not have a known cause (Murray State University, 2005).

In sum, voice typically is defined by the elements of pitch (frequency), loudness (intensity), and quality (complexity). By varying the pitch, loudness, rate, and rhythm of voice (prosody), the speaker can convey additional meaning and emotion to words. A voice disorder exists when the quality, pitch, or volume differs from that of other persons of similar age, culture, and geographical location (Melfi & Garrison, 2004).

Types of Voice Disorders (Dysphonia)

SL 5.01 Muscle Tension Dysphonia

Definition A type of voice disorder specifically associated with strained, effortful phonation, usually causing vocal fatigue if used extensively (Columbia University College of Physicians and Surgeons, 2005).

Explanation Muscle tension dysphonia occurs when the vocal folds typically fail to come completely together because two muscles are pulling in opposite directions simultaneously. The vocal folds have the capacity and ability to assume the correct position for a task, but do not because they are pulling against one another in an inefficient fashion. This is most likely a learned behavior (Thomas, 2004).

SL 5.01a **Primary Muscle Tension Dysphonia** A type of vocalizing or speaking in which the muscles in the neck are tense and no lesion or paralysis is seen (Columbia University College of Physicians and Surgeons, 2005).

SL 5.01b **Secondary Muscle Tension Dysphonia** A compensatory method of vocalizing due to a paralysis, paresis, or muscular weakness, causing the person to squeeze other parts of the larynx to help produce sound (Columbia University College of Physicians and Surgeons, 2005).

SL 5.02 Resonance Disorders

Definition A type of voice disorder specifically associated with sound quality of speech. Resonance is defined as the vocal quality associated with the vibration of air in the oral and nasal cavities (American Cleft Palate-Craniofacial Association, 2004).

Explanation A voice with a resonance disorder suffers from either too many sounds coming out through the air passages of the nose (hypernasality) or, conversely, not enough resonance of the nasal pages (hyponasality).

SL 5.02a **Hypernasality Resonance Disorder** Hypernasality resonance disorder occurs when too much air passes through the nasal cavities during production of sounds, giving the speaker a distinctive nasal quality or twang. Hypernasality is a speech disorder that occurs when the palate and pharynx tissues do not close properly. This inadequate closure causes air to escape through the nose during speech instead of coming out of the sides and back of the throat, particularly with certain sounds such as *p, b, s,* and *k* (American Academy of Otolaryngology, 2002).

Hypernasality is the most common resonance disorder in children. It occurs most frequently in children born with a cleft palate or other craniofacial anomalies (Children's Hospital of New York, 2005).

It also can occur after cleft palate surgery, from a deformation of the face (such as Down syndrome), or from neurological problems. This condition rarely occurs after surgery to remove the adenoids and in otherwise healthy children. It can also be a learned behavior (American Academy of Otolaryngology, 2002). Hypernasality is often found in children with motor-based speech disturbances. Sluggish movements of the lips, tongue, or soft palate can result in airflow that is directed more toward the nasal cavity (Children's Hospital Medical Center of Akron, 2004).

SL 5.02b **Hyponasality Resonance Disorder** Hyponasality resonance disorder occurs when too much air passes through the nasal cavities during production of sounds. Nasal congestion from a cold or allergies or sometimes enlarged adenoids cause hyponasality (Children's Hospital Medical Center of Akron, 2004). The speaker may sound as if his or nose is being held or he or she has a cold.

SL 5.03 Spasmodic Dysphonia (Laryngeal Dystonia)

Definition A type of neurological voice disorder specifically associated with involuntary spasms of the vocal cords causing interruptions of speech and affecting the voice quality. Spasmodic dysphonia can cause the voice to break up or to have a tight, strained, or strangled quality (National Spasmodic Dysphonia Association, 2000).

Explanation Spasmodic dysphonia (or laryngeal dystonia) is a neurological voice disorder that involves involuntary spasms of the vocal cords causing interruptions of speech and affecting the voice quality. Individuals who have spasmodic dysphonia may have occasional difficulty saying a word or two or may experience sufficient difficulty to interfere with communication.

SL 5.03a **Adductor Spasmodic Dysphonia** In adductor spasmodic dysphonia, sudden involuntary muscle movements or spasms cause the vocal folds (or vocal cords) to slam together and stiffen. These spasms make it difficult for the vocal folds to vibrate and produce voice. Words are often cut off or difficult to start because of the muscle spasms. Therefore, speech may be choppy and sound similar to stuttering (Baylor College of Medicine, 2006; National Institute on Deafness and Other Communication Disorders, 2002g).

SL 5.03b **Abductor Spasmodic Dysphonia** in abductor spasmodic dysphonia, sudden involuntary muscle movements or spasms cause the vocal folds to open. The vocal folds cannot vibrate when they are open. The open position of the vocal folds also allows air to escape from the lungs during speech. As a result, the voices of these individuals often sound weak, quiet, and breathy or whispery (Baylor College of Medicine, 2006; National Institute on Deafness and Other Communication Disorders, 2002b).

SL 5.03c **Mixed Spasmodic Dysphonia** Mixed spasmodic dysphonia involves muscles that open the vocal folds as well as muscles that close the vocal folds and therefore has features of both adductor and abductor spasmodic dysphonia (National Institute on Deafness and Other Communication Disorders, 2002c).

SL 5.04 Other Types of Voice Disorders

SL 6.00 Dysarthria

Definition Dysarthria is a collective name for a group of related speech disorders that are due to disturbances in muscular control of the speech mechanism resulting from impairment of any of the basic motor processes involved in the execution of speech. It is the outcome of a motoric impairment, or a fundamental disturbance of movement, of the muscles of the speech production mechanism (Anderson & Shames, 2006).

Diagnostic Symptoms According to American-Speech-Language-Hearing Association (2006), a person with dysarthria may experience any of the following symptoms, depending on the extent and location of damage to the nervous system:

- "Slurred" speech
- Speaking softly or barely able to whisper
- Slow rate of speech
- Rapid rate of speech with a "mumbling" quality
- Limited tongue, lip, and jaw movement
- Abnormal intonation (rhythm) when speaking
- Changes in vocal quality ("nasal" speech or sounding "stuffy")

- Hoarseness
- Breathiness
- Drooling or poor control of saliva
- Chewing and swallowing difficulty

Further Key Points Dysarthria can be caused by dysfunction in the nervous pathways affecting any of the muscles of the tongue and mouth, the voice box, and the respiratory system. In multiple sclerosis it is often caused by lesions in the connecting pathways.

Therapy for dysarthria focuses on maximizing the function of all systems. Compensatory strategies are often used. Individuals with dysarthria may be advised to take frequent pauses for breath, to overarticulate, or to pause before important words to make them stand out. If there is muscle weakness, they may benefit from performing oro-facial exercises. This helps to strengthen the muscles of the face and mouth that are used for speech (*Dysarthria*, 1999).

Types of Dysarthria

SL 6.01 Ataxic Dysarthria

Definition Damage to the cerebellum or its connection leads to a condition called *ataxia* in which movements become uncoordinated. If the ataxia affects the muscles of the speech mechanism, production of speech may become abnormal lead ing to a cluster of deviant speech dimensions referred to as Ataxic Dysarthria (Anderson & Shames, 2006).

Explanation Ataxic dysarthria results from lesions. Such damage could be caused by stroke, trauma or by neurological disorders like muscular sclerosis. The cerebellum plays an important role in the coordination of motor movement due to its integration of sensory and motor information. Due to its connections with the vestibular system, it also affects equilibrium (McCaffrey, 2001).

SL 6.02 Flaccid Dysarthria

Definition Dysarthria resulting from a stroke is generally broken into two categories based on the site of the lesion. Damage to the lower motor neurons, LMN, those running from the spine to the muscle, results in Flaccid Dysarthria (Center for Speech, Language and Occupational Therapy, 2000).

Explanation Speech is characterized by a nasal quality (sounding as if "speaking through your nose") and a "breathy" voice due to poor closure of the vocal cords (resulting in low volume). Consonant sounds are especially difficult to articulate.

SL 6.03 Hyperkinetic Dysarthria

Definition Hyperkinetic dysarthria is usually thought to be due to lesions of the basal ganglia. Its predominant symptoms are associated with involuntary movement. There may be unilateral or bilateral damage.

Explanation As with spastic dysarthria, vocal quality may be described as harsh, strained, or strangled. Voice stoppages may occur in dysarthria associated with dystonia. Hypernasality is common. When voluntary speech movements are made there is often a super-imposition of involuntary movements. Speech can range from total lack of intelligability to a mild problem. There are many syndromes associated with this problem, several of which are described previously (McCaffrey, 2001).

SL 6.04 Hypokinetic Dysarthria

Definition Hypokinetic dysarthria involves a lack of movement, usually caused by Parkinson's disease. As once described, this disorder, "it puts you in a box"—in other words, it limits the patient's amount, range, and force of movement (Morales, 2006).

Explanation Features include monotony of pitch and loudness, breathy and hash vocal quality, reduced vocal intensity, consonant imprecision, reduction in phonation time, difficulty in the initiation of speech activities, and inappropriate silences (Anderson & Shames, 2006).

SL 6.05 Mixed dysarthria

Definition This type of dysarthria results from dysfunction in more than one speech motor system. Characteristics will vary depending on whether the upper or lower motor neurons remain most intact.

Explanation If upper motor neurons are most damaged initially, the voice will sound harsh. However, if lower motor neurons are most affected, the voice will sound breathy (Anderson & Shames, 2006).

SL 6.06 Spastic dysarthria

Definition This type occurs when the muscles involved in speech are impaired, creating speech problems (*Dysarthria,* 2006).

Explanation Spastic dysarthria involves excessive muscle tension and overly sensitive reflexes. This patient's voice often sounds strained or strangled and reflexes are so easily elicited that these extraneous movements interfere with speech production (Morales, 2006).

Language Disorders

SL 7.00 Aphasia

Definition Aphasia is a language disorder that results from damage to portions of the brain that are responsible for language (Anderson & Shames, 2006). For most people, these are parts of the left side (hemisphere) of the brain. Aphasia usually occurs suddenly, often as the result of a stroke or head injury, but it may also develop slowly, as in the case of a brain tumor. The disorder impairs both the expression and understanding of language, as well as reading and writing. Aphasia is an impairment of language, affecting the production or comprehension of speech and the ability to read or write (National Aphasia Association, 1999).

Diagnostic Symptoms The diagnostic symptoms of aphasia may be temporary or permanent, depending on the amount of brain damage (Penn State-Milton Hershey Medical Center College of Medicine, 2005). Symptoms vary based on the type of aphasia. Common symptoms include:

- Difficulty expressing oneself
- Difficulty reading
- Difficulty speaking
- Difficulty writing
- Inability to form sentences
- Jumbled speech
- Language problems
- Trouble understanding speech
- Unrelated words though clearly articulated

Further Key Points Aphasia may co-occur with speech disorders, which also result from brain damage (National Institute of Deafness and Other Communication Disorders, 2005). Aphasia's onset is usually abrupt, occurring without warning (Anderson & Shames, 2006).

Types of Aphasia

SL 7.01 Anomic Aphasia (Nominal Aphasia or Subcortical Aphasia)

Definition A type of aphasia specifically associated with either partial or total loss of the ability to recall the names of persons or things as a result of a stroke, head injury, brain tumor, or infection (National Institute on Deafness and Other

Communication Disorders, 2002a). Individuals with anomic aphasia have language marred by word-retrieval difficulties, but otherwise it is normal (Anderson & Shames, 2006).

Explanation Anomic aphasia primarily influences an individual's ability to find the right name for a person or object. As a result, an object may be described rather than named. Hearing comprehension, repetition, reading, and writing are not affected other than by this inability to find the right name. Speech is fluent, except for pauses as the individual tries to recall the right name. Physical symptoms are variable, and some individuals have no symptoms of one-sided weakness or sensory loss (National Institute on Deafness and Other Communication Disorders, 2005).

SL 7.02 Broca's Aphasia (Motor Aphasia)

Definition A type of aphasia specifically associated with damage to the frontal lobe of the brain. Individuals with Broca's aphasia frequently speak in short, meaningful phrases that are produced with great effort. Broca's aphasia is thus characterized as a nonfluent aphasia (National Institute on Deafness and Other Communication Disorders, 2002a).

Explanation Individuals with Broca's aphasia often omit small words such as *is, and,* and *the* (Anderson & Shames, 2006). For example, a person with Broca's aphasia may say, "Walk dog," meaning, "I will take the dog for a walk." The same sentence could also mean, "You take the dog for a walk" or "The dog walked out of the yard," depending on the circumstances (National Institute on Deafness and Other Communication Disorders, 2002c).

Individuals with Broca's aphasia may not be able to speak at all, or they may be able to use single-word statements or full sentences after great effort. They frequently omit words that are conjunctions and articles (*and, or, but, the, a*), which results in speech that sounds abrupt and choppy. People with Broca's aphasia can understand and process what others are saying, so they often become depressed and frustrated by their own inability to communicate. They may have difficulty reading, and weakness on the right side of the body may make writing difficult (Penn State-Milton Hershey Medical Center College of Medicine, 2005).

SL 7.03 Conduction Aphasia (Associative Aphasia)

Definition A type of aphasia specifically associated with an inability to repeat words, sentences, or phrases as a result of a stroke, head injury, brain tumor, or infection (Joseph F. Smith Medical Library, 2003).

Explanation Conduction aphasia is rather uncommon. Individuals with this disorder are unable to repeat words, sentences, and phrases. Speech is fairly unbroken, although individuals may frequently correct themselves and skip or repeat words (Anderson & Shames, 2006). Although they are able to understand spoken language, it may be difficult for them to find the right word to describe a person or object. The impact of this condition on reading and writing ability varies. As with other types of aphasia, right-sided weakness or sensory loss may be present (National Institute on Deafness and Other Communication Disorders, 2002c).

People with conduction aphasia cannot repeat words, sentences, and phrases. Although they can understand what others say, they may have difficulty finding the right words when speaking and so may correct themselves frequently and skip or repeat words. Conduction aphasia is uncommon (Penn State-Milton Hershey Medical Center College of Medicine, 2005).

SL 7.04 Global Aphasia

Definition A type of aphasia specifically associated with partial or total loss of the ability to communicate verbally or using written words as a result of widespread injury to the language areas of the brain (National Institute on Deafness and Other Communication Disorders, 2002a).

Explanation Global aphasia results from damage to extensive portions of the language areas of the brain. Individuals have severe communication difficulties and may be extremely limited in their ability to speak or comprehend language (National Institute on Deafness and Other Communication Disorders, 2002a). Because it affects more than one area of the brain, it can affect all language areas and is the most severe form of aphasia. Nevertheless, symptoms vary depending on the location and extent of injury (Penn State Milton Hershey Medical Center College of Medicine, 2005).

SL 7.05 Landau-Kleffner Syndrome

Definition Landau-Kleffner syndrome (LKS; also called infantile acquired aphasia, acquired epileptic aphasia, or aphasia with convulsive disorder) is characterized by the gradual or sudden loss of the ability to use or comprehend spoken language (New York-Presbyterian Hospital, 2003).

Explanation LKS occurs most frequently in normally developing children who are between three and seven years of age. For no apparent reason, these children begin having trouble understanding what is said to them. Doctors often refer to this problem as auditory agnosia, or word deafness. The auditory agnosia may occur slowly or very quickly. Parents often think that the child is developing a hearing problem or has become suddenly deaf. Hearing tests, however, show normal hearing. Children may also appear to be autistic or developmentally delayed (National Institute of Neurological Disorders and Stroke, 2005; National Institute on Deafness and Other Communication Disorders National Institutes of Health, 2002d; New York-Presbyterian Hospital, 2003).

SL

The inability to understand language eventually affects the child's spoken language, which may progress to a complete loss of the ability to speak (mutism). Children who have learned to read and write before the onset of auditory agnosia can often continue communicating through written language. Some children develop a type of gestural communication or signlike language.

The loss of language may be preceded by an epileptic seizure, which usually occurs at night. At some time, 80 percent of children with LKS have one or more seizures. The seizures usually stop by the time the child becomes a teenager. All LKS children have abnormal electrical brain activity on both sides of the brain (National Institute of Neurological Disorders and Stroke, 2005; National Institute on Deafness and Other Communication Disorders National Institutes of Health, 2002d).

SL 7.06 Transcortical Aphasia

Definition A type of aphasia specifically associated with partial or total loss of the ability to communicate verbally or using written words that does not affect an individual's ability to repeat words, phrases, and sentences (National Institute on Deafness and Other Communication Disorders, 2002a). Transcortical aphasia is caused by damage to the language areas of the left hemisphere that are outside the primary language areas (Penn State-Milton Hershey Medical Center College of Medicine, 2005).

Explanation People with transcortical aphasia suffer partial or total loss of the ability to communicate verbally or use written words but can still repeat words, phrases, or sentences (Penn State-Milton Hershey Medical Center College of Medicine, 2005). Other language functions may also be impaired to varying degrees, depending on the extent and particular location of brain damage.

There are three types of transcortical aphasia:

- Transcortical motor aphasia
- Transcortical sensory aphasia
- Mixed transcortical aphasia.

SL 7.06a **Transcortical Motor Aphasia** Transcortical motor aphasia is different from Broca's aphasia in that repetition ability is intact. Patients who demonstrate transcortical motor aphasia have the same halting, agrammatical speech of Broca's but may be echolalic, or able to repeat complex words and phrases (DaVanzo, 2005).

SL 7.06b **Transcortical Sensory Aphasia** This occurs when the speech areas are disconnected from the posterior association cortex. Patients can recognize words and can talk, but they cannot understand what people are saying to them and have no spontaneous speech of their own (DaVanzo, 2005).

SL 7.06c **Mixed Transcortical Mixed Aphasia** A rare aphasic disorder involves the isolation of both Broca's and Wernicke's areas. The patient has a virtual compulsion to repeat utterances to the point of appearing echolalic. Other language abilities, such as comprehension, naming, expression, and reading, are impaired. The individual might not utter any language unless spoken to (DaVanzo, 2005).

SL 7.07 Wernicke's Aphasia

Definition A type of aphasia specifically associated with damage to the temporal lobe of the brain (typically the left hemisphere), thought to be important for the comprehension of spoken language (Hedge & Maul, 2006).

Explanation Individuals with Wernicke's aphasia may speak in long sentences that have no meaning, add unnecessary words, and even create new "words" (Anderson & Shames, 2006). For example, someone with Wernicke's aphasia may say, "You know that smoodle pinkered and that I want to get him round and take care of him like you want before," meaning, "The dog needs to go out, so I will take him for a walk." Individuals with Wernicke's aphasia usually have great difficulty understanding speech and are therefore often unaware of their mistakes. They usually have no body weakness because their brain injury is not near the parts of the brain that control movement (National Institute of Neurological Disorders and Stroke, 2005).

People with Wernicke's aphasia often speak with words that are not needed, difficult to understand, or simply made up. They are often completely unaware of their language difficulties and may not even understand what other people say at all. Although they may be able to write, what they write may not be understandable. People with Wernicke's aphasia also have difficulty reading (Penn State-Milton Hershey Medical Center College of Medicine, 2005).

SL 7.08 Other Types of Aphasia

SL 8.00 Central Auditory Processing Disorders

Definition The American Speech-Language-Hearing Association (1996) defines central auditory processing disorder (CAPD) as a disorder with problems in one of six areas:

- Sound localization and lateralization (knowing where in space a sound source is located).
- Auditory discrimination (usually with reference to speech, but the ability to tell that one sound is different from another).
- Auditory pattern recognition (musical rhythms are one example of an auditory pattern).

- Temporal aspects of audition (auditory processing relies on making fine discriminations of timing changes in auditory input, especially differences in timing between the way input comes through one ear as opposed to the other).
- Auditory performance decrements with competing acoustic signals (listening in noise).
- Auditory performance decrements with degraded acoustic signals, for example, listening to sounds that are muffled or unclear, or missing information. An example is trying to listen to speech taking place on the other side of a wall. The wall filters or blocks out certain parts of the speech, but a typical listener can often understand the conversation.

Diagnostic Symptoms Children with central auditory processing difficulty typically have normal hearing and intelligence (National Institute on Deafness and Other Communication Disorders, 2004). However, they have also been observed to have:

- Trouble paying attention to and remembering information presented orally
- Problems carrying out multistep directions
- Poor listening skills
- A need for more time to process information
- Low academic performance
- Behavior problems
- Language difficulty (for example, confusing syllable sequences and problems developing vocabulary and understanding language)
- Difficulty with reading, comprehension, spelling, and vocabulary

Further Key Points Approximately 10 to 20 percent of students with communication disorders have difficulty with central auditory processing, which is the ability to track individual and group conversations that occur in both quiet and noisy backgrounds (Cockrell & Nickel, 2000, cited in Turnbull, Turnbull, & Wehmeyer, 2006).

The cause of CAPD is often unknown. In children, auditory processing difficulty may be associated with conditions such as dyslexia, attention deficit disorder, autism, autism spectrum disorder, specific language impairment, pervasive developmental disorder, or developmental delay. Sometimes this term has been misapplied to children who have no hearing or language disorder but have challenges in learning (National Institute on Deafness and Other Communication Disorders, 2004).

Since speech and language skills are developed most efficiently through the auditory sensory modality, it is not unusual to observe speech and language problems, as well as academic problems (many of them language based), in children with CAPD. A child who experiences difficulty in processing the brief and rapidly changing acoustics of spoken speech is likely to have problems recognizing the speech sounds of language (Schminky & Baran, 2004).

SL 9.00 Language Delay

See also Chapter Thirteen on infants, toddlers, and preschool language delays.

Definition Language delay occurs when a child's language is developing in the right sequence but at a slower-than-normal rate (University of Michigan Health Systems, 2006). A child with a language delay is often very late in beginning to talk or lags well behind peers in language development (Boyse & Solomon, 2005).

Language delay occurs when the normal rate of developmental progress is interrupted but the systematic sequence of development remains essentially intact. For individuals with a language delay, the development follows a normal pattern or course of growth but is substantially slower than in most other children of the same age; in other words, affected children use the language rules typical of a younger child (Hardman, Drew, and Egan, 2005).

Diagnostic Symptoms The National Institute on Deafness and Other Communication Disorders (2001) and various children's hospitals list the following age-appropriate speech and language milestones:

Birth to Five Months

- Coos
- Vocalizes pleasure and displeasure sounds (laughs, giggles, cries, or fusses)
- Makes noise when talked to

Six to Eleven Months

- Understands "no-no"
- Babbles (says "ba-ba-ba")
- Says "ma-ma" or "da-da" without meaning
- Tries to communicate by actions or gestures
- Tries to repeat another person's sounds
- First word

Twelve to Seventeen Months

- Answers simple questions nonverbally
- Follows simple directions
- Says two to three words to label a person or object (pronunciation may not be clear)
- Tries to imitate simple words
- Vocabulary of four to six words

Eighteen to Twenty-Three Months

- Correctly pronounces most vowels and *n, m, p, h,* especially at the beginning of syllables and short words; also begins to use other speech sounds
- Vocabulary of at least fifty words; pronunciation often unclear
- Asks for common foods by name
- Makes animal sounds such as "moo"
- Starting to combine words such as "more milk"
- Begins to use pronouns such as "mine"
- Uses two-word phrases

Two to Three Years

- Knows some spatial concepts such as "in," "on"
- Knows pronouns such as "you," "me," "her"
- Knows descriptive words such as "big," "happy"
- Vocabulary of 250 to 900 words
- Uses three-word sentences
- Speech is becoming more accurate but may still leave off ending sounds; strangers may not be able to understand much of what is said
- Answers simple questions
- Begins to use more pronouns such as "you," "I"
- Uses question inflection and question words to ask for something such as, "My ball?"
- Begins to use plurals such as "shoes" or "socks" and regular past-tense verbs such as "jumped"

Three to Four Years

- Groups objects such as foods and clothes
- Identifies colors
- Uses most speech sounds but may distort some of the more difficult sounds such as *l, r, s, sh, ch, y, v, z, th;* these sounds may not be fully mastered until age seven or eight
- Uses consonants in the beginning, middle, and ends of words; some of the more difficult consonants may be distorted, but attempts to say them
- Strangers are able to understand much of what is said
- Able to describe the use of objects such as "fork," "car"
- Has fun with language; enjoys poems and recognizes language absurdities such as, "Is that an elephant on your head?"

- Expresses ideas and feelings rather than just talking about the world around him or her
- Uses verbs that end in "-ing," such as "walking" and "talking"
- Answers simple questions such as, "What do you do when you are hungry?"
- Repeats sentences

Four to Five Years

- Understands spatial concepts such as "behind," "next to"
- Understands complex questions
- Speech is understandable but makes mistakes pronouncing long, difficult, or complex words such as "hippopotamus"
- Vocabulary of about 1,500 words
- Uses some irregular past tense verbs such as "ran," "fell"
- Describes how to do things such as painting a picture
- Defines words
- Lists items that belong in a category such as animals, vehicles
- Answers "why" questions
- Can have simple conversation

Five Years

- Understands more than 2,000 words
- Understands time sequences (what happened first, second, third)
- Carries out a series of three directions
- Understands rhyming
- Engages in more extensive conversation
- Can use sentences of eight or more words in length
- Uses compound and complex sentences
- Describes objects
- Uses imagination to create stories
- May have beginning reading skills

Further Key Points Children vary in their development of speech and language. There is, however, a natural progression or timetable for mastery of these skills for each language. The milestones are identifiable skills that can serve as a guide to normal development. Typically simple skills need to be reached before the more complex skills can be learned. There is a general age and time when most children pass through these periods. These milestones help doctors and other health professionals determine when a child may need extra help to learn to speak or use language (National Institute on Deafness and Other Communication Disorders, 2001).

Types of Language Delays

SL 9.01 Acquired Language Delay

Definition A type of language delay specifically associated with injury or illness as its cause (Royal College of Speech and Language Therapists, 2001).

Explanation A language delay can be thought of as a delay resulting from something traumatic occurring to the individual. Examples include a car accident, sickness, or other type of situation that has a direct cause-and-effect relationship to the language delay of the individual.

SL 9.02 Developmental Language Delay

Definition A type of language delay specifically occurring when language is not achieved at the expected time and is not due to injury or illness (Royal College of Speech and Language Therapists, 2001).

Explanation Children acquire language at tremendously variable rates during the first four years of life, yet some children are clearly behind by age two or three. This is an important signal. Delayed language development can be the first warning of a pervasive developmental disability, hearing impairment, or neurological problem. Any of these conditions puts a child at risk of future reading difficulties. Often an evaluation by a speech-language professional reveals that these children have early language impairment. About 40 to 75 percent of preschoolers with such an impairment develop reading difficulties later, often along with other academic problems (North Central Regional Educational Laboratory, 2005).

SL 9.03 Other Types of Language Delays

SL 10.00 Expressive Language Disorders

Definition Expressive spoken language disorders are characterized by difficulties using spoken or written language. These types of language disorders involve problems associated with verbal or written expression (Hunt & Marshall, 2005).

Individuals with expressive language disorders have difficulty in language production or formulating and using spoken or written language. Those with expressive language disorders may have limited vocabularies and use the same array of words regardless of the situation. Expressive language disorders may appear as immature speech, often resulting in interaction difficulties (Vicari et al., 2000;

cited in Hardman et al., 2005). People with expressive disorders may also use hand signals and facial expressions to communicate.

Diagnostic Symptoms Children with expressive spoken language disorders have a vocabulary that tends to be smaller compared with other children of the same age. They are usually also below the average level for their age in producing sentences, putting words together to formulate thoughts, recalling words, and using language appropriately in different settings with different people (Hedge & Maul, 2006; Better Health Channel, 2005). Other common symptoms include:

- Below-average vocabulary skills
- Difficulty with oral and written work and school assignments in older children
- Frequent trouble finding the right word
- Improper use of tenses (past, present, future)
- Inability to come to the point or talking in circles
- Inability to start or hold a conversation
- Learning problems
- Low self-esteem
- Grammatical mistakes and using poor sentence structure
- Misnaming items (dysnomia)
- Problems in recalling words
- Problems in the production of complex sentences
- Problems with retelling a story or relaying information
- Problems with socialization
- Reliance on short, simple sentence construction
- Reliance on stock standard phrases and limited content in speech
- Using the wrong words in sentences or confusing meaning in sentences

Further Key Points Expressive language disorders are characterized by difficulty formulating ideas and information (Turnbull et al., 2007). Children with expressive language delays often do not talk much or often, although they generally understand language addressed to them. These are children who may have a lot to say but are unable to retrieve the words they need to speak. Some may have no problem in simple expression but difficulty retrieving and organizing words and sentences when expressing more complicated thoughts and ideas. This may occur when they are trying to describe, define, or explain information or retell an event or activity (Morales, 2005a).

An expressive language disorder could occur in a child of normal intelligence, or it could be a component of a condition affecting mental functioning more broadly such as mental retardation or autism. The disturbance may be manifest clinically by symptoms that include having a markedly limited vocabulary, making errors in tense, or having difficulty recalling words or producing sentences with developmentally appropriate length or complexity (Morales, 2005a).

Types of Expressive Language Disorders

SL 10.01 Expressive Morphological Language Disorder

Definition An expressive language disorder specifically associated with difficulties in the use of grammar in words.

Explanation Morphology is the set of rules that govern the parts of words that form the basic elements of meanings and structures of words (Deutsch Smith, 2004). For example, prefixes and suffixes change the meaning of the roots of specific words: An "-ed" at the end of a verb changes the tense to past (cover and covered); an "un-" at the beginning of a word means that something is not (cover and uncover). For example, children with this disorder might say:

"I win the game yesterday"

"We goed to the store"

"They played baseball tomorrow"

Children with expressive language morphological disorder may also exhibit more grammatical errors than peers, slow development of grammatical morphemes, or many pronoun errors (Hunt and Marshall, 2005).

SL 10.02 Expressive Phonological Language Disorder

Definition An expressive language disorder specifically associated with difficulties in the use of sounds to create meaningful syllables and words. Individuals with expressive phonological language disorder have great difficulties articulating speech sounds and using the sounds of language correctly (Friend, 2005).

Explanation Phonology is the sound system of language that includes rules that govern various sound combinations (Hunt & Marshall, 2005). Examples of expressive language phonological disorder include saying *bunk* for *dunk, pan* for *pen,* or *sin* for *sun.* Children with expressive language phonological disorder may also exhibit a failure to capitalize on regularities across words, slow development of phonological processes, or unusual errors across sound categories (Hunt & Marshall, 2005).

SL 10.03 Expressive Pragmatic Language Disorder

Definition An expressive language disorder specifically associated with difficulties in the use of language in a social context (Gargiulo, 2004; Friend, 2005).

Explanation Pragmatics is the study of language in context and focuses in part on the intention of the communication (Turnbull et al., 2004). The context of discussion between two children talking to each other during free play is quite different from the context of discussion between a teacher and a child (Deutsch Smith, 2004). Children with expressive pragmatic language disorder often lack the understanding for the subtleties and intricacies of humor or slang, which can present social as well as communication problems for such children (Gargiulo, 2004). These children may also exhibit:

- Difficulty gaining access into conversations
- Less effective means at negotiating disputes
- Less use of the naming function
- Difficulty tailoring the message to the listener
- Difficulty repairing communication breakdowns

SL 10.04 Expressive Syntax Language Disorder

Definition An expressive language disorder specifically associated with difficulties in the use of the rules that govern sentence structure (Hunt & Marshall, 2005). Individuals with expressive syntax language disorder have great difficulties using grammar in phrases and sentences.

Explanation Syntax determines where a word is placed in a sentence. Students with problems in syntax use may have difficulty organizing and expressing complex ideas since the placement of words in a sentence can change their meaning (Gargiulo, 2004)—for example:

"The boy hit the ball" has a different meaning from "The ball hit the boy."

"I hardly studied for this test" has a different meaning from "I studied hard for this test" (Deutsch-Smith, 2004).

"Will you help Ted?" has a different meaning from "You will help Ted."

An individual with expressive syntax language disorder may often speak in a manner that makes no sense to the listener. For example, he or she might say, "The yellow beautiful sun" instead of "The beautiful yellow sun."

SL 10.05 Expressive Semantics Language Disorder

Definition An expressive language disorder specifically associated with difficulties in the use of word meanings and word relationships (Gargiulo, 2004).

Explanation Semantics is the system where the intent and meaning of the words used affect the meaning of the message (Deutsch-Smith, 2004). It represents the understanding of language, the component most concerned with meaning.

Individuals with expressive semantics language disorder are characterized by poor vocabulary development and inappropriate use of word meanings (Gargiulo, 2004).

An individual with this disorder might say, when describing his or her day, "It was fun," while his or her peers might say, "We spent the day at the beach and had a lot of fun and many laughs." The meaning and the precision of the words of the individual with expressive language semantics disorder are not nearly as accurate and detailed as those of his or her peers. He or she may also exhibit delayed acquisition of first words, slower rate of vocabulary acquisition, and less diverse repertoire of verb types (Hunt & Marshall, 2005)

SL 10.06 Other Types of Expressive Language Disorders

SL 11.00 Receptive Language Disorders

Definition Individuals with receptive language disorders have difficulty comprehending what others say. They have great difficulty understanding other people's messages and may process only part or none of what is being said to them. Their problems are associated with language processing, which is essentially listening to and interpreting spoken language (Hardman et al., 2005). Receptive language disorders involve difficulties in the ability to attend to, process, comprehend, retain, or integrate spoken language.

Diagnostic Symptoms There is no standard set of symptoms that indicates receptive language disorder, since it varies from one child to the next. However, symptoms may include (Friend, 2005; Kauffman Children's Center, 2004):

- Difficulty responding appropriately to yes/no questions, either/or questions, who/what/where questions and when/why/how questions
- Echolalia (repeating back words or phrases either immediately or at a later time)
- Short attention span
- Problems with multiple word meanings
- High activity level and not attending to spoken language
- Inability to follow directions (following of routine, repetitive directions may be okay)
- Inability to follow verbal instructions
- Inability to understand complicated sentences
- Lack of interest when storybooks are read to them
- Language skills below the expected level for the person's age
- Not attending to spoken language
- Not seeming to listen when spoken to

- Reauditorization (repeating back a question first and then responding to it)
- Responding inconsistently to sounds or speech
- Seems to be easily distracted
- Sometimes looking blank when spoken to
- Using memorized phrases and sentences

Further Key Points Students with receptive language disorders often experience significant academic performance problems and difficulties with social situations and interactions. Receptive language disorders appear as a high-risk indicator of other disabilities and may frequently remain undiagnosed because they are not as evident as problems in language production (Toppleberg & Shapiro, 2001).

SL 11.01 Receptive Morphological Language Disorder

Definition A type of receptive language disorder specifically associated with difficulties in the understanding of grammatical structure of words (Gargiulo, 2004).

Explanation Morphology is the set of rules governing the parts of words that form the basic elements of meanings and structures of words (Deutsch-Smith, 2004). For example, prefixes and suffixes change the meaning of the roots of specific words. An "-ed" at the end of a verb changes the tense to past (cover and covered); an "un-" at the beginning of a word means that something is not (cover and uncover). A student with receptive morphological language disorder may not understand that something will occur in the future or has already occurred because he or she has difficulties understanding tenses.

SL 11.02 Receptive Phonological Language Disorder

Definition A type of receptive language disorder specifically associated with difficulties in the discrimination of speech sounds (Friend, 2005).

Explanation Phonology is the sound system of language that includes rules that govern various sound combinations (Turnbull et al., 2004; Deutsch-Smith, 2004). Students with receptive phonological language disorder may have difficulties processing decoding the spoken language, or make substitutions for sounds they hear, such as hearing *blink* for *drink.* Other examples include hearing *bunk* for *dunk, pan* for *pen,* or *sin* for *sun.*

SL 11.03 Receptive Pragmatic Language Disorder

Definition A type of receptive language disorder specifically associated with difficulties in understanding contextual language cues (Hardman et al., 2005).

Explanation Pragmatics is the study of language in context and focuses in part on the intention of the communication (Hallahan & Kauffman, 2006). Children

SL

with receptive pragmatic language disorder often lack the understanding for the subtleties and intricacies of humor or slang, which can present social as well as communication problems for them (Gargiulo, 2004).

SL 11.04 Receptive Syntax Language Disorder

Definition A type of receptive language disorder specifically associated with difficulties in understanding phrases and sentences (Hunt & Marshall, 2005).

Explanation Syntax determines where a word is placed in a sentence. Students with syntactical deficits may have difficulty organizing and expressing complex ideas (Gargiulo, 2004) since the placement of words in a sentence can change their meaning. For example, a student with receptive language syntax disorder may hear:

"The boy hit the ball" instead of, "The ball hit the boy."

"I hardly studied for this test" instead of, "I studied hard for this test" (Deutsch-Smith, 2004).

"Will you help Ted?" instead of, "You will help Ted."

SL 11.05 Receptive Semantics Language Disorder

Definition A type of receptive language disorder specifically associated with difficulties in understanding word meanings and word relationships (Gargiulo, 2004).

Explanation Semantics is the system where the intent and meaning of all the words used affect the meaning of the message (Deutsch Smith, 2004). It represents the understanding of language, the component most concerned with meaning (Friend, 2005). Individual with receptive semantics language disorder often have difficulty organizing complex ideas and putting together a series of words to determine how such order will later be used in the communication process (Gargiulo, 2004).

SL 11.06 Other Types of Receptive Language Disorders

SL 12.00 Medically Based Language Disorders or Other Types of Speech and Language Disorders-Be Specific

---

References

American Academy of Neurology. (2001). *Study ties stuttering to anatomical differences in the brain.* Retrieved August 1, 2005, from http://www.sciencedaily.com/releases/2001/07/010730075359.htm.

American Academy of Otolaryngology. (2002). *Hypernasality: A treatable speech disorder.* Retrieved August 1, 2005, from http://www.entnet.org/healthinfo/throat/hypernasality.cfm.

American Cleft Palate-Craniofacial Association. (2004). *Glossary of terms.* Retrieved August 1, 2005, from http://www.cleftline.org/aboutclp/glossary.htm.

American Speech-Language-Hearing Association. (1996). Central auditory processing: Current status of research and implications for clinical practice. *American Journal of Audiology, 5(*2), 41–54.

American Speech-Language-Hearing Association. (2002). *Communication facts: Incidence and prevalence of communication disorders and hearing loss in children.* Retrieved April 18, 2005, from www.professional.asha.org/resources/factsheets/children.cfm.

American Speech-Language-Hearing Association. (2005). *Speech-language disorders and the speech-language pathologist.* Retrieved August 1, 2005, from http://www.asha.org/students/professions/overview/sld.htm.

American Speech-Language-Hearing Association. (2006). *Dysarthria.* Retrieved November 5, 2006, from http://www.asha.org/public/speech/disorders/dysarthria.htm.

Anderson, N. B., & Shames, G. H. (2006). *Human communication disorders: An introduction.* Needham Heights, MA: Allyn & Bacon.

Barlow, J. A., & Gierut, J. A. (2002). Minimal pair approaches to phonological remediation. *Seminars in Speech and Language, 23*(1), 57–67.

Baylor College of Medicine. (2006). *Adductor spasmodic dysphonia.* Retrieved February 3, 2006, from http://www.bcm.edu/oto/grand/71391.html.

Better Health Channel. (2005). *Expressive language disorder.* Retrieved August 1, 2005, from http://www.betterhealth.vic.gov.au/bhcv2/bhcarticles.nsf/pages/Expressive_language_disorder?OpenDocument.

Boston College. (2005). *Fluency disorders.* Retrieved August 1, 2005, from http://www2.bc.edu/~tougher/fluencydisorders.html.

Bowen, C. (2005). *Children's speech sound disorders: Questions and answers.* Retrieved August 1, 2005, from http://members.tripod.com/Caroline_Bowen/phonol-and-artic.htm.

Boyse, K., & Solomon, R. (2005). *Speech and language delays and disorders.* University of Michigan Health System. Retrieved August 1, 2005, from http://www.med.umich.edu/1libr/yourchild/speech.htm.

Brice, A. (2001). *Children with communication disorders.* Arlington, VA: ERIC Clearinghouse on Disabilities and Gifted Education.

Burgess, J. (2005). *Developing literacy—phonological processing.* Retrieved August 1, 2005, from http://curry.edschool.virginia.edu/go/edis771/98webquests/professional/pkathieburgess/litindex.html.

Caruso, A., & Strand, E. A. (Eds.). (1999). *Clinical management of motor speech disorders of children.* New York: Thieme Publishing.

Center for Speech, Language and Occupational Therapy. (2000). *What is dysarthria?* Retrieved November 1, 2006 from http://www.cslot.com/adults/dysarthria_art.htm.

Child Development Institute. (2005). *Children with communication disorders.* Retrieved August 1, 2005, from http://www.childdevelopmentinfo.com/.

Childhood Apraxia of Speech Association. (2005). *Understanding apraxia.* Retrieved August 1, 2005, from http://www.childhoodanxietynetwork.org/htdocs/newest1.htm.

Children's Hospital of New York. (2005). *Craniofacial speech disorders.* Retrieved August 1, 2005, from http://entcolumbia.org/Craniofacial%20Speech%20Disorder-%20 GENERAL.pdf.

Children's Hospital Medical Center of Akron. (2004). *Voice disorders.* Retrieved August 1, 2005, from http://www.voiceandswallowing.com/Voicedisorders_mtd.htm.

Columbia University College of Physicians and Surgeons. (2005). *Muscle tension dysphonia.* Retrieved August 1, 2005, from http://www.entcolumbia.org/hearloss.htm.

DaVanzo, J. (2005). *Aphasia.* Retrieved August 1, 2005, from http://www.people.virginia.edu/~jpd3n/aphasia.html.

Deutsch-Smith, D. (2004). *Introduction to special education: Teaching in an age of opportunity* (5th ed.). Needham Heights, MA: Allyn & Bacon.

Dodd, B., & Bradford, A. (2000). A comparison of three therapy methods for children with different types of developmental phonological disorder. *International Journal of Language and Communication Disorders, 35,* 189–209.

Downey, A. (2004). *The physiology of speech/language disorders in children.* Retrieved August 1, 2005, from http://www.vh.org/pediatric/provider/pediatrics/speechdelay/physiology.html.

Durkel, J. (2002). *Central auditory processing disorder and auditory neuropathy.* Retrieved August 1, 2005, from http://www.tsbvi.edu/Outreach/seehear/winter01/capd.htm.

Dysarthria. (1999). Speech Language Pathology Web site. Retrieved November 1, 2006, from http://home.ica.net/~fred/anch10-1.htm.

Dysarthria. (2006). All About Multiple Sclerosis. Retrieved November 15, 2006, from http://www.mult-sclerosis.org/dysarthria.html.

Encyclopedia of Neurological Disorders. (2006). *Ataxic dysarthria.* Retrieved October 23, 2006, from http://health.enotes.com/neurological-disorders-encyclopedia/dysarthria.

Fackler, A. (2005). *What is stuttering?* Retrieved August 1, 2005, from http://www.healthbanks.com/PatientPortal/Public/ArticlePromoted.aspx?ArticleID=HW5ue5032.

Forrest, K. (2002). Are oral-motor exercises useful in the treatment of phonological/articulatory disorders? *Seminars in Speech and Language, 23,* 15–25.

Forrest, K., Elbert, M., & Dinnsen, D. (2002). The effect of substitution patterns on phonological treatment outcomes. *Clinical Linguistics and Phonetics, 14,* 519–531.

Friend, M. (2005). *Special education: Contemporary perspectives for school professionals.* Needham Heights, MA: Allyn & Bacon.

Gargiulo, R. M. (2004). *Special education in contemporary society: An introduction to exceptionality.* Belmont, CA: Thompson-Wadsworth.

Gierut, J. A. (2001). Complexity in phonological treatment: Clinical factors. *Language, Speech and Hearing Services in Schools, 32*(4), 229–241.

Gierut, J. A., & Champion, A. H. (2001). Syllable onsets II: Three-element clusters in phonological treatment. *Journal of Speech, Language and Hearing Research, 44,* 886–904.

Goldstein, B., Fabiano, L., & Iglesias. A. (2004). Spontaneous and imitated productions in Spanish-speaking children with phonological disorders. *Language, Speech, and Hearing Services in Schools, 35,* 5–15.

Golisano Children's Hospital. (2005). *Pediatric speech pathology—apraxia.* Retrieved August 1, 2005, from http://www.stronghealth.com/services/childrens/conditions/apraxia.cfm.

Hall, B. J., Oyer, H. J., & Haas, W. H. (2001). *Speech, language, and hearing disorders: A guide for the teacher.* Needham Heights, MA: Allyn & Bacon.

Hallahan, D. P., & Kauffman, J.M. (2006). *Exceptional learners: An introduction to special education* (10th ed.). Needham Heights, MA: Allyn & Bacon.

Hamaguchi, P. M. (2001). *Childhood speech, language, and listening problems: What every parent should know* (2nd ed.). Hoboken, NJ: Wiley.

Hardman, M. L., Drew, C. J., & Egan, M. W. (2005). *Human exceptionality: School, community, and family.* Needham Heights, MA: Allyn & Bacon.

Hearing, Speech & Deafness Center. (2005). *Developmental apraxia of speech.* Retrieved August 1, 2005, from http://www.hsdc.org/Child/Speech/devapraxia.htm.

Hedge, M. N., & Maul, C. A. (2006). *Language disorders in children: An evidence-based approach to assessment and treatment.* Needham Heights, MA: Allyn & Bacon.

Heward, J. (2006). *Exceptional children: An introduction to special education* (8th ed.). Upper Saddle River, NJ: Pearson Education Inc.

Hulit, H., & Howard, M. (2002). *Born to talk: An introduction to speech and language development* (3rd ed.). Needham Heights, MA: Allyn & Bacon.

Hunt, N., & Marshall, K. (2005). *Exceptional children and youth* (5th ed.). Boston: Houghton Mifflin.

Irishhealth.com. (2005). *Cluttering.* Retrieved August 1, 2005, from http://www.irishhealth.com/?level=4&con=93.

Jacobsen, K. (n.d.). *Auditory and language processing disorders.* Retrieved August 1, 2005, from http://pcs.mgh.harvard.edu/heal_lang_art3.htm.

Joseph F. Smith Medical Library. (2003). *Conduction aphasia.* Retrieved September 4, 2005, from http://www.aspiruslibrary.org/.

Kauffman Children's Center. (2004). *Receptive language disorders: Signs and symptoms.* Retrieved August 1, 2005, from http://www.kidspeech.com/index.php?page=79.

Kim, O. H., & Kaiser, A. P. (2000). Language characteristics of children with ADHD [electronic version]. *Communication Disorders Quarterly, 21,* 154–165.

Lahey Clinic Foundation. (2005). *Voice disorders.* Retrieved August 1, 2005, from http://www.lahey.org/Medical/VoiceCenter/VoiceCenter_VoiceSymptoms.asp.

Learning Disabilities of Ontario. (2005). *Phonological processes.* Retrieved August 1, 2005, from http://learn-ontario.ca/dyslexia.htm#td.

LinguaLinks Library. (2005). *What is phonology?* Retrieved August 1, 2005, from http://www.sil.org/linguistics/GlossaryOfLinguisticTerms/WhatIsPhonology.htm.

Magee, K. (2003). *Stuttering.* Retrieved August 1, 2005, from http://health.yahoo.com/ency/healthwise/ue5064/popup/ue5064-sec.

Marshall University. (2005). *Disorders of articulation.* Retrieved August 1, 2005, from http://webpages.marshall.edu/~lynch4/articulation.html.

McCaffrey, P. (2001). *Neuropathologies of swallowing and speech.* Retrieved October 28, 2006, from http://www.csuchico.edu/~pmccaff/syllabi/SPPA342/index.html.

McCormick, L., Loeb, D. F., & Schiefelbusch, R. L. (2003). *Supporting children with communication difficulties in inclusive settings* (2nd ed.) Needham Heights, MA: Allyn & Bacon.

Melfi, R., & Garrison, S. (2004). *Communication disorders.* Retrieved August 1, 2005, from http://www.emedicine.com/pmr/topic153.htm.

Morales, S. (2005a). *Expressive language disorder.* Retrieved August 1, 2005, from http://www.childspeech.net/u_iv_h.html.

Morales, S. (2005b). *Overview of speech and language impairments.* Retrieved August 1, 2005, from http://www.childspeech.net/u_i.html.

Morales, S. (2006). *Dysarthria.* Children's Speech Care Center. Retrieved November 8, 2006, from www.childspeech.net/u_iv_g.html.

Murray State University. (2005). *Voice disorders.* Retrieved August 1, 2005, from http://mick.murraystate.edu/cdi624/fall97/disords.htm.

National Aphasia Association. (1999). *Aphasia fact sheet.* Retrieved August 1, 2005, from http://www.aphasia.org/NAAfactsheet.html.

National Dissemination Center for Children with Disabilities. (2004). *Speech and language impairments.* Retrieved August 1, 2005, from http://nichcy.org/pubs/factshe/fs11txt.htm

National Institute of Neurological Disorders and Stroke. (2005). *Aphasia information page.* Retrieved August 1, 2005, from http://www.ninds.nih.gov/disorders/aphasia/aphasia.htm.

National Institute on Deafness and Other Communication Disorders. (2001). *Speech and language developmental milestones.* Bethesda, MD: NIH Publication No. 00-478.

National Institute on Deafness and Other Communication Disorders. (2002a). *Aphasia information page.* Retrieved August 1, 2005, from http://www.nidcd.nih.gov/health/voice/aphasia.asp.

National Institute on Deafness and Other Communication Disorders. (2002b). *Apraxia of speech.* Retrieved April 12, 2006, from http://www.nidcd.nih.gov/health/voice/apraxia.asp.

National Institute on Deafness and Other Communication Disorders. (2002c). *Auditory processing disorder in children.* Retrieved on April 12, 2006, from http://www.nidcd.nih.gov/health/voice/auditory.asp.

National Institute on Deafness and Other Communication Disorders National Institutes of Health. (2002d). *Landau-Kleffner syndrome.* Bethesda, MD: National Institutes of Health.

National Institute on Deafness and Other Communication Disorders. (2002e). *Speech and language developmental milestones.* Retrieved on April 12, 2006 from:http://www.nidcd.nih.gov/health/voice/speechandlanguage.asp.

National Institute on Deafness and Other Communication Disorders. (2002f). *Stuttering.* Retrieved on April 12, 2006 from: http://www.nidcd.nih.gov/health/voice/stutter.htm.

National Institute on Deafness and Other Communication Disorders. (2002g). *What is voice? What is speech? What is language*? Retrieved on April 12, 2006 from: http://www.nidcd.nih.gov/health/voice/whatis_vsl.asp.

SL

National Institute on Deafness and Other Communication Disorders. (2004). *Auditory processing disorder in children.* Bethesda, MD: NIH Pub. No. 01-4949.

National Spasmodic Dysphonia Association. (2000). *Spasmodic dysphonia.* Retrieved August 1, 2005, from http://www.dysphonia.org.

New Jersey Speech and Hearing Association. (2005). *FAQ about articulation disorders.* Retrieved August 1, 2005, from http://www.njsha.org/faq/articulation.htm.

New York-Presbyterian Hospital. (2003). Landau-Kleffner Syndrome. Retrieved January 17, 2006, from http://wo-pub2.med.cornell.edu/cgi-bin/WebObjects/PublicA.woa/4/wa/viewHContent?website=nyp&contentID=454&wosid=TtLtiWpnOFgOxFv1fT5m60.

Nipold, M. A. (2001). Phonological disorders and stuttering in children: What is the frequency of co-occurrence [electronic version]? *Clinical Linguistics and Phonetics, 15,* 219–228.

North Central Regional Educational Laboratory. (2005). *Language development delays.* Retrieved August 1, 2005, from http://www.ncrel.org/sdrs/areas/issues/content/cntareas/reading/li1lk36.htm.

Novita Children's Services. (2005). *Speech.* Retrieved August 1, 2005, from http://www.novita.org.au/content.asp?p=62.

Oswego Community Unit. (2005). *Speech and language services.* Retrieved August 1, 2005, from http://www.oswego308.org/308/speechAndLanguageServices.htm.

Penn State-Milton Hershey Medical Center College of Medicine. (2005). *Aphasia.* Retrieved August 1, 2005, from http://www.hmc.psu.edu/healthinfo/a/aphasia.htm.

PsychNet-UK (2005). *Speech articulation disorders.* Retrieved August 1, 2005, from http://www.psychnet-uk.com/dsm_iv/speech_articulation_disorder.htm.

Psychology Today. (2005). *Communication disorders.* Retrieved August 1, 2005, from http://cms.psychologytoday.com/conditions/commdisorde.html.

Roberts, J. E., & Zeisel, S. A. (2002). *Ear infections and language development.* Washington, DC: U.S. Department of Education and American Speech-Language-Hearing Association.

Royal College of Speech and Language Therapists. (2001). *Delayed language.* Retrieved August 1, 2005, from http://www.rcslt.org/leaflet-delayed.shtml.

Schminky, M. M., & Baran, J. A. (2004). Central auditory processing disorders: An overview of assessment and management practices. Retrieved on April 3, 2006, from http://www.tsbvi.edu/Outreach/seehear/spring00/centralauditory.htm.

Shames, G. H., & Anderson, N. B. (2002). *Human communication disorders: An introduction.* Needham Heights, MA: Allyn & Bacon.

Speech-Language Pathology. (2005). *Articulation/phonology.* Retrieved August 1, 2005, from http://home.ica.net/~fred/anch10–2.htm.

St. Louis, K. O., Raphael, L. J., Myers, F. L., & Baker, K. (2003). Cluttering updated. *ASHA Leader, 4–5,* 20–22.

Stuart, S. (2002). Communication: Speech and language. In M. Batshaw (Ed.), *Children with disabilities* (5th ed., pp. 229–241). Baltimore, MD: Brookes.

Thomas, J. (2004). V*ocal hyperfunction and muscle tension dysphonia.* Retrieved August 1, 2005, from http://www.voicedoctor.net/therapy/hyperfunction.html.

Toppleberg, C. O., & Shapiro, T. (2001). Language disorders: A 10-year research update review. *Journal of the Academy of Child and Adolescent Psychiatry, 39,* 143–152.

Turnbull, A., Turnbull, R., Shank, M., & Smith, S. J. (2004). *Exceptional lives: Special education in today's schools* (4th ed.). Upper Saddle River, NJ: Prentice Hall.

Turnbull, A., Turnbull, H. R., & Wehmeyer, M. L. (2006). *Exceptional lives: Special education in today's schools* (5th ed.). Upper Saddle River, NJ: Prentice Hall.

University of Michigan Health Systems. (2006). Speech and language delays. Retrieved February 12, 2006, from http://www.med.umich.edu/1libr/yourchild/speech.htm.

University of Virginia. (2004). *Otolaryngology.* Retrieved August 1, 2005, from http://www.healthsystem.virginia.edu/UVAHealth/adult_ent/glossary.cfm.

U.S. Department of Education. (2004). *Twenty-Sixth Annual Report to Congress on the Implementation of the Individuals with Disabilities Education Act.* Washington, DC: Author.

Van Riper, C., & Erickson, R. L. (1996). *Speech correction: An introduction to speech pathology and audiology* (9th ed.). Needham Heights, MA: Allyn & Bacon.

Vicari, S., Albertoni, A., Chilosi, A. M., Cipriani, P., Cioni, G., & Bates, E. (2000). Plasticity and reorganization during language development in children with early brain injury. *Cortex, 36,* 31–46.

CHAPTER 3

MENTAL RETARDATION

MR

EDM CODE: MR

- MR 1.00 Mental Retardation Due to Chromosomal Abnormalities
  - MR 1.01 Mental Retardation Due to Cornelia de Lange Syndrome
  - MR 1.02 Mental Retardation Due to Cri-du-Chat Syndrome
  - MR 1.03 Mental Retardation Due to Down Syndrome
    - MR 1.03a Down Syndrome Due to Mosaic Trisomy 21
    - MR 1.03b Down Syndrome Due to Translocation Trisomy 21
    - MR 1.03c Down Syndrome Due to Trisomy 21
  - MR 1.04 Mental Retardation Due to Fragile X Syndrome
  - MR 1.05 Mental Retardation Due to Klinefelter Syndrome
  - MR 1.06 Mental Retardation Due to Prader-Willi Syndrome
  - MR 1.07 Mental Retardation Due to Turner Syndrome
  - MR 1.08 Mental Retardation Due to Williams Syndrome
  - MR 1.09 Other Types of Mental Retardation Due to Chromosomal Abnormalities
- MR 2.00 Mental Retardation Due to Developmental Disorders of Brain Formation
  - MR 2.01 Mental Retardation Due to Anencephaly
  - MR 2.02 Mental Retardation Due to Colpocephaly
  - MR 2.03 Mental Retardation Due to Holoprosencephaly
  - MR 2.04 Mental Retardation Due to Hydranencephaly
  - MR 2.05 Mental Retardation Due to Hydrocephalus
  - MR 2.06 Mental Retardation Due to Iniencephaly
  - MR 2.07 Mental Retardation Due to Lissencephaly
  - MR 2.08 Mental Retardation Due to Megalencephaly
  - MR 2.09 Mental Retardation Due to Microcephaly
  - MR 2.10 Mental Retardation Due to Porencephaly
  - MR 2.11 Mental Retardation Due to Less Common Cephalies
    - MR 2.11a Mental Retardation Due to Acephaly
    - MR 2.11b Mental Retardation Due to Exencephaly
    - MR 2.11c Mental Retardation Due to Macrocephaly
    - MR 2.11 d Mental Retardation Due to Micrencephaly
    - MR 2.11e Mental Retardation Due to Octocephaly
    - MR 2.11f Mental Retardation Due to Brachycephaly
    - MR 2.11g Mental Retardation Due to Oxycephaly
    - MR 2.11h Mental Retardation Due to Plagiocephaly
    - MR 2.11i Mental Retardation Due to Scaphocephaly
    - MR 2.11j Mental Retardation Due to Trigoncephaly
  - MR 2.12 Mental Retardation Due to Other Types of Cephalic Disorders
- MR 3.00 Mental Retardation Due to Metabolic Disorders
  - MR 3.01 Mental Retardation Due to Galactosemia
  - MR 3.02 Mental Retardation Due to Hunter Syndrome
  - MR 3.03 Mental Retardation Due to Phenylketonuria (PKU)

- MR 3.04 Mental Retardation Due to Tay-Sachs Disease
- MR 3.05 Mental Retardation Due to Other Types of Metabolic Disorders

MR 4.00 Mental Retardation Due to Maternal Infections
- MR 4.01 Mental Retardation Due to Maternal Cytomegalovirus Infection
- MR 4.02 Mental Retardation Due to Maternal Rubella
- MR 4.03 Mental Retardation Due to Rh Disease (Rhesus Hemolytic Disease)
- MR 4.04 Mental Retardation Due to Maternal Syphilis
- MR 4.05 Mental Retardation Due to Maternal Toxoplasmosis
- MR 4.06 Mental Retardation Due to Maternal Meningitis and Encephalitis
- MR 4.07 Mental Retardation Due to Other Types of Maternal Infections

MR 5.00 Mental Retardation Due to Fetal Intoxicant Exposure
- MR 5.01 Mental Retardation Due to Fetal Exposure to Drugs
- MR 5.02 Mental Retardation Due to Fetal Alcohol Syndrome
- MR 5.03 Mental Retardation Due to Fetal Lead Exposure
- MR 5.04 Mental Retardation Due to Other Types of Fetal Intoxicant Exposure

MR 6.00 Mental Retardation Due to Gestational Disorders
- MR 6.01 Mental Retardation Due to Low Birth Weight
- MR 6.02 Mental Retardation Due to Premature Birth
- MR 6.03 Mental Retardation Due to Other Types of Gestational Disorders

MR 7.00 Mental Retardation Due to Postnatal Environmental Prob lems
- MR 7.01 Mental Retardation Due to Child Abuse and Neglect
- MR 7.02 Mental Retardation Due to Malnutrition
- MR 7.03 Mental Retardation Due to Psychosocial Disadvantage
- MR 7.04 Mental Retardation Due Traumatic Brain Injury
- MR 7.05 Mental Retardation Due to Postnatal Meningitis or Encephalitis
- MR 7.06 Mental Retardation Due to Lead Poisoning
- MR 7.07 Mental Retardation Due to the Effects of Other Forms of Postnatal Environmental Prob lems

MR 8.00 Mental Retardation Due to Other Causes
- MR 8.01 Mental Retardation Due to Other Prenatal Disorders or Exposure—Be Specific
- MR 8.02 Mental Retardation Due to Pregnancy Complications During Childbirth—Be Specific
- MR 8.03 Mental Retardation Due to Other Postnatal Conditions, Intoxicants, or Brain Diseases—Be Specific

IDEA 2004 Definition of Mental Retardation

Under IDEA 2004, mental retardation is defined as "significantly subaverage general intellectual functioning, existing concurrently with deficits in adaptive behavior and manifested during the developmental period, that adversely affects a child's educational performance" (34 C.F.R. 300.7(c)(6)).

Overview of Mental Retardation

According to the American Association on Mental Retardation (AAMR), "Mental retardation is a disability characterized by significant limitations both in intellectual functioning and in adaptive behavior as expressed in conceptual and practical adaptive skills. The disability originates before age 18 (AAMR Ad Hoc Committee on Terminology and Classification, 2002, p. 1).

Adaptive behavior is defined as "the collection of conceptual, social, and practical skills that people have learned so that they can function in their everyday lives. Significant limitations in adaptive behavior impact a person's daily life and affect the ability to respond to a particular situation or to the environment (AAMR, 2002).

Mental retardation is a term used when a person has certain limitations in mental functioning and in skills such as communicating, taking care of himself or herself, and social skills. These limitations cause a child to learn and develop more slowly than a typical child (Joseph F. Smith Library, 2005b).

Children with mental retardation may take longer to learn to speak, walk, and take care of their personal needs such as dressing or eating. They are likely to have trouble learning in school; they will learn, but it will take them longer. There may be some concepts that those with mental retardation cannot learn (National Dissemination Center for Children with Disabilities, 2004).

Today, the field of mental retardation continues to evolve (Baroff, 2000), with an emphasis on inclusive practices, recommended strategies, and decreasing the stigma for those diagnosed with mental retardation.

Causes-Etiology of Mental Retardation

Researchers in the field of mental retardation have suggested many possible causes. The most common are:

- *Genetic conditions.* Sometimes mental retardation is due to the effects of abnormal genes inherited from parents, errors when genes combine, or other reasons. For example, fragile X syndrome, identified in 1991, is now recognized as the most commonly known inherited cause of mental retardation, affecting about one in four thousand males (Mazzocco, 2000; Sudhalter & Belser, 2001). Other genetic conditions that may cause mental retardation are Down syndrome, Williams syndrome, and Turner syndrome.
- *Infections.* Infections such as syphilis and herpes simplex can be passed from mother to child during childbirth. These venereal diseases can potentially result in mental retardation (Hallahan & Kauffman, 2006).
- *Problems at birth.* Low birth weight is a major risk factor for numerous disabilities, including mental retardation (Deutsch-Smith, 2004). Also, a baby who has problems during labor and birth, such as not getting enough oxygen (anoxia), may be mentally retarded (Taylor, Klein, Minich, & Hack, 2000).
- *Health problems and malnutrition.* Diseases like whooping cough, the measles, and meningitis can cause mental retardation. Mental retardation can also be due to not getting enough medical care or extreme malnutrition (not eating right). Malnutrition remains one of the most prevalent conditions affecting children. Periods of mild to moderate malnutrition prior to two years of age are associated with delays in cognitive development and poor performance in school later in life (National Institute of Child Health and Human Development, 2005c)
- *Environmental influences.* Exposures to toxins such as lead harm children and are a source of disabilities (Deutsch-Smith, 2004). We are much more aware

now than in the past of the harmful effects of a variety of substances ranging from cocaine and heroin to more subtle potential poisons such as tobacco and alcohol (in particular, the effects on intellectual ability of children suffering from fetal alcohol syndrome).

- *Child abuse and neglect.* Abused children have lower IQs and reduced response rates to cognitive stimuli (Children's Defense Fund, 2001). The connection between neglect and mental retardation has long been recognized and is part of the early history and documentation of their field (Deutsch-Smith, 2004).

Prevalence of Mental Retardation

According to the *Twenty-Sixth Annual Report* (U.S. Department of Education, 2004), 570,642 students between the ages of six and twenty-one years of age were identified as having mental retardation. This represents approximately 10 percent of all students having a classification in special education, or about 1.5 percent of all school-age students.

The prevalence estimate of mental retardation varies in research studies. The American Association on Mental Retardation estimates that 2.5 percent of the population has this disability (Luckasson, 2002).

One rationale for the differences in prevalence estimates is the idea that sometimes school officials and committees on special education have to make a decision on whether a child has a serious learning disability or mental retardation. In this situation, they more often select Specific Learning Disability as the IDEA classification for the child rather than Mental Retardation because the former is a "less stigmatizing label" (MacMillan, Gresham, Bocian, & Lambros, 1998).

Age of Onset of Mental Retardation

The age of onset of mental retardation depends on the etiology (cause) of the disability. In general, mental retardation is a developmental disability that can appear from birth through the age of eighteen years of age (AAMR Ad Hoc Committee on Terminology and Classification, 2002, p. 1).

Gender Features of Mental Retardation

There is limited research on the prevalence of mental retardation and gender (Dembro, 2003). In general, boys are thought to have mental retardation at a slightly higher prevalence rate than girls. The Centers for Disease Control (2005a) also suggests this to be the case, stating that their research indicates mental retardation being more common in boys than in girls. However, according to Penn State Children's Hospital, the research indicates that there is no connection between mental retardation and gender (Penn State Children's Hospital, 2007). Based on the information regarding gender and research, it is an area of research where the views of various professionals differ in their determination of prevalence.

Cultural Features of Mental Retardation

One of the most disturbing aspects of data available on the prevalence of mental retardation relates to students who are African American (Jones & Menchetti, 2001). African American students are more than twice as likely as European American children to be identified as having mental retardation. African American students account for 14.8 percent of the general student population in the United States, but they account for a greater percentage (18.9 percent) of the population of students identified as having mental retardation (U.S. Department of Education, 2002).

Familial Patterns of Mental Retardation

No information is available on this topic.

Characteristics of Mental Retardation

Although every person is an individual and stereotypes can be unfair and inaccurate when applied to individual people, it is helpful to understand some characteristics educators frequently encounter when working with students with mental retardation There are many signs of mental retardation. For example, children with mental retardation may (Hallahan & Kauffman, 2006; Deutsch-Smith, 2004):

- Sit up, crawl, or walk later than other children
- Learn to talk later or have trouble speaking
- Find it hard to remember things
- Not understand how to pay for things
- Have trouble understanding social rules
- Have trouble seeing the consequences of their actions
- Have trouble solving problems
- Have trouble thinking logically

About 87 percent of people with mental retardation are only a little slower than average in learning new information and skills. When they are children, their limitations may not be obvious. They may not even be diagnosed as having mental retardation until they get to school (National Dissemination Center for Children with Disabilities, 2004). The remaining 13 percent of people with mental retardation score below 50 on IQ tests. They have more difficulty in school, at home, and in the community. Those with more severe retardation will need intensive support during their entire life.

Educational Implications of Mental Retardation

Most students with mental retardation have mild disabilities. Increasingly, these students are included in general education classes (Deutsch-Smith, 2004). A child with mental retardation can do well in school but is likely to need individualized help. Educational programming for students with mental retardation involves a number of interrelated and mutually influencing components (National Dissemination Center for Children with Disabilities, 2004).

Many children with mental retardation need help with adaptive skills, which are skills needed to live, work, and play in the community. Teachers and parents can help a child work on these skills at both school and home. Some of these skills include:

- Communicating with others
- Taking care of personal needs (dressing, bathing, going to the bathroom)
- Health and safety
- Home living (helping to set the table, cleaning the house, cooking dinner)
- Social skills (manners, knowing the rules of conversation, getting along in a group, playing a game)
- Reading, writing, and basic math
- As they get older, skills that will help them in the workplace

Supports or changes in the classroom (called adaptations) help most students with mental retardation (National Dissemination Center for Children with Disabilities, 2004).

Permissions and Authorization to Use Proprietary and Nonproprietary Sources

Due to the scientific and detailed nature of certain Level II, Level III, and Level IV disorders described in this chapter, we thought that some were best explained by national institutes and centers that conduct comprehensive scientific research in respective fields of study. The sources obtained were all written with explicit permission that the scientific and diagnostic information they prepared was in the public domain and can be used without restriction.

We thank the following national research offices for the opportunity to freely disseminate their scientific research and writing in this chapter:

- Centers for Disease Control
- National Center for Infectious Diseases of the Centers for Disease Control Prevention
- National Dissemination Center for Children with Disabilities
- National Human Genome Research Institute

- National Institute of Allergy and Infectious Diseases
- National Institute of Child Health and Human Development
- National Institutes of Health
- National Institute of Neurological Disorders and Stroke
- U.S. Department of Education
- U.S. National Library of Medicine

EDM Codes, Definitions, and Explanations of Mental Retardation

This section of the EDM is set up according to prenatal (occurring before birth) contributions, perinatal (occurring during birth) conditions, and postnatal (occurring after birth) factors associated with mental retardation. The types of mental retardation addressed are:

- Chromosomal Abnormalities (MR 1.00)
- Cephalic Disorders (MR 2.00)
- Metabolic Disorders (MR 3.00)
- Maternal Infections (MR 4.00)
- Metal Intoxicant Exposure (MR 5.00)
- Gestational Disorders (MR 6.00)
- Postnatal Conditions Associated with Mental Retardation (MR 7.00)
- Mental Retardation Due to other Prenatal, Perinatal, Postnatal causes (MR 8.00)

MR 1.00 Mental Retardation Due to Chromosomal Abnormalities

Definition A chromosome abnormality reflects an abnormality of chromosome number or structure. Chromosomes are the threadlike or rodlike structures that hold our genes. Genes are the individual instructions that tell our bodies how to develop and function; they govern our physical and medical characteristics, such as hair color, blood type, and susceptibility to disease (National Human Genome Research Institute, 2005). Genes occupy specific positions on chromosomes.

A person's genes may be damaged prior to or during conception, and abnormal genes may be passed down through a family (National Human Genome

Research Institute, 2005; Sunnybrook and Women's College Health Sciences Centre, 2005).

Numerous research studies done on the genetic causes of mental retardation, and at least 750 genetic syndromes have been identified (Dykens, Hodapp, & Finucane, 2000).

Diagnostic Symptoms According to the National Human Genome Research Institute (2005), there are many types of chromosome abnormalities. However, they can be organized into two basic groups.

Numerical abnormalities occur when an individual is missing a chromosome from a pair (monosomy) or has more than two chromosomes of a pair (trisomy). An example of a condition due to the effects of numerical abnormalities is Down syndrome, also known as trisomy 21 (an individual with Down syndrome has three copies of chromosome 21, rather than two). Turner syndrome is an example of monosomy 13, when the individual is born with only one sex chromosome, an X.

Structural abnormalities occur when the chromosome's structure is altered. This can take several forms (National Institute of Child Health and Human Development, 2005a):

- Deletions: A portion of the chromosome is missing or deleted.
- Duplications: A portion of the chromosome is duplicated, resulting in extra genetic material.
- Translocations: A portion of one chromosome is transferred to another chromosome.
- Inversions: A portion of the chromosome has broken off, turned upside down, and reattached; therefore, the genetic material is inverted.
- Rings: A portion of a chromosome has broken off and formed a circle or ring. This can happen with or without loss of genetic material.

Further Key Points Most chromosome abnormalities occur as an accident in the egg or sperm. Therefore, the abnormality is present in every cell of the body (National Human Genome Research Institute, 2005). Some abnormalities, however, can happen after conception, resulting in mosaicism (some cells have the abnormality, and some do not).

Chromosome abnormalities can be inherited from a parent (such as a translocation) or be de novo (new to the individual). This is why chromosome studies are often performed on parents when a child is found to have an abnormality. The precise and rather fragile roles of genes and chromosomes as building blocks of development are dramatically represented in mental retardation research (National Institute of Child Health and Human Development, 2005a).

MR 1.01 Mental Retardation Due to Cornelia de Lange Syndrome

Definition Cornelia de Lange syndrome (CdLS), also known as Bachmann-de Lange syndrome, is a rare genetic disorder that is apparent at birth (congenital).

As with other syndromes, individuals with CdLS strongly resemble one another. Common characteristics include low birth weight (often under five pounds), slow growth and small stature, and small head size (microcephaly). Typical facial features include thin eyebrows, which frequently meet at midline; long eyelashes; short, upturned nose; and thin and downturned lips (Cornelia de Lange Syndrome Foundation, 2005).

Explanation Named for the Dutch physician who first described it in 1933, Cornelia de Lange syndrome involves a complex of symptoms. These include mental retardation, self-injurious behavior, impaired growth, heart defects, hearing loss, and abnormalities of the fingers and hands. This syndrome occurs in one of every ten thousand individuals (National Institutes of Health, 2004).

MR 1.02 Mental Retardation Due to Cri-du-Chat Syndrome

Definition Cri-du-chat syndrome is a group of symptoms that result from missing a piece of chromosome number 5. The syndrome's name is based on the infant's cry, which is high-pitched and sounds like a cat (U.S. National Library of Medicine, 2005a).

Explanation Cri du chat is a rare syndrome (one in fifty thousand live births) caused by a deletion on the short arm of chromosome 5. The name of this syndrome is French for "cry of the cat," referring to the distinctive cry of children with this disorder. The cry is caused by abnormal larynx development, which becomes normal within a few weeks of birth. Infants with cri du chat have low birth weight and may have respiratory problems. Some people with this disorder have a shortened life span, but most have a normal life expectancy (Genetic Science Learning Center, 2006). They also have an extensive grouping of abnormalities, with severe mental retardation being the most important (U.S. National Library of Medicine, 2005a).

Symptoms of cri-du-chat syndrome include:

- High-pitched cry sounds like a cat
- Low birth weight and slow growth
- Small head (microcephaly)
- Wide-set eyes (hypertelorism)
- Downward slant to the eyes (palpebral fissures)
- Small jaw (micrognathia)
- Low-set ears (may be malformed)
- Skin tags just in front of the ear
- Partial webbing or fusing of fingers or toes
- Single line in the palm of the hand (simian crease)

- Mental retardation
- Slow or incomplete development of motor skills (U.S. National Library of Medicine, 2005a)

MR 1.03 Mental Retardation Due to Down Syndrome

Definition Down syndrome is a chromosomal disorder due to the effects of an error in cell division that results in the presence of an anomaly at the twenty-first pair of chromosomes (National Institute of Child Health and Human Development, 2005a). In the majority of cases, the twenty-first set of chromosomes is a triplet pair rather than a pair (Hallahan & Kauffman, 2006). Estimated to account for about 5 to 6 percent of all cases of mental retardation (Beirne-Smith, Ittenbach, & Patton, 2002), Down syndrome is the most common form of mental retardation that is present at birth.

Down syndrome is probably the best-known of the genetic disorders (Friend, 2005). Research suggests that approximately one in every eight hundred to one thousand children is born with Down syndrome (National Down Syndrome Society, 2003).

Explanation Named after John Langdon Down, the first physician to identify the syndrome, Down syndrome is the most common and readily identifiable chromosomal condition associated with mental retardation (Hunt & Marshall, 2006). It is caused by a chromosomal abnormality: an accident in cell development results in forty-seven instead of the usual forty-six chromosomes. This extra chromosome changes the orderly development of the body and brain. In most cases, the diagnosis of Down syndrome is made according to results from a chromosome test administered shortly after birth (National Dissemination Center for Children with Disabilities, 2004).

There are over fifty clinical signs of Down syndrome, but it is rare to find all or even most of them in one person (National Dissemination Center for Children with Disabilities, 2004). Some common characteristics are:

- Poor muscle tone
- Slanting eyes with folds of skin at the inner corners (called epicanthal folds)
- Hyperflexibility (excessive ability to extend the joints)
- Short, broad hands with a single crease across the palm on one or both hands
- Broad feet with short toes
- Flat bridge of the nose
- Short, low-set ears
- Short neck
- Small head
- Small oral cavity

- Short, high-pitched cries in infancy (Taylor, Richards, & Brady, 2005; Beirne-Smith et al., 2002)

Individuals with Down syndrome are usually smaller than their nondisabled peers, and their physical as well as intellectual development is slower. Besides having a distinct physical appearance, children with Down syndrome frequently have specific health-related problems. A lowered resistance to infection makes these children more prone to respiratory problems. Visual problems such as crossed eyes and far- or nearsightedness are higher in those with Down syndrome, as are mild to moderate hearing loss and speech difficulty. Approximately one-third of babies born with Down syndrome have heart defects, most of which are now correctable. Some individuals are born with gastrointestinal tract problems that can be surgically corrected (March of Dimes, 2003).

Children with Down syndrome may have a tendency to become obese as they grow older. Besides having negative social implications, this weight gain threatens these individuals' health and longevity. A supervised diet and exercise program may help reduce this problem (National Dissemination Center for Children with Disabilities, 2004).

Finally, research suggests that that the chance of having a second child with Down syndrome is about one in one hundred. The incidence is higher if one parent is a carrier of a translocated cell (National Down Syndrome Society, 2006).

MR 1.03a **Down Syndrome Due to Mosaic Trisomy 21** In approximately 2 to 4 percent of cases, Down syndrome is due to mosaic trisomy 21. This situation is similar to simple trisomy 21, but in this instance, the extra chromosome 21 is present in some, but not all, cells of the individual (Hunt & Marshall, 2006). For example, the fertilized egg may have the right number of chromosomes, but due to an error in chromosome division early in embryonic development, some cells acquire an extra chromosome 21. Thus, an individual with Down syndrome due to mosaic trisomy 21 will typically have forty-six chromosomes in some cells but forty-seven chromosomes (including an extra chromosome 21) in others. In this situation, the range of the physical problems may vary, depending on the proportion of cells that carry the additional chromosome 21 (National Institute of Child Health and Human Development, 2005a).

MR 1.03b **Down Syndrome Due to Translocation Trisomy 21** Approximately 3 to 4 percent of individuals with Down syndrome have cells containing forty-six chromosomes, but still have the features associated with Down syndrome. In such cases, material from one chromosome 21 gets stuck or translocated onto another chromosome, either prior to or at conception. In such situations, cells from individuals with Down syndrome have two normal chromosomes 21, but also have additional chromosome 21 material on the translocated chromosome. Thus, there is still too much material from chromosome 21, resulting in the features associated with Down syndrome. In such situations, the individual with Down syndrome is said to have translocation trisomy 21 (National Institute of Child Health and Human Development, 2005a).

MR 1.03c **Down Syndrome Due to Trisomy 21** Approximately 92 percent of the time, Down syndrome is caused by the presence of an extra chromosome 21 in all cells of the individual. In such cases, the extra chromosome originates in the development of the egg or the sperm. Consequently, when the egg and sperm unite to form the fertilized egg, three—rather than two—chromosomes 21 are present. As the embryo develops, the extra chromosome is repeated in every cell. This condition, in which three copies of chromosome 21 are present in all cells of the individual, is called trisomy 21 (Taylor et al., 2005; National Institute of Child Health and Human Development, 2005a).

MR 1.04 Mental Retardation Due to Fragile X Syndrome

Definition A genetic condition involving changes in which the bottom of the X chromosome in the twenty-third pair of chromosomes is pinched off, which can result in a number of physical anomalies as well as mental retardation (Hallahan & Kauffman, 2006; Taylor et al., 2005; U.S. National Library of Medicine, 2005b). The mutation, occurring when a gene segment that is repeated in most people about thirty times is repeated fifty-five to two hundred times, causes the gene to turn off, that is, to stop producing a chemical present in the cells of people who do not have this disorder (Fast, 2003, cited in Friend, 2005).

Explanation Fragile X syndrome (also called fragile X) is the most common inherited form of mental retardation (Taylor et al., 2005). It results from a change, or mutation, in a single gene, which can be passed from one generation to the next (National Institute of Child Health and Human Development, 2005b). In association with mental retardation, it occurs in one in four thousand males and at least half as many females (Turner, Webb, Wake, & Robinson, 1996).

Symptoms of fragile X syndrome occur because the mutated gene cannot produce enough of a protein that is needed by the body's cells, especially cells in the brain, to develop and function normally. The amount and usability of this protein in part determine how severe the effects of fragile X are in the individual (National Institute of Child Health and Human Development, 2005b).

The most noticeable and consistent effect of fragile X is on intelligence. More than 80 percent of males with fragile X have an IQ (intelligence quotient) of 75 or less. The effect of fragile X on intelligence is more variable in females. Some females have mental impairment, some have learning disabilities, and some have a normal IQ (Dykens et al., 2000). Fragile X occurs less often in females because they have an extra X chromosome, giving them better protection if one of their X chromosomes is damaged (Hallahan & Kauffman, 2006).

People with fragile X syndrome also share certain medical problems as well as many common physical characteristics, such as large ears, large head, narrow face, prominent forehead, broad nose, square chin, large testicles, large hands, and a long face (Dykens et al., 2000). In addition, having fragile X is often associated with problems with sensation, emotion, and behavior. Students with this syndrome also are likely to become anxious when routines are changed, and they often have poor social skills (Symons, Clark, Roberts, & Bailey, 2001).

MR 1.05 Mental Retardation Due to Klinefelter Syndrome

Definition Klinefelter syndrome is a chromosomal condition related to chromosomes X and Y. The syndrome is caused by the presence of one or more extra copies of the X chromosome in a male's cells. Extra copies of genes on the X chromosome interfere with male sexual development, preventing the testicles from functioning normally and reducing the levels of testosterone (U.S. National Library of Medicine, 2005e).

Explanation Most often, Klinefelter syndrome is caused by a single extra copy of the X chromosome, for a total of forty-seven chromosomes per cell. Males normally have one X chromosome and one Y chromosome in each cell (XY), but males with Klinefelter syndrome have two X chromosomes and one Y chromosome (XXY). Some males with Klinefelter syndrome have the extra X chromosome in only some of their cells; these cases are called mosaic XY/XXY (National Institute of Child Health and Human Development, 2005c).

The most common characteristic of men with Klinefelter syndrome is sterility. Adolescents and adults with this syndrome have normal sexual function but cannot produce sperm for fathering children. It is presumed that all men with Klinefelter syndrome are infertile.

No one knows what puts a couple at risk for conceiving an XXY child. Advanced maternal age increases the risk for the XXY chromosome count, but only slightly (American Association for Klinefelter Syndrome Information and Support, 2006).

Variants of Klinefelter syndrome, which involve more than one extra X chromosome or extra copies of both sex chromosomes in each cell, tend to have more severe signs and symptoms. These disorders affect male sexual development but may also cause decreased IQ, distinctive facial features, skeletal abnormalities, poor coordination, and more severe problems with speech (U.S. National Library of Medicine, 2005e).

MR 1.06 Mental Retardation Due to Prader-Willi Syndrome

Definition Prader-Willi syndrome is a chromosomal disorder caused by inheriting from one's father a lack of genetic material on the fifteenth pair of chromosomes (Dykens et al., 2000). It is a complex genetic disorder that typically causes low muscle tone, short stature, incomplete sexual development, cognitive disabilities, problem behaviors, and a chronic feeling of hunger that can lead to excessive eating and life-threatening obesity (Hallahan & Kaufmann, 2003; National Center for Biotechnology Information, 2005). Children who have Prader-Willi syndrome have mild or moderate mental retardation, and some of them have abilities in the low-average range (Prader-Willi Syndrome Association, 2003).

Explanation Prader-Willi syndrome is a complex genetic condition that affects many parts of the body. This condition is due to the effects of the loss of active genes in a specific region of chromosome 15. People normally have two copies of this chromosome in each cell—one copy from each parent. Some genes on this chromosome, however, are active only when they are inherited from a person's father (the paternal copies). Prader-Willi syndrome occurs when the region of paternal chromosome 15 containing these genes is missing (U.S. National Library of Medicine, 2005g).

The condition is characterized in infancy by weak muscle tone (hypotonia), feeding difficulties, poor growth, and delayed development (Taylor et al., 2005). Beginning in childhood, features of the disorder include excessive eating (hyperphagia), obesity, short stature, scoliosis, mental retardation or learning disabilities, and behavioral problems. Some affected individuals also have unusually fair skin and light-colored hair (Taylor et al., 2005; U.S. National Library of Medicine, 2005g).

MR 1.07 Mental Retardation Due to Turner Syndrome

Definition Turner syndrome (TS) is a chromosomal condition that describes girls and women with common features that are caused by complete or partial absence of the second sex chromosome. TS occurs when one of the two X chromosomes normally found in females is missing or contains certain structural defects. The syndrome is named after Henry Turner, who was among the first to describe its features in the 1930s. TS occurs in approximately one in two thousand live female births (Turner Syndrome Society, 2006).

Other features of Turner syndrome vary among affected females and can include webbing of the neck, puffiness or swelling (lymphedema) of the hands and feet, skeletal abnormalities, heart defects, and kidney problems (U.S. National Library of Medicine, 2005i).

Explanation About half of individuals with Turner syndrome have monosomy X, which means each cell in a woman's body has only one copy of the X chromosome instead of the usual two copies. Turner syndrome can also occur if one of the sex chromosomes is partially missing or rearranged rather than completely missing. Some women with Turner syndrome have a chromosomal change in only some of their cells, which is known as X-chromosome mosaicism (U.S. National Library of Medicine, 2005i).

MR 1.08 Mental Retardation Due to Williams Syndrome

Definition A chromosomal disorder resulting from deletion of genetic material on the seventh pair of chromosomes (Semel & Rosner, 2003). It is characterized by mild mental retardation, distinctive facial appearance, problems with calcium balance, and blood vessel disease (U.S. National Library of Medicine, 2005j). Although individuals with Williams syndrome may show competence in areas such as language, music, and interpersonal relations, their IQs are usually below average, and they are often considered to have moderate to mild mental retardation (Semel & Rosner, 2003).

Explanation Williams syndrome is a rare congenital (present at birth) disorder characterized by physical and developmental problems including an impulsive and outgoing (excessively social) personality, limited spatial skills and motor control, and intellectual disability (developmental delay, learning disabilities, mental retardation, or attention deficit disorder).

Other features include characteristic elfin-like facial features, heart and blood vessel problems, hypercalcemia (elevated blood calcium levels), low birth weight, slow weight gain, feeding problems, irritability during infancy, dental and kidney abnormalities, hyperacusis (sensitive hearing), and musculoskeletal problems (Semel & Rosner, 2003).

The prognosis for individuals with Williams syndrome varies. Some may be able to master self-help skills, complete academic or vocational school, and live in supervised homes or on their own, while others may not progress to this level (National Institute of Neurological Disorders and Stroke, 2006).

MR 1.09 Other Types of Mental Retardation Due to Chromosomal Abnormalities

MR 2.00 Mental Retardation Due to Developmental Disorders of Brain Formation (Cephalic Disorders or Cranial Malformations)

Definition Most cephalic disorders are caused by a disturbance that occurs very early in the development of the fetal nervous system (Cleveland Clinic, 2003). Damage to the developing nervous system is a major cause of chronic, disabling disorders, and sometimes death in infants, children, and even adults. Cephalic disorders may be influenced by hereditary or genetic conditions or by environmental exposures during pregnancy (National Institute of Neurological Disorders and Stroke, 2005a).

Diagnostic Symptoms Due to the various types of cephalic disorders, symptoms vary based on the diagnosis. Consequently, no generalizations about symptoms regarding individuals with cephalic disorders are made. However, symptoms of cephalic disorders may include:

- Unusual facial appearance
- Difficulty swallowing
- Failure to thrive
- Severe psychomotor retardation
- Anomalies of the hands, fingers, or toes, muscle spasms, and sometimes seizures (Hydrocephalus Association, 2004; National Institute of Neurological Disorders and Stroke, 2005a)

Further Key Points Scientists are rapidly learning how harmful insults at various stages of pregnancy can lead to developmental disorders. For example, a critical nutritional deficiency or exposure to an environmental insult during the first month of pregnancy (when the neural tube is formed) can produce neural tube defects. (Cleveland Clinic, 2003).

Several conditions associated with mental retardation manifest themselves as cranial malformations (AAMR, 2002). The degree to which damage to the developing nervous system harms the mind and body varies enormously. Many disabilities are mild enough to allow those afflicted to eventually function independently in society. Others are not. Some infants, children, and adults die, others remain totally disabled, and an even larger population is partially disabled, functioning well below normal capacity throughout life (National Institute of Neurological Disorders and Stroke, 2005a).

MR 2.01 Mental Retardation Due to Anencephaly

Definition A type of cephalic disorder characterized by a neural tube defect that occurs when the cephalic (head) end of the neural tube fails to close, usually between the twenty-third and twenty-sixth days of pregnancy, resulting in the absence of a major portion of the brain, skull, and scalp (National Institute of Neurological Disorders and Stroke, 2005a). Infants with this disorder are born without a forebrain—the largest part of the brain consisting mainly of the cerebrum, which is responsible for thinking and coordination (Anencephaly Awareness, 2006; National Institute of Neurological Disorders and Stroke, 2005a).

Explanation Infants born with anencephaly are usually blind, deaf, unconscious, and unable to feel pain (National Institute of Neurological Disorders and Stroke, 2005a). Although some individuals with anencephaly may be born with a rudimentary brain stem, the lack of a functioning cerebrum permanently rules out the possibility of ever gaining consciousness. Reflex actions such as breathing and responses to sound or touch may occur (Anencephaly Awareness, 2006). The disorder is one of the most common disorders of the fetal central nervous system.

Approximately one thousand to two thousand American babies are born with anencephaly each year. The disorder affects females more often than males (Anencephaly Awareness, 2006).

The cause of anencephaly is unknown. Although it is believed that the mother's diet and vitamin intake may play a role, scientists agree that many other factors are also involved. There is no cure or standard treatment for anencephaly, and the prognosis for affected individuals is poor. Most infants do not survive infancy. If the infant is not stillborn, then he or she usually dies within a few hours or days after birth (National Institute of Neurological Disorders and Stroke, 2005a).

MR 2.02 Mental Retardation Due to Colpocephaly

Definition A type of cephalic disorder characterized by an abnormal enlargement of the occipital horns—the posterior or rear portion of the lateral ventricles (cavities or chambers) of the brain. This enlargement occurs when there is an underdevelopment or lack of thickening of the white matter in the posterior cerebrum (Cerebral Palsy Network, 1999; National Institute of Neurological Disorders and Stroke, 2005a).

Explanation Colpocephaly is characterized by microcephaly (abnormally small head) and mental retardation. Other features may include motor abnormalities, muscle spasms, and seizures. Although the cause is unknown, researchers believe that the disorder results from an intrauterine disturbance that occurs between the second and sixth months of pregnancy. Colpocephaly may be diagnosed late in pregnancy, although it is often misdiagnosed as hydrocephalus (excessive accumulation of cerebrospinal fluid in the brain). It may be more accurately diagnosed after birth when signs of mental retardation, microcephaly, and seizures are present. The prognosis for individuals with colpocephaly depends on the severity of the associated conditions and the degree of abnormal brain development (Cerebral Palsy Network, 1999; National Institute of Neurological Disorders and Stroke, 2005a).

MR 2.03 Mental Retardation Due to Holoprosencephaly

Definition Holoprosencephaly (HPE) is a birth defect that occurs during the first few weeks of intrauterine life (Carter Centers for Brain Research in Holosencephaly and Related Malformations, 2002). It is a type of cephalic disorder characterized by the failure of the prosencephalon (the forebrain of the embryo) to develop. During normal development, the forebrain is formed, and the face begins to develop in the fifth and sixth weeks of pregnancy. Holoprosencephaly is caused by a failure of the embryo's forebrain to divide to form bilateral cerebral hemispheres (the left and right halves of the brain), causing defects in the development of the face and in brain structure and function (National Institute of Neurological Disorders and Stroke, 2005a).

MR

Explanation Although the causes of most cases of holoprosencephaly remain unknown (Carter Centers for Brain Research in Holosencephaly and Related Malformations, 2002), researchers know that approximately half of all cases have a chromosomal cause.

Holoprosencephaly, once called arhinencephaly, consists of a spectrum of defects or malformations of the brain and face. At the most severe end of this spectrum are cases involving serious malformations of the brain, malformations so severe that they are incompatible with life and often cause spontaneous intrauterine death. At the other end of the spectrum are individuals with facial defects—which may affect the eyes, nose, and upper lip—and normal or near-normal brain development. Seizures and mental retardation may occur. Other common problems include slowness in eating, frequent pauses, and vomiting with risk of aspiration (Gropman & Muenke, 2005).

There is no treatment for holoprosencephaly, and the prognosis for individuals with the disorder is poor. Most of those who survive show no significant developmental gains. For children who survive, treatment is symptomatic (Gropman & Muenke, 2005; National Institute of Neurological Disorders and Stroke, 2005a).

MR 2.04 Mental Retardation Due to Hydranencephaly

Definition A rare type of cephalic disorder in which the cerebral hemispheres are absent and replaced by sacs filled with cerebrospinal fluid (Cleveland Clinic, 2003). Usually the cerebellum and brain stem are formed normally (National Institute of Neurological Disorders and Stroke, 2005a). It is a central nervous system disorder characterized by an enlarged head and neurological deficits (National Organization for Rare Disorders, 1999).

Explanation An infant with hydranencephaly may appear normal at birth. The infant's head size and spontaneous reflexes such as sucking, swallowing, crying, and moving the arms and legs may all seem normal. However, after a few weeks, the infant usually becomes irritable and has increased muscle tone (hypertonia). After several months of life, seizures and hydrocephalus may develop. Other symptoms may include visual impairment, lack of growth, deafness, blindness, spastic quadriparesis (paralysis), and intellectual deficits.

Hydranencephaly is an extreme form of porencephaly (a rare disorder characterized by a cyst or cavity in the cerebral hemispheres) and may be caused by vascular insult (such as stroke) or injuries, infections, or traumatic disorders after the twelfth week of pregnancy (Cleveland Clinic, 2003; National Institute of Neurological Disorders and Stroke, 2005a; National Organization for Rare Disorders, 1999).

There is no standard treatment for hydranencephaly. Treatment is symptomatic and supportive. Hydrocephalus may be treated with a shunt. The outlook for children with hydranencephaly is generally poor, and many children with this disorder die before age one. However, in rare cases, children with hydranencephaly may survive for several years or more (National Institute of Neurological Disorders and Stroke, 2005a).

MR 2.05 Mental Retardation Due to Hydrocephalus

Definition A type of cephalic disorder characterized by excessive accumulation of fluid in the brain (Hydrocephalus Association, 2004; National Institute of Neurological Disorders and Stroke, 2005a).

Explanation Although hydrocephalus was once known as "water on the brain," the "water" is actually cerebrospinal fluid (CSF)—a clear fluid surrounding the brain and spinal cord. The excessive accumulation of CSF results in an abnormal dilation of the spaces in the brain called ventricles. This dilation causes potentially harmful pressure on the tissues of the brain (National Hydrocephalus Foundation, 2006).

The causes of hydrocephalus are not well understood. Symptoms vary with age, disease progression, and individual differences in tolerance to CSF. In infancy, the most obvious indication of hydrocephalus is often the rapid increase in head circumstance or an unusually large head size (National Institute of Neurological Disorders and Stroke, 2005a). In older children and adults, symptoms may include headache followed by vomiting, nausea, papilledema (swelling of the optic disk, which is part of the optic nerve), downward deviation of the eyes (called "sunsetting"), problems with balance, poor coordination, gait disturbance, urinary incontinence, slowing or loss of development, lethargy, drowsiness, irritability, or other changes in personality or cognition, including memory loss (National Institute of Neurological Disorders and Stroke, 2005a).

MR 2.06 Mental Retardation Due to Iniencephaly

Definition A rare type of cephalic disorder characterized by is a neural tube defect that combines extreme retroflexion (backward bending) of the head with severe defects of the spine (National Institute of Neurological Disorders and Stroke, 2005a).

Explanation Infants with iniencephaly tend to be short, with a disproportionately large head. Diagnosis can be made immediately after birth because the head is so severely retroflexed that the face looks upward. The skin of the face is connected directly to the skin of the chest and the scalp is directly connected to the skin of the back. Generally the neck is absent.

Most individuals with iniencephaly have other associated anomalies such as anencephaly, cephalocele (a disorder in which part of the cranial contents protrudes from the skull), hydrocephalus, cyclopia, absence of the mandible (lower jaw bone), cleft lip and palate, cardiovascular disorders, diaphragmatic hernia, and gastrointestinal malformation. The disorder is more common among females.

The prognosis for those with iniencephaly is extremely poor. Newborns with iniencephaly seldom live more than a few hours (Dobyns, 1991; National Institute of Neurological Disorders and Strokes, 2005a).

MR 2.07 Mental Retardation Due to Lissencephaly

Definition Lissencephaly is a malformation of the brain in which the brain surface is smooth rather than convoluted. The name comes from the Greek words *lissos,* which means smooth, and *enkephalos,* which means brain. It is caused by defective neuronal migration, the process in which nerve cells move from their place of origin to their permanent location. In humans, the surface of the brain is formed by a complex series of ridges and valleys. The ridges are called gyri or convolutions, and the valleys are called sulci. In children with lissencephaly, the normal convolutions are absent or only partly formed, so the surface is smooth (Dobyns, 1991).

Explanation In infants with classical lissencephaly, the head circumference may be smaller than would otherwise be expected (microcephaly). Additional abnormalities may include sudden episodes of uncontrolled electrical activity in the brain (seizures), severe or profound mental retardation, feeding difficulties, growth retardation, and impaired motor abilities. If an underlying syndrome is present, there may be additional symptoms and physical findings (National Organization of Rare Disorders, 2002).

The prognosis for children with lissencephaly varies depending on the degree of brain malformation. Many individuals show no significant development beyond a three- to five-month-old level. Some may have near-normal development and intelligence. Many die before the age of two. Respiratory problems are the most common causes of death (National Institute of Neurological Disorders and Stroke, 2005a).

MR 2.08 Mental Retardation Due to Megalencephaly (Macrencephaly)

Definition Megalencephaly, also called macrencephaly, is a condition in which there is an abnormally large, heavy, and usually malfunctioning brain. By definition, the brain weight is greater than average for the age and gender of the individual. Head enlargement may be evident at birth, or the head may become abnormally large in the early years of life (Cleveland Clinic, 2003).

Explanation Megalencephaly is thought to be related to a disturbance in the regulation of cell reproduction or proliferation. In normal development, neuron proliferation—the process in which nerve cells divide to form new generations of cells—is regulated so that the correct number of cells is formed in the proper place at the appropriate time.

Symptoms of megalencephaly may include delayed development, convulsive disorders, corticospinal (brain cortex and spinal cord) dysfunction, and seizures. Megalencephaly affects males more often than females.

The prognosis for individuals with megalencephaly largely depends on the underlying cause and the associated neurological disorders. Treatment is symptomatic. Unilateral megalencephaly or hemimegalencephaly is a rare condition characterized by the enlargement of half of the brain. Children with this disorder may have a large, sometimes asymmetrical head. Often they suffer from intractable seizures and mental retardation (National Institute of Neurological Disorders and Stroke, 2005).

MR 2.09 Mental Retardation Due to Microcephaly

Definition A type of cephalic disorder in which the circumference of the head is smaller than average for the age and gender of the infant or child. Microcephaly may be congenital, or it may develop in the first few years of life. The disorder may stem from a wide variety of conditions that cause abnormal growth of the brain or from syndromes associated with chromosomal abnormalities (National Institute of Neurological Disorders and Stroke, 2005a).

Explanation Infants with microcephaly are born with a normal or reduced head size. They are characterized by a small, conical skull and a curved spine that typically leads to a stooping posture (National Institute of Neurological Disorders and Stroke, 2005a). Subsequently the head fails to grow while the face continues to develop at a normal rate, producing a child with a small head, a large face, a receding forehead, and a loose, often wrinkled scalp. As the child grows older, the smallness of the skull becomes more obvious, although the entire body also is often underweight and dwarfed. Development of motor functions and speech may be delayed. Hyperactivity and mental retardation are common occurrences, although the degree of each varies.

In general, life expectancy for individuals with microcephaly is reduced and the prognosis for normal brain function is poor. The prognosis varies depending on the presence of associated abnormalities (National Institute of Neurological Disorders and Stroke, 2005a).

MR 2.10 Mental Retardation Due to Porencephaly

Definition A type of cephalic disorder characterized by a cyst or cavity in a cerebral hemisphere. The cysts or cavities are usually the remnants of destructive lesions but are sometimes the result of abnormal development. The disorder can occur before or after birth (Medical College of Wisconsin, 2003).

Explanation Porencephaly most likely has a number of different, often unknown causes, including absence of brain development and destruction of brain tissue. More severely affected infants show symptoms of the disorder shortly after birth, and the diagnosis is usually made before age one. Signs may include delayed growth and development, spastic paresis (slight or incomplete paralysis), hypotonia (decreased muscle tone), seizures (often infantile spasms), and macrocephaly or microcephaly.

Individuals with porencephaly may have poor or absent speech development, epilepsy, hydrocephalus, spastic contractures (shrinkage or shortening of muscles), and mental retardation (National Institute of Neurological Disorders and Stroke, 2005a).

MR 2.11 Mental Retardation Due to Less Common Cephalies

MR 2.11a **Mental Retardation Due to Acephaly** *Acephaly* literally means absence of the head. It is a much rarer condition than anencephaly. The acephalic fetus is a parasitic twin attached to an otherwise intact fetus. The acephalic fetus has a body but lacks a head and a heart; the fetus's neck is attached to the normal twin. The blood circulation of the acephalic fetus is provided by the heart of the twin. The acephalic fetus cannot exist independent of the fetus to which it is attached (National Institute of Neurological Disorders and Stroke, 2005a).

MR 2.11b **Mental Retardation Due to Exencephaly** Exencephaly is a condition in which the brain is located outside the skull. This condition is usually found in embryos as an early stage of anencephaly. As an exencephalic pregnancy progresses, the neural tissue gradually degenerates. It is unusual to find an infant carried to term with this condition because the defect is incompatible with survival (National Institute of Neurological Disorders and Stroke, 2005a).

MR 2.11c **Mental Retardation Due to Macrocephaly** Macrocephaly is a condition in which the head circumference is larger than average for the age and gender of the infant or child. It is a descriptive rather than a diagnostic term and is a characteristic of a variety of disorders. Macrocephaly also may be inherited. Although one form of macrocephaly may be associated with mental retardation, mental development is normal in approximately half of cases. Macrocephaly may be caused by an enlarged brain or hydrocephalus. It may be associated with other disorders such as dwarfism, neurofibromatosis, and tuberous sclerosis (National Institute of Neurological Disorders and Stroke, 2005a).

MR 2.11d **Mental Retardation Due to Micrencephaly** Micrencephaly is a disorder characterized by a small brain and may be caused by a disturbance in the proliferation of nerve cells. Micrencephaly may also be associated with maternal problems such as alcoholism, diabetes, or rubella (German measles). A genetic factor may play a role in causing some cases of micrencephaly. Affected newborns generally have striking neurological defects and seizures. Severely impaired intellectual development is common, but disturbances in motor functions may not appear until later in life (National Institute of Neurological Disorders and Stroke, 2005a).

MR 2.11e **Mental Retardation Due to Octocephaly** Octocephaly is a lethal condition in which the primary feature is agnathia: a developmental anomaly characterized by total or virtual absence of the lower jaw. The condition is considered lethal because of a poorly functioning airway. In octocephaly, agnathia may occur alone or together with holoprosencephaly (National Institute of Neurological Disorders and Stroke, 2005a).

MR 2.11f **Mental Retardation Due to Brachycephaly** Brachycephaly occurs when the coronal suture fuses prematurely, causing a shortened front-to-back diameter of the skull. The coronal suture is the fibrous joint that unites the frontal bone with the two parietal bones of the skull. The parietal bones form the top and sides of the skull (National Institute of Neurological Disorders and Stroke, 2005a).

MR 2.11g **Mental Retardation Due to Oxycephaly** *Oxycephaly* is a term sometimes used to describe the premature closure of the coronal suture plus any other suture, or it may be used to describe the premature fusing of all sutures (National Institute of Neurological Disorders and Stroke, 2005a).

MR 2.11h **Mental Retardation Due to Plagiocephaly** Plagiocephaly results from the premature unilateral fusion (joining of one side) of the coronal or lambdoid sutures. The lambdoid suture unites the occipital bone with the parietal bones of the skull. Plagiocephaly is a condition characterized by an asymmetrical distortion (flattening of one side) of the skull. It is a common finding at birth and may be the result of brain malformation, a restrictive intrauterine environment, or torticollis (a spasm or tightening of neck muscles) (National Institute of Neurological Disorders and Stroke, 2005a).

MR 2.11i **Mental Retardation Due to Scaphocephaly** Scaphocephaly applies to premature fusion of the sagittal suture, which joins together the two parietal bones of the skull. Scaphocephaly is the most common of the craniostenoses and is characterized by a long, narrow head (National Institute of Neurological Disorders and Stroke, 2005a).

MR 2.11j **Mental Retardation Due to Trigoncephaly** Trigoncephaly is the premature fusion of the metopic suture (part of the frontal suture that joins the two halves of the frontal bone of the skull) in which a V-shaped abnormality occurs at the front of the skull. It is characterized by the triangular prominence of the forehead and closely set eyes (National Institute of Neurological Disorders and Stroke, 2005a).

MR 2.12 Mental Retardation Due to Other Types of Cephalic Disorders

MR 3.00 Mental Retardation Due to Metabolic Disorders

Definition *Metabolism* refers to all the physical and chemical processes within the body that create and use energy, such as:

- Digesting food and nutrients
- Eliminating waste through urine and feces

- Breathing
- Circulating blood
- Regulating temperature (U.S. National Library of Medicine, 2005f)

Inborn errors of metabolism result from inherited deficiencies in enzymes used to metabolize basic substances in the body, such as amino acids, carbohydrates, vitamins, or trace elements (Hallahan & Kauffman, 2006).

Certain metabolic disorders have a significant impact on cognitive abilities, potentially causing mental retardation (and often severe physical disabilities) as well (Texas Department of Aging and Disability, 2005).

Diagnostic Symptoms Due to the numerous types of metabolic and nutritional disorders, no general statement about symptoms can be made regarding either for specific diagnostic purposes.

Further Key Points *Metabolic disorder* is a generic term for disorders caused by an abnormal metabolic process. It can be congenital due to inherited enzyme abnormality (metabolism, inborn errors) or acquired due to disease of an endocrine organ or failure of a metabolically important organ such as the liver (U.S. National Library of Medicine, 2005f).

Metabolic disorders are characterized by the body's inability to process (metabolize) certain substances that can then become poisonous and damage tissue in the central nervous system (Hardman, Drew, & Egan, 2005).

MR 3.01 Mental Retardation Due to Galactosemia

Definition Galactosemia is the inability of the body to use (metabolize) the simple sugar galactose (causing the accumulation of galactose 1-phosphate), which then reaches high levels in the body, causing damage to the liver, central nervous system, and various other body systems (U.S. National Library of Medicine, 2005f).

Diagnostic symptoms include:

- Jaundice (yellowish discoloration of the skin and the whites of the eyes)
- Vomiting
- Poor feeding (baby refusing to drink milk-containing formula)
- Poor weight gain
- Lethargy
- Irritability
- Convulsions (U.S. National Library of Medicine, 2005f)

Explanation Galactosemia is a rare genetic metabolic disorder. The child with classic galactosemia inherits a gene for galactosemia from both parents, who are carriers. Patients who inherit the classic galactosemia gene from each parent are sometimes described as having the genetic makeup G/G. Normally when a person consumes a product that contains lactose (for example, dairy products such as milk, cheese, or butter), the body breaks the lactose down into galactose and glucose (Parents of Galactosemic Children, 2006).

Galactosemia is an inherited disorder (transmitted as an autosomal-recessive, which means abnormal gene on one of the autosomal chromosomes, trait). It occurs at a rate of approximately one out of sixty thousand births.

MR 3.02 Mental Retardation Due to Hunter Syndrome

Definition Hunter syndrome is a rare inherited metabolic disorder in which the breakdown of the chemical mucopolysaccharide (a chemical that is widely distributed in the body outside cells) is defective. This chemical builds up and causes a characteristic facial appearance, abnormal function of multiple organs, and, in severe cases, early death (Mayo Clinic, 2005).

Explanation Hunter syndrome is inherited as an X-linked recessive disease. This means that women carry the disease and can pass it on to their sons but are not themselves affected.

Because girls have two X chromosomes, their normal X can provide a functioning gene even if their other X is defective. But because boys have an X and a Y, there is no normal X gene to fix the problem if the X is defective.

Affected children may develop an early-onset type (severe form) shortly after age two that causes a large skull, coarse facial features, profound mental retardation, spasticity, aggressive behavior, joint stiffness, and death before age twenty. A late-onset type (mild form) causes later and less severe symptoms (U.S. National Library of Medicine, 2005d).

MR 3.03 Mental Retardation Due to Phenylketonuria (PKU)

Definition Phenylketonuria (PKU) is a metabolic genetic disorder caused by the inability of the body to convert phenylalanine (a common dietary substance) to tyrosine. The consequent accumulation of phenylalanine results in abnormal brain development (ARC, 2001).

Explanation Phenylalanine is one of the eight essential amino acids found in protein-containing foods. In PKU, phenylalanine cannot be used in a normal fashion because of the missing enzyme. Subsequently, high levels of phenylalanine and two closely related phenylalanine derivatives build up in the body. These compounds are toxic to the central nervous system and cause brain damage (Hallahan & Kauffman, 2006; U.S. National Library of Medicine, 2005f; The Arc, 2001).

PKU is a treatable disease that can be easily detected by a simple blood test. Most states require a PKU screening test for all newborns shortly after birth. If the infant is diagnosed with PKU, potential damage to the brain can cause marked mental retardation by the end of the first year of life if the offending proteins are not scrupulously avoided. Consequently, babies with PKU are immediately put on a special diet, which prevents the occurrence of mental retardation (The Arc, 2001).

By analyzing the concentration of phenylalanine in a newborn's blood plasma, doctors can diagnose PKU and treat it with a phenylalanine-restricted diet. Most children with PKU who receive treatment have normal intellectual development (U.S. National Library of Medicine, 2005f).

MR 3.04 Mental Retardation Due to Tay-Sachs Disease

Definition Tay-Sachs disease is caused by the absence of hexosaminidase A (Hex-A), a vital enzyme. Without Hex-A, a fatty substance or lipid called GM2 ganglioside accumulates abnormally in cells, especially in the nerve cells of the brain. This ongoing accumulation causes progressive damage to the cells. The destructive process begins in the fetus early in pregnancy, although the disease is not clinically apparent until the child is several months old. By the time a child with TSD is three or four years old, the nervous system is so badly affected that life itself cannot be supported. Even with the best of care, all children with classical TSD die early in childhood, usually by the age of five (National Tay-Sachs & Allied Diseases Association, 2006).

Explanation Infants with Tay-Sachs disease appear to develop normally for the first few months of life. As nerve cells become distended with fatty material, a relentless deterioration of mental and physical abilities occurs. The child becomes blind, deaf, and unable to swallow. Muscles begin to atrophy, and paralysis sets in. Other neurological symptoms include dementia, seizures, and an increased startle reflex to noise (National Institute of Neurological Disorders and Stroke, 2005c).

When both parents are carriers of the inactive Tay-Sachs gene, they have a one in four chance (25 percent) with each pregnancy that their child will have Tay-Sachs disease, and a three in four chance (75 percent) that their child will be healthy. Of their unaffected children, there is a two in three chance that each child will be a carrier, like the parents. This pattern of inheritance is called autosomal recessive (National Tay-Sachs & Allied Diseases Association, 2006).

MR 3.05 Mental Retardation Due to Other Types of Metabolic Disorders

MR 4.00 Mental Retardation Due to Maternal Infections

Definition Infections can be passed from mother to child during fetal development or during childbirth. These infections in the mother during pregnancy can sometimes have the potential to injure the unborn child (Deutsch-Smith, 2004). Specific types of infections, such as syphilis and cytomegalovirus (a member of the herpes virus family), can result in mental retardation (Hallahan & Kauffman, 2006).

Diagnostic Symptoms Due to the numerous types of maternal infections, no general statement about symptoms can be made regarding either for specific diagnostic purposes.

Further Key Points According to Gargiulo (2004), "While pregnant, a woman and her developing child are very susceptible to a wide variety of potential infections. Exposure during the first trimester of pregnancy usually results in severe consequences" (p. 165).

MR 4.01 Mental Retardation Due to Maternal Cytomegalovirus Infection

Definition CMV, or cytomegalovirus, is a common virus that infects people of all ages. Once CMV is in a person's body, it stays there for life (American Pregnancy Association, 2006). Most infections with CMV are silent, meaning most people who are infected with the virus have no signs or symptoms. However, CMV can cause disease in unborn babies and in people with a weakened immune system. For infants who are infected by their mothers before birth, symptoms may range from moderate enlargement of the liver and spleen (with jaundice) to fatal illness. With supportive treatment, most infants with CMV disease usually survive. However, from 80 to 90 percent have complications within the first few years of life that may include hearing loss, vision impairment, and varying degrees of mental retardation (Centers for Disease Control, 2006).

Explanation CMV infection is important to certain high-risk groups. One major area of concern is the risk of infection to the unborn baby during pregnancy (National Center for Infectious Diseases, 2005). Approximately ten out of every thousand babies born in the United States have CMV infection. Nine of these babies have no symptoms, and one may have significant illness involving nervous system damage or developmental disabilities (NYS Department of Health, 2005).

CMV is a member of the herpes virus family, which includes the herpes simplex viruses and the viruses that cause chickenpox (varicella-zoster virus) and infectious mononucleosis (Epstein-Barr virus). Like other herpes viruses, CMV infection can become dormant for a while and may reactivate later. The virus is carried by people and is not associated with food, water, or animals (NYS Department of Health, 2005).

MR 4.02 Mental Retardation Due to Maternal Rubella

Definition Rubella (German measles) is an acute viral disease that can affect susceptible persons of any age. Although it is generally a mild rash illness, if contracted in the early months of pregnancy it is associated with a high rate of fetal loss or a constellation of birth defects known as congenital rubella syndrome (Centers for Disease Control, 2005b).When rubella is contracted by mothers during the first three months of pregnancy, it causes severe damage in 10 to 40 percent of unborn children, with mental retardation being a possibility (Heward, 2006).

Explanation Probably the most significant single preventative strike against mental retardation was the development of an effective rubella vaccine in 1962. Rubella is caused by a virus that is spread through the air or by close contact. It is a serious viral disease when occurring in the first trimester of pregnancy. If it occurs during this time, it is likely to cause a deformity in the fetus, potentially leading to mental retardation.

Congenital rubella syndrome occurs in 25 percent or more of infants born to women who acquired rubella during the first trimester of pregnancy. Defects are rare if the infection occurs after the twentieth week of pregnancy. One or more defects may occur in an infected fetus and include deafness, cataracts, microcephaly, mental retardation, congenital heart defects, and other problems (Centers for Disease Control, 2005b; Heward, 2006).

MR 4.03 Mental Retardation Due to Rh Disease (Rhesus Hemolytic Disease)

Definition Rh disease is a condition caused by an incompatibility between the blood of a mother and that of her fetus (ARC, 2005). It is a hemolytic disease—that is, it causes destruction of fetal red blood cells (March of Dimes Birth Defect Foundation, 2005b).

Explanation Rh disease once affected about twenty thousand babies in the United States each year. Since 1968, however, there has been a treatment that usually can prevent it, and the number of babies born with the disease has declined dramatically since then. Today, doctors are able to detect and treat Rh disease in the fetus, so about 95 percent of babies with severe Rh disease survive. But not all women who need the treatment get it, and a small number of women cannot benefit from it. As a result, there are still some four thousand infants born each year with Rh disease (March of Dimes Birth Defect Foundation, 2005b).

Very few first-pregnancy babies are damaged, as the Rh antibodies have not formed sufficiently to harm the first baby. However, a previous miscarriage, abortion, or amniocentesis in which the fetus's blood was Rh positive might have sensitized the woman. During subsequent pregnancies, antibodies can cross the placenta and attack the fetal blood cells. Rh disease destroys an unborn baby's blood cells, potentially resulting in newborns being born with jaundice (yellowing of the skin and eyes) and anemia. In some cases the results are brain damage, heart failure, and even death.

MR 4.04 Mental Retardation Due to Maternal Syphilis

Definition Syphilis is a sexually transmitted disease (STD) caused by the bacterium *Treponema pallidum.* It has often been called "the great imitator" because so many of the signs and symptoms are indistinguishable from those of other diseases (Centers for Disease Control, 2005c).

Explanation A pregnant woman with untreated, active syphilis is likely to pass the infection to her unborn child. In addition, miscarriage may occur in as many as 25 to 50 percent of women acutely infected with syphilis during pregnancy. Between 40 and 70 percent of women with active syphilis give birth to a syphilis-infected infant.

Some infants with congenital syphilis may have symptoms at birth, but most develop symptoms between two weeks and three months later. These symptoms may include:

- Skin ulcers
- Rashes
- Fever
- Weakened or hoarse crying sounds
- Swollen liver and spleen
- Yellowish skin (jaundice)
- Anemia (low red blood cell count)
- Various deformities

People who care for infants with congenital syphilis must use special caution because the moist sores are infectious. Rarely, the symptoms of syphilis go undetected in infants. As infected infants become older children and teenagers, they may develop the symptoms of late-stage syphilis, including damage to their bones, teeth, eyes, ears, and brain (National Institute of Allergy and Infectious Diseases, 2005).

MR 4.05 Mental Retardation Due to Maternal Toxoplasmosis

Definition A single-celled parasite called *Toxoplasma gondii,* which is found throughout the world, causes a disease known as toxoplasmosis. More than 60 million people in the United States may be infected with the Toxoplasma parasite. Of those who are infected, very few have symptoms because a healthy person's immune system usually keeps the parasite from causing illness. However, pregnant women and individuals who have compromised immune systems should be cautious; for them, a Toxoplasma infection could cause serious health problems (National Center for Infectious Diseases of the Centers for Disease Control and Prevention, 2004).

Explanation Infants born to mothers who became infected with Toxoplasma for the first time during or just before pregnancy are at risk for developing severe toxoplasmosis. According to the National Center for Infectious Diseases of the Centers for Disease Control and Prevention, Division of Parasitic Diseases (2004), symptoms of the infection vary.

Most people who become infected with Toxoplasma are not aware of it.

Most infants who are infected while still in the womb have no symptoms at birth, but they may develop symptoms later in life. A small percentage of infected newborns have serious eye or brain damage at birth (National Center for Infectious Diseases of the Centers for Disease Control and Prevention, 2004).

MR 4.06 Mental Retardation Due to Maternal Meningitis and Encephalitis

Definition Infections in the brain and spinal cord can cause dangerous inflammation that can produce a wide range of symptoms, including fever, headache, or confusion and, in extreme cases, can cause brain damage, stroke, seizures, or even death.

Infection of the meninges, the membranes that surround the brain and spinal cord, is called meningitis, and inflammation of the brain itself is called encephalitis. Myelitis is an infection of the spinal cord. When both the brain and the spinal cord become inflamed, the condition is called encephalomyelitis (National Institute of Neurological Disorders and Stroke, 2005b).

Explanation Viral meningitis is sometimes called aseptic meningitis to indicate it is not the result of bacterial infection and cannot be treated with antibiotics. Symptoms of encephalitis include sudden fever, headache, vomiting, heightened sensitivity to light, stiff neck and back, confusion and impaired judgment, drowsiness, weak muscles, a clumsy and unsteady gait, and irritability. Symptoms that might require emergency treatment include loss of consciousness, seizures, muscle weakness, or sudden and severe dementia.

Symptoms of meningitis, which may appear suddenly, often include high fever, severe and persistent headache, stiff neck, nausea, and vomiting. Changes in behavior such as confusion, sleepiness, and difficulty waking up may occur. In infants, symptoms of meningitis may include irritability or fatigue, lack of appetite, and fever. Viral meningitis usually resolves in ten days or less, but other types of meningitis can be deadly if not treated promptly. Anyone experiencing symptoms of meningitis or encephalitis should see a doctor immediately (National Institute of Neurological Disorders and Stroke, 2005b).

MR 4.07 Mental Retardation Due to Other Types of Maternal Infections

MR 5.00 Mental Retardation Due to Fetal Intoxicant Exposure

Definition A type of mental retardation believed to be caused by the fetus's being prenatally exposed to a toxin or toxins, including drugs, alcohol, or lead (Hallahan & Kauffman, 2006; Gargiulo, 2004).

Diagnostic Symptoms Although the symptoms of fetal exposure to toxins vary based on the nature of the exposure, the research suggests that mothers who drink, smoke, or take illegal substances place their unborn children at serious risk for premature birth, low birth weight, and mental retardation (Ball, 1999).

Further Key Points Experts estimate that one-half to three-quarters of a million infants are born each year who have been exposed to one or more illicit drugs in utero. When the legal drugs—alcohol and tobacco—are added, the figure rises to considerably more than 1 million substance-exposed infants (Brady, Posner, Lang, & Rosati, 1994).

MR 5.01 Mental Retardation Due to Fetal Exposure to Drugs

Definition A type of mental retardation believed to be caused by the fetus's being prenatally exposed to illicit drugs (U.S. National Library of Medicine, 2005h).

Explanation Long-term studies using sophisticated assessment techniques indicate that prenatally exposed children may have subtle but significant impairments in their ability to regulate emotions and focus and sustain attention on a task. These neurobehavioral deficits may place these children on a developmental pathway that leads to poor school performance and other adverse consequences over time.

Generally most studies of physical and neurobehavioral outcomes in newborn infants have shown that prenatal exposure to marijuana, cocaine, or opiates increases the risk that exposed infants will be born prematurely, weigh less, have smaller heads, and be shorter than unexposed infants (National Institute on Drug Abuse, 2005).

The difficulty that some drug-exposed infants have in achieving a quiet, alert state may also affect their intellectual development because it can affect their ability to respond to new stimuli, focus and sustain attention, and process information. These abilities are critical components of learning. Cocaine-exposed children appear to be more impulsive than nonexposed children and have more difficulty screening out distractions and focusing their attention (National Institute on Drug Abuse, 2005).

MR 5.02 Mental Retardation Due to Fetal Alcohol Syndrome

Definition Fetal alcohol syndrome (FAS) is the manifestation of specific growth, mental, and physical birth defects associated with the mother's high levels of alcohol use during pregnancy (U.S. National Library of Medicine, 2005h). Students with fetal alcohol syndrome often have mild or moderate mental retardation. FAS is considered the leading cause of mental retardation and the only one that is clearly preventable (University of South Dakota Center for Disabilities, 2002).

Explanation Alcohol use or abuse by the pregnant woman subjects her to the same range of risks that alcohol has in the general population. However, it poses extreme and unique risks to the fetus and is associated with fetal alcohol syndrome (National Organization on Fetal Alcohol Syndrome, 2006).

A pregnant woman who drinks any amount of alcohol is at risk, since a safe level of alcohol ingestion during pregnancy has not been established. However, larger amounts appear to cause increased problems. Multiple birth defects associated with classic fetal alcohol syndrome are more commonly associated with heavy alcohol use or alcoholism (National Organization on Fetal Alcohol Syndrome, 2006).

Fetal alcohol syndrome consists of the following abnormalities (Fetal Alcohol Disorders Society, 2006; National Organization on Fetal Alcohol Syndrome, 2006):

- Intrauterine growth retardation: growth deficiency in the fetus and newborn in all parameters—head circumference, weight, and height
- Delayed development with decreased mental functioning (mild to severe)
- Facial abnormalities, including small head (microcephaly); small maxilla (upper jaw); short, upturned nose; smooth philtrum (groove in upper lip); smooth and thin upper lip; and narrow, small, and unusual-appearing eyes with prominent epicanthal folds
- Heart defects such as ventricular septal defect or atrial septal defect
- Limb abnormalities of joints, hands, feet, fingers, and toes

Consumption of alcohol by a pregnant woman may be the first indicator of potential fetal alcohol syndrome. Other symptoms include (U.S. National Library of Medicine, 2005h):

- Slow intrauterine and neonatal growth with occasional diagnosis of failure to thrive
- Delayed development and evidence of mild to moderate mental retardation (IQ range from 50 to 85, with reported average in the mid-60s)
- Facial abnormalities, skeletal (limb) abnormalities, tremor (in the newborn infant), and agitation and crying (in the newborn infant).

MR 5.03 Mental Retardation Due to Fetal Lead Exposure

Definition One of the toxins or poisons that has been linked to mental retardation is lead (Hallahan & Kauffman, 2006). Fetal lead exposure is associated with delayed embryonic development of several organ systems and cognitive deficiencies in early childhood. Infants and children are more susceptible to the metal's effects than adults, and women exposed to high levels of lead decades ago may still pass the toxic metal to their unborn children.

Explanation Lead exposure can be harmful to fetuses because lead is able to cross the placenta, causing the amount of lead ingested by the child to be up to 50 percent attributed to the fetal absorption. Any exposure to lead during the prenatal period hurts the development of the child after birth, making it especially important for pregnant women to avoid lead ingestion and exposure (Lead Poisoning News, 2005). Although lead is now prohibited in paint, infants still become poisoned by eating lead-based paint chips, particularly in impoverished areas.

MR 5.04 Mental Retardation Due to Other Types of Fetal Intoxicant Exposure

MR 6.00 Mental Retardation Due to Gestational Disorders

Definition Gestation refers to the period from conception to birth. Gestational age is the time measured from the first day of the woman's last menstrual cycle to the current date and is measured in weeks. A pregnancy of normal gestation is approximately 40 weeks, with a normal range of thirty-eight to forty-two weeks (Heward, 2006).

Diagnostic Symptoms Due to the numerous types of gestational disorders and the areas of the body that they affect, no general statement about symptoms can be made regarding gestational disorders for specific diagnostic purposes.

Further Key Points Medical advances have greatly increased the likelihood that infants born weighing less than two pounds will survive, and this has led to both a new cause of mental retardation and increased numbers of individuals with mental retardation (Deutsch-Smith, 2004).

In the majority of instances, low-birth-weight infants are premature. Not all babies with gestational disorders will have a disability or will encounter future problems in school. However, some of these children may develop subtle learning problems, some may have mental retardation, and still others may have sensory of motor impairments (Gargiulo, 2004). Low-birth-weight babies are 50 percent more likely to be enrolled in special education when they reach school age, and 31 percent will have repeated a grade by age ten (Deutsch-Smith, 2004).

MR 6.01 Mental Retardation Due to Low Birth Weight

Definition According to the March of Dimes Birth Defects Foundation (2005a), low birth weight is a weight of less than five pounds, eight ounces (twenty-five hundred grams) at birth. Very low birth weight is a weight of less than three pounds, five ounces (fifteen hundred grams).

Explanation Low birth weight affects about one in every thirteen babies born each year in the United States. It is a factor in 65 percent of infant deaths. Low-birth-weight babies may face serious health problems as newborns and are at increased risk of long-term disabilities (Hallahan & Kauffman, 2006).

Advances in newborn medical care have greatly reduced the number of infant deaths associated with low birth weight, as well as the number of disabilities survivors of low birth weight experience. Still, a small percentage of survivors are left with problems such as mental retardation, cerebral palsy, and impairments in lung function, sight, and hearing (March of Dimes Birth Defects Foundation, 2005a).

MR 6.02 Mental Retardation Due to Premature Birth (Premature Infant)

Definition A premature infant is any infant born before thirty-seven weeks' gestation (U.S. National Library of Medicine, 2005h).

Explanation Every newborn is classified at birth as one of the following: premature (less than thirty-seven weeks gestation), full term (thirty-seven to forty-two weeks gestation), or postterm (born after forty-two weeks gestation). A premature infant is particularly vulnerable to brain damage (Texas Department of Aging and Disability, 2005).

The problems that premature infants encounter are related to the immaturity of the organ systems. These infants require specialized care in a nursery until their organ systems have developed enough to sustain life without specialized support. Depending on the extent of prematurity, this may take weeks to months.

The smaller and less mature the premature baby is at birth, the greater will be its problems in the long run. These babies can develop cerebral palsy, mental retardation, learning disorders, and vision, speech, and hearing problems.

MR 6.03 Mental Retardation Due to Other Types of Gestational Disorders

MR 7.00 Mental Retardation Due to Postnatal Environmental Problems

Definition According to Gargiulo (2004, p. 167), "A wide variety of environmental or psychosocial influences are often associated with mental retardation, especially instances of mild mental retardation. Debilitating factors may include nutritional problems, adverse living conditions, inadequate health care, and a lack of early cognitive stimulation. Many of these factors are associated with lower socioeconomic factors. . . . These illustrations only represent evident correlated with, but necessarily causes of, mental retardation. It is perhaps best to think of these variables as interacting risk factors, with some children being more vulnerable than others. Fortunately, most children exposed to these unfavorable circumstances develop normally."

Diagnostic Symptoms Children who are exposed to environmental deprivation resulting in mental retardation may exhibit the following symptoms:

- Failure to meet intellectual developmental markers
- Persistence of infantile behavior
- Lack of curiosity

- Decreased learning ability
- Inability to meet educational demands of school (U.S. National Library of Medicine, 2004)

Further Key Points Ignored or neglected infants who are not provided the mental and physical stimulation required for normal development may suffer irreversible learning impairments. Children who live in poverty and suffer from malnutrition, unhealthy living conditions, and improper or inadequate medical care are at a higher risk. Exposure to lead can also cause mental retardation (Joseph F. Smith Library, 2005a).

MR 7.01 Mental Retardation Due to Child Abuse and Neglect

Definition Federal legislation provides a foundation for states by identifying a minimum set of acts or behaviors that define child abuse and neglect. The Federal Child Abuse Prevention and Treatment Act (CAPTA), as amended by the Keeping Children and Families Safe Act of 2003, defines child abuse and neglect as, at minimum, "Any recent act or failure to act on the part of a parent or caretaker which results in death, serious physical or emotional harm, sexual abuse or exploitation; or an act or failure to act which presents an imminent risk of serious harm."

Explanation The exact number of abuse-caused disabilities is unknown, but it is estimated to represent 25 percent of all developmental disabilities. In addition, more than 50 percent of the child victims of severe neglect sustain permanent disabilities, including mental retardation and other forms of learning and cognitive disabilities.

According to a 1990 study, 53 percent of child abuse–related fatalities were children under one year of age, and 90 percent of the children were under five years of age (ARCH National Resource Center for Respite and Crisis Care Services, 1994). Head trauma is the leading cause of death for children who die from child abuse. It is unknown how many more children who do not die as a result of the abuse retain serious permanent disabilities due to head and neck trauma. Specific causes of brain and other central nervous system injuries may result from the shaken baby syndrome, blows to the head (such as slapping, hitting, child tossing), as well as asphyxiation due to suffocation or strangling.

MR 7.02 Mental Retardation Due to Malnutrition

Definition Malnutrition is an imbalance or deficiency of nutrients. This can come from not eating enough healthy foods or by using up too many nutrients through activities. Malnutrition can be identified by using body weight, body fat, protein stores, and laboratory values (North Memorial Medical Center, 2002).

Explanation Malnutrition is the condition that develops when the body does not get the right amount of the vitamins, minerals, and other nutrients it needs to maintain healthy tissues and organ function (Joseph F. Smith Library, 2005a). The absence of adequate nutrition can lead to meningitis and encephalitis, which can damage the brain of a growing child. Symptoms vary with the specific malnutrition-related disorder. Some general symptoms are fatigue, dizziness, weight loss, and decreased immune response (U.S. National Library of Medicine, 2004).

MR 7.03 Mental Retardation Due to Psychosocial Disadvantage (Developmental Retardation)

Definition A type of mental retardation that occurs when no demonstrable evidence of organic pathology (no brain damage or other biological problem) exists (Heward, 2006).

Explanation According to Heward (2006), the term *developmental retardation* is often used as a synonym for *psychosocial disadvantage* to refer to mental retardation thought to be caused primarily by environmental influences such as minimal opportunities to develop language, child abuse, and neglect, and/or chronic social or sensory deprivation (p. 151)."

According to McDermott (1994), a large percentage of mental retardation is based on environmental causes, most notably deprivation in the early years of life. Research suggests that children who live in poverty have a higher-than-normal chance of being identified as mentally retarded (Fujiura & Yamaki, 2000).

MR 7.04 Mental Retardation Due to Traumatic Brain Injury

Definition Traumatic brain injury (TBI), also called acquired brain injury or simply head injury, occurs when a sudden trauma causes damage to the brain. TBI can result when the head suddenly and violently hits an object or when an object pierces the skull and enters brain tissue (National Institute of Neurological Disorders and Stroke, 2005d).

Explanation Symptoms of a TBI can be mild, moderate, or severe, depending on the extent of the damage to the brain. A person with a mild TBI may remain conscious or may experience a loss of consciousness for a few seconds or minutes. Other symptoms of mild TBI are headache, confusion, lightheadedness, dizziness, blurred vision or tired eyes, ringing in the ears, bad taste in the mouth, fatigue or lethargy, a change in sleep patterns, behavioral or mood changes, and trouble with memory, concentration, attention, or thinking. (See Chapter Eleven for more details on traumatic brain injury.)

MR 7.05 Mental Retardation Due to Postnatal Meningitis or Encephalitis

Definition Meningitis is an infection of the covering of the brain that may be caused by a variety of bacterial or viral agents. Encephalitis, an inflammation of the brain, results more often in mental retardation and usually affects intelligence more severely (Hallahan & Kauffman, 2006).

Explanation Infection of the meninges, the membranes that surround the brain and spinal cord, is called meningitis, and inflammation of the brain itself is called encephalitis. Myelitis is an infection of the spinal cord. When both the brain and the spinal cord become inflamed, the condition is called encephalomyelitis (National Institute of Neurological Disorders and Stroke, 2006).

Meningitis and encephalitis are usually caused by viruses or bacteria. Most often, the body's immune system is able to contain and defeat an infection. But if the infection passes into the blood stream and then into the cerebrospinal fluid that surrounds the brain and spinal cord, it can affect the nerves and travel to the brain or surrounding membranes, causing inflammation. This swelling can harm or destroy nerve cells and cause bleeding in the brain.

MR 7.06 Mental Retardation Due to Lead Poisoning

Definition Lead is toxic to many of the body's tissues and enzymes. Children particularly are susceptible to lead poisoning because lead can accumulate in their nervous system as their bodies grow and develop. Death by lead poisoning is uncommon, but dangerous levels of lead in children may cause serious health problems, including lower intelligence and poor school performance (Mayo Clinic, 2006).

Explanation Lead is a soft, heavy, blue-gray metal. It occurs naturally in the earth's crust, and human activities such as burning fossil fuels, mining, and manufacturing have spread it throughout the environment, including homes and workplaces.

Lead is highly toxic to humans, especially young children (Centers for Disease Control, 2007). It has no known physiological value to the human body. Nearly half a million children living in the United States have blood lead levels high enough to cause irreversible damage to their health.

The effects of lead are the same whether it enters the body through breathing or swallowing. Lead can affect almost every organ and system in the body. The main target for lead toxicity is the nervous system. Exposure to lead can happen from breathing workplace air or dust, eating contaminated foods, or drinking contaminated water. Children can be exposed from eating lead-based paint chips or playing in contaminated soil. Lead can damage the nervous system, kidneys, and reproductive system (Agency for Toxic Substances and Disease Registry, 2006).

MR 7.07 Mental Retardation Due to the Effects of Other Forms of Postnatal Environmental Problems

MR 8.00 Mental Retardation Due to Other Causes

MR

MR 8.01 Mental Retardation Due to Other Prenatal Disorders or Exposure—Be Specific

MR 8.02 Mental Retardation Due to Pregnancy Complications During Childbirth (For Example, Breech Delivery, Prolonged Delivery, Respiratory Distress)—Be Specific

MR 8.03 Mental Retardation Due to Other Postnatal Conditions, Intoxicants, or Brain Diseases—Be Specific

---

References

AAMR Ad Hoc Committee on Terminology and Classification. (2002). *Mental retardation: Definition, classification, and systems of support* (10th ed.). Washington, DC: American Association on Mental Retardation.

Agency for Toxic Substances and Disease Registry. (2006). ToxFAQ for lead. Retrieved on April 6, 2006, from http://www.atsdr.cdc.gov/tfacts13.html.

American Association for Klinefelter Syndrome Information and Support. (April 2006). Understanding Klinefelter syndrome. Retrieved April 18, 2006, from http://www.aaksis.org/bock.cfm#xcauses.

American Pregnancy Association (2006). *Cytomegalovirus infection.* Retrieved March 21, 2006, from http://www.americanpregnancy.org/pregnancycomplications/cytomegalovirusinfection.html.

Anecephaly Awareness. (2006). *Everything you ever wanted to know about anencephaly, but couldn't find!* Retrieved February 11, 2006, from http://www.angelfire.com/mb/jessicasjourney/info.html.

ARC. (2001, April 10). *Phenylketonuria (PKU).* Retrieved April 6, 2006, from www.thearc.org/faqs/pku.html.

ARC. (2005). *Rh disease of newborns.* Retrieved July 28, 2005, from http://www.prevention-news.com/disorders/rh-newborns.htm.

ARCH National Resource Center for Respite and Crisis Care Services. (1994). *Abuse and neglect of children with disabilities.* Retrieved July 28, 2005, from http://www.archrespite.org/archfs36.htm.

Ball, W. (1999). Examining the link between tobacco use and low birth weight. *Early Childhood Reports, 10,* 3.

Baroff, G. S. (2000). Eugenics, "Baby Doe," and Peter Singer: Toward a more "perfect" society. *Mental Retardation, 38,* 73–77.

Beirne-Smith, M., Ittenbach, R. F., & Patton, J. R. (2002). *Mental retardation: An introduction to intellectual disabilities* (6th ed.). Upper Saddle River, NJ: Merrill/Prentice Hall.

Brady, J. P., Posner, M., Lang, C., & Rosati, M. J. (1994). *Risk and reality: The implications of prenatal exposure to alcohol and other drugs.* Rockville, MD: U.S. Department of Health.

Carter Centers for Brain Research in Holosencephaly and Related Malformations. (2002). *Information about holosencephaly.* Retrieved April 20, 2006, from http://hpe.stanford.edu/about/.

Centers for Disease Control. (2005a). *Mental retardation: How common is it?* Retrieved January 22, 2007, from http://www.cdc.gov/ncbddd/dd/mr3.htm.

Centers for Disease Control. (2005b). *Rubella.* Retrieved July 28, 2005, from http://www2.ncid.cdc.gov/travel/yb/utils/ybGet.asp?section=dis&obj=rubella.htm.

Centers for Disease Control. (2005c). *Syphilis.* Retrieved July 28, 2005, from http://www.clevelandclinic.org/health/health-info/docs/1200/1240.asp?index=5998&src=news.

Centers for Disease Control. (2006). *CMV.* Retrieved January 28, 2006, from http://www.cdc.gov/cmv/faqs.htm.

Centers for Disease Control. (2007). *Lead: Topic home.* Retrieved January 24, 2007, from http://www.cdc.gov/lead/default.htm.

Cerebral Palsy Network. (1999). *Cephalic disorders.* Retrieved March 15, 2006, from http://thecpnetwork.netfirms.com/colpocephaly.html.

Cerullo, A., Marini, C., Cevoli, S., Carelli, V., Montagna, P., & Tinuper, P. (2000). Colpocephaly in two siblings: Further evidence of a genetic transmission. *Developmental Medicine and Child Neurology, 42*(4), 280–282.

Children's Defense Fund. (2001). *The state of America's children.* Washington, DC: Children's Defense Fund.

Cleveland Clinic. (2003, September). *Cephalic disorders.* Retrieved April 18, 2006, from http://www.clevelandclinic.org/health/health-info/docs/1200/1240.asp?index=5998&src=newsp.

Cornelia de Lange Syndrome Foundation (2005). *FAQ about Cornelia de Lange.* Retrieved July 2, 2005, from http://www.cdlsusa.org/about_cdls/faq.html.

Dembro, M. R. (2003, September). *Five-minute clinical consult: A reference for clinicians* (12th ed.). Retrieved July 28, 2005, from www.5mcc.com/Assets/SUMMARY/TPO583.html.

Deutsch-Smith, D. (2004). *Introduction to special education: Teaching in an age of opportunity* (5th ed.). Needham Heights, MA: Allyn & Bacon.

Dobyns, W. (1991). *What is lissencephaly?* Retrieved April 18, 2006, from http://www.ghg.net/lissnet/about/lissen.htm#types.

Dykens, E. M., Hodapp, R. M., & Finucane, B. M. (2000). *Genetics and mental retardation syndromes: A new look at behavior and interventions.* Baltimore, MD: Paul H. Brookes.

Fast, D. (2003, April). *What is the molecular cause of fragile X syndrome?* Retrieved April 10, 2006, from http://fragilex.org/html/molecular.htm.

Fetal Alcohol Disorders Society. (2006). *Overview of FAS.* Retrieved January 3, 2006, from http://www.faslink.org/.

MR

Friend, M. (2005). *Special education: Contemporary perspectives for school professionals.* Boston: Pearson Educational.

Fujiura, G. T., & Yamaki, K. (2000). Analysis of ethnic variations in developmental disability prevalence and household economic status. *Mental Retardation, 35,* 286–294.

Gargiulo, R. M. (2004). *Special education in contemporary society: An introduction to exceptionality.* Belmont, CA: Thompson-Wadsworth.

Genetic Science Learning Center. (2006, April). *Cri du chat syndrome.* Retrieved April 18, 2006, from .

Gropman, A., & Muenke, M. (2005). Holoprosencephaly. In S. B. Cassidy & J. Allanson (Eds.), *Management of genetic syndromes* (2nd ed., pp. 291–308). New York: Wiley-Liss.

Hallahan, D., & Kauffman, J. (2006). *Exceptional learners: Introduction to special education* (9th ed.). Boston: Allyn & Bacon.

Hardman, M. L., Drew, C. J., & Egan, M. W. (2005). *Human exceptionality: School, community, and family.* Needham Heights, MA: Allyn & Bacon.

Heward, W. L. (2006). *Exceptional children: An introduction to special education* (8th ed.). Upper Saddle River, NJ: Pearson Education.

Hunt, N., & Marshall, K. (2006). *Exceptional children and youth: An introduction to special education* (4th ed.). Boston: Houghton Mifflin.

Hydrocephalus Association. (2004). *Information about hydrocephalus.* Retrieved April 21, 2006, from http://www.hydroassoc.org/information/information.htm.

Jones, L., & Menchetti, B. M. (2001). Identification of variables contributing to definitions of mild and moderate mental retardation in Florida [electronic version]. *Journal of Black Studies, 31,* 619–634.

Joseph F. Smith Library. (2005a). *Malnutrition.* Retrieved July 2, 2005, from http://www.chclibrary.org/micromed/00055940.html.

Joseph F. Smith Library. (2005b). *Mental retardation.* Retrieved July 2, 2005, from http://www.chclibrary.org/micromed/00056550.html.

Kleinfelter Syndrome and Associates. (2006, April). *Sex chromosome variations: About 47XXY.* Retrieved April 18, 2006, from http://www.genetic.org/ks/scvs/47xxy.htm.

Lead Poisoning News. (2005). *Lead poisoning dangers.* Retrieved July 2, 2005, from http://www.lead-poisoning-news.com/html/dangers.html.

Luckasson, R. (2002). *Mental retardation: Definition, classification, and systems of supports* (10th ed.). Washington, DC: American Association on Mental Retardation.

MacMillan, D. L., Gresham, F. M., Bocian, K. M., & Lambros, K. M. (1998). Current plight of borderline students: Where do they belong? *Education and Training in Mental Retardation and Developmental Disabilities, 33,* 83–94.

March of Dimes. (2003). *Quick reference: Birth defects and genetics—Down syndrome.* New York: National Down Syndrome Society.

March of Dimes Birth Defect Foundation. (2005a). *Low birthweight.* Retrieved July 2, 2005, from http://www.marchofdimes.com/professionals/681_1153.asp.

March of Dimes Birth Defect Foundation. (2005b). *Rh disease.* Retrieved July 2, 2005, from http://www.marchofdimes.com/professionals/681_1220.asp.

Mayo Clinic. (2005). *Hunter's syndrome.* Retrieved April 18, 2006, from http://www.mayoclinic.com/health/hunters-syndrome/AN01100.

Mayo Clinic. (2006). *Lead poisoning.* Retrieved April 6, 2006, from http://www.mayoclinic.com/health/lead-poisoning/FL00068.

Mazzocco, M. (2000). Advances in research on the fragile X syndrome. *Mental retardation and developmental disabilities research reviews, 6*(2), 96–106.

McDermott, S. (1994). Explanatory model to describe school district prevalence rates for mental retardation and learning disabilities. *American Journal on Mental Retardation, 99,* 175–185.

Medical College of Wisconsin. (2003). *Porencephaly.* Retrieved April 22, 2006, from http://healthlink.mcw.edu/article/921449639.html.

National Center for Biotechnology Information. (2005). *Prader-Willi syndrome.* Retrieved July 20, 2005, from http://www.ncbi.nlm.nih.gov/books/bv.fcgi?call=bv.Vie.ShowSection&rid=gnd.section.182.

National Center for Infectious Diseases of the Centers for Disease Control Prevention. (2004). *Toxoplasmosis.* Retrieved July 21, 2005, from http://www.cdc.gov/ncidod/dpd/parasites/toxoplasmosis/factsht_toxoplasmosis.htm.

National Center for Infectious Diseases of the Centers for Disease Control Prevention. (2005). *Cytomegalovirus (CMV) infection.* Retrieved July 12, 2005, from http://www.cdc.gov/ncidod/diseases/cmv.htm.

National Dissemination Center for Children with Disabilities. (2004). *Mental retardation.* Retrieved July 13, 2005, from http://www.nichcy.org/pubs/factshe/fs8txt.htm.

National Down Syndrome Society. (2003, October). *Questions and answers about Down syndrome.* Retrieved April 3, 2006, from www.ndss.org.

National Down Syndrome Society. (2006, April). *Incidence of Down syndrome.* Retrieved April 18, 2006, from http://www.ndss.org/content.cfm?fuseaction=InfoRes.Generalarticle&article=27.

National Human Genome Research Institute. (2005). *Chromosomal abnormalities.* Retrieved July 24, 2005, from http://www.genome.gov/11508982.

National Hydrocephalus Foundation. (2006). *What is hydrocephalus?* Retrieved April 3, 2006, from http://www.nhfonline.org/aboutus.php.

National Institute of Allergy and Infectious Diseases. (2005). *Syphilis.* Retrieved July 29, 2005, from http://www.niaid.nih.gov/factsheets/stdsyph.htm.

National Institute of Child Health and Human Development. (2005a). *Facts about Down syndrome.* Retrieved July 24, 2005, from http://www.nih.gov/.

National Institute of Child Health and Human Development. (2005b). *What is fragile-X syndrome?* http://www.nichd.nih.gov/publications/pubs/fragileX/sub1.htm.

National Institute of Child Health and Human Development. (2005c). *Mental retardation and developmental disabilities.* Retrieved July 27, 2005, from http://www.nichd.nih.gov/crmc/mrdd/#genetics.

National Institute of Neurological Disorders and Stroke. (2005a). *Cephalic disorders information page.* Retrieved July 16, 2005, from http://www.ninds.nih.gov/disorders/cephalic_disorders/cephalic_disorders.htm.

National Institute of Neurological Disorders and Stroke. (2005b). *Meningitis and encephalitis information page.* Retrieved July 20, 2005, from http://www.ninds.nih.gov/disorders/encephalitis_meningitis/encephalitis_meningitis.htm.

National Institute of Neurological Disorders and Stroke. (2005c). *Tay-Sachs disease information page.* Retrieved July 22, 2005, from http://www.ninds.nih.gov/disorders/taysachs/taysachs.htm.

National Institute of Neurological Disorders and Stroke. (2005d). *Traumatic brain injury information page.* Retrieved July 8, 2005, from http://www.ninds.nih.gov/disorders/tbi/tbi.htm.

National Institute of Neurological Disorders and Stroke. (2006a). *Meningitis and encephalitis fact sheet.* Bethesda, MD: National Institutes of Health.

National Institute of Neurological Disorders and Stroke. (2006b). *Williams syndrome.* Retrieved January 4, 2007, from http://www.ninds.nih.gov/disorders/williams/williams.htm.

National Institute on Drug Abuse. (2005). *Prenatal exposure to drugs of abuse may affect later behavior and learning.* Retrieved July 6, 2005, from http://www.drugabuse.gov/NIDA_Notes/NNVol13N4/Prenatal.html.

National Institutes of Health. (2004). *NICHD funded researchers discover gene for Cornelia de Lange syndrome: Discovery may lead to prenatal test for debilitating disorder.* Retrieved July 6, 2005, from http://www.nih.gov/.

National Organization for Rare Disorders. (1999). *Hydrancephaly.* Retrieved April 19, 2006, from, http://www.rarediseases.org/search/rdbdetail_abstract.html?disname=Hydranencephaly.

National Organization for Rare Disorders. (2002). *Lissencephaly.* Retrieved April 18, 2006 from http://www.rarediseases.org/search/rdbdetail_abstract.html?disname=Lissencephaly.

National Organization on Fetal Alcohol Syndrome. (2006). *Fetal alcohol syndrome.* Retrieved March 12, 2006, from http://www.nofas.org/educator/.

National Tay-Sachs & Allied Diseases Association. (2006). *Tay-Sachs disease-Classical infantile form.* Retrieved February 16, 2006, from http://www.ntsad.org/pages/t-sachs.htm#What percent20is percent20Tay-Sachs percent20Disease?

North Memorial Medical Center. (2002). *Malnutrition.* Retrieved July 28, 2005, from http://www.northmemorial.com/HealthEncyclopedia/content/1921.asp.

NYS Department of Health. (2005). *Cytomegalovirus.* Retrieved July 23, 2005, from http://www.health.state.ny.us/nysdoh/communicable_diseases/en/cytomega.htm.

Parents of Galactosemic Children. (2006, April). *What is classic galactosemic?* Retrieved April 18, 2006, from http://www.galactosemia.org/galactosemia.htm.

Penn State Children's Hospital. (2007). *A to Z topics: Mental retardation.* Retrieved January 22, 2007, from http://www.hmc.psu.edu/childrens/healthinfo/m/mental retardation.htm.

Prader-Willi Syndrome Association. (2003). *Questions and answers about Prader-Willi syndrome.* Retrieved March 15, 2006, from www.pwsausa.org/faq.htm.

Semel, E., & Rosner, S. R. (2003). *Understanding Williams syndrome: Behavioral patterns and interventions.* Mahwah, NJ: Erlbaum.

Sudhalter V., & Belser, R. (2001). Conversational characteristics of children with fragile X syndrome: Tangential language. *American Journal of Retardation, 106*(5), 389–400.

Sunnybrook and Women's College Health Sciences Centre. (2005). *Glossary-Pregnancy health care.* Retrieved July 23, 2005, from http://www.womenshealthmatters.ca/centres/pregnancy/glossary/index.html.

Symons, F. J., Clark, R. D., Roberts, J. P., & Bailey, D. B. (2001). Classroom behavior of elementary school-age boys with fragile X syndrome. *Journal of Special Education, 34,* 194–202.

Taylor, H. G., Klein, N., Minich, N. M., & Hack, M. (2000). Middle-school-age outcomes in children with very low birthweight. *Child Development, 71,* 1495–1511.

Taylor, R. L., Richards, S. B., & Brady, M. P. (2005). *Mental retardation: Historical perspectives, current practices, and future directions.* Needham Heights, MA: Allyn & Bacon.

Texas Department of Aging and Disability. (2005). *Mental retardation. The implications of prenatal exposure to alcohol and other drugs.* Retrieved July 3, 2005, from http://www.come-over.to/FAS/RiskReality.htm.

Turner, G., Webb, T., Wake, S., & Robinson, H. (1996). Prevalence of fragile X syndrome. *American Journal of Medical Genetics, 64,* 196–199.

Turner Syndrome Society of the United States. (2006, April). About Turner Syndrome. Retrieved April 18, 2006, from http://www.turner-syndrome-us.org/about/.

University of South Dakota Center for Disabilities. (2002). *Fetal alcohol syndrome handbook.* Sioux Falls, SD: Author.

U.S. Department of Education. (2002). *The Twenty-Fourth Annual Report to Congress on the Implementation of IDEA.* Washington, DC: U.S. Department of Education.

U.S. Department of Education. (2004). *The Twenty-Sixth Annual Report to Congress on the Implementation of IDEA.* Washington, DC: U.S. Department of Education.

U.S. National Library of Medicine. (2004). *Mental retardation.* Retrieved July 2, 2005, from http://www.nlm.nih.gov/medlineplus/ency/article/001523.htm.

U.S. National Library of Medicine. (2005a). *Cri du chat syndrome.* Retrieved July 23, 2005, from http://www.nlm.nih.gov/medlineplus/ency/article/001593.htm.

U.S. National Library of Medicine. (2005b). *Fragile X syndrome.* Retrieved July 23, 2005, from http://www.nlm.nih.gov/medlineplus/ency/article/001668.htm.

U.S. National Library of Medicine. (2005c). *Galactosemia.* Retrieved July 1, 2005, from http://www.nlm.nih.gov/medlineplus/ency/article/000366.htm.

U.S. National Library of Medicine. (2005d). *Hunter syndrome.* Retrieved July 30, 2005, from http://www.nlm.nih.gov/medlineplus/ency/article/001203.htm.

U.S. National Library of Medicine. (2005e). *Klinefelter syndrome-Genetics home reference.* Retrieved July 9, 2005, from http://ghr.nlm.nih.gov/condition=klinefeltersyndrome.

U.S. National Library of Medicine. (2005f). *Metabolism.* Retrieved July 23, 2005, from http://www.nlm.nih.gov/medlineplus/ency/article/002257.htm.

U.S. National Library of Medicine. (2005g). *Prader-Willi syndrome.* http://ghr.nlm.nih.gov/condition=praderwillisyndrome.

U.S. National Library of Medicine. (2005h). *Premature infant.* Retrieved July 23, 2005, from http://www.nlm.nih.gov/medlineplus/ency/article/001562.htm.

U.S. National Library of Medicine. (2005i). *Turner syndrome.* Retrieved July 18, 2005, from http://ghr.nlm.nih.gov/condition=turnersyndrome/show/Educational+resources.

U.S. National Library of Medicine. (2005j). *Williams syndrome.* Retrieved July 23, 2005, from http://www.nlm.nih.gov/medlineplus/ency/article/001562.htm.

ED

CHAPTER 4

EMOTIONAL DISTURBANCE

EDM CODE: ED

ED

- ED 1.00 Emotional Disturbance by Exclusion
- ED 2.00 Relationship Prob lems Disorder
- ED 3.00 Inappropriate Behavior or Feelings Disorder
  - ED 3.01 Inappropriate Behavior or Feelings Disorder— Aggressive Interactive Type
  - ED 3.02 Inappropriate Behavior or Feelings Disorder—Disruptive Behavior Type
  - ED 3.03 Inappropriate Behavior or Feelings Disorder—Immaturity Type
  - ED 3.04 Inappropriate Behavior or Feelings Disorder-Impulse Control Type
  - ED 3.05 Inappropriate Behavior or Feelings Disorder—Self-Destructive Behavior Type
  - ED 3.06 Other Types of Inappropriate Feelings and Behavior Disorders Not Otherwise Listed
- ED 4.00 Pervasive Mood Disorder
- ED 5.00 Physical Complaints Disorder
- ED 6.00 Anxiety Reactive Disorder
  - ED 6.01 Panic Reactive Disorder
  - ED 6.02 School Avoidance Anxiety Reactive Disorder
  - ED 6.03 School-Related Anxiety Reactive Disorder
    - ED 6.03a Test Anxiety Reactive Disorder
  - ED 6.04 Separation Anxiety Reactive Disorder
  - ED 6.05 Social Avoidance Anxiety Reactive Disorder
  - ED 6.06 Social-Related Anxiety Reactive Disorder
  - ED 6.07 Unfounded Anxiety Reactive Disorder
- ED 7.00 Schizophrenia
- ED 8.00 Psychological and Psychiatric Disorders Already Diagnosed by Mental Health Professionals—Be Very Specific

IDEA 2004 Definition of Emotional Disturbance

Under IDEA 2004, an emotional disturbance is defined as:

> a condition exhibiting one or more of the following characteristics over a long period of time and to a marked degree that adversely affects a child's educational performance:
>
> (a) An inability to learn that cannot be explained by intellectual, sensory, or health factors.
>
> (b) An inability to build or maintain satisfactory interpersonal relationships with peers and teachers.
>
> (c) Inappropriate types of behavior or feelings under normal circumstances.
>
> (d) A general pervasive mood of unhappiness or depression.

(e) A tendency to develop physical symptoms or fears associated with personal or school problems.

The term includes schizophrenia. The term does not apply to children who are socially maladjusted, unless it is determined that they have an emotional disturbance [34 C.F.R. 300.7(c)(4)].

Overview of Emotional Disturbance

Individuals with emotional disorders or behavior disorders experience great difficulties in relating appropriately to peers, siblings, parents, and teachers (Jensen, 2005). They also have difficulty responding to academic and social tasks that are essential parts of their schooling. Sometimes they may exhibit too much behavior, or they may be deficient in important academic and social behaviors. In other cases, individuals with emotional or behavioral disorders may not have learned the essential skills necessary for successful participation in school settings (Hardman, Drew, & Egan, 2005).

According to Hunt and Marshall (2005),

> The definition of emotional disturbance, like most definitions in special education, is the source of much debate and discussion, and the term "emotional disturbance" is being challenged at the federal level. A number of professionals are urging that the term "emotional or behavioral disorder" be used instead and are also proposing several changes to the definition. Some states have adopted the term "behavior disordered" because of its more direct relationship to assessment and identification procedures.
>
> In defining behavioral disorders or emotional disturbance, no single measure of social or emotional functioning is sufficiently reliable and valid to serve in the way that intelligence tests and other measures do in defining mental retardation and achievement tests in being part of the definition of learning disabilities (Rosenberg, Mueser, & Jankowski, 2004). Further, much of the controversy revolves around the ambiguity of the terms used as diagnostic markers and concern that this ambiguity excludes children who require services. For example, phrases such as "inappropriate types of behavior" or "satisfactory interpersonal relationships" are difficult to translate into clear-cut measures of performance. There is also much concern over the exclusion of children identified as "socially maladjusted." The term is considered difficult to define, particularly in view of the possible overlap with behaviors (such as aggression, poor peer relationships) that would qualify a child for special education services [p. 236].

Causes-Etiology of Emotional Disturbance

The causes of emotional disturbance have not been adequately determined. However, research suggests that emotional disturbances are caused by a combination of biological, psychological and environmental factors.

Biological Factors That May Result in Mental Illness

Some types of mental illnesses have been linked to an abnormal balance of special chemicals in the brain called neurotransmitters. A neurotransmitter is a chemical that helps transmit nerve impulses through the nervous system. There are many different neurotransmitters used by the body, and these can have an adverse affect on the individual's mental state (Kirk, Gallagher, & Anastasiow, 2003). For example, the neurotransmitter chemicals known as norepinephrine, serotonin, acetylchlorine, dopamine, and gamma-aminobutryric acid seemed to be lower in some depressed people or higher in nondepressed people (Harper, 2003). If these chemicals are out of balance or are not working properly, messages may not make it through the brain correctly, leading to symptoms of mental illness.

Other biological factors may be involved in the development of mental illness:

- *Genetics* (heredity). Many mental illnesses run in families, suggesting that people who have a family member with a mental illness are more susceptible (have a greater likelihood of being affected) to developing a mental illness. Susceptibility is passed on in families through genes. Experts believe many mental illnesses are linked to abnormalities in many genes, not just one (Kauffman, 2005). That is why a person inherits a susceptibility to a mental illness and does not necessarily develop the illness. Mental illness itself occurs from the interaction of multiple genes and other factors—such as stress, abuse, or a traumatic event—that can influence, or trigger, an illness in a person who has an inherited susceptibility to it (Jensen, 2005).
- *Infections.* Certain infections have been linked to brain damage and the development of mental illness or the worsening of its symptoms. For example, a condition known as pediatric autoimmune neuropsychiatric disorder associated with the Streptococcus bacterium has been linked to the development of obsessive-compulsive disorder and other mental illnesses in children (Cleveland Clinic Department of Psychiatry and Psychology, 2005).
- *Brain defects or injury.* Defects in or injury to certain areas of the brain have been linked to some mental illnesses (Jensen, 2005; Kauffman, 2005).
- *Prenatal damage.* Some evidence suggests that a disruption of early fetal brain development or trauma that occurs at the time of birth—for example, loss of oxygen to the brain—may be a factor in the development of certain conditions such as autism (Cleveland Clinic Department of Psychiatry and Psychology, 2005; Kauffman, 2005).
- *Other factors.* Poor nutrition and exposure to toxins such as lead may play a role in the development of mental illnesses (Jensen, 2005; Kauffman, 2005).

Psychological Factors That May Result in Mental Illness

A number of psychological factors may contribute to an emotional or behavioral disorder (Hallahan & Kauffman, 2006; Jensen, 2005; Kauffman, 2005; Gargiulo, 2005):

- Trauma experienced as a child, such as emotional, physical, or sexual abuse
- Early loss of an important person, such as the loss of a parent
- Emotional, physical, or educational neglect
- Substance abuse
- Poor relations with peers and adults
- High levels of stress
- Educational failure
- Dysfunctional family life
- Feelings of inadequacy, low self-esteem, anxiety, anger, or loneliness

Prevalence of Emotional Disturbance

According to the *Twenty-Sixth Annual Report* (U.S. Department of Education, 2004), 482,597 students between the ages of six and twenty-one years of age were identified as having emotional disturbances. This represents slightly more than 8 percent of all students having a classification in special education, or less than 1 percent of all school-age students.

According to the National Alliance for the Mentally Ill (2003), an American advocacy organization, approximately 9 to 13 percent of children under the age of eighteen experience serious emotional disturbance with substantial functional impairment; 5 to 9 percent have serious emotional disturbance with extreme functional impairment due to a mental illness. Many of these young people will recover from their illnesses before reaching adulthood and go on to lead normal lives uncomplicated by illness.

Age of Onset of Emotional Disturbance

There is relatively little emotional disturbance reported in the early grades, with a sharp increase and peak during the middle grades and a decline in prevalence beginning in middle school and continuing through high school (U.S. Department of Education, 2004).

Gender Features of Emotional Disturbance

Males are significantly more likely than females to fall within each major disability group. The largest disparity is within the category of emotionally disturbance, where boys comprise some 80 percent of the population. Among the general population of students in grades 1 to 8, there are more boys with emotional disturbance (7 percent of all boys in special education are classified as emotionally disturbed) than girls (4 percent of all girls in special education are so classified). Sources document that boys outnumber girls at about five to one (Hallahan & Kauffman, 2003; Hardman et al., 2005; Heward, 2006; Turnbull et al., 2004).

Cultural Features of Emotional Disturbance

According to Turnbull et al. (2004), "African American males are overrepresented in the category of emotional or behavioral disorders. The special education community faces three challenges in terms of this high identification rate: (1) unavailability of culturally appropriate assessment instruments, (2) concern about teacher expectations regarding appropriate behavior, and (3) building respectful family-professional partnerships that may prevent identification. Ethnically diverse groups are more likely to experience stressors such as 'poverty, discrimination, violence, violent death, drug and alcohol abuse, and teenage pregnancy' that can contribute to mental health problems" (p. 144). Although African Americans comprise 14.8 percent of the school population, they comprise nearly 27 percent of the students who receive special education services as having and emotional disturbance (U.S. Department of Education, 2004).

Familial Pattern of Emotional Disturbance

Patterns such as parental discord, a parent's mental illness or criminal behavior, overcrowding in the same home, and large family size may result in conditions conducive to the development of emotional disturbance, especially if the child does not have a loving, nurturing relationship with at least one parent (Gargiulo, 2004).

Characteristics of Emotional Disturbance

The causes of emotional disturbance have not been adequately determined. Although various factors such as heredity, brain disorder, diet, stress, and family functioning have been suggested as possible causes, research has not shown any of these factors to be the direct cause of behavior or emotional problems (Jensen, 2005). Some of the characteristics and behaviors seen in children who have emotional disturbances include:

- Hyperactivity (short attention span, impulsiveness)
- Aggression or self-injurious behavior (acting out, fighting); classmates of students with emotional or behavioral disorders tend to reject them (Bullis, Walker, & Sprague, 2001)
- Withdrawal (failure to initiate interaction with others; retreat from exchanges of social interaction, excessive fear or anxiety)
- Immaturity (inappropriate crying, temper tantrums, poor coping skills)
- Learning difficulties (academically performing below grade level)

Children with the most serious emotional disturbances may exhibit distorted thinking, excessive anxiety, bizarre motor acts, and abnormal mood swings. Some are identified as children who have a severe psychosis or schizophrenia (Jensen, 2005).

Many children who do not have emotional disturbances may display some of these same behaviors at various times during their development. However, when children have an emotional disturbance, these behaviors continue over long periods of time. Their behavior thus signals that they are not coping with their environment or peers (Turnbull, Turnbull, Shank, & Smith, 2004).

Possibly more than any other group of children with disabilities, children with emotional or behavior disorders present problems with social skills to themselves, their families, their peers, and their teachers (U.S. Department of Education, 2001; Gresham, Lane, MacMillian, & Boscian, 1999).

Educational Implications of Emotional Disturbance

"School failure is the common link between delinquency and disability" (OSEP, 2001, p. II-3). Regardless of intellectual potential, students with emotional or behavioral disorders typically do not perform well academically.

The educational programs for children with an emotional disturbance need to include attention to providing emotional and behavioral support as well as helping them master academics, develop social skills, and increase self-awareness, self-control, and self-esteem. A large body of research exists regarding methods of providing students with positive behavioral support (PBS) in the school environment, so that problem behaviors are minimized and positive, appropriate behaviors are fostered (Heward, 2006; Hunt & Marshall, 2005; Turnbull et al., 2004). It is also important to know that within the school setting:

- For a child whose behavior impedes learning (including the learning of others), the team developing the child's Individualized Education Program (IEP) needs to consider, if appropriate, strategies to address that behavior, including positive behavioral interventions, strategies, and supports.
- Students eligible for special education services under the category of emotional disturbance may have IEPs that include psychological or counseling services. These are important related services that are available under law and are provided by a qualified social worker, psychologist, guidance counselor, or other qualified personnel.
- Career education (both vocational and academic) is a major part of secondary education and should be a part of the transition plan included in every adolescent's IEP.

There is growing recognition that families, as well as their children, need support, respite care, intensive case management, and a collaborative, multiagency approach to services. Many communities are working toward providing these wraparound services. A growing number of agencies and organizations are actively involved in establishing support services in the community (National Dissemination Center for Children with Disabilities, 2004).

IDEA Exclusion of Students Who Are "Socially Maladjusted"

Students who are "socially maladjusted" do not qualify for special education under IDEA unless they meet the criteria for an emotional disturbance in another way. Social maladjustment without a linkage to an emotional disorder is often characterized by deviant behavior with conscious control. Emotional overreactions may occur when the behavior is criticized or punishment is applied. Anger is a frequent reaction, but the thoughts are related to the situation.

The student's perceptions are logically related to the situation and consistent with other people's perceptions (Hallahan & Kauffman, 2006; Jensen, 2005). The following indicators are often associated with a social maladjustment and lack the emotional disorder:

- Signs of depression may be present, but are not pervasive.
- Problem behaviors are goal directed, self-serving, and manipulative.
- Actions are based on perceived self-interest even though others may consider the behavior to be self-defeating.
- Inappropriate behaviors are displayed in selected settings or situations (for example, only at home, in school, or in selected classes), while most behavior is controlled.
- Problem behaviors are frequently exhibited by and encouraged by the peer group, and the actions are intentional with understanding of the consequences.
- General social conventions and behavioral standards are understood but are not accepted; countercultural standards of the neighborhood and peers are accepted and followed.
- Problem behaviors have escalated during preadolescence or adolescence (Hallahan & Kauffman, 2006; Kauffman, 2005; Jensen, 2005).

The exclusion of students who are socially maladjusted but not emotionally disturbed is one of the most heavily criticized parts of IDEA's definition of an emotional disturbance (Hallahan & Kauffman, 2006).

Eligibility Criteria for Emotional Disturbance Under IDEA

In determining eligibility under IDEA, the IEP team must decide if a student has an emotional condition that is manifested by one or more of the five characteristics listed in the definition of emotional disturbance. These characteristics must meet the qualifying conditions of adverse effect on educational performance, occurring over a long period of time (chronicity) and to a marked degree (severity):

- *Long period of time.* The standard for duration is not precisely specified. The literature frequently makes reference to several months as an appropriate standard. The intention is to avoid labeling a student who is temporarily reacting to a situational trauma. The characteristics must also be evident over time and situations (Connecticut Department of Education, 1997).

- *Marked degree.* The problems are significant and apparent to school staff members who observe the student in a variety of settings and situations. A comparison is made with the student's appropriate peer group; the problems must be more severe or frequent than the normally expected range of behavior for individuals of the same age, gender, and cultural group. The characteristics must be persistent and generalized across environments (Connecticut Department of Education, 1997).

Permissions and Authorization to Use Proprietary and Nonproprietary Sources

Due to the detailed nature of certain Level II and Level III disorders described in this chapter, we felt that some were best explained by state departments of education that had done extensive research in creating evaluation guidelines on emotional disturbance. The sources obtained were all in the public domain. We thank the following state departments of education for the opportunity to freely disseminate their information:

- Connecticut State Department of Education
- Wisconsin State Department of Education

EDM Codes, Definitions, and Explanations of Emotional Disturbance

All of the categories listed below come directly from the language of IDEA 2004. It should also be noted that the team that is determining an emotional disturbance using the following categories should include a psychologist.

ED 1.00 Emotional Disturbance by Exclusion

Under IDEA 2004, one of the criteria for a classification of emotional disturbance is "an inability to learn that cannot be explained by intellectual, sensory, or health factors." This criterion will be termed Emotional Disturbance by Exclusion in the EDM classification system.

Definition A type of emotional disturbance that is characterized by an inability to learn that cannot be explained by intellectual, sensory, or health factors. Inability to learn means that the condition must significantly interfere with the ability to benefit from instruction. It does not necessarily mean a total inability to learn.

Diagnostic Symptoms For these particular criteria for an emotional disturbance, the determination is that the child's emotional and behavioral problems are not due to intellectual, sensory, or health factors. Consequently, the following symptoms should be present:

- Academic history and data on current academic assessment indicate an adverse effect on a child's educational performance over a long period of time and to a marked degree.
- Achievement scores are incompatible with IQ scores.
- The student is disorganized.
- The student has been retained.
- IQ testing or other information shows clear evidence of at least average potential cognitive ability.
- The student may be learning to some extent, but there is a significant difference between potential and demonstrated learning.
- Medical history rules out any primary health–related issues that are associated with emotional and behavioral problems.
- No health or sensory impairments have been found by a physician, or any identified impairments are not significant enough to explain the discrepancy.
- The student quits or gives up easily.
- Vision and hearing screening do not indicate a primary cause that might account for the emotional behavior.
- The student has difficulty retaining material.

Further Key Points This characteristic requires documentation that a student is not able to learn despite appropriate instructional strategies and support services. A comprehensive and differential assessment is performed to establish an inability to learn. The assessment should rule out any other primary reasons for the suspected disability, such as mental retardation, speech and language disorders, autism, learning disability, hearing or vision impairment, multihandicapping conditions, traumatic brain injury, neurological impairment, or other medical conditions (Pierangelo & Giuliani, 2006). If any of these other conditions is the primary cause, then the student may be deemed eligible for special education under that category of disability. Such a determination does not necessarily rule out emotional disturbance as a concomitant disability, since emotional and behavioral problems may also be associated with one of the above conditions (Wisconsin Department of Instruction, 2002; Connecticut Department of Education, 1997).

There are problems inherent in the use of the phrase "inability to learn" as found in both the federal and state regulations. Inability to learn is inconsistent with a philosophy that all children can be characterized as learners (Kauffman, 2005). Therefore, the "inability to learn" characteristic should be appropriately interpreted as serious difficulties in learning. The sole selection of this characteristic must be supported by evidence of a serious emotional disturbance. It would expectedly be used only in rare cases such as elective mutism or multiple personality disorder (Wisconsin Department of Instruction, 2002; Connecticut Department of Education, 1997).

ED 2.00 Relationship Problems Disorder

Under IDEA 2004, one of the criteria for a classification of emotional disturbance is "an inability to build or maintain satisfactory interpersonal relationships with peers and teachers." This criterion will be termed Relationship Problems Disorder in the EDM classification system.

Definition A type of emotional disturbance that is characterized by patterns and problems of interpersonal relationships that result in an inability to build or maintain satisfactory relationships with peers, teachers, and others. This also includes individuals who are profoundly withdrawn, have poor reality contact, or lack social skills but have the ability to learn them.

Diagnostic Symptoms Symptoms of a relationship problems disorder may include:

- Demands for constant attention from others
- Difficulty attaching to others
- Difficulty separating from caregivers
- Excessively controlling
- Excessively dependent
- Inappropriate sexual behavior
- Frequent teasing by peers
- Ignored or rejected by peers
- Inability to interact with a group or play by the rules
- Too easily influenced by peers
- Lack of affect or disorganized or distorted emotions toward others
- Lack of social awareness—(may not understand social conventions)
- Lacking trust in others or fearful of others
- Neglect by peers
- Overly affectionate
- Painful shyness in social situations

- Peer avoidance
- Physical or verbal aggression when others approach him or her
- Poor reality contact
- Sees self as a victim
- Teacher avoidance in general
- Using or manipulating others
- Victimization by peers
- Seeking constant attention or approval
- Withdrawal from all social interactions
- Withdrawal from social activities or interaction on the playground, physical education, and other social interactions with peers

Further Key Points EDM 2.00 requires documentation that the student is unable to initiate or maintain satisfactory interpersonal relationships with peers and teachers. Satisfactory interpersonal relationships include the ability to demonstrate sympathy, warmth, and empathy toward others; establish and maintain friendships; be constructively assertive; and work and play independently. These abilities should be considered when observing the student's interactions with both peers and teachers. This characteristic does not refer to the student who has conflict with only one teacher or with certain peers. Rather, it is a pervasive inability to develop relationships with others across settings and situations (Wisconsin Department of Instruction, 2002; Connecticut Department of Education, 1997).

ED 3.00 Inappropriate Behavior or Feelings Disorder

Under IDEA 2004, one of the criteria for a classification of emotional disturbance is "inappropriate types of behavior or feelings under normal circumstances." This criterion will be termed Inappropriate Behavior or Feelings Disorder in the EDM classification system.

This category is set aside for diagnoses made by the multidisciplinary team that have not been previously diagnosed by an outside mental health professional. For example, if a child has been previously diagnosed with, say, oppositional defiant disorder, conduct disorder, or a disruptive behavior disorder, he or she does not receive a diagnosis of ED 3.00. In this case, the team would refer to ED 8.00: Psychological and Psychiatric Disorders Already Diagnosed by Mental Health Professionals and specifically state the medical diagnosis.

ED 3.00, Inappropriate Behavior or Feelings Disorder, as defined in EDM is associated with symptoms of disruptive behavior disorders. However, it is not the responsibility of the multidisciplinary and IEP team to diagnose a child with these disorders. The role of the multidisciplinary and IEP team should be to determine whether the child meets the criteria for an emotional disturbance as defined by IDEA. Then, if the child exhibits symptoms associated with EDM's description of inappropriate behavior or feelings disorder, the child receives an EDM diagnosis of ED 3.00. This diagnosis represents a child with an emotional disturbance who exhibits symptoms similar to disruptive behavior disorders but not previously diagnosed by an outside professional. If a child receives a diagnosis of ED 3.00, the team should seriously consider an outside referral for a more specific diagnosis.

Definition A type of emotional disturbance that is characterized by behaviors inappropriate to the situation or highly volatile. This characteristic requires documentation that the student's inappropriate behavior or feelings deviate significantly from expectations for the student's age, gender, and culture across different environments.

Diagnostic Symptoms Behavior include bizarre verbalization, overreaction, repeated recitation of words, fetishes, and obsessive and compulsive behaviors. Other actions may include inappropriate sexual behaviors such as inappropriate touching of others, public masturbation, or unusual or provocative sexual verbalization. Inappropriate feelings include negative self-statements as well as feelings that are reflected in and inferred from observable behavior. Other diagnostic symptoms include:

- Antisocial behaviors
- Apparent remorseless
- Becoming defensive without provocation
- Disorganized or scattered thought processes
- Excessive dependence and overcloseness, or inappropriate rebellion and defiance
- Excessive emotional responses
- Flat affect
- Extreme responses to changes in routine or schedule
- Impulsivity; lack of self control
- Inability to make changes or transitions
- Inappropriately laughing or crying
- Lack of assertiveness
- Lack of empathy
- Lying, cheating, or stealing
- Limited ability to predict consequences of behavior
- Limited or excessive self-control

- Limited premeditation or planning
- Low frustration tolerance, emotional overreactions, and impulsivity
- Low-self-esteem or distorted self-concept
- Noncompliant or passive-aggressive behavior
- Overly perfectionistic or hard on self
- Overreacting
- Rapid changes in behavior or mood
- Refusing to do school work
- Refusing to respond to others
- Wide mood swings

Further Key Points Once it is established that the inappropriate behaviors are significantly deviant, it must also be determined that they are due to an emotional condition. The condition is documented by a comprehensive assessment. The IEP team must determine whether the student's inappropriate responses are occurring under normal circumstances. When considering "normal circumstances," the team should take into account whether a student's home or school situation is disrupted by stress, recent changes, or unexpected events. Such evidence does not preclude an eligibility determination (Wisconsin Department of Instruction, 2002; Connecticut Department of Education, 1997).

Types of Inappropriate Behavior or Feelings Disorder

ED 3.01 Inappropriate Behavior or Feelings Disorder—Aggressive Interactive Type

Definition A type of inappropriate behavior or feelings disorder characterized by extreme out-of-control behavior patterns that result in intimidation, confrontation, and verbal or physical aggression.

Explanation Symptoms of inappropriate behavior or feelings disorder aggressive interactive type include:

- Verbal or physical hostility
- Verbal threats of physical harm to people or animals
- Cursing
- Verbal confrontation
- Physical confrontation
- Fighting
- Biting

- Kicking
- Throwing objects
- Temper tantrums with directed aggression

ED 3.02 Inappropriate Behavior or Feelings Disorder—Disruptive Behavior Type

Definition A type of inappropriate behavior or feelings disorder characterized by behaviors that disrupt the educational process for students and teachers. These behaviors are the result of emotional disturbance, and the intensity, frequency, and duration of the behaviors are severe.

Explanation Symptoms of inappropriate behavior or feelings disorder–disruptive behavior type include:

- Repeatedly leaving and entering the classroom without authorization
- Making loud or distracting noises
- Persisting in speaking without being recognized
- Repeatedly answering a cellular phone or allowing pagers to beep
- Resorting to physical threats or personal insults
- Behaviors of defiance
- Touching other people or other people's property
- Showing a complete disregard for the rights and property of others
- Unwillingness to follow classroom or school rules
- Lack of personal boundaries
- Not taking responsibility for inappropriate behaviors or feelings
- Open violation of societal norms and rules
- Causing property loss or damage
- Stealing
- Oppositional behavior
- Disturbance of conduct
- Nonconforming behavior to the rules of authority

ED 3.03 Inappropriate Behavior or Feelings Disorder–Immaturity Type

Definition A type of inappropriate behavior or feelings disorder characterized by behaviors that require an inordinate amount of attention, focus, and concentration by the teacher or school staff. These behaviors are considered inappropriate and infantile for a child of the individual's age.

Explanation Symptoms of inappropriate behavior or feelings disorder–immature type include:

- Temper tantrums without physical aggression
- Using lewd or obscene gestures
- Whining
- Frequent crying
- Demanding
- Ignoring the teacher or others
- Making noises in class (for example, burping)
- Needing to be the center of attention
- Constant clinging behavior to the teacher and other adults

ED 3.04 Inappropriate Behavior or Feelings Disorder–Impulse Control Type

Definition A type of inappropriate behavior or feelings disorder where children act on a certain impulse that is potentially harmful to themselves or others but they cannot resist. The child with this disorder does not learn from his or her mistakes or incorporate boundaries resulting from discipline or consequences.

Explanation Impulsive children seem unable to curb their immediate reactions or think before they act. They often blurt out inappropriate comments, display their emotions without restraint, and act without regard for the later consequences of their conduct. Their impulsivity may make it hard for them to wait for things they want or take their turn in games. They may grab a toy from another child or hit when they are upset. Even as teenagers or adults, they may impulsively choose to do things that have an immediate but small payoff rather than engage in activities that may take more effort yet provide much greater but delayed rewards.

ED 3.05 Inappropriate Behavior or Feelings Disorder–Self-Destructive Behavior Type

Definition A type of inappropriate behavior or feelings disorder characterized by destructive behaviors to oneself that not only affect the child exhibiting the behavior but also the lives of family members and others around the child.

Explanation The effects of destructive behaviors may have a short life span or may have damaging effects that last a lifetime. Identifying whether children's misbehavior is destructive may be relatively easy if the behavior exhibits obvious damaging results affecting the individual socially, academically, emotionally, and physically. Symptoms of this disorder may include (Ferentz, 2002):

- High-risk behavior patterns resulting in injury
- Self-sabotaging behavior
- Overuse of drugs

- Overuse of alcohol
- Shoplifting
- Putting oneself down in public
- Setting oneself up for failure
- Deliberately and repeatedly hurting one's body: cutting oneself, picking or pulling skin and hair, burning the skin, limb hitting and bruising, picking at wounds
- Sexual promiscuity or unprotected sex
- Head banging
- Pulling out hair
- Reckless driving
- Eating-disordered behaviors

ED 3.06 Other Types of Inappropriate Feelings and Behavior Disorders Not Otherwise Listed

ED 4.00 Pervasive Mood Disorder

Under IDEA 2004, one of the criteria for a classification of emotional disturbance is "a general pervasive mood of unhappiness or depression." This criterion will be termed Pervasive Mood Disorders in the EDM classification system.

This category is set aside for diagnoses made by the multidisciplinary team that have not been previously diagnosed by an outside mental health professional. For example, if a child has been previously diagnosed by a medical professional with bipolar disorder or depression, he or she does not receive a diagnosis of ED 4.00. In this case, you would refer to ED 8.00-Psychological and Psychiatric Disorders Already Diagnosed by Mental Health Professionals and specifically state the medical diagnosis.

Pervasive Mood Disorder as defined in EDM is associated with symptoms of depression and bipolar depression (manic depression). However, it is not the responsibility of the multidisciplinary and IEP team to diagnose a child with this disorder. The role of the team should be to determine whether the child meets the criteria for an emotional disturbance as defined by IDEA 2004. Then if the child exhibits symptoms associated with EDM's description of Pervasive Mood Disorder, the child receives an EDM diagnosis of ED 4.00.

A diagnosis of ED 4.00 represents a child with an emotional disturbance who exhibits symptoms similar to depression or bipolar disorder but not previously diagnosed by an outside professional.

If a child receives a diagnosis of ED 4.00, the team should seriously consider an outside referral for a more specific diagnosis.

Definition Mood disorders are mental disorders characterized by periods of depression, sometimes alternating with periods of elevated mood. They are serious disorders that can affect people of all ages. They cause significant changes in mood, energy, and behavior, which can make it difficult or impossible for the affected individual to function effectively in everyday life (National Institute of Mental Health, 2004).

EDM 4.00 requires documentation that the student's unhappiness or depression is occurring across most, if not all, of the student's life situations. The student must demonstrate a consistent pattern of depression or unhappiness in keeping with the criterion "long period of time" (that is, several months). In other words, this pattern is not a temporary response to situational factors or to a medical condition (Connecticut State Department of Education, 1997).

Diagnostic Symptoms Children, depending on their age and the type of mood disorder present, may exhibit different symptoms of depression. The following are the most common symptoms of a mood disorder. However, each child and adolescent may experience symptoms differently. Symptoms may include (National Institute of Mental Health, 2001):

- A decrease in the ability to make decisions
- Anxious habits such as nail biting or hair pulling
- Blaming self; extremely self-critical
- Changes in appetite or weight
- Decreased energy
- Difficulty concentrating
- Difficulty with relationships
- Excessive guilt
- Expressing feelings of worthlessness, hopelessness
- Feeling hopeless or helpless
- Feeling inadequate
- Feelings of wanting to die
- Frequent physical complaints (for example, headache, stomachache, fatigue)
- Having low self-esteem
- Hi
- Hypersensitivity to failure or rejection
- Irritability, hostility, aggression
- Lack of interest in surroundings, activities
- Listlessness or apathy

- Loss of interest in activities
- Loss of interest in usual activities or activities once enjoyed
- Obsessive/compulsive
- Overly pessimistic
- Persistent feelings of sadness
- Preoccupations
- Preoccupation with negative feelings
- Running away or threats of running away from home
- Running away from home
- Sleep disturbances (for example, insomnia, hypersomnia)
- Thinking or talking repeatedly of suicide
- Volatile temper or excessive anger

In mood disorders, these feelings appear more intense than adolescents normally feel from time to time. It is also of concern if these feelings continue over a period of time or interfere with an adolescent's interest in being with friends or taking part in daily activities at home or school. Any adolescent who expresses thoughts of suicide should be evaluated immediately.

Further Key Points Only in the past two decades have mood disorders in children been taken very seriously. A child with a mood disorder may pretend to be sick, refuse to go to school, cling to a parent, or worry that the parent may die. Older children may sulk, get into trouble at school, be negative, act grouchy, and feel misunderstood. Because normal behaviors vary from one childhood stage to another, it can be difficult to tell whether a child is going through a temporary phase or is suffering from a mood disorder (National Institute of Mental Health, 2001). Understanding age-appropriate behaviors and the symptoms of mood disorders are critical in asking a correct diagnosis of Pervasive Mood Disorder. Furthermore, feeling depressed about a death in the family or the divorce of parents is situation specific and for the most part a normal feeling that tends to be resolvable and not pervasive.

ED 5.00 Physical Complaints Disorder

Under IDEA 2004, one of the criteria for a classification of emotional disturbance is "a tendency to develop physical symptoms . . . associated with personal or school problems." This criterion will be termed Physical Complaints Disorder in the EDM classification system.

This category is set aside for diagnoses made by the multidisciplinary team that have not been previously diagnosed by an outside professional.

For example, a child who has been previously diagnosed by a medical professional with Somatoform Disorders does not receive a diagnosis of EDM 5.00. In this case, you would refer to ED 8.00-Psychological and Psychiatric Disorders Already Diagnosed by Mental Health Professionals and specifically state the medical diagnosis.

Physical Complaints Disorder as defined in EDM is associated with symptoms of somatoform disorders (disorders that suggest a medical condition but in actuality are psychologically based). However it is not the responsibility of the multidisciplinary and IEP team to diagnose a child with somataform disorders.

The role of the multidisciplinary and IEP team should be to determine whether the child meets the criteria for an emotional disturbance as defined by IDEA 2004. If the child exhibits symptoms associated with EDM's description of Physical Complaints Disorder, he or she receives an EDM diagnosis of ED 5.00. This diagnosis represents a child with an emotional disturbance who exhibits symptoms similar to a somatoform disorder but not previously diagnosed by an outside professional.

If a child receives a diagnosis of ED 5.00 the team should seriously consider an outside referral for a more specific diagnosis.

Definition EDM 5.00 requires documentation that the student exhibits physical symptoms or fears associated with his or her personal or school life. Persistent physical symptoms are chronic, as opposed to acute reactions to some situation at home or school, and must have a negative impact on learning (Connecticut State Department of Education, 1997).

Diagnostic Symptoms Diagnostic symptoms associated with Physical Complaints disorders include:

- Auditory or visual hallucinations
- Cardiopulmonary symptoms
- Eating disorders
- Excessive absences, tardiness, truancy
- Excessively fearful in response to new situations
- Flinches or cowers
- Frequently requests visits to the school nurse
- Gastrointestinal problems
- Has atypical physical reactions (i.e., sweaty palms, dizziness, voice)
- Headaches
- Incapacitating feelings of anxiety often accompanied by trembling, hyperventilating and/or dizziness
- Intense fears or irrational thoughts related to separation from parent(s)

- Neglects self-care and hygiene
- Panic attacks characterized by physical symptoms, for example, when an object, activity, individual or situation cannot be avoided or is confronted
- Persistent and irrational fears of particular objects or situations
- Physical complaints that cannot be easily checked or verified
- Psychosomatic illnesses (stomach aches, nausea, dizziness, headaches)
- Refuses to attend school ("school phobic")
- Self-mutilating
- Unusual sleeping or eating patterns

Further Key Points Physical symptoms that qualify under EDM 5.00 should adhere to the following conditions:

- Symptoms suggesting physical disorders are present with no demonstrable medical findings.
- Positive evidence or a strong presumption exists that these symptoms are linked to psychological factors or conflict.
- The person is not conscious of intentionally producing the symptoms.
- The symptoms are not a culturally sanctioned response pattern (Connecticut Department of Education, 1997).

ED 6.00 Anxiety Reactive Disorder

Under IDEA, one of the criteria for a classification of emotional disturbance is "a tendency to develop . . . fears associated with personal or school problems." This criterion will be termed Anxiety Reactive Disorders in the EDM classification system.

This category is set aside for diagnoses made by the multidisciplinary team that have not been previously diagnosed by an outside mental health professional. For example, a child who has been previously diagnosed by a medical professional with an anxiety disorder (for example, generalized anxiety disorder, obsessive compulsive disorder, panic disorder, posttraumatic stress disorder, or social anxiety disorder) does not receive a diagnosis of ED 6.00. In this case you would refer to ED 8.00-Psychological and Psychiatric Disorders Already Diagnosed by Mental Health Professionals and specifically state the medical diagnosis.

Anxiety Reactive Disorder as defined in EDM is associated with symptoms of anxiety. However, it is not the responsibility of the multidisciplinary and IEP team to diagnose a child with an anxiety disorder. The role of the team should be to determine whether the child meets the criteria for an Emotional Disturbance as defined by IDEA. Then if the child exhibits symptoms associated with EDM's description of Anxiety Reactive Disorder, the child receives an EDM diagnosis of

ED 6.00. This diagnosis represents a child with an emotional disturbance who exhibits symptoms similar to an anxiety disorder but not previously diagnosed by an outside professional.

If a child receives a diagnosis of ED 6.00 the team should seriously consider an outside referral for a more specific diagnosis.

Definition A type of emotional disturbance characterized by a tendency to develop symptoms or fears associated with personal or school problems. However, it is much more than the normal anxiety many people experience day to day. It is chronic and fills one's day with exaggerated worry and tension, even though there is little or nothing to provoke it. Having this disorder means always anticipating disaster, often worrying excessively about health, family, or school. Sometimes the source of the worry is hard to pinpoint. Simply the thought of getting through the day provokes anxiety. It is similar to the symptoms associated with generalized anxiety disorder (National Institute of Mental Health, 2004).

Diagnostic Symptoms Individuals with anxiety reactive disorder cannot seem to shake their concerns, even though they usually realize that their anxiety is more intense than the situation warrants. Their worries are accompanied by physical symptoms, especially fatigue, headaches, muscle tension, muscle aches, difficulty swallowing, trembling, twitching, irritability, sweating, and hot flashes. Individuals with this disorder may feel lightheaded or out of breath. They also may feel nauseated or have to go to the bathroom frequently.

They seem unable to relax and may startle more easily than other individuals. They tend to have difficulty concentrating in school or at home and often have trouble falling or staying asleep.

Unlike individuals with several other anxiety disorders, people with this disorder do not characteristically avoid certain situations as a result of their disorder. When their impairment is mild, students with the disorder may be able to function in social settings or in school. If symptoms are severe, this disorder can be debilitating, making it difficult to carry out even the most ordinary daily activities, such as attending school or functioning in social situations.

Further Key Points The mind of a person with anxiety reactive disorder is constantly racing: the person's thoughts keep running and running, with worrisome thoughts being repeated endlessly. Even if the person realizes these thoughts are irrational, he or she seems unable to stop them. At other times, thoughts may be blocked out by an overwhelming sense of worry and dread.

An individual with an anxiety reactive disorder may have better and worse times of the day or better and worse days. As with other anxiety disorders, he or she may also suffer symptoms of other disorders as well, such as depression, social anxiety, or panic disorder. Anxiety Reactive Disorder can be treated, though, and learning ways of dealing with the sources of anxiety can give an individual a stronger and more resilient attitude toward future trials.

Types of Anxiety Reactive Disorders

ED

ED 6.01 Panic Reactive Disorder

Definition A type of anxiety reactive disorder characterized by unexpected and repeated episodes of intense fear accompanied by physical symptoms that may include chest pain, heart palpitations, shortness of breath, dizziness, or abdominal distress.

Explanation Students with panic reactive disorder have feelings of terror that strike suddenly and repeatedly with no warning. They cannot predict when an attack will occur, and many develop intense anxiety between episodes, worrying when and where the next one will strike.

They may feel intense heart pounding or feel sweaty, weak, faint, or dizzy. Their hands may tingle or feel numb and might feel flushed or chilled. They may experience nausea, chest pain or smothering sensations, a sense of unreality, or fear of impending doom or loss of control. They may genuinely believe they are having a heart attack, or losing their mind, or on the verge of death.

The lives of some students with panic anxiety reactive disorder become so restricted that they avoid normal, everyday activities such as going outside and playing with friends or hanging out at the mall. In some cases, they become housebound and cannot attend school. Or they may be able to confront a feared situation only if accompanied by a trusted person (for example, being able to drive to a school-related function with parents and a few friends but never being able to stay by themselves).

ED 6.02 School Avoidance Anxiety Reactive Disorder

Definition A type of anxiety reactive disorder characterized by extreme anxiety manifested in an avoidance of school.

Explanation Individuals with this disorder may become very upset or ill when forced to go to school. They may stay in close contact with their parents or caregivers and are frequently (although not always) anxious and fearful. Truants may be distinguished from this group by their antisocial or delinquent behaviors, their lack of anxiety about missing school, and the fact that they are not in contact with parents or caregivers when they are avoiding school.

ED 6.03 School-Related Anxiety Reactive Disorder

Definition A type of anxiety reactive disorder characterized by excessive worry about school-related issues.

Explanation Individuals with this disorder may tend to worry excessively about school-related issues such as grades, work completion, being called on in class, fear of failure, fear of authority, changing in gym, and using the school bathroom.

ED 6.03a **Test Anxiety Reactive Disorder** An anxiety reactive disorder characterized by overwhelming anxiety or stress related to classroom tests or testing situations in general. This stress is so excessive that it hinders the individual's ability to prepare properly and test effectively.

Many students experience some nervousness or apprehension before, during, or after an exam, and this kind of anxiety can be a powerful motivator. However, some students experience test-related anxiety to such a degree that it can lead to poor performance and interfere with their learning. Symptoms of test anxiety include:

- Physical—headaches, nausea or diarrhea, extreme body temperature changes, excessive sweating, shortness of breath, lightheadedness or fainting, rapid heart beat, dry mouth
- Emotional—excessive feelings of fear, disappointment, anger, depression, uncontrollable crying or laughing, feelings of helplessness
- Behavioral—fidgeting, pacing, substance abuse, avoidance
- Cognitive—racing thoughts, going blank, difficulty concentrating, negative self talk, feelings of dread, comparing self to others, difficulty organizing thoughts (University of Cincinnati, 2004)

ED 6.04 Separation Anxiety Reactive Disorder

Definition A type of anxiety reactive disorder characterized by extreme anxiety over separation from parents in the transition to school. Furthermore, the child often fears for the safety of the parent, cries, withdraws from activities, and seems inconsolable.

Explanation Separation anxiety reactive disorder affects children who are afraid to be separated from the main caretakers in their lives, even to go to a friend's house or school. When separated, they are constantly afraid that something horrible will happen to either themselves or their primary caretaker (they or the caretaker will die, for instance). When the subject of separating is brought up, the child begins to present with somatic symptoms ranging from headaches to nausea and vomiting, with anxiety.

ED 6.05 Social Avoidance Anxiety Reactive Disorder

Definition A type of anxiety reactive disorder characterized by a complete unwillingness, fear, hesitation, or withdrawal from social situations.

Explanation These children do not respond to reason or logic and have no real evidence or experiences that may result in such a level of social withdrawal.

ED 6.06 Social-Related Anxiety Reactive Disorder

Definition A type of anxiety reactive disorder characterized by an overwhelming anxiety and excessive self-consciousness in social situations. While anxious, students with this disorder do attend school.

Explanation Students with social-related anxiety disorder have a persistent, intense, and chronic fear of being scrutinized by others and of being embarrassed or humiliated by their own actions. Although it is common for many students to experience some anxiety before or during certain social situations, anxiety levels in students with social anxiety reactive disorder can become so high that they begin to avoid social situations. They may also have a fear of speaking in class and in public, fear of eating or drinking in the cafeteria, excessive fear of rejection, fear of social activities, fear of group interaction, and fear of performance in physical education class.

ED 6.07 Unfounded Anxiety Reactive Disorder

Definition A type of anxiety reactive disorder characterized by extreme anxiety and irrational fears of an object or situation. It is an unreasonable fear caused by the presence or thought of a specific object or situation that usually poses little or no actual danger and impedes one's ability to function.

Explanation These irrational fears include fear of dying, thunder, elevators, animals, spiders and insects, and germs. These may include excessive fears of dogs, snakes, insects or mice, flying, riding in a car or on public transportation, driving, going over bridges or in tunnels, of being in a closed-in place, storms, heights or water, being injured, seeing blood, invasive medical procedures such as blood tests or injections, falling down, loud sounds, and costumed characters such as clowns.

ED 7.00 Schizophrenia

Neither the multidisciplinary team, committee on special education, nor IEP team should ever diagnose a student with schizophrenia. This is the responsibility of an outside mental health professional.

If the student had received an outside diagnosis of schizophrenia, the EDM classification is ED 7.00.

Definition Contrary to the common misconception, schizophrenia does not mean "split or multiple personality." And although people with schizophrenia often are portrayed as violent on television and in movies, that is seldom the case. Schizophrenia is one of the most disabling and puzzling mental disorders. Many researchers now consider schizophrenia to be a group of mental disorders rather than a single illness (National Mental Health Information Center, 2003).

Diagnostic Symptoms Diagnostic symptoms for schizophrenia include:

- Excessive fatigue and sleepiness or an inability to sleep
- Social withdrawal, isolation, and reclusiveness
- Deteriorating social relationships
- Inability to concentrate or cope with minor problems
- Apparent indifference, even in highly important situations
- Dropping out of activities (skipping classes)
- Decline in academic and athletic performance
- Deteriorating personal hygiene; eccentric dress
- Frequent moves or trips or long walks leading nowhere
- Drug or alcohol abuse
- Undue preoccupation with spiritual or religious matters
- Bizarre behavior
- Inappropriate laughter
- Strange posturing
- Low tolerance of irritation
- Excessive writing without apparent meaning
- Inability to express emotion
- Irrational statements
- Peculiar use of words or language structure
- Conversation that seems deep but is not logical or coherent
- Staring, vagueness
- Unusual sensitivity to stimuli (noise, light)
- Forgetfulness

Further Key Points Students properly diagnosed with schizophrenia do not automatically meet the characteristics and conditions of the emotionally disturbed criteria. Such students are entitled to services if they need special education or related services.

The reference to schizophrenia is included in the definition of emotional disturbance for the purpose of illustrating one example of a psychiatric (medical) diagnosis of an emotional disturbance. However, a student diagnosed with schizophrenia or comparably serious psychiatric disorders is eligible for special education and related services under the Individuals with Disabilities Education Act only if the ED definition criteria are met. When the IEP team has a physician's diagnosis of schizophrenia or a comparable serious emotional disorder, the team must then answer the following two questions:

- Is the student's educational performance adversely affected?
- Has the student been exhibiting the condition for a long period of time and to a marked degree? (Connecticut State Department of Education, 1997).

ED 8.00 Psychological and Psychiatric Disorders Already Diagnosed by Mental Health Professionals—Be Very Specific

ED

References

Bullis, M., Walker, H.M., & Sprague, J. R. (2001). A promise unfulfilled: Social skills training with at-risk and antisocial children and youth. *Exceptionality, 9,* 67–90.

Cleveland Clinic Department of Psychiatry and Psychology. (2005). *Mental health: Causes of mental illness.* Retrieved October 31, 2006, from http://www.webmd.com/content/article/60/67140.htm.

Connecticut Department of Education. (1997). *Guidelines for identifying students with a serious emotional disturbance.* Hartford: State of Connecticut.

Ferentz, L. (2002). *Understanding self-injurious behavior.* Retrieved May 6, 2005, from http://www.prponline.net/School/SAJ/Articles/understanding_self_injurious_behavior.htm.

Gargiulo, R. M. (2004). *Special education in contemporary society: An introduction to exceptionality.* Belmont, CA: Thompson-Wadsworth.

Gresham, F. M., Lane, K. L., MacMillan, D. L., & Boscian, K. M. (1999). Social and academic profiles of externalizing and internalizing groups. Risk factors for emotional and behavioral disorders. *Behavioral Disorders, 24,* 231–245.

Hallahan, D. P., & Kauffman, J. M. (2006). *Exceptional learners: An introduction to special education* (10th ed.). Needham Heights, MA: Allyn & Bacon.

Hardman, M. L., Drew, C. J., & Egan, M. W. (2005). *Human exceptionality: School, community, and family* (8th ed.) Needham Heights, MA: Allyn & Bacon.

Harper, J. (2003). *Depression facts: What depression is not, what depression really is.* Retrieved May 4, 2005, from http://www.freedomhealthrecovery.com/depression.html.

Heward, W. L. (2006). *Exceptional children: An introduction to special education* (8th ed.). Upper Saddle River, NJ: Merrill/Prentice Hall.

Hunt, N., & Marshall, K. (2005). *Exceptional children and youth* (5th ed.). Boston: Houghton Mifflin.

Jensen, M. (2005). *Introduction to emotional and behavioral disorders: Recognizing and managing problems in the classroom.* Upper Saddle River, NJ: Merrill/Prentice Hall.

Kauffman, J. M. (2005). *Characteristics of emotional and behavioral disorders of children and youth* (8th ed.). Upper Saddle River: Pearson.

Kirk, S. A., Gallagher, J. J., & Anastasiow, N. J. (2003). *Educating exceptional children* (10th ed.). Boston: Houghton Mifflin.

National Alliance for the Mentally Ill. (2003). *Mental illness.* Retrieved May 7, 2005, from www.nami.org.

National Dissemination Center for Children with Disabilities. (2004). *Emotional disturbance-Fact sheet #5.* Retrieved May 20, 2005, from http://www.nichcy.org/pubs/factshe/fs5txt.htm.

National Institute of Mental Health. (2001). *The invisible disease: Depression.* Retrieved May 5, 2005, from http://www.nimh.nih.gov/publicat/invisible.cfm.

National Institute of Mental Health. (2004). *Anxiety disorders.* Retrieved May 9, 2005, from http://www.nimh.nih.gov/healthinformation/anxietymenu.cfm.

National Mental Health Information Center. (2003). *Schizophrenia.* Retrieved May 20, 2005, from http://www.mentalhealth.samhsa.gov/publications/allpubs/ken98–0052/default.asp.

Office of Special Education Programs (OSEP). (2001). *The Twenty-Third Annual Report to Congress on the Implementation of IDEA.* Washington, DC: U.S. Department of Education.

Pierangelo, R., & Giuliani, G. (2006). *Assessment in special education: A practical approach* (2nd ed.). Needham Heights, MA: Allyn & Bacon.

Rosenberg, S. D., Mueser, K. T., & Jankowski, M. K. (2004). Cognitive behavioral treatment of PTSD in severe mental illness: Results of a pilot study. *American Journal of Psychiatric Rehabilitation, 7,* 171–186.

Turnbull, R., Turnbull, A., Shank, M., & Smith, S. J. (2004). *Exceptional lives: Special education in today's schools* (4th ed.). Upper Saddle River, NJ: Prentice Hall.

University of Cincinnati. (2004). *Test anxiety.* Retrieved May 7, 2005, from http://www.campusblues.com/test.asp.

U.S. Department of Education. (2001). *The Twenty-Third Annual Report to Congress on the Implementation of IDEA.* Washington, DC: U.S. Department of Education.

U.S. Department of Education. (2004). *The Twenty-Sixth Annual Report to Congress on the Implementation of IDEA.* Washington, DC: U.S. Department of Education.

Wisconsin Department of Instruction. (2002). *Evaluation guide for emotional behavioral disability.* Madison: Author.

Chapter 5

Other Health Impairments

EDM Code: OHI

OHI

- OHI 1.00 Aicardi Syndrome (Aicardi-Goutieres Syndrome)
- OHI 2.00 Alcohol Dependency
- OHI 3.00 Alexander Disease
- OHI 4.00 Allergies (Allergic Reaction)
  - OHI 4.01 Drug-Medication Allergies (Drug Allergies)
    - OHI 4.01a Drug/Medication Allergies—Antiseizure Drugs
    - OHI 4.01b Drug/Medication Allergies—Insulin
    - OHI 4.01c Drug/Medication Allergies—Local Anesthetics
    - OHI 4.01d Drug/Medication Allergies—Penicillin-Related Antibiotics
    - OHI 4.01e Drug/Medication Allergies—Sulfa Drugs
    - OHI 4.01f Other Drug/Medication Allergies—Be Specific
  - OHI 4.02 Dust Mites Allergies
  - OHI 4.03 Food Allergies
    - OHI 4.03a Food Allergies–Egg
    - OHI 4.03b Food Allergies–Exercise Induced
    - OHI 4.03c Food Allergies–Milk
    - OHI 4.03d Food Allergies–Peanut
    - OHI 4.03e Food Allergies–Shellfish
    - OHI 4.03f Food Allergies–Soy
    - OHI 4.03g Food Allergies–Tree Nut
    - OHI 4.03h Food Allergies–Wheat, Rye, Barley
    - OHI 4.03i Other Types of Food Allergies—Be Specific
  - OHI 4.04 Hayfever/Pollen and Mold
  - OHI 4.05 Lactose Intolerance
  - OHI 4.06 Latex Allergies
  - OHI 4.07 Pet Allergies
  - OHI 4.08 Other Types of Allergies
- OHI 5.00 Alpers Disease
- OHI 6.00 Angelman Syndrome
- OHI 7.00 Asthma
  - OHI 7.01 Cough Variant Asthma
  - OHI 7.02 Exercise-Induced Asthma
  - OHI 7.03 Extrinsic Asthma
  - OHI 7.04 Intrinsic Asthma
  - OHI 7.05 Nocturnal Asthma
  - OHI 7.06 Seasonal Asthma
  - OHI 7.07 Silent Asthma
  - OHI 7.08 Other Types of Asthma Not Otherwise Listed—Be Specific
- OHI 8.00 Attention Deficit–Hyperactivity Disorder
- OHI 9.00 Autoimmune Diseases
  - OHI 9.01 Autoimmune Thyroid Diseases
    - OHI 9.01a Grave's Disease
    - OHI 9.01b Hashimoto's Thyroiditis
  - OHI 9.02 Immune-Mediated or Type 1 Diabetes Mellitus
  - OHI 9.03 Inflammatory Bowel Diseases
  - OHI 9.04 Multiple Sclerosis
  - OHI 9.05 Psoriasis
    - OHI 9.05a Erythrodermic Psoriasis
    - OHI 9.05b Guttate Psoriasis
    - OHI 9.05d Inverse Psoriasis
    - OHI 9.05e Plaque Psoriasis
    - OHI 9.05f Psoriatic Arthritis
    - OHI 9.05g Pustular Psoriasis
    - OHI 9.05g Other Forms of Psoriasis Not Otherwise Listed
  - OHI 9.06 Lupus
    - OHI 9.06a Systemic Lupus Erythematosus

OHI 9.06b Discoid Lupus Erythematosus
OHI 9.06c Drug-Induced Lupus
OHI 9.07 Other Autoimmune Disorders
OHI 10.00 Hematologic Diseases (Blood Disorders)
OHI 10.01 Anemia
OHI 10.01a Anemia Due to the Effects of Blood Loss
OHI 10.01b Anemia Due to the Effects of Inadequate Red Blood Cell Production
OHI 10.01c Aplastic Anemia
OHI 10.01d Autoimmune Hemolytic Anemia
OHI 10.01e Iron-Deficiency Anemia
OHI 10.01f Pernicious Anemia
OHI 10.01g Sickle Cell Anemia
OHI 10.01h Thalassemia
OHI 10.02 Hemophilia
OHI 10.03 von Willebrand Disease
OHI 10.04 Other Blood Disorders Not Otherwise Listed
OHI 11.00 Cancers of Childhood
OHI 11.01 Bone Cancers
OHI 11.01a Chondrosarcoma
OHI 11.01b Ewing's Sarcoma
OHI 11.01c Osteosarcoma or Osteogenic Sarcoma
OHI 11.02 Leukemia
OHI 11.02a Chronic Lymphocytic Leukemia
OHI 11.02b Chronic Myeloid Leukemia
OHI 11.02c Acute Lymphocytic Leukemia
OHI 11.02d Acute Myeloid Leukemia
OHI 11.03 Liver Cancers
OHI 11.03a Hepatob lastoma
OHI 11.03b Hepatocellular Cancer
OHI 11.04 Soft Tissue Sarcoma
OHI 11.05 Lymphoma
OHI 11.05a Burkitt's Lymphoma
OHI 11.05b Hodgkin's Disease
OHI 11.05c Non-Hodgkin's Lymphoma
OHI 11.06 Other Types of Cancers—Be Specific
OHI 12.00 Congenital Heart Disease
OHI 12.01 Cyanotic Congenital Heart Disease
OHI 12.02 Noncyanotic Congenital Heart Diseases
OHI 12.03 Other Congenital Heart Diseases Not Otherwise Listed—Be Specific
OHI 13.00 Diabetes
OHI 13.01 Type 1 Diabetes
OHI 13.02 Type 2 Diabetes
OHI 13.03 Other Types of Diabetes Not Otherwise Listed
OHI 14.00 Endocrine-Metabolic Disorders
OHI 14.01 Acromegaly
OHI 14.02 Addison's Disease
OHI 14.03 Cushing's Syndrome
OHI 14.04 Cystic Fibrosis
OHI 14.05 Hyperparathyroidism
OHI 14.06 Multiple Endocrine Neoplasia Type 1
OHI 14.07 Other Endocrine-Metabolic Diseases Not Otherwise Listed
OHI 15.00 Ehlers-Danlos Syndrome
OHI 16.00 Epidermolysis Bullosa
OHI 17.00 Epilepsy
OHI 17.01 Epilepsy with Absence Seizures
OHI 17.02 Epilepsy with Atonic Seizures
OHI 17.03 Epilepsy with Complex Partial Seizures
OHI 17.04 Epilepsy with Generalized Seizures
OHI 17.05 Epilepsy with Myoclonic Seizures
OHI 17.06 Epilepsy with Nocturnal Seizures
OHI 17.07 Epilepsy with Partial Seizures
OHI 17.08 Epilepsy with Secondarily Generalized Seizure
OHI 17.09 Epilepsy with Simple Partial Seizures
OHI 17.10 Epilepsy with Tonic-Clonic Convulsive Seizure
OHI 17.11 Epilepsy with Tonic Seizures
OHI 17.12 Other Types of Epilepsy
OHI 18.00 Lead Poisoning
OHI 19.00 Lyme Disease
OHI 20.00 Marfan Syndrome
OHI 21.00 Oral-Facial Clefts
OHI 21.01 Cleft Lip
OHI 21.01a Bilateral Cleft Lip
OHI 21.01b Unilateral Cleft Lip
OHI 21.02 Cleft Palate
OHI 21.02a Bilateral Cleft Lip
OHI 21.02b Unilateral Cleft Palate
OHI 22.00 Osteogenesis Imperfecta
OHI 23.00 Rheumatic Fever
OHI 24.00 Tuberculosis
OHI 25.00 Viral Hepatitis
OHI 25.01 Hepatitis A
OHI 25.02 Hepatitis B
OHI 25.03 Hepatitis C
OHI 25.04 Hepatitis D
OHI 25.05 Hepatitis E
OHI 25.06 Other Forms of Hepatitis Not Otherwise Listed
OHI 26.00 Other Types of Health Impairments

IDEA 2004 Definition of Other Health Impairments

According to IDEA 2004, "other health impairment" means:

> having limited strength, vitality or alertness, including a heightened alertness to environmental stimuli, that results in limited alertness with respect to the educational environment, that is due to chronic or acute health problems such as asthma, attention deficit disorder or attention deficit hyperactivity disorder, diabetes, epilepsy, a heart condition, hemophilia, lead poisoning, leukemia, nephritis, rheumatic fever, and sickle cell anemia; and adversely affects a child's educational performance [34 C.F.R. 300.7(c)(9)].

Overview of Other Health Impairments

Many conditions and diseases can significantly affect a child's health and ability to function successfully in school. Most health impairments are chronic conditions; that is, they are always present, or they recur. By contrast, an acute condition develops quickly with intense symptoms that last for a relatively short period of time. To be served under the OHI category, the student's health condition must limit strength, vitality, or alertness to such a degree that the student's educational progress is adversely affected. More than two hundred specific health impairments exist, and most are rare (Turnbull, Turnbull, & Wehmeyer, 2007).

It should be noted that within the category of OHI is attention deficit–hyperactive disorder (ADHD). Only time will tell whether ADHD finds its way to another special education category or whether it becomes a category of its own in the future. Currently, the inclusion of ADHD has caused a significant increase in the size of the category (U.S. Department of Education, 2001).

Causes-Etiology of Other Health Impairments

The etiology of specific health impairments varies. Most result from infections, genetic factors, environmental influences, prenatal influences, perinatal influences, and postnatal influences. However, they can be grouped into some general areas (Deutsch Smith, 2004):

- Allergies
- Heredity
- Accidents
- Multiple factors
- Unknown

Prevalence of Other Health Impairments

According to the *Twenty-Sixth Annual Report* (U.S. Department of Education, 2004), 449,093 students between the ages of six and twenty-one years of age were identified as having other health impairments. This represents approximately 7.5 percent of all students having a classification in special education, or less than 1 percent of all school-age students.

Age of Onset of Other Health Impairments

Due to the various types of health impairments that adversely affect children's performances in school, no specific age of onset can be generalized to the entire school-age population that receives special education services. Some health impairments are congenital (present at birth), and other conditions are acquired during the child's development as a result of accident, illness or unknown cause.

Gender Features of Other Health Impairments

Due to the number and specific types of health impairments covered in this section, no statement concerning gender patterns can be generalized.

Cultural Features of Other Health Impairments

Information on this topic is not available.

Familial Patterns of Other Health Impairments

Due to the number and specific types of health impairments covered in this section, no statement concerning familial patterns can be generalized.

Characteristics of Other Health Impairments

According to the Starbright Foundation (2002), there are numerous complex challenges facing children with health impairments. Common issues are "loss of sense of control, lack of understanding about the condition, fear, worry, anxiety, stress, anger, and guilt, changes in family dynamics, isolation, isolation, medical noncompliance, boredom, depression, pain, decreased self-esteem, negative body image, and impact on identity and social interactions, including those at school" (p. 313).

Some general characteristics faced by individuals with other health impairments include these:

- Fatigue
- Mobility issues
- Issues involving attention
- Coordination difficulties
- Muscle weakness
- Frequent absences or lateness to school
- Stamina
- Inability to concentrate for long periods of time

Educational Implications of Other Health Impairments

When responsible educators encounter diseases and conditions they know little about, they seek out all the information they need to provide an appropriate education to students involved (Deutsch Smith, 2004). One of the main considerations in the education of these students is the use of the team approach in developing and carrying out a child's educational program. The team generally includes the parents, teachers, medical professionals, and health-related professionals such as a physical therapist.

Parents are critical members of the team and should be involved in all educational decisions. Sirvis (1988) noted that the team should design a program that meets the needs of the student in five basic goal areas: "(a) physical independence, including mastery of daily living skills; (b) self-awareness and social maturation; (c) communication; (d) academic growth; and (e) life skills training" (p. 400). Interdisciplinary services such as occupational and physical therapy and speech and language therapy are of prime importance for youngsters who have physical disabilities.

It is often necessary to modify and adapt the school environment to make it accessible, safe, and less restrictive since good architecture does not have to discriminate (Leibrock & Terry, 1999). Accessibility guidelines are readily available, and when these guidelines are followed, the environment becomes easier for the child to manage independently.

Finally, what role teachers should play in the medical management of children is an ongoing and contentious issue (Temple, 2000) since teachers are being called on to assume more responsibilities for the medical management of their students (Heller, Frederic, Best, Dykes, & Cohen, 2000).

Permissions and Authorization to Use Proprietary and Nonproprietary Sources

Due to the scientific and detailed nature of certain Level II disorders, Level III types of disorders, and Level IV subtypes of disorders described in this chapter, we thought that some were best explained by national institutes and centers that conduct comprehensive scientific research in respective fields of study. The sources obtained were all written with explicit permission that the scientific and diagnostic information they prepared was in the public domain and can be used without restriction.

We thank the following national research offices for the opportunity to freely disseminate their scientific research and writing in this chapter:

- Centers for Disease Control
- Endocrine and Metabolic Diseases Information Service
- National Cancer Institute
- National Center for Infectious Diseases
- National Diabetes Information Clearinghouse

- National Digestive Diseases Information Clearinghouse
- National Heart, Lung and Blood Institute
- National Institute for Occupational Safety and Health
- National Institute of Allergy and Infectious Diseases
- National Institute of Arthritis and Musculoskeletal and Skin Diseases
- National Institute of Child Health and Human Development
- National Institute of Diabetes and Digestive and Kidney Diseases
- National Institute of Neurological Disorders and Stroke
- National Institute of Mental Health
- National Institute on Alcohol Abuse and Alcoholism
- National Institute on Drug Abuse
- National Institutes of Health Osteoporosis and Related Bone Diseases
- U.S. Department of Education
- U.S. Department of Health and Human Services
- U.S. Food and Drug Administration
- U.S. National Library of Medicine

EDM Codes, Definitions, and Explanations of Other Health Impairments

When using the following OHI codes in a student's IEP, it is necessary to refer to state, local and district policies concerning confidentiality regarding release of medical information. The team should also be aware that these diagnoses are made by outside qualified medical professionals.

No health impairments listed or discussed in this chapter should ever be diagnosed by an IEP team. If a child suffers symptoms of any of these conditions, an outside referral to a qualified medical professional should be made by the team.

OHI 1.00 Aicardi Syndrome (Aicardi-Goutieres Syndrome)

Definition Aicardi syndrome is a rare genetic disorder identified by the French neurologist Jean Aicardi in 1965 (Aicardi Syndrome Foundation, 2006). It is characterized by the partial or complete absence of the structure that links the two hemispheres of the brain, the corpus callosum. The disorder affects only girls (National Institute of Neurological Disorders and Stroke, 2005a).

Diagnostic Symptoms According to the Aicardi Syndrome Foundation (2006), Aicardi syndrome is characterized by the following markers:

- Absence of the corpus callosum, either partial or complete (the corpus callosum is the part of the brain that sits between the right and left sides of the brain and allows the right side to communicate with the left)
- Infantile spasms (a form of seizures)
- Lesions or "lacunae" of the retina of the eye that are specific to this disorder
- Other types of defects of the brain such as microcephaly (small brain), enlarged ventricles, or porencephalic cysts (a gap in the brain where there should be healthy brain tissue)

Further Key Points Children are most commonly identified with Aicardi syndrome before the age of five months (U.S. National Library of Medicine, 2005a). A significant number of these girls are products of normal births and seem to be developing normally until around the age of three months, when they begin to have infantile spasms (Aicardi Syndrome Foundation, 2006). Aicardi syndrome may be associated with other brain defects such as a smaller-than-average brain and cavities or gaps in the brain filled with cerebrospinal fluid (National Institute of Neurological Disorders and Stroke, 2005a).

Treatment primarily involves management of seizures and early and continuing intervention programs for developmental delays. Prognosis for these children varies, though all experience developmental delays, typically moderate to severe mental retardation (Aicardi Syndrome Foundation, 2005).

OHI

OHI 2.00 Alcohol Dependency

Definition Alcohol is one of the most often abused substances for adolescents (National Institute on Drug Abuse, 2003, cited in Jensen, 2005). Alcohol dependence is a chronic pattern of alcohol abuse.

Diagnostic Symptoms Diagnostic symptoms of alcohol dependence include (National Institute on Alcohol Abuse and Alcoholism, 2003):

- Alcohol withdrawal when drinking stops suddenly, with symptoms that include nervousness, shaking, irritability, and nausea
- Increased tolerance to alcohol
- Alcohol consumed in larger amounts or over a longer period than was intended
- Considerable time devoted to activities associated with alcohol use or obtaining alcohol
- Neglected daily activities
- Disregard for consequences of negative behavior
- Loss of control—the inability to limit one's drinking on any given occasion

Further Key Points An alcoholic gets used to the effects of alcohol and requires more alcohol to get the desired effect. This is called tolerance. A person with alcohol dependence may experience an uncontrollable need for alcohol. The risk for developing alcoholism is influenced by both a person's genes and his or her lifestyle (National Institute on Alcohol Abuse and Alcoholism, 2003).

More than 150 medications interact harmfully with alcohol. These interactions may result in increased risk of illness, injury, and even death. Alcohol's effects are heightened by medicines that depress the central nervous system, such as sleeping pills, antihistamines, antidepressants, antianxiety drugs, and some painkillers. In addition, medicines for certain disorders, including diabetes, high blood pressure, and heart disease, can have harmful interactions with alcohol (National Institute on Alcohol Abuse and Alcoholism, 2003).

OHI 3.00 Alexander Disease

Definition Alexander disease is a rare, genetically determined degenerative disorder of the central nervous system. It is one of a group of disorders known as the leukodystrophies, diseases that result from imperfect growth or development of the myelin sheath, the fatty covering that acts as an insulator around nerve fibers in the brain (Medical College of Wisconsin, 2003). Alexander usually begins before two years of age (infantile form). Onset can also occur, although less commonly, later in childhood (juvenile form) or adulthood (U.S. National Library of Medicine, 2005b).

Diagnostic Symptoms Diagnostic symptoms of Alexander disease include (National Institute of Neurological Disorders and Stroke, 2005b; U.S. National Library of Medicine, 2005b; National Organization for Rare Disorders, 2005):

- A failure to grow and gain weight at the expected rate (failure to thrive)
- Delays in the development of certain physical, mental, and behavioral skills that are typically acquired at particular stages (psychomotor retardation)
- Progressive neurological deterioration
- Mental and physical retardation
- Dementia
- Enlargement of the brain and head (megalencephaly)
- Spasticity (stiffness of arms and/or legs)
- Seizures

If Alexander disease onset occurs later in childhood, common problems include speech abnormalities, swallowing difficulties, and poor coordination (ataxia).

Further Key Points There is no cure for Alexander disease and no standard course of treatment. Treatment of Alexander disease is symptomatic and supportive. The prognosis for individuals with Alexander disease is generally poor. Most children with the infantile form do not survive past the age of six. Juvenile- and adult-onset forms of the disorder have a slower, lengthier course (Medical College of Wisconsin, 2003; National Institute of Neurological Disorders and Stroke, 2005b).

OHI 4.00 Allergies (Allergic Reaction)

Definition An allergy is an exaggerated immune response or reaction to substances that are generally not harmful. Allergy refers to an acquired potential to develop immunologically mediated adverse reactions to normally innocuous substances, and many agents commonly found in the environment can provoke an allergic response (U.S. National Library of Medicine, 2005c; American Academy of Allergy, Asthma and Immunology, 2005b).

Diagnostic Symptoms Diagnostic symptoms of allergies include (Cleveland Clinic, 2006; U.S. National Library of Medicine, 2005c):

- Coughing
- Diarrhea
- Difficulty breathing
- Headache
- Hives (skin wheals)
- Hoarseness
- Itching nose, mouth, throat, skin, or any other area
- Red eyes, conjunctivitis
- Repeated ear and sinus infections
- Runny nose
- Skin rashes
- Stomach cramps
- Swollen eyes
- Tearing, burning, or itching eyes
- Throat clearing
- Vomiting
- Wheezing

Further Key Points Allergic disorders affect more than 20 percent of adults and children (40 to 50 million people) and are the sixth leading cause of chronic illness in the United States, according to the American Academy of Allergy, Asthma and Immunology (2005b).

4.01 Drug-Medication Allergies (Drug Allergies)

Definition A type of allergy characterized by an allergic reaction to a drug (medication). In general, adverse reactions to drugs are not uncommon, and almost any drug can cause an adverse reaction (U.S. National Library of Medicine, 2005c).

Explanation A drug allergy is caused by an overly sensitive immune system. People with drug allergies have an immune system that attacks the drug as if it were a harmful substance, leading to hives, itching, and other allergic symptoms.

In contrast, most drug side effects are not related to the immune system; they are caused by a drug's general effect on various organs throughout the body. For example, a nasal decongestant works because it constricts the capillaries in the nose, which reduces nasal swelling and opens the airway. But an unwanted side effect is that it also constricts the capillaries throughout the body, which may lead to an increased heart rate, headaches, and dizziness. A decongestant is not specific enough to one part of the body or one single action, so just about anyone can experience these side effects. This has nothing to do with whether the person has an immune system that is sensitive to the drug (University of Maryland Medical Center, 2002).

4.01a Drug/Medication Allergies—Antiseizure Drugs

4.01b Drug/Medication Allergies—Insulin

4.01c Drug/Medication Allergies—Local Anesthetics

4.01d Drug/Medication Allergies—Penicillin-Related Antibiotics

4.01e Drug/Medication Allergies—Sulfa Drugs

4.01f Other Drug/Medication Allergies—Be Specific

4.02 Dust Mites Allergies

Definition A type of allergy that is characterized by an abnormal response to dust mites (National Institute of Allergy and Infectious Diseases, 2005).

Explanation The dust mite, a microscopic, eight-legged insect, is the most common cause of allergic rhinitis and asthma. More than 100,000 dust mites can be in a single gram of dust. People are not allergic to the dust mite itself but to dust mite feces. Dust mites eat the microscopic skin dander found on people and animals and then leave droppings. Each dust mite can produce approximately twenty droppings each day. Dust mites are found on people, animals, and on almost every surface in homes, including carpet, upholstered furniture, mattresses and box springs, sheets and blankets, pillows, and stuffed animals. When dead dust mites and dust mite droppings become airborne and are inhaled, they may produce an allergic reaction (Allergy Relief Center, 2006).

If an individual has asthma, high concentrations of dust mite residue can trigger frequent and severe asthma signs and symptoms such as lung congestion, wheezing, and shortness of breath. He or she may be especially prone to asthma attacks at night, when he or she is lounging on a mite-infested sofa or sleeping in a mite-infested bed (Mayo Clinic, 2004d).

4.03 Food Allergies

Definition A food allergy, or hypersensitivity, is an abnormal response to a food triggered by the immune system (U.S. Food and Drug Administration, 2001; National Institute of Allergy and Infectious Diseases, 2005).

Explanation Sometimes a reaction to food is not an allergy at all but another type of reaction called food intolerance. Food intolerance is more common than food allergy. The immune system does not cause the symptoms of food intolerance, though these symptoms can look and feel like those of a food allergy (National Institute of Allergy and Infectious Diseases, 2005).

4.03a Food Allergies—Egg

4.03b Food Allergies—Exercise Induced At least one situation may require more than the simple ingestion of a food allergen to provoke a reaction: exercise. People who experience this reaction eat a specific food before exercising. As they exercise and their body temperature goes up, they begin to itch, get lightheaded, and soon have allergic reactions such as hives or even anaphylaxis. The cure for exercised-induced food allergy is not eating for a couple of hours before exercising (National Institute of Allergy and Infectious Diseases, 2005).

4.03c Food Allergies—Milk

4.03d Food Allergies—Peanut

4.03e Food Allergies—Shellfish

4.03f Food Allergies—Soy

4.03g Food Allergies—Tree Nut (Walnut, Cashew, etc.)

4.03h Food Allergies—Wheat, Rye, Barley (Gluten)

4.03i Other types of food allergies—Be specific

OHI 4.04 Hayfever/Pollen and Mold

Definition A type of allergy that is characterized by an abnormal response to pollen. *Hay fever* is the commonly used term for pollen allergy, a type of seasonal allergic rhinitis (runny nose). Pollen grains can be dispersed into the air in the spring, summer, and fall, depending on the type of tree, grass, or weed (National Institute of Allergy and Infectious Diseases, 2005).

Explanation Sneezing that is repeated and prolonged is the most common mark of the hay fever sufferer. A stuffy and watery nose is also a main sign of hay fever. Other symptoms are redness, swelling, and itching of the eyes; itching of the nose, throat, and mouth; and itching of the ears or other ear problems. Breathing difficulties at night due to obstruction of the nose may interfere with sleep (American Lung Association, 2005).

OHI 4.05 Lactose Intolerance

Definition A type of allergy that is characterized by an abnormal response to lactose-related products. Lactose intolerance is the inability to digest significant amounts of lactose, the predominant sugar of milk. This inability results from a shortage of the enzyme lactase, which is normally produced by the cells that line the small intestine (National Digestive Diseases Information Clearinghouse, 2003).

Explanation Lactose intolerance results from a shortage of the enzyme lactase, which is normally produced by the cells that line the small intestine. Lactase breaks down milk sugar into simpler forms that can be absorbed into the blood stream. When there is not enough lactase to digest the amount of lactose consumed, the results, although not usually dangerous, may be very distressing (American Gastroenterological Association, 2006).

Common symptoms are nausea, cramps, bloating, gas, and diarrhea, which begin about thirty minutes to two hours after eating or drinking foods containing lactose. Many people who have never been diagnosed as lactose intolerant or lactase deficient may notice that milk and other dairy products cause problems that do not occur when eating other foods. The severity of symptoms varies depending on the amount of lactose each individual can tolerate (American Gastroenterological Association, 2006; National Digestive Diseases Information Clearinghouse, 2003).

OHI 4.06 Latex Allergies

Definition A type of allergy that is characterized by an abnormal response to latex and latex-related products. The protein in rubber can cause an allergic reaction in some people. The thin, stretchy latex rubber in gloves, condoms, and balloons is high in this protein. It causes more allergic reactions than products made of hard rubber like tires. Also, because some latex gloves are coated with cornstarch powder, the latex protein particles stick to the cornstarch and fly into the air when the gloves are taken off. In places where gloves are being put on and removed frequently, the air may contain many latex particles (American Academy of Family Physicians, 2005).

Explanation The amount of latex exposure needed to produce sensitization or an allergic reaction is unknown. Increasing the exposure to latex proteins increases the risk of developing allergic symptoms. In sensitized persons, symptoms usually begin within minutes of exposure, but they can occur hours later and can be quite varied. Mild reactions are skin redness, rash, hives, or itching. More severe reactions may involve respiratory symptoms such as runny nose, sneezing, itchy eyes, scratchy throat, and asthma (difficult breathing, coughing spells, and wheezing (National Institute for Occupational Safety and Health, 1999).

The most serious allergic reaction to latex is an anaphylactic response, which can be deadly. Anaphylactic reactions develop immediately after latex exposure in highly sensitive individuals and cause the airway tubes (bronchi) to constrict, making it hard to breathe. Blood pressure may drop to life-threatening levels, making the person feel dizzy or causing him or her to lose consciousness (Mayo Clinic, 2005c).

OHI 4.07 Pet Allergies

Definition A type of allergy that is characterized by an abnormal response to certain types of pets (Nemours Foundation, 2004).

Explanation Studies show that approximately 15 percent of the population is allergic to dogs or cats. An estimated one-third of Americans who are allergic to cats (about 2 million people) live with at least one cat in their household anyway (Humane Society of the United States, 2006). Cats cause the most allergies because the protein from their saliva is extremely tiny and they tend to lick themselves more than other animals as part of grooming (Nemours Foundation, 2004).

In a study of 341 adults who were allergic to cats or dogs and had been advised by their physicians to give up their pets, only one out of five did. And 122 of them obtained another pet after a previous one had died. It is clear the benefits of pet companionship outweigh the drawbacks of pet allergies for many owners. Living comfortably with a companion animal despite being allergic requires a good understanding of the allergic condition and adherence to a few rules (Humane Society of the United States, 2006).

OHI 4.08 Other Types of Allergies

OHI 5.00 Alpers Disease

Definition Alpers disease is a rare, genetically determined disease of the brain that causes progressive degeneration of gray matter in the cerebrum (National Institute of Neurological Disorders and Stroke, 2005c). It is a progressive neurological disorder that begins during childhood (University Health Systems of Eastern Carolina, 2000).

Diagnostic Symptoms Diagnostic symptoms of Alpers disease include (Loyola University Health System, 2000):

- Convulsions early in a child's development
- Developmental delay

- Progressive mental retardation
- Hypotonia (low muscle tone)
- Spasticity (stiffness of the limbs)
- Dementia
- Liver conditions such as jaundice and cirrhosis that can lead to liver failure

Further Key Points The prognosis for individuals with Alpers disease is poor. Those with the disease usually die within the first decade of life. Continuous, unrelenting seizures often lead to death. Liver failure and cardiorespiratory failure may also occur. (National Institute of Neurological Disorders and Stroke, 2005c).

OHI 6.00 Angelman Syndrome

Definition Angelman syndrome is a chromosomal (gene-linked) disease that causes neurological problems. The physician Harold Angelman first identified the syndrome in 1965, when he described several children in his practice as having "flat heads, jerky movements, protruding tongues, and bouts of laughter." Infants with Angelman syndrome appear normal at birth, but begin to have feeding problems at one to two months and noticeable developmental delays by six to twelve months (National Institute of Neurological Disorders and Stroke, 2005d).

Diagnostic Symptoms Diagnostic symptoms of Angelman syndrome include (Williams & Driscoll, 2005):

- Normal prenatal and birth history, normal head circumference at birth, no major birth defects
- Normal metabolic, hematologic, and chemical laboratory profiles
- Structurally normal brain by magnetic resonance imaging or computer tomography, although mild cortical atrophy or dysmyelination may be observed
- Delayed attainment of developmental milestones without loss of skills
- Evidence of developmental delay by six to twelve months of age, eventually classified as severe
- Speech impairment, with minimal to no use of words; receptive language skills and nonverbal communication skills higher than expressive language skills
- Movement or balance disorder, usually ataxia (meaning without coordination) of gait or tremulous movement of the limbs, or both
- Behavioral uniqueness, including any combination of frequent laughter and smiling; apparent happy demeanor; excitability, often with hand-flapping movements; hypermotoric behavior; short attention span

Further Key Points Most individuals with Angelman syndrome have severe developmental delays, speech limitations, and problems with walking and staying upright. Early diagnosis and tailored interventions and therapies help improve their quality of life. Angelman syndrome has confused the medical community and parents of children with this disorder for hundreds of years. Initially presumed to be rare, it is now believed that thousands of Angelman syndrome cases have gone undiagnosed or misdiagnosed as cerebral palsy, autism, or other childhood disorders (Angelman Syndrome Foundation, 2004).

OHI 7.00 Asthma

Definition *Bronchial asthma* is the more correct name for the common form of asthma. The term *bronchial* is used to differentiate it from cardiac asthma, a separate condition that is caused by heart failure. Although the two types of asthma have similar symptoms, including wheezing (a whistling sound in the chest) and shortness of breath, they have quite different causes (MIMS Consumer Health Group, 2005).

Asthma is a chronic disease that affects the airways, which are the tubes that carry air in and out of the lungs. The inside walls of the airways are inflamed (swollen) in those who have asthma. The inflammation makes the airways very sensitive, and they tend to react strongly to things to which the person is allergic or finds irritating. When the airways react, they get narrower and less air flows through to the lung tissues (National Heart, Lung, and Blood Institute, 2006a). Patients with asthma may respond to factors in the environment, called triggers, that do not affect nonasthmatics. In response to a trigger, an asthmatic's airways become narrowed and inflamed, resulting in wheezing or coughing symptoms (American Academy of Allergy Asthma and Immunology, 2005a).

Diagnostic Symptoms Diagnostic symptoms of asthma include (Asthma and Allergy Foundation of America, 2005; National Heart, Lung, and Blood Institute, 2006a):

- Frequent coughing, especially at night (sometimes the only sign of asthma in a child)
- Wheezing
- Chest tightness
- Shortness of breath
- Faster breathing or noisy breathing

Further Key Points According to the Asthma and Allergy Foundation of America (2005), more than an estimated 20 million people in the United States have asthma. This health problem is the reason for nearly 500,000 hospital stays each year. People with asthma can be of any race, age or sex. Its treatment costs billions of dollars each year.

Types of Asthma

OHI 7.01 Cough Variant Asthma

Definition A type of asthma that is characterized by a chronic, persistent cough without shortness of breath (American Academy of Allergy Asthma and Immunology, 2005a).

Explanation Asthma has been shown in many studies to be one of the most common causes of chronic cough in all age groups. If cough is the only symptom of the asthma, this is referred to as cough variant asthma (Zwolski, 2005).

Cough variant asthma is difficult to diagnose. Children with this type of asthma are often treated for allergies, bronchitis, or colds. Typically a cough is the sole or at least most predominant symptom, and it is at its worst at night and after exertion. Wheezing or shortness of breath is not common in cough variant asthma.

OHI 7.02 Exercise-Induced Asthma

Definition Exercise-induced asthma (EIA) is a narrowing of the airways that causes difficulty moving air out of the lungs. Chronic asthma is an inflammatory disorder. Most patients with chronic asthma have a flare when they exercise. Other individuals appear to have a flare of asthma only when they exercise and do not otherwise have chronic asthma.

Explanation Running can trigger an episode in over 80 percent of children with asthma. Bronchodilator medications used before exercise can prevent most of these episodes. With proper control of asthma, most children with asthma can participate fully in physical activities.

There might be exceptions, such as prolonged running, especially during cold weather, allergy season, or illness from a cold. Swimming seems to be the least asthma-provoking form of exercise (American Lung Association, 2005).

OHI 7.03 Extrinsic Asthma

Definition A type of asthma that is triggered by external agents such as pollen or chemicals. Most cases of extrinsic asthma have an allergic origin and are due to the effects of an IgE-mediated response (allergic reaction) to an inhaled allergen. This is the type of asthma commonly diagnosed in early life. Many patients with extrinsic asthma respond to immunotherapy.

Explanation Cigarette smoke, air pollution, strong odors, aerosol sprays, and paint fumes are some of the substances that irritate the tissues of the lungs and upper airways. The reaction (cough, wheeze, runny nose, watery eyes) produced by these irritants can be identical to those produced by allergens.

Cigarette smoke is a good example, because it is highly irritating and can trigger asthma. Most people are not allergic to cigarette smoke; that is, there is no known immunological reaction. Nevertheless, this irritant can be more significant than any allergen (American Lung Association, 2005).

OHI 7.04 Intrinsic Asthma

Definition A type of asthma that is triggered by boggy membranes, congested tissues, and other native causes such as adrenalin stress or exertion (Health on the Net Foundation, 2002).

Explanation Intrinsic asthma generally develops later in life, and virtually nothing is known of its causes. It carries a worse prognosis than extrinsic asthma and tends to be less responsive to treatment. Intrinsic bronchial hyperactivity can be triggered by infection, exercise, or drugs such as aspirin (Health on the Net Foundation, 2002).

OHI 7.05 Nocturnal Asthma

Definition A type of asthma that suddenly worsens in the middle of the night, typically between 2:00 and 4:00 A.M.

Explanation It is common to experience a worsening of asthma symptoms at night (National Jewish Medical and Research Center, 2005). With nocturnal asthma, asthmatics often fall asleep quickly because they are physically exhausted, only to wake some three to four hours later with breathing difficulties.

This type of asthmatic frequently feels totally exhausted during the day and needs catnaps to keep functioning at an adequate level. Nocturnal asthma should be taken seriously: there is a high frequency of respiratory arrest and death due to asthma in the early hours of the morning (Buteyko Asthma Management, 1999).

OHI 7.06 Seasonal Asthma

Definition A type of asthma that is triggered by trees, grasses, or flowers releasing pollen to the atmosphere or by a particular climate (Buteyko Asthma Management, 1999).

Explanation With seasonal asthma, some people find the summer heat makes their asthma worse, while others find spring is particularly bad with the increase in flowering plants (Buteyko Asthma Management, 1999).

OHI 7.07 Silent Asthma

Definition A type of asthma that is characterized by little or no prior warning and very little wheezing. The episodes are usually severe and can be life threatening (Buteyko Asthma Management, 1999).

Explanation Signs of silent asthma (when no wheezing is heard) include persistent cough at night, cough with exercise, cough with laughter, cough when consuming cold foods or drinks, prolonged cough following or accompanying a cold, feeling of a tight chest, or difficulty breathing (Yamamoto, 2002).

OHI 7.08 Other Types of Asthma Not Otherwise Listed—Be Specific

OHI 8.00 Attention Deficit Hyperactivity Disorder

Definition Attention deficit hyperactivity disorder (ADHD) is a biologically based condition causing a persistent pattern of difficulties resulting in inattention, hyperactivity, or impulsivity or any combination of these (National Institute of Mental Health, 2005).

OHI

Diagnostic Symptoms According to the National Institute of Mental Health (2005), the principal characteristics of ADHD are inattention, hyperactivity, and impulsivity. These symptoms appear early in a child's life. Because many normal children may have these symptoms but at a low level or the symptoms may be caused by another disorder, it is important that the child receive a thorough examination and appropriate diagnosis by a well-qualified professional.

Symptoms of ADHD appear over the course of many months, often with the symptoms of impulsiveness and hyperactivity preceding those of inattention, which may not emerge for a year or more. Different symptoms may appear in different settings, depending on the demands the situation may pose for the child's self-control. A child who "can't sit still" or is otherwise disruptive will be noticeable in school, but the inattentive daydreamer may be overlooked.

Further Key Points According to the most recent edition of the American Psychiatric Association's (2003) *Diagnostic and Statistical Manual of Mental Disorders* (DSM-IV-TR), there are three patterns of behavior that indicate ADHD. People with ADHD may show several signs of being consistently inattentive. They may have a pattern of being hyperactive and impulsive far more than others of their age. Or they may show all three types of behavior. This means that there are three subtypes of ADHD recognized by professionals: the predominantly hyperactive-impulsive type (which does not show significant inattention); the predominantly inattentive type (which does not show significant hyperactive-impulsive behavior), sometimes called ADD—an outdated term for this entire disorder; and the combined type (which displays both inattentive and hyperactive-impulsive symptoms).

OHI 9.00 Autoimmune Diseases

Definition One of the functions of the immune system is to protect the body by responding to invading microorganisms, such as viruses or bacteria, by producing antibodies or sensitized lymphocytes (types of white blood cells). Under normal conditions, an immune response cannot be triggered against the cells of one's own body. In certain cases, however, immune cells make a mistake and attack the very cells that they are meant to protect. This can lead to a variety of autoimmune diseases. They encompass a broad category of related diseases in which the person's immune system attacks his or her own tissue (American Autoimmune Related Services Association, 2003).

Diagnostic Symptoms Autoimmunity can affect almost any organ or body system. The exact problem one has with autoimmunity (or its diseases) depends on which tissues are targeted.

If the skin is the target, an individual may have skin rashes, blisters, or color changes. If it is the thyroid gland, the individual may be tired, gain weight, be sensitive to cold, and have muscle aches. If it is the joints, the individual may have joint pain, stiffness, and loss of function (National Institute of Arthritis and Musculoskeletal and Skin Diseases, 2002a).

Further Key Points Approximately 50 million Americans, 20 percent of the population, suffer from autoimmune diseases. Women are more likely than men to be affected; some estimates say that 75 percent of those affected—some 30 million people—are women. Still, with these statistics, autoimmunity is rarely discussed as a women's health issue (American Autoimmune Related Services Association, 2003).

Types of Autoimmune Diseases

OHI 9.01 Autoimmune Thyroid Diseases

Definition An autoimmune disease characterized by disease of the thyroid gland (U.S. National Library of Medicine, 2004k).

Explanation It is common for people to develop thyroid diseases, such as hyperthyroidism (hyper means "too much") and hypothyroidism (hypo means "too little.) The two main types of autoimmune thyroid disease fall into hyperthyroidism (Graves' disease), and hypothyroidism (Hashimoto's thyroiditis) (U.S. National Library of Medicine, 2004j).

OHI 9.01a **Graves' Disease** Graves' disease is thought to be an autoimmune disorder of the thyroid that causes overproduction of thyroid hormones. Hallmarks of the condition are bulging eyes (exophthalmos), heat intolerance, increased energy, difficulty sleeping, diarrhea, and anxiety (U.S. National Library of Medicine, 2004d).

OHI 9.01b **Hashimoto's Thyroiditis** Hashimoto's thyroiditis is a type of autoimmune thyroid disease in which the immune system attacks and destroys the thyroid gland. The thyroid helps set the rate of metabolism—the rate at which the body uses energy. Hashimoto's prevents the gland from producing enough thyroid hormones for the body to work correctly. It is the most common form of hypothyroidism (underactive thyroid).

Some patients with Hashimoto's thyroiditis may have no symptoms. However, the common symptoms are fatigue, depression, sensitivity to cold, weight gain, muscle weakness, coarsening of the skin, dry or brittle hair, constipation, muscle cramps, increased menstrual flow, and goiter (enlargement of the thyroid gland) (U.S. Department of Health and Human Services, 2001).

OHI 9.02 Immune-Mediated or Type 1 Diabetes Mellitus

See Diabetes OHI 13.00.

OHI 9.03 Inflammatory Bowel Diseases

Definition Inflammatory bowel disease (which is not the same as irritable bowel syndrome) refers to two chronic diseases that cause inflammation of the intestines: ulcerative colitis and Crohn's disease. Although the diseases have some features in common, there are some important differences (Nemours Foundation, 2005d). Ulcerative colitis causes inflammation and sores, called ulcers, in the lining of the large intestine. Ulcerative colitis may also be called colitis or proctitis (National Digestive Diseases Information Clearinghouse, 2003). Crohn's disease is a chronic (ongoing) disorder that causes inflammation of the digestive or gastrointestinal (GI) tract. Although it can involve any area of the GI tract from the mouth to the anus, it most commonly affects the small intestine or colon, or both (Crohn's & Colitis Foundation of America, 2005).

Explanation The most common symptoms of ulcerative colitis and Crohn's disease are diarrhea and abdominal pain. Diarrhea can range from mild to severe (as many as twenty or more trips to the bathroom a day). If the diarrhea is extreme, it can lead to dehydration, rapid heartbeat, and a drop in blood pressure, and continued loss of small amounts of blood in the stool can lead to anemia.

At times, those with inflammatory bowel disease may also have constipation. With Crohn's disease, this can happen as a result of a partial obstruction (called stricture) in the intestines. In ulcerative colitis, constipation may be a symptom of inflammation of the rectum, also known as proctitis (Nemours Foundation, 2005b).

OHI 9.04 Multiple Sclerosis

Definition Multiple sclerosis (MS) is a chronic, potentially debilitating disease that affects the central nervous system, which is made up of the brain and spinal cord. Doctors and researchers think the illness is probably an autoimmune disease, which means that an individual's immune system attacks part of the body as if it is a foreign substance (Mayo Clinic, 2004e).

Explanation Most people experience their first symptoms of MS between the ages of twenty and forty; the initial symptom is often blurred or double vision, red-green color distortion, or even blindness in one eye. Most patients experience muscle weakness in their extremities and difficulty with coordination and balance. These symptoms may be severe enough to impair walking or even standing. In the worst cases, MS can produce partial or complete paralysis.

Most people with MS also exhibit paresthesias, transitory abnormal sensory feelings such as numbness, prickling, or "pins and needles" sensations. Some may experience pain. Speech impediments, tremors, and dizziness are other frequent complaints. Occasionally people with MS have hearing loss. Approximately half of all people with MS experience cognitive impairments such as difficulties with concentration, attention, memory, and poor judgment, but such symptoms are usually mild and are frequently overlooked. Depression is another common feature of MS (National Institute of Neurological Disorders and Stroke, 2005g).

OHI 9.05 Psoriasis

Definition Psoriasis is a chronic (long-lasting) skin disease of scaling and inflammation that affects 2.0 to 2.6 percent of the U.S. population, or between 5.8 and 7.5 million people. Although the disease occurs in all age groups, it primarily affects adults. It appears about equally in males and females. Psoriasis occurs when skin cells quickly rise from their origin below the surface of the skin and pile up on the surface before they have a chance to mature. Usually this movement (also called turnover) takes about a month, but in psoriasis it may occur in only a few days (National Institute of Arthritis and Musculoskeletal and Skin Diseases, 2003c).

Explanation Psoriasis is almost unnoticeable in its early stages (American Academy of Dermatology, 2005). There is an itching or burning sensation as the disease progresses. In particular, plaque psoriasis usually begins with small, red bumps on the skin that progress to bigger ones. Scaly patches appear that may become itchy and uncomfortable. As the scales accumulate, pink to deep-red plaques with a white crust of silvery scales appear on the skin surface.

OHI 9.05a **Erythrodermic Psoriasis** Widespread reddening and scaling of the skin may be a reaction to severe sunburn or to taking corticosteroids (cortisone) or other medications. It can also be due to the effects of a prolonged period of increased activity of psoriasis that is poorly controlled (National Institute of Arthritis and Musculoskeletal and Skin Diseases, 2003c).

OHI 9.05b **Guttate Psoriasis** Guttate psoriasis is most often triggered by upper respiratory infections, for example, a sore throat due to the effects of streptococcal bacteria (National Institute of Arthritis and Musculoskeletal and Skin Diseases, 2003c).

OHI 9.05c **Inverse Psoriasis** A type of psoriasis characterized by smooth, red patches in the folds of the skin near the genitals, under the breasts, or in the armpits. The symptoms may be worsened by friction and sweating (National Institute of Arthritis and Musculoskeletal and Skin Diseases, 2003c).

OHI 9.05d **Plaque Psoriasis** Skin lesions are red at the base and covered by silvery scales (National Institute of Arthritis and Musculoskeletal and Skin Diseases, 2003c).

OHI 9.05e **Psoriatic Arthritis** Joint inflammation that produces symptoms of arthritis in patients who have or will develop psoriasis (National Institute of Arthritis and Musculoskeletal and Skin Diseases, 2003c).

OHI 9.05f **Pustular Psoriasis** Blisters of noninfectious pus appear on the skin. Attacks of pustular psoriasis may be triggered by medications, infections, stress, or exposure to certain chemicals (National Institute of Arthritis and Musculoskeletal and Skin Diseases, 2003c).

OHI 9.05g **Other Forms of Psoriasis Not Otherwise Listed**

OHI 9.06 Lupus

Definition Lupus is an autoimmune disease that can affect almost any part of the body, most often the joints, skin, kidneys, heart, lungs, blood, or brain. Normally the immune system produces proteins called antibodies that protect the body from viruses and bacteria. In autoimmune diseases, the immune system instead produces antibodies directed against the healthy cells and tissues it is designed to protect. These autoantibodies (*auto* means *self*) cause inflammation and damage in various parts of the body. Inflammation is considered the hallmark, or primary feature, of lupus; the word is from the Latin word for "set on fire," so lupus is characterized by pain, heat, redness, swelling, and loss of function, either on the inside or on the outside of the body (or both) (Lupus Foundation of America, 2006).

Explanation In almost all cases, lupus will follow an irregular pattern of remission (times when symptoms disappear) and flare (times when the disease is more active). These periods of wellness and remission are most often reached with medication.

There is no cure for lupus, which is why it is called a chronic disease—*chronic* means ongoing or lifelong. However, lupus can be successfully treated, and 80 to 90 percent of people with a lupus that does not involve any major organs can lead active, normal lives.

Since lupus can affect so many different organs, there are many different symptoms that can occur. Table 5.1 gives the most common symptoms of lupus and the percentage of people with lupus who have that particular symptom. Most of these symptoms are obvious to the person who is experiencing them, but some can only be detected with laboratory tests.

In lupus, symptoms may come and go, and different symptoms may appear at different times during the course of the disease. Many of these symptoms—aching joints, headaches, fever, fatigue, rashes—are not unique to lupus; in fact, lupus is sometimes called a "great imitator" because its symptoms are often like the symptoms of rheumatoid arthritis, blood disorders, kidney problems caused

Table 5.1 Common Lupus Symptoms and Percentage of Occurrence.

Lupus Symptom	Percentage of Persons with Symptom
Achy joints (arthralgia)	95
Fever more than 100 degrees F (38 degrees C)	90
Swollen joints (arthritis)	90
Prolonged or extreme fatigue	81
Skin rashes	74
Anemia	71
Kidney involvement	50
Pain in the chest on deep breathing (pleurisy)	45
Butterfly-shaped rash across the cheeks and nose	42
Sun- or light-sensitivity (photosensitivity)	30
Hair loss	27
Abnormal blood-clotting problems	20
Fingers turning white and/or blue in the cold (Raynaud's phenomenon)	17
Seizures	15
Mouth or nose ulcers	12

Robert J. Lahita, M.D., Ph.D. ©2006.

by fibromyalgia, diabetes, thyroid problems, Lyme disease, and a number of heart, lung, muscle, and bone diseases. (Lupus Foundation of America, Inc. 2006).

According to the National Institute of Arthritis and Musculoskeletal and Skin Diseases (2002b), there are three forms of lupus.

OHI 9.06a **Systemic Lupus Erythematosus** Systemic lupus erythematosus (SLE) is the most common form. The word *systemic* means that the disease can involve many parts of the body, such as the heart, lungs, kidneys, and brain. Symptoms can be mild or serious.

OHI 9.06b **Discoid Lupus Erythematosus** Discoid lupus erythematosus mainly affects the skin. A red rash may appear, or the skin on the face, scalp, or elsewhere may change color. It is diagnosed by examining a biopsy of the rash. In discoid lupus, the biopsy will show abnormalities that are not found in skin without the rash (National Lupus Foundation, 2001).

OHI 9.06c **Drug-Induced Lupus** Drug-induced lupus is triggered by a few medicines. It is like SLE, but symptoms are usually milder. Most of the time, the disease goes away when the medicine is stopped. More men than women develop drug-induced lupus because the drugs that cause it, hydralazine and procainamide, are used to treat heart conditions that are more common in men.

OHI 9.07 Other Autoimmune Disorders

OHI 10.00 Hematologic Diseases (Blood Disorders)

Definition Disorders of the blood and blood-forming tissues (Medical Webends.com, 2005).

Diagnostic Symptoms Symptoms vary based on the type of blood disorder. Accordingly, no generalization about the symptoms of blood disorders can be made.

Further Key Points Two types of blood vessels carry blood throughout our bodies. The arteries carry oxygenated blood (blood that has received oxygen from the lungs) from the heart to the rest of the body. The blood then travels through the veins back to the heart and lungs, where they receive more oxygen. As the heart beats, you can feel blood traveling through the body at your pulse points, like the neck and the wrist, where large, blood-filled arteries run close to the surface of the skin.

The blood that flows through this network of veins and arteries is called *whole blood.* Whole blood contains three types of blood cells: red blood cells, white blood cells, and platelets.

Most of the time, blood functions without problems, but sometimes blood disorders or diseases can cause illness in children and teens. Diseases of the blood that commonly affect children can involve any or all of the three types of blood cells (red blood cells, white blood cells, or platelets). Other types of blood diseases affect the proteins and chemicals in the plasma that are responsible for clotting (Nemours Foundation, 2005a).

OHI 10.01 Anemia

Definition Anemia occurs when there is a lower-than-normal number of red blood cells (erythrocytes) in the blood, usually measured by a decrease in the amount of hemoglobin. Hemoglobin is the red pigment in red blood cells that transports oxygen (U.S. National Library of Medicine, 2004a).

Explanation The main symptom of most types of anemia is fatigue. Other signs and symptoms of anemia include:

- Weakness
- Pale skin
- A fast heartbeat
- Shortness of breath
- Chest pain
- Dizziness

- Cognitive problems
- Numbness or coldness in the extremities
- Headache

Initially, anemia can be so mild it goes unnoticed, but signs and symptoms increase as the condition progresses

OHI 10.01a Anemia Due to the Effects of Blood Loss

OHI 10.01b Anemia Due to the Effects of Inadequate Red Blood Cell Production

OHI 10.01c Aplastic Anemia Aplastic anemia occurs when the bone marrow is unable to produce sufficient numbers of blood cells.

OHI 10.01d Autoimmune Hemolytic Anemia In autoimmune hemolytic anemia, the immune system mistakes red blood cells for foreign invaders and begins destroying them.

OHI 10.01e Iron-Deficiency Anemia

OHI 10.01f Pernicious Anemia Anemia can be due to the effects of deficiency in the nutrients folic acid and vitamin B_{12}, both of which are necessary for normal blood production.

OHI 10.01g Sickle Cell Anemia Sickle cell anemia is a serious disease in which the body makes abnormally shaped red blood cells. Normal red blood cells are smooth and round like a doughnut without a hole. They move easily through blood vessels to carry oxygen to all parts of the body. In sickle cell anemia, the body produces red blood cells that are shaped like a sickle (or crescent). These "sickle cells" are hard and sticky and they don't move easily through blood vessels. They tend to get stuck and block the flow of blood to the limbs and organs. This can cause pain, organ damage, and a low blood count.

Sickle cell anemia is an inherited (genetic) disorder. It is a lifelong disease (National Heart, Lung, and Blood Institute, 2006b).

OH 10.01h Thalassemia People with thalassemia have an inherited blood disorder that causes mild or severe anemia. The genes that code for hemoglobin are missing or variant (different from the normal genes). Severe forms of thalassemia are usually diagnosed in early childhood and are lifelong conditions.

OHI 10.02 Hemophilia

Definition Hemophilia is a rare inherited bleeding disorder in which the blood does not clot normally. Persons with hemophilia may bleed for a longer time following an injury or accident than others. They also may bleed internally, especially in the joints (knees, ankles, and elbows) (National Heart, Lung, and Blood Institute, 2004).

Explanation People with severe hemophilia usually bleed frequently into their muscles or joints. They may bleed one to two times per week. Bleeding is often spontaneous, which means the bleeding happens with no obvious cause.

People with moderate hemophilia bleed less frequently, usually after an injury, perhaps once a month. Cases of hemophilia vary, however, and a person with moderate hemophilia can bleed spontaneously.

People with mild hemophilia usually bleed only as a result of surgery or major injury. They may never have a bleeding problem (World Federation of Hemophilia, 2005).

OHI10.03 Von Willebrand Disease

Definition Von Willebrand disease is an inherited bleeding disorder. Children born with the disease have one or both of the following: (1) low levels of a protein that helps the blood to clot and (2) the protein does not work as it should.

This clotting protein is called von Willebrand factor. When some of this factor is missing or defective, it can cause prolonged bleeding after an injury or accident (National Heart, Lung, and Blood Institute, 2004).

Explanation The signs and symptoms depend on the type and severity of the disease. Some people have the gene for the disease but do not have bleeding symptoms. Patients with type 1 and type 2 disease may have the following mild to moderate bleeding symptoms:

- Easy bruising
- Nosebleeds
- Bleeding from the gums after a dental procedure
- Heavy menstrual bleeding
- Blood in their stools (from bleeding in the intestines or stomach)
- Blood in their urine (from bleeding in the kidneys or bladder)
- Excessive bleeding after a cut or other accident
- Excessive bleeding after surgery

Heavy menstrual bleeding is the most common symptom in women. If untreated, it can lead to iron deficiency and anemia. Doctors usually test for the disease in women who have heavy menstrual bleeding. Some people may be diagnosed only after an episode of prolonged bleeding after an accident or surgery (National Heart, Lung, and Blood Institute, 2004).

OHI 10.04 Other Blood Disorders Not Otherwise Listed

OHI 11.00 Cancers of Childhood

Definition Cancer is a disease in which abnormal cells divide without control. The body is made up of many types of cells. Normally, cells grow and divide to produce more cells only when the body needs them. This orderly process helps keep the body healthy. Sometimes, however, cells keep dividing when new cells are not needed. These extra cells form a mass of tissue called a growth or tumor.

Tumors can be benign or malignant. Benign tumors are not cancer. They can often be removed and in most cases do not come back. Cells from benign tumors do not spread to other parts of the body. Most important, they are rarely a threat to life.

Malignant tumors are cancer. Cells in these tumors are abnormal and divide without control or order. They can invade and damage nearby tissues and organs. Also, cancer cells can break away from a malignant tumor and enter the bloodstream or the lymphatic system. That is how cancer spreads from the original cancer site to form new tumors in other organs. Cancer that has spread is called metastatic cancer.

Cancer cells can invade nearby tissues and spread through the bloodstream and lymphatic system to other parts of the body (National Cancer Institute, 2006).

Diagnostic Symptoms Diagnostic symptoms for childhood cancer include (National Cancer Institute, 2006):

- Bleeding, including nosebleeds; red or black bowel movements; pink, red, or brown urine; or many bruises
- Blurred or double vision
- Constipation that lasts more than two days
- Depression or a sudden change in behavior
- Diarrhea
- Difficulty chewing
- Dizziness
- Fever (100.4°F or 38°C) or other sign of infection, especially if the child's white count is low
- Mouth sores that keep the child from eating
- Pain anywhere in the body
- Painful urination or bowel movements
- Red or swollen areas
- Severe or continuing headaches
- Digestive tract problems

- Eating difficulties
- changes in mobility or mood
- Trouble talking
- Trouble walking or bending
- Vomiting

Further Key Points Because of better research and treatment, children who have cancer are living longer than they used to, and their quality of life is better than in the past. Although they lead normal lives, survivors of cancer have some concerns that other people may not have. For example, they must take special care of their health and may have problems obtaining insurance. Cancer is more curable when detected early (eMedicine, 2005).

OHI 11.01 Bone Cancers

Definition A tumor is a lump or mass of tissue that forms when cells divide uncontrollably. For most bone tumors, the cause is unknown (National Cancer Institute, 2002a). A growing tumor may replace healthy tissue with abnormal tissue. It may weaken the bone, causing it to break (fracture). Aggressive tumors can lead to disability or death, particularly if signs and symptoms are ignored.

Explanation Most patients with a bone tumor experience pain in the area of the tumor. The pain is generally described as dull and achy. It may or may not get worse with activity. The pain often awakens the patient at night. Although tumors are not caused by trauma, occasionally injury can cause a tumor to start hurting. Injury can cause a bone weakened by tumor to break, which often leads to severe pain. Some tumors can also cause fevers and night sweats. Many patients do not experience any symptoms but instead note a painless mass (American Academy of Orthopaedic Surgeons, 2004).

OHI 11.01a **Chondrosarcoma** Chondrosarcoma forms in cartilage, the rubbery tissue around the joints. It is found mainly in adults, although it can occur in children (National Cancer Institute, 2006).

OHI 11.01b **Ewing's Sarcoma** The most common sites for Ewing's sarcoma are the hip bones, long bones in the thigh (femur) and upper arm (humerus), and ribs. It occurs between ages ten and twenty-five (National Cancer Institute, 2006).

OHI 11.01c **Osteosarcoma or Osteogenic Sarcoma** Osteosarcoma is the sixth most common malignancy in children and the most common type of bone cancer in children. It usually affects the thigh bone (femur), upper arm bone (humerus), or one of the long bones of the lower leg (tibia). It occurs between ages ten and twenty-five (National Cancer Institute, 2006).

OHI 11.02 Leukemia

Definition Leukemia is a malignant disease (cancer) of the bone marrow and blood. It is characterized by the uncontrolled accumulation of blood cells (Leukemia and Lymphoma Society, 2006).

Explanation The types of leukemia are grouped by how quickly the disease develops and worsens. Leukemia is either chronic (gets worse slowly) or acute (gets worse quickly).

Early in chronic leukemia, the abnormal blood cells can still do their work, and people with this leukemia may not have any symptoms. Slowly, it gets worse and causes symptoms as the number of leukemia cells in the blood rises.

In acute leukemia, the blood cells are very abnormal and cannot carry out their normal work. The number of abnormal cells increases rapidly. Acute leukemia worsens quickly (National Cancer Institute, 2003). There are four common types of leukemia (National Cancer Institute, 2003).

OHI 11.02a **Chronic Lymphocytic Leukemia (Chronic Lymphoblastic Leukemia)** This accounts for about 7,000 new cases of leukemia each year. Most often people diagnosed with the disease are over age fifty-five. It almost never affects children.

OHI 11.02b **Chronic Myeloid Leukemia (Chronic Myelogenous Leukemia)** This accounts for about 4,400 new cases of leukemia each year. It affects mainly adults.

OHI 11.02c **Acute Lymphocytic Leukemia (Acute Lymphoblastic Leukemia)** This accounts for about 3,800 new cases of leukemia each year. It is the most common type of leukemia in young children. It also affects adults.

OHI 11.02d **Acute Myeloid Leukemia (Acute Myelogenous Leukemia)** This accounts for about 10,600 new cases of leukemia each year. It occurs in both adults and children.

OHI 11.03 Liver Cancers

Definition Primary liver cancer begins in the cells of the liver itself. Although many cancers are declining in the United States, new cases of primary liver cancer are increasing and are likely to continue to increase for the next two decades. Liver cancer also occurs as metastatic cancer, which happens when tumors from other parts of the body spread (metastasize) to the liver. In the United States, most cancer found in the liver has originated elsewhere (Mayo Clinic, 2005d).

Explanation Also called hepatoma, liver cancer is a rare disease. Most people do not have signs and symptoms in the early stages of liver cancer, which means the disease may not be detected until it is quite advanced. When symptoms do appear, they may include some or all of the following:

- Loss of appetite and weight

- Abdominal pain, especially in the upper right part of the abdomen, that may extend into the back and shoulder
- Nausea and vomiting
- General weakness and fatigue
- An enlarged liver
- Abdominal swelling
- A yellow discoloration of the skin and the whites of the eyes (jaundice) (Mayo Clinic, 2005d)

These symptoms are not sure signs of liver cancer. Other liver diseases and other health problems can also cause these symptoms. When the tumor is solely in the liver and can be removed with surgery, the cancer is highly curable (National Cancer Institute, 2002c).

OHI 11.03a **Hepatoblastoma** Hepatoblastoma, a very rare cancerous tumor that originates in the liver, affects children from infancy to about five years of age, with most cases appearing during the first eighteen months of life.

OHI 11.03b **Hepatocellular Cancer** Children infected with hepatitis B or C (viral infections of the liver) are more likely to get this type of cancer. It occurs most often in children age four or younger and those between ages twelve and fifteen.

OHI 11.04 Soft Tissue Sarcomas

Definition Malignant (cancerous) tumors that develop in soft tissue are called sarcomas, a term that comes from the Greek word meaning "fleshy growth." There are many different kinds of soft tissue sarcomas. They are grouped together because they share certain microscopic characteristics, produce similar symptoms, and are generally treated in similar ways (National Cancer Institute, 2002b). Bone tumors (osteosarcomas) are also called sarcomas, but they are in a separate category because they have different clinical and microscopic characteristics and are treated differently.

Explanation When sarcomas develop on the arms or legs, most people notice a lump that has grown over a period of time (weeks to months). Although it can be painful, generally it does not hurt.

When sarcomas grow in the abdomen, the symptoms they cause are not very specific. About a third of the time, they can cause pain. Sometimes they are found because they cause blockage or bleeding of the stomach or bowels. They can also be found because they have grown large enough to be felt in the abdomen.

Since symptoms of soft tissue sarcomas often do not appear until the disease is advanced, only about 50 percent of soft tissue sarcomas are found in the early stages, before they have spread (American Cancer Society, 2005).

OHI 11.05 Lymphoma

Definition Lymphoma is a cancer that begins in the cells of the immune system. There are two basic categories of lymphomas: either Hodgkin's disease or non-Hodgkin's lymphoma (National Cancer Institute, 2005).

Explanation Lymphoma is a tumor of the lymph tissue. Because lymph tissue is in many parts of the body, they can start almost anywhere. In most cases, patients seek attention because of the appearance of swollen glands in the neck, armpits, or groin. These swollen lymph nodes are mostly painless. They are present for several weeks before attention is directed toward them. They are unresponsive to treatment with antibiotics.

General symptoms may include feeling tired, having a flulike syndrome, or aching all over. Fatigue may be the result of anemia. Others experience night sweats, and some may have recurring high-grade or constant low-grade fevers. Since all these symptoms are common to many illnesses, from minor ailments to serious disorders, the correct diagnostic procedures must be performed in order to confirm or rule out the diagnosis of lymphoma (Leukemia & Lymphoma Society, 2005).

OHI 11.05a **Burkitt's Lymphoma** This is a type of non Hodgkin's lymphoma. In Americans, the usual site is the abdomen. The age range is two to sixteen years.

OHI 11.05b **Hodgkin's Disease** Hodgkin's disease is a cancer that tends to affect the lymph nodes that are close to the body's surface, such as those in the neck, armpit, or groin area. It occurs mainly in young adults and in people over age sixty-five but can affect teenagers and children. Lymphomas are the third most common childhood cancer. They are rare under age five.

OHI 11.05c **Non-Hodgkin's Lymphoma** In children, non-Hodgkin's lymphoma affects lymph nodes that are found deeper in the body. The bowel is the most frequent spot, often in the area next to the appendix, or in the upper part of the chest. It occurs most often between ages ten to twenty and is unusual under age three.

OHI 11.06 Other Types of Cancers—Be Specific

OHI 12.00 Congenital Heart Disease

Definition The term *congenital heart disease* (or congenital heart *defect*) indicates that a structural problem (or defect) in a baby's heart is present at birth (National Heart, Lung and Blood Institute, 2005b).

It can be inherited or caused by disease or distress of the embryo during its development. It is usually characterized by:

- A hole between the right and left sides of the heart
- An abnormal number of heart chambers

- Abnormalities of the heart valves or major blood vessels near the heart
- Abnormal placement or twisting of the heart
- Other variations from normal (Maine School Health Advisory Committee, 2006)

Diagnostic Symptoms A baby's heart begins to form shortly after conception. By the end of the second month of pregnancy, the heart is completely formed. It is during this time that a congenital heart defect can occur. In this case, a part of the heart, heart valves, or blood vessels near the heart does not develop properly. When this happens, blood flow can slow down, go in the wrong direction or to the wrong place, or be blocked completely (National Heart, Lung and Blood Institute, 2005b). About eight out of every thousand infants are born with one or more heart or circulatory problems (Texas Heart Institute of St. Luke's Hospital, 2006).

Further Key Points More than 32,000 infants (one out of every 125 to 150) are born with heart defects each year in the United States. The defect may be so slight that the baby appears healthy for many years after birth, or so severe that his or her life is in immediate danger. Heart defects are among the most common birth defects and the leading cause of birth defect–related deaths. Advances in diagnosis and surgical treatment over the past forty years have led to dramatic increases in survival for children with serious heart defects. Between 1987 and 1997, the death rate from congenital heart defects dropped 23 percent (March of Dimes, 2005a).

OHI 12.01 Cyanotic Congenital Heart Diseases

Definition Heart disorders that cause a decreased, inadequate amount of oxygen in blood pumped to the body are called *cyanotic defects.* In people with congenital heart defects, cyanosis can happen if the defect allows oxygen-poor blood from the right side of the heart to enter the left side of the heart directly instead of traveling to the lungs for more oxygen. In the left side of the heart, the oxygen-poor blood mixes with oxygen-rich blood to be pumped through the body (U.S. National Library of Medicine, 2004i; Texas Heart Institute, 2004).

Explanation Cyanosis is a condition in which the lips, fingers, and toes appear blue. It happens in some people with congenital heart defects that cause the blood to circulate abnormally. In people with congenital heart defects, cyanosis can happen if the defect allows oxygen-poor blood from the right side of the heart to enter the left side of the heart directly, instead of traveling to the lungs for more oxygen. In the left side of the heart, the oxygen-poor blood mixes with oxygen-rich blood to be pumped through the body (Texas Heart Institute of St. Luke's Hospital, 2006; Heart Center Online, 2005).

OHI 12.02 Noncyanotic Congenital Heart Diseases

Definition Noncyanotic heart diseases are congenital heart problems where the blood receives all the oxygen it requires and hence does not go blue but where there is abnormal leakage between different sides of the heart or blockages in blood vessels (U.S. National Library of Medicine, 2004i).

Explanation In many cases, noncyanotic heart disease causes no symptoms in childhood. As the child grows older, the heart gets abnormally large because of the extra workload of having to pump a larger than normal volume of blood. The enlarged heart is weak and eventually decompensates (fails). When this happens, the child begins to show many of the same symptoms as the child with cyanotic heart disease (Maine School Health Advisory Committee, 2006).

OHI 12.03 Other Congenital Heart Diseases Not Otherwise Listed—Be Specific

OHI 13.00 Diabetes

Definition Diabetes is a disease in which blood glucose levels are above normal. People with diabetes have problems converting food to energy. After a meal, food is broken down into a sugar called glucose, which is carried by the blood to cells throughout the body. Cells use insulin, a hormone made in the pancreas, to help them convert blood glucose into energy (Centers for Disease Control, 2005a).

People develop diabetes because the pancreas does not make enough insulin or because the cells in the muscles, liver, and fat do not use insulin properly, or both. As a result, the amount of glucose in the blood increases, while the cells are starved of energy. Over the years, high blood glucose, also called hyperglycemia, damages nerves and blood vessels, which can lead to complications such as heart disease and stroke, kidney disease, blindness, nerve problems, gum infections, and amputation (National Diabetes Information Clearinghouse, 2005b).

Diagnostic Symptoms Diagnostic symptoms for diabetes include (American Diabetes Association, 2005; National Diabetes Information Clearinghouse, 2005b; Centers for Disease Control, 2005a):

- Frequent urination
- Excessive thirst
- Extreme hunger
- Unusual weight loss
- Increased fatigue
- Irritability
- Blurry vision

Further Key Points People with diabetes must take responsibility for their day-to-day care. Much of the daily care involves keeping blood glucose levels from going too low or too high. When blood glucose levels drop too low, a condition known as hypoglycemia, the person can become nervous, shaky, and confused. Judgment can be impaired, and if blood glucose falls too low, fainting can occur (National Diabetes Information Clearinghouse, 2005b).

There are 18.2 million people in the United States, or 6.3 percent of the population, who have diabetes. While an estimated 13 million have been diagnosed with diabetes, 5.2 million people (or nearly one-third) are unaware that they have the disease (American Diabetes Foundation, 2005).

OHI 13.01 Type 1 Diabetes

Definition Type 1 diabetes is an autoimmune disease. An autoimmune disease results when the body's system for fighting infection (the immune system) turns against a part of the body. In diabetes, the immune system attacks the insulin-producing beta cells in the pancreas and destroys them. The pancreas then produces little or no insulin. A person who has type 1 diabetes must take insulin daily to live (Centers for Disease Control, 2005a).

Explanation Scientists do not know exactly what causes the body's immune system to attack the beta cells (cells that make insulin), but they believe that autoimmune, genetic, and environmental factors, possibly viruses, are involved. Type 1 diabetes accounts for about 5 to 10 percent of diagnosed diabetes in the United States. It develops most often in children and young adults but can appear at any age.

Symptoms of type 1 diabetes usually develop over a short period, although beta cell destruction (destruction of the cells that produce insulin) can begin years earlier. Symptoms may include increased thirst and urination, constant hunger, weight loss, blurred vision, and extreme fatigue. If type 1 diabetes is not diagnosed and treated with insulin, a person with this disease can lapse into a life-threatening diabetic coma, known as diabetic ketoacidosis (National Diabetes Informational Clearinghouse, 2005a).

OHI 13.02 Type 2 Diabetes

Definition The most common form of diabetes is type 2 diabetes. About 90 to 95 percent of people with diabetes have type 2. This form is associated with older age, obesity, family history of diabetes, previous history of gestational diabetes, physical inactivity, and ethnicity. About 80 percent of people with type 2 diabetes are overweight (National Diabetes Informational Clearinghouse, 2005b).

Explanation Type 2 diabetes is increasingly being diagnosed in children and adolescents. When it is diagnosed, the pancreas is usually producing enough insulin, but for unknown reasons the body cannot use the insulin effectively, a condition called insulin resistance. After several years, insulin production decreases. The result is the same as for type 1 diabetes: glucose builds up in the blood, and the body cannot make efficient use of its main source of fuel (Centers for Disease Control, 2005a).

The symptoms of type 2 diabetes develop gradually. Their onset is not as sudden as in type 1 diabetes. Symptoms may include fatigue, frequent urination, increased thirst and hunger, weight loss, blurred vision, and slow healing of wounds or sores. Some people have no symptoms (U.S. Department of Health and Human Services, 2002).

OHI 13.03 Other Types of Diabetes Not Otherwise Listed

OHI 14.00 Endocrine-Metabolic Disorders

Definition The endocrine system is a complex collection of hormone-producing glands that control basic body functions such as metabolism, growth, and sexual development. The amount of hormones produced by each gland is carefully balanced. Too much or too little of a certain hormone can have effects throughout the body and cause endocrine disorders. Many of the hormones produced by the endocrine glands interact with each other to maintain balance (University of Maryland Medical Center, 2006).

Endocrine disorders happen when one or more of the endocrine systems in the body is not working well. Hormones may be released in amounts that are too great or too small for the body to work normally. There may not be enough receptors, or binding sites, for the hormones so that they can direct the work that needs to be done. There could be a problem with the system regulating the hormones in the blood stream, or the body may have difficulty controlling hormone levels because of problems clearing hormones from the blood (Hormone Foundation, 2005).

Diagnostic Symptoms Symptoms vary based on the type of endocrine disorder. Accordingly, no generalization about the symptoms of endocrine disorders can be made.

Further Key Points Hormones are chemical substances created by the body that control numerous body functions. They act as messengers to coordinate functions of various body parts. Most hormones are proteins consisting of amino acid chains. Some hormones are steroids, fatty cholesterol–produced substances.

Functions controlled by hormones include:

- Activities of entire organs
- Growth and development
- Reproduction
- Sexual characteristics
- Usage and storage of energy
- Levels of fluid, salt, and sugar in the blood (University of Virginia Health System, 2004)

OHI

OHI 14.01 Acromegaly

Definition *Acromegaly* is the Greek word for "extremities" and "enlargement." When the pituitary gland produces excess growth hormones, this results in excessive growth, called acromegaly. The excessive growth occurs first in the hands and feet, as soft tissue begins to swell. Acromegaly affects mostly middle-aged adults. Untreated, the disease can lead to severe illness and death (University of Maryland Medical Center, 2004). Acromegaly is a serious systemic condition caused in over 98 percent of cases by an adenoma (a benign tumor) of the pituitary gland that secretes excessive growth hormone (Pituitary Network Association, 2005).

Explanation Symptoms of acromegaly vary depending on how long the patient has had the disease. The following are the most common symptoms. However, each individual may experience symptoms differently (Pituitary Network Association, 2005; University of Maryland Medical Center, 2004):

- Arthritis
- Carpal tunnel syndrome
- Colon polyps and colon cancer
- Diabetes mellitus
- Enlargement of forehead (frontal bossing) and jaw (prognathism) with pronounced under- or overbite, spreading teeth, and enlarging tongue
- Enlargement of hands (ring size), feet (shoe size), and head (hat size)
- Headaches
- Heart disease and heart enlargement (cardiomegaly and left ventricular hypertrophy)
- Hypertension
- Impotence, loss of libido
- Interrupted menstrual cycle (amenorrhea)
- Lactation (galactorrhea)
- Loss of vision
- Oily skin and excessive sweating
- Sleep apnea
- Soft tissue thickening of the palms of the hands and soles of the feet
- Fatigue
- Depression

OHI 14.02 Addison's Disease

Definition Addison's disease occurs when the body produces insufficient amounts of certain important hormones (Mayo Clinic, 2005a). It is an endocrine or hormonal disorder that occurs in all age groups and afflicts men and women equally. The disease is characterized by weight loss, muscle weakness, fatigue, low blood pressure, and sometimes darkening of the skin in both exposed and unexposed parts of the body. It occurs when the adrenal glands do not produce enough of the hormone cortisol and, in some cases, the hormone aldosterone. The disease is also called adrenal insufficiency or hypocortisolism (Endocrine and Metabolic Diseases Information Service, 2004).

Explanation Because the symptoms progress slowly, they are usually ignored until a stressful event like an illness or an accident causes them to become worse. This is called an addisonian crisis, or acute adrenal insufficiency. In most cases, symptoms are severe enough that patients seek medical treatment before a crisis occurs. However, in about 25 percent of patients, symptoms first appear during an addisonian crisis. The symptoms of adrenal insufficiency usually begin gradually. Characteristics of the disease are:

- Chronic, worsening fatigue
- Diarrhea
- Loss of appetite
- Low blood pressure that falls further when standing, causing dizziness or fainting
- Muscle weakness
- Nausea
- Skin changes
- Vomiting
- Weight loss (Endocrine and Metabolic Diseases Information Service, 2004).

OHI

OHI 14.03 Cushing's Syndrome

Definition Cushing's syndrome, also called hypercortisolism, is a rare endocrine disorder caused by chronic exposure of the body's tissues to excess levels of cortisol, a hormone naturally produced by the adrenal gland. Exposure to too much cortisol can occur from long-term use of synthetic glucocorticoid hormones to treat inflammatory illnesses (National Institute of Neurological Disorders and Stroke, 2005e).

Explanation Cushing's syndrome occurs when the body's tissues are exposed to excessive levels of cortisol for long periods of time. Many people suffer from the symptoms because they take glucocorticoid hormones such as prednisone for asthma, rheumatoid arthritis, lupus, and other inflammatory diseases, or for immunosuppression after transplantation.

Others develop Cushing's syndrome because of overproduction of cortisol by the body. Normally the production of cortisol follows a precise chain of events.

First, the hypothalamus, a part of the brain about the size of a small sugar cube, sends corticotropin-releasing hormone (CRH) to the pituitary gland. CRH causes the pituitary to secrete ACTH (adrenocorticotropin), a hormone that stimulates the adrenal glands. When the adrenals, which are located just above the kidneys, receive the ACTH, they respond by releasing cortisol into the bloodstream (Endocrine and Metabolic Diseases Information Service, 2002).

OHI 14.04 Cystic Fibrosis

Definition Cystic fibrosis (CF) is an inherited disease of the mucus and sweat glands. It affects mostly the lungs, pancreas, liver, intestines, sinuses, and sex organs. Normally mucus is watery. It keeps the linings of certain organs moist and prevents them from drying out or getting infected. But in CF, an abnormal gene causes mucus to become thick and sticky. The mucus builds up in the lungs and blocks the airways. This makes it easy for bacteria to grow and leads to repeated serious lung infections. Over time, these infections can cause serious damage to the lungs. The thick, sticky mucus can also block tubes, or ducts, in the pancreas. As a result, digestive enzymes that are produced by the pancreas cannot reach the small intestine. These enzymes help break down the food that an individual eats. Without them, the intestines cannot absorb fats and proteins fully (National Heart, Lung, and Blood Institute, 2005a).

Explanation Cystic fibrosis (CF), a life-threatening disorder that causes severe lung damage and nutritional deficiencies, used to be a genetic mystery, and most people with the disease did not live beyond their teens (Mayo Clinic, 2004b). Although someone with cystic fibrosis is born with it, it is not always obvious at birth. It may take a while for symptoms to develop. Doctors may suspect that a baby has CF if he or she coughs a lot and gets a lot of lung infections. The baby also might have unusual large, bulky bowel movements or may not gain weight as expected (Nemours Foundation, 2005c).

The symptoms and severity of CF vary from person to person. Some people with CF have serious lung and digestive problems. Other people have a more mild disease that does not show up until they are adolescents or young adults. Respiratory failure is the most common cause of death in people with CF (National Heart, Lung, and Blood Institute, 2005a).

OHI 14.05 Hyperparathyroidism

Definition Hyperparathyroidism is a disorder in which the parathyroid glands produce too much parathyroid hormone. The resulting imbalance in calcium and phosphorus can create a multitude of health problems, affecting the teeth, bones, nervous system, and muscles (Mayo Clinic, 2005b).

Explanation Symptoms of hyperparathyroidism include (U.S. National Library of Medicine, 2004i):

- Fatigue
- Depression
- Memory problems
- Abdominal pain
- Pain in other areas of the body
- Muscular weakness
- Muscle pain
- Depression
- Personality changes
- Constipation (Journal of American Medical Association, 2005)

OHI 14.06 Multiple Endocrine Neoplasia Type 1

Definition In Multiple Endocrine Neoplasia Type 1 (MEN1), all four parathyroid glands tend to be overactive. They release too much parathyroid hormone, leading to excess calcium in the blood. High blood calcium, known as hypercalcemia, can exist for many years before it is found by accident or by family screening. Unrecognized hypercalcemia can cause excess calcium to spill into the urine, leading to kidney stones or kidney damage (National Institute of Diabetes and Digestive and Kidney Diseases, 2002).

Explanation In patients with MEN1, sometimes multiple endocrine glands, such as the parathyroid, the pancreas, and the pituitary, become overactive at the same time. Most people who develop overactivity of only one endocrine gland do not have MEN1 (National Institute of Diabetes and Digestive and Kidney Diseases, 2002).

OHI 14.07 Other Endocrine-Metabolic Diseases Not Otherwise Listed

OHI 15.00 Ehlers-Danlos Syndrome (EDS)

Definition Ehlers-Danlos syndrome (EDS) is a group of disorders that affect connective tissue—the tissue that supports skin, bones, tendons, ligaments, blood vessels, and other organs. Defects in connective tissue cause the signs and symptoms of Ehlers-Danlos syndrome, which vary from mildly loose joints to life-threatening complications (U.S. National Library of Medicine, 2005d).

Diagnostic Symptoms According to the Ehlers Danlos Foundation (2006), clinical manifestations of EDS are most often joint and skin related and may include:

- Joints: Joint hypermobility; loose or unstable joints that are prone to frequent dislocations or subluxations (when one or more of the bones in the spine move out of position and create pressure on or irritate spinal nerves); joint pain;

hyperextensible joints (they move beyond the joint's normal range); early onset of osteoarthritis

- Skin: Soft, velvet–like skin; variable skin hyperextensibility; fragile skin that tears or bruises easily (bruising may be severe); severe scarring; slow and poor wound healing; development of molluscoid pseudo tumors (fleshy lesions associated with scars over pressure areas)
- Miscellaneous/less common: Chronic, early-onset, debilitating musculoskeletal pain; arterial, intestinal, uterine fragility or rupture (usually associated with the vascular type); scoliosis at birth and scleral fragility; poor muscle tone; mitral valve prolapse; gum disease

Further Key Points Some forms of EDS can present problems with the spine, including curved spine; the eyes; and internal organs, including the uterus, intestines, and large blood vessels. Mutations in several different genes are responsible for different symptoms in the several types of EDS. In most cases, the genetic defect involves collagen, the major protein-building material of bone (National Institute of Arthritis and Musculoskeletal and Skin Diseases, 2001a).

OHI 16.00 Epidermolysis Bullosa

Definition Epidermolysis bullosa (EB) is a group of blistering skin conditions. The skin is so fragile in people with EB that even minor rubbing may cause blistering. At times, the person may not be aware of rubbing or injuring the skin even though blisters develop. In severe EB, blisters are not confined to the outer skin. They may develop inside the body, in such places as the linings of the mouth, esophagus, stomach, intestines, upper airway, bladder, and the genitals (National Institute of Arthritis and Musculoskeletal and Skin Diseases, 2003a).

Diagnostic Symptoms One of the most common diagnostic symptoms of all forms of EB is fragile skin that blisters, which can lead to serious complications. For example, blistering areas may become infected, and blisters in the mouth or parts of the gastrointestinal tract may interfere with proper nutrition (National Institute of Arthritis and Musculoskeletal and Skin Diseases, 2003a).

Further Key Points Most forms of EB are evident at birth. This disorder can be both disabling and disfiguring, and some forms may lead to early death. The disease results when skin layers separate after minor trauma. Defects of several proteins within the skin are at fault (National Institute of Arthritis and Musculoskeletal and Skin Diseases, 2003a).

OHI 17.00 Epilepsy

Definition Epilepsy is a neurological condition that makes people susceptible to seizures. A seizure is a change in sensation, awareness, or behavior brought about by a brief electrical disturbance in the brain.

Seizures vary from a momentary disruption of the senses, to short periods of unconsciousness or staring spells, to convulsions. Some people have just one type of seizure. Others have more than one type(Epilepsy Foundation, 2005b).

Diagnostic Symptoms Diagnostic symptoms of epilepsy include (National Institute of Neurological Disorders and Stroke, 2005f):

- Strange sensations
- Strange emotions
- Strange behavior
- Convulsions
- Muscle spasms
- Loss of consciousness

Further Key Points Epilepsy affects people of all ages, races, and ethnic backgrounds. More than 2.5 million Americans of all ages are living with epilepsy. Every year, 181,000 Americans will develop seizures and epilepsy for the first time. The condition can develop at any time of life, especially in early childhood and old age.

It is not uncommon for people with epilepsy, especially children, to develop behavioral and emotional problems, sometimes the consequence of embarrassment and frustration or bullying, teasing, or avoidance in school and other social setting. For many people with epilepsy, the risk of seizures restricts their independence (some states refuse driver's licenses to people with epilepsy) and recreational activities. People with epilepsy are at special risk for two life-threatening conditions: status epilepticus (any continuing type of seizure lasting longer than thirty minutes without gaining consciousness) and sudden unexplained death (National Institute of Neurological Disorders and Stroke, 2005f).

Types of Epilepsy

OHI 17.01 Epilepsy with Absence Seizures

Definition Seizure activity varies for different persons with epilepsy. Absence seizures, formally called petit mal, involve staring off into space for a few moments (Journal of the American Medical Association, 2004a). These seizures almost always begin in childhood or adolescence, and they tend to run in families, suggesting that they may be at least partially due to a defective gene or genes (National Institute of Neurological Disorders and Stroke, 2005f]).

Explanation Some people with absence seizures have purposeless movements during their seizures, such as a jerking arm or rapidly blinking eyes. Others have no noticeable symptoms except for brief times when they are "out of it." Immediately after a seizure, the person can resume whatever he or she was doing. However, these seizures may occur so frequently that the person cannot concentrate in school or other situations. Childhood absence epilepsy usually stops when the child reaches puberty. Absence seizures usually have no lasting effect on intelligence or other brain functions (National Institute of Neurological Disorders and Stroke, 2005f).

OHI 17.02 Epilepsy with Atonic Seizures

Definition Atonic seizures, also known as drop attacks, involve a sudden loss of muscle tone, causing the person to fall. There is consequent risk of injury, but recovery is generally rapid. (Epilepsy.com, 2004).

Explanation *Atonic* means "without tone," so in an atonic seizure, muscles suddenly lose strength. The eyelids may droop, the head may nod, and the person may drop things and often fall to the ground. These seizures are also called "drop attacks" or "drop seizures." The person usually remains conscious (Epilepsy.com, 2004).

OHI 17.03 Epilepsy with Complex Partial Seizures

Definition In a complex focal seizure, the person has a change in or loss of consciousness. His or her consciousness may be altered, producing a dreamlike experience (National Institute of Neurological Disorders and Stroke, 2005f).

Explanation Typically a complex partial seizure starts with a blank stare and loss of contact with surroundings. This is often followed by chewing movements with the mouth, picking at or fumbling with clothing, mumbling, and performing simple, unorganized movements over and over again.

Sometimes people wander around. For example, a person might leave a room, go downstairs, and walk out into the street, completely unaware of what he or she was doing. In rare cases, a person might try to undress during a seizure or become very agitated, screaming, running, or making flailing movements with arms or bicycling movements with legs.

Other complex partial seizures may cause a person to run in apparent fear, cry out, or repeat the same phrase over and over again. Actions and movements are typically unorganized, confused, and unfocused during a complex partial seizure (Epilepsy Foundation, 2005a).

OHI 17.04 Epilepsy with Generalized Seizures

Definition In these seizures the whole of the brain is involved, and consciousness is lost. They often occur with no warning and the person will have no memory of the event. Generalized seizures are more common in children under the age of ten; afterward, more than half of those newly diagnosed with epilepsy will have partial seizures (Epilepsy Foundation, 2005c).

Explanation Generalized seizures are a result of abnormal neuronal activity on both sides of the brain. These seizures may cause loss of consciousness, falls, or massive muscle spasms (National Institute of Neurological Disorders and Stroke, 2005f).

OHI 17.05 Epilepsy with Myoclonic Seizures

Definition Juvenile myoclonic epilepsy (also called Janz's syndrome, impulsive petit mal, myoclonic epilepsy of adolescence, and jerk epilepsy) was first described in 1956 by Dieter Janz, who called it impulsive petit mal because of the sudden jerking (myoclonic) seizures that are a prominent part of the syndrome. The syndrome is characterized by myoclonic seizures of arms and legs, especially on awakening (Epilepsy Foundation, 2005c).

Explanation Juvenile myoclonic epilepsy generally appears at puberty but may have existed prior to that time. It is usually not outgrown and is associated with generalized tonic-clonic seizures (see OHI 17.10). Seizures may be precipitated by sleep deprivation, early awakening, alcohol and drug use, stress, strong emotion, photic stimulation, and menstruation (Epilepsy Foundation, 2005c).

OHI 17.06 Epilepsy with Nocturnal Seizures

Definition Some people experience seizures only during sleep; these are called nocturnal seizures. They could also occur during the day if the person were to fall asleep. This does not describe the form that the seizures take, only the time when they occur.

Explanation Nocturnal seizures are usually tonic-clonic. They might occur just after a person has fallen asleep, just before waking, during daytime sleep, or while in a state of drowsiness. People who experience nocturnal seizures may find it difficult to wake up or stay awake. Although unaware of having had a seizure while asleep, they may arise with a headache, have temper tantrums, or engage in destructive behavior throughout the day.

Nocturnal seizures are highly uncommon, and their mechanisms are poorly understood. The majority of people with nocturnal seizures have idiopathic epilepsy, and there is evidence in the electroencephalogram that sleep enhances epileptic discharges, though daytime recordings may appear to be normal. However, if a pattern of limiting seizures to the hours of slumber is maintained, the chance of their occurring during the daytime is greatly reduced (Epilepsy Ontario, 2005).

OHI 17.07 Epilepsy with Partial Seizures

Definition During partial seizures, the disturbance in brain activity begins in or involves one part of the brain. These seizures are sometimes known as focal seizures. A person's experiences during the seizure depend on which part of the brain is being affected (National Society for Epilepsy, 2002).

Simple partial seizures are sometimes called *warnings* or *auras*. For some people, a simple partial seizure is a warning to the person that another type of seizure is going to happen (National Society for Epilepsy, 2005).

Explanation Patients with simple focal seizures do not lose consciousness and are aware and remember the events that occur at the time. Patients with complex partial seizures have abnormal consciousness and may or may not remember any or all of the symptoms or events surrounding the seizure (National Society for Epilepsy, 2005).

OHI 17.08 Epilepsy with Secondarily Generalized Seizure

Definition For some people, either of these partial seizures may spread to involve the entire brain. This is called a secondarily generalized seizure, and the person will lose consciousness. If this spread is rapid, the person may not be aware of the partial seizure onset. The whole of the brain is involved, and consciousness is lost. These seizures often occur with no warning, and the person will have no memory of the event (National Society for Epilepsy, 2005).

Explanation Secondarily generalized seizures are predominant in 16 percent of all children and 9 percent of all adults with seizure disorders. Most people with complex partial seizures and many with simple partial seizures experience a secondarily generalized seizure at some point. When they occur frequently, the chances for future partial seizures may be increased. Secondarily generalized seizures occur infrequently and are easily controlled by antiepileptic medication (Epilepsy Ontario, 2005).

OHI17.09 Epilepsy with Simple Partial Seizures

Definition In simple partial seizures, consciousness is not impaired. The seizure may be confined to rhythmical twitching of one limb or part of a limb, or to unusual tastes or sensations such as pins and needles in a specific part of the body. Simple partial seizures sometimes develop into other sorts of seizures and may be referred to as a warning or aura (National Society for Epilepsy, 2005).

Explanation People experiencing a simple partial seizure can talk and answer questions. They will remember what went on during the seizure. Simple partial seizures take different forms in different people (Epilepsy Ontario, 2005).

OHI 17.10 Epilepsy with Tonic-Clonic Convulsive Seizure

Definition The most recognized type of seizure is the generalized tonic-clonic convulsive seizure, sometimes called a grand mal seizure (National Society for Epilepsy, 2002).

Explanation In the first part of the seizure, the person becomes rigid and may fall. The muscles then relax and tighten rhythmically, causing the person to convulse. At the start of the seizure, the person may cry out, become stiff (if they are still standing they usually fall backwards), and may bite their tongue or cheek (National Society for Epilepsy, 2005). Breathing may become labored, and the person may be incontinent. After the seizure, the person may feel tired, confused, or have a headache and may need to rest to recover fully (National Society for Epilepsy, 2005).

OHI 17.11 Epilepsy with Tonic Seizures

Definition In tonic seizures, there is general stiffening of the muscles without rhythmical jerking. The person may fall to the ground with consequent risk of injury, but generally recovery is quick.

Explanation Tonic seizures are characterized by facial and truncal muscle spasms, flexion or extension of the upper and lower extremities, and impaired consciousness. Several types of tonic seizures exist. Those grouped with absence, myoclonic, and atonic seizures are nonconvulsive and tend to be brief. The more prolonged seizures usually are convulsive and may manifest pupillary dilation, tachycardia, apnea, cyanosis, salivation, and the loss of bladder or bowel control (Epilepsy Ontario, 2005).

OHI 17.12 Other Types of Epilepsy

OHI 18.00 Lead Poisoning

Definition Lead is a metal that can make infants and young children ill, though many of those affected never look sick. Sometimes children with lead poisoning can have learning disabilities and other health problems. Lead poisoning can be detected and it can be prevented (U.S. Environmental Protection Agency, 2005).

Diagnostic Symptoms Lead can harm virtually every system in the human body. It is particularly harmful to the developing brain and nervous system of fetuses and young children. In many cases. there are no visible symptoms of elevated blood lead levels or lead poisoning (U.S. Environmental Protection Agency, 2005).

The accumulation of lead usually is gradual, building up unnoticed until levels become dangerous and cause signs and symptoms. The signs and symptoms of lead poisoning in children are nonspecific and may include (Mayo Clinic, 2004d):

- Irritability
- Loss of appetite
- Weight loss
- Sluggishness
- Abdominal pain
- Vomiting
- Constipation
- Pallor from anemia

Further Key Points The main treatment for lead poisoning is to stop the exposure. Removing the lead from a person's environment helps to ensure a decline in blood lead levels. The longer a person is exposed to lead, the greater the likelihood is that damage to the person's health will result. In some cases, medications are used to lower blood lead levels U.S. Environmental Protection Agency, 2005).

OHI 19.00 Lyme Disease

Definition Lyme disease is caused by a bacterial organism that is transmitted to humans by the bite of an infected tick. Most people bitten by an infected tick develop a characteristic skin rash around the area of the bite (National Institute of Neurological Disorders and Stroke, 2005h).

Diagnostic Symptoms Diagnostic symptoms of Lyme disease include (National Institute of Neurological Disorders and Stroke, 2005i; U.S. Department of Health and Human Services, 2003):

- A flat or slightly raised red lesion at the site of the tick bite (can be larger than one to three inches in diameter, often with a clear area in the center)
- Fever
- Headache
- Lethargy
- Muscle pain
- Stiff neck
- Joint inflammation in the knees and other large joints

Further Key Points Most individuals with Lyme disease respond well to antibiotics and have full recovery. In a few patients symptoms of persisting infection may continue or recur, requiring additional antibiotic treatment. Varying degrees of permanent joint or nervous system damage may develop in patients with late chronic Lyme disease. In rare cases, some individuals may die from Lyme disease and its complications.

OHI 20.00 Marfan Syndrome

Definition Marfan syndrome is a heritable condition that affects the connective tissue. The primary purpose of connective tissue is to hold the body together and provide a framework for growth and development. In Marfan syndrome, the connective tissue is defective and does not act as it should. Because connective tissue is found throughout the body, Marfan syndrome can affect many body systems, including the skeleton, eyes, heart and blood vessels, nervous system, skin, and lungs (National Institute of Arthritis and Musculoskeletal and Skin Diseases, 2001b).

Diagnostic Symptoms Diagnostic symptoms of Marfan syndrome include (U.S. National Library of Medicine, 2004h):

- Abnormally shaped chest
- Arms, legs, fingers, and toes often long compared to the rest of the body
- Curvature of the spine (scoliosis)
- Flat feet
- Loose joints
- Nearsightedness (myopia)
- Oversized or malfunctioning heart valves, especially the mitral valve
- Problems with the lens of the eye not being centered correctly
- Stretch marks, even without weight gain
- Arched roof of mouth crowding the teeth
- Typically tall and slender
- Weakened walls of major arteries
- Weakness in abdominal wall
- Widening (dilation) of aorta

Further Key Points This condition is inherited in an autosomal-dominant pattern, which means one copy of the altered gene is sufficient to cause the disorder. About 75 percent of people with Marfan syndrome inherit the mutation from one affected parent. About 25 percent of Marfan cases result from a new mutation in the gene. These cases occur in people with no history of the disorder in their family (U.S. National Library of Medicine, 2005h).

OHI 21.00 Oral-Facial Clefts

Definition An oral-facial cleft is a birth defect. A cleft lip is an opening in the upper lip, usually just below the nose. A cleft palate is an opening in the roof of the mouth (hard palate) or in the soft tissue at the back of the mouth (soft palate).

Two major types of oral-facial clefts are cleft lip/palate and isolated cleft palate. Babies with cleft lip/palate have a cleft lip. which usually is accompanied by cleft palate. In isolated cleft palate, the cleft palate occurs by itself, without cleft lip or other malformations. These two forms of oral-facial clefts are considered separate birth defects. Here we refer to each specific type of cleft by name and use the term *oral-facial cleft* when the information applies to both (March of Dimes, 2005b).

Diagnostic Symptoms A doctor can diagnose cleft lip or cleft palate by examining the newborn baby. A newborn with an oral-facial cleft may be referred to a team of medical specialists soon after birth. Rarely, a partial, or "submucous," cleft palate may not be diagnosed for several months or even years.

The major symptom of a cleft lip or cleft palate is a visible opening in the lip or palate. Other symptoms can occur as a result of an oral-facial cleft (Somerset Medical Center 2005):

- Feeding problems (especially with cleft palate)
- Problems with speech development
- Dental problems, including missing teeth, especially when the cleft lip extends to the upper gum area
- Recurrent middle ear infections
- Hearing problems

Further Key Points Cleft palate occurs alone less often, appearing in approximately 1 in 2,000 babies. Unlike the risk for cleft lip/palate, the risk for isolated cleft palate appears to be similar across all racial groups. Another difference from cleft lip/palate is that females are affected more often than males (March of Dimes, 2005b).

OHI 21.01 Cleft Lip

Definition Cleft lip and palate are congenital (present from before birth) abnormalities that affect the upper lip and the hard and soft palate of the mouth. Severity of the abnormalities may range from a small notch in the lip to a complete fissure (groove) extending into the roof of the mouth and nose. These features may occur separately or together (U.S. National Library of Medicine, 2004b).

Explanation The symptoms of cleft lip include:

- Separation of the lip alone
- Separation of the palate
- Separation of the lip and palate
- Varying amounts of nasal distortion
- Recurrent ear infections
- Failure to gain weight
- Nasal regurgitations during bottle feeding
- Growth retardation
- Misaligned teeth
- Poor speech
- Feeding problems (U.S. National Library of Medicine, 2004b)

OHI 21.01a **Bilateral Cleft Lip** A cleft lip that occurs on both sides is referred to as a bilateral cleft lip.

OHI 21.01b **Unilateral Cleft Lip** A cleft lip on only one side is referred to as a unilateral cleft lip.

OHI 21.02 Cleft Palate

Definition A cleft palate is an opening in the roof of the mouth (hard palate) or in the soft tissue at the back of the mouth (soft palate). In the majority of cases, a cleft lip and cleft palate occur together (Somerset Medical Center, 2005).

Explanation The major symptom of a cleft palate is a visible opening in the palate. Other symptoms can occur as a result of an oral-facial cleft:

- Feeding problems (especially with cleft palate)
- Problems with speech development
- Dental problems, including missing teeth, especially when the cleft lip extends to the upper gum area
- Recurrent middle ear infections
- Hearing problems (Somerset Medical Center, 2005).

OHI 21.02a **Bilateral Cleft Lip** A cleft palate on both sides is referred to as a bilateral cleft palate.

OHI 21.02b **Unilateral Cleft Palate** A cleft palate on only one side is referred to as a unilateral cleft palate.

OHI 22.00 Osteogenesis Imperfecta

Definition Osteogenesis imperfecta (OI) is a genetic disorder characterized by bones that break easily, often from little or no apparent cause. There are at least four recognized forms of the disorder, representing a range of severities. For example, a person may have just a few or as many as several hundred fractures in a lifetime (National Institutes of Health Osteoporosis and Related Bone Diseases, 2004). Type I osteogenesis imperfecta is the mildest form of the disorder, and type II is the most severe.

Diagnostic Symptoms Diagnostic symptoms of osteogenesis imperfecta include (U.S. National Library of Medicine, 2005f).

- Fragile bones
- Frequent bone fractures
- Brittle teeth
- Hearing loss in some cases
- A blue or gray tint to the part of the eye that is usually white (the sclera)
- Curvature of the spine (scoliosis)
- Loose joints

Further Key Points The prognosis for an individual with OI varies greatly depending on the number and severity of symptoms. Despite numerous fractures, restricted activity, and short stature, most adults and children with OI lead productive and successful lives.

OHI 23.00 Rheumatic Fever

Definition Rheumatic fever is an inflammatory disease that may develop after an infection with streptococcus bacteria (such as strep throat or scarlet fever) and can involve the heart, joints, skin, and brain (U.S. National Library of Medicine, 2005h). Although rheumatic fever can occur at any age, it most frequently occurs in children between the ages of six and fifteen years. The disease is twice as common in females as it is in males (Mayo Clinic, 2005e). At present, it is considered a rare complication of strep throat in the United States, although it used to be much more common. It is still not known what the mechanism causing disease is, but it is likely to be mediated by the immune system (Karibean, 2000).

Diagnostic Symptoms Diagnostic symptoms of rheumatic fever include (Mayo Clinic, 2005e; U.S. National Library of Medicine, 2005d):

- Abdominal pain
- Cardiac (heart) involvement that may be asymptomatic or may result in shortness of breath or chest pain
- Epistaxis (nosebleeds)
- Fever
- Joint pain, migratory arthritis—involving primarily knees, elbows, ankles, and wrists
- Joint swelling; redness or warmth
- Skin nodules
- Skin rash (erythema marginatum)
- Sydenham's chorea—emotional instability, muscular weakness, and rapid, uncoordinated jerky movements affecting primarily the face, feet, and hands

Further Key Points Rheumatic fever is not as common in the United States today as it was at the start of the twentieth century, before the widespread use of the antibiotic penicillin. Outbreaks do occur periodically, however. Rheumatic fever is still common in developing countries.

OHI 24.00 Tuberculosis

Definition Tuberculosis (TB) is a disease caused by bacteria called *Mycobacterium tuberculosis.* The bacteria usually attack the lungs. But TB bacteria can attack any part of the body, such as the kidney, spine, and brain. If not treated properly, TB can be fatal. In fact, it was once the leading cause of death in the United States (National Center for HIV, STD, and TB Prevention, 2005).

Diagnostic Symptoms Diagnostic symptoms of TB depend on where in the body the TB bacteria are growing. TB bacteria usually grow in the lungs. TB in the lungs may cause symptoms such as:

- A bad cough that lasts longer than two weeks
- Pain in the chest
- Coughing up blood or sputum (phlegm from deep inside the lungs)

Other symptoms of active TB disease are:

- Weakness or fatigue
- Weight loss
- No appetite
- Chills
- Fever
- Sweating at night (National Center for HIV, STD, and TB Prevention, 2005).

Further Key Points Many people think tuberculosis is a disease of the past, but it is still a leading killer of young adults worldwide. Some 2 billion people (one-third of the world's population) are infected with *M. tuberculosis*. TB is a chronic bacterial infection that is spread through the air and usually infects the lungs, although other organs are sometimes involved. Most persons who are infected with *M. tuberculosis* harbor the bacterium without symptoms, but many develop active TB disease. Each year, 8 million people worldwide develop active TB, and 3 million die (World Health Organization, 2005).

OHI 25.00 Viral Hepatitis

Definition Hepatitis is inflammation of the liver. Several different viruses cause viral hepatitis. They are named the hepatitis A, B, C, D, and E viruses. All viruses cause acute, or short-term, viral hepatitis. The hepatitis B, C, and D viruses can also cause chronic hepatitis, in which the infection is prolonged, and sometimes lifelong (National Digestive Diseases Information Clearinghouse, 2003).

Diagnostic Symptoms Diagnostic symptoms of viral hepatitis include (National Center for Infectious Diseases, 2005; National Digestive Diseases Information Clearinghouse, 2003):

- Abdominal pain
- Dark urine

- Diarrhea
- Fatigue
- Headache
- Jaundice (yellowing of the skin and eyes)
- Loss of appetite
- Low grade fever
- Nausea
- Vomiting

Further Key Points The number of new infections per year has declined from an average of 240,000 in the 1980s to about 30,000 in 2003. Most infections are due to illegal injection drug use.

Transfusion-associated cases occurred prior to blood donor screening; it now occurs in less than one per million transfused units of blood. An estimated 3.9 million (1.8 percent) Americans have been infected with Hepatitis C Virus (HCV), of whom 2.7 million are chronically infected (Centers for Disease Controls and Prevention, 2005b).

Types of Viral Hepatitis

OHI 25.01 Hepatitis A

Definition Hepatitis A is transmitted by contaminated food or water or contact with a person who is ill with the disease. The hepatitis A virus is shed in the stools of an infected person during the incubation period of fifteen to forty-five days before symptoms occur and during the first week of illness. Blood and other bodily secretions may also be infectious (U.S. National Library of Medicine, 2004e).

Explanation Symptoms of hepatitis A include:

- Jaundice
- Fatigue
- Loss of appetite
- Nausea and vomiting
- Low-grade fever
- Pale or clay-colored stools
- Dark urine
- Generalized itching (U.S. National Library of Medicine, 2004e)

OHI

OHI 25.02 Hepatitis B

Definition Disease spread through contact with infected blood, through sex with an infected person, and from mother to child during childbirth. Most people who become infected with hepatitis B get rid of the virus within six months. A short infection is known as an acute case of hepatitis B.

Approximately 10 percent of people infected with the hepatitis B virus develop a chronic, lifelong infection. People with chronic infection may have symptoms, but many of these patients never develop symptoms. These patients are sometimes referred to as carriers and can spread the disease to others. Having chronic hepatitis B increases the chance of permanent liver damage, including cirrhosis (scarring of the liver) and liver cancer (U.S. National Library of Medicine, 2005f).

Explanation Symptoms of hepatitis B include:

- Fatigue
- Malaise
- Joint aches
- Low-grade fever
- Nausea
- Vomiting
- Loss of appetite
- Abdominal pain
- Jaundice
- Dark urine

OHI 25.03 Hepatitis C

Definition Hepatitis C is an inflammation of the liver caused by infection with the hepatitis C virus. (U.S. National Library of Medicine, 2004g). This disease spreads primarily through contact with infected blood and, less commonly, sexual contact and childbirth. People at risk are injection drug users, people who have sex with an infected person, people who have multiple sex partners, health care workers, infants born to infected women, hemodialysis patients, and people who received a transfusion of blood or blood products before July 1992 or clotting factors made before 1987.

Explanation Many people who are infected with the hepatitis C do not have symptoms. Hepatitis C is often detected during blood tests for a routine physical or other medical procedure. If the infection has been present for many years, the liver may be permanently scarred—a condition called cirrhosis. In many cases, there may be no symptoms of the disease until cirrhosis has developed (U.S. National Library of Medicine, 2004g).

OHI 25.04 Hepatitis D

Definition Hepatitis D (HDV) is a viral infection of the liver that can be acquired only if a person has active hepatitis B (HBV) (American Social Health Association, 2005a).

Explanation Many with both HBV and HDV may or may not develop symptoms. When present, symptoms are similar to those of HBV. People with both HBV and HDV are more likely to have sudden, severe symptoms, called fulminant hepatitis. Those who are infected with both HBV and HDV are at greater risk for developing serious complications associated with chronic liver disease. People infected with HBV and HDV may become chronically infected and may be contagious from time to time for the rest of their lives (American Social Health Association, 2005a).

OHI 25.05 Hepatitis E

Definition Hepatitis E, known as enteric non-A, non-B, is a viral hepatitis most commonly found in geographical areas lacking clean water and sanitation. This disease is spread through food or water contaminated by feces from an infected person. This disease is uncommon in the United States. People at risk are international travelers, people living in areas where hepatitis E outbreaks are common, and people who live or have sex with an infected person (American Social Health Association, 2005b).

Explanation Symptoms of hepatitis E resemble those of hepatitis A:

- Low-grade fever
- Malaise (feeling of ill health)
- Anorexia (lack of appetite)
- Nausea
- Abdominal discomfort
- Dark-colored urine
- Jaundice

OHI 25.06 Other Forms of Hepatitis Not Otherwise Listed

OHI 26.00 Other Types of Health Impairments

References

Aicardi Syndrome Foundation. (2006). *Aicardi syndrome: General information.* Retrieved April 4, 2006, from http://www.aicardisyndrome.org/index.php?pname=whatis.

Allergy Relief Center. (2006). *Information on dust mite allergies allergy, dust mite spray, and house dust mites.* Retrieved April 23, 2006, from http://www.theallergyrelief center.com/dust_mite_allergy.htm.

American Academy of Allergy, Asthma and Immunology. (2002). *Exercise induced asthma.* Retrieved April 8, 2006 from http://www.aaaai.org/patients/allergic_ conditions/exercise_induced_asthma.stm.

American Academy of Allergy, Asthma and Immunology. (2005a). *Do you have good asthma control?* Retrieved April 5, 2005, from http://www.aaaai.org/patients/topicof themonth/0505/.

American Academy of Allergy, Asthma and Immunology. (2005b). *The allergy report page.* Retrieved April 5, 2005, from http://www.theallergyreport.org/.

American Academy of Dermatology. (2005). *Psoriasis.* Retrieved April 15, 2005, from http://www.aad.org/default.htm.

American Academy of Family Physicians. (2005). *Allergies.* Retrieved April 25, 2005, from http://www.aafp.org/.

American Academy of Orthopaedic Surgeons. (2004). *Bone tumor.* Retrieved April 18, 2005, from http://orthoinfo.aaos.org/fact/thr_report.cfm?Thread_ID=278&top category=About%20Orthopaedics.

American Autoimmune Related Diseases Association. (2003). *Autoimmune related diseases.* Retrieved April 16, 2005, from http://www.aarda.org/qa_frames.html.

American Cancer Society. (2005). *How is sarcoma diagnosed?* Retrieved April 17, 2005, from http://www.cancer.org/docroot/cri/content/cri_2_4_3x_how_is_sarcoma_ diagnosed_38.asp?sitearea=cri.

American Diabetes Association. (2005). *Overview of diabetes.* Retrieved April 16, 2005, from http://www.diabetes.org/home.jsp.

American Gastroenterological Association. (2006). *Lactose intolerance.* Retrieved January 7, 2006, from http://www.gastro.org/wmspage.cfm?parm1=854.

American Lung Association. (2005). *Asthma.* Retrieved April 19, 2005, from http:// www.lungusa.org/site/pp.asp?c=dvLUK9O0E&b=33276.

American Psychiatric Association. (2003). *Diagnostic and statistical manual of mental disorders* (DSM-IV-TR). Washington, DC: Author.

American Social Health Association. (2005a). *Facts and answers about STD's: Information to live by—Hepatitis D.* Retrieved April 19, 2005, from http://www.ashastd.org/stdfaqs/hepd.html#what.

American Social Health Association. (2005b). *Facts and answers about STD's: Information to live by-Hepatitis E.* Retrieved April 16, 2005, from http://www.ashastd.org/stdfaqs/hepe.html#what.

Angelman Syndrome Foundation. (2004). *Angelman syndrome.* Retrieved April 23, 2005, from http://www.angelman.org/angel/.

Asthma and Allergy Foundation of America. (2005). *Asthma: An overview.* Retrieved April 19, 2005, from http://www.aafa.org/display.cfm?id=8.

Buteyko Asthma Management. (1999). *Types of asthma.* Retrieved April 16, 2005, from http://www.beaconliteracy.com/r_dyslexia.html.

Centers for Disease Control and Prevention. (2005a). *FAQ about diabetes.* Retrieved January 13, 2006, from http://www.cdc.gov/diabetes/faq/basics.htm.

Centers for Disease Control and Prevention. (2005b). *Viral hepatitis.* Retrieved April 16, 2005, from http://www.cdc.gov/.

Cleveland Clinic. (2006). *Allergies.* Retrieved April 13, 2006, from http://www.clevelandclinic.org/health/health-info/docs/1900/1958.asp?index=8632.

Crohn's & Colitis Foundation of America. (2005). *Crohn's disease.* Retrieved April 11, 2005, from http://www.ccfa.org/.

Deutsch Smith, S. (2004). *Introduction to special education: Teaching in the age of opportunity* (4th ed.). Boston: Allyn & Bacon.

Ehlers Danlos Foundation. (2006). *Ehlers Danlos syndrome.* Retrieved April 13, 2006, from http://www.ednf.org/abouteds/content/view/12/30/.

eMedicine. (2005). *Cancer.* Retrieved April 11, 2005, from http://www.emedicine.com/cgi-bin/foxweb.exe/searchengine@/em/searchengine?boolean=and&book=all&maxhits=100&HiddenURL=&query=cancer.

Endocrine and Metabolic Diseases Information Service. (2002). *Cushing's syndrome.* Bethesda, MD: National Institutes of Health. NIH Publication No. 02–3007.]

Endocrine and Metabolic Diseases Information Service. (2004). *Addison's disease.* Bethesda, MD: National Institutes of Health.

Epilepsy Foundation. (2005a). *Complex partial seizures.* Retrieved April 19, 2005, from http://www.epilepsyfoundation.org/answerplace/Medical/seizures/types/partialSeizures/complex.cfm.

Epilepsy Foundation. (2005b). *Epilepsy and seizure statistics.* Retrieved April 19, 2005, from http://www.epilepsyfoundation.org/answerplace/statistics.cfm.

Epilepsy Foundation. (2005c). *Juvenile myoclonic epilepsy.* Retrieved April 11, 2005, from http://www.epilepsyfoundation.org/answerplace/Medical/seizures/syndromes/juvenilemyoclonic.cfm.

Epilepsy Ontario. (2005). *Epilepsy.* Retrieved April 19, 2005, from http://www.epilepsyontario.org/.

Epilepsy.com. (2004). *Epilepsy.* Retrieved April 19, 2005, from http://epilepsy.com/.

Health on the Net Foundation. (2002). *Allergy glossary.* Retrieved April 29, 2005, from http://www.hon.ch/Library/Theme/Allergy/Glossary/intrinsic_asthma.html.

Heart Center Online. (2005). *Congenital heart disease.* Retrieved April 29, 2005, from http://heart.healthcentersonline.com/congenitalheartdisease/congenitalheart.cfm.

Heller, K. W., Frederic, L. D., Best, S., Dykes, M. K., & Cohen, E. T. (2000). Specialized health care procedures in the schools: Training and service delivery. *Exceptional Children, 66,* 173–186.

Hormone Foundation. (2005). *Endocrine disorders.* Retrieved April 29, 2005, from http://www.hormone.org/.

Humane Society of the United States. (2006). *Pet allergies.* Retrieved February 22, from http://www.hsus.org/pets/pet_care/allergies_to_pets/index.html.

Jensen, M. (2005). *Introduction to emotional and behavioral disorders: Recognizing and managing problems in the classroom.* Upper Saddle River, NJ: Pearson.

Journal of the American Medical Association. (2004a, February 4). *Epilepsy, 291* (4). Retrieved April 29, 2005, from http://jama.ama-assn.org/cgi/content/full/291/4/514.

Journal of the American Medical Association. (2004b, January 28). *Childhood leukemia, 291*(5), 514.

Journal of the American Medical Association. (2005, April 13). *Hyperparathyroidism, 293(*14). Retrieved April 29, 2005, from http://jama.ama-assn.org/cgi/content/full/293/14/1818.

Karibean, A. (2000). *Rheumatic fever.* Retrieved April 29, 2005, from http://www.keepkidshealthy.com/welcome/conditions/rheumaticfever.html.

Leibrock, C., & and Terry, J. E. (1999). *Beautiful universal design.* Hoboken, NJ: Wiley

Leukemia & Lymphoma Society. (2005). *Non-Hodgkin lymphoma.* Retrieved April 9, 2005, from http://www.leukemia.org/hm_lls.

Leukemia & Lymphoma Society. (2006). *Leukemia facts and statistics.* Retrieved March 30, 2006, from http://www.leukemia-lymphoma.org/all_page?item_id=9346.

Loyola University Health System. (2000). *Alpers disease.* Retrieved February 11, 2006, from http://www.luhs.org/HEALTH/kbasc/htm/nord/610/nord610.htm.

Lupus Foundation of America. (2006). *FAQ about lupus.* Retrieved April 9, 2005, from http://www.lupus.org/education/faq.html#1.

Maine School Health Advisory Committee. (2006). *Congenital heart disease.* Augusta: Maine Department of Education.

March of Dimes. (2005a). *Congenital heart defects.* Retrieved April 9, 2005, from http://www.marchofdimes.com/professionals/681_1212.asp.

March of Dimes. (2005b). *Oral-facial clefts.* Retrieved April 9, 2005, from http://marchofdimes.org/.

Mayo Clinic. (2004a). *Anemia.* Retrieved April 24, 2005, from http://www.mayoclinic.com/invoke.cfm?id=DS00321.

Mayo Clinic. (2004b). *Cystic fibrosis.* Retrieved April 24, 2005, from http://www.mayoclinic.com/invoke.cfm?id=DS00287.

Mayo Clinic. (2004c). *Hay fever.* Retrieved April 24, 2005, from http://www.mayoclinic.com/invoke.cfm?id=DS00174.

Mayo Clinic. (2004d). *Lead poisoning.* Retrieved April 24, 2005, from http://www.mayoclinic.com/invoke.cfm?id=FL00068.

Mayo Clinic. (2004e). *Multiple sclerosis.* Retrieved April 14, 2005, from http://www.mayoclinic.com/invoke.cfm?id=DS00188.

Mayo Clinic. (2005a). *Addisons disease.* Retrieved April 24, 2005, from http://www.mayoclinic.com/invoke.cfm?id=DS00361.

Mayo Clinic. (2005b). *Hyperparathyroidism.* Retrieved April 4, 2005, from http://www.mayoclinic.com/invoke.cfm?id=DS00396.

Mayo Clinic (2005c). *Latex allergy.* Retrieved November 3, 2006, from http://www.mayoclinic.com/health/latex/-allergy/DS00621.

Mayo Clinic. (2005d). *Liver cancer.* Retrieved April 14, 2005, from http://www.mayoclinic.com/invoke.cfm?id=DS00399.

Mayo Clinic. (2005e). *Rheumatic fever.* Retrieved April 4, 2005, from http://www.mayoclinic.com/invoke.cfm?id=DS00250.

Medical College of Wisconsin. (2003). *Alexander disease.* Retrieved March 13, 2006, from http://healthlink.mcw.edu/article/921383447.html.

Medical Webends.com. (2005). *Blood disorders.* Retrieved April 4, 2005, from http://medical.webends.com/r/Blood%20Physiology.

MIMS Consumer Health Group. (2005). *Bronchial asthma and cardiac asthma.* Retrieved April 4, 2005, from http://www.mydr.com.au/default.asp?article=2709.

National Cancer Institute. (2002a). *Bone cancer: Q&A.* Retrieved May 12, 2005, from http://cis.nci.nih.gov/fact/6_26.htm.

National Cancer Institute. (2002b). *Soft tissue sarcomas: Questions and answers.* Retrieved May 12, 2005, from http://www.leukemia-lymphoma.org/all_page?item_id=7087.

National Cancer Institute. (2002c). *What you need to know about liver cancer.* Retrieved May 12, 2005, from http://www.cancer.gov/cancertopics/wyntk/liver/page5.

National Cancer Institute. (2003). *What is leukemia*? Retrieved May 12, 2005, from http://www.cancer.gov/cancertopics/wyntk/leukemia/page2.

National Cancer Institute. (2005). *Non-Hodgkin's lymphoma.* Retrieved August 20, 2005, from http://www.nci.nih.gov/cancertopics/types/non-hodgkins-lymphoma.

National Cancer Institute. (2006). *Young people with cancer: A handbook for parents.* Retrieved March 3, 2006, from http://www.cancer.gov/cancertopics/youngpeople/page2.

National Center for HIV, STD, and TB Prevention. (2005). *Tuberculosis.* Retrieved May 22, 2005, from http://marchofdimes.org/.

National Center for Infectious Diseases. (2005). *Viral hepatitis.* Retrieved May 22, 2005, from http://www.cdc.gov/ncidod/.

National Diabetes Information Clearinghouse. (2005a). *What diabetes is.* Retrieved May 22, 2005, from http://www.diabetes.niddk.nih.gov/dm/pubs/type1and2/what.htm.

National Diabetes Information Clearinghouse. (2005b). *Diabetes: An overview.* Retrieved May 22, 2005, from http://diabetes.niddk.nih.gov/dm/pubs/overview/index.htm#types.

National Digestive Diseases Information Clearinghouse. (2003). *Crohn's disease-ulcerative colitis.* Retrieved May 2, 2005, from

National Heart, Lung and Blood Institute. (2004). *What is hemophilia*? Retrieved May 2, 2005, from http://www.nhlbi.nih.gov/health/dci/Diseases/hemophilia/hemophilia_what.html.

National Heart, Lung, and Blood Institute. (2005a). *Cystic fibrosis.* Retrieved April 3, 2006, from http://www.nhlbi.nih.gov/health/dci/Diseases/cf/cf_what.html.

National Heart, Lung, and Blood Institute. (2005b). *What is acongenital heart defect*? Retrieved June 12, 2005, from http://www.nhlbi.nih.gov/health/dci/Diseases/chd/chd_what.html.

National Heart, Lung, and Blood Institute. (2006a). *What is asthma?* Retrieved November 1, 2006, from http://www.nhlbi.nih.gov/health/dci/Diseases/Asthma/Asthma_WhatIs.html.

National Heart Lung and Blood Institute. (2006b). *What is sickle cell anemia?* Retrieved November 2, 2006, from http://www.nhlbi.nih.gov/health/dci/diseases/sca/SCA_whatis.html.

National Institute for Occupational Safety and Health. (1999). *Allergies.* Retrieved June 16, 2005, from http://www.cdc.gov/niosh/homepage.html.

National Institute of Allergy and Infectious Diseases. (2005). *Allergies.* Retrieved June 16, 2005, from http://www3.niaid.nih.gov/.

National Institute of Arthritis and Musculoskeletal and Skin Diseases. (2001a). *Ehlers-Danlos syndrome.* Retrieved June 16, 2005, from http://www.niams.nih.gov/hi/topics/connective/connective.htm.

National Institute of Arthritis and Musculoskeletal and Skin Diseases. (2001b). *Marfan syndrome: Q&A.* Retrieved June 26, 2005, from http://www.niams.nih.gov/hi/topics/marfan/marfan.htm.

National Institute of Arthritis and Musculoskeletal and Skin Diseases. (2002a). *Questions and answers about autoimmunity.* Retrieved October 20, 2006, from http://www.niams.nih.gov/hi/topics/autoimmune/autoimmunity.htm.

National Institute of Arthritis and Musculoskeletal and Skin Diseases. (2002b). *The many shades of lupus.* National Institute of Health Publication No: 01-4958. Washington, DC: Author.

National Institute of Arthritis and Musculoskeletal and Skin Diseases. (2003a). *Epidermolysis bullosa.* Bethesda, MD: National Institutes of Health.

National Institute of Arthritis and Musculoskeletal and Skin Diseases. (2003b). *Questions and answers about epidermolysis bullosa.* Bethesda, MD: National Institutes of Health.

National Institute of Arthritis and Musculoskeletal and Skin Diseases. (2003c). *Questions and answers about psoriasis.* Bethesda, MD: National Institutes of Health.

National Institute of Diabetes and Digestive and Kidney Diseases. (2002). *Multiple endocrine neoplasia MEN1.* Retrieved June 26, 2005, from http://www.niddk.nih.gov/health/endo/pubs/men1/men1.htm.

National Institute of Mental Health. (2005). *Attention deficit hyperactivity disorder (ADHD).* Retrieved June 29, 2005, from http://www.nimh.nih.gov/health information/adhdmenu.cfm.

National Institute of Neurological Disorders and Stroke. (2005a). *Aicardi syndrome.* Retrieved September 1, 2005, from http://www.ninds.nih.gov/disorders/aicardi/aicardi.htm.

National Institute of Neurological Disorders and Stroke. (2005b). *Alexander disease.* Retrieved September 1, 2005, from http://www.ninds.nih.gov/disorders/alexander_disease/alexander_disease.htm.

National Institute of Neurological Disorders and Stroke. (2005c). *Alpers disease.* Retrieved June 29, 2005, from http://www.ninds.nih.gov/disorders/alpersdisease/alpers disease.htm.

OHI

National Institute of Neurological Disorders and Stroke. (2005d). *Angelman syndrome.* Retrieved June 29, 2005, from http://www.ninds.nih.gov/disorders/angelman/angelman.htm.

National Institute of Neurological Disorders and Stroke. (2005e). *Cushing's syndrome information page.* Retrieved September 2, 2005, from http://www.ninds.nih.gov/disorders/cushings/cushings.htm.

National Institute of Neurological Disorders and Stroke. (2005f). *Epilepsy.* Retrieved September 2, 2005, from http://www.ninds.nih.gov/disorders/epilepsy/epilepsy.htm.

National Institute of Neurological Disorders and Stroke. (2005g). *Multiple sclerosis information page.* Retrieved September 2, 2005, from http://www.ninds.nih.gov/disorders/multiple_sclerosis/multiple_sclerosis.htm.

National Institute of Neurological Disorders and Stroke. (2005h). *Neurological complications of Lyme disease.* Retrieved September 2, 2005, from http://www.ninds.nih.gov/disorders/lyme/lyme.htm.

National Institute on Alcohol Abuse and Alcoholism. (2003). *Alcoholism.* Retrieved March 2, 2005, from http://www.niaaa.nih.gov/.

National Institute on Drug Abuse. (2003). *Commonly abused drugs.* Retrieved April 3, 2006, from www.nida.nih.gov/DrugPages/DrugsofAbuse.html.

National Institutes of Health Osteoporosis and Related Bone Diseases. (2004). *Facts about osteogenesis imperfecta.* Retrieved September 2, 2005, from http://www.osteo.org/newfile.asp?doc=i101i&doctype=HTML+Fact+Sheet&doctitle=Fast+Facts+on+Osteogenesis+Imperfecta.

National Jewish Medical and Research Center. (2005). *Nocturnal asthma.* Retrieved May 5, 2005, from http://www.nationaljewish.org/disease-info/diseases/asthma/about/types/nocturnal.aspx.

National Lupus Foundation. (2001). *Lupus.* Retrieved May 5, 2005, from http://www.lupus.org/.

National Organization for Rare Disorders. (2005). *Alexander disease.* Retrieved May 5, 2005, from http://www.rarediseases.org/.

National Society for Epilepsy. (2002). *Epilepsy: Information on seizures.* Retrieved May 5, 2005, from http://www.epilepsynse.org.uk/pages/info/leaflets/seizures.cfm.

National Society for Epilepsy. (2005). *Epilepsy: An introduction to epileptic seizures.* Chalfont St. Peter, Bucks, Great Britain: Author.

Nemours Foundation. (2004). *Pet allergies.* Retrieved March 3, 2006, from http://kidshealth.org/teen/diseases_conditions/allergies_immune/allergies.html.

Nemours Foundation. (2005a). *Blood.* Retrieved May 15, 2005, from http://kidshealth.org/parent/general/body_basics/blood.html.

Nemours Foundation. (2005b). *Crohns disease.* Retrieved May 15, 2005, from http://www.kidshealth.org/teen/diseases_conditions/digestive/ibd.html

Nemours Foundation. (2005c). *Cystic fibrosis.* Retrieved May 5, 2005, from http://kidshealth.org/kid/health_problems/heart/cystic_fibrosis.html.

Nemours Foundation. (2005d). *Inflammatory bowel diseases.* Retrieved May 15, 2005, from http://www.kidshealth.org/teen/diseases_conditions/digestive/ibd.html.

Pituitary Network Association. (2005). *Acromegaly.* Retrieved May 15, 2005, from http://www.pituitary.com/.

Sirvis, B. (1988). Physical disabilities. In E. Meyen & T. Skrtic (Eds.), *Exceptional children and youth: An introduction* (3rd ed.). Denver: Love Publishing.

Somerset Medical Center. (2005). *Oral-facial clefts (cleft lip and cleft palate).* Retrieved May 15, 2005, from http://www.somersetmedicalcenter.com/1300.cfm?InFrame.

Starbright Foundation. (2002). *STARBRIGHT healthcare goals.* Retrieved May 18, 2005, from http://www.starbright.org/about/goals.html.

Temple, L. (2000, February 15). Disputed health duties injected into teaching of disabled. *USA Today,* p. 9D.

Texas Heart Institute of St. Luke's Hospital. (2004). *Cyanosis.* Retrieved June 11, 2005, from http://www.texasheartinstitute.org/cyanosis.html.

Texas Heart Institute of St. Luke's Hospital. (2006). *Congenital heart disease.* Retrieved March 3, 2006, from http://www.tmc.edu/thi/congenit.html.

Turnbull, R., Turnbull, A., Shank, M., & Smith, S. J. (2004). *Exceptional lives: Special education in today's schools* (4th ed.). Upper Saddle River, NJ: Prentice Hall.

Turnbull, R., Turnbull, A., & Wehmeyer, M. (2007). *Exceptional lives: Special education in today's schools* (5th ed.). Upper Saddle River, NJ: Prentice Hall.

University Health Systems of Eastern Carolina. (2000). *Alpers disease.* Retrieved March 30, 2006, from http://www.uhseast.com/111961.cfm.

University of Maryland Medical Center. (2002). *Drug allergies.* Retrieved April 3, 2006, from http://www.umm.edu/careguides/allergy/allergy_drugallergies.html.

University of Maryland Medical Center. (2006). *Endocrinology health guide.* Retrieved November 1, 2006, from http://www.umm.edu/endocrine.

University of Virginia Health System. (2004). *Anatomy of the endocrine system.* Retrieved August 30, 2005, from http: www.healthsystem.virginia.edu/uvahealth/adult_endocrine/anatomy.cfm.

U.S. Department of Education. (2001). *The Twenty-Third Annual Report to Congress on the Implementation of IDEA.* Washington, DC: U.S. Department of Education.

U.S. Department of Education. (2004). *The Twenty-Sixth Annual Report to Congress on the Implementation of IDEA.* Washington, DC: U.S. Department of Education.

U.S. Department of Health and Human Services. (2001). *Hashimoto's thyroiditis.* Retrieved June 11, 2005, from http://www.4woman.gov/faq/hashimoto.htm.

U.S. Department of Health and Human Services. (2002). *Diabetes.* Retrieved April 11, 2005, from http://www.hhs.gov/diseases/index.shtml.

U.S. Department of Health and Human Services. (2003). *Lyme disease.* Retrieved June 19, 2005, from http://www.os.dhhs.gov/.

U.S. Environmental Protection Agency. (2005). *Lead poisoning.* Retrieved June 1, 2005, from http://www.epa.gov/lead/.

U.S. Food and Drug Administration. (2001, July-August). Food allergies: When food becomes the enemy. *FDA Consumer Magazine.*

U.S. National Library of Medicine. (2004a). *Anemia.* Retrieved April 30, 2006, from http://www.nlm.nih.gov/medlineplus/ency/article/000560.htm#

U.S. National Library of Medicine. (2004b). *Cleft lip.* Retrieved June 11, 2005, from http://www.nlm.nih.gov/medlineplus/cleftlipandpalate.html.

U.S. National Library of Medicine. (2004c). *Epilepsy.* Retrieved June 1, 2005, from http://www.nlm.nih.gov/medlineplus/epilepsy.html.

U.S. National Library of Medicine (2004d). *Graves' disease.* Retrieved June 11, 2005, from http://search.nlm.nih.gov/medlineplus/query?DISAMBIGUATION=true &FUNCTION=search&SERVER2=server2&SERVER1=server1&PARAMETER= Graves+disease.

U.S. National Library of Medicine. (2004e). *Hepatitis A.* Retrieved June 11, 2005, from http://www.nlm.nih.gov/medlineplus/ency/article/000278.htm.

U.S. National Library of Medicine. (2004f). *Hepatitis B.* Retrieved June 13, 2005, from http://www.nlm.nih.gov/medlineplus/ency/article/000279.htm.

U.S. National Library of Medicine. (2004g). *Hepatitis C.* Retrieved June 11, 2005, from http://www.nlm.nih.gov/medlineplus/hepatitisc.html.

U.S. National Library of Medicine. (2004h). *Marfan syndrome.* Retrieved June 17, 2005, from http://www.nlm.nih.gov/medlineplus/marfansyndrome.html.

U.S. National Library of Medicine. (2004i). *Non-cyanotic heart disease.* Retrieved June 11, 2005, from http://www.nlm.nih.gov/medlineplus/heartdiseases.html.

U.S. National Library of Medicine. (2004j). *Primary hyperparathyroidism.* Retrieved June 11, 2005, from http://www.nlm.nih.gov/medlineplus/ency/article/000384.htm# definition.

U.S. National Library of Medicine. (2004k). *Thyroid diseases.* Retrieved May 5, 2005, from http://www.nlm.nih.gov/medlineplus/thyroiddiseases.html.

U.S. National Library of Medicine. (2005a). *Aicardi syndrome.* Retrieved June 1, 2005, from http://search.nlm.nih.gov/medlineplus/query?DISAMBIGUATION=true &FUNCTION=search&SERVER2=server2&SERVER1=server1&PARAMETER= Aicardi+Syndrome&x=114&y=11.

U.S. National Library of Medicine. (2005b). *Alexander disease.* Retrieved June 1, 2005, from http://search.nlm.nih.gov/medlineplus/query?DISAMBIGUATION=true& FUNCTION=search&SERVER2=server2&SERVER1=server1&PARAMETER= Alexander+Disease&x=83&y=11.

U.S. National Library of Medicine. (2005c). *Allergies.* Retrieved June 13, 2005, from http://www.nlm.nih.gov/medlineplus/allergy.html.

U.S. National Library of Medicine. (2005d). *Ehlers-Danlos syndrome.* Retrieved June 13, 2005, from http://search.nlm.nih.gov/medlineplus/query?DISAMBIGUATION= true&FUNCTION=search&SERVER2=server2&SERVER1=server1&PARA METER=Ehlers-Danlos+syndrome&x=65&y=10.

U.S. National Library of Medicine. (2005e). *Marfan syndrome.* Retrieved June 13, 2005, from http://search.nlm.nih.gov/medlineplus/query?MAX=500&SERVER1=server1 &SERVER2=server2&PARAMETER=Marfan+syndrome&DISAMBIGUATION= true&FUNCTION=search&x=44&y=2.

U.S. National Library of Medicine. (2005f). *Osteogenesis imperfecta.* Retrieved June 13, 2005, from http://www.nlm.nih.gov/medlineplus/osteogenesisimperfecta.html.

U.S. National Library of Medicine. (2005g). *Psoriasis.* http://www.nlm.nih.gov/medlineplus/psoriasis.html.

U.S. National Library of Medicine. (2005h). *Rheumatic fever.* Retrieved June 13, 2005, from http://search.nlm.nih.gov/medlineplus/query?DISAMBIGUATION=true&FUNCTION=search&SERVER2=server2&SERVER1=server1&PARAMETER=Rheumatic+fever.

Williams, C. A., & Driscoll, D. J. (2005). Angelman syndrome. *Gene Reviews.* University of Washington.

World Federation of Hemophilia. (2005). *FAQ about hemophilia.* Retrieved June 13, 2005, from http://www.wfh.org/ShowDoc.asp?Rubrique=28&Document=42&ContentId=42#What_is_hemophilia?

World Health Organization. (2005). *Tuberculosis.* Retrieved June 1, 2005, from http://www.who.int/en/.

Yamamoto, F. (2002). *Case based pediatrics for medical students and residents.* Honolulu: University of Hawaii, John A. Burns School of Medicine.

Zwolski, R. (2005). *Tutorial on cough: Cough variant asthma.* Retrieved June 13, 2005, from http://www.pathoplus.com/cough.htm.

CHAPTER 6

MULTIPLE DISABILITIES

EDM CODE: MD

IDEA 2004 Definition of Multiple Disabilities

Under IDEA 2004, multiple disabilities:

> means concomitant [simultaneous] impairments (such as mental retardation-blindness, mental retardation-orthopedic impairment, etc.), the combination of which causes such severe educational needs that they cannot be accommodated in a special education program solely for one of the impairments. The term does not include deaf-blindness [34 C.F.R., sec. 300.7 (c)(7)]].

Overview of Multiple Disabilities

According to Deutsch-Smith (2004), people with multiple disabilities require ongoing and intensive supports across their school years and typically across their lives. For some, these supports may well be in only one life activity, but for many of these individuals, supports are needed for access and participation in mainstream society. Supports are necessary because most individuals with multiple disabilities require assistance in many adaptive areas.

No single definition covers all the conditions associated with severe and multiple disabilities. Schools usually link the two areas (severe disabilities and multiple disabilities) into a single category for students who have the most significant cognitive, physical, or communication impairments (Turnbull, Turnbull, & Wehmeyer, 2006).

Causes-Etiology of Multiple Disabilities

Multiple factors can cause disabilities. Heredity, problems during pregnancy, problems at birth, and incidents after birth can all lead to a lifelong set of challenges and sometimes even to multiple disabilities. In addition, it can be difficult to recognize early signs of illness or disability among children with multiple disabilities, which can result in permanent sensory impairment (Royal Institute for Deaf and Blind Children, 2005).

Prevalence of Multiple Disabilities

According to the U.S. Department of Education (2004), 131,225 children between the ages of six and twenty-one received special education services under the category of multiple disabilities. This makes up 2.2 percent of all school-age children receiving special education services

Age of Onset of Multiple Disabilities

Due to the various causes of multiple disabilities, no specific age of onset can be generalized to the entire school-age population that receives special education services. Some students classified with multiple disabilities have had this condition since birth (congenital), and other students attained this diagnosis during their development (acquired) as a result of accident, illness, or unknown cause.

Gender Features of Multiple Disabilities

Information on this topic is not available.

Cultural Features of Multiple Disabilities

Information on this topic is not available.

Familial Patterns of Multiple Disabilities

Information on this topic is not available.

Characteristics of Multiple Disabilities

Individuals with severe or multiple disabilities may exhibit a wide range of characteristics, depending on the combination and severity of disabilities and the person's age. There are, however, some traits they may share, including:

- Limited speech or communication
- Difficulty in basic physical mobility
- Tendency to forget skills through disuse
- Trouble generalizing skills from one situation to another
- A need for support in major life activities (for example, domestic, leisure, community, vocational; National Dissemination Center for Children with Disabilities, 2004).

Medical Implications of Multiple Disabilities

Multiple disabilities in an infant or young child require the coordinated efforts of multiple experts (one from every identified disability area). Because of the interactive, multiplicative effects of multiple disabilities, it is essential that intervention and programming efforts be focused cooperatively on functional tasks. Whenever possible, intervention should be aimed toward minimizing or preventing developmental delays. Since there seems to be increasing numbers of infants and young children with multiple disabilities, the cooperative approach to early intervention appears to have the best potential for enhancing the potential of these children (Texas School for the Blind and Visually Impaired, 2003).

A variety of medical problems may accompany severe disabilities. Examples include seizures, sensory loss, hydrocephalus, and scoliosis. These conditions should be considered when establishing school services (National Dissemination Center for Children with Disabilities, 2004).

Educational Implications of Multiple Disabilities

Early intervention, preschool, and educational programs with the appropriate support services are important to children with sensory and additional disabilities (NEC Foundation of America, 2001).

Students with severe and multiple disabilities are taught in a variety of settings, from totally segregated to fully inclusive. The doctrine of the least restrictive environment, as applied to students with severe and multiple disabilities, has usually resulted in placement in a special education classroom within a regular school. Now an increasing number of leaders in the field of severe and multiple disabilities are advocating for full inclusion for these students. Successful collaboration is essential if students are to be fully included in schools and community settings. Because the students' needs can be extensive, families, educators, physical and occupational therapists, speech and language pathologists, and medical personnel need to work closely with each other to ensure that students receive an appropriate and inclusive education. In addition, students without disabilities and community members need to understand their roles in the collaborative planning process (Turnbull, Turnbull, Shank, & Smith 2002).

In order to effectively address the considerable needs of individuals with sensory and additional disabilities, educational programs need to incorporate a variety of components, including language and communication development, social skill development, functional skill development (self-help skills), and vocational skill development.

Related services are of great importance, and the appropriate therapists need to work closely with classroom teachers and parents. Best practices indicate that related services are best offered during the natural routine of the school and community rather than by removing the student from class for isolated therapy (Ohio Coalition for the Education of Children with Disabilities, 2005).

Classroom arrangements must take into consideration students' needs for medications, special diets, or special equipment. Adaptive aids and equipment enable students to increase their range of functioning. The use of computers, augmentative and alternative computer communication systems, communication boards, head sticks, and adaptive switches are some of the technological advances that enable students with sensory and additional disabilities to participate more fully in integrated settings.

Integration or inclusion with peers without disabilities is important for the development of social skills and friendships for children with sensory and additional disabilities.

These conditions should be considered when establishing school services. A multidisciplinary team consisting of the student's parents, educational specialists, and medical therapeutic specialists in the areas in which the individual demonstrates problems should work together to plan and coordinate necessary services (National Dissemination Center for Children with Disabilities, 2004).

EDM Codes, Definitions, and Explanations of Multiple Disabilities

MD

Since the coding system for Multiple Disabilities requires two or more diagnoses, please refer to page 22 for examples on coding this category.

References

Deutsch-Smith, D. (2004). *Introduction to special education: Teaching in an age of opportunity* (5th ed.). Needham Heights, MA: Allyn & Bacon.

National Dissemination Center for Children with Disabilities (2004). *Severe and/or Multiple disabilities—Fact sheet #10.* Retrieved April 5, 2005, from http://www.nichcy.org/pubs/factshe/fs10txt.htm.

NEC Foundation of America. (2001). *Multiple disabilities: Educational implications.* Retrieved on February 4, 2006, from http://www.teachersandfamilies.com/sped/prof/multdis/education.html.

Ohio Coalition for the Education of Children with Disabilities. (2005). *What are multiple disabilities*? Retrieved March 18, 2006, from http://www.ocecd.org/ocecd/h_docs/whataremult.cfm.

Royal Institute for Deaf and Blind Children. (2005). *Causes of multiple disabilities.* Retrieved March 2, 2006, from http://www.ridbc.org.au/resources/md_causes.asp.

Texas School for the Blind and Visually Impaired. (2003). *Multiple disabilities.* Retrieved March 2, 2006, from http://www.tsbvi.edu/Education/infant/page5.htm.

Turnbull, A., Turnbull, R., Shank, M., & Smith, S. J. (2002). *Exceptional lives: Special education in today's schools* (3rd ed.). Upper Saddle River, NJ: Pearson

Turnbull, A., Turnbull, A., & Wehmeyer, M. L. (2006). *Exceptional lives: Special education in today's schools* (4th ed.). Upper Saddle River, NJ: Pearson.

U.S. Department of Education. (2004). *Twenty-Sixth Annual Report to Congress on the Implementation of the Individuals with Disabilities Education Act.* Washington, DC: Author.

CHAPTER 7
AUTISM

EDM CODE: AU

AU 1.00	**Asperger's Syndrome**	**AU 5.00**	**Hyperlexia**
AU 2.00	**Autistic Disorder**	**AU 6.00**	**Multiplex Developmental Disorder**
AU 3.00	**Childhood Disintegrative Disorder**	**AU 7.00**	**Rett Syndrome**
AU 4.00	**High-Functioning Autism**	**AU 8.00**	**Other Types of Autism-Be Specific**

IDEA 2004 Definition of Autism

Under IDEA 2004, autism is defined as:

> a developmental disability significantly affecting verbal and nonverbal communication and social interaction, usually evident before age 3 that adversely affects a child's educational performance. Other characteristics often associated with autism are engagement in repetitive activities and stereotyped movements, resistance to environmental change or change in daily routines, and unusual responses to sensory experiences. The term does not apply if a child's educational performance is adversely affected because the child has an emotional disturbance [34 C.F.R. 300.7(c)(1)].

Overview of Autism

Originally described in 1943 by Leo Kanner (Colarusso & O'Rourke, 2004), *autism,* also referred to as pervasive developmental disorder and autism spectrum disorder (ASD), is an increasingly popular term that refers to a broad definition of autism, including the classical form of the disorder, as well as closely related disabilities that share many of the core characteristics. The terms *autism spectrum disorders* and *pervasive developmental disorders* are used synonymously. Besides the classic form of autism (often referred to as autistic disorder; Turnbull, Turnbull, & Wehmeyer, 2007), ASD also includes the following diagnoses and classifications:

- Pervasive developmental disorder—not otherwise specified (PDD-NOS), which refers to a collection of features that resemble autism but may not be as severe or extensive (Westling & Fox, 2004; National Institute of Neurological Disorders and Stroke, 2005b)

- Rett's syndrome, which affects girls and is a genetic disorder with hard neurological signs (meaning those that are observable and indicative of brain damage), including seizures, that become more apparent with age (Colarusso & O'Rourke, 2004; Vaughn, Bos, & Schumm, 2003)
- Asperger's syndrome, which refers to individuals with autistic characteristics but relatively intact language abilities (Westling & Fox, 2004)
- Childhood disintegrative disorder, which refers to children whose development appears normal for the first few years, but then regresses with the loss of speech and other skills until the characteristics of autism are conspicuous (Kutscher, 2003)

Although the classical form of autism can be readily distinguished from other forms of ASD, the terms *autism* and *ASD* are often used interchangeably (Hunt & Marshall, 2005).

Individuals with autism and ASD vary widely in ability and personality. Individuals can exhibit severe mental retardation or be extremely gifted in their intellectual and academic accomplishments (Vaughn et al., 2003). Although many individuals prefer isolation and tend to withdraw from social contact, others show high levels of affection and enjoyment in social situations. Some people with autism appear lethargic and slow to respond, with more focus on objects instead of other people (Scott, Clark, & Brady, 2000). Others are very active and seem to interact constantly with preferred aspects of their environment.

Autism is a behavioral syndrome, which means that its definition is based on patterns of behaviors that a person exhibits.

Causes-Etiology of Autism

Autism is a neurological disability that is presumed to be present from birth and is always apparent before the age of three. Most researchers agree that the collection of symptoms constituting autism arises from a set of inherited factors (Rodier, 2000). Although autism affects the functioning of the brain, the specific cause of autism is unknown. In fact, it is widely assumed that there are likely multiple causes, each of which may be manifested in different forms, or subtypes, of autism.

In the majority of cases, no specific underlying cause can be identified. However, a variety of infectious, metabolic, genetic, and environmental factors are being investigated. Professionals generally agree that symptoms of autism are triggered by malfunctions in the brain (Szatmari, Jones, Zwaigenbaum, & MacLean, 1998) and that trauma related to abuse or neglect by caregivers is not the cause (Gillberg & Coleman, 2000).

The search for physiological causes of autism began in the 1960s (Scott et al., 2000). A working group convened by the National Institutes of Health in 1995 reached a consensus that autism probably results from a genetic susceptibility that involves multiple genes. However, the research on chromosomal abnormalities in autism shows no agreement as to what chromosome or chromosomes are implicated as a cause of autism (International Molecular Genetic Study of Autism Consortium, 1998; Konstantareas & Homatidis, 1999).

To date there is no conclusive evidence that any vaccine increases the risk of developing autism or any other behavior disorder. Currently, no study provides definitive evidence of an association between autism and vaccines (Dales, Hammer, & Smith, 2001; Stratton, Gable, Shetty, & McCormick, 2001). However, continued research is needed to examine the mechanisms of autism and any possible relationship to vaccines.

Prevalence of Autism

According to the *Twenty-Sixth Annual Report* (U.S. Department of Education, 2004), 140,473 students between the ages of six and twenty-one years of age were identified as having autism. This represents approximately 2.3 percent of all students having a classification in special education, and approximately 0.12 percent of all school-age students.

AU

A controversial finding is that prevalence figures for autism have increased dramatically over the past thirty to forty years, leading some to claim that there is an "autism epidemic." However, most authorities think that such claims are exaggerated (Hallahan & Kauffman, 2006).

Finally, the Centers for Disease Control (2006) suggests that in 2006, data from several studies found prevalence rates for autism between 2 and 6 per 1,000 individuals. Therefore, it can be summarized that between 1 in 500 (2 out of every 1,000) to 1 in 166 children (6 out of every 1,000) have an ASD.

Age of Onset of Autism

Symptoms of autism usually appear during the first three years of childhood and continue throughout life (Friend, 2005). Interestingly, in close to 50 percent of children diagnosed with autism, the defining characteristics do not become evident until the child is a toddler, at which point some of the children begin to regress markedly in communication and social abilities.

Gender Features of Autism

According to the American Psychiatric Association's *Diagnostic and Statistical Manual of Mental Disorders-Text Revision* (2000), the prevalence rate of autism in males is about four times higher than females. Other studies have found ratios as high (Kadesjo, Gillberg, & Hagberg, 1999) or higher (Scott et al., 2002). Although debate exists on this issue, it is clear that autism is diagnosed much more often in males rather than females. When females do have autism, however, they are more likely to have cognitive deficits (National Research Council on Autism, 2001).

Cultural Features of Autism

Autism has been found throughout the world in people of all racial and social backgrounds. It exists at approximately the same level in all racial and ethnic groups and among individuals at all income levels (U.S. Department of Education, 2004).

Familial Pattern of Autism

Recent studies strongly suggest that some people have a genetic predisposition to autism. Scientists estimate that in families with one autistic child, the risk of having a second child with the disorder is approximately 5 percent, or one in twenty, which is greater than the risk for the general population (Yirmiya, Shaked, & Erel, 2001).

Characteristics of Autism

Individuals with autism are characterized primarily by developmental difficulties in verbal and nonverbal communication, social relatedness, and leisure and play activities. All individuals with autism experience substantial problems with social interactions. In addition, they often exhibit unusual, repetitive, and perseverative movements (including stereotyped and self-stimulatory behaviors), resistance to changes in routines and in other features of their environments, apparent oversensitivity or undersensitivity to specific kinds of stimulation, and extreme tantrums, aggression, or other forms of acting-out behavior. It is also observed that individuals with autism have uneven patterns of skill development. Some people display superior abilities in particular areas such as music, mechanics, and arithmetic calculations, while other areas show significant delay (Scheuermann & Webber, 2002).

Recent research and literature on dual diagnosis suggests that 50 percent of people with autism have some form of mental retardation (Freeman, 2000). Furthermore, approximately half of individuals with autism are nonverbal (Scheuermann & Webber, 2002).

Some or all of the following characteristics may be observed in mild to severe forms:

- Communication problems (for example, using and understanding language)
- Difficulty in relating to people, objects, and events
- Unusual play with toys and other objects
- Difficulty with changes in routine or familiar surroundings
- Sleeping problems (Rapin & Katzman, 1998)

- Playing alone rather than in groups (Sigman & Ruskin, 1999)
- Repetitive body movements or behavior patterns

Children with autism vary widely in abilities, intelligence, and behaviors. Some children do not speak; others have limited language that often includes repeated phrases or conversations. People with more advanced language skills tend to use a small range of topics and have difficulty with abstract concepts. Repetitive play skills, a limited range of interests, and impaired social skills are generally evident as well. Unusual responses to sensory information—for example, loud noises, lights, certain textures of food or fabrics—are also common (Edelson, 1999; Friend, 2005; Krajer, 2000; Scott et al., 2000).

Some individuals with autism exhibit self-injurious behaviors or self-abusive behaviors. These can range from hand biting or hand slapping to life-threatening behaviors such as head banging (Hunt & Marshall, 2005). Research suggests that these types of behaviors are efforts to manipulate the environment or avoid demanding or stressful situations (Sigafoos, 2000).

Educational Implications of Autism

The question as to whether a student with autism should be fully included in the general education classroom is a subject of great controversy. There are many studies supporting full inclusion (Kliewer & Biklen, 1996; Stainback & Stainback, 1990), as there are studies indicating the need for a full continuum of services (Klingner, Vaughn, Schumm, Cohen, & Forgan, 1998; Padeliadu & Zigmond, 1996). Today, more than half the students (57 percent) with autism receive services in a self-contained classroom or more restrictive environment; approximately 25 percent are assigned to the general education classroom (U.S. Department of Education, 2004).

Appropriate educational programs and determining a diagnosis early are critical to children with autism. Students with autism need educational curriculums and programs that focus on improving numerous types of skills. These include communication, social, academic, behavioral, and daily living skills (National Dissemination Center for Children with Disabilities, 2006).

Appropriate educational programs need to be designed for children with autism to afford them the greatest possible opportunities for future transition to live and work in the community and secure paid employment in competitive settings (Bock & Myles, 1999; Cowley, 2000; Bowe, 2005).

Permissions and Authorization to Use Proprietary and Nonproprietary Sources

Due to the scientific and detailed nature of certain Level II disorders described in this chapter, we thought that some were best explained by national institutes and centers that conduct comprehensive scientific research in respective fields of study. The sources obtained were all written with explicit permission that the scientific and diagnostic information they prepared was in the public domain and can be used without restriction.

We thank the following national research offices for the opportunity to freely disseminate their scientific research and writing in this chapter:

- National Dissemination Center for Children with Disabilities
- National Institute of Neurological Disorders and Strokes
- U.S. Department of Education
- U.S. Library of Medicine

EDM Codes, Definitions, and Explanations of Autism

AU

AU 1.00 Asperger's Syndrome

Definition In Asperger's syndrome, a young child experiences impaired social interactions and develops limited repetitive patterns of behavior (Nemours Foundation, 2005). Motor milestones may be delayed, and clumsiness is often observed (U.S. National Library of Medicine, 2004a). However, people with this syndrome usually have fewer problems with language than those with autism, often speaking fluently, though their words can sometimes sound formal or stilted. People with Asperger's syndrome do not usually have the accompanying learning disabilities associated with autism; in fact, they are often of average or above-average intelligence (National Autistic Society, 2005).

Diagnostic Symptoms School-age children with Asperger's syndrome exhibit a range of characteristics, with varying degrees of severity. Diagnostic symptoms include (Hallahan & Kauffman, 2006; Turnbull et al., 2006; Friend, 2005; Westling & Fox, 2004; National Institute of Neurological Disorders and Stroke, 2005a; U.S. National Library of Medicine, 2004a; Mayo Clinic, 2005):

Social skills

- Has difficulty making friends
- Engages in one-sided, long-winded conversations without noticing if the listener is listening or trying to change the subject
- Displays unusual nonverbal communication, such as lack of eye contact, few facial expressions, or awkward body postures and gestures
- Does not empathize with or seem sensitive to others' feelings and has a hard time reading other people or understanding humor

- Does not understand the give-and-take of conversation or engage in small talk
- Seems egocentric or self-absorbed
- May speak in a voice that is monotone, rigid, jerky, or unusually fast
- Can be extremely literal or have difficulty understanding the nuances of language, despite having a good vocabulary

Behavior

- Shows an intense obsession with one or two specific, narrow subjects, such as baseball statistics, train schedules, weather, or snakes
- Likes repetitive routines or rituals
- May memorize information and facts easily, especially information related to a topic of interest
- May have clumsy, uncoordinated movements, an odd posture, or a rigid gait
- May perform repetitive movements, such as hand or finger flapping
- May engage in violent outbursts, self-injurious behaviors, and tantrums
- May be hypersensitive to sensory stimulation, such as light, sound, and texture

Further Key Points Asperger's syndrome is a neurobiological disorder named for a Viennese physician, Hans Asperger, who in 1944 published a paper that described a pattern of behaviors in several young boys who had normal intelligence and language development, but also exhibited autistic-like behaviors and marked deficiencies in social and communication skills (National Institute of Neurological Disorders and Stroke, 2005a).

Overall, people with this syndrome are quite capable of functioning in everyday life, but they tend to be somewhat socially immature and may be seen by others as odd or eccentric (Nemours Foundation, 2005). They have higher intelligence and communication skills than those with classic or more severe forms of autism, but they display most, if not all, of the other characteristics of autism spectrum disorders, with their primary difficulties manifested in poor social interactions (Hallahan & Kauffman, 2006).

AU 2.00 Autistic Disorder (Classic Autism)

Definition Autistic disorder (sometimes called classical autism) is the most common condition in a group of developmental disorders known as the autism spectrum disorders (ASDs). Autism is characterized by impaired social interaction, problems with verbal and nonverbal communication, and unusual, repetitive, or severely limited activities and interests (National Institute of Neurological Disorders and Stroke, 2005a).

Diagnostic Symptoms Three distinctive behaviors characterize autism: autistic children have difficulties with social interaction, problems with verbal and nonverbal communication, and repetitive behaviors or narrow, obsessive interests. These behaviors can range in impact from mild to disabling. Other common symptoms of classic autism include (Westling & Fox, 2004; Heward, 2006; Gargiulo, 2004):

- Difficulty in expressing needs; using gestures or pointing instead of words
- Difficulty in relating to and mixing in with others
- Lack of response to normal teaching methods
- Lack of response verbal cues
- Exhibiting minimal or no eye contact
- Exhibiting oversensitivity or undersensitivity to pain
- Exhibiting physical overactivity or extreme underactivity
- Difficulty expressing and receiving physical affection
- No real fears of danger
- Inappropriate attachments to objects
- Uneven motor skills
- Often exhibiting tantrums
- Preference to be alone; an aloof manner
- Repeating words or phrases in place of normal, responsive language
- Resistance to change
- Spinning objects
- Engaging in sustained odd play

Further Key Points According to the Autism Society of America (2005), there is no known single cause for autism, but it is generally accepted that it is caused by abnormalities in brain structure or function. Brain scans show differences in the shape and structure of the brain in autistic versus nonautistic children. Researchers are investigating a number of theories, including the link between heredity, genetics, and medical problems. In many families, there appears to be a pattern of autism or related disabilities, further supporting a genetic basis to the disorder (National Institute of Neurological Disorders and Stroke, 2005a). Although no one gene has been identified as causing autism, researchers are searching for irregular segments of genetic code that autistic children may have inherited. It also appears that some children are born with a susceptibility to autism, but researchers have not yet identified a single trigger that causes autism to develop.

AU 3.00 Childhood Disintegrative Disorder

Definition Childhood disintegrative disorder is a condition occurring in three- and four-year-olds who have developed normally to age two. Over several months, a child with this disorder deteriorates in intellectual, social, and language functioning from previously normal behavior (U.S. National Library of Medicine 2004b).

Diagnostic Symptoms Childhood disintegrative disorder develops in children who have previously seemed perfectly normal. Typically language, interest in the social environment, and often toileting and self-care abilities are lost, and there may be a general loss of interest in the environment. The child usually comes to look very "autistic"; the clinical presentation (but not the history) is then typical of a child with autism (Yale Developmental Disabilities Clinic, 2005a). An affected child shows a loss of communication skills, has regression in nonverbal behaviors, and has significant loss of previously acquired skills. The condition is similar to classic autism.

Symptoms of childhood disintegrative disorder may include (U.S. National Library of Medicine 2004b):

- Loss of social skills
- Loss of bowel and bladder control
- Loss of expressive or receptive language
- Loss of motor skills
- Lack of play
- Failure to develop peer relationships
- Impairment in nonverbal behaviors
- Delay or lack of spoken language
- Inability to start or sustain a conversation

Further Key Points Childhood disintegrative disorder must be differentiated from both childhood schizophrenia and pervasive developmental disorder (autism). The most important signs of childhood disintegrative disorder are loss of developmental milestones (U.S. National Library of Medicine, 2004b). The child tends to have normal development through age three or four and then over a few months undergoes a gradual loss of previously established abilities such as language, motor, or social skills. The cause is unknown, but it has been linked to neurological problems (Yale Developmental Disabilities Clinic, 2005a).

AU 4.00 High-Functioning Autism

Definition According to the Cure Autism Now Foundation (2005), "high-functioning autism" is not an official medical term. It has come to refer to people with autism who have average or above-average intelligence and can function in typical settings, such as school or the workplace, with minimal assistance.

Some experts have questioned the differentiation between high-functioning autism and Asperger's, noting that there are some people with Asperger's whose speech did not develop normally, while there are people with high-functioning autism who demonstrate the same high level of self-care and cognitive skills. This topic will likely be the subject of debate until more is known about the physiological causes that lead people to exhibit the symptoms of autism.

Diagnostic Symptoms Children with high-functioning autism are much more efficient with expressive and receptive speech, less likely to suffer from epilepsy, and have IQ scores of 71 or above. Although too much sensory input can overload them, they have a higher tolerance and learn to desensitize themselves. These children have a stronger grasp on the theory of mind and can empathize with the feelings and reactions of others (Autism and PDD Support Network, 2005).

Further Key Points Autism is diagnosed on the basis of abnormalities in the areas of social development, communicative development, and imagination, together with marked repetitive or obsessional behavior or unusual, narrow interests. Individuals with autism may have an IQ at any level. By convention, an individual with autism who has an IQ in the normal range (or above) is said to have high-functioning autism (HFA). If an individual meets all of the criteria for HFA except communicative abnormality or history of language delay, he or she is said to have Asperger's syndrome (Cohen, 2000).

AU 5.00 Hyperlexia

Definition A type of syndrome often associated with autistic features characterized by above-normal ability to read coupled with a below-normal ability to understand spoken language (American Hyperlexia Association, 2005).

Diagnostic Symptoms Hyperlexia is a syndrome with three main characteristics (Autism Support Network, 2002):

- Early precocious or intense fascination with letters or numbers
- Delays in verbal language
- Social skills deficits

Examples of the these characteristics include (American Hyperlexia Association, 2005):

- Learning expressive language in a peculiar way, echoing or memorizing the sentence structure without understanding the meaning (echolalia)

- Listening selectively, appearing to be deaf
- Showing normal development until eighteen to twenty-four months, then regressing
- Rarely initiating conversations
- Engaging in self-stimulatory behavior
- Significant difficulty in understanding verbal language
- Specific, unusual fears
- Strong auditory and visual memory
- Thinking in concrete and literal terms, difficulty with abstract concepts

Further Key Points Hyperlexia has characteristics similar to autism, behavior disorder, language disorder, emotional disorder, attention deficit disorder, hearing impairment, giftedness, and, paradoxically, mental retardation.

To develop effective teaching strategies and more typical childhood development, it is important to differentiate hyperlexia from other disorders. Thorough psychological evaluation by a psychologist who is familiar with the syndrome of hyperlexia is a crucial first step. Hearing, neurological, psychiatric, blood chemistry, speech and language, and genetic evaluations can be performed to rule out other disorders but are not needed to identify hyperlexia (Kay, 2004).

According to the American Hyperlexia Association (2005), "Hyperlexia's place on or outside of the autistic spectrum is a matter of much debate. Be that as it may, hyperlexia is a trait commonly seen in autistic spectrum disorders. Autistics with hyperlexia have a unique learning style and a better prognosis than those without this reading skill. Hyperlexia is often written off as a 'meaningless splinter skill' but it is much more than that even if comprehension lags because reading can be a very useful tool for learning other skills and can be the doorway to language in general" (p. 1).

AU 6.00 Multiplex Developmental Disorder

Definition Multiplex developmental disorder is a proposed developmental disorder (or syndrome) designed to encompass preschool and early-school-age children who have consistent and enduring deficits in affect regulation, relatedness, and thought. Such children are thought to represent another variant in the spectrum of pervasive developmental disorders (Demb & Noskin, 2001).

Diagnostic Symptoms Symptoms emerge in earliest childhood, often in the first years of life, and persist throughout development. Diagnostic criteria include (Yale Developmental Disabilities Clinic, 2005b):

- Impaired social behavior or sensitivity, similar to that seen in autism, such as:
  - Social disinterest
  - Detachment, avoidance of others, or withdrawal
  - Impaired peer relations
  - Highly ambivalent attachments
  - Limited capacity for empathy or understanding what others are thinking or feeling
- Affective symptoms, including:
  - Impaired regulation of feelings
  - Intense, inappropriate anxiety
  - Recurrent panic
  - Emotional liability, without obvious cause
- Thought disorder symptoms, such as:
  - Sudden, irrational intrusions on normal thoughts
  - Magical thinking
  - Confusion between reality and fantasy
  - Delusions such as paranoid thoughts or fantasies of special powers

Further Key Points Some children who display the severe, early-appearing social and communicative deficits characteristic of autism also display some of the emotional instability and disordered thought processes that resemble schizophrenic symptoms. Cohen, Paul, and Volkmar (1986) coined the term *multiplex developmental disorder* (MDD) to describe these children, although they are often given a diagnosis of Pervasive Developmental Disorder-Not Otherwise Specified (PDD-NOS) by clinicians who may be unfamiliar with this terminology (Yale Developmental Disabilities Clinic, 2005b).

AU 7.00 Rett Syndrome

Definition Rett syndrome (RS) is a neurological disorder seen almost exclusively in females and found in a variety of racial and ethnic groups worldwide (International Rett Syndrome Association, 2005).

Diagnostic Symptoms An inability to perform motor functions is perhaps the most severely disabling feature of Rett syndrome, interfering with every body movement, including eye gaze and speech. Other diagnostic symptoms of Rett syndrome include (International Rett Syndrome Association, 2005; National Institute on Neurological Disorders and Stroke, 2005c):

- An early period of apparently normal or near-normal development until six to eighteen months of life
- A following period of temporary stagnation or regression during which the child loses communication skills and purposeful use of the hands
- Stereotyped hand movements
- Gait disturbances
- Slowing of the rate of head growth
- Seizures
- Disorganized breathing patterns that occur when awake
- Compulsive hand movements such as wringing and washing following the loss of functional use of the hands

Further Key Points There are four stages to this syndrome (National Institute for Neurological Disorders and Stroke, 2004c).

Stage I, called *early onset*, generally begins between six and eighteen months of age. Quite frequently this stage is overlooked because symptoms of the disorder may be somewhat vague, and parents and doctors may not notice the subtle slowing of development at first. The infant may begin to show less eye contact and have reduced interest in toys. There may be delays in gross motor skills such as sitting or crawling. Hand-wringing and decreasing head growth may occur, but not enough to draw attention. This stage usually lasts for a few months but can persist for more than a year.

Stage II, the *rapid destructive stage,* usually begins between ages one and four and may last for weeks or months. This stage may have either a rapid or a gradual onset as purposeful hand skills and spoken language are lost. The characteristic hand movements begin to emerge during this stage and often include wringing, washing, clapping, or tapping, as well as repeatedly moving the hands to the mouth. Hands are sometimes clasped behind the back or held at the sides, with random touching, grasping, and releasing. The movements persist while the child is awake but disappear during sleep. Breathing irregularities such as episodes of apnea and hyperventilation may occur, although breathing is usually normal during sleep. Some girls display autistic-like symptoms such as loss of social interaction and communication. General irritability and sleep irregularities may be seen. Gait patterns are unsteady, and initiating motor movements can be difficult. Slowing of head growth is usually noticed during this stage.

Stage III, the *plateau* or *pseudostationary stage,* usually begins between ages two and ten and can last for years. Apraxia, motor problems, and seizures are prominent during this stage. However, there may be improvement in behavior, with less irritability, crying, and autistic-like features. An individual in stage III may show more interest in her surroundings, and her alertness, attention span, and communication skills may improve. Many girls remain in this stage for most of their lives.

Stage IV, the *late motor deterioration stage,* can last for years or decades and is characterized by reduced mobility. Muscle weakness, rigidity (stiffness), spasticity, dystonia (increased muscle tone with abnormal posturing of extremity or trunk), and scoliosis (curvature of the spine) are other prominent features. Girls who were previously able to walk may stop walking. Generally there is no decline in cognition, communication, or hand skills in this stage. Repetitive hand movements may decrease, and eye gaze usually improves.

AU 8.00 Other Types of Autism—Be Specific

References

American Hyperlexia Association. (2005). *Semantic pragmatic disorder.* Retrieved June 10, 2005, from http://www.hyperlexia.org/sp1.html.

American Psychiatric Association. (2000). *Diagnostic and statistical manual of mental disorders DSM-IV-TR* (4th ed). Washington, DC: Author.

Autism and PDD Support Network. (2005). *Low/high functioning autism.* Retrieved July 10, 2005, from http://www.autism-pdd.net/testdump/test259.htm.

Autism Society of America. (2005). *Autistic disorder.* Retrieved July 10, 2005, from http://www.autism-society.org/site/PageServer.

Autism Support Network. (2002) *Hyperlexia.* Retrieved April 1, 2006, from http://www.bbbautism.com/other_conditions.htm.

Bock, S. J., & Myles, B. S. (1999). An overview of characteristics of Asperger syndrome. *Education and Training in Mental Retardation and Developmental Disabilities, 34*(4), 511–520.

Bowe, F. (2005). *Making inclusion work.* Upper Saddle River, NJ: Merrill Pearson.

Centers for Disease Control. (2006). *How common are autism spectrum disorders (ASD)?* Retrieved November 10, 2006, from http://www.cdc.gov/ncbddd/autism/asd_common.htm.

Cohen, D. J., Paul, R., & Volkmar, F. R. (1986). Issues in the classification of pervasive and other developmental disorders: Toward DSM-IV. *Journal of the American Academy of Child Psychiatry, 25,* 213–220.

Cohen, S. B. (2000, Jan. 5). *Is Asperger's syndrome/high-functioning autism necessarily a disability?* Invited submission for Special Millennium Issue of Developmental and Psychopathology Draft.

Colarusso, R., & O'Rourke, C. (2004). *Special education for all teachers.* Dubuque, IA: Kendall Hunt.

Cowley, G. (2000, July 31). The challenge of "mindblindness." *Newsweek,* 46–54.

Cure Autism Now Foundation. (2005). *High functioning autism.* Retrieved June 1, 2005, from http://www.cureautismnow.org/kb/subcat/3232.jsp.

Dales, L., & Hammer, S. J., & Smith, N. J. (2001). Time trends in autism and in MMR immunization coverage in California. *Journal of the American Medical Association, 285,* 1183–1185.

Demb, H. B., & Noskin, O. (2001). The use of the term multiple complex developmental disorder in a diagnostic clinic serving young children with developmental disabilities: A report of 15 cases. *Mental Health Aspects of Developmental Disabilities, 2,* 49–60.

Edelson, S. (1999). *Overview of autism.* Salem, OR: Center for Study of Autism.

Freeman, B. (2000, March). *Autism: What we know.* Paper presented at a meeting of the Alabama Autism Academy, Birmingham, AL.

Friend, M. (2005). *Special education: Contemporary perspectives for school professionals.* Needham Heights, MA: Allyn & Bacon.

Gargiulo, R. M. (2004). *Special education in contemporary society: An introduction to exceptionality.* Belmont, CA: Wadsworth-Thompson.

Gillberg, C., & Coleman, M. (2000). *The biology of the autistic syndromes* (3rd ed.). London: MacKeith Press.

Hallahan, D. P., & Kauffman, J. M. (2006). *Exceptional learners: An introduction to special education* (10th ed.) Needham Heights, MA: Allyn & Bacon.

Heward, W. L. (2006). *Exceptional children: An introduction to special education.* Upper Saddle River, NJ: Pearson Education.

Hunt, N., & Marshall, K. (2005). *Exceptional children and youth* (5th ed.). Boston: Houghton Mifflin.

International Molecular Genetic Study of Autism Consortium. (1998). A full gene screen for autism with linkage to a region on chromosome 7q. *Human Molecular Genetics, 7*(3), 571–578.

International Rett Syndrome Foundation. (2005). *Overview of Rett syndrome.* Retrieved June 10, 2005, from http://www.rettsyndrome.org/main/overview.htm.

Kadesjo, B., Gillberg, C., & Hagberg, B. (1999). Brief report: Autism and Asperger syndrome in seven-year-old children: A total population study. *Journal of Autism and Developmental Disorders, 29,* 327–331.

Kay, M. J. (2004). *What is hyperlexia*? Retrieved June 15, 2005, from http://www.margaretkay.com/Hyperlexia.htm.

Kliewer, C., & Biklen, D. (1996). Labeling: Who wants to be called retarded? In W. Stainback & S. Stainback (Eds.), *Controversial issues confronting special education: Divergent perspectives* (2nd ed., pp. 83–95). Needham Heights, MA: Allyn & Bacon.

Klingner, J. K., Vaughn, S., Schumm, J. S., Cohen, P., & Forgan, J. W. (1998). Inclusion or pullout? Which do students prefer? *Journal of Learning Disabilities, 31,* 148–158.

Konstantareas, M. M., & Homatidis, S. (1999). Chromosomal abnormalities in a series of children with autistic disorder. *Journal of Autism and Developmental Disorders, 29*(4), 275–285.

Krajer, D. (2000). Review of adaptive behavior studies in mentally retarded persons with autism/pervasive developmental disorder. *Journal of Autism and Developmental Disorders, 30,* 39–47.

Kutscher, M. L. (2003, Nov. 23). *Autism spectrum disorders: Sorting it out.* Retrieved June 17, 2005, from http://www.pediactricneurology.com/autism.htm.

Mayo Clinic. (2005). *Asperger syndrome.* Retrieved July 1, 2005, from http://www.mayoclinic.com/invoke.cfm?objectid=8F748903–096F-475C-9D715967183034B0&dsection=2.

National Autistic Society. (2005). *What is Asperger syndrome?* Retrieved June 27, 2005, from http://www.nas.org.uk/nas/jsp/polopoly.jsp?d=212&a=3580.

National Dissemination Center for Children with Disabilities. (2006). *Autism and pervasive developmental disorder.* Retrieved November 4, 2006, from http://www.nichcy.org/pubs/factshe/fs1txt.htm.

National Institute of Neurological Disorders and Stroke. (2005a). *Asperger syndrome fact sheet from the NINDS.* Bethesda, MD: National Institutes of Health.

National Institute of Neurological Disorders and Stroke. (2005b). *Pervasive developmental disorders information page.* Retrieved June 8, 2005, from http://www.ninds.nih.gov/disorders/pdd/pdd.htm.

National Institute of Neurological Disorders and Stroke. (2005c). *Rett syndrome information page.* Retrieved June 7, 2005, from http://www.ninds.nih.gov/disorders/rett/rett.htm.

National Research Council on Autism. (2001). *Educating children with autism.* Washington, DC: National Academies Press.

Nemours Foundation. (2005). *Asperger syndrome.* Retrieved June 15, 2005, from http://kidshealth.org/parent/medical/brain/asperger.html.

Padeliadu, S., & Zigmond, N. (1996). Perspectives of students with learning disabilities about special education placement. *Learning Disabilities Research and Practice, 11,* 15–23.

Prizant, B. M., Wetherby, A. M., & Rydell, P. J. (2000). Communication intervention issues for young children with autism spectrum disorders. In A. M. Wetherby & B. M. Prizant (Eds.), *Children with autism spectrum disorders: A developmental, transactional perspective.* Baltimore, MD: Paul Brookes.

Rapin, I., & Katzman, R. (1998). Neurobiology of autism. *Annals of Neurology, 43(1),* 7–14.

Rodier, P. (2000). The early origins of autism. *Scientific American, 282(2),* 56–63.

Scheuermann, B., & Webber, J. (2002). Level systems: Problems and solutions. *Beyond Behavior, 7*(2), 12–17.

Scott, J., Clark, C., & Brady, M. (2000). *Students with autism: Characteristics and instructional programming.* San Diego: Singular.

Sigafoos, J. (2000). Communication development and aberrant behavior in children with developmental disabilities. *Education and Training in Mental Retardation and Developmental Disabilities, 35*(2), 168–176.

Sigman, M., & Ruskin, E. (1999). Continuity and change in the social competence of children with autism, Down syndrome, and developmental delays. *Journal of Autism and Developmental Disorders, 24,* 647–657.

Stainback, W., & Stainback, S. (1990). Inclusive schooling. In W. Stainback & S. Stainback (Eds.), *Support networks for inclusive schooling* (pp. 51–63). Baltimore, MD: Brookes Publishing.

Stratton, K., Gable, A., Shetty, P., & McCormick, M. C. 741(Eds.). (2001). *Immunization safety review: Measles-mumps-rubella vaccine and autism.* Washington DC: National Academy Press.

Szatmari, P., Jones, M. B., Zwaigenbaum, L., & MacLean, J. E. (1998). Genetics of autism: Overview and new directions. *Journal of Autism and Developmental Disorders, 28,* 351–368.

Turnbull, A., Turnbull, R., & Wehmeyer, M. (2006). Exceptional lives: *Special education in today's schools* (5th ed.). Upper Saddle River, NJ: Pearson.

U.S. Department of Education. (2004). *The Twenty-Sixth Annual Report to Congress on the Implementation of IDEA.* Washington, DC: U.S. Department of Education.

U.S. National Library of Medicine. (2004a). *Asperger syndrome.* Retrieved June 30, 2005, from http://www.nlm.nih.gov/medlineplus/ency/article/00154.htm.

U.S. National Library of Medicine. (2004b). *Childhood disintegrative disorder.* Retrieved July 2, 2005, from http://search.nlm.nih.gov/medlineplus/query?DISAMBIGUATION=true&FUNCTION=search&SERVER2=server2&SERVER1=server1&PARAMETER=Childhood+Disintegrative+disorder.

Vaughn, S., Bos, C., & Schumm, J. S. (2003). *Teaching exceptional and diverse at-risk students in the general education classroom* (3rd ed.). Needham Heights, MA: Allyn & Bacon.

Westling, D. L., & Fox, L. (2004). *Teaching students with severe disabilities* (3rd ed.). Upper Saddle River, NJ: Pearson.

Yale Developmental Disabilities Clinic. (2005a). *Childhood disintegrative disorder.* Retrieved April 3, 2006, from http://info.med.yale.edu/chldstdy/autism/mdd.html.

Yale Developmental Disabilities Clinic. (2005b). *Multiplex developmental disorder.* Retrieved June 28, 2005, from http://info.med.yale.edu/chldstdy/autism/mdd.html.

Yirmiya, N., Shaked, M., & Erel, O. (2001). Comparison of siblings of individuals with autism and siblings of individuals with other diagnoses: An empirical summary. In E. Schoper, N. Yirmiya, & C. Shulman (Eds.), *The research basis for autism intervention* (pp. 59–73). New York: Kluwer Academic/Plenum Publishers.

AU

Chapter 8

Orthopedic Impairments

EDM Code: OI

OI 1.00 Bone Diseases
- OI 1.01 Fibrous Dysplasia
- OI 1.02 Klippel-Feil Syndrome
- OI 1.03 Marfan Syndrome
- OI 1.04 McCune-Albright Syndrome
- OI 1.05 Osteogenesis Imperfecta-Brittle Bone Disease
  - OI 1.05a Type I Osteogenesis Imperfecta
  - OI 1.05b Type II Osteogenesis Imperfecta
  - OI 1.05c Type III Osteogenesis Imperfecta
  - OI 1.05d Type IV Osteogenesis Imperfecta
- OI 1.06 Osteopetrosis
  - OI 1.06a Adult Form
  - OI 1.06b Intermediate Form
  - OI 1.06c Malignant Infantile Form
- OI 1.07 Idiopathic Juvenile Osteoporosis
  - OI 1.08 Renal Osteodystrophy

OI 2.00 Cerebral Palsy
- OI 2.01 Ataxic Cerebral Palsy
- OI 2.02 Athetoid Cerebral Palsy
- OI 2.03 Mixed Cerebral Palsy
- OI 2.04 Spastic Cerebral Palsy

OI 3.00 Hydrocephalus
- OI 3.01 Acquired Hydrocephalus
- OI 3.02 Communicating Hydrocephalus
- OI 3.03 Congenital Hydrocephalus
- OI 3.04 Hydrocephalus Ex Vacuo
- OI 3.05 Noncommunicating Hydrocephalus

OI 4.00 Limb Deficiency
- OI 4.01 Amputation
  - OI 4.01a Major Amputation
  - OI 4.01b Minor Amputation
  - OI 4.01c Traumatic Amputation
- OI 4.02 Clubfoot
- OI 4.03 Contracture Deformity
  - OI 4.03a Clawfoot
  - OI 4.03b Clawhand
  - OI 4.03c Dupuytren's Contracture
  - OI 4.03d Foot-Drop
  - OI 4.03e Volkmann's Contracture
  - OI 4.03f Wrist-Drop
- OI 4.04 Other Types of Loss or Deformity of Limbs

OI 5.00 Muscular Dystrophy
- OI 5.01 Becker Muscular Dystrophy
- OI 5.02 Congenital Muscular Dystrophy
- OI 5.03 Duchenne Muscular Dystrophy
- OI 5.04 Emery-Dreifuss Muscular Dystrophy
- OI 5.05 Facioscapulohumeral Muscular Dystrophy
- OI 5.06 Limb-Girdle Muscular Dystrophy
- OI 5.07 Myotonic Muscular Dystrophy
- OI 5.08 Other Types of Muscular Dystrophy

OI 6.00 Poliomyelitis
- OI 6.01 Abortive Poliomyelitis
- OI 6.02 Paralytic Polio
  - OI 6.02a Bulbar Polio
  - OI 6.02b Bulbospinal Polio
  - OI 6.02c Spinal Polio
- OI 6.03 Post-Polio Syndrome
- OI 6.04 Other Types of Poliomyelitis

OI 7.00 Scoliosis
- OI 7.01 Adolescent Idiopathic Scoliosis
- OI 7.02 Early-Onset or Infantile Idiopathic Scoliosis
- OI 7.03 Juvenile Idiopathic Scoliosis
  - OI 7.03a Nonstructural (Functional) Scoliosis

OI 7.03b Structural Scoliosis
OI 7.04 Other Types of Scoliosis
OI 8.00 Spina Bifida
OI 8.01 Meningocele
OI 8.02 Myelomeningocele
OI 8.03 Spina Bifida Occulta
OI 8.04 Other Types of Spina Bifida
OI 9.00 Spinal Cord Injury
OI 9.01 Incomplete Injury
OI 9.02 Complete injury
OI 9.03 Other Types of Spinal Cord Injuries
OI 10.00 Spinal Muscular Atrophies
OI 10.01 Amyotrophic Lateral Sclerosis—Adult Spinal Muscular Atrophies
OI 10.02 Congenital Spinal Muscular Atrophies with Arthrogryposis
OI 10.03 Kennedy Syndrome or Progressive Spinobulbar Muscular atrophy
OI 10.04 Spinal Muscular Atrophies, Type I
OI 10.05 Spinal Muscular Atrophies, Type II
OI 10.06 Juvenile Spinal Muscular Atrophy
OI 11.00 Stroke
OI 12.00 Other Types of Orthopedic Impairments—Be Specific

IDEA 2004 Definition of Orthopedic Impairments

Under IDEA 2004, orthopedic impairment:

> means a severe orthopedic impairment that adversely affects a child's educational performance. The term includes impairments due to the effects of congenital anomaly (e.g., clubfoot, absence of some member, etc.), impairments due to the effects of disease (e.g., poliomyelitis, bone tuberculosis, etc.), and impairments from other causes (e.g., cerebral palsy, amputations, and fractures or burns that cause contractures) [C.F.R. 300.7(c)(8)].

Overview of Orthopedic Impairments

Although IDEA uses the term *orthopedic impairments,* educators typically use the term *physical disabilities* when referring to these same conditions (Turnbull, Turnbull, & Wehmeyer, 2006). A physical disability is a condition that interferes with a child's ability to use his or her body. Physical disabilities are conditions that affect movement, that is, an individual's motor control (for example, walking, standing) and fine motor control (for example, writing, holding, or manipulating small objects using the hands and oral motor skills; Friend, 2005).

Many physical disabilities are orthopedic impairments (Kirk, Gallagher, & Anastasiow, 2003). According to Heward (2006), although IDEA uses the term *orthopedic impairments,* children with physical disabilities may have orthopedic impairments or neuromotor impairments. An orthopedic impairment involves the skeletal system: bones, joints, limbs, and associated muscles. A neuromotor impairment involves the central nervous system, affecting the ability to move, use, feel, or control certain parts of the body. Although orthopedic and neurological impairments are two distinct and separate types of disabilities, they may cause similar limitations in movement.

Students with orthopedic impairments, although few in number, comprise one of the most diverse group of exceptional individuals due to the many types of diseases and disorders that interfere with the normal functioning of the muscles or bones (Colarusso & O'Rourke, 2004). Individuals with physical disabilities often require highly specialized interventions to realize their maximum potential. Moreover, "the range of medical services, educational placements, and therapies is extremely diverse and highly specific to the person and his or her needs" (Hardman, Drew, & Egan, 2005, p. 473).

Causes-Etiology of Orthopedic Impairments

Physical disabilities and orthopedic impairments occur with tremendous range and variety. Children may have congenital anomalies (defects they are born with) or may acquire disabilities through accident or disease after birth (Hallahan & Kauffman, 2006).

The causes of orthopedic impairments vary greatly according to the specific disease or disorder (Gargiulo, 2004). Orthopedic problems may result from deformities, diseases, injuries, or surgeries. Problems a child might be born with include cerebral palsy, osteogenesis imperfecta, joint deformities, or muscular dystrophy. Injuries or surgeries may result in the loss of a bone or muscle tissue and may include the amputation of a limb. Burns and broken bones can also result in damage to both bones and muscles.

Potential causes of orthopedic impairments include motor vehicle accidents, water and diving accidents, gunshot wounds, sports injuries, child abuse, poisoning or toxins, disease, premature birth, genetic disabilities, seizures, and hydrocephaly, to name a few (Deutsch-Smith, 2004). However, since the disability category of orthopedic impairments includes students with many different types of disorders, the causes obviously vary (Friend, 2005).

Prevalence of Orthopedic Impairments

According to the *Twenty-Sixth Annual Report* from the U.S. Department of Education (2004), 74,000 students between the ages of six and twenty-one received special education services under the disability category of orthopedic impairments. This represents approximately 1.1 percent of all school-age children receiving special education services.

Age of Onset of Orthopedic Impairments

Due to the various types of orthopedic impairments that adversely affect children's performances in school, no specific age of onset can be generalized to the entire school-age population that receives special education services. Children with orthopedic impairments may have congenital anomalies (defects they are born with) or may acquire disabilities through accident or disease after birth (Hallahan & Kauffman, 2006).

Gender Features of Orthopedic Impairments

Information on this topic is not available.

Cultural Features of Orthopedic Impairments

Information on this topic is not available.

Familial Pattern of Orthopedic Impairments

Information on this topic is not available.

Characteristics of Orthopedic Impairments

The characteristics of children with physical disabilities are so varied that attempting to describe them is nearly impossible (Heward, 2006). The reality is that it is difficult to generalize about such a broad spectrum of limitations (Bowe, 2005).

Orthopedic impairments are often divided into three main areas:

- Neuromotor impairments—An abnormality of or damage to the brain, spinal cord, or nerves that send impulses to the muscles of the body (Gargiulo, 2004).
- Degenerative diseases—Diseases that affect motor movement (Gargiulo, 2004).
- Musculoskelatal disorders—Defects or diseases of the muscles or bones (Hallahan & Kauffman, 2006)

Educational Implications of Orthopedic Impairments

A critical educational consideration for students with orthopedic impairments is placement. Educational services for these students may be provided in a variety of settings depending on the type and severity of the condition, the services available in the community, and the medical prognosis for the condition (Hallahan & Kauffman, 2006). Educational placement options include general education classrooms, resource rooms, special classes, and more restrictive settings such as special classrooms, special schools, residential facilities, or hospital and homebound programs.

Most children with orthopedic or physical impairments spend at least part of the day in regular classrooms (Bowe, 2005). According to the U.S. Department of Education (2004), approximately 46 percent of all school-age students who received special education services under the disability category of orthopedic impairment were educated in regular classrooms. Twenty-three percent received resource room services. And almost one-third received their education in a special classroom or more restrictive environment (U.S. Department of Education, 2004).

Maintaining strong peer relationships can be very anxiety provoking, especially when these students often have to leave the room to participate in certain forms of treatment, have prolonged absences (Olsen & Sutton, 1998), and have concerns about their physical appearance. These concerns are reasons for emotional difficulties and feelings of depression (Sexson & Dingle, 2001).

It is often necessary to modify and adapt the school environment to make it accessible, safe, and less restrictive. Accessibility guidelines are readily available, and when these guidelines are followed, the environment becomes easier for the child to manage independently. Environmental modifications include adaptations to provide increased access to a task or an activity, changing the way instruction is delivered, and changing the manner in which the task is done (Best, Heller, & Bigge, 2005; Heward, 2006; Heller, Dangel, & Sweatman, 1995).

It is important that modifications be no more restrictive than absolutely necessary so that the student's school experiences can be as normal as possible. Many authorities stress the importance of avoiding overprotection of students with physical or health impairments. It is also important to permit students with disabilities to take risks just as their able-bodied cohorts do. It is essential that students with physical disabilities be encouraged to develop as much independence as possible (McGill & Vogle, 2001).

Teachers are being called on to perform duties that historically have not been considered part of their role in school (Heller et al., 2000). They need to be familiar with the orthotics, prosthetics, and adaptive devices their students use. They should also have a good working knowledge of the specialists who frequently provide related services to children with physical disabilities (Downing, 2004; Etzel-Wise & Mears, 2004; Neal, Bigby, & Nicholson, 2004).

In conclusion, it is impossible to specify the content of the educational curriculum for learners with physical disabilities because there is so much variation with regard to need. Some students need only minor modifications, while others with more severe disabilities will require extensive adaptations. However, it should be emphasized that teachers will need to work closely with professionals from other disciplines to meet the needs of these learners. In most cases, educating students with physical disabilities is not so much a matter of special instruction for children with disabilities as it is of educating the nondisabled population (Closs, 2000).

Permissions and Authorization to Use Proprietary and Nonproprietary Sources

Due to the scientific and detailed nature of certain Level II, Level II, and Level IV disorders described in this chapter, we thought that some were best explained by national institutes and centers that conduct comprehensive scientific research in respective fields of study. The sources obtained were all written with explicit permissions that the scientific and diagnostic information they prepared was in the public domain and can be used without restriction.

We thank the following national research offices for the opportunity to freely disseminate their scientific research and writing in this chapter:

- National Dissemination Center for Children with Disabilities
- National Institute of Arthritis and Musculoskeletal and Skin Diseases

- National Institutes of Health
- National Institute of Neurological Disorders and Stroke
- National Kidney and Urologic Diseases Information Clearinghouse
- U.S. Department of Education
- U.S. National Library of Medicine

EDM Codes, Definitions, and Explanations of Orthopedic Impairments

OI 1.00 Bone Diseases

Definition Bone diseases are any of the diseases and injuries that affect human bones (National Resource Center of the National Institutes of Health, 2005).

Diagnostic Symptoms Diseases and injuries of bones are major causes of abnormalities of the locomotor system. Although physical injury, causing fracture, dominates over disease, fracture is but one of several common causes of bone disease, and disease in fact is a common cause of fracture. Each disorder has specific symptoms so a generalized list of symptoms is not made.

Further Key Points Bone is living tissue that provides shape and support for the body, as well as protection for some organs. It also serves as a storage site for minerals and provides the medium—marrow—for the development and storage of blood cells. Because the functions of bone are numerous and complex, there are many disorders that require clinical care by a physician or other health care professional. These conditions include benign (noncancerous) disorders, cancers that occur in bone, and cancers that affect bone (University of Virginia Health Systems, 2005).

Types of Bone Diseases

OI 1.01 Fibrous Dysplasia

Definition Fibrous dysplasia is a chronic disorder in which bone expands due to abnormal development of fibrous tissue, often resulting in one or more of the following:

- Uneven growth of bones
- Pain
- Brittle bones
- Bone deformity (University of Maryland Medical System, 2003)

Some patients have only one bone affected (monostotic), whereas other patients have numerous bones affected (polyostotic) (NIH Osteoporosis and Related Bone Diseases, 2000).

Explanation The following are the most common symptoms for fibrous dysplasia, although each individual may experience symptoms differently:

- A waddling walk
- Bone pain (as a consequence of the expanding fibrous tissue in the bone)
- Bone deformity
- Bone pain
- Bone fractures
- Scoliosis—a lateral, or sideways, curvature and rotation of the back bones (vertebrae), giving the appearance that the person is leaning to one side

The symptoms of fibrous dysplasia may resemble other bone disorders or medical problems. A physician should always be consulted for a diagnosis (U.S. National Library of Medicine, 2003a; University of Maryland Medical Center, 2003).

OI 1.02 Klippel-Feil Syndrome

Definition Klippel-Feil syndrome is a rare disorder characterized by the congenital fusion of any two of the seven cervical (neck) vertebrae. It is caused by a failure in the normal segmentation or division of the cervical vertebrae during the early weeks of fetal development (National Institute of Neurological Disorders and Stroke, 2005e).

Type I is described as a massive fusion of the cervical spine. Type II is present when the fusion of one or two vertebrae occurs. Type III occurs when thoracic and lumbar spine anomalies are associated with type I or type II Klippel-Feil syndrome (Klippel & Feil, 1975).

Explanation The most common signs of the disorder are short neck, low hairline at the back of the head, and restricted mobility of the upper spine. Associated abnormalities may include scoliosis (curvature of the spine), spina bifida (a birth defect of the spine), anomalies of the kidneys and the ribs, cleft palate, respiratory problems, and heart malformations. The disorder may be associated with abnormalities of the head and face, skeleton, sex organs, muscles, brain and spinal cord, arms, legs, and fingers (National Institute of Neurological Disorders and Stroke, 2005e).

OI 1.03 Marfan Syndrome

Definition Marfan syndrome is inherited as an autosomal-dominant trait. However, up to 30 percent of cases have no family history and are so-called sporadic cases. In sporadic cases, Marfan syndrome is believed to result from a spontaneous new mutation. Marfan syndrome is caused by mutations in the gene fibrillin-1, which plays an important role as the scaffolding for elastic tissue in the body. Disruption of such scaffolding (by mutations in fibrillin-1) results in changes in elastic tissues, particularly in the aorta, eye, and skin. Mutations in fibrillin-1 also cause overgrowth of the long bones of the body, resulting in the tall stature and long limbs seen in Marfan patients (U.S. National Library of Medicine, 2005c).

Explanation A matter of debate among medical historians is whether Abraham Lincoln had Marfan syndrome, an inherited connective tissue disorder. Lincoln's famously gaunt appearance is far from definitive proof, but he did have certain physical traits commonly associated with the disease: an extremely tall, slender build; a narrow face, loose joints; and spinal or chest wall abnormalities.

Signs and symptoms of Marfan syndrome can vary greatly from person to person. The disorder affects connective tissue—the fibers that provide the framework and support for the body. As a result, Marfan syndrome can harm many different body systems, including the heart and blood vessels, eyes, skin, and skeleton. In some cases, the damage may be relatively mild, but in others, it can be severe (Mayo Clinic, 2004a).

OI 1.04 McCune-Albright Syndrome

Definition McCune-Albright syndrome is a genetic disease affecting the bones and pigmentation of the skin, which also causes hormonal problems and premature sexual development (U.S. National Library of Medicine, 2004g).

Explanation Symptoms of McCune-Albright include:

- Irregular, patchy café-au-lait spots, especially on the back
- Vaginal bleeding (first menstruation) at a very early age
- Premature puberty
- Early breast development
- Early pubic and armpit hair development
- More than the usual number of broken bones
- Rarely, a form of gigantism (overgrowth of the body caused by excess hormones)

OI 1.05 Osteogenesis Imperfecta-Brittle Bone Disease

Definition Osteogenesis imperfecta (OI) is a genetic disorder characterized by bones that break easily, often from little or no apparent cause. There are at least four recognized forms of the disorder, representing a range of severities. For example, a person may have just a few or as many as several hundred fractures in a lifetime (National Institute of Arthritis and Musculoskeletal and Skin Diseases, 2004a).

Explanation This inherent weakness of the bones is due to a malfunction in the body's production of the protein collagen. Collagen, of which there are at least ten identifiable subtypes, is found in the connective tissues of the body and makes up a large portion of the bones and cartilage. It is the substance that holds the tissues together, providing strength and mass to the bones. For a person with OI, either the amount of collagen being produced is too little or the quality being produced is poor. Either way, the bones of a person with OI are less dense than normal and break easily. It is estimated that OI affects between twenty thousand and fifty thousand people in the United States (Cleveland Clinic, 2004).

At least four types of OI have been identified:

OI 1.05a **Type I Osteogenesis Imperfecta** Type I is the most common form of OI. People with this type of the disease tend to fracture easily and exhibit other features, such as blue sclera, hearing loss, a triangular face, spinal curvature, and dental problems.

OI 1.05b **Type II Osteogenesis Imperfecta** Type II, though less common, is a severe form of the disease. Newborns with type II often fracture before birth and usually die shortly after birth.

OI 1.05c **Type III Osteogenesis Imperfecta** Individuals with type III OI tend to be very small in stature, experience hearing loss at a young age, and have a barrel-shaped rib cage.

OI 1.05d **Type IV Osteogenesis Imperfecta** Type IV OI individuals tend to fracture easily and often have spinal curvature and significant dental problems.

OI 1.06 Osteopetrosis

Definition Generalized hereditary condition consisting of excessive bone mineralization, resulting in altered stature and frequent fractures. They also lack bone marrow hematopoietic function. (A hematopoietic stem cell is one that is isolated from the blood or bone marrow that can renew itself, can differentiate to a variety of specialized cells, can mobilize out of the bone marrow into circulating blood, and can undergo programmed cell death, called apoptosis—a process by which cells that are detrimental or unneeded self-destruct.) Finally, they have a tendency for severe osteomyelitis (an acute or chronic bone infection, usually caused by bacteria) of the jaws (Marquette University School of Dentistry, 2001).

Explanation Osteopetrosis is a congenital disease characterized in each of its forms by defective osteoclast function. Osteoclasts are the cells responsible for bone resorption. They are necessary for the formation of bone marrow. In people with osteopetrosis, osteoclasts do not function normally, and the cavity for bone marrow does not form. This causes bones that appear dense on X-ray and cannot resist average stressors and therefore break easily. The condition is quite rare; incidences have been reported at 1 in 20,000 to 500,000 for the dominant form and 1 in 200,000 for the recessive.

Symptoms include:

- Pain
- Frequent fractures, especially of the long bones, which often do not heal
- Nerve compression, leading to headache, blindness, and deafness
- Enlarged spleen
- Osteomyelitis
- Frontal bossing of the skull
- Unusual dentition, including malformed and unerupted teeth
- Infection
- Bleeding
- Stroke (Osteopetrosis.org, 2002)

There are three major types of osteopetrosis.

OI 1.06a **Adult Form** A milder type of osteopetrosis that is found in adults between twenty and forty years old. This form rarely causes a significant reduction in life expectancy.

OI 1.06b **Intermediate Form** A type of osteopetrosis that is less severe than the malignant infantile form. Found in children younger than ten years old, it is more severe than the adult form of osteopetrosis but usually does not shorten life expectancy.

OI 1.06c **Malignant Infantile Form** A severe type of osteopetrosis. It is inherited when both parents have an abnormal gene that is passed to the child. The disease is apparent from birth and frequently ends in death. Despite its name, the disease is not related to cancer.

OI 1.07 Idiopathic Juvenile Osteoporosis

Definition *Osteoporosis* literally means "porous bone." It is a disease characterized by too little bone formation or excessive bone loss or a combination of both. People with osteoporosis have an increased risk of fractures. It is most common in older people, especially older women.

Osteoporosis is rare in children and adolescents. When it does occur, it is usually caused by an underlying medical disorder or by medications used to treat the disorder. This is called *secondary osteoporosis.* Sometimes, however, there is no identifiable cause of osteoporosis in a child. This is known as *idiopathic osteoporosis* (National Institute of Arthritis and Musculoskeletal and Skin Diseases, 2005).

Explanation Idiopathic juvenile osteoporosis (IJO) is diagnosed after excluding other causes of juvenile osteoporosis (primary diseases or medical therapies known to cause bone loss, as discussed above). It was identified in the medical literature in 1965 (Dent & Friedman, 1965). Since then, fewer than one hundred cases have been reported.

This rare form of osteoporosis typically occurs in previously healthy children just before the onset of puberty (U.S. National Library of Medicine, 2003b). The average age of onset is between eight and fourteen years, but it may also occur in younger children during periods of rapid growth.

OI 1.08 Renal Osteodystrophy

Definition The word *renal* describes things related to the kidneys. Renal osteodystrophy is a bone disease that occurs when the kidneys fail to maintain the proper levels of calcium and phosphorus in the blood. It is a common problem in people with kidney disease and affects 90 percent of dialysis patients (National Kidney and Urologic Diseases Information Clearinghouse, 2005).

Explanation Renal osteodystrophy is most serious in children because their bones are still growing. The condition slows bone growth and causes deformities. One such deformity occurs when the legs bend inward toward each other or outward away from each other; this deformity is referred to as renal rickets. Another important consequence is short stature. Symptoms can be seen in growing children with renal disease even before they start dialysis (National Kidney and Urologic Diseases Information Clearinghouse, 2005).

OI 2.00 Cerebral Palsy

Definition *Cerebral palsy* is an umbrella term used to describe a group of chronic disorders impairing control of movement that appear in the first few years of life and generally do not worsen over time. The disorders are caused by faulty development of or damage to motor areas in the brain that disrupts the brain's ability to control movement and posture (National Institute of Neurological Disorders and Stroke, 2005b). Individuals with cerebral palsy have abnormal, involuntary, or uncoordinated motor movements (Hunt & Marshall, 2006).

Diagnostic Symptoms According to United Cerebral Palsy (2006),

> Early signs of cerebral palsy usually appear before 18 months of age, and parents are often the first to suspect that their infant is not developing motor skills normally. Infants with cerebral palsy are frequently slow to reach developmental milestones, such as learning to roll over, sit, crawl, smile, or walk. This is sometimes called developmental delay.
>
> Some affected children have abnormal muscle tone. Decreased muscle tone is called hypotonia; the baby may seem flaccid and relaxed, even floppy. Increased muscle tone is called hypertonia, and the baby may seem stiff or rigid. In some cases, the baby has an early period of hypotonia that progresses to hypertonia

> after the first 2 to 3 months of life. Affected children may also have unusual posture or favor one side of their body [p. 1].

Further diagnostic symptoms of cerebral palsy include (National Institute of Neurological Disorders and Stroke, 2005b; Mayo Clinic, 2005a):

- Difficulty with fine motor tasks (such as writing or using scissors)
- Difficulty maintaining balance or walking, involuntary movements.
- Possible seizures or mental impairment, but cerebral palsy does not always cause profound handicap
- Early signs (usually before three years of age)
- Infants who are frequently slow to reach developmental milestones such as learning to roll over, sit, crawl, smile, or walk
- Lack of muscle coordination when performing voluntary movements (ataxia)
- Stiff muscles and exaggerated reflexes (spasticity)
- Asymmetrical walking gait, with one foot or leg dragging
- Variations in muscle tone, from too stiff to too floppy
- Excessive drooling or difficulties swallowing, sucking, or speaking
- Tremors
- Difficulty with precise motions, such as writing or buttoning a shirt

Further Key Points In about 70 percent of cases, cerebral palsy results from events occurring before birth that can disrupt normal development of the brain. Contrary to common belief, lack of oxygen reaching the fetus during labor and delivery contributes to only a small minority of cases of cerebral palsy, according to a 2003 report by the American College of Obstetricians and Gynecologists and the American Academy of Pediatrics The American College of Obstetricians and Gynecologists (Task Force on Neonatal Encephalopathy . . . , 2003). A small number of babies also develop brain injuries in the first months or years of life that can result in cerebral palsy. In many cases, the cause of cerebral palsy in a child is not known (March of Dimes, 2006).

There is no standard therapy that works for all patients. Drugs can be used to control seizures and muscle spasms, and special braces can compensate for muscle imbalance. Surgery, mechanical aids to help overcome impairments, counseling for emotional and psychological needs, and physical, occupational, speech, and behavioral therapy may be employed. At this time, cerebral palsy cannot be cured, but many patients can enjoy near-normal lives if their neurological problems are properly managed.

Types of Cerebral Palsy

OI 2.01 Ataxic Cerebral Palsy

Definition A type of cerebral palsy characterized by low muscle tone and poor coordination of movements. Ataxic cerebral palsy involves tremors, unsteady gait, loss of coordination, and abnormal movements. Children often walk with feet wide apart, trunk weaving back and forth, and arms held out (Colarusso & O'Rourke, 2004; U.S. National Library of Medicine, 2004c).

Explanation Children with ataxic CP look unsteady and shaky, especially when they are trying to write or turn a page or cut with scissors. They often have poor balance and may be unsteady when they walk. Because of the shaky movements and problems coordinating their muscles, they may take longer to finish writing or art projects (Turnbull et al., 2006; Colarusso & O'Rourke, 2004; University of Virginia Children's Hospital, 2003).

OI 2.02 Athetoid Cerebral Palsy (Dyskinetic Cerebral Palsy)

Definition A type of cerebral palsy occurring when muscle tone is mixed—sometimes too high and sometimes too low (University of Virginia Children's Hospital, 2003). In athetoid cerebral palsy, there is fluctuating muscle tone, resulting in slow, abnormal writhing movements in which the limb rotates back and forth (Colarusso & O'Rourke, 2004).

Explanation Children with athetoid CP have trouble holding themselves in an upright, steady position for sitting or walking and often show random, involuntary movements of their face, arms, and upper body that they do not mean to make. These movements are usually big. For some, it takes a lot of work and concentration to get their hand to a certain spot (for example, to scratch their nose or reach for a cup). Because of their mixed tone and trouble keeping a position, they may not be able to hold on to things like a toothbrush or fork or pencil. About one-fourth of all people with CP have athetoid CP (University of Virginia Children's Hospital, 2003).

Dyskinetic (athetoid) cerebral palsy affects about 20 percent of all cases of CP (United Cerebral Palsy, 2006). It involves development of abnormal movements (twisting, jerking, or other movements) (U.S. National Library of Medicine, 2004c).

OI 2.03 Mixed Cerebral Palsy

Definition A type of cerebral palsy occurring when muscle tone is too low in some muscles and too high in other muscles (University of Virginia Children's Hospital, 2003). It combines spastic muscle tone and the involuntary movements of athetoid cerebral palsy (Turnbull et al., 2006).

Explanation It is common for patients to have symptoms of more than one of the three forms described in this section. The most common mixed form includes spasticity and athetoid movements, but other combinations are also possible (National Institute of Neurological Disorders and Stroke, 2005b).

OI 2.04 Spastic Cerebral Palsy

Definition A type of cerebral palsy characterized by muscle tone that is too high or too tight (University of Virginia Children's Hospital, 2003). It involves a mild to severe exaggerated contraction of muscles when the muscle is stretched (Hunt & Marshall, 2005).

Explanation Children with spastic CP have stiff and jerky movements because their muscles are too tight. They often have a hard time moving from one position to another or letting go of something in their hand (University of Virginia Children's Hospital, 2003). This is the most common type of CP, occurring in 70 to 80 percent of all cases (Hunt & Marshall, 2005).

OI 3.00 Hydrocephalus

Definition Hydrocephalus is a condition in which the primary characteristic is excessive accumulation of fluid in the brain. Although hydrocephalus was once known as "water on the brain," the "water" is actually cerebrospinal fluid (CSF), a clear fluid surrounding the brain and spinal cord (National Institute of Neurological Disorders and Stroke, 2005c). The excessive accumulation of CSF results in an abnormal dilation of the spaces in the brain called ventricles. This dilation causes potentially harmful pressure on the tissues of the brain and can cause brain damage or mental retardation (Hunt & Marshall, 2006).

Diagnostic Symptoms Diagnostic symptoms of hydrocephalus include (U.S. National Library of Medicine, 2005b):

Early Symptoms in Infants

- Enlarged head (increased head circumference)
- Bulging fontanelles (soft spots of the head) with or without enlargement of the head size
- Separated sutures
- Vomiting

Symptoms of Continued Hydrocephalus

- Irritability, poor temper control
- Muscle spasticity (spasm)

Late Symptoms

- Decreased mental function
- Delayed development
- Slow or restricted movement
- Difficulty feeding
- Lethargy, excessive sleepiness
- Urinary incontinence (loss of control over bladder)
- Brief, shrill, high-pitched cry
- Slow growth (child from birth to five years)

The symptoms vary depending on the amount of damage caused by pressure in the brain. The symptoms may include the following or other symptoms:

In Older Infants and Children

- Headache
- Vomiting
- Vision changes
- Crossed eyes
- Uncontrolled eye movements
- Loss of coordination
- Poor gait (walking pattern)
- Mental aberrations (such as confusion or psychosis)
- Changes in facial and brow contours, eye spacing, or protrusion

Further Key Points The prognosis for patients diagnosed with hydrocephalus is difficult to predict (National Institute of Neurological Disorders and Stroke, 2005c). Hydrocephalus often results in motor language or perceptual disabilities and seizure disorders. Usually the condition is treated immediately on its discovery during the first year of life using a shunting procedure (Westling & Fox, 2004).

Types of Hydrocephalus

OI 3.01 Acquired Hydrocephalus

Definition Acquired hydrocephalus develops at the time of birth or at some point afterward. It can affect individuals of all ages and may be due to the effects of injury or disease (National Institute for Neurological Disorders and Stroke, 2005c).

Explanation Acquired hydrocephalus can occur at any age. The following conditions may cause CSF obstruction and subsequently acquired hydrocephalus:

- Bleeding (hemorrhage)
- Brain trauma (the result of injury)
- Brain tumor
- Cyst (a fluid-filled sac)
- Infection (for example, cerebral abscess, bacterial meningitis)
- Hemorrhaging, traumatic brain injury, and infection in some premature births
- Premature birth (Neurology Channel, 2005)

OI 3.02 Communicating Hydrocephalus

Definition Communicating hydrocephalus occurs when the flow of CSF is blocked after it exits the ventricles. This form is called *communicating* because the CSF can still flow between the ventricles, which remain open (National Institute for Neurological Disorders and Stroke, 2005c).

Explanation Communicating hydrocephalus (or nonobstructive hydrocephalus) is caused by impaired CSF resorption, in the absence of any CSF flow obstruction. Communicating hydrocephalus is, by definition, a hydrocephalus in an individual whose CSF circulation pathways are competent from the ventricles inside the brain to the fluid spaces just below the third ventricle, the so-called basilar cisterns (Hyman-Newman Institute for Neurology and Neurosurgery, 2005).

OI 3.03 Congenital Hydrocephalus

Definition Congenital hydrocephalus is present at birth and may be due to the effects of either environmental influence during fetal development or genetic predisposition (National Institute for Neurological Disorders and Stroke, 2005c).

Explanation By definition, congenital means present at birth. Congenital hydrocephalus is hydrocephalus that is present at a child's birth.

Congenital hydrocephalus is caused by an imbalance between the brain's production of cerebrospinal fluid (CSF) and the body's ability to distribute or absorb it properly. Normally, CSF flows through and out of chambers in the brain called ventricles, and then around the brain and spinal cord, providing nutrition and a protective cushion. It is then reabsorbed by the thin tissue that surrounds the brain and spinal cord.

In infants whose bones have not yet reached mature size or have hardened, hydrocephalus causes the skull to swell and enlarge unless immediate treatment is sought; otherwise, there is an increasing likelihood that the swelling will become fatal. The swelling creates pressure on the brain, which becomes compressed and shrunken unless the pressure is released, and can cause brain damage that may not be reversible. In older adolescents and adults who develop hydrocephalus, the skull has by now hardened and the pressure will be directed inwards onto the brain. The fluid can also collect in the ventricles and hollows of the brain, forcing the tissues of the brain outward against the inside of the cranium. Some symptoms may include intense headaches or migraines, memory problems, blurred vision, and loss of consciousness (BBC, 2006).

OI 3.04 Hydrocephalus Ex Vacuo

Definition Hydrocephalus ex vacuo occurs when there is damage to the brain due to the effects of stroke or traumatic injury. In these cases, there may be actual shrinkage (atrophy or wasting) of brain tissue (National Institute for Neurological Disorders and Stroke, 2005c).

Explanation Hydrocephalus ex vacuo occurs when there is damage to the brain caused by stroke or injury and there may be an actual shrinkage of brain substance. This disorder is essentially hydrocephalus only by default; the CSF pressure itself is normal (Medicine.net, 2004).

OI 3.05 Noncommunicating Hydrocephalus

Definition Noncommunicating hydrocephalus—also called obstructive hydrocephalus—occurs when the flow of CSF is blocked along one or more of the narrow pathways connecting the ventricles (National Institute for Neurological Disorders and Stroke, 2005c).

Explanation In most cases, this disorder refers to a blockage between the third and fourth ventricles at the level of the aqueduct of Sylvius, so-called aqueductal obstruction. This can be due to scarring of this passage (aqueductal stenosis) or a tumor (in most cases, a tectal glioma). When the obstruction is due to a tectal glioma, it is important to realize that the tumor has only a 10 percent chance for growth and the only treatment required is for the hydrocephalus. Additional treatments for the tumor are delivered only if growth is documented (Hyman-Newman Institute for Neurology and Neurosurgery, 2005).

OI 4.00 Limb Deficiency

Definition A limb deficiency refers to any number of skeletal abnormalities in which one or more limbs is partially or totally missing (Gargiulo, 2004).

Diagnostic Symptoms The diagnostic symptoms for these disorders vary, so no generalized list of symptoms will be made.

Further Key Points There were 1,285,000 persons in the United States living with the limb loss (excluding fingers and toes) in 1996. The prevalence rate in 1996 was 4.9 per 1,000 persons. The incidence rate was 46.2 per 100,000 persons with dysvascular disease, 5.86 per 100,000 persons secondary to trauma, and 0.35 per 100,000 secondary to malignancy of a bone or joint. The birth prevalence of congenital limb deficiency in 1996 was 25.64 per 100,000 live births. The prevalence rate is highest among people aged sixty-five years and older: 19.4 per 1,000 (Amputee Coalition of America, 2006).

OI 4.01 Amputation

Definition Amputation is the intentional surgical removal of a limb or body part. It is performed to remove diseased tissue or relieve pain (Joseph Smith Medical Library, 2005).

Explanation If an accident or trauma results in complete amputation (the body part is totally severed), the part sometimes can be reattached, especially when proper care is taken of the severed part and stump.

In a partial amputation, some soft-tissue connection remains. Depending on the severity of the injury, the partially severed extremity may or may not be able to be reattached (U.S. National Library of Medicine, 2004a).

An amputation usually refers to the removal of the whole or part of an arm/hand or a leg/foot. Amputations can be divided into major and minor.

OI 4.01a **Major Amputation** A type of amputation where part of the leg is removed. The amputation is usually below the knee or above the knee.

OI 4.01b **Minor Amputation** A type of amputation where a toe or part of the foot is removed.

OI 4.01c **Traumatic Amputation** A type of amputation caused by a traumatic loss of a body part—usually a finger, toe, arm, or leg—that occurs as the result of an accident or trauma. If an accident or trauma results in complete amputation (the body part is totally severed), the part sometimes can be reattached, especially when proper care is taken of the severed part and stump. In a partial amputation, some soft tissue connection remains. Depending on the severity of the injury, the partially severed extremity may or may not be able to be reattached. There are various complications associated with amputation of a body part. The most important of these are bleeding, shock, and infection.

OI 4.02 Clubfoot

Definition A clubfoot is a foot disorder where the foot turns inward and downward at birth and remains tight in this position, resisting realignment. Clubfoot is the most common disorder of the legs that children are born with. It can range from mild and flexible to severe and rigid (U.S. National Library of Medicine, 2004d).

Explanation With clubfoot, the appearance is unmistakable: the foot is turned to the side and may even appear that the top of the foot is where the bottom should be. The involved foot, calf, and leg are smaller and shorter than the normal side. It is not a painful condition, but if it is not treated, clubfoot leads to significant discomfort and disability by the teenage years (American Academy of Orthopedic Surgeons, 2004).

OI 4.03 Contracture Deformity

Definition A contracture is a permanent tightening of muscle, tendons, ligaments, or skin that prevents normal movement of the associated body part and can cause permanent deformity (U.S. National Library of Medicine, 2004e).

Explanation Contracture deformity develops when the normally elastic connective tissues are replaced by inelastic fibrous tissue. This makes the affected area resistant to stretching and prevents normal movement. Contractures occur primarily in the skin, underlying tissues, muscle, tendons and joint areas (University of Maryland Medical Center, 2005). The most common causes are scarring and lack of use due to immobilization or inactivity.

OI 4.03a **Clawfoot** A type of contracture deformity of the toes in which the toe joint nearest the foot is bent upward (from contracture) and the other toe joints bend downward (also from contracture). Claw foot can be something that a child is born with (congenital) or can develop as a consequence of disorders (acquired).

OI 4.03b **Clawhand** A type of contracture deformity characterized by curved or bent fingers, which makes it appear like the claw of an animal. Clawhand can be something that a child is born with (congenital), or it can develop as a consequence of certain disorders (acquired).

OI 4.03c **Dupuytren's Contracture** A type of contracture deformity characterized by a painless thickening and contracture of tissue beneath the skin on the palm of the hand and fingers. Progressive contracture may result in deformity and loss of function of the hand (Union Memorial Hospital, 2004a).

OI 4.03d **Foot-Drop** A type of contracture deformity where the foot points downward.

OI 4.03e **Volkmann's Contracture (Ischemic Contracture)** A type of contracture deformity resulting in the deformity of the hand, fingers, and wrist due to the effects of injury to the muscles of the forearm. Volkmann's contracture occurs when there is a lack of blood flow (ischemia) to the forearm, usually due to the effects of increased pressure that results from swelling (Union Memorial Hospital, 2004b).

OI 4.03f **Wrist-Drop** A type of contracture deformity where the wrist cannot be lifted.

OI 4.04 Other Types of Loss or Deformity of Limbs

OI 5.00 Muscular Dystrophy

Definition Muscular dystrophy refers to a group of genetic diseases marked by progressive weakness and degeneration of the skeletal or voluntary muscles that control movement (Muscular Dystrophy Family Foundation, 2005; Hardman et al., 2005).

Diagnostic Symptoms Symptoms vary with the different types of muscular dystrophy. Some types, such as Duchenne muscular dystrophy, are ultimately fatal, while other types have associated muscle weakness but cause little disability and are associated with normal life expectancy.

The muscles primarily affected vary, but can be around the pelvis, shoulder, face, or elsewhere. The age of onset can vary as well, with more severe subtypes tending to occur earlier in childhood. Other symptoms include:

- Muscle weakness
- Progressive symptoms
- Frequent falls
- Delayed development of muscle motor skills
- Problems walking (delayed walking)
- Difficulty using one or more muscle groups (the specific muscles affected depends on the type of disorder)
- Eyelid drooping (ptosis)
- Drooling
- Mental retardation (present only in some types)
- Hypotonia (low muscle tone)
- Joint contractures (clubfoot, clawhand, or others)
- Scoliosis (curved spine)

Further Key Points *Muscular dystrophy* (MD) is the common term for several progressive hereditary diseases that cause muscles to weaken and degenerate. Each type has its own hereditary pattern, age of onset, and rate of muscle loss. Most muscular dystrophies are inherited and caused by alterations in specific genes. Genes are found on the chromosomes in the cells and provide the instructions for how a person will grow and develop. Different genetic alterations cause different types of muscular dystrophies (Muscular Dystrophy Family Foundation, 2005).

The prognosis of MD varies according to the type and the progression of the disorder. Some cases may be mild and very slowly progressive, with normal life span, while other cases may have more marked progression of muscle weakness, functional disability, and loss of ambulation. It is a progressive disorder that may affect the muscles of the hips, legs, shoulders, and arms, progressively causing these individuals to lose their ability to walk and use their arms and hands effectively (Hardman et al., 2005).

Types of Muscular Dystrophy

OI 5.01 Becker Muscular Dystrophy

Definition Becker muscular dystrophy is similar to Duchenne MD, but it progresses more slowly. Symptoms typically begin during adolescence but can begin as early as age five or as late as age twenty-five (U.S. National Library of Medicine, 2004b). Muscle weakness first occurs in the legs, so most children eventually lose the ability to walk. As the disease progresses, they also lose strength in their shoulders and back. It tends to affect older boys and young men (Milton S. Hershey Medical Center of Penn State University, 2006a).

Explanation Symptoms of Becker muscular dystrophy include:

- Slowly progressive muscle weakness, causing difficulty with muscle skills (running, hopping, jumping)
- Progressive difficulty walking, although ability to walk may continue into adulthood (up to age forty)
- Frequent falls
- Problems breathing
- Enlarged calves (Muscular Dystrophy Association, 2004)
- Cognitive dysfunction
- Skeletal deformities of the chest and back (scoliosis)
- Muscle deformities
- Contractures of heels and legs
- Fatigue
- Heart disease (U.S. National Library of Medicine, 2004b)

OI 5.02 Congenital Muscular Dystrophy

Definition Congenital muscular dystrophy is a rare form of MD present from birth. It is really a group of diseases, not a single disease. These diseases are called congenital because symptoms can be noted from birth.

Explanation Joint contractures occur when muscles attached to a joint have unequal strength; the stronger muscle pulls and bends the joint into a locked and nonfunctional position. A combination of the facial, arm and leg, pelvic, respiratory, and shoulder muscles can be weak at birth, but this muscle weakness rarely gets worse. Some types of congenital muscular dystrophy affect the brain, causing tissue abnormalities and seizures (U.S. National Library of Medicine, 2004e).

OI 5.03 Duchenne Muscular Dystrophy

Definition Duchenne muscular dystrophy is the most severe form of muscular dystrophy and the most common form of MD that affects children (Mayo Clinic, 2005). It is a rapidly progressive form of the disease.

Explanation Duchenne muscular dystrophy is caused by a defective gene, but it often occurs in people from families without a known history of the condition. It is marked by progressive loss of muscle function, which begins in the lower limbs (U.S. National Library of Medicine, 2004f).

Symptoms of Duchenne muscular dystrophy include (Mayo Clinic, 2005; U.S. National Library of Medicine, 2004f):

- Muscle weakness
- Waddling gait
- Large calf muscles
- Rapid progression
- Frequent falls
- Difficulty with motor skills (running, hopping, jumping)
- Progressive difficulty walking or lost ability to walk (may occur by age twelve)
- Fatigue
- Intellectual retardation (possible)
- Skeletal deformities of the chest and back (scoliosis)
- Muscle deformities
- Contractures of heels or legs

OI 5.04 Emery-Dreifuss Muscular Dystrophy

Definition Emery-Dreifuss muscular dystrophy typically starts causing symptoms in late childhood to the early teens and sometimes as late as age twenty-five. It is another form of muscular dystrophy that affects mostly boys. It involves muscles in the shoulders, upper arms, and shins, and it often causes joint problems (joints can become tighter in people with EDMD). The heart muscle may also be affected (Nemours Foundation, 2005a).

Explanation The symptoms of Emery-Dreifuss muscular dystrophy include weakness and wasting of shoulder, upper arm, and shin muscles; joint deformities; and slow progress slow. Sudden death may occur from cardiac problems (Mayo Clinic, 2005). Muscle weakness and wasting generally start in the shoulders, upper arms, and lower legs. Weakness may later spread to involve the muscles of the chest and pelvic area.

Contractures appear early in the disease, usually involving the ankle and elbow. Unlike other forms of muscular dystrophy, contractures in Emery-Dreifuss dystrophy often appear before the person experiences significant muscle weakness. Physical therapy is beneficial in minimizing the contractures (Muscular Dystrophy Association, 2001).

OI 5.05 Facioscapulohumeral Muscular Dystrophy (Landouzy-Dejerine Dystrophy)

Definition Facioscapulohumeral muscular dystrophy is a type of muscular dystrophy that affects the upper body, unlike some other types that affect primarily the lower body (including Duchenne muscular dystrophy and Becker muscular dystrophy). It is a genetic disorder with an autosomal-dominant inheritance pattern. This means the disorder appears in both men and women and may develop in a child if either parent carries the gene for the disorder (U.S. National Library of Medicine, 2005a).

Explanation Onset of facioscapulohumeral muscular dystrophy usually occurs during the teen to early adult years. Symptoms are usually mild and slowly progressive. Facial muscle weakness and shoulder muscle weakness are common. There is difficulty raising the arms because of shoulder and arm muscle weakness. Weakness of the lower legs is possible as the disorder progresses and can be severe enough to interfere with walking. Other body systems are usually not affected, and intellectual function is normal (Mayo Clinic, 2004b; U.S. National Library of Medicine, 2005a).

OI 5.06 Limb-Girdle Muscular Dystrophy

Definition Limb-girdle muscular dystrophies encompass at least ten different inherited disorders that initially affect the muscles around the shoulder girdle and the hips. The limb-girdle group of muscular dystrophies is so-called because generally weakness occurs in the shoulder and pelvic girdle (Bushby, 2004).

Explanation Typically, onset of pelvic muscle weakness (difficulty standing from a sitting position without using arms, difficulty climbing stairs) starts in childhood to young adulthood. Later there is the onset of shoulder weakness with progression to significant loss of mobility or wheelchair dependence over the next twenty to thirty years (Bushby, 2004).

OI 5.07 Myotonic Muscular Dystrophy

Definition Myotonic dystrophy is the most common adult form of muscular dystrophy and is caused by a defective gene. Unlike any of the other muscular dystrophies, the muscle weakness is accompanied by myotonia (delayed relaxation of muscles after contraction) and a variety of abnormalities in addition to those of muscle. The disorder is also known as Steinert's disease and dystrophia myotonica (Muscular Dystrophy Association, 2003a).

Explanation The following can be symptoms of myotonic MD:

- Slack jaw
- Drooping eyelids
- Difficulty swallowing
- Difficulty in relaxing grasp (especially if an object is cold)
- Weakened grip (110 pounds is normal grip strength for an unaffected man and 10 pounds for a person with myotonic MD)
- Cataracts
- Constipation
- Frontal balding
- Sleep apnea
- Testicular atrophy
- Insulin resistance
- Arrhythmias
- Reduced fertility (Cleveland Clinic, 2001)

OI 5.08 Other Types of Muscular Dystrophy

OI 6.00 Poliomyelitis

Definition Poliomyelitis is a disorder caused by a viral infection (poliovirus) that can affect the whole body, including muscles and nerves. Severe cases may cause permanent paralysis or death.

Diagnostic Symptoms The polio virus attacks the nerve cells that control muscle movements. Many people infected with the virus have few or no symptoms. Others have short-term symptoms, such as headache, fatigue, fever, stiff neck and back, and muscle pain. More serious problems happen when the virus invades nerves in the brain and causes paralysis of the muscles used in swallowing and breathing. Invasion of the nerves in the spinal cord can cause paralysis of the arms, legs, or trunk (Directors of Health Promotion and Education, 2006).

Further Key Points Poliomyelitis is a communicable disease caused by infection with the poliovirus. Transmission occurs by direct person-to-person contact, contact with infected secretions from the nose or mouth, or contact with infected feces.

The virus enters through the mouth and nose, multiplies in the throat and intestinal tract, and then is absorbed and spread through the blood and lymph system. Incubation (the time from being infected with the virus to developing symptoms of disease) ranges from five to thirty-five days (the average is seven to fourteen days).

Between 1840 and the 1950s, polio was a worldwide epidemic. Since the development of polio vaccines, the incidence is much reduced. Outbreaks still occur, usually in unimmunized groups (U.S. National Library of Medicine, 2004b). It once affected mostly infants and children, but now is mostly seen in people over fifteen years old. Adults and young girls are more likely to be infected, but infection in young boys is more likely to result in paralysis.

Types of Poliomyelitis

OI 6.01 Abortive Poliomyelitis

Definition Abortive poliomyelitis is a mild and short course of the disease (University of Utah Health Sciences Center, 2001). It may simulate acute respiratory infection or gastroenteritis and is usually not dangerous.

Explanation Most people with this form of polio may not even suspect they have it because their sickness is limited to mild flulike symptoms such as mild upper respiratory infection, diarrhea, fever, sore throat, and a general feeling of being ill (Nemours Foundations, 2005b). Other symptoms may include:

- Fever (up to 103°F or 38.5°C)
- Decreased appetite
- Nausea or vomiting
- Sore throat
- Generally not feeling well
- Constipation
- Abdominal pain (University of Utah Health Sciences Center, 2001).

OI 6.02 Paralytic Polio

Definition Paralytic polio is the most serious type of polio associated with aseptic meningitis (1 to 5 percent show neurological symptoms such as sensitivity to light and neck stiffness) (Nemours Foundation, 2005b).

Explanation The symptoms of paralytic poliomyelitis include those of nonparalytic and abortive poliomyelitis. In addition, the following symptoms may occur:

- Muscle weakness all over
- Severe constipation
- Muscle wasting

- Weakened breathing
- Difficulty swallowing
- Weak cough
- Flushed or blotchy skin
- Hoarse voice
- Bladder paralysis
- Muscle paralysis (University of Virginia Health System, 2004)

Paralytic polio, which occurs in less than 1 percent of all cases, is classified into three types according to level of involvement.

OI 6.02a **Bulbar Polio** A type of paralytic polio characterized by weakness of muscles controlled by cranial nerves.

OI 6.02b **Bulbospinal Polio** A type of paralytic polio characterized by a combination of spinal and bulbar paralysis.

OI 6.02c **Spinal Polio** In spinal polio, the most common type of paralytic polio, asymmetric paralysis, most often involving the legs, is typical.

OI 6.03 Post-Polio Syndrome

Definition Post-polio syndrome (PPS) is a condition that affects polio survivors anywhere from ten to forty years after recovery from an initial paralytic attack of the poliomyelitis virus. It is characterized by a further weakening of muscles that were previously affected by the polio infection (National Institute of Neurological Disorders and Stroke, 2005f).

Explanation Symptoms include fatigue, slowly progressive muscle weakness, and, at times, muscular atrophy. Joint pain and increasing skeletal deformities such as scoliosis are common. Some patients experience only minor symptoms, while others develop spinal muscular atrophy and, very rarely, what appears to be, but is not, a form of amyotrophic lateral sclerosis (ALS), also called Lou Gehrig's disease. PPS is rarely a life-threatening infection (National Institute of Neurological Disorders and Stroke, 2005f).

OI 6.04 Other Types of Poliomyelitis

OI 7.00 Scoliosis

Definition Scoliosis is a lateral deviation of the normal vertical line of the spine that, when measured by X-ray, is greater than ten degrees. Scoliosis consists of a lateral curvature of the spine with rotation of the vertebrae within the curve (National Scoliosis Foundation, 2005).

Diagnostic Symptoms Diagnostic symptoms of scoliosis include (U.S. National Library of Medicine, 2004j):

- The spine curving abnormally to the side (laterally)
- Shoulders or hips, or both, that appear uneven
- Backache or low back pain
- Fatigue

Further Key Points The outcome for individuals with scoliosis depends on the cause, location, and severity of the curve. The greater the curve, the greater the chance of progression after growth has stopped. Scoliosis affects a small percentage of the population, approximately 2 percent. However, it runs in families. If someone in a family has scoliosis, the likelihood of an incidence is much higher—approximately 20 percent.

The vast majority of scoliosis is idiopathic, meaning its cause is unknown. It usually develops in middle or late childhood, before puberty, and is seen more often in girls than boys. Although scoliosis can occur in children with cerebral palsy, muscular dystrophy, spinal bifida, and other miscellaneous conditions, most scoliosis is found in otherwise healthy youngsters (American Academy of Orthopaedic Surgeons, 2000).

Types of Scoliosis

OI 7.01 Adolescent Idiopathic Scoliosis (Scoliosis of Unknown Cause)

Definition Adolescent idiopathic scoliosis is present in 2 to 4 percent of children between ten and sixteen years of age. It is defined as a lateral curvature of the spine greater than ten degrees accompanied by vertebral rotation appearing in a previously straight spine (U.S. National Library of Medicine, 2004j).

Explanation In 80 to 85 percent of people, the cause of scoliosis is unknown; this is called idiopathic scoliosis. It is the most common type and occurs after the age of ten. Girls are more likely than boys to have this type of scoliosis. Since scoliosis can run in families, a child who has a parent, brother, or sister with idiopathic scoliosis should be checked regularly for scoliosis by the family physician. Idiopathic scoliosis can also occur in children younger than ten years of age but is very rare (National Institute of Arthritis and Musculoskeletal and Skin Diseases, 2001).

OI 7.02 Early-Onset or Infantile Idiopathic Scoliosis

Definition Infantile idiopathic scoliosis is extremely rare. It occurs from birth to three years of age and is found mostly in males and usually results in a left thoracic (upper spine) curve (National Scoliosis Foundation, 2003).

Explanation Many infantile idiopathic curves correct themselves spontaneously without treatment but should be monitored (National Scoliosis Foundation, 2003).

OI 7.03 Juvenile Idiopathic Scoliosis

Definition Juvenile idiopathic scoliosis usually occurs from about age three to the onset of puberty-roughly age ten to eleven for girls, age twelve for boys (National Scoliosis Foundation, 2003).

Explanation This disorder is a relatively uncommon condition. Spinal fusion may be necessary before puberty. The prognosis is worse for younger children.

OI 7.03a **Nonstructural (Functional) Scoliosis** A type of juvenile idiopathic scoliosis characterized by a structurally normal spine that appears curved. This is a temporary, changing curve. It is due to the effects of an underlying condition such as a difference in leg length, muscle spasms, or inflammatory conditions such as appendicitis. Doctors treat this type of scoliosis by correcting the underlying problem.

OI 7.03b **Structural Scoliosis** A type of juvenile idiopathic scoliosis characterized by a fixed curve that doctors treat case by case. Sometimes structural scoliosis is one part of a syndrome or disease such as Marfan's syndrome, an inherited connective tissue disorder. In other cases, it occurs by itself.

OI 7.04 Other Types of Scoliosis

OI 8.00 Spina Bifida

OI

Definition Spina bifida (SB) is a neural tube defect (a disorder involving incomplete development of the brain, spinal cord, or their protective coverings) caused by the failure of the fetus's spine to close properly during the first month of pregnancy (Spina Bifida Association, 2006; National Institute of Neurological Disorders and Stroke, 2005g; U.S. National Library of Medicine, 2004k). It is the most frequently occurring permanently disabling birth defect (Hardman, Drew, & Egan, 2005).

Diagnostic Symptoms Infants born with spina bifida sometimes have an open lesion on their spine where significant damage to the nerves and spinal cord has occurred. Although the spinal opening can be surgically repaired shortly after birth, the nerve damage is permanent, resulting in varying degrees of paralysis of the lower limbs. Even when no lesion is present, there may be improperly formed or missing vertebrae and accompanying nerve damage. In addition to physical and mobility difficulties, most individuals have some form of learning disability (National Institute of Neurological Disorders and Stroke, 2005g).

Further Key Points An estimated seventy thousand people in the United States are currently living with spina bifida. There are 60 million childbearing-aged women at risk of having a baby born at risk for spina bifida and about three thousand pregnancies are affected by these birth defects each year (Spina Bifida Association, 2006).

Types of Spina Bifida

OI 8.01 Meningocele

Definition Meningocele occurs when the spinal cord develops normally but the meninges protrude from a spinal opening (National Institute of Neurological Disorders and Stroke, 2005g). *Meningocele* is the term used when just the meninges—no nerves—push through the opening in the vertebrae. The meninges form a fluid-filled sac that is usually covered with skin (Nemours Foundation, 2005c).

Explanation With this disorder, the spinal cord is normal, and a person with a meningocele usually has no mobility impairments (Turnbull et al., 2006). A person with meningocele will need surgery to prevent any nerve damage later (Nemours Foundation, 2005c).

OI 8.02 Myelomeningocele

Definition Myelomeningocele is one of the most common birth defects of the central nervous system. It is a neural tube defect in which the bones of the spine do not completely form, and the spinal canal is incomplete. This allows the spinal cord and meninges (the membranes covering the spinal cord) to protrude out of the child's back (U.S. National Library of Medicine, 2004h).

Explanation The symptoms of this disorder include:

- Visible sac-like protrusion on the mid- to lower back of a newborn
- Not translucent when a light is shone from behind the sac
- Weakness of the hips, legs, or feet of a newborn

This is the most serious form of spina bifida and results in varying degrees of leg weakness, inability to control bowels or bladder, and a variety of physical problems such as dislocated hips or clubfeet (Turnbull et al., 2006).

OI 8.03 Spina Bifida Occulta

Definition Occulta is the mildest and most common form in which one or more vertebrae are malformed. The name *occulta,* which means "hidden," indicates that the malformation, or opening in the spine, is covered by a layer of skin. This form of spina bifida rarely causes disability or symptoms (National Institute of Neurological Disorders and Stroke, 2005g).

Explanation Because the spinal nerves are not involved, most children with this form of spina bifida have no signs or symptoms and experience no neurological problems. An abnormal tuft of hair, a collection of fat, a small dimple, or a birthmark may be seen on the newborn's skin above the spinal defect and may be the only indication of the condition. In fact, most people who have spina bifida occulta do not even know it, unless the condition is discovered during an X-ray for unrelated reasons (Mayo Clinic, 2003).

OI 8.04 Other Types of Spina Bifida

OI 9.00 Spinal Cord Injury

Definition The term *spinal cord injury* (SCI) refers to any injury of the neural (pertaining to nerves) elements within the spinal canal. It can occur from trauma or disease to the vertebral column or the spinal cord itself. Most spinal cord injuries are the result of trauma to the vertebral column. Such trauma can cause a fracture of bone or tearing of ligaments with displacement of the bony column. This causes a pinching of the spinal cord (Spinal Cord Injury Information Network, 2000).

Diagnostic Symptoms Damage to the spinal cord interrupts the signals from the sensory and motor nerves, resulting in varying degrees of paralysis and loss of sensation. Symptoms depend on the severity and location of the injury. A completely severed spinal cord causes paralysis and loss of sensation below the severed section. Patients with the cord partially severed may have some function below the injury. Damage to the front portion of the cord causes paralysis and loss of the ability to feel pain and changes in temperature. Damage to the center of the cord may paralyze the arms but not the legs. Damage to the right or left half of the spinal cord causes paralysis on the side of the injury, loss of pain and temperature sensation, on the opposite side of the injury, and loss of the ability to sense position (Milton S. Hershey Medical College of Penn State University, 2006b).

Further Key Points There are currently over a quarter-million people with spinal cord injury living in the United States. For some of these people, the injury is the result of a disease such as polio or spina bifida. However, for a vast majority, the spinal cord injury is the result of trauma. The leading traumatic cause of spinal cord injuries is automobile accidents, causing 44 percent of all injuries. Other causes, in descending order of frequency, are violence (such as gunshot wounds), falls, and sports. While sports account for only 8 percent of all spinal cord injuries, 60 percent of those sports-related injuries are a result of diving accidents (National Institute of Neurological Disorders and Stroke, 2005h).

Types of Spinal Cord Injury

OI 9.01 Incomplete Injury

Definition A type of spinal cord injury where the ability of the spinal cord to convey messages to or from the brain is not completely lost (Spinal Cord Injury Resource Center, 2005).

Explanation An incomplete injury means that there is some functioning below the primary level of the injury. The person may be able to move one limb more than another, may be able to feel parts of the body that cannot be moved, or may have more functioning on one side of the body than the other. With the advances in acute treatment of SCI, incomplete injuries are becoming more common (Spinal Cord Injury Resource Center, 2005).

OI 9.02 Complete Injury

Definition A type of spinal cord injury indicated by a total lack of sensory and motor function below the level of injury (Spinal Cord Injury Resource Center, 2005).

Explanation A complete injury means that there is no function below the level of the injury, that is, no sensation and no voluntary movement. Both sides of the body are equally affected (Spinal Cord Injury Resource Center, 2005). Almost half of all spinal cord injuries are complete: there is no function below the level of the injury. About 3 percent of patients with complete injuries show some improvement over the first twenty-four hours after injury. After twenty-four hours postinjury, improvement is almost never seen (Chicago Institute of Neurosurgery and Neuroresearch, 2005).

OI 9.03 Other Types of Spinal Cord Injuries

OI 10.00 Spinal Muscular Atrophies

Definition Spinal muscular atrophy (SMA) is a genetic motor neuron disease caused by progressive degeneration of motor neurons in the spinal cord. The disorder causes weakness and wasting of the voluntary muscles. Weakness is often more severe in the legs than in the arms (National Institute of Neurological Disorders and Stroke, 2005i).

Diagnostic Symptoms An individual with SMA has a missing or mutated gene (SMN1, or survival motor neuron 1) that produces a protein in the body called survival motor neuron (SMN) protein. This protein deficiency has its most severe effect on motor neurons, nerve cells in the spinal cord that send out nerve fibers to muscles throughout the body. Since SMN protein is critical to the survival and health of motor neurons, cells without this protein nerve may atrophy, shrink, and eventually die, resulting in muscle weakness.

As children with SMA grow, their bodies are doubly stressed, first by the decrease in motor neurons and then by the increased demands on the nerve and muscle cells as their bodies grow larger. The resulting muscle atrophy can cause weakness and bone and spinal deformities that may lead to further loss of function, as well as additional compromise of the respiratory (breathing) system (Families of Spinal Muscular Atrophy, 2004).

Further Key Points Children with SMA who have difficulty swallowing are at risk for aspirating when eating. Sometimes the child may aspirate his or her own secretions. The child may choke while eating and may also experience weight loss as swallowing becomes more difficult (Families of Spinal Muscular Atrophy, 2004).

Types of Spinal Muscular Atrophies

OI 10.01 Amyotrophic Lateral Sclerosis–Adult Spinal Muscular Atrophies

Definition Amyotrophic lateral sclerosis (ALS), sometimes called Lou Gehrig's disease, is a rapidly progressive, invariably fatal neurological disease that attacks the nerve cells (neurons) responsible for controlling voluntary muscles. In ALS, both the upper motor neurons and the lower motor neurons degenerate or die, ceasing to send messages to muscles. Unable to function, the muscles gradually weaken, waste away, and twitch. Eventually the ability of the brain to start and control voluntary movement is lost (National Institute of Neurological Disorders and Stroke, 2005a).

Explanation Individuals with ALS lose their strength and the ability to move their arms, legs, and body. When muscles in the diaphragm and chest wall fail, they lose the ability to breathe without ventilatory support. In most cases, the disease does not impair a person's mind, personality, intelligence, or memory, nor does it affect the ability to see, smell, taste, hear, or recognize touch. A small percentage of patients may experience problems with memory or decision making, and there is growing evidence that some may develop a form of dementia. The cause of ALS is not known (National Institute of Neurological Disorders and Stroke, 2005a).

OI 10.02 Congenital Spinal Muscular Atrophies with Arthrogryposis

Definition Congenital spinal muscular atrophies (SMA) with arthrogryposis (persistent contracture of joints with fixed abnormal posture of the limb) is a rare disorder (National Institute of Neurological Disorders and Stroke, 2005i).

Explanation Manifestations include severe contractures, curvature of the spine, chest deformity, respiratory problems, an unusually small jaw, and drooping upper eyelids (National Institute of Neurological Disorders and Stroke, 2005i).

OI 10.03 Kennedy Syndrome or Progressive Spinobulbar Muscular Atrophy

Definition Kennedy syndrome or progressive spinobulbar muscular atrophy is a motor neuron disease caused by progressive degeneration of motor neurons in the spinal cord that occurs between fifteen and sixty years of age (National Institute of Neurological Disorders and Stroke, 2005d).

Explanation Features of this type may include weakness of muscles in the tongue and face, difficulty swallowing, speech impairment, and excessive development of the mammary glands in males. The course of the disorder is usually slowly progressive. Kennedy syndrome is an X-linked recessive disorder, which means that women carry the gene but the disorder occurs only in men (National Institute of Neurological Disorders and Stroke, 2005d).

OI 10.04 Spinal Muscular Atrophies, Type I (Infantile)

Definition Infantile spinal muscular atrophy (also called Werdnig-Hoffmann disease) is the most severe form of SMA. It usually becomes evident in the first six months of life. The child is unable to roll or sit unsupported, and the severe muscle weakness eventually causes feeding and breathing problems. These children usually do not live beyond about eighteen months of age (Muscular Dystrophy Association, 2003b).

Explanation Symptoms of this disorder include floppiness of the limbs and trunk, feeble movements of the arms and legs, swallowing and feeding difficulties, and impaired breathing. Affected children never sit or stand and usually die before the age of two (National Institute of Neurological Disorders and Stroke, 2005i).

OI 10.05 Spinal Muscular Atrophies, Type II (Intermediate)

Definition This is the largest SMA group (45 percent) and may represent an overlap between arrested types I and III. It is transmitted by autosomal-recessive inheritance. Most children develop normally for the first six months of life, with onset of motor arrest before eighteen months (Tsao & Armon, 2003).

Explanation A child with the intermediate form of SMA often reaches six to twelve months of age, sometimes later, and learns to sit unsupported before symptoms are noticed. Weakness of the muscles in the legs and trunk develops, and this makes it difficult for the child to crawl properly or walk normally, if at all. Weakness in the muscles of the arms occurs as well, although this is not as severe as in the legs. Usually the muscles used in chewing and swallowing are not significantly affected early on. The muscles of the chest wall are affected, causing poor breathing function. Parents notice that the child is "floppy" or limp (the medical term is *hypotonia;* Muscular Dystrophy Association, 2003a).

OI 10.06 Juvenile Spinal Muscular Atrophy-Type III

Definition Juvenile spinal muscular atrophy (Kugelberg-Welander disease) usually has its onset after two years of age. It is considerably milder than the infantile or intermediate forms. In juvenile spinal muscular atrophy, children are able to walk, although with difficulty (Muscular Dystrophy Association, 2003a).

Explanation Weakness is most severe in muscles closest to the center of the body, such as those of the shoulders, hips, thighs, and upper back. Respiratory muscle weakness and spinal curvature sometimes develop. This disease progresses slowly, with walking ability usually maintained until at least adolescence. A wheelchair is often required later in life. Life span usually is not affected.

OI 11.00 Stroke

Definition Stroke occurs when the blood supply to part of the brain is suddenly interrupted or a blood vessel in the brain bursts, spilling blood into the spaces surrounding brain cells. Brain cells die when they no longer receive oxygen and nutrients from the blood or there is sudden bleeding into or around the brain (National Institute of Neurological Disorders and Stroke, 2005j).

Diagnostic Symptoms The symptoms of a stroke include sudden numbness or weakness, especially on one side of the body; sudden confusion or trouble speaking or understanding speech; sudden trouble seeing in one or both eyes; sudden trouble with walking, dizziness, or loss of balance or coordination; or sudden severe headache with no known cause. There are two forms of stroke: ischemic—(blockage of a blood vessel supplying the brain) and hemorrhagic—(bleeding into or around the brain; National Institute of Neurological Disorders and Stroke, 2005j).

Further Key Points Every forty-five seconds, someone in the United States has a stroke. If blood flow is stopped for longer than a few seconds, the brain cannot get blood and oxygen. Brain cells can die, causing permanent damage (U.S. National Library of Medicine, 2005).

OI 12.00 Other Types of Orthopedic Impairments—Be Specific

OI

References

American Academy of Orthopaedic Surgeons. (2000). Scoliosis. Retrieved March 18, 2006 from http://orthoinfo.aaos.org/brochure/thr_report.cfm?Thread_ID=14&top category=Spine.

American Academy of Orthopedic Surgeons. (2004). *Club foot.* Retrieved June 13, 2005, from http://orthoinfo.aaos.org/fact/thr_report.cfm?Thread_ID=161&top category=Children.

Amputee Coalition of America. (2006). *Limb loss.* Retrieved February 6, 2006 from http://www.amputee-coalition.org/.

BBC. (2006). *Congenital hydrocephalus.* Retrieved November 13, 2006, from http://www.bbc.co.uk/dna/h2g2/A540541.

Best, S. J., Heller, K. W., & Bigge, J. L. (2005). *Teaching individuals with physical or multiple disabilities* (5th ed.). Upper Saddle River, NJ: Merrill/Prentice Hall.

Bowe, F. (2005). *Making inclusion work.* Upper Saddle River, NJ: Merrill/Pearson.

Bushby, K.M.D. (2004). *Limp-girdle MD.* Retrieved March 3, 2006, from http://www.muscular-dystrophy.org/information_resources/factsheets/medical_conditions_factsheets/limb_girdle.html#Whatislimbgirdlemusculardystrophy.

Chicago Institute of Neurosurgery and Neuroresearch. (2005). *Spinal cord injury and spine injury.* Retrieved June 13, 2005, from http://www.cinn.org/isc/spinalcord injury.html.

Cleveland Clinic. (2001). *Myotonic muscular dystrophy.* Retrieved July 1, 2005, from http://www.clevelandclinic.org/health/health-info/docs/2100/2113.asp?index=8884&src=news.

Cleveland Clinic. (2004). *Osteogenesis imperfecta.* Retrieved May 13, 2005, from http://www.clevelandclinic.org/health/health-info/docs/2600/2610.asp?index=9500.

Closs, A. (2000). *The education of children with medical conditions.* London: David Fulton Publishers.

Colarusso, R., & O'Rourke, C. (2004). *Special education for all teachers.* Dubuque, IA: Kendall/Hunt.

Dent, C. E., & Friedman, M. (1965, April). Idiopathic juvenile osteoporosis. *Medicine, 34,* 177–210.

Deutsch-Smith, D. (2004). *Introduction to special education: Teaching in an age of opportunity* (5th ed.). Needham Heights, MA: Allyn & Bacon.

Directors of Health Promotion and Education. (2006). *Polio.* Retrieved January 7, 2006, from http://www.dhpe.org/infect/polio.html.

Downing, J. A. (2004). Related services for students with disabilities: Introduction to the special issue. *Intervention in School and Clinic, 39,* 195–208.

Etzel-Wise, D., & Mears, B. (2004). Adapted physical education and therapeutic recreation in schools. *Intervention in School and Clinic, 39,* 223–232.

Families of Spinal Muscular Atrophy. (2004). *Understanding SMA.* Retrieved July 13, 2005, from http://www.fsma.org/booklet.shtml.

Friend, M. (2005). *Special education: Contemporary perspectives for school professionals.* Needham Heights, MA: Allyn & Bacon.

Gargiulo, R. M. (2004). *Special education in contemporary society: An introduction to exceptionality.* Belmont, CA: Thompson-Wadsworth.

Hallahan, D. P., & Kauffman, J. M. (2006). *Exceptional learners: Introduction to special education* (10th ed.). Needham Heights, MA: Allyn & Bacon.

Hardman, M. L., Drew, C. J., & Egan, M. W. (2005). *Human exceptionality: School, community, and family* (8th ed.). Needham Heights, MA: Allyn & Bacon.

Heller, K. W., Dangel, H., & Sweatman, L. (1995). Systematic selection of adaptations for students with muscular dystrophy. *Journal of Developmental and Physical Disabilities, 7,* 253–265.

Heller, K. W., Frederick, L. D., Best, S., Dykes, M. K., & Cohen, E. T. (2000). Specialized health care procedures in the schools: Training and service delivery. *Exceptional Children, 66,* 173–186.

Heward, W. L. (2006). *Exceptional children: An introduction to special education* (8th ed.). Upper Saddle River, NJ: Pearson Education.

Hunt, N., & Marshall, K. (2006). *Exceptional children and youth: An introduction to special education* (4th ed.). Boston: Houghton Mifflin.

Hyman-Newman Institute for Neurology and Neurosurgery. (2005). *Obstructive hydrocephalus.* Retrieved June 1, 2005, from http://nyneurosurgery.org/hydroobstruct.htm.

Joseph Smith Medical Library. (2005). *Amputation.* Retrieved June 18, 2005, from http://www.chclibrary.org/micromed/00037150.html.

Kirk, S. A. Gallagher, J. J. & Anastasiow, N. J. (2003). *Educating exceptional children* (10th ed.). Boston: Houghton Mifflin.

Klippel, M., & Feil, A. (1975). The classic: A case of absence of cervical vertebrae with the thoracic cage rising to the base of the cranium (cervical thoracic cage). *Clinical Orthopedics, 109,* 3–8.

March of Dimes. (2006). *Cerebral palsy.* Retrieved March 23, 2006 from http://www.marchofdimes.com/professionals/681_1208.asp.

Marquette University School of Dentistry. (2001). *Oral pathology glossary.* Retrieved June 26, 2005, from http://www.dental.mu.edu/oralpath/opgloss2.html#ojump.

Mayo Clinic. (2003). *Spina bifida.* Retrieved June 10, 2005, from http://www.mayoclinic.com/invoke.cfm?objectid=CB5F085A-6152–42FC-8CFC55380EF705A2&dsection=2.

Mayo Clinic. (2004a). *Marfan syndrome.* Retrieved June 11, 2005, from http://www.mayoclinic.com/invoke.cfm?id=DS00540.

Mayo Clinic. (2004b). *Muscular dystrophy.* Retrieved July 13, 2005, from http://www.mayoclinic.com/invoke.cfm?id=DS00200.

Mayo Clinic. (2005a). *Cerebral palsy.* Retrieved July 13, 2005, from http://www.mayoclinic.com/invoke.cfm?id=DS00302.

Mayo Clinic. (2005b). *Muscular dystrophy.* Retrieved April 13, 2006 from http://www.mayoclinic.com/health/muscular-dystrophy/DS00200/DSECTION=2.

McGill, T., & Vogle, L. K. (2001). Driver's education for students with physical disabilities. *Exceptional Children, 67,* 455–466.

Medicine.net. (2004). *Definition of water on the brain.* Retrieved July 23, 2005, from http://www.medterms.com/script/main/art.asp?articlekey=8476.

Milton S. Hershey Medical Center of Penn State University. (2006a). *Muscular dystrophy.* Retrieved March 10, 2006, from http://www.hmc.psu.edu/healthinfo/m/musculardystrophy.htm.

Milton S. Hershey Medical Center College of Medicine at Penn State. (2006b). *Spinal cord injury.* Retrieved April 1, 2006, from.

Muscular Dystrophy Association. (2003a). *Myotonic dystrophy.* Retrieved July 29, 2005, from http://www.mda.org.au/specific/mdamyt.html.

Muscular Dystrophy Association. (2003b). *Spinal muscularatrophy: A fact sheet.* Retrieved July 1, 2005, from http://www.mda.org.au/specific/mdasma.html.

Muscular Dystrophy Association. (2004). *Becker muscular dystrophy.* Retrieved July 29, 2005, from http://www.mda.org.au/specific/.html.

Muscular Dystrophy Family Foundation. (2005). *Muscular dystrophy.* Retrieved July 1, 2005, from http://www.mdff.org/.

National Institute of Arthritis and Musculoskeletal and Skin Diseases. (2001). *Questions and answers about scoliosis in children and adolescents.* Retrieved November 1, 2005, from http://www.niams.nih.gov/hi/topics/scoliosis/scochild.htm.

National Institute of Arthritis and Musculoskeletal and Skin Diseases. (2004a). *Osteogenesis imperfecta.* Retrieved June 13, 2005, from http://www.niams.nih.gov/bone/hi/osteogenesis/oi.htm.

National Institute of Arthritis and Musculoskeletal and Skin Diseases. (2005). *Juvenile osteoporosis.* Retrieved March 1, 2006, from http://www.niams.nih.gov/bone/hi/osteoporosis_juv.htm.

National Institute of Neurological Disorders and Stroke. (2005a). *Amyotrophic lateral sclerosis information page.* Retrieved March 8, 2005, from http://www.ninds.nih.gov/disorders/amyotrophiclateralsclerosis/amyotrophiclateralsclerosis.htm.

National Institute of Neurological Disorders and Stroke. (2005b). *Cerebral palsy: Hope through research.* Bethesda, MD: National Institutes of Health.

National Institute of Neurological Disorders and Stroke. (2005c). *Hydrocephalus fact sheet.* Retrieved July 1, 2005, from http://www.ninds.nih.gov/disorders/hydro cephalus/detail_hydrocephalus.htm.

National Institute of Neurological Disorders and Stroke. (2005d). *Kennedy's disease information page.* Retrieved March 8, 2005, from http://www.ninds.nih.gov/disorders/kennedys/kennedys.htm.

National Institute of Neurological Disorders and Stroke. (2005e). *Klippel-Feil syndrome information page.* http://www.ninds.nih.gov/disorders/klippel_feil/klippel_feil.htm.

National Institute of Neurological Disorders and Stroke. (2005f). *Post-polio syndrome fact sheet.* Bethesda, MD: National Institutes of Health.

National Institute of Neurological Disorders and Stroke. (2005g). *Spina bifida information page.* Retrieved July 1, 2005, from http://www.ninds.nih.gov/disorders/spina_bifida/spina_bifida.htm.

National Institute of Neurological Disorders and Stroke. (2005h). *Spinal cord injury information page.* Retrieved July 1, 2005, from http://www.ninds.nih.gov/disorders/sci/sci.htm.

National Institute of Neurological Disorders and Stroke. (2005i). *Spinal muscular atrophy information page.* Retrieved July 14, 2005, from http://www.ninds.nih.gov/disorders/sma/sma.htm.

National Institute of Neurological Disorders and Stroke. (2005j). *Stroke information page.* Retrieved March 18, 2005, from http://www.ninds.nih.gov/disorders/stroke/stroke.htm.

National Kidney and Urologic Diseases Information Clearinghouse. (2005). *Renal osteodystrophy.* Bethesda, MD: National Institutes of Health.

National Resource Center. (2005). *Osteoporosis overview.* Retrieved February 22, 2006, from http://www.osteo.org/about.html.

National Scoliosis Foundation. (2005). *Scoliosis.* Retrieved March 28, 2005, from http://www.scoliosis.org/index.php.

Neal, J., Bigby, L., & Nicholson, R. (2004). Occupational therapy, physical therapy, and orientation and mobility services in public schools. *Intervention in School and Clinic, 39,* 218–222.

Nemours Foundation. (2005a). *Muscular dystrophy.* Retrieved March 8, 2005, from http://kidshealth.org/teen/diseases_conditions/bones/muscular_dystrophy.html.

Nemours Foundation. (2005b). *Polio.* Retrieved June 3, 2005, from http://kidshealth.org/parent/infections/bacterial_viral/polio.html.

Nemours Foundation. (2005c). *Spina bifida.* Retrieved March 8, 2005, from http://kidshealth.org/kid/health_problems/bone/spina_bifida.html.

Neurology Channel. (2005). *Hydrocephalus.* Retrieved March 13, 2005, from http://www.neurologychannel.com/hydrocephalus/causes.shtml.

NIH Osteoporosis and Related Bone Diseases. (2000). *Osteoporosis prevention, diagnosis, and therapy.* Retrieved November 4, 2005, from http://consensus.nih.gov/2000/2000Osteoporosis111html.htm.

Olsen, R., & Sutton, J. (1998). More hassle, more alone: Adolescents with diabetes. The role of formal and informal support. *Child, Care, Health and Development, 24,* 31–40.

Osteopetrosis.org. (2002). *Osteopetrosis.* Retrieved March 8, 2005, from http://www.osteopetrosis.org/home.html.

Sexson, S. B., & Dingle, A. D. (2001). Medical disorders. In F. M. Kilne, L. B. Silver, & S. C. Russell (Eds.), *The educator's guide to medical issues in the classroom* (pp. 29–48). Baltimore: Brookes.

Spina Bifida Association. (2006). *Overview of spina bifida.* Retrieved March 3, 2006, from http://www.sbaa.org/site/PageServer?pagename=about_sb.

Spinal Cord Injury Information Network. (2000). *Spinal cord injury overview.* Retrieved March 18, 2006, http://www.spinalcord.uab.edu/show.asp?durki=22409.

Spinal Cord Injury Resource Center. (2005). *Spinal cord 101.* Retrieved March 28, 2005, from http://www.spinalinjury.net/html/_spinal_cord_101.html.

Task Force on Neonatal Encephalopathy and Cerebral Palsy Staff American College of Obstetricians and Gynecologists with American Academy of Pediatrics Staff. (2003). *Neonatal Encephalopathy and Cerebral Palsy: Defining the Pathogenesis and Pathophysiology.* Washington, DC: The American College of Obstetricians and Gynecologists.

Tsao, B., & Armon, C. (2003). *Spinal muscular atrophy.* Retrieved March 6, 2005, from http://www.emedicine.com/neuro/topic631.htm.

Turnbull, A., Turnbull, R., & Wehmeyer, L. (2006). *Exceptional lives: Special education in today's schools* (5th ed.). Upper Saddle River, NJ: Merrill Pearson.

Union Memorial Hospital. (2004a). *Dupuytren's contracture.* Retrieved February 2, 2006 from http://www.unionmemorial.org/body.cfm?xyzpdqabc=0&id=555608&a.ction=detail&AEProductIDSRC=Adam2004_1&AEArticleID=001233.

Union Memorial Hospital. (2004b). *Volkmann's ischemic contracture.* Retrieved February 19, 2006, from http://www.unionmemorial.org/body.cfm?xyzpdqabc=0&id=555608&action=detail&AEProductIDSRC=Adam2004_1&AEArticleID=001221.

United Cerebral Palsy. (2006). *Cerebral palsy overview.* Retrieved January 19, 2006 from http://www.ucp.org/.

University of Maryland Medical System. (2003). *Fibrous dysplasia.* Retrieved March 8, 2005, from http://www.umm.edu/bone/fibrdys.htm.

University of Maryland Medical System. (2005). *Contracture deformity.* Retrieved March 22, 2006 from http://www.umm.edu/ency/article/003185.htm.

University of Utah Health Sciences Center. (2001). *Poliomyelitis.* Retrieved March 28, 2005, from http://uuhsc.utah.edu/healthinfo/adult/infectious/polio.htm.

University of Virginia Children's Hospital. (2003). *Tutorialfor cerebral palsy.* Retrieved March 8, 2005, from http://www.healthsystem.virginia.edu/home.html.

University of Virginia Health Systems. (2004). *Poliomyelitis.* Retrieved March 18, 2005, http://www.healthsystem.virginia.edu/uvahealth/peds_infectious/polio.cfm.

University of Virginia Health Systems. (2005). *Bone disorders.* Retrieved March 18, 2005, from http://www.healthsystem.virginia.edu/uvahealth/adult_bone/index.cfm.

U.S. Department of Education. (2004). *Twenty-Sixth Annual Report to Congress on the Implementation of the Individuals with Disabilities Education Act.* Washington, DC: Author.

U.S. National Library of Medicine. (2003a). *Fibrous dysplasia.* Retrieved May 4, 2005, from http://search.nlm.nih.gov/medlineplus/query?DISAMBIGUATION=true &FUNCTION=search&SERVER2=server2&SERVER1=server1&PARAMETER= Fibrous+Dysplasia.

U.S. National Library of Medicine. (2003b). *Osteoporosis.* Retrieved March 28, 2005, from http://www.nlm.nih.gov/medlineplus/ency/article/000360.htm#Definition.

U.S. National Library of Medicine. (2004a). *Amputation.* Retrieved July 8, 2005, from http://search.nlm.nih.gov/medlineplus/query?MAX=500&SERVER1=server1&SER VER2=server2&PARAMETER=amputation&DISAMBIGUATION=true& FUNCTION=search.

U.S. National Library of Medicine. (2004b). *Becker's muscular dystrophy.* Retrieved March 8, 2005, from http://www.nlm.nih.gov/medlineplus/ency/article/000706. htm#Definition.

U.S. National Library of Medicine. (2004c). *Cerebral palsy.* Retrieved March 3, 2005, from http://www.nlm.nih.gov/medlineplus/cerebralpalsy.html.

U.S. National Library of Medicine. (2004d). *Club foot.* Retrieved March 30, 2005, from http://www.nlm.nih.gov/medlineplus/ency/article/001228.htm#Definition

U.S. National Library of Medicine. (2004e). *Contractures.* Retrieved September 1, 2005, from http://www.nlm.nih.gov/medlineplus/ency/article/003185.htm#Definition.

U.S. National Library of Medicine. (2004f). *Duchenne muscular dystrophy.* Retrieved April 16, 2005, from http://www.nlm.nih.gov/medlineplus/ency/article/000705. htm#Symptoms.

U.S. National Library of Medicine. (2004g). *McCune-Albright syndrome.* Retrieved March 21, 2005, from http://search.nlm.nih.gov/medlineplus/query?DISAM BIGUATION=true&FUNCTION=search&SERVER2=server2&SERVER1=server 1&PARAMETER=McCune-Albright+Syndrome&x=80&y=6.

U.S. National Library of Medicine. (2004h). *Myelomeningocele.* Retrieved March 18, 2005, from http://www.nlm.nih.gov/medlineplus/ency/article/001558.htm# Definition.

U.S. National Library of Medicine. (2004i). *Primary hyperparathyroidism.* Retrieved May 11, 2005, from http://www.nlm.nih.gov/medlineplus/ency/article/000384.htm# Definition.

OI

U.S. National Library of Medicine. (2004j). *Scoliosis.* Retrieved March 8, 2005, from http://www.nlm.nih.gov/medlineplus/ency/article/001241.htm#Definition.

U.S. National Library of Medicine. (2004k). *Spina bifida.* Retrieved April 12, 2005, from http://www.nlm.nih.gov/medlineplus/spinabifida.html.

U.S. National Library of Medicine. (2005a). *Facioscapulohumeral muscular dystrophy (Landouzy-Dejerine).* Retrieved March 18, 2005, from http://www.nlm.nih.gov/medlineplus/ency/article/000707.htm#Definition.

U.S. National Library of Medicine. (2005b). *Hydrocephalus.* Retrieved May 1, 2005, from http://www.nlm.nih.gov/medlineplus/hydrocephalus.html.

U.S. National Library of Medicine. (2005c). *Marfan syndrome.* Retrieved March 18, 2005, from http://www.nlm.nih.gov/medlineplus/marfansyndrome.html.

U.S. National Library of Medicine. (2005d). *Stroke.* Retrieved March 28, 2005, from http://www.nlm.nih.gov/medlineplus/ency/article/000726.htm#Causes, percent20 incidence, percent20and percent20risk percent20factors.

Westling, D. L., & Fox, L. (2004). *Teaching students with severe disabilities* (3rd ed.). Upper Saddle River, NJ: Pearson.

CHAPTER 9

HEARING IMPAIRMENTS

EDM CODE: HI

HI 1.00 Central Hearing Loss
- HI 1.01 Auditory Agnosia
  - HI 1.01a Auditory/Verbal Information Agnosia
  - HI 1.01b Cortical Deafness
  - HI 1.01c Nonverbal Auditory Agnosia
  - HI 1.01dc Receptive Amusia
- HI 1.02 Pure Word Deafness
- HI 1.03 Tinnitus
  - HI 1.03a Objective Tinnitus
  - HI 1.03b Subjective Tinnitus
- HI 1.04 Other Types of Central Hearing Loss Not Otherwise Listed

HI 2.00 Conductive Hearing Loss
- HI 2.01 Cholesteatoma
  - HI 2.01a Acquired Cholesteatoma
  - HI 2.01b Congenital Cholesteatoma
- HI 2.02 Otitis Media
  - HI 2.02a Acute Otitis Media
  - HI 2.02b Otitis Media with Effusion
- HI 2.03 Otosclerosis
  - HI 2.03a Classic Otosclerosis
  - HI 2.03b Cochlea Otosclerosis
  - HI 2.03c Stapedial Otosclerosis
- HI 2.04 Other Types of Conductive Hearing Losses Not Otherwise Listed

HI 3.00 Mixed Hearing Loss

HI 4.00 Neurodegenerative Disorders
- HI 4.01 Neurodegenerative Disorders Associated with Hunter Syndrome
- HI 4.02 Auditory Neuropathy
- HI 4.03 Other Types of Neurodegenerative Disorders Not Otherwise Listed

HI 5.00 Sensorineural Hearing Loss
- HI 5.01 Acquired Sensorineural Hearing Loss
  - HI 5.01a Acquired Sensorineural Hearing Loss Due to Acoustic Tumor
  - HI 5.01b Acquired Sensorineural Hearing Loss Due to Head Injury
  - HI 5.01c Acquired Sensorineural Hearing Loss Due to Infection
  - HI 5.01d Acquired Sensorineural Hearing Loss Due to Noise Exposure-Noise Induced Hearing Loss)
  - HI 5.01e Acquired Sensorineural Hearing Loss Due to Toxic Drug Effects
  - HI 5.01f Acquired Sensorineural Hearing Loss Due to Vascular Disease
  - HI 5.01g Acquired Sensorineural Hearing Loss Due Ménière's Disease
- HI 5.02 Congenital Sensorineural Hearing Loss
  - HI 5.02a Congenital Sensorineural Hearing Loss Due to Birth Trauma
  - HI 5.02b Congenital Sensorineural Hearing Loss Due to Hereditary Factors
  - HI 5.02c Congenital Sensorineural Hearing Loss Due to Intrauterine Viral Infections
  - HI 5.02d Congenital Sensorineural Hearing Loss Due to Malformation of the Cochlea
- HI 5.03 Sudden Sensorineural Hearing Loss
- HI 5.04 Other Types of Sensorineural Hearing Loss Not Otherwise Listed

HI 6.00 Syndromic Hearing Losses
- HI 6.01 Aplasia
  - HI 6.01a Michel Aplasia

HI 6.01b Mondini Aplasia
HI 6.01c Scheibe Aplasia
HI 7.00 Vestibular Schwannoma (Acoustic Neuroma)
HI 7.01 Bilateral Vestibular Schwannomas
HI 7.02 Other Vestibular Schwannoma (Acoustic Neuromas) Not Otherwise Listed
HI 8.00 Other Types of Hearing Impairments—Be Specific

IDEA 2004 Definition of Hearing Impairments

Under IDEA, a *hearing impairment* is defined as "an impairment in hearing, whether permanent or fluctuating, that adversely affects a child's educational performance" (C.F.R. 300.7(c)(5)).

Deafness is defined as "a hearing impairment that is so severe that the child is impaired in processing linguistic information through hearing, with or without amplification" (C.F.R. 300.7(c)(3)).

Overview of Hearing Impairments

Deafness and hearing loss may be defined according to the degree of hearing impairment, which is determined by assessing an individual's sensitivity to loudness (sound intensity) and pitch (sound frequency). Sound is measured by its loudness or intensity (measured in units called decibels, dB) and its frequency or pitch (measured in units called hertz, Hz). The range of human hearing is approximately 0 to 130 dB.

Hearing loss is generally described as slight, mild, moderate, severe, or profound, depending on how well a person can hear the intensities or frequencies most greatly associated with speech (Gargiulo, 2004). Generally only children whose hearing loss is greater than 90 decibels (dB) are considered deaf for the purposes of educational placement (Hardman, Drew, & Egan, 2005).

There are four types of hearing loss (Friend, 2007; Gargiulo, 2004; Hallahan & Kauffman, 2006; National Dissemination Center for Children and Youth with Disabilities, 2004).

Conductive hearing losses are due to the effects of diseases or obstructions in the outer or middle ear (the conduction pathways for sound to reach the inner ear). Conductive hearing losses usually affect all frequencies of hearing evenly and do not result in severe losses. A person with a conductive hearing loss usually is able to use a hearing aid well or can be helped medically or surgically.

Sensorineural hearing losses result from damage to the delicate sensory hair cells of the inner ear or the nerves which supply it. These hearing losses can range from mild to profound. They often affect the person's ability to hear certain frequencies more than others. Thus, even with amplification to increase the sound level, a person with a sensorineural hearing loss may perceive distorted sounds, sometimes making the successful use of a hearing aid impossible.

Mixed hearing losses refer to a combination of conductive and sensorineural loss and mean that a problem occurs in both the outer or middle and the inner ear.

Central hearing losses result from damage or impairment to the nerves or nuclei of the central nervous system, either in the pathways to the brain or in the brain itself. For babies who are born deaf or with a hearing impairment, the earliest possible detection and intervention are crucial. Currently, a child's hearing loss is usually diagnosed between the ages of fourteen months and three years, resulting in the loss of a significant window of opportunity for acquiring language, whether spoken or signed. A delayed diagnosis can also affect a child's social skills. The research strongly suggests that children with a hearing loss must receive intervention as soon as possible if they are to learn the language skills necessary for reading and other academic subjects as they approach the school years (Calderon & Naidu, 2000).

According to Hallahan and Kauffman (2006), research suggests that the earlier the hearing impairment occurs in the child's life, the more difficulty the child will have developing language of the hearing society. For this reason, professionals frequently use the terms *congenitally deaf* (those who are born deaf) and *adventitiously deaf* (those who acquire deafness some time after birth).

Two terms are often used when describing individuals who are deaf. *Prelingual deafness* refers to deafness that occurs at birth or early in life before speech and language develop. *Postlingual deafness* is deafness that occurs after the development of speech and language. Experts differ about the dividing point between prelingual and postlingual deafness. Some believe that it should be at about eighteen months; others think it should be lower, at about twelve months or even six months (Hallahan & Kauffman, 2006).

Research suggests that 33 percent of all students with hearing impairments or deafness have one or more additional educationally significant disabilities. The most frequently reported conditions are learning disabilities, cognitive disabilities, attention deficit–hyperactive disorder, cerebral palsy, and emotional and behavioral disorders (Friend, 2006).

Causes-Etiology of Hearing Impairments

In general, professionals tend to classify causes of hearing impairments on the basis of the location of the problem within the hearing mechanism. There are three major classifications: conductive, sensorineural, and mixed hearing impairments (Hallahan & Kauffman, 2006). These are addressed in the "Types of Hearing Impairments" section of this chapter.

Although more than two hundred types of deafness have been related to heredity factors, the cause of 33 percent of prelingual hearing loss remains unknown (Center for Assessment and Demographic Studies, 2002).

Causes of congenital hearing loss include genetic factors, maternal rubella, heredity, congenital cytomegalovirus, congenital cytomegalovirus (Pediatric Bulletin, 2000), and prematurity. Common causes of acquired hearing loss include otitis media, meningitis, Ménière's disease, and noise exposure.

Prevalence of Hearing Impairments

Hearing loss and deafness affect individuals of all ages and may occur at any time from infancy through old age. Hearing impairment and deafness affect approximately 28 million Americans. Of these 28 million, approximately 11 million have significant irreversible hearing loss, and 1 million are deaf. Only 5 percent of people with hearing loss are under the age of seventeen (Deaf World Web, 2000).

The U.S. Department of Education (2004) reports that during the 2003–2004 school year, 71,118 students aged six to twenty-one (or 1.2 percent of all students with disabilities) received special education services under the category of "hearing impairment." However, the number of children with hearing loss and deafness is undoubtedly higher, since many of these students may have other disabilities as well and may be served under other categories (Holden-Pitt & Diaz, 1998). Also, these figures represent only students who receive special services; a number of students with hearing loss who could benefit from additional services do not receive them (U.S. Department of Education, 2004).

Age of Onset of Hearing Impairments

It is important to consider the age of onset with a hearing impairment. Hearing loss can be congenital (present at birth) or acquired (appears after birth). Prelingual hearing loss occurs prior to the age of two, or before speech development. Postlingual hearing loss identifies any hearing loss occurring after the development of spoken language. Of the deaf and hard-of-hearing children served in special education programs, 90 percent have a prelingual hearing loss. A person who is born with hearing loss has significantly more challenges, particularly in the areas of communication and social adaptation (Magnuson, 2000).

Gender Features of Hearing Impairments

Males at all ages are more likely than females to be deaf or hard of hearing; the gap widens after age eighteen.

Cultural Features of Hearing Impairments

According to the U.S. Department of Education (2000, cited in Bowe, 2005), there is no disproportionate representation of racial or ethnic groups among individuals with hearing impairments. That is, the same percentages are of Hispanic origin, white, and so on as obtained in the general population. However, an important statistic to note is that almost 23 percent of students who are deaf in the

United States come from Hispanic-speaking homes (Gallaudet Research Institute, 2003). In addition, there are relatively large numbers of other non-English-speaking immigrants who are deaf (Hallahan & Kauffman, 2006).

Familial Pattern of Hearing Impairments

Of those children with hearing loss associated with a known syndrome, advancement in the fields of genetics and molecular biology have allowed us to identify many of these syndromes. Sixty to 70 percent of these children have autosomal-recessive hearing impairment, making it the most common pattern of transmission. In these cases, the parents have normal hearing but carry the recessive gene, and there is a 25 percent chance of the children being affected.

A small percentage of hereditary hearing impairment is due to X-linked abnormalities. Because girls have two X chromosomes and boys only have one, X-linked disorders are carried by girls and show up in boys (Children's Hospital of Michigan, 2006).

Characteristics of Hearing Impairments

According to Heward (2006), any discussion of characteristics of students who are deaf or have hearing impairments should include three qualifications:

- Students who receive special education services comprise an extremely heterogeneous group (Easterbrooks, 1999).
- The effects of hearing loss on a child's communication and language skills, academic achievement, and social functioning are influenced by many factors (Mores, 2001).
- Generalizations about how deaf people are supposed to act and feel must be viewed with extreme caution (Andrews, Leigh, & Weiner, 2004).

Hardman et al. (2005) note other significant characteristics of students with hearing impairments or who are deaf:

- Research on the intellectual characteristics of children with hearing loss has suggested that distribution of IQ scores for these individuals is similar to that of hearing children (Mores, 2001).
- Speech and language skills are the areas of development most severely affected for individuals with hearing losses, particularly for those who are born deaf.
- The educational achievement of students with hearing loss may be significantly delayed compared to that of students who can hear. Low achievement is characteristic of students who are deaf (Mores, 2001); they average three to four years below their age-appropriate grade levels.
- Reading is the academic area that gives these students the greatest difficulties (Kuntz & Hesslar, 1998).

- Students with hearing impairments go through a different social development from that of children who can hear (Easterbrook, 1999). Delayed language development may lead to more limited opportunities for social interaction.

Educational Implications of Hearing Impairments

Hearing loss or deafness does not affect a person's intellectual capacity or ability to learn (Mores, 2001). However, children who are hard of hearing or deaf generally require some form of special education services in order to receive an adequate education (U.S. Department of Education, 2004). Such services may include:

- Regular speech, language, and auditory training from a specialist
- Amplification systems
- Services of an interpreter for students who use sign language
- Favorable seating in the class to facilitate lip reading
- Captioned films and videos
- Assistance of a note taker who takes notes for the student with a hearing loss so that the student can fully attend to instruction
- Instruction for the teacher and peers in alternate communication methods, such as sign language
- Counseling

Children who are hard of hearing find it much more difficult than children who have normal hearing to learn vocabulary, grammar, word order, idiomatic expressions, and other aspects of verbal communication. For children who are deaf or have severe hearing losses, early, consistent, and conscious use of visible communication modes (such as sign language, finger spelling, and cued speech), amplification, and aural and oral training can help reduce this language delay.

It is important for teachers and audiologists to work together to teach the child to use his or her residual hearing to the maximum extent possible, even if the preferred means of communication is manual. Since the great majority of deaf children (over 90 percent) are born to hearing parents, programs should provide instruction for parents on implications of deafness within the family (National Dissemination Center for Children and Youth with Disabilities, 2004).

Permissions and Authorization to Use Proprietary and Nonproprietary Sources

Due to the scientific and detailed nature of certain Level II, Level III, and Level IV disorders described in this chapter, we thought that some were best explained by national institutes and centers that conduct comprehensive scientific research in respective fields of study. The sources obtained were all written with explicit permissions that the scientific and diagnostic information they prepared was in the public domain and can be used without restriction. We thank the following national research offices for the opportunity to freely disseminate their scientific research and writing in this chapter:

- National Dissemination Center for Children and Youth with Disabilities
- National Institute of Neurological Disorders and Stroke
- National Institute on Deafness and Other Communication Disorders
- U.S. Department of Education
- U.S. National Library of Medicine

EDM Codes, Definitions, and Explanations of Hearing Impairments

Note for Deafness

The Individuals with Disabilities Education Act of 2004 (IDEA) includes "hearing impairment" and "deafness" as two of the categories under which children with disabilities may be eligible for special education and related services programming. While the term *hearing impairment* is often used generically to describe a wide range of hearing losses, including deafness, the regulations for IDEA 2004 define hearing loss and deafness separately.

Based on this categorization, EDM suggests use of the following notation for Level I if a child is deaf. After HI, simply put *–D,* for example, HI-*D.* This indicates that the disorder the child has been diagnosed with a particular disorder and is deaf. For example, a child with a diagnosis of HI-D 5.00 indicates that the child has a sensorineural hearing loss and the child is deaf. Any HI without a *–D* indicates the child is not deaf but has a hearing impairment as defined under IDEA.

HI

Acoustic Neuroma

HI 1.00 Central Hearing Loss

Definition Central hearing loss is caused by a problem along the pathway from the inner ear to the auditory region of the brain or in the brain itself (National Center on Birth Defects and Developmental Disabilities, 2004).

Diagnostic Symptoms Central hearing loss occurs when auditory centers of the brain are affected by injury, disease, tumor, hereditary, or unknown causes. Loudness of sound is not necessarily affected, although understanding of speech, also thought of as clarity of speech, may be affected. Certainly both loudness and clarity may be affected too (Deafness Research Foundation, 2002).

Further Key Points Central hearing loss is generally thought to be extremely rare compared to the sensorineural or conductive types of hearing loss, but recent studies has shown that central components to hearing loss are much more common than previously appreciated (Gates et al., 1996).

Patients with central hearing loss typically have inconsistent auditory behavior that may cause them to be misdiagnosed as having functional or psychogenic hearing disturbances. Cortically deaf patients may have reactions to environmental sounds, despite absence of reaction to loud noises. As in patients with cortical visual disturbances, patients may consider themselves deaf in spite of having reactions to sounds in the room (Hain, 2004).

HI 1.01 Auditory Agnosia

Definition Auditory agnosia refers to the inability to recognize specific sounds in the context of intact hearing. There is a distinction in this syndrome between pure word deafness, which is considered an agnosia for auditory and verbal information, and auditory agnosia, which involves an agnosia for environmental, nonverbal sounds. *Cortical deafness* is also a term applied to patients who essentially do not respond to any auditory information even when hearing is intact. Finally, *receptive amusia* is a term that refers to agnosia for music (National Academy of Neuropsychology, 2000).

Explanation Agnosia is a rare disorder characterized by an inability to recognize and identify objects or persons despite having knowledge of the characteristics of the objects or persons. People with agnosia may have difficulty recognizing the geometric features of an object or face or may be able to perceive the geometric features but not know what the object is used for or whether a face is familiar.

HI

Agnosia can be limited to one sensory modality such as vision or hearing. For example, a person may have difficulty in recognizing an object as a cup or identifying a sound as a cough. Agnosia can result from strokes, dementia, or other neurological disorders. It typically results from damage to specific brain areas in the occipital or parietal lobes of the brain. People with agnosia may retain their cognitive abilities in other areas (National Institute of Neurological Disorders and Stroke, 2005).

HI 1.01a **Auditory/Verbal Information Agnosia** A type of auditory agnosia characterized by an inability to hear words.

HI 1.01b **Cortical Deafness** A type of auditory agnosia characterized by an inability to respond to any auditory information even when hearing is intact.

HI 1.01c **Nonverbal Auditory Agnosia** The inability to hear environmental sounds such as a car starting or a dog barking.

HI 1.01d **Receptive Amusia** A type of auditory agnosia characterized by the inability to hear music.

HI 1.02 Pure Word Deafness

Definition Pure word deafness is a specific deficit of perception of spoken language while other auditory perception is intact. The individual's speech is intact, but some garbled language may be present at the onset of illness. Writing is normal, while reading may be impaired (National Academy of Neuropsychology, 2000). Comprehension and repetition of speech are impaired, but reading, writing, and spontaneous speech are preserved (Coslett, Brashear, & Heilman, 1984).

Explanation Pure word deafness is a subtype of central deafness. This disorder is defined as disturbed auditory comprehension without difficulties with visual comprehension. Patients characteristically have fluent verbal output, severe disturbance of spoken language comprehension and repetition, and no problems with reading or writing (Hain, 2004).

HI 1.03 Tinnitus

Definition *Tinnitus* is the medical term for "hearing" noises in one's ears when there is no outside source of the sounds. The noises heard can be soft or loud. They may sound like ringing, blowing, roaring, buzzing, hissing, humming, whistling, or sizzling. The person may even think he or she is hearing air escaping, water running, the inside of a seashell, or musical notes (U.S. National Library of Medicine, 2005a). The word comes from Latin and means "to tinkle or to ring like a bell" (American Tinnitus Association, 2005).

Explanation Tinnitus, often described as a ringing or buzzing sound in the ear, is a symptom that can be related to almost every known hearing problem. Tinnitus is not a disease, but it can be caused by exposure to loud sounds, middle or inner ear infections, tumors on the hearing nerve, and even wax on the eardrum. Sometimes tinnitus can be medically or surgically treated. All patients with tinnitus should consult an ear, nose, and throat physician (otolaryngologist) before seeking treatment (Oregon Health and Science University, 2006).

HI 1.03a **Objective Tinnitus (Nontonal)** A type of tinnitus that is quite rare is when the noise is heard not only by the affected individual but also by others. Usually the tinnitus here is described as being pulsatile or clicking. Causes for objective tinnitus include the presence of vascular middle ear tumors (glomus tumors), aneurysms near the inner ear or skull base, or the repetitive contractions of the middle ear muscles (so-called middle ear myoclonus).

HI 1.03b **Subjective Tinnitus (Tonal)** A type of tinnitus that can be appreciated only by the affected individual. It is usually associated with a sensorineural hearing loss of some type and is the most common type noted. It is usually described as a constant sound (for example, a ring, buzz, or hum) that is worse in the absence of competing background noise such as at night.

HI 1.04 Other Types of Central Hearing Loss Not Otherwise Listed

HI 2.00 Conductive Hearing Loss

Definition Conductive hearing loss results from abnormalities or complications of the outer or middle ear (Heward, 2006). It is referred to as a conductive loss because sound is not conducted normally through the mechanical sound-conducting mechanisms in the disordered outer or middle ear (Gargiulo, 2004).

Diagnostic Symptoms Diagnostic symptoms of conductive hearing loss include (University of Rochester Medical Center, 2005):

- Agreeing or nodding the head during conversations when not sure what has been said
- Difficulty hearing certain environmental sounds, such as birds chirping
- Difficulty hearing conversations, especially in the presence of background noise
- Difficulty hearing on the telephone
- Feeling that people are mumbling when they are talking
- Frequently asking others to repeat what they have said
- Misunderstanding what people say
- Reading lips to try to follow what people are saying
- Removing oneself from conversations because it is too difficult to hear
- Requiring the TV or radio volume to be louder than others in the room prefer
- Straining to hear or keep up with conversations
- Tinnitus

Further Key Points Conductive hearing losses are due to the effects of diseases or obstructions in the outer or middle ear (the conduction pathways for sound to reach the inner ear). Other causes are scarring, narrowing of the ear canal, tumors in the middle ear, and perforation of the tympanic membrane. Once the cause is found and removed or treated, hearing usually is restored (Columbia University College of Physicians and Surgeons, 2002).

Conductive hearing losses usually affect all frequencies of hearing evenly and do not result in severe losses. A person with a conductive hearing loss usually is able to use a hearing aid well or can be helped medically or surgically.

HI 2.01 Cholesteatoma

Definition Cholesteatoma can be a congenital (present at birth) defect, but it more commonly occurs as a complication of chronic ear infection. Long-term inflammation and malfunction of the eustachian tube lead to chronic negative pressure in the middle ear (U.S. National Library of Medicine, 2004).

Explanation According to the American Academy of Otolaryngology (2004), a cholesteatoma is a skin growth that occurs in an abnormal location, the middle ear behind the eardrum. It is usually due to repeated infection, which causes an ingrowth of the skin of the eardrum.

Cholesteatomas often take the form of a cyst or pouch that sheds layers of old skin that builds up inside the ear. Over time, the cholesteatoma can increase in size and destroy the surrounding delicate bones of the middle ear. Hearing loss, dizziness, and facial muscle paralysis are rare but can result from continued cholesteatoma growth.

HI 2.01a **Acquired Cholesteatoma** A type of cholesteatoma that occurs after birth.

HI 2.01b **Congenital Cholesteatoma** A type of cholesteatoma that is present from birth.

HI 2.02 Otitis Media

Definition Otitis media is an infection or inflammation of the middle ear (Heward, 2006).

Explanation These problems can be viral or bacterial infections. Seventy-five percent of children experience at least one episode of otitis media by their third birthday. Almost half of these children have three or more ear infections during their first three years. Nearly 90 percent of all children experience otitis media at least once, and about one-third of children under age five have recurrent episodes (Bluestone & Klein, 2001).

Otitis media not only causes severe pain but may result in serious complications if it is not treated. An untreated infection can travel from the middle ear to the nearby parts of the head, including the brain. Although the hearing loss due to the effects of otitis media is usually temporary, untreated otitis media may lead to permanent hearing impairment.

Persistent fluid in the middle ear and chronic otitis media can reduce a child's hearing at a time that is critical for speech and language development. Children who have early hearing impairment from frequent ear infections are likely to have speech and language disabilities (National Institute on Deafness and Other Communication Disorders, 2002).

HI 2.02a **Acute Otitis Media** A type of otitis media that is characterized by an inflammation of the area behind the eardrum (tympanic membrane) in the chamber called the middle ear. Acute otitis media is an infection that produces pus, fluid, and inflammation within the middle ear. Older children often complain about ear pain, ear fullness, or hearing loss. Younger children may demonstrate irritability, fussiness, or difficulty in sleeping, feeding, or hearing. Fever may be present (Nemours Foundation, 2004).

HI 2.02b Otitis Media with Effusion A type of otitis media that is characterized by fluid in the middle (inner) ear and the inner ear is inflamed (swollen). (*Effusion* is another word for fluid.) This fluid usually does not bother children and almost always goes away on its own. This problem does not have to be treated with antibiotics unless the fluid does not go away (American Academy of Family Physicians, 2004).

HI 2.03 Otosclerosis

Definition Otosclerosis is a condition of the middle ear that causes progressive hearing loss. Unlike hearing loss resulting from damage to the inner ear, the hearing loss from otosclerosis is often reversible. The name otosclerosis comes from the Greek words for "hard" (*sclero*) and "ear" (*oto*). This is because otosclerosis is a disorder that causes a hardening of the bones of the middle ear (Harris, 2000).

Explanation Otosclerosis can cause different types of hearing loss, depending on which structure within the ear is affected. It usually affects the last bone in the chain, the stapes, which rests in the entrance to the inner ear (the oval window). The abnormal bone fixates the stapes in the oval window and interferes with sound passing waves to the inner ear.

Hearing loss is the most frequent symptom of otosclerosis. The loss may appear very gradually. Many people with otosclerosis first notice that they cannot hear low-pitched sounds or that they can no longer hear a whisper. In addition to hearing loss, some people with otosclerosis may experience dizziness, balance problems, or tinnitus (National Institute on Deafness and Other Communication Disorders, 1999).

HI 2.03a Classic Otosclerosis A type of otosclerosis in which the stapes (one of the three bones in the middle ear) is immobilized by a spongiotic growth. Classic otosclerosis has traditionally been addressed through surgical management (Bukowski, 2004).

HI 2.03b Cochlea Otosclerosis A type of otosclerosis that spreads to the inner ear. A sensorineural hearing impairment may result from interference with the nerve function (New York Eye and Ear Infirmary, 2005).

HI 2.03c Stapedial Otosclerosis A type of otosclerosis that spreads to the stapes or stirrup bone, the final link in the middle ear transformer chain. The stapes rests in a small groove, the oval window, in intimate contact with the inner ear fluids. Anything that interferes with its motion results in a conductive hearing impairment (New York Eye and Ear Infirmary, 2005).

HI 2.04 Other Types of Conductive Hearing Losses Not Otherwise Listed

HI 3.00 Mixed Hearing Loss

Definition Mixed hearing loss results when a conductive hearing loss occurs in combination with a sensorineural hearing loss. In other words, there may be damage in the outer or middle ear and in the inner ear (cochlea) or auditory nerve. When this occurs, the hearing loss is referred to as a mixed hearing loss (American Speech-Language Hearing Association, 2005a).

Diagnostic Symptoms See the sections on Conductive Hearing Loss and Sensorineural Hearing Loss.

Further Key Points With mixed hearing loss, the conductive part may be treated, but the sensorineural part is usually permanent.

HI 4.00 Neurodegenerative Disorders

Definition Neurodegenerative diseases are a varied assortment of central nervous system disorders characterized by the gradual and progressive loss of neural tissue or nerve cells (Kennedy Krieger Institute, 2005). These diseases can result from genetic problems, biochemical defects, viral infections, or toxic substances (Green, 2003).

Diagnostic Symptoms The hallmark of these diseases is a progressive loss of speech, hearing, vision, and strength. Seizures, feeding difficulties, and loss of intellect often accompany this downhill course (Green, 2003).

Further Key Points Until recently, the majority of the concerns about environmental agents have centered on their potential for causing cancer. Cancer and neurodegeneration represent opposite ends of a spectrum: whereas cancer is an uncontrolled proliferation of cells, neurodegeneration is the result of the death of cells whether due to direct killing of cells by necrosis or the delayed process of apoptosis. Attention is now being focused on environmental agents' potential for damaging the developing and mature nervous system, resulting in neurodegenerative diseases.

HI

Types of Neurodegenerative Disorders

HI 4.01 Neurodegenerative Disorders Associated with Hunter Syndrome

Definition Hunter syndrome is a hereditary disease in which the breakdown of a mucopolysaccharide (a chemical that is widely distributed in the body outside of cells) is defective. This chemical builds up and causes a characteristic facial appearance, abnormal function of multiple organs, and, in severe cases, early death (U.S. National Library of Medicine, 2005b).

Explanation Hunter syndrome is inherited as an X-linked recessive disease. This means that women carry the disease and can pass it on to their sons but are not themselves affected. Because females have two X chromosomes, their normal X can provide a functioning gene even if their other X is defective, but because males have an X and a Y, there is no normal gene to fix the problem if the X is defective (U.S. National Library of Medicine, 2005b).

HI 4.02 Auditory Neuropathy

Definition Auditory neuropathy, also known as auditory dyssynchrony, is a hearing disorder in which sound enters the inner ear normally, but the transmission of signals from the inner ear to the brain is impaired. It can affect people of all ages, from infancy through adulthood. The number of people affected by auditory neuropathy is not known, but the condition affects a relatively small percentage of people who are deaf or hearing impaired (National Institute on Deafness and Other Communication Disorders, 2003).

Explanation Several factors have been linked to auditory neuropathy in children. However, a clear cause-and-effect relationship has not been proven. Some children who have been diagnosed with auditory neuropathy experienced certain health problems as newborns or during or shortly before birth. These problems include jaundice, premature birth, low birth weight, and an inadequate supply of oxygen to the unborn baby. In addition, some drugs that have been used to treat medical complications in pregnant women or newborns may damage the inner hair cells in the baby's ears, causing auditory neuropathy (National Institute on Deafness and Other Communication Disorders, 2003).

HI 4.03 Other Types of Neurodegenerative Disorders Not Otherwise Listed

HI 5.00 Sensorineural Hearing Loss

Definition A hearing loss caused by a problem in the inner ear or auditory nerve. A sensorineural loss often affects a person's ability to hear some frequencies more than others. This means that sounds are distorted, even with the use of a hearing aid. Sensorineural losses can range from mild to profound (National Center on Birth Defects and Developmental Disabilities, 2005).

HI

Diagnostic Symptoms According to the American Speech-Language-Hearing Association (2005b), a sensorineural hearing loss not only involves a reduction in sound level or ability to hear faint sounds, but also affects speech understanding or the ability to hear clearly.

Sensorineural hearing loss can be caused by disease, birth injury, drugs that are toxic to the auditory system, and genetic syndromes. It may also occur as a result of noise exposure, viruses, head trauma, aging, and tumors.

Further Key Points Various infections can cause damage to the nerves in the cochlea, such as spinal meningitis or syphilis. The most common viruses that cause hearing loss are measles (rubella) and mumps. Viral infections in a pregnant mother can also affect the fetus. Damage to the cochlea of an unborn child can take place when there is an Rh incompatibility with the mother or the mother has a fever (House Ear Institute, 2004). Although a small percentage of sensorineural hearing losses can be medically or surgically treated, most cannot and are permanent in nature (Bess & Humes, 1990).

Types of Sensorineural Hearing Loss

HI 5.01 Acquired Sensorineural Hearing Loss

Definition A type of sensorineural hearing loss that occurs after birth and is a result of damage to, or malfunction of, the cochlea (the sensory part) or the hearing nerve (the neural part) (MIMS Consumer Health Groups, 2005).

Explanation Acquired sensorineural hearing loss may be caused by autoimmune disorders; ototoxic substances such as aminoglycosides, cisplatin, and aspirin (whose effect is reversible); bacterial meningitis; congenital and acquired viral infections, such as congenital rubella, cytomegalovirus, and mumps; bacterial endotoxins and exotoxins; sound trauma, which can result from exposure to loud music, firearms, engine noise, or loud toys; or head trauma resulting in temporal bone concussion or fracture (the fractures can have a conductive component to the hearing loss because of the traumatic disruption of the middle ear) (Merck, 2005).

HI 5.01a Acquired Sensorineural Hearing Loss Due to Acoustic Tumor

HI 5.01b Acquired Sensorineural Hearing Loss Due to Head Injury

HI 5.01c Acquired Sensorineural Hearing Loss Due to Infection

HI 5.01d Acquired Sensorineural Hearing Loss Due to Noise Exposure-Noise Induced Hearing Loss

HI 5.01e Acquired Sensorineural Hearing Loss Due to Toxic Drug Effects

HI 5.01f Acquired Sensorineural Hearing Loss Due to Vascular Disease

HI 5.01g Acquired Sensorineural Hearing Loss Due to Ménière's Disease

HI 5.02 Congenital Sensorineural Hearing Loss

Definition A type of sensorineural hearing loss that is not hereditary in nature. These may include prenatal infections, illnesses, or conditions occurring at the time of birth or shortly after. These conditions typically cause sensorineural hearing loss ranging from mild to profound in degree (American Speech-Language-Hearing Association, 2005b).

Explanation Sensorineural hearing loss, also known as nerve deafness, typically occurs when part of the inner ear (cochlea, hair cells, hearing nerve) is damaged or destroyed. It may have a variety of causes, such as heredity, aging, disease, and infection.

HI 5.02a Congenital Sensorineural Hearing Loss Due to Birth Trauma

HI 5.02b Congenital Sensorineural Hearing Loss Due to Hereditary Factors

HI 5.02c Congenital Sensorineural Hearing Loss Due to Intrauterine Viral Infections

HI 5.02d Congenital Sensorineural Hearing Loss Due to Malformation of the Cochlea

HI 5.03 Sudden Sensorineural Hearing Loss (Sudden Deafness)

Definition Sudden sensorineural hearing loss (SSHL), or sudden deafness, is a rapid loss of hearing. It can happen to a person all at once or over a period of up to three days. It should be considered a medical emergency. A person who experiences SSHL should visit a doctor immediately (National Institute on Deafness and Other Communication Disorders, 2005b).

Explanation It is now clear, based on abundance of scientific evidence, that the vast majority of cases of sudden sensorineural hearing loss are caused by a viral infection of either the inner ear or nerve of hearing. While it was once felt that this problem was caused by a decrease in blood flow to the inner ear (analogous to a stroke of the inner ear), it is now felt that only a small number of patients with this form of hearing loss suffer from a loss of blood flow to the inner ear (University of Tennessee Department of Otolaryngology, 2006).

HI 5.04 Other Types of Sensorineural Hearing Loss Not Otherwise Listed

HI 6.00 Syndromic Hearing Losses

Definition Syndromic hearing impairment is associated with malformations of the external ear or other organs or with medical problems involving other organ systems (Smith, Green, & Van Camp, 2005).

Diagnostic Symptoms The symptoms for syndromic hearing loss vary by disorder, and as a result, no general symptoms can be reported.

Further Key Points Genetic causes of hearing loss can be syndromic or nonsyndromic. *Syndromic* means that a person has other related symptoms besides hearing loss. For example, some people with hearing loss are also blind. Usher's syndrome is one example. There are many different syndromes that have hearing loss as one of the symptoms. *Nonsyndromic* means that the person does not have any other symptoms related to the hearing loss. Whatever caused the hearing loss does not cause any other symptoms. The more common type of genetic hearing loss is nonsyndromic, which includes two-third of all genetic hearing losses. A common nonsyndromic hearing loss is caused by one gene known as Connexin 26 (CX26). CX26 alone is the cause in about one-third of all children with a nonsyndromic genetic hearing loss (National Center on Birth Defects and Developmental Disabilities, 2005).

Types of Syndromic Hearing Losses

HI 6.01 Aplasia

Definition An aplasia is an abnormal development of the bony or membranous portion of the inner ear (cochlea) (League for the Hard of Hearing, 2005; MedicineNet.com, 2005).

Explanation The disorders discussed in this section have a variety of symptoms. Therefore, no generalized list of diagnostic symptoms can be made.

HI 6.01a **Michel Aplasia** A type of aplasia characterized by the complete absence of the inner ear and auditory nerve, resulting in total absence of hearing. It may appear in one ear (unilaterally) or both ears (bilaterally). Patients cannot be helped by either a hearing aid or a cochlear implant if the hearing nerve is absent. They may be assisted by a vibrotactile device (a device that augments remote voice communication with touch, by converting hand pressure into vibrational intensity between users in real time).

HI 6.01b **Mondini Aplasia** A type of aplasia characterized by an abnormal development of the cochlea. It may occur unilaterally or bilaterally. Hearing loss can range from moderate to profound and is often progressive in cases where residual hearing is present. In less severe cases, hearing aids are beneficial. If the loss is too profound to be helped by hearing aids, cochlear implants are an option.

HI 6.01c **Scheibe Aplasia** A type of aplasia characterized by an abnormal formation of the cochlear membrane. The defect may be unilateral or bilateral. There may be residual low-frequency hearing that can be helped by a hearing aid. If not, a cochlear implant is an option.

HI 7.00 Vestibular Schwannoma (Acoustic Neuroma)

HI

Definition Vestibular schwannoma (also known as acoustic neuroma, acoustic neurinoma, and acoustic neurilemoma) is a benign, usually slow-growing tumor that develops from the balance and hearing nerves supplying the inner ear. The tumor comes from an overproduction of Schwann cells—the cells that normally wrap around nerve fibers like onion skin to help support and insulate nerves. As the vestibular schwannoma grows, it presses against the hearing and balance nerves, usually causing unilateral (one-sided) or asymmetrical hearing loss, tinnitus (ringing in the ear), and dizziness or loss of balance (National Institute on Deafness and Other Communication Disorders, 2005a).

Diagnostic Symptoms Diagnostic symptoms of vestibular schwannoma include (Mayo Clinic, 2006):

- Hearing loss in one ear
- Ringing (tinnitus) in the affected ear

- Dizziness
- Loss of balance

Further Key Points Scientists are working to better understand how the gene works so they can begin to develop gene therapy to control the overproduction of Schwann cells in individuals with vestibular schwannoma. Also, learning more about the way genes help control Schwann cell growth may help prevent other brain tumors.

HI 7.01 Bilateral Vestibular Schwannomas

Definition A type of vestibular schwannomas that affects both hearing nerves and is usually associated with a genetic disorder called neurofibromatosis type 2 (NF 2). Half of affected individuals have inherited the disorder from an affected parent, and half seem to have a mutation for the first time in their family (National Institute and Other Communication Disorders, 2004).

Explanation Each child of an affected parent has a 50 percent chance of inheriting the disorder. Unlike those with a unilateral vestibular schwannoma, individuals with NF2 usually develop symptoms in their teens or early adulthood. In addition, patients with NF2 usually develop multiple brain and spinal cord–related tumors. They also can develop tumors of the nerves important for swallowing, speech, eye and facial movement, and facial sensation (National Institute and Other Communication Disorders, 2004).

HI 7.02 Other Vestibular Schwannoma (Acoustic Neuromas) Not Otherwise Listed

HI 8.00 Other Types of Hearing Impairments—Be Specific

HI

References

American Academy of Family Physicians. (2004). *Ear infections: Otitis media with effusion.* Retrieved November 1, 2006, from http://www.familydoctor.org/330.xml.

American Academy of Otolaryngology. (2004). *Cholesteatoma.* Retrieved May 7, 2005, from http://www.entnet.org/healthinfo/ears/cholesteatoma.cfm.

American Speech-Language-Hearing Association. (2005a). *Causes of hearing loss in children.* Retrieved May 17, 2005, from http://www.asha.org/default.htm.

American Speech-Language-Hearing Association. (2005b). *Type, degree, and configuration of hearing loss.* Retrieved May 7, 2005, from http://www.asha.org/public/hearing/disorders/types.htm.

American Tinnitus Association. (2005). *About tinnitus.* Retrieved February 9, 2006, from http://www.ata.org/about_tinnitus/.

Andrews, J. F., Leigh, I. W., & Weiner, M. T. (2004). *Deaf people: Evolving perspectives from psychology, education, and sociology.* Needham Heights, MA: Allyn & Bacon.

Bess, F. H., & Humes, L. E. (1990). *Audiology: The fundamentals.* Baltimore, MD: Williams and Wilkins.

Bluestone, C. D., & Klein, J. O. (2001). *Otitis media in infants and children* (3rd ed.). Philadelphia: Saunders.

Bowe, F. (2005). *Making inclusion work.* Upper Saddle River, NJ: Pearson.

Bukowski, J. (2004). *Classic otosclerosis.* Retrieved May 7, 2005, from Audiology Online. http://www.audiologyonline.com/interview/displayarchives.asp?interview_id=271.

Calderon, R., & Naidu, S. (2000). Further support for the benefits of early identification and intervention for children with hearing loss. *Volta Review, 100*(5), 53–84.

Center for Assessment and Demographic Studies. (2002). *Annual survey of deaf and hard-of-hearing children & youth.* Washington DC: Gallaudet University.

Children's Hospital of Michigan. (2006). *Hearing loss in kids.* Retrieved November 2, 2006, from http://www.chmkids.org/default.aspx?id=193&sid=1.

Columbia University College of Physicians and Surgeons. (2002). *Hearing loss.* Retrieved May 17, 2005, from http://www.entcolumbia.org/hearloss.htm.

Coslett, H. B., Brashear, H. R., & Heilman, K. M. (1984). Pure word deafness after bilateral primary auditory cortex infarcts. *Neurology, 34*(3), 347–352.

Deafness Research Foundation. (2002). *Hearing loss.* Retrieved March 7, 2006, from http://www.drf.org/hh_dictionary/hearing_loss.htm.

Deaf World Web. (2000). *Deaf America Web* [Online]. Retrieved May 17, 2005, from http://deafworldweb.org/int/us.

Easterbrook, S. (1999). Improving practices for students with hearing impairments. *Exceptional Children, 65,* 537–554.

Friend, M. (2006). *Introduction to special education: Making a difference.* Needham Heights, MA: Allyn & Bacon.

Gates, G. A., Cobb, J., Linn, R., Rees, T., Wolf, P., & D'Agostino, R. (1996). Central auditory dysfunction, cognitive dysfunction, and dementia in older people. *Archives of Otolaryngeal Head Neck Surgery, 122*(2), 166–167.

Gallaudet Research Institute. (2003). *Regional and national summary report of data from 2001–2002 Annual Survey of Deaf and Hard of Hearing Children and Youth.* Washington, DC: Gallaudet University.

Gargiulo, R. M. (2004). *Special education in contemporary society: An introduction to exceptionality.* Belmont, CA: Wadsworth.

Green, G. (2003). *Neurodegenerative diseases.* Retrieved May 7, 2005, from http://drgreene.org/body.cfm?id=21&action=detail&ref=525.

Hain, T. C. (2004). *Central hearing loss.* Retrieved May 7, 2005, from http://www.dizziness-and-balance.com/disorders/hearing/cent_hearing.html.

Hallahan, D., & Kauffman, J. (2006). *Exceptional learners: Introduction to special education* (10th ed.). Needham Heights, MA: Allyn & Bacon.

Hardman, M. L., Drew, C. J., & Egan, M. W. (2005). *Human exceptionality: School, community, and family.* Needham Heights, MA:: Allyn & Bacon.

HI

Harris, J. P. (2000). *What is otosclerosis?* Retrieved April 24, 2004, from http://www-surgery.ucsd.edu/ent/PatientInfo/info_otosclerosis.html.

Heward, W. L. (2006). *Exceptional children: An introduction to special education* (8th ed.). Upper Saddle River, NJ: Pearson Education.

Holden-Pitt, L., & Diaz, J. (1998). Thirty years of the Annual Survey of Deaf and Hard-Of-Hearing Children and Youth: A glance over the decades. *American Annals of the Deaf, 142*(2), 72–76.

House Ear Institute. (2004). *Sensorineural hearing loss.* Retrieved May 7, 2005, from http://www.hei.org/about/contact/contact.htm.

Kennedy Krieger Institute. (2005). *Neurodegenerative disorders.* Retrieved May 7, 2005, from http://www.kennedykrieger.org/kki_diag.jsp?pid=1096.

Kuntz, S., & Hesslar, A. (1998). *Bridging the gap between theory and practice: Fostering active learning through the case method.* Annual Meeting of the Association of American Colleges and Universities, p. 23.

League for the Hard of Hearing. (2005). *What parents should know about hearing loss.* Retrieved September 2, 2005, from http://www.lhh.org/earlyid/parents.htm.

Magnuson, M. (2000). Infants with congenital deafness: On the importance of early sign language acquisition. *American Annals of the Deaf, 145*(1), 6–14.

Mayo Clinic. (2006). *Acoustic neuroma.* Retrieved January 4, 2007, from http://www.mayoclinic.com/health/acoustic-neuroma/DS00803.

MedicineNet.com. (2005). *Aplasia.* Retrieved September 2, 2005, from http://www.medicineNet.com.

Merck. (2005). *Sensorineural hearing loss.* Retrieved May 7, 2005, from http://www.merck.com/.

MIMS Consumer Health Groups. (2005). *Causes of hearing loss.* Retrieved May 9, 2005, from http://www.mydr.com.au/default.asp?Article=3246.

Mores, D. F. (2001). *Educating the deaf: Psychology, principles, and practices* (5th ed.). Boston: Houghton Mifflin.

National Academy of Neuropsychology. (2000). *Aphasia.* Retrieved May 7, 2005, from http://nanonline.org/nandistance/mtbi/ClinNeuro/aphasia.html.

National Center on Birth Defects and Developmental Disabilities. (2004). *Hearing loss.* Retrieved May 18, 2005, from http://www.cdc.gov/ncbddd/dd/ddhi.htm.

National Center on Birth Defects and Developmental Disabilities. (2005). *Hearing loss-FAQ.* Retrieved September 10, 2005, from http://www.cdc.gov/ncbddd/ehdi/FAQ/questionsgeneralHL.htm.

National Dissemination Center for Children and Youth with Disabilities. (2004). *Deafness and hearing loss—Fact sheet #3.* Retrieved May 7, 2005, from http://www.nichcy.org/pubs/factshe/fs3txt.htm.

National Institute of Neurological Disorders and Stroke. (2005). *Auditory agnosia.* Retrieved May 21, 2005, from http://www.ninds.nih.gov/disorders/agnosia/agnosia.htm.

National Institute on Deafness and Other Communication Disorders. (1999). *Otosclerosis.* Retrieved May 7, 2005, from http://www.nidcd.nih.gov/health/hearing/otosclerosis.asp.

National Institute on Deafness and Other Communication Disorders. (2002). *Otitis media (ear infection).* Bethesda, MD: National Institutes of Health.

National Institute on Deafness and Other Communication Disorders. (2003). *Auditory neuropathy.* Bethesda, MD: National Institutes of Health.

National Institute on Deafness and Other Communication Disorders. (2004). *Vestibular schwannoma (acoustic neuroma) and neurofibromatosis.* Retrieved May 7, 2005, from http://www.nicd.gov.

National Institute on Deafness and Other Communication Disorders. (2005a). *Acoustic neuroma.* Retrieved May 7, 2005, from http://www.nidcd.nih.gov/health/hearing/acoustic_neuroma.asp.

National Institute on Deafness and Other Communication Disorders. (2005b). *Sudden deafness.* Bethesda, MD: National Institutes of Health.

Nemours Foundation. (2004). *Otitis media.* Retrieved May 7, 2005, from http://www.healthfinder.gov/orgs/HR2778.htm.

New York Eye and Ear Infirmary. (2005). *Otosclerosis.* Retrieved May 23, 2005, from http://www.nyee.edu/.

Oregon Health and Science University. (2006). *What is tinnitus.* Retrieved April 23, 2006, from http://www.ohsu.edu/ohrc/tinnitusclinic/factSheet.html#what% percent20is% percent20tinnitus.

Pediatric Bulletin. (2000). *Congenital cytomegalovirus infection and disease* [Online]. Retrieved May 17, 2005, from http//home.coqui.net/myrna/cmv.htm.

Smith, J. H., Green, G. E., & Van Camp, G. (2005). *Deafness and hereditary hearing loss—Overview.* Retrieved May 7, 2005, from http://www.geneclinics.org/profiles/deafness-overview/details.html.

University of Rochester Medical Center. (2005). *Conductive hearing loss.* Retrieved May 7, 2005, from http://www.urmc.rochester.edu/.

University of Tennessee Department of Otolaryngology. (2006). *Sudden hearing loss.* Retrieved March 16, 2006, from http://www.utmem.edu/otolaryngology/Patients&Public/Ear&BalanceCenter/SuddenHearingLoss.html.

U.S. Department of Education. (2004). *Twenty-Sixth Annual Report to Congress on the Implementation of the Individuals with Disabilities Education Act (IDEA).* Washington, DC: Author.

U.S. National Library of Medicine. (2004). *Cholesteatoma.* Retrieved May 7, 2005, from http://www.nlm.nih.gov/medlineplus/ency/article/001050.htm#Definition.

U.S. National Library of Medicine. (2005a). *Ear noises or buzzing.* Retrieved May 7, 2005, from http://www.nlm.nih.gov/medlineplus/ency/article/003043.htm#Definition.

U.S. National Library of Medicine. (2005b). *Hunter syndrome.* Retrieved May 7, 2005, from http://www.nlm.nih.gov/medlineplus/ency/article/001203.htm.

CHAPTER 10

VISUAL IMPAIRMENTS

EDM CODE: VI

VI 1.00 Corneal Disease
- VI 1.01 Allergies
- VI 1.02 Conjunctivitis (Pink Eye)
- VI 1.03 Corneal Infections
- VI 1.04 Dry Eye
- VI 1.05 Ocular Herpes
- VI 1.06 Pterygium
- VI 1.07 Stevens-Johnson Syndrome
- VI 1.08 Other Types of Corneal Diseases Not Otherwise Listed

VI 2.00 Corneal Dystrophies of the Eye
- VI 2.01 Bietti's Crystalline Dystrophy
- VI 2.02 Lattice Dystrophy
- VI 2.03 Keratoconus
- VI 2.04 Map-Dot-Fingerprint Dystrophy
- VI 2.05 Noncorneal Dystrophy-Retinal Stargardt's Macular Dystrophy
- VI 2.06 Other Types of Corneal Dystrophies Not Otherwise Listed

VI 3.00 Commonly Named Conditions for Causes of Visual Impairment
- VI 3.01 Albinism
  - VI 3.01a Oculocutaneous Albinism
  - VI 3.01b Ocular Albinism
- VI 3.02 Amb lyopia ("Lazy Eye")
  - VI 3.02a Anisometropic Amb lyopia
  - VI 3.02b Strabismic Amb lyopia
- VI 3.03 Aniridia
  - VI 3.03a Familial Aniridia
  - VI 3.03b Gillespie Syndrome
  - VI 3.03c Sporadic Aniridia
  - VI 3.03d WAGR Syndrome
- VI 3.04 Anophthalmia
  - VI 3.04a Consecutive or Degenerative Anophthalmia
  - VI 3.04b Primary Anophthalmia
  - VI 3.04c Secondary Anophthalmia
- VI 3.05 Microphthalmia
- VI 3.06 Cataracts
  - VI 3.06a Congenital Cataract
  - VI 3.06b Radiation Cataract
  - VI 3.06c Secondary Cataract
  - VI 3.06d Traumatic cataract
- VI 3.07 Coloboma
- VI 3.08 Color Blindness
  - VI 3.08a Blue-Yellow Color Blindness
  - VI 3.08b Maskun
  - VI 3.08c Red-Green Color Blindness
- VI 3.09 Diabetic retinopathy
  - VI 3.09a Mild Nonproliferative Retinopathy
  - VI 3.09b Moderate Nonproliferative Retinopathy
  - VI 3.09c Proliferative Retinopathy
  - VI 3.09d Severe Nonproliferative Retinopathy
- VI 3.10 Glaucoma
  - VI 3.10a Angle-Closure Glaucoma
  - VI 3.10b Congenital Glaucoma
  - VI 3.10c Low-Tension Glaucoma
  - VI 3.10d Neovascular Glaucoma
  - VI 3.10e Open Angle Glaucoma
  - VI 3.10f Pigmentary Glaucoma
  - VI 3.10g Secondary Glaucomas
- VI 3.11 Nystagmus
  - VI 3.11a Acquired Nystagmus
  - VI 3.11b Congenital Nystagmus
  - VI 3.11c Jerk Nystagmus
  - VI 3.11d Latent Nystagmus
  - VI 3.11e Pendular Nystagmus
- VI 3.12 Optic Nerve Atrophy
- VI 3.13 Optic Nerve Hypoplasia

VI 3.14 Retinitis Pigmentosa)
VI 3.14a Autosomal-Dominant Inheritance
VI 3.14b Autosomal-Recessive Inheritance
VI 3.14c X-Linked Inheritance
VI 3.15 Retinob lastoma
VI 3.15a Bilateral Retinob lastoma
VI 3.15b Unilateral Retinob lastoma
VI 3.16 Retinopathy of Prematurity
VI 3.16a Stage I—Mildly Abnormal Blood Vessel Growth.
VI 3.16b Stage II—Moderately Abnormal Blood Vessel Growth.
VI 3.16c Stage III—Severely Abnormal Blood Vessel Growth
Vi 3.16d Stage IV—Partially Detached Retina
Vi 3.16e Stage V—Completely Detached Retina and the End Stage of the Disease
VI 3.17 Strabismus
VI 3.17a Constant Strabismus
VI 3.17b Duane's Syndrome
VI 3.17c Esotropia
VI 3.17d Exotropia
VI 3.17e Hypertropia
VI 3.17f Intermittent Strabismus
VI 3.18 Vision Loss Due to Disease or Infection
VI 3.19 Xerophthalmia
VI 3.20 Retinal detachment
VI 3.20a Exudative Retinal Detachment
VI 3.20b Rhegmatogenous Retinal Detachment
VI 3.20c Tractional Retinal Detachment
VI 3.21 Other Types of Eye Conditions Not Otherwise Listed
VI 4.00 Neurological Visual Impairment
VI 4.01 Cortical Blindness
VI 4.02 Cortical Visual Impairment
VI 4.03 Delayed Visual Maturation
VI 4.04 NVI Associated with Cerebral Palsy
VI 4.05 NVI Associated with Epilepsy
VI 4.06 NVI Associated with Hydrocephalus
VI 4.07 NVI Associated with Severe to Mild Learning Disabilities
VI 4.08 NVI Associated with Seizures
VI 4.09 Other Types of NVI Not Otherwise Listed
VI 5.00 Ocular Motor Impairments
VI 6.00 Other Vision Loss Impairments
VI 6.01 Acute Posterior Multifocal Placoid Pigment Epitheliopathy
VI 6.02 Behçet's Disease
VI 6.03 Blepharitis
VI 6.03a Anterior Blepharitis
VI 6.03b Posterior Blepharitis
VI 6.04 Blepharospasm
VI 6.05 Blurred Vision
VI 6.06 Extreme Light Sensitivity
VI 6.07 Fundus Flavimaculatus
VI 6.08 Generalized Haze
VI 6.09 Histoplasmosis Maculopathy
VI 6.10 Night Blindness
VI 6.11 Other Types of Vision Loss Impairments Not Otherwise Listed
VI 7.00 Refractive Errors
VI 7.01 Astigmatism
VI 7.01a Compound Astigmatism
VI 7.01b Mixed Astigmatism
VI 7.01c Simple Astigmatism
VI 7.02 Hyperopia
VI 7.02a Axial Hyperopia
VI 7.02b Curvature Hyperopia
VI 7.02c Refractive Hyperopia
VI 7.03 Myopia
VI 7.03a Axial Myopia
VI 7.03b Curvature myopia
VI 7.03c Refractive Myopia
VI 7.04 Other Types of Refractive Vision Errors Not Otherwise Listed
VI 8.00 Visual Field Disorders
VI 8.01 Central Visual Field Disorder
VI 8.02 Hemianopsia
VI 8.02a Absolute Hemianopsia
VI 8.02b Bitemporal Hemianopsia
VI 8.02c Congruous Hemianopsia
VI 8.02d Homonymous Hemianopsia
VI 8.02e Incongruous Hemianopsia
VI 8.02f Relative Hemianopsia
VI 8.03 Scotomas Disorder
VI 8.03a Absolute Scotoma
VI 8.03b Deep Scotoma
VI 8.03c Relative Scotoma
VI 8.03d Shallow Scotoma
VI 8.04 Tunnel Vision
VI 8.05 Other Types of Visual Field Disorders Not Otherwise Listed
VI 9.00 Other Types of Visual Impairments—Be Specific

IDEA 2004 Definition of Visual Impairments

Visual impairment including blindness means "an impairment in vision that, even with correction, adversely affects a child's educational performance. The term includes both partial sight and blindness" (C.F.R. 300.7(c)(13)).

Overview of Visual Impairments

The terms *partially sighted, low vision, legally blind,* and *totally blind* are used in the educational context to describe students with visual impairments.

Partially sighted indicates that some type of visual problem has resulted in a need for special education (National Dissemination Center for Children with Disabilities, 2004).

Low vision generally refers to a severe visual impairment, not necessarily limited to distance vision. It indicates that some functional vision exists to be used for gaining information through written means with or without the assistance of optical, nonoptical, or electronic devices (Kirk, Gallagher, & Anastasiow, 2000).

Low vision applies to all individuals with sight who are unable to read the newspaper at a normal viewing distance, even with the aid of eyeglasses or contact lenses. They use a combination of vision and other senses to learn, although they may require adaptations in lighting or the size of print and sometimes Braille.

Legal blindness is defined as visual acuity of 20/200 or less in the person's eye after correction, resulting in some confusion (National Dissemination Center for Children with Disabilities, 2004).

Blindness implies that a student must learn and use learn Braille (a system of raised dots that the student reads tactilely), aural methods in order to receive instruction, or other nonvisual media (Heward, 2006; National Dissemination Center for Children with Disabilities, 2004). It refers to a person with "no vision or only light perception" (the ability to determine the presence or absence of light) (Huebner, 2000, p. 58).

Causes-Etiology of Visual Impairments

The etiologies of visual impairment have changed over time as medical treatments evolve and new conditions arise that result from medical conditions or complex premature births. The most common causes of visual impairment in children in the United States vary according to reporting sources and extent of other disabilities.

Prevalence of Visual Impairments

The U.S. Department of Education (2004) reports that during the 2003–2004 school year, 25,294 students aged six to twenty-one (or 0.4 percent of all students with disabilities) received special education services under the category of visual impairment. However, this number is not representative of the total number of students with visual impairments. This is due to the fact that students with visual impairments often have other disabilities as well, thereby being reported in another IDEA disability category (Mason, Davidson, & McNerney, 2000).

Visual impairment is considered a low-incidence disability because it occurs infrequently in the general population and in less than 5 percent of all children with disabilities (Mason et al., 2000). The rate at which visual impairments occur in individuals under the age of eighteen is 12.2 per 1,000. Severe visual impairments (legally or totally blind) occur at a rate of 0.06 per 1,000.

Age of Onset of Visual Impairments

In schools, students with visual impairments can often be easily identified if their visual loss is severe. However, many students have milder losses that are much more difficult to identify and may continue over several years without being recognized (Smith, Polloway, Patton, & Dowdy, 2004). Students with visual impairments can be grouped by their age of onset. Individuals who are born with visual impairments at birth or during infancy are considered to have congenital visual impairments, while those with visual impairments after the age of two years old are considered to have adventitious visual impairments (Huebner, 2000).

Gender Features of Visual Impairments

According to the U.S. Department of Education (2004), more boys than girls are visually impaired. In addition, the increasing numbers of infants are born very prematurely and survive are at high risk for multiple disabilities, including visual deficits, and will substantially increase the number of Americans with visual impairment.

Cultural Features of Visual Impairments

Information on this topic is not available.

Familial Pattern of Visual Impairments

Information on this topic is not available.

Characteristics of Visual Impairments

The effect of visual problems on a child's development depends on the severity, type of loss, age at which the condition appears, and overall functioning level of the child. Many children who have multiple disabilities may also have visual impairments resulting in motor, cognitive, or social developmental delays.

Cognitive Effects

Visual impairments directly influence development and learning in a variety of significant ways. As a group, students with visual impairments exhibit a wide range of cognitive and intellectual abilities.

Blindness and low vision can have an impact on the child's cognitive experience in many ways, including limited range and variety of experience, restriction of movement within the environment, and limited interaction with the environment itself. When the absence of normal experiences with the environment is limited, the effect on a child's development is significant (Pogrund & Fazzi, 2002). A young child with visual impairments has little reason to explore interesting objects in the environment and thus may miss opportunities to have experiences and learn. This lack of exploration may continue until learning becomes motivating or until intervention begins (National Dissemination Center for Children with Disabilities, 2004).

Academic Effects

Visual impairments can have a significant effect on the academic performance of a child, particularly in the areas of reading and writing. Students with visual impairments may use a variety of alternative media and tools for reading and writing, depending on their individual needs. They may use Braille or an alternative form of print (Friend, 2005).

Social and Emotional Effects

Since so much of social development is developed by observing social events and customs and imitating them (Sacks & Silberman, 2000), students with visual impairments are often restricted from learning through observation and imitation. Socially appropriate behaviors can be problematic for them, as many of these behaviors that we learn are through modeling and demonstration.

Behavior Effects

Visual handicaps can create obstacles to a growing child's independence (National Dissemination Center for Children with Disabilities, 2004). Children with visual impairments, especially those who are totally blind, may be unable to imitate social behavior or understand nonverbal cues. Tuttle and Tuttle (1996) found that students with visual impairments may be socially immature, may be more isolated, and may be less assertive than other children. Also, sometimes students with visual impairments are viewed as less capable of taking care of daily needs, so others tend to do things for them. When this happens, students can become even more passive (Friend, 2005).

VI

Educational Implications of Visual Impairments

In the mid-1900s, most students with visual impairments were educated in residential schools or separate classrooms. Now the trend is reversed: about 90 percent of these students are educated in public schools, and most of these children spend some time in the regular classroom with students their own age (U.S. Department of Education, 2004).

The most common model for providing necessary adaptations is the assignment of an itinerant teacher to serve the student directly in the regular classroom or provide consultation to the educational team. This professional is also responsible for obtaining specialized materials and textbooks, conducting assessments related to the visual impairment such as the functional visual evaluation, and collaborating with the educational team to ensure that team members understand the child's educational needs.

In some cases, children with visual impairments are educated in separate classrooms or specialized schools. A specialized placement may be due to the presence of additional disabilities that create complex educational needs or to the preference of the student's family. Some specialized schools encourage short-term placements for students with visual impairments who need to work on a specific skill such as orientation and mobility or assistive technologies (Lewis, 2002). This option may be especially worthwhile after a student experiences a decrease in vision and needs an intensive opportunity to learn adaptive skills. Some specialized schools offer summer programs that allow students with visual impairments to socialize with peers who have common experiences, and many students remember such programs as valuable in helping them develop an understanding of the effects of their own low vision or blindness.

The National Agenda for the Education of Children and Youth with Visual Impairments, Including Those with Multiple Disabilities, a set of goals established by families and professionals in 1995, has provided a framework for advocacy for a continuum of high-quality educational services for learners who are visually impaired (Corn, Hatlen, Huebner, Ryan, & Siller, 1995).

Most students with visual impairments are able to use vision for some activities. Families and professionals can encourage use of vision for activities where it is more efficient or can provide information. Use of vision in regular activities can be determined by administration of a functional vision evaluation, an observational assessment completed by a certified teacher of visually impaired children. This assessment should include recommendations for adaptations, services, and instructional skills that will help the student learn to use vision appropriately (Erin, 2003).

Students who are blind need opportunities for direct experiences with materials and objects because they do not gain information from pictures. Opportunities to pat a cow, stand in the ocean, or climb a tree are more valuable for young children who are blind than relying on verbal descriptions. As children grow older, they will understand raised-line representations of concepts such as maps, charts, and other graphics that can be reproduced through technology to allow tactile examination (Steinkuller et al., 1999).

Most students with visual impairments rely on auditory information for some part of their learning. Books on tape or CD, spoken output from the computer, and use of tape recorders provide a quick means of access that has the advantage of being meaningful to sighted peers as well (National Dissemination Center for Children with Disabilities, 2004; Koenig & Holbrook, 1995).

Children with visual impairments vary widely in their learning abilities and needs, and educational support from a professional in visual impairment is vital in their learning. As they grow older, it is important for them to have contact with adults who are visually impaired and to have the opportunity to participate in regular work experiences. Not only must education provide information access, but it must also help them develop the skills needed to make decisions and experience the results of these decisions (Erin, 2003). Educators and families should resist the temptation to provide assistance where it is not needed. Only through initiative and experience will students understand their own capabilities and develop a realistic plan for his future.

Permissions and Authorization to Use Proprietary and Nonproprietary Sources

Due to the scientific and detailed nature of certain Level II, Level III, and Level IV disorders described in this chapter, we thought that some were best explained by national institutes and centers that conduct comprehensive scientific research in respective fields of study. The sources obtained were all written with explicit permissions that the scientific and diagnostic information they prepared was in the public domain and can be used without restriction.

We thank the following national research offices for the opportunity to freely disseminate their scientific research and writing in this chapter:

- National Dissemination Center for Children and Youth with Disabilities
- National Eye Institute
- U.S. Department of Education
- U.S. National Library of Medicine

VI

EDM Codes, Definitions, and Explanations of Visual Impairments

VI 1.00 Corneal Disease (Not Including Dystrophies of the Eye)

Definition The cornea is the clear, protective outer layer of the eye. Along with the sclera (white of the eye), it serves as a barrier against dirt, germs, and other particles that can harm the eye's delicate components. The cornea is also capable of filtering out some of the sun's ultraviolet light (Cleveland Clinic, 2005).

The cornea plays a key role in vision. As light enters the eye, it is refracted, or bent, by the outside shape of the cornea. The curvature of this outer layer helps determine how well the eye can focus on objects close up and far away.

The term *corneal disease* refers to a variety of conditions that affect mainly the cornea. These include infections, degenerations, and many other disorders of the cornea that may arise mostly as a result of heredity.

Diagnostic Symptoms Due to the fact that the various conditions differ in diagnostic symptoms, no generalization about symptomatology should be made.

Further Key Points The cornea copes very well with minor injuries or abrasions. If the highly sensitive cornea is scratched, healthy cells slide over quickly and patch the injury before infection occurs and vision is affected. If the scratch penetrates the cornea more deeply, the healing process will take longer, at times resulting in greater pain, blurred vision, tearing, redness, and extreme sensitivity to light. These symptoms require professional treatment. Deeper scratches can also cause corneal scarring, resulting in a haze on the cornea that can greatly impair vision. In this case, a corneal transplant may be needed (National Eye Institute, 2005j).

Types of Corneal Diseases

VI 1.01 Allergies

Definition An allergy is an exaggerated immune response or reaction to substances that are generally not harmful (National Eye Institute, 2004j).

Explanation Symptoms of allergies can include redness, itching, tearing, burning, stinging, and watery discharge, although they are not usually severe enough to require medical attention. Antihistamine decongestant eyedrops can effectively reduce these symptoms, as do rain and cooler weather, which decrease the amount of pollen in the air.

An increasing number of eye allergy cases are related to medications and contact lens wear. Also, animal hair and certain cosmetics, such as mascara, face creams, and eyebrow pencil, can cause allergies that affect the eye. Touching or rubbing eyes after handling nail polish, soaps, or chemicals may cause an allergic reaction. Some people have sensitivity to lip gloss and eye makeup. Allergy symptoms are temporary and can be eliminated by not having contact with the offending cosmetic or detergent (National Eye Institute, 2005j).

VI 1.02 Conjunctivitis (Pink Eye)

Definition Conjunctivitis describes a group of diseases that cause swelling, itching, burning, and redness of the conjunctiva, the protective membrane that lines the eyelids and covers exposed areas of the sclera, or white of the eye (National Eye Institute, 2005j).

Explanation At its onset, conjunctivitis is usually painless and does not adversely affect vision. The infection clears in most cases without requiring medical care. But for some forms of conjunctivitis, treatment will be needed. If treatment is delayed, the infection may worsen and cause corneal inflammation and a loss of vision (National Eye Institute, 2005j).

VI 1.03 Corneal Infections

Definition Sometimes the cornea is damaged after a foreign object has penetrated the tissue, such as from a poke in the eye. At other times, bacteria or fungi from a contaminated contact lens can pass into the cornea. Situations like these can cause painful inflammation and corneal infections called keratitis (National Eye Institute, 2005j).

Explanation These infections can reduce visual clarity, produce corneal discharges, and perhaps erode the cornea. Corneal infections can also lead to corneal scarring, which can impair vision and may require a corneal transplant.

As a general rule, the deeper the corneal infection, the more severe the symptoms and complications are. It should be noted that corneal infections, although relatively infrequent, are the most serious complication of contact lens wear. Minor corneal infections are commonly treated with antibacterial eyedrops. If the problem is severe, it may require more intensive antibiotic or antifungal treatment to eliminate the infection, as well as steroid eyedrops to reduce inflammation. Frequent visits to an eye care professional may be necessary for several months to eliminate the problem (National Eye Institute, 2005j).

VI1.04 Dry Eye

Definition The continuous production and drainage of tears is important to the eye's health. Tears keep the eye moist, help wounds heal, and protect against eye infection. In people with dry eye, the eye produces fewer or lower-quality tears and is unable to keep its surface lubricated and comfortable (National Eye Institute, 2005j).

Explanation The tear film consists of three layers: an outer oily (lipid) layer that keeps tears from evaporating too quickly and helps tears remain on the eye; a middle (aqueous) layer that nourishes the cornea and conjunctiva; and a bottom (mucin) layer that helps to spread the aqueous layer across the eye to ensure that the eye remains wet. As we age, the eyes usually produce fewer tears. Also, in some cases, the lipid and mucin layers produced by the eye are of such poor quality that tears cannot remain in the eye long enough to keep the eye sufficiently lubricated.

The main symptom of dry eye is usually a scratchy or sandy feeling, as if something is in the eye. Other symptoms may include stinging or burning of the eye; episodes of excess tearing that follow periods of very dry sensation; a stringy discharge from the eye; and pain and redness of the eye. Sometimes people with dry eye experience heaviness of the eyelids or blurred, changing, or decreased vision, although loss of vision is uncommon.

Dry eye is more common in women, especially after menopause. Surprisingly, some people with dry eye may have tears that run down their cheeks. This is because the eye may be producing less of the lipid and mucin layers of the tear film, which help keep tears in the eye. When this happens, tears do not stay in the eye long enough to thoroughly moisten it.

Dry eye can occur in climates with dry air, as well as with the use of some drugs, including antihistamines, nasal decongestants, tranquilizers, and antidepressants. People with dry eye should let their health care providers know all the medications they are taking, since some of them may intensify dry eye symptoms.

People with connective tissue diseases, such as rheumatoid arthritis, can also develop dry eye. It is important to note that dry eye is sometimes a symptom of Sjögren's syndrome, a disease that attacks the body's lubricating glands, such as the tear and salivary glands. A complete physical examination may diagnose underlying disease.

Artificial tears, which lubricate the eye, are the principal treatment for dry eye. They are available over the counter as eyedrops. Sterile ointments are sometimes used at night to help prevent the eye from drying. Using humidifiers, wearing wraparound glasses when outside, and avoiding outside windy and dry conditions may bring relief. For people with severe cases of dry eye, temporary or permanent closure of the tear drain (small openings at the inner corner of the eyelids where tears drain from the eye) may be helpful (National Eye Institute, 2005j).

VI 1.05 Ocular Herpes

Definition Herpes of the eye, or ocular herpes, is a recurrent viral infection that is due to the effects of the herpes simplex virus and is the most common infectious cause of corneal blindness in the United States (National Eye Institute, 2005j).

Explanation Previous studies show that once people develop ocular herpes, they have up to a 50 percent chance of having a recurrence. This second flare-up could come weeks or even years after the initial occurrence.

Ocular herpes can produce a painful sore on the eyelid or surface of the eye and cause inflammation of the cornea. Prompt treatment with antiviral drugs helps to stop the herpes virus from multiplying and destroying epithelial cells. However, the infection may spread more deeply into the cornea and develop into a more severe infection called stromal keratitis, which causes the body's immune system to attack and destroy stromal cells. Stromal keratitis is more difficult to treat than less severe ocular herpes infections. Recurrent episodes of stromal keratitis can cause scarring of the cornea, which can lead to loss of vision and possibly blindness.

Like other herpetic infections, herpes of the eye can be controlled. An estimated 400,000 Americans have had some form of ocular herpes. Each year, nearly 50,000 new and recurring cases are diagnosed in the United States, with the more serious stromal keratitis accounting for about 25 percent. In one large study, researchers found that the recurrence rate of ocular herpes was 10 percent within one year, 23 percent within two years, and 63 percent within twenty years. Some factors believed to be associated with recurrence are fever, stress, sunlight, and eye injury (National Eye Institute, 2005j).

VI 1.06 Pterygium

Definition A pterygium is a pinkish, triangular-shaped tissue growth on the cornea. Some pterygia grow slowly throughout a person's life, while others stop growing after a certain point. A pterygium rarely grows so large that it begins to cover the pupil of the eye (National Eye Institute, 2005j).

Explanation Pterygia are more common in sunny climates and in the between twenty and forty years old. Scientists do not know what causes pterygia to develop. However, since people who have pterygia usually have spent a significant time outdoors, many doctors believe ultraviolet light from the sun may be a factor. In areas where sunlight is strong, wearing protective eyeglasses, sunglasses, or hats with a brim are suggested. While some studies report a higher prevalence of pterygia in men than in women, this may reflect different rates of exposure to ultraviolet light.

Because a pterygium is visible, many people want to have it removed for cosmetic reasons. It is usually not too noticeable unless it becomes red and swollen from dust or air pollutants. Surgery to remove a pterygium is not recommended unless it affects vision. If a pterygium is surgically removed, it may grow back, particularly if the patient is less than forty years of age. Lubricants can reduce the redness and provide relief from the chronic irritation (National Eye Institute, 2005j).

VI 1.07 Stevens-Johnson Syndrome

Definition Stevens-Johnson Syndrome (SJS), also called erythema multiform major, is a disorder of the skin that can also affect the eyes (National Eye Institute, 2005j).

VI

Explanation SJS is characterized by painful, blistery lesions on the skin and the mucous membranes (the thin, moist tissues that line body cavities) of the mouth, throat, genital region, and eyelids. It can cause serious eye problems, such as severe conjunctivitis; iritis, an inflammation inside the eye; corneal blisters and erosions; and corneal holes. In some cases, the ocular complications from SJS can be disabling and lead to severe vision loss.

Scientists are not certain why SJS develops. The most commonly cited cause is an adverse allergic drug reaction. Almost any drug, but most particularly sulfa drugs, can cause SJS. The allergic reaction to the drug may not occur until seven to fourteen days after first using it. SJS can also be preceded by a viral infection, such as herpes or the mumps, and its accompanying fever, sore throat, and sluggishness. Treatment for the eye may include artificial tears, antibiotics, or corticosteroids. About one-third of all patients diagnosed with SJS have recurrences of the disease.

SJS occurs twice as often in men as women, and most cases appear in children and young adults under age thirty, although it can develop in people at any age (National Eye Institute, 2005j).

VI 1.08 Other Types of Corneal Diseases Not Otherwise Listed

VI 2.00 Corneal Dystrophies of the Eye

Definition Corneal dystrophies form a group of rare disorders that usually affect both eyes. They may be present at birth, but more frequently develop during adolescence and progress gradually throughout life. Some forms are mild and others severe (Royal National Institute for the Blind, 2005).

Diagnostic Symptoms Corneal dystrophies affect vision in widely differing ways. Some cause severe visual impairment, while a few cause no vision problems and are discovered during a routine eye examination. Other dystrophies may cause repeated episodes of pain without leading to permanent loss of vision (National Eye Institute, 2005h).

Further Key Points These diseases share many traits, including:

- They are usually inherited.
- They affect the right and left eyes equally.
- They are not due to the effects of outside factors, such as injury or diet.
- Most progress gradually.
- Most usually begin in one of the five corneal layers and may later spread to nearby layers.
- Most do not affect other parts of the body, and they are not related to diseases affecting other parts of the eye or body.
- Most can occur in otherwise totally healthy people, male or female.

Corneal dystrophies affect vision in widely differing ways. Some cause severe visual impairment, while a few cause no vision problems and are discovered during a routine eye examination. Other dystrophies may cause repeated episodes of pain without leading to permanent loss of vision.

Types of Corneal Dystrophies of the Eye

VI 2.01 Bietti's Crystalline Dystrophy

Definition Bietti's crystalline dystrophy is an inherited eye disease (National Eye Institute, 2005e).

Explanation Bietti's crystalline dystrophy (BCD) is named for G. B. Bietti, an Italian ophthalmologist, who described three patients with similar symptoms in 1937. The symptoms include crystals in the cornea (the clear covering of the eye); yellow, shiny deposits on the retina; and progressive atrophy of the retina, choriocapillaries, and choroid (the back layers of the eye). This tends to lead to progressive night blindness and visual field constriction. BCD is a rare disease and appears to be more common in people with Asian ancestry.

People with BCD have crystals in some of their white blood cells (lymphocytes) that can be seen by using an electron microscope. Researchers have been unable to determine exactly what substance makes up these crystalline deposits. Their presence does not appear to harm the patient in any other way except to affect vision.

BCD is inherited primarily in an autosomal-recessive fashion. This means that an affected person receives one nonworking gene from each parent. A person who inherits a nonworking gene from only one parent will be a carrier but will not develop the disease. A person with BCD syndrome will pass on one gene to each of his or her children. However, unless the person has children with another carrier of BCD genes, the individual's children are not at risk for developing the disease (National Eye Institute, 2005e).

VI 2.02 Lattice Dystrophy

Definition Lattice dystrophy gets its name from an accumulation of amyloid deposits, or abnormal protein fibers, throughout the middle and anterior stroma (National Eye Institute, 2005j).

Explanation During an eye examination, the doctor sees these deposits in the stroma as clear, comma-shaped overlapping dots and branching filaments, creating a lattice effect. Over time, the lattice lines grow opaque and involve more of the stroma. They also gradually converge, giving the cornea a cloudiness that may also reduce vision.

In some people, these abnormal protein fibers can accumulate under the cornea's outer layer—the epithelium. This can cause erosion of the epithelium. This condition is known as recurrent epithelial erosion. These erosions alter the cornea's normal curvature, resulting in temporary vision problems and expose the nerves that line the cornea, causing severe pain. Even the involuntary act of blinking can be painful.

Although lattice dystrophy can occur at any time in life, the condition usually arises in children between the ages of two and seven (National Eye Institute, 2005j).

VI 2.03 Keratoconus

Definition Keratoconus, a progressive thinning of the cornea, is the most common corneal dystrophy in the United States, affecting one in every two thousand Americans (National Eye Institute, 2005j).

Explanation It is more prevalent in teenagers and adults in their twenties. Keratoconus arises when the middle of the cornea thins and gradually bulges outward, forming a rounded cone shape. This abnormal curvature changes the cornea's refractive power, producing moderate to severe distortion (astigmatism) and blurriness (nearsightedness) of vision. Keratoconus may also cause swelling and a sight-impairing scarring of the tissue.

In most cases, the cornea stabilizes after a few years without ever causing severe vision problems. But in about 10 to 20 percent of people with keratoconus, the cornea will eventually become too scarred or will not tolerate a contact lens. If either of these problems occurs, a corneal transplant may be needed. This operation is successful in more than 90 percent of those with advanced keratoconus. Several studies have also reported that 80 percent or more of these patients have 20/40 vision or better after the operation (National Eye Institute, 2005j).

VI 2.04 Map-Dot-Fingerprint Dystrophy

Definition This dystrophy occurs when the epithelium's basement membrane develops abnormally (the basement membrane serves as the foundation on which the epithelial cells, which absorb nutrients from tears, anchor, and organize themselves). When this happens, the epithelial cells cannot properly adhere to it. This causes recurrent epithelial erosions, in which the epithelium's outermost layer rises slightly, exposing a small gap between the outermost layer and the rest of the cornea (National Eye Institute, 2005j).

Explanation Epithelial erosions can be a chronic problem. They may alter the cornea's normal curvature, causing periodic blurred vision. They may also expose the nerve endings that line the tissue, resulting in moderate to severe pain lasting as long as several days. Generally the pain is worse on awakening in the morning. Other symptoms include sensitivity to light, excessive tearing, and foreign body sensation in the eye (National Eye Institute, 2005j).

VI 2.05 Noncorneal Dystrophy–Retinal Stargardt's Macular Dystrophy

Definition Stargardt's macular dystrophy is an inherited condition that affects the macula, an area of the central retina (Royal National Institute of the Blind, 2005).

Explanation Conditions involving the macula affect central vision. Decreased central vision is usually the first symptom of Stargardt's macular dystrophy and visual loss is progressive over a period of years, sometimes to a level of 6/60 (Royal National Institute of the Blind, 2005).

VI 2.06 Other Types of Corneal Dystrophies Not Otherwise Listed

VI 3.00 Commonly Named Conditions for Causes of Visual Impairment

Definition The disorders discussed in this section vary in definition and diagnostic symptoms.

Diagnostic Symptoms Due to the fact that the various conditions differ in diagnostic symptoms, no generalization about symptomatology should be made.

Further Key Points Some of the conditions involve hereditary factors. However, there are many patterns of heredity, even for a single disorder. If there is any questions about the inheritance of a particular characteristic in an individual or family, family members should be directed to a genetic specialist. A family physician can usually provide the proper referral.

Types of Eye Conditions

VI 3.01 Albinism

Definition Albinism refers to a group of related conditions that are the result of altered genes that cause a defect of melanin production. This defect results in the partial or full absence of pigment from the skin, hair, and eyes (U.S. National Library of Medicine, 2006).

Explanation Albinism results when the body is unable to produce or distribute pigment, called melanin, because of one of several possible genetic defects. In type 1 albinism, defects in the metabolism of tyrosine lead to failure in converting this amino acid to melanin. This is due to a genetic defect in tyrosinase—the enzyme responsible for metabolizing tyrosine. Type 2 albinism is due to a defect in the P gene. Those with this type have slight pigmentation at birth.

In the most severe form of albinism (called *oculocutaneous albinism*), those affected appear to have hair, skin, and iris color that are white or pink, as well as vision defects. This is inherited by an autosomal-recessive process.

Many types of albinism exist, all of which involve lack of pigment in varying degrees; however, there are two main categories of albinism: oculocutaneous albinism and ocular albinism.

VI 3.01a **Oculocutaneous Albinism** Oculocutaneous albinism involves the eyes, hair, and skin. It is the most common form of albinism. People with ocular albinism may have slight lightening of hair and skin color compared to other family members. This form of albinism makes up a group of different types of albinism based on the specific albinism gene involved. Oculocutaneous albinism type 1 and type 2 are the most common types.

VI 3.01b **Ocular Albinism** Melanin pigment is mainly missing from the eyes; the skin and hair appear normal or only slightly lighter. It accounts for 10 to 15 percent of all albinism cases.

VI 3.02 Amblyopia (Lazy Eye)

Definition *Amblyopia* is the medical term used when the vision in one of the eyes is reduced because the eye and the brain are not working together properly (National Eye Institute, 2005a).

Explanation Amblyopia is the most common cause of visual impairment in childhood. This condition, sometimes called lazy eye, affects approximately two to three out of every one hundred children. Unless it is successfully treated in early childhood, amblyopia usually persists into adulthood and is the most common cause of monocular (one-eye) visual impairment among children and young and middle-aged adults.

Amblyopia may be due to the effects of any condition that affects normal visual development or use of the eyes. Amblyopia can be due to the effects of strabismus, an imbalance in the positioning of the two eyes. Strabismus can cause the eyes to cross in (esotropia) or turn out (exotropia). Sometimes amblyopia is caused when one eye is more nearsighted, farsighted, or astigmatic than the other eye. Occasionally amblyopia is due to the effects of other eye conditions such as cataract (National Eye Institute, 2005a).

VI 3.02a **Anisometropic Amblyopia** With anisometropic amblyopia, the eyes have different refractive powers. For example, one eye may be nearsighted and the other farsighted. It may be difficult for the brain to balance the difference, and it favors the stronger eye.

VI 3.02b **Strabismic Amblyopia** In strabismic amblyopia, strabismus is present, and the eyes are not aligned properly, resulting in one eye being used less than the other. The nonpreferred eye is not adequately stimulated, and the visual brain cells do not develop normally.

VI 3.03 Aniridia

Definition Aniridia is a congenital malformation of the eye in which the iris is not completely formed and that results in cataract formation and congenital glaucoma (Office of Rare Diseases, 2005).

Explanation If there is no iris in the eye, it is impossible to control the inlet of light—(the iris is an analogue to the aperture of the camera). The pupil stands wide open, no matter how light it is. The only treatment of aniridia is the use of colored eye lenses in order to reduce the light inlet.

Aniridia literally means "without iris." In most cases, this is the most visible sign of the condition. However, aniridia is caused when the gene responsible for eye development—the PAX6 gene—does not function correctly. This causes the eye to stop developing too early, and when the baby is born, most of the eye is underdeveloped to some degree.

There are four basic types of aniridia.

VI 3.03a **Familial Aniridia (Autosomal Dominant)** This is the most common form of aniridia, and it is inherited directly from a parent who has this disorder. It is the result of a mutation in the PAX6 gene. Familial aniridia is associated with many serious ocular conditions, including cataracts, glaucoma, and corneal pannus. Close follow-up by an experienced ophthalmologist is very important. Each child of a person with familial aniridia will have a 50 percent chance of inheriting the gene mutation.

VI 3.03b **Gillespie Syndrome (Autosomal Recessive)** This type of aniridia is extremely rare. It may be inherited through parents who do not have aniridia themselves but who both have one normal copy of the PAX6 gene and one mutated copy. This type of aniridia is associated with a particular appearance of the iris remnant (described as having a "scalloped" border), mental retardation, and cerebellar ataxia (muscle incoordination). There are reports of more than one case of Gillespie syndrome in a family and reports of people with Gillespie syndrome whose children also have the disorder.

VI 3.03c **Sporadic Aniridia (No Deletion Detected)** This type of aniridia is the second most common form. Both parents have normal chromosomes. The affected person has a new mutation of the PAX6 gene (a mutation that occurred before or very soon after conception). It is not known what causes this mutation. People with sporadic aniridia are at risk for the same eye complications as those with familial aniridia.

VI 3.03d **WAGR Syndrome** This type of aniridia is rare. Both parents have normal chromosomes, and the affected person has a new mutation (as in sporadic aniridia, VI 3.03c). Unlike sporadic aniridia, however, this new mutation involves not only the PAX6 gene but a large number of neighboring genes as well. This genetic abnormality is a deletion, or set of missing genes, located on the short arm of chromosome number 12. In addition to aniridia, children with WAGR syndrome have a high risk for Wilms tumor (a type of cancer of the kidney) and other medical complications such as genital abnormalities and learning and behavior difficulties.

VI 3.04 Anophthalmia

Definition Anophthalmia is the absence of one or both eyes. This rare disorder develops during pregnancy and can be associated with other birth defects (National Eye Institute, 2005c).

Explanation Causes of this condition may include genetic mutations and abnormal chromosomes. Researchers also believe that environmental factors, such as exposure to X-rays, chemicals, drugs, pesticides, toxins, radiation, or viruses, increase the risk of anophthalmia and microphthalmia, but research is not conclusive. Sometimes the cause in an individual patient cannot be determined (National Eye Institute, 2005c).

VI 3.04a **Consecutive or Degenerative Anophthalmia** In degenerative anophthalmia, the eye started to form and then degenerated. One possible reason is a lack of blood supply to the eye.

VI 3.04b **Primary Anophthalmia** Primary anophthalmia is a complete absence of eye tissue due to a failure of the part of the brain that forms the eye.

VI 3.04c **Secondary Anophthalmia** In secondary anophthalmia, the eye starts to develop and then stops, leaving the infant with only residual eye tissue or extremely tiny eyes that can be seen only under close examination.

VI 3.05 Microphthalmia

Definition Microphthalmia is a disorder in which one or both eyes are abnormally small (National Eye Institute, 2005c).

Explanation Children with microphthalmia may have some residual vision (limited sight). In these cases, the good eye can be patched to strengthen vision in the microphthalmic eye. A prosthesis can be made to cap the microphthalmic eye to help with cosmetic appearance while preserving the remaining sight (National Eye Institute, 2005c).

VI 3.06 Cataracts

Definition A cataract is a clouding of the lens in the eye that affects vision (National Eye Institute, 2005h).

Explanation Most cataracts are related to aging and are common in older people. A cataract can occur in either or both eyes but cannot spread from one eye to the other. The most common symptoms of a cataract are:

- Cloudy or blurry vision.
- Colors seem faded.
- Glare. Headlights, lamps, or sunlight may appear too bright. A halo may appear around lights.

- Poor night vision.
- Double vision or multiple images in one eye. (This symptom may clear as the cataract gets larger.)
- Frequent prescription changes in eyeglasses or contact lenses (National Eye Institute, 2005h).

VI 3.06a **Congenital Cataract** Some babies are born with cataracts or develop them in childhood, often in both eyes. These cataracts may be so small that they do not affect vision. If they do, the lenses may need to be removed.

VI 3.06b **Radiation Cataract** Cataracts can develop after exposure to some types of radiation.

VI 3.06c **Secondary Cataract** Cataracts can form after surgery for other eye problems such as glaucoma. They also can develop in people who have other health problems such as diabetes. Cataracts are sometimes linked to steroid use.

VI 3.06d **Traumatic Cataract** Cataracts can develop after an eye injury, sometimes years later.

VI 3.07 Coloboma

Definition The word *coloboma* comes from the Greek word that literally translates to "mutilation." Coloboma describes a situation where the patient has a portion of the structure of the eye lacking. This gap can occur in a range of areas and be large or small.

Coloboma of the iris is a congenital (present since birth) defect of the iris of the eye. It is visible as a hole, split, or cleft in the iris (Micro & Anophthalmic Children's Society, 2005).

Explanation In this condition, there has been a failure of the closure of the optic fissure, leaving a gap in some or all of the structures of the eye. This condition is usually (but not always) apparent because the pupil is misshaped. It can often be a "cat's eye" or "keyhole" shape.

Although no specific pattern has been identified, there appears to be a strong hereditary factor in the incidence of this condition, which is sometimes linked to chromosomal disorders (Micro & Anophthalmic Children's Society, 2005).

VI 3.08 Color Blindness (Color Deficiency)

Definition Color blindness may be a hereditary condition or caused by disease of the optic nerve or retina (St. Luke's Cataract & Laser Institute, 2004a).

Explanation Color blindness is the inability to perceive differences between some colors that other people can distinguish. Approximately one out of every twelve males and less than 1 percent of females are color-blind. *Color blindness* is the term used to describe mild to severe difficulties with identifying various colors and shades of colors. It is a misleading term because color-blind people are not blind.

Rather, they tend to confuse some colors, and a rare few may not see colors at all. The English chemist John Dalton in 1794 published the first scientific paper on the subject, "Extraordinary Facts Relating to the Vision of Colours," after the realization of his own color blindness.

VI 3.08a **Blue-Yellow Color Blindness (Tritanopia)** Tritanopia describes mild to severe difficulties with identifying colors and shades of the colors blue and yellow.

VI 3.08b **Maskun (Achromatopsia)** Maskun, also called achromatopsia, is a medical condition characterized by the inability to perceive any colors, a severe and rare form of color blindness.

VI 3.08c **Red-Green Color Blindness** Red-green color blindness describes mild to severe difficulties with identifying colors and shades of the colors red and green.

VI 3.09 Diabetic Retinopathy

Definition Diabetic retinopathy is a complication of diabetes and a leading cause of blindness. It occurs when diabetes damages the tiny blood vessels inside the retina, the light-sensitive tissue at the back of the eye. A healthy retina is necessary for good vision (National Eye Institute, 2005i).

Explanation Diabetic retinopathy has four stages (National Eye Institute, 2005g).

VI 3.09a **Mild Nonproliferative Retinopathy** At this earliest stage, microaneurysms occur. They are small areas of balloon-like swelling in the retina's tiny blood vessels.

VI 3.09b **Moderate Nonproliferative Retinopathy** As the disease progresses, some blood vessels that nourish the retina are blocked.

VI 3.09c **Proliferative Retinopathy** At this advanced stage, the signals sent by the retina for nourishment trigger the growth of new blood vessels. These new blood vessels are abnormal and fragile. They grow along the retina and along the surface of the clear, vitreous gel that fills the inside of the eye.

VI

VI 3.09d **Severe Nonproliferative Retinopathy** Many more blood vessels are blocked, depriving several areas of the retina with their blood supply. These areas of the retina send signals to the body to grow new blood vessels for nourishment.

VI 3.10 Glaucoma

Definition Glaucoma is a group of diseases that can damage the eye's optic nerve and result in vision loss and blindness (National Eye Institute, 2005k).

Explanation Vision loss is due to the effects of damage to the optic nerve. As glaucoma remains untreated, people may miss objects to the side and out of the corner of their eye. Without treatment, they slowly lose their peripheral (side) vision. They seem to be looking through a tunnel. Over time, straight-ahead vision may decrease, until no vision remains. There is no cure for glaucoma. Vision lost from the disease cannot be restored (National Eye Institute, 2005k).

VI 3.10a **Angle-Closure Glaucoma** In angle-closure glaucoma, the fluid at the front of the eye cannot reach the angle and leave the eye. The angle gets blocked by part of the iris. People with this type of glaucoma have a sudden increase in eye pressure. Symptoms include severe pain and nausea, as well as redness of the eye and blurred vision.

VI 3.10b **Congenital Glaucoma** In congenital glaucoma, children are born with a defect in the angle of the eye that slows the normal drainage of fluid. These children usually have obvious symptoms, such as cloudy eyes, sensitivity to light, and excessive tearing.

VI 3.10c **Low-Tension Glaucoma (Normal-Tension Glaucoma)** In low-tension or normal-tension glaucoma, optic nerve damage and narrowed side vision occur in people with normal eye pressure. Lowering eye pressure at least 30 percent through medicine slows the disease in some people.

VI 3.10d **Neovascular Glaucoma** Neovascular glaucoma, a severe form of the disease, is linked to diabetes. Corticosteroid drugs used to treat eye inflammations and other diseases can trigger glaucoma in some people. Treatment includes medicines, laser surgery, or conventional surgery.

VI 3.10e **Open Angle Glaucoma** In the front of the eye is a space called the anterior chamber. A clear fluid flows continuously in and out of the chamber and nourishes nearby tissues. The fluid leaves the chamber at the open angle where the cornea and iris meet. When the fluid reaches the angle, it flows through a spongy meshwork, like a drain, and leaves the eye.

Sometimes when the fluid reaches the angle, it passes too slowly through the meshwork drain. As the fluid builds up, pressure inside the eye rises to a level that may damage the optic nerve. When the optic nerve is damaged from increased pressure, open-angle glaucoma—and vision loss—may result.

VI 3.10f **Pigmentary Glaucoma** Pigmentary glaucoma occurs when pigment from the iris flakes off and blocks the meshwork, slowing fluid drainage.

VI 3.10g **Secondary Glaucomas** Secondary glaucoma can develop as complications of other medical conditions. These types of glaucoma are sometimes associated with eye surgery or advanced cataracts, eye injuries, certain eye tumors, or uveitis (eye inflammation).

VI 3.11 Nystagmus

Definition Nystagmus is generally described as an involuntary movement of the eyes, which reduces vision. The movement is usually side to side (but can be up and down or circular motion) (National Eye Institute, 2005m).

Explanation Nystagmus, thought to sometimes be hereditary, is neither contagious nor infectious, but it often seriously reduces vision. Nystagmus affects people in many ways, and the effects vary from person to person. Most people who have had the condition since childhood do not suffer from a constantly moving image (known as oscillopsia) most of the time, as their brains adapt to the movement of the eyes. However, people who acquire nystagmus in later life are unlikely to adjust so well and suffer much more from the effects of oscillopsia. People with nystagmus may be slow readers because of the extra time they need to scan. This should not be taken as a sign of poor reading ability, but students with nystagmus may need extra time when they are taking exams (National Eye Institute, 2005m).

VI 3.11a **Acquired Nystagmus** Acquired nystagmus occurs later than six months of age and can be due to the effects of a stroke, a disease such as multiple sclerosis, or even a heavy blow to the head.

VI 3.11b **Congenital Nystagmus** Nystagmus that appears in the first six months of life is called early-onset nystagmus or congenital or infantile nystagmus.

VI 3.11c **Jerk Nystagmus** Jerk nystagmus consists of two movements: (1) a slow drift of the eyes and (2) a rapid corrective movement back to the point of fixation. This is the most common form of nystagmus.

VI 3.11d **Latent Nystagmus** Latent nystagmus is defined clinically as nystagmus that appears only when occluding one eye.

VI 3.11e **Pendular Nystagmus** Pendular nystagmus consists of movement that occurs at roughly the same velocity in both directions.

VI 3.12 Optic Nerve Atrophy (Second Cranial Nerve Atrophy)

Definition Optic nerve atrophy involves tissue death of the nerve that carries the information of vision from the eye to the brain (U.S. National Library of Medicine, 2004a).

Explanation There are many unrelated causes of optic atrophy. The optic nerve can also be damaged by shock, toxic substances, radiation, or trauma. Various eye diseases, glaucoma most commonly, can also cause optic nerve atrophy. In addition, the condition can be due to the effects of diseases of the brain and central nervous system, such as multiple sclerosis, brain tumor, and stroke. Several rare forms of hereditary optic nerve atrophy affect children and young adult. Optic nerve atrophy causes dimming of vision and reduction of the field of vision (U.S. National Library of Medicine, 2004a).

VI 3.13 Optic Nerve Hypoplasia

Definition *Hypoplasia* means smaller than normal. Optic nerve hypoplasia (ONH) refers to underdevelopment of the nerve that transmits vision signals from the eye to the brain. This is usually associated with permanent vision loss, which may be mild or severe and may affect one or both eyes (American Association for Pediatric Ophthalmology and Strabismus, 2005a).

Explanation Vision can range from near-normal levels to severe impairment. Children with ONH may have difficulty locating objects due to a constricted visual field or impaired depth perception. Some children have light sensitivity.

If vision is significantly affected in both eyes, an infant will present with poor vision or shaking of the eyes (nystagmus). If only one optic nerve is small, the eye may cross in or drift out (American Association for Pediatric Ophthalmology and Strabismus, 2005a).

VI 3.14 Retinitis Pigmentosa

Definition Retinitis pigmentosa (RP) is a progressive degeneration of the retina (part of the eye) that affects night vision and peripheral vision (U.S. National Library of Medicine, 2004b).

Explanation Retinitis pigmentosa commonly runs in families. The disorder can be caused by defects in a number of different genes that have recently been identified.

The cells controlling night vision, called rods, are most likely to be affected. However, in some cases, retinal cone cells are most damaged. The hallmark of the disease is the presence of dark pigmented spots in the retina (U.S. National Library of Medicine, 2004b).

VI 3.14a **Autosomal-Dominant Inheritance** In families with the autosomal-dominant RP, an affected parent can have both affected and unaffected children. The patient has one gene for retinitis pigmentosa paired with one normal gene and has a 50 percent chance of passing the disease to the child, even if the other parent is unaffected.

VI 3.14b **Autosomal-Recessive Inheritance** In families with autosomal-recessive RP, unaffected parents can have both affected and unaffected children. There may not be a known family history of the disorder. Both parents have normal retinas and carry a defective gene. There is a 25 percent chance that their child will be afflicted.

VI 3.14c **X-Linked Inheritance** In families with the X-linked type, only males are affected. Females carry the genetic trait but do not experience serious vision loss.

VI 3.15 Retinoblastoma

Definition Retinoblastoma is a malignant (cancerous) tumor of the retina. The retina is the thin nerve tissue that lines the back of the eye that senses light and forms images (National Cancer Institute, 2004).

Explanation Although retinoblastoma may occur at any age, it most often occurs in younger children, usually before the age of five years. The tumor may be in one or both eyes. Retinoblastoma is usually confined to the eye and does not spread to nearby tissue or other parts of the body.

This disease is caused by mutations in the Retinoblastoma-1 (RB1) gene. These mutations are either inherited (passed from the parents to the children) or new (not passed from the parents to the children) mutations. Some new mutations may become inherited, that is, the new mutation is passed from the parents to the children. Tumors caused by inherited mutations are called hereditary retinoblastomas. Tumors caused by new mutations are called sporadic retinoblastomas. Hereditary retinoblastomas may form in one or both eyes and are generally found in younger children (National Cancer Institute, 2004).

VI 3.15a **Bilateral Retinoblastoma** When the tumors are present in both eyes, the condition is referred to as bilateral retinoblastoma.

VI 3.15b **Unilateral Retinoblastoma** When the tumors are present in one eye, the condition is referred to as unilateral retinoblastoma.

VI 3.16 Retinopathy of Prematurity (Retrolental Fibroplasias)

Definition Retinopathy of prematurity (ROP) is a potentially blinding eye disorder that primarily affects premature infants weighing about 2_ pounds (1,250 grams) or less who are born before thirty-one weeks of gestation (a full-term pregnancy has a gestation of thirty-eight to forty-two weeks) (National Eye Institute, 2005p).

Explanation The smaller a baby is at birth, the more likely that baby is to develop ROP. This disorder, which usually develops in both eyes, is one of the most common causes of visual loss in childhood and can lead to lifelong vision impairment and blindness. In a small number of babies, ROP worsens, sometimes very rapidly. Untreated ROP threatens to destroy vision (National Eye Institute, 2005p).

ROP, first diagnosed in 1942, occurs when abnormal blood vessels grow and spread throughout the retina, the tissue that lines the back of the eye. These abnormal blood vessels are fragile and can leak, scarring the retina and pulling it out of position. This causes a retinal detachment. Retinal detachment is the main cause of visual impairment and blindness in ROP.

ROP is classified in five stages, ranging from mild (stage I) to severe (stage V). Most babies who develop ROP have stages I or II.

VI 3.16a **Stage I: Mildly Abnormal Blood Vessel Growth** Many children who develop stage I improve with no treatment and eventually develop normal vision. The disease resolves on its own.

VI 3.16b **Stage II: Moderately Abnormal Blood Vessel Growth** Many children who develop stage II improve with no treatment and eventually develop normal vision. The disease resolves on its own.

VI 3.16c **Stage III: Severely Abnormal Blood Vessel Growth** The abnormal blood vessels grow toward the center of the eye instead of following their normal growth pattern along the surface of the retina. Some infants who develop stage III improve with no treatment and eventually develop normal vision.

VI 3.16d **Stage IV: Partially Detached Retina** Traction from the scar produced by bleeding, abnormal vessels pulls the retina away from the wall of the eye.

VI 3.16e **Stage V: Completely Detached Retina and the End Stage of the disease** If the eye is left alone at this stage, the baby can have severe visual impairment and even blindness.

VI 3.17 Strabismus

Definition Strabismus involves deviation of the alignment of one eye in relation to the other (U.S. National Library of Medicine, 2004c).

Explanation Strabismus is due to the effects of a lack of coordination between the eyes. As a result, the eyes look in different directions and do not focus simultaneously on a single point. In most cases of strabismus in children, the cause is unknown. In more than half of these cases, the problem is present at or shortly after birth (congenital strabismus). In children, when the two eyes fail to focus on the same image, the brain may learn to ignore the input from one eye. If this is allowed to continue, the eye that the brain ignores will never see well. This loss of vision is called amblyopia and is frequently associated with strabismus.

Some other disorders associated with strabismus in children include retinopathy of prematurity, retinoblastoma, traumatic brain injury, hemangioma near the eye during infancy, Apert syndrome, Noonan syndrome, Prader-Willi syndrome, trisomy 18, congenital rubella, incontinentia pigmenti syndrome, and cerebral palsy.

A family history of strabismus is a risk factor. Farsightedness may be a contributing factor. In addition, any other disease causing visual loss may produce strabismus as a complication. Symptoms include eyes that appear crossed, eyes that do not align in the same direction, uncoordinated eye movements, double vision, and vision in only one eye with loss of depth perception (U.S. National Library of Medicine, 2004c).

VI

VI 3.17a **Constant Strabismus** When the eye turn occurs all of the time, the condition is called constant strabismus.

VI 3.17b **Duane's Syndrome** Duane's syndrome is made up of three disorders. Duane's syndrome (type I) is made up of three parts: an inability to move an eye laterally away from the nose with widening of the eyes (palpebral fissure), retraction of the eye when attempting to look close or toward one's nose, and retraction of the eye. In Duane II, the eye has trouble looking toward the nose (opposite of Duane's I). Duane III is made up of a combination of types I and II.

VI 3.17c **Esotropia** Esotropia, the inward turning of the eyes, is by far the most common type of strabismus and is divided into two types: paretic esotropia due to paralysis of one or more of the nerves or muscles that turn the eye out and nonparetic (nondominant), the more common type of strabismus seen in infants and children. Nonparetic esotropia can be uncommon in childhood but accounts for most new cases of strabismus in adults.

VI 3.17d **Exotropia** Exotropia is the outward deviation (turn) of an eye. The deviation may occur while fixating (looking at) distant objects, near objects, or both. Exotropia is much less common than esotropia. It tends to begin very gradually and is initially noted only when the child is very tired, daydreaming, or sick. With time, the out-turning becomes more evident during the day and may eventually become constant. Children with exotropia often squint or close one eye in the bright sunlight.

VI 3.17e **Hypertropia** Hypertropia is a vertical deviation of the eyes. This condition is much less common than the horizontal deviations seen in childhood. There are many causes for a vertical deviation. Sometimes there is a genetic tendency for one eye to be higher than the other. In other instances, children are born with eye muscles or nerves that do not work properly. In addition, trauma to the head, tumors in the brain or around the eye, and certain diseases can produce hypertropia. The first line of remediation is to treat the underlying problem if one is present.

VI 3.17f **Intermittent Strabismus** When the eye turn occurs only some of the time, it is called intermittent strabismus or alternating strabismus.

VI 3.18 Vision Loss Due to Disease or Infection

VI 3.19 Xerophthalmia

Definition Xerophthalmia, or dry eye syndrome, occurs when the tear glands produce fewer tears than usual. The symptoms range from mild irritation and a sensation of something in the eye, to severe discomfort and sensitivity to light (U.S. National Library of Medicine, 2004e).

VI

Explanation Dry eye syndrome often occurs in people who are otherwise healthy. It is more common with older age because fewer tears are produced with age. In rare cases, it can be associated with rheumatoid arthritis, lupus erythematosus, and other similar diseases. It may also be caused by thermal or chemical burns.

In areas of the world where malnutrition is common, vitamin A deficiency is a common cause. This is rare in the United States (U.S. National Library of Medicine, 2004e).

VI 3.20 Retinal Detachment (Detached Retina, Retinal Tear)

Definition The retina is the light-sensitive layer of tissue that lines the inside of the eye and sends visual messages through the optic nerve to the brain. When the retina detaches, it is lifted or pulled from its normal position. If not promptly treated, retinal detachment can cause permanent vision loss (National Eye Institute, 2005o).

Explanation In some cases, there may be small areas of the retina that are torn. These areas, called retinal tears or retinal breaks, can lead to retinal detachment. Symptoms include a sudden or gradual increase in either the number of floaters, which are little "cobwebs" or specks that float about in the field of vision, or light flashes in the eye. Another symptom is the appearance of a curtain over the field of vision. A retinal detachment is a medical emergency. Anyone experiencing the symptoms of a retinal detachment should see an eye care professional immediately (National Eye Institute, 2005o).

There are three different types of retinal detachment.

VI 3.20a **Exudative Retinal Detachment** Frequently due to the effects of retinal diseases, including inflammatory disorders and injury or trauma to the eye. In this type, fluid leaks into the area underneath the retina, but there are no tears or breaks in the retina.

VI 3.20b **Rhegmatogenous Retinal Detachment** A tear or break in the retina allows fluid to get under the retina and separate it from the retinal pigment epithelium, the pigmented cell layer that nourishes the retina. These types of retinal detachments are the most common.

VI 3.20c **Tractional Retinal Detachment** Scar tissue on the retina's surface contracts and causes the retina to separate from the RPE. This type of detachment is less common than the others.

VI 3.21 Other Types of Eye Conditions Not Otherwise Listed

VI 4.00 Neurological Visual Impairment

Definition *Neurological visual impairment* (NVI) is the preferred name for a type of vision impairment that has been and is still referred to as cortical visual impairment or cortical blindness.

Diagnostic Symptoms NVI is divided into three categories: cortical visual impairment, delayed visual maturation, and cortical blindness. These divisions are made according to what area of the brain has been affected.

Further Key Points A variety of studies indicate that between 3.6 and 21 percent of children with vision impairments have NVI, making it the major cause of vision impairment in children who are deaf-blind. NVI occurs when the part of the brain that is responsible for seeing is damaged. The eye itself is normal, but the brain does not process the information properly. NVI has a variety of causes, including lack of oxygen before, during, and after birth; viral or bacterial illness such as meningitis and cytomegalovirus; and traumatic brain injury. Children with NVI can but do not always have additional disabilities. Other types of vision impairments such as optic atrophy (defect of the optic nerve resulting in the inability of the nerve to conduct images to the brain) and optic nerve hypoplasia (a vision impairment due to the effects of a congenital defect of the optic disk) are more common in children with NVI.

NVI affects vision in a variety of ways and causes vision loss that can range from mild to severe and be temporary or permanent. There is no way to predict what a young child's vision will be like as he or she matures, but many children with NVI experience improvement in their vision. Fluctuating vision is common. This is most pronounced in children with seizure disorders or those on certain medications such as dilantin, tegretol, or phenobarbital. A child may be able to see an object one day but be unable to the next. These children may also have better peripheral than central vision and thus look at objects out of the side of their eye. They may have visual field losses that are not symmetrical (one eye may be worse than the other). This uneven loss does not necessarily correspond to hand function. If the left eye is better than the right, the left hand is not necessarily stronger than the right.

Children with NVI experience problems with specific types of visual tasks. They have difficulty with figure-ground (seeing an object instead of the background) and complex visual displays such as cluttered pictures (a picture of five different animals instead of two, for example). Spatial confusion is common, for example, being unable to locate their chair even though they can see it. They may also be visually inattentive, not wanting to look at objects, and may prefer their sense of touch. It is common to see a child turn his or her head away while exploring an object with his or her hands. Seeing with NVI can be compared with trying to listen to one voice in a noisy room or to speaking a foreign language.

Types of Neurological Visual Impairment

VI 4.01 Cortical Blindness

Definition A term used to describe an apparent lack of visual functioning in spite of anatomically and structurally intact eyes.

Explanation The cause is assumed to be a lack of cortical functioning (the visual cortex of the brain is nonfunctional).

VI 4.02 Cortical Visual Impairment

Definition Cortical visual impairment (CVI) is a temporary or permanent visual impairment due to the effects of the disturbance of the posterior visual pathways or the occipital lobes of the brain.

Explanation The degree of vision impairment can range from severe visual impairment to total blindness. The degree of neurological damage and visual impairment depends on the time of onset, as well as the location and intensity of the insult. It is a condition that indicates that the visual systems of the brain do not consistently understand or interpret what the eyes see. The presence of CVI is not an indicator of the child's cognitive ability.

VI 4.03 Delayed Visual Maturation

Definition Delayed visual maturation is one of three categories of neurological visual impairment (NVI), now the preferred name for a type of vision impairment that has been and is still referred to as cortical visual impairment or cortical blindness. NVI is divided into three categories: cortical visual impairment, delayed visual maturation, and cortical blindness. These divisions are made according to what area of the brain has been effected (Morgan, 2002).

Explanation Vision and its manifestations—such as following objects, recognizing faces, smiling, and grasping—are part of a normal developmental picture. If there are no other abnormalities and the condition simply is a delay, we refer to it as delayed visual maturation.

VI 4.04 NVI Associated with Cerebral Palsy

VI 4.05 NVI Associated with Epilepsy

VI 4.06 NVI Associated with Hydrocephalus

VI 4.07 NVI Associated with Severe to Mild Learning Disabilities

VI 4.08 NVI Associated with Seizures

VI 4.09 Other Types of NVI Not Otherwise Listed

VI

VI 5.00 Ocular Motor Impairments

Definition Ocular motor impairment or difficulties with motor control in the eye can also affect a child's vision. The muscles of the eye control how well a child is able to fixate, follow, search, and converge with the eyes. When the muscles work together, they allow the child to see a three-dimensional image. Difficulties with ocular skills affect how well the eyes work. In some cases, surgery may help with ocular motor difficulties.

Diagnostic Symptoms Because the various conditions differ in diagnostic symptoms, no generalization about symptomatology should be made.

VI 6.00 Other Vision Loss Impairments

Definition The disorders discussed in this section vary in definition and diagnostic symptoms. These conditions represent disorders not otherwise specified in this chapter.

Diagnostic Symptoms Because the conditions differ in diagnostic symptoms, no generalization about symptomatology should be made.

Further Key Points Nearly two-thirds of children with vision impairment also have one or more other developmental disabilities, such as mental retardation, cerebral palsy, hearing loss, or epilepsy. Children with more severe vision impairment are more likely to have additional disabilities than are children with milder vision impairment (National Center on Birth Defects and Developmental Disabilities, 2005).

Types of Other Vision Loss Impairments

VI 6.01 Acute Posterior Multifocal Placoid Pigment Epitheliopathy

Definition Multifocal placoid pigment epitheliopathy was first described by Gass in 1966. Acute posterior multifocal placoid pigment epitheliopathy is an acquired inflammatory disorder affecting the retina, retinal pigment epithelium, and choroid of otherwise young healthy adults.

Explanation Acute posterior multifocal placoid pigment epitheliopathy (APMPPE) is a rare eye disorder of unknown (idiopathic) cause. The disorder is characterized by the impairment of central vision in one eye (unilateral), but within a few days, the second eye may also become affected (bilateral). In most cases, the disorder resolves within a few weeks without loss of clearness of vision (acuity).

VI 6.02 Behçet's Disease

Definition Behçet's disease is a rare, chronic inflammatory disorder. The cause is unknown, although there have been reports of a virus found in some individuals with the disease (National Institute of Neurological Disorders and Stroke, 2005).

Explanation Behçet's disease generally begins when individuals are in their twenties or thirties, although it can happen at any age. It tends to occur more often in men than in women. Symptoms include recurrent ulcers in the mouth (resembling canker sores) and on the genitals, and eye inflammation. The disorder may cause skin lesions, arthritis, bowel inflammation, meningitis (inflammation of the membranes of the brain and spinal cord), and cranial nerve palsies.

Behçet's is a multisystem disease; it may involve all organs and affect the central nervous system, causing memory loss and impaired speech, balance, and movement.

The effects of the disease may include blindness, stroke, swelling of the spinal cord, and intestinal complications. The disease is common in Japan, Turkey, and Israel and less common in the United States (National Institute of Neurological Disorders and Stroke, 2005).

VI 6.03 Blepharitis (Granulated Eyelids)

Definition Blepharitis is a common condition that causes inflammation of the eyelids. The condition can be difficult to manage because it tends to recur (National Eye Institute, 2005).

Explanation Symptoms include a foreign body or burning sensation, excessive tearing, itching, sensitivity to light (photophobia), red and swollen eyelids, redness of the eye, blurred vision, frothy tears, dry eye, or crusting of the eyelashes on awakening.

Complications from blepharitis include:

- Stye: A red tender bump on the eyelid that is due to the effects of an acute infection of the oil glands of the eyelid.
- Chalazion: A usually painless firm lump due to the effects of inflammation of the oil glands of the eyelid. Chalazion can be painful and red if there is also an infection. This condition can follow the development of a stye.
- Problems with the tear film: Abnormal or decreased oil secretions that are part of the tear film can result in excess tearing or dry eye. Because tears are necessary to keep the cornea healthy, tear film problems can make people more at risk for corneal infections (National Eye Institute, 2005j).

Blepharitis occurs in two forms.

VI 6.03a **Anterior Blepharitis** Anterior blepharitis affects the outside front of the eyelid, where the eyelashes are attached. The two most common causes are bacteria (Staphylococcus) and scalp dandruff.

VI 6.03b **Posterior Blepharitis** Posterior blepharitis affects the inner eyelid (the moist part that makes contact with the eye) and is due to the effects of problems with the oil (meibomian) glands in this part of the eyelid. Two skin disorders can cause this form of blepharitis: acne rosacea, which leads to red and inflamed skin, and scalp dandruff (seborrheic dermatitis).

VI 6.04 Blepharospasm

Definition Blepharospasm, also referred to as benign essential blepharospasm or hemifacial spasm, is an abnormal, involuntary blinking or spasm of the eyelids (National Eye Institute, 2005g).

Explanation Blepharospasm is associated with an abnormal function of the basal ganglion from an unknown cause. The basal ganglion is the part of the brain responsible for controlling the muscles. In rare cases, heredity may play a role in the development of blepharospasm.

Most people develop blepharospasm without any warning symptoms. It may begin with a gradual increase in blinking or eye irritation. Some people may also experience fatigue, emotional tension, or sensitivity to bright light. As the condition progresses, the symptoms become more frequent, and facial spasms may develop. Blepharospasm may decrease or cease while a person is sleeping or concentrating on a specific task (National Eye Institute, 2005g).

VI 6.05 Blurred Vision

Definition Blurred vision is the loss of sharpness of vision and the inability to see small details. Blurred vision causes both near and far objects to appear to be out of focus, even with the best conventional spectacle correction possible (U.S. National Library of Medicine, 2005d).

Explanation Changes in vision, blurriness, blind spots, halos around lights, or dimness of vision should always be evaluated by a medical professional. Such changes may represent an eye disease, aging, eye injury, or a condition like diabetes that affects many organs (U.S. National Library of Medicine, 2005d).

VI 6.06 Extreme Light Sensitivity

Definition Photophobia, or light sensitivity, is an intolerance of light. Sunlight, fluorescent light, and incandescent light—can all be bothersome. Sometimes light-sensitive people are bothered only by bright light. In extreme cases, any light can be irritating (All About Vision, 2005).

Explanation Extreme light sensitivity exists when standard levels of illumination overwhelm the visual system, producing a washed-out image or glare disability. People with extreme light sensitivity may suffer pain or discomfort from relatively normal levels of illumination.

VI 6.07 Fundus Flavimaculatus (Stargardt's Disease)

Definition Fundus Flavimaculatus (also known as Stargardt's disease) is a type of macular degeneration that typically surfaces before the age of twenty. This disease causes a progressive loss of central vision of both eyes but does not affect peripheral vision (St. Luke's Cataract & Laser Institute, 2004b).

Explanation Stargardt's is a progressive disease. Initially the symptoms may be mild, but they worsen over time. The progression of Stargardt's varies with the individual. Studies show that after visual acuity decreases below 20/40, deterioration may be rapid until visual acuity reaches 20/200. At this level, the patient's vision typically becomes more stable.

VI 6.08 Generalized Haze

Definition Generalized haze causes the sensation of a film or glare that may extend over the entire viewing field (American Optometric Association, 2005).

VI 6.09 Histoplasmosis Maculopathy

Definition Histoplasmosis is a disease caused when airborne spores of the fungus *Histoplasma capsulatum* are inhaled into the lungs, the primary infection site. This microscopic fungus, which is found throughout the world in river valleys and soil where bird or bat droppings accumulate, is released into the air when soil is disturbed by plowing fields, sweeping chicken coops, or digging holes (National Eye Institute, 2005l).

Explanation Histoplasmosis is often so mild that it produces no apparent symptoms. Any symptoms that might occur are often similar to those from a common cold. In fact, a person with histoplasmosis symptoms might dismiss them as those from a cold or flu, since the body's immune system normally overcomes the infection in a few days without treatment. Histoplasmosis, even mild cases, can later cause a serious eye disease, ocular histoplasmosis syndrome (OHS), a leading cause of vision loss in Americans ages twenty to forty.

Scientists believe that *Histoplasma capsulatum* (histo) spores spread from the lungs to the eye, lodging in the choroid, a layer of blood vessels that provides blood and nutrients to the retina. The retina is the light-sensitive layer of tissue that lines the back of the eye. Scientists have not yet been able to detect any trace of the histo fungus in the eyes of patients with ocular histoplasmosis syndrome. Nevertheless, there is good reason to suspect the histo organism as the cause of OHS.

VI 6.10 Night Blindness

Definition Night blindness is poor vision at night or in dim light.

Explanation Common causes of night blindness include:

- Cataracts (usually in older persons)
- Retinitis pigmentosa (may be the first sign of the disease in a young person)
- Poor adaptation to darkness (not caused by any disease), often accompanied by myopia (nearsightedness)
- Vitamin A deficiency
- Certain drugs
- Birth defect (U.S. National Library of Medicine, 2005)

VI 6.11 Other Types of Vision Loss Impairments Not Otherwise Listed

VI 7.00 Refractive Errors

Definition A refractive error means that the shape of the eye does not refract the light properly, so that the image seen is blurred. Although refractive errors are called eye disorders, they are not diseases (American Academy of Ophthalmology, 2003).

Diagnostic Symptoms Refractive errors occur when the curve of the cornea is irregularly shaped (too steep or too flat). When the cornea is of normal shape and curvature, it bends, or refracts, light on the retina with precision. However, when the curve of the cornea is irregularly shaped, the cornea bends light imperfectly on the retina. This affects good vision. The refractive process is similar to the way a camera takes a picture. The cornea and lens in the eye act as the camera lens. The retina is similar to the film. If the image is not focused properly, the film (or retina) receives a blurry image. The image that the retina "sees" then goes to the brain, which tells the viewer what the image is (National Eye Institute, 2005n).

Further Key Points There is no best method for correcting refractive errors. The most appropriate correction depends on the individual's eyes and lifestyle. The individual should discuss his or her refractive errors and lifestyle with an ophthalmologist to decide which correction will be most effective.

Types of Refractive Errors

VI 7.01 Astigmatism (Distorted Vision)

Definition Astigmatism is a condition in which the uneven curvature of the cornea blurs and distorts both distant and near objects (National Eye Institute, 2005n).

Explanation A normal cornea is round, with even curves from side to side and top to bottom. With astigmatism, the cornea is shaped more like the back of a spoon, curved more in one direction than in another. This causes light rays to have more than one focal point and focus on two separate areas of the retina, distorting the visual image. Two-thirds of Americans with myopia also have astigmatism (National Eye Institute, 2005n).

VI 7.01a Compound Astigmatism Compound astigmatism occurs when an eye has both myopia and astigmatism or hyperopia and astigmatism.

VI 7.01b Mixed Astigmatism Mixed astigmatism occurs when myopia is combined with hyperopic astigmatism or hyperopia is combined with myopic astigmatism.

VI 7.01c Simple Astigmatism Astigmatism is considered simple astigmatism when it is not combined with hyperopia or myopia.

VI 7.02 Hyperopia (Farsightedness)

Definition Hyperopia, or farsightedness, is the opposite of myopia. Distant objects are clear, and close-up objects appear blurry. With hyperopia, images focus on a point beyond the retina. Hyperopia results from an eye that is too short (National Eye Institute, 200n).

Explanation People with hyperopia can see distant objects very well but have difficulty seeing objects that are up close. Distant light rays focus behind the retina, and optically everything is blurred.

VI 7.02a **Axial Hyperopia** In axial hyperopia, the refractive power of the eye is normal, but the length of the eye is shorter than normal. Axial hyperopia is due to shortening of the anteroposterior diameter of the globe of the eye. It is the most frequent type of hyperopia.

VI 7.02b **Curvature Hyperopia** In curvature hyperopia, the length of the eye is normal, but the decrease in the curvature of the cornea, or the lens, causes the light rays to be refracted insufficiently and focused behind the retina.

VI 7.02c **Refractive Hyperopia** In refractive hyperopia, the size of the eye is normal, but the refractive power of the lens is less than normal.

VI 7.03 Myopia (Nearsightedness)

Definition Myopia occurs when the cornea is curved too much or if the eye is too long. Faraway objects appear blurry because they are focused in front of the retina. This is called myopia, or nearsightedness. Myopia affects over 25 percent of all adult Americans (National Eye Institute, 2005n).

Explanation The cause of myopia is still unknown, although a genetic component is postulated, as it is commonly seen in the same family.

VI 7.03a **Axial Myopia** Axial myopia is nearsightedness due to the elongation of the axis of the eye (the eyeball is too long).

VI 7.03b **Curvature Myopia** In curvature myopia, the length of the eye is normal, but an increase in the curvature of the cornea or the lens causes the light rays to be refracted more and focused in front of the retina.

VI 7.03c **Refractive Myopia** In refractive myopia, the size of the eye is normal, but the refractive power of the lens is greater than normal.

VI 7.04 Other Types of Refractive Vision Errors Not Otherwise Listed

VI 8.00 Visual Field Disorders

Definition The visual field is the total area in which objects can be seen in the peripheral vision while the eye is focused on a central point. Abnormal test results may indicate diseases or central nervous system problems such as tumors that damage or compress the parts of the brain that deal with vision. Other diseases that may affect the visual field of the eye include diabetes, hyperthyroidism (a condition where the thyroid produces an excess of hormones), hypertension, diseases of the pituitary gland, and multiple sclerosis.

Diagnostic Symptoms Visual acuity alone cannot tell you how much a person's life will be affected by his or her vision loss. It is important to also assess how well a person uses the vision he or she has. Two people may have the same visual acuity, but one may be able to use vision better to do everyday tasks. Most people who are blind have at least some usable vision that can help them move around in their environment and do things in their daily lives.

A person's functional vision can be evaluated by observing him or her in different settings to see how he or she uses the vision. A functional vision evaluation can answer questions such as these:

- Can the person scan a room to find someone or something?
- What lighting is best for the person to do different tasks?
- How does the person use his or her vision to move around in a room or outside?

Vision impairment changes how a child understands and functions in the world. Impaired vision can affect a child's cognitive, emotional, neurological, and physical development by possibly limiting the range of experiences and the kinds of information a child is exposed to (National Center on Birth Defects and Developmental Disabilities Vision Impairment, 2005).

Further Key Points Vision impairment means that a person's eyesight cannot be corrected to a normal level. It may be caused by a loss of visual acuity, where the eye does not see objects as clearly as usual. It may also be caused by a loss of visual field, where the eye cannot see as wide an area as usual without moving the eyes or turning the head.

There are different ways of describing how severe a person's vision loss is. The World Health Organization defines low vision as visual acuity between 20/70 and 20/400, with the best possible correction, or a visual field of 20 degrees or less (Centers for Disease Control, 2004). Blindness is defined as a visual acuity worse than 20/400, with the best possible correction, or a visual field of 10 degrees or less. Someone with a visual acuity of 20/70 can see at twenty feet what someone with normal sight can see at seventy feet. Someone with a visual acuity of 20/400 can see at twenty feet what someone with normal sight can see at four hundred feet. A normal visual field is about 160 to 170 degrees horizontally (National Center on Birth Defects and Developmental Disabilities Vision Impairment, 2005).

Types of Visual Field Disorders

VI 8.01 Central Visual Field Disorder

Definition A central visual field disorder is a loss of an individual's central visual field.

Explanation With a visual field loss, the patient is literally blind to half of his or her field of vision. This places the person at increased risk of injury and harm from bumping into objects, being struck by approaching objects, and falls (Neuro-Optometric Rehabilitation Association, 2005).

VI 8.02 Hemianopsia (Hemianopia)

Definition A homonymous hemianopsia is the loss of half of the field of view on the same side in both eyes (Windsor & Windsor, 2005).

Explanation Common causes of hemianopsia are stroke, trauma (injury), or tumors. A stroke occurs when there is a sudden disturbance in the blood supply to the brain, and in 75 percent of cases this will be due to the effects of a blocked blood vessel. The other major cause of stroke is a leaking blood vessel. The majority of people who experience stroke are over retirement age.

People with high blood pressure are at higher risk of stroke and heart-related illnesses. People with an abnormal heart rhythm may be at risk. Where there is identifiable change, hemianopsia will affect both eyes, and sight loss can be severe or so slight that many people do not notice the changes (Royal National Institute of the Blind, 2005).

There are several types of field loss in this condition.

VI 8.02a Absolute Hemianopsia In absolute hemianopsia, the affected part of the retina is totally blind to light, form and color.

VI 8.02b Bitemporal Hemianopsia In bitemporal hemianopsia, the visual the field loss consists of both temporal (outside edge) halves of visual field. This is typical of pituitary tumors.

VI 8.02c Congruous Hemianopsia In congruous hemianopsia, there are identical defects in the visual fields of each eye.

VI 8.02d Homonymous Hemianopsia In homonymous hemianopsia, the visual field loss consists of the nasal half of one eye and temporal (or outer) half of the other. This is typical of stroke patients.

VI 8.02e Incongruous Hemianopsia In incongruous hemianopsia, both visual fields are differently affected in one or more ways.

VI 8.02f Relative Hemianopsia In relative hemianopsia, there is a loss of form and color but not of light.

VI 8.03 Scotomas Disorder

Definition Scotomas disorder occurs when portions of the retinal field are nonfunctional (there are blind areas) (Special Education Exchange, 2005).

Explanation Scotomas may be central, and caused by macular or optic nerve disease, or peripheral, if the result of chorioretinal lesions or retinal holes. Field testing, if carefully done, can identify the areas affected (Special Education Exchange, 2005).

VI 8.03a **Absolute Scotoma** An absolute scotoma refers to an area that cannot see any of the stimuli, not even the brightest.

VI 8.03b **Deep Scotoma** A deep scotoma refers to a defective area of retina that cannot see any but the brightest stimuli.

VI 8.03c **Relative Scotoma** Relative scotomas are insensitive to a light level relatively less than the very bright object.

VI 8.03d **Shallow Scotoma** A shallow scotoma marks an area of retina that is not sensitive to relatively dim stimuli but is sensitive to brighter stimuli.

VI 8.04 Tunnel Vision

Definition Tunnel vision, also called tubular vision (MedicineNet.com, 2005), is defined as a loss of peripheral vision (side vision) with retention of central vision (straight-ahead vision), resulting in a constricted circular tunnel-like field of vision and, by extension, any very narrow point of view. Those with tunnel vision often can read small print but not large print (Tiresias.org, 2005).

Explanation Tunnel vision can be associated with a late stage of glaucoma or some forms of retinitis pigmentosa. With glaucoma, the pressure inside the eye is raised; this damages the fragile head of the optic nerve where it enters the eye, causing classic loss of nerve fibers.

Retinitis pigmentosa covers a group of hereditary disorders that affect the retina; one effect is problems in low illumination and very slow light adaptation, and often problems reading displays at the red end of the visible spectrum.

VI

VI 8.05 Other Types of Visual Field Disorders Not Otherwise Listed

VI 9.00 Other Types of Visual Impairments—Be Specific

References

All About Vision. (2005). *Photophobia.* Retrieved September 6, 2005, from http://www.allaboutvision.com/conditions/lightsensitive.htm.

American Academy of Ophthalmology. (2003). *Refractive errors.* Retrieved March 15, 2005, from http://www.medem.com/medlb/article_detaillb.cfm?article_ID=ZZZYXB80Z9C&sub_cat=2017.

American Association for Pediatric Ophthalmology and Strabismus (2005a). *Optic nerve hypoplasia.* Retrieved February 18, 2006, from http://www.aapos.org/pubresources/FAQs-Optic+Nerve+Hipoplasia.htm.

American Association for Pediatric Ophthalmology and Strabismus. (2005b). *Optic nerve hypoplasia.* Retrieved March 6, 2005, from http://www.aapos.org/.

American Optometric Association. (2005). *Stargardt's disease.* Retrieved March 14, 2005, from http://www.aoa.org/.

Centers for Disease Control. (2004). *Vision impairment.* Retrieved November 28, 2006, from http://www.cdc.gov/ncbddd/dd/vision2.htm.

Cleveland Clinic. (2005). *Corneal disease.* Retrieved April 24, 2006, from http://www.medicinenet.com/corneal_disease/article.htm.

Corn, A. L., Hatlen, P., Huebner, K. M., Ryan, F., & Siller, M. A. (1995). *The national agenda for the education of children and youth with visual impairments, including those with multiple disabilities.* New York: American Foundation for the Blind.

Erin, J. N. (December, 2003). Educating students with visual impairments. *Eric Digest, 53.*

Friend, M. (2005). *Special education: Contemporary perspectives for school professionals.* Needham Heights, MA: Allyn & Bacon.

Heward, W. L. (2006). *Exceptional children: An introduction to special education* (8th ed.). Upper Saddle River, NJ: Pearson Education, Inc.

Huebner, K. M. (2000). Visual impairment. In M. C. Holbrook & A. J. Koenig (Eds.), *Foundations of education: History and theory of teaching children and youths with visual impairments* (2nd ed., pp. 55–76). New York: American Foundation for the Blind Press.

Kirk, S., Gallagher, J., & Anastasiow, N. (2000). *Educating exceptional children.* Boston: Houghton Mifflin.

Koenig, A. J., & Holbrook, M. C. (1995). *Learning media assessment of students with visual impairments: A resource guide for teachers* (2nd ed.). Austin: Texas School for the Blind and Visually Impaired.

Lewis, S. (2002). Some thoughts on inclusion, alienation, and meeting the needs of children with visual impairments. RE:*view, 34,* 99–101.

Mason, C., Davidson, R., & McNerney, C. (2000). *National plan for training personnel to serve children with blindness and low vision.* Reston, VA: Council for Exceptional Children.

MedicineNet.com. (2005). *Visual field test.* Retrieved September 3, 2005, from http://www.medicinenet.com/visual_field_test/article.htm.

Micro & Anophthalmic Children's Society. (2005). *Coloboma.* Retrieved March 6, 2005, from http://www.macs.org.uk/detailed.html#colo.

Morgan, S. (2002). *Neurological visual impairments fact sheet*: California Deaf-Blind Services. Retrieved March 6, 2005, from http://www.tsbvi.edu/Outreach/seehear/winter01/nvi.htm.

National Cancer Institute. (2004). *Retinoblastoma (PDQ®): Treatment.* Retrieved February 23, 2006, from http://www.cancer.gov/cancerinfo/pdq/treatment/retinoblastoma/patient/.

National Center on Birth Defects and Developmental Disabilities. (2005). *Vision impairment.* Retrieved September 10, 2005, from http://www.cdc.gov/ncbddd/dd/ddvi.htm.

National Dissemination Center for Children with Disabilities. (2004). *Visual impairments.* Retrieved March 7, 2006 from http://nichcy.org/pubs/factshe/fs13txt.htm.

National Eye Institute. (2005a). *Amblyopia.* Retrieved March 18, 2005, from http://www.nei.nih.gov/health/amblyopia/index.asp.

National Eye Institute. (2005b). *Aniridia.* Retrieved March 16, 2005, from http://www.nei.nih.gov/

National Eye Institute. (2005c). *Anophthalmia and microphthalmia.* Retrieved March 18, 2005, from http://www.nei.nih.gov/health/anoph/index.asp.

National Eye Institute. (2005d). *Astigmatism.* Retrieved March 17, 2005, from http://www.nei.nih.gov/.

National Eye Institute. (2005e). *Bietti's crystalline dystrophy.* Retrieved March 14, 2005, from http://www.nei.nih.gov/health/biettis/index.asp

National Eye Institute. (2005f). *Blepharitis.* Retrieved February 23, 2006, from http://www.nei.nih.gov/health/blepharitis/index.asp.

National Eye Institute. (2005g). *Blepharospasm.* February 3, 2006, from http://search.nlm.nih.gov/medlineplus/query?MAX=500&SERVER1=server1&SERVER2=server2&PARAMETER=Blepharospasm+&DISAMBIGUATION=true&FUNCTION=search.

National Eye Institute. (2005h). *Cataract: What you should know.* Retrieved March 18, 2005, from http://www.nei.nih.gov/health/cataract/cataract_facts.asp.

National Eye Institute. (2005i). *Diabetic retinopathy: What you should know.* Retrieved March 18, 2005, from http://www.nei.nih.gov/health/diabetic/retinopathy.asp.

National Eye Institute. (2005j). *Facts about the cornea and corneal disease.* Retrieved February 3, 2006, from http://www.nei.nih.gov/health/cornealdisease/index.asp#i.

National Eye Institute. (2005k). *Glaucoma: What you should know.* Retrieved March 18, 2005, from http://www.nei.nih.gov/health/glaucoma/glaucoma_facts.asp.

National Eye Institute. (2005l). *Histoplasmosis.* Retrieved March 18, 2005, from http://www.nei.nih.gov/health/histoplasmosis/index.asp.

National Eye Institute. (2005m). *Nystagmus.* Retrieved March 18, 2005, from http://www.nei.nih.gov/health/examples/.

National Eye Institute. (2005n). *Questions and answers about refractive errors.* Retrieved March 18, 2005, from www.nei.nih.gov/canwesee/qa_refractive.asp

National Eye Institute. (2005o). *Retinal detachment.* Retrieved February 23, 2006, from http://www.nei.nih.gov/health/retinaldetach/index.asp.

National Eye Institute. (2005p). *Retinopathy of Prematurity.* Retrieved January 23, 2006, from http://www.nei.nih.gov/health/rop/index.asp.

National Institute of Neurological Disorders and Stroke. (2005). *NINDS Behcet's disease information page.* Retrieved February 3, 2006, from http://www.ninds.nih.gov/disorders/behcet/behcet.htm.

Neuro-Optometric Rehabilitation Association. (2005). *Introduction to vision and brain injury.* Retrieved September 4, 2005, from http://www.nora.cc/patient_area/vision_and_brain_injury.html.

Office of Rare Diseases. (2005). *Aniridia.* Retrieved September 4, 2005, from http://rarediseases.info.nih.gov/asp/diseases/diseaseinfo.asp?ID=5816.

Pogrund, R. L., & Fazzi, D. L. (2002). Motor focus: Promoting movement experiences and motor development. In R. L. Pogrund & D. L. Fazzi (Eds.), *Early focus: Working with young children who are blind or visually impaired and their families.* New York: AFB.

Royal National Institute of the Blind. (2005). *Corneal dystrophy.* Retrieved September 14, 2005, from http://www.rnib.org.uk/xpedio/groups/public/documents/PublicWebsite/public_rnib003645.hcsp.

Sacks, S. Z., & Silberman, R. K., (2000). Social skills. In A. J. Koenig & M. C. Holbrook (Eds.), *Foundations of education: Vol. 2. Instructional strategies for teaching children and youths with visual impairments.* New York: American Foundation for the Blind Press.

Smith, T.E.C., Polloway, E. A., Patton, J. R., & Dowdy, C. A. (2004). *Teaching students with special needs in inclusive settings* (4th ed.). Needham Heights, MA: Allyn & Bacon.

Special Education Exchange. (2005). *Scotoma.* Retrieved February 3, 2006, from http://www.spedex.com/main_graphics.htm.

Steinkuller, P. G., Du, L., Gilbert, C., Foster, A., Collins, M. L., & Coats, D. K. (1999). Childhood blindness. *Journal of AAPOS, 3,* 26–32.

St. Luke's Cataract & Laser Institute. (2004a). *Cataracts.* Retrieved September 14, 2005, from http://www.stlukeseye.com/.

St. Luke's Cataract & Laser Institute. (2004b). *Stargardt's disease.* Retrieved February 3, 2006, from http://www.stlukeseye.com/Conditions/Stargardts.asp.

Tiresias.org. (2005). *Tunnel vision.* Retrieved September 4, 2005, from http://www.tiresias.org/.

Tuttle, D. W., & Tuttle, N. R. (1996). *Self-esteem and adjusting with blindness* (2nd ed.) Springfield, IL: Charles C. Thomas.

U.S. Department of Education. (2004). *Twenty-Sixth Annual Report to Congress on the Implementation of the Individuals with Disabilities Education Act.* Washington, DC: Author.

U.S. National Library of Medicine. (2004a). *Optic nerve atrophy.* Retrieved February 18, 2006, from http://www.nlm.nih.gov/medlineplus/ency/article/001622.htm#Definition.

U.S. National Library of Medicine. (2004b). *Retinitis pigmentosa.* Retrieved February 18, 2006, from http://www.nlm.nih.gov/medlineplus/ency/article/001029.htm#Definition.

U.S. National Library of Medicine. (2004c). *Strabismus.* Retrieved February 23, 2006, from http://www.nlm.nih.gov/medlineplus/ency/article/001004.htm#Definition.

U.S. National Library of Medicine. (2004d). *Visual field disorders.* Retrieved February 23, 2006, from http://www.nlm.nih.gov/medlineplus/ency/article/003879.htm#.

U.S. National Library of Medicine. (2004e). *Xerophthalmia-Dry eye syndrome.* Retrieved February 23, 2006, from www. www.nim.nih.gov/medlineplus/ency/article/000426.htm.

U.S. National Library of Medicine (2005). *Vision-night blindness.* Retrieved November 11, 2006, from www.nim.nih.gov/medlineplus/ency/article/003039.htm.

U.S. National Library of Medicine. (2006). *Albinism.* Retrieved November 11, 2006, from http://www.nlm.nih.gov/medlineplus/ency/article/001479.htm.

Windsor, L. K., & Windsor, R.L. (2005). *Hemianopsia: Loss of half of the visual field.* Retrieved February 3, 2006, from http://www.eyeassociates.com/hemianopsia_article_blue.htm.

VI

Chapter 11

Traumatic Brain Injury

EDM Code: TBI

TBI 1.00 Concussion
- TBI 1.01 Concussion with Academic Prob lem Impairments Associated with Traumatic Brain Injury
- TBI 1.02 Concussion with Behavior or Mental Health Impairments Associated with Traumatic Brain Injury
- TBI 1.03 Concussion with Cognition Impairments Associated with Traumatic Brain Injury
- TBI 1.04 Concussion with Communication Impairments Associated with Traumatic Brain Injury
- TBI 1.05 Concussion with Functional Impairments Associated with Traumatic Brain Injury
- TBI 1.06 Concussion with Motor Impairments Associated with Traumatic Brain Injury
- TBI 1.07 Concussion with Physical/Medical/Regulatory Impairments Associated with Traumatic Brain Injury
- TBI 1.08 Concussion with Sensory Processing Impairments Associated with Traumatic Brain Injury
- TBI 1.09 Concussion with Social Impairments Associated with Traumatic Brain Injury

TBI 2.00 Contrecoup
- TBI 2.01 Contrecoup with Academic Prob lem Impairments Associated with Traumatic Brain Injury
- TBI 2.02 Contrecoup with Behavior or Mental Health Impairments Associated with Traumatic Brain Injury
- TBI 2.03 Contrecoup with Cognition Impairments Associated with Traumatic Brain Injury
- TBI 2.04 Contrecoup with Communication Impairments Associated with Traumatic Brain Injury
- TBI 2.05 Contrecoup with Functional Impairments Associated with Traumatic Brain Injury
- TBI 2.06 Contrecoup with Motor Impairments Associated with Traumatic Brain Injury
- TBI 2.07 Contrecoup with Physical/Medical/Regulatory Impairments Associated with Traumatic Brain Injury
- TBI 2.08 Contrecoup with Sensory Processing Impairments Associated with Traumatic Brain Injury
- TBI 2.09 Contrecoup with Social Impairments Associated with Traumatic Brain Injury

TBI 3.00 Contusion
- TBI 3.01 Contusion with Academic Prob lem Impairments Associated with Traumatic Brain Injury.
- TBI 3.02 Contusion with Behavior or Mental Health Impairments Associated with Traumatic Brain Injury
- TBI 3.03 Contusion with Cognition Impairments Associated with Traumatic Brain Injury
- TBI 3.04 Contusion with Communication Impairments Associated with Traumatic Brain Injury
- TBI 3.05 Contusion with Functional Impairments Associated with Traumatic Brain Injury
- TBI 3.06 Contusion with Motor Impairments Associated with Traumatic Brain Injury
- TBI 3.07 Contusion with Physical/Medical/Regulatory Impairments Associated with Traumatic Brain Injury

TBI 3.08 Contusion with Sensory Processing Impairments Associated with Traumatic Brain Injury
TBI 3.09 Contusion with Social Impairments Associated with Traumatic Brain Injury

TBI 4.00 Depressed Skull Fracture
TBI 4.01 Depressed Skull Fracture with Academic Prob lem Impairments Associated with Traumatic Brain Injury
TBI 4.02 Depressed Skull Fracture with Behavior or Mental Health Impairments Associated with Traumatic Brain Injury
TBI 4.03 Depressed Skull Fracture with Cognition Impairments Associated with Traumatic Brain Injury
TBI 4.04 Depressed Skull Fracture with Communication Impairments Associated with Traumatic Brain Injury
TBI 4.05 Depressed Skull Fracture with Functional Impairments Associated with Traumatic Brain Injury
TBI 4.06 Depressed Skull Fracture with Motor Impairments Associated with Traumatic Brain Injury
TBI 4.07 Depressed Skull Fracture with Physical/Medical/Regulatory Impairments Associated with Traumatic Brain Injury
TBI 4.08 Depressed Skull Fracture with Sensory Processing Impairments Associated with Traumatic Brain Injury
TBI 4.09 Depressed Skull Fracture with Social Impairments Associated with Traumatic Brain Injury

TBI 5.00 Diffuse Axonal Injury (Shearing)
TBI 5.01 Diffuse Axonal Injury with Academic Prob lem Impairments Associated with Traumatic Brain Injury
TBI 5.02 Diffuse Axonal Injury with Behavior or Mental Health Impairments Associated with Traumatic Brain Injury
TBI 5.03 Diffuse Axonal Injury with Cognition Impairments Associated with Traumatic Brain Injury
TBI 5.04 Diffuse Axonal Injury with Communication Impairments Associated with Traumatic Brain Injury
TBI 5.05 Diffuse Axonal Injury with Functional Impairments Associated with Traumatic Brain Injury
TBI 5.06 Diffuse Axonal Injury with Motor Impairments Associated with Traumatic Brain Injury
TBI 5.07 Diffuse Axonal Injury with Physical/Medical/Regulatory Impairments Associated with Traumatic Brain Injury
TBI 5.08 Diffuse Axonal Injury with Sensory Processing Impairments Associated with Traumatic Brain Injury
TBI 5.09 Diffuse Axonal Injury with Social Impairments Associated with Traumatic Brain Injury

TBI 6.00 Locked-In Syndrome Resulting from TBI
TBI 6.01 Locked-In Syndrome with Academic Prob lem Impairments Associated with Traumatic Brain Injury
TBI 6.02 Locked-In Syndrome with Behavior or Mental Health Impairments Associated with Traumatic Brain Injury
TBI 6.03 Locked-In Syndrome with Cognition Impairments Associated with Traumatic Brain Injury
TBI 6.04 Locked-In Syndrome with Communication Impairments Associated with Traumatic Brain Injury
TBI 6.05 Locked-In Syndrome with Functional Impairments Associated with Traumatic Brain Injury
TBI 6.06 Locked-In Syndrome with Motor Impairments Associated with Traumatic Brain Injury
TBI 6.07 Locked-In Syndrome with Physical/Medical/Regulatory Impairments Associated with Traumatic Brain Injury
TBI 6.08 Locked-In Syndrome with Sensory Processing Impairments Associated with Traumatic Brain Injury
TBI 6.09 Locked-In Syndrome with Social Impairments Associated with Traumatic Brain Injury

TBI 7.00 Penetrating Skull Fracture (Open Head Injuries)
TBI 7.01 Penetrating Skull Fracture with Academic Prob lem Impairments Associated with Traumatic Brain Injury
TBI 7.02 Penetrating Skull Fracture with Behavior or Mental Health Impairments Associated with Traumatic Brain Injury
TBI 7.03 Penetrating Skull Fracture with Cognition Impairments Associated with Traumatic Brain Injury

- TBI 7.04 Penetrating Skull Fracture with Communication Impairments Associated with Traumatic Brain Injury
- TBI 7.05 Penetrating Skull Fracture with Functional Impairments Associated with Traumatic Brain Injury
- TBI 7.06 Penetrating Skull Fracture with Motor Impairments Associated with Traumatic Brain Injury
- TBI 7.07 Penetrating Skull Fracture with Physical/ Medical/Regulatory Impairments Associated with Traumatic Brain Injury
- TBI 7.08 Penetrating Skull Fracture with Sensory Processing Impairments Associated with Traumatic Brain Injury
- TBI 7.09 Penetrating Skull Fracture with Social Impairments Associated with Traumatic Brain Injury

TBI 8.00 Shaken Baby Syndrome

- TBI 8.01 Shaken Baby Syndrome with Academic Prob lem Impairments Associated with Traumatic Brain Injury
- TBI 8.02 Shaken Baby Syndrome with Behavior or Mental Health Impairments Associated with Traumatic Brain Injury
- TBI 8.03 Shaken Baby Syndrome with Cognition Impairments Associated with Traumatic Brain Injury
- TBI 8.04 Shaken Baby Syndrome with Communication Impairments Associated with Traumatic Brain Injury
- TBI 8.05 Shaken Baby Syndrome with Functional Impairments Associated with Traumatic Brain Injury
- TBI 8.06 Shaken Baby Syndrome with Motor Impairments Associated with Traumatic Brain Injury
- TBI 8.07 Shaken Baby Syndrome with Physical/ Medical/Regulatory Impairments Associated with Traumatic Brain Injury
- TBI 8.08 Shaken Baby Syndrome with Sensory Processing Impairments Associated with Traumatic Brain Injury
- TBI 8.09 Shaken Baby Syndrome with Social Impairments Associated with Traumatic Brain Injury

TBI 9.00 Other Types of TBI Not Otherwise Listed—Be Specific

IDEA 2004 Definition of Traumatic Brain Injury

Under IDEA 2004, Traumatic Brain Injury is:

> an acquired injury to the brain caused by an external physical force, resulting in total or partial functional disability or psychosocial impairment, or both, that adversely affects a child's educational performance. The term applies to open or closed head injuries resulting in impairments in one or more areas, such as cognition; language; memory; attention; reasoning; abstract thinking; judgment; problem-solving; sensory, perceptual, and motor abilities; psychosocial behavior; physical functions; information processing; and speech. The term does not apply to brain injuries that are congenital or degenerative, or to brain injuries induced by birth trauma [34 C.F.R. 300.7 (c)(12)].

Overview of Traumatic Brain Injury

During the reauthorization of IDEA in 1990, traumatic brain injury was added as a separate disability category, in part because of its unique and multiple characteristics that can interfere with learning and functioning (Gargiulo, 2004).

Traumatic brain injury (TBI), also referred to as acquired brain injury (ABI; Brain Injury Association of America, 2004), is sudden physical damage to the brain. The damage may be due to the effects of the head forcefully hitting an object such as the dashboard of a car (closed head injury) or by something passing through the skull and piercing the brain (penetrating head injury or open head injury), as in a gunshot wound (Michaud, Semel-Concepcion, Duhaime, & Lazar, 2002).

The term *traumatic brain injury* is not used for a person who is born with a brain injury or for brain injuries that occur during birth. It is used for head injuries that can cause changes in one or more areas, such as thinking and reasoning, understanding words, remembering, paying attention, solving problems, thinking abstractly, talking, behaving, walking and other physical activities, seeing, hearing, and learning (Hallahan & Kauffman, 2006).

The physical, behavioral, or mental changes that may result from head trauma depend on the areas of the brain that are injured. Nearly any domain of functioning can be affected by TBI (Keyser-Marcus et al., 2002; Clark, Russman, & Orme, 1999).

Most injuries cause focal brain damage, that is, damage confined to a small area in the brain. The focal damage is most often at the point where the head hits an object or where an object, such as a bullet, enters the brain.

In addition to focal damage, closed head injuries frequently cause diffuse brain injuries or damage to several other areas of the brain. The diffuse damage occurs when the impact of the injury causes the brain to move back and forth against the inside of the bony skull. The frontal and temporal lobes of the brain, the major speech and language areas, often receive the most damage in this way because they sit in pockets of the skull that allow more room for the brain to shift and sustain injury. Because these major speech and language areas often receive damage, communication difficulties frequently occur following closed head injuries. Other problems may include voice, swallowing, walking, balance, and coordination difficulties, as well as changes in the ability to smell and in memory and cognitive (or thinking) skills.

Causes-Etiology of Traumatic Brain Injury

In many instances, the causes of TBI are for the most part preventable (Youse, Le, Cannizzaro, & Coelho, 2002). TBI is the most common cause of disability and death among children in the United States, affecting more than 1 million of them each year (Keyser-Marcus et al., 2002). Falls around the home are the leading cause of injury for infants and toddlers. The leading causes for adolescents and adults are automobile and motorcycle accidents. Half of all TBIs are due to transportation accidents involving automobiles, motorcycles, bicycles, and pedestrians. Other causes of head trauma and TBI are violent shaking of an infant or toddler, especially shaken baby syndrome; child abuse; and injuries that occur during violent crimes. TBI can change how the person acts, moves, and thinks. A traumatic brain injury can also change how a student learns and acts in school.

Prevalence of Traumatic Brain Injury

The U.S. Department of Education (2004) reports that, during the 2003–2004 school year, 22,459 students aged six to twenty-one (0.4 percent of all students with disabilities) received special education services under the IDEA category of traumatic brain injury.

TBI is the most common cause of disability and death in the United States. More than 1 million children receive brain injuries each year (Keyser-Marcus et al., 2002). More than 30,000 of these children have lifelong disabilities as a result of the brain injury. Other statistics dramatically tell the story of head injury in the United States. Each year:

- Approximately 270,000 people experience a moderate or severe TBI.
- Approximately 70,000 people die from head injury.
- Approximately 1 million head-injured people are treated in hospital emergency rooms.
- Approximately 60,000 new cases of epilepsy occur as a result of head trauma.
- Approximately 230,000 people are hospitalized for TBI and survive (National Dissemination Center for Children with Disabilities, 2004).

Age of Onset of Traumatic Brain Injury

Head trauma can affect anyone at any age. Traumatic brain injury is a major public health problem, especially among male adolescents and young adults ages fifteen to twenty-four. Children aged five years and younger are also at high risk for TBI (National Dissemination Center for Children with Disabilities, 2004).

Gender Features of Traumatic Brain Injury

Traumatic brain injuries occur most often in males. The most common ages of occurrence are before age ten and from fifteen to twenty-four years (Colarusso & O'Rourke, 2004).

Cultural Features of Traumatic Brain Injury

The information on this topic is not available.

Familial Pattern of Traumatic Brain Injury

The information on this topic is not available.

Characteristics of Traumatic Brain Injury

According to Hallahan and Kauffman (2006), the possible effects of TBI include a long list of learning and psychosocial problems, such as the following:

- Problems remembering
- Problems learning new information

- Speech or language problems
- Difficulty sequencing things
- Difficulty processing information
- Extremely uneven progress
- Inappropriate manners or mannerisms
- Failure to understand humor or social situations
- Becoming easily tired, frustrated, or angered
- Unreasonable fear or anxiety
- Irritability
- Sudden, exaggerated swings of mood
- Depression
- Aggression
- Perseveration

Educational Implications of Traumatic Brain Injury

The difficulty experienced by children with TBI returning to school is that their educational and emotional needs vary greatly. Although their disability has happened suddenly and traumatically, individuals with TBI can often remember how they were before the brain injury. Consequently, this awareness of loss can bring on many emotional and social changes and adverse reactions. Besides the child, the child's family, friends, and teachers also recall what the child was like before the injury. The differences in the child's behavior and medical condition usually lead to difficulties in changing or adjusting their expectations of the child (Hibbard, Gordon, Martin, Rashkin, & Brown, 2001). Therefore, it is extremely important to plan carefully for the child's return to school.

It is important that the school play a proactive role in assisting parents with the child's transition back to school. The planning of such a return should be a process that begins weeks before the child returns. As part of this process, the school will need to evaluate the child thoroughly so that the school and parents know what the student's educational needs are. The school and parents will then develop an Individualized Education Program (IEP) that addresses those educational needs (National Dissemination Center for Children with Disabilities, 2004; DePompei, Blosser, Savage, & Lash, 1998).

Permissions and Authorization to Use Proprietary and Nonproprietary Sources

Due to the detailed nature of certain Level II disorders described in this chapter, we thought that some were best explained by national institutes and centers that conduct comprehensive scientific research in respective fields of study. The sources obtained were all written with explicit permission that the scientific and diagnostic information they prepared was in the public domain and can be used without restriction.

We thank the following national research offices for the opportunity to freely disseminate their scientific research and writing in this chapter:

- National Center for Injury Prevention and Control
- National Dissemination Center for Children with Disabilities
- National Institute of Neurological Disorders and Stroke
- U.S. Department of Education
- U.S. National Library of Medicine

EDM Codes, Definitions, and Explanations of Traumatic Brain Injury

To diagnose a traumatic brain injury with the EDM coding system, the following steps should be taken:

1 Determine the type of traumatic brain injury that is appropriate for the individual (for example, concussion, contrecoup, depressed skull fracture).

2 Determine the impairments that the individual is experiencing: academic problems, behavioral or mental health impairments, cognitive impairments, communication impairments, physical or medical impairments, sensory processing impairments, and social impairments. These seven types of impairments are labeled .01 to .07, respectively.

3 Combine the type of traumatic brain injury with the specific impairments for a formal diagnosis.

For example, an individual with a depressed skull fracture with academic problems and communication problems would receive diagnoses of TBI 4.01 and TBI 4.04. An individual with a penetrating skull fracture with physical problems and social problems would receive diagnoses of TBI 7.07 and TBI 7.09.

Possible Codes to Be Used with TBI Diagnoses

TBI ___.01: Academic Problem Impairments Associated with Traumatic Brain Injury.

Individuals with this diagnosis may exhibit problems in reading, writing, spelling, and mathematics to a marked degree.

TBI ___.02: Behavior or Mental Health Impairments Associated with Traumatic Brain Injury.

Individuals with this diagnosis may exhibit depression, apathy, anxiety, irritability, anger, paranoia, confusion, frustration, agitation, insomnia or other sleep problems, and mood swings. Problem behaviors may include aggression and violence, impulsivity, disinhibition, acting out, noncompliance, social inappropriateness, emotional outbursts, childish behavior, impaired self-control, impaired self-awareness, inability to take responsibility or accept criticism, egocentrism, inappropriate sexual activity, and alcohol or drug abuse/addiction.

TBI ___.03: Cognition Impairments Associated with Traumatic Brain Injury.

Individuals with this diagnosis may have impairments in the processes of thinking, reasoning, problem solving, information processing, and memory.

TBI ___.04: Communication Impairments Associated with Traumatic Brain Injury.

Individuals with this diagnosis may have difficulty understanding and producing spoken and written language; difficulty with the more subtle aspects of communication, such as body language and emotional, nonverbal signals; difficulty in recalling words and speaking in complete sentences; apraxia (choosing the right words); and difficulty identifying objects and their function and decreased language.

TBI ___.05: Functional Impairments Associated with Traumatic Brain Injury.

Individuals with this diagnosis may have difficulty with activities of daily living such as dressing, bathing, and eating; problems with organization, shopping, or paying bills; problems with vocational issues; and an inability to drive a car.

TBI ___.06: Motor Impairments Associated with Traumatic Brain Injury.

Individuals with this diagnosis may have difficulty with paralysis or weakness, spasticity, poor balance, decreased endurance, inability to plan motor movements, delays in initiation, tremors, swallowing problems, and poor coordination.

TBI ___.07: Physical/Medical/Regulatory Impairments Associated with Traumatic Brain Injury.

Individuals with this diagnosis have difficulty and suffer from fatigue, seizures, headaches, and problems with regulation of various functions such as growth, eating, body temperature, and blurred vision.

TBI ___.08: Sensory Processing Impairments Associated with Traumatic Brain Injury.

Individuals with this diagnosis may have impairments in sight, hearing, touch, taste, and smell; may not be able to register what they are seeing or may be slow to recognize objects; and have difficulty with hand-eye coordination.

TBI ___.09: Social Impairments Associated with Traumatic Brain Injury.

Individuals with this diagnosis may exhibit problems in social functioning, social interaction with peers, inappropriate social responses, inability to set social boundaries, inability to properly interpret social cues, and difficulty making and keeping friends.

TBI 1.00 Concussion

Definition A concussion is a significant blow to the head that may result in unconsciousness. It may result from a fall in which the head strikes against an object or a moving object strikes the head. Significant jarring in any direction can produce unconsciousness. It is thought that there may be microscopic shearing of nerve fibers in the brain from the sudden acceleration or deceleration resulting from the injury to the head (National Institute of Neurological Disorders and Stroke, 2005).

A concussion is the most minor and the most common type of TBI. Technically, a concussion is a short loss of consciousness in response to a head injury, but in common language, the term has come to mean any minor injury to the head or brain (National Institute of Neurological Disorders and Stroke, 2005).

Diagnostic Symptoms Diagnostic symptoms of a concussion include:

- Persistent low-grade headaches
- More trouble than usual remembering, concentrating, or making decisions
- Feeling tired all the time
- Feeling sad, anxious, or listless
- Becoming easily irritated for little or no reason
- Convulsions
- Repeated vomiting
- Unequal pupils
- Unusual eye movements
- Muscle weakness on one or both sides
- Gait or walking abnormalities (National Center for Injury Prevention and Control, 2006)

Further Key Points The length of unconsciousness may relate to the severity of the concussion. Often victims have no memory of events preceding the injury or immediately after regaining consciousness, with worse injuries causing longer periods of amnesia. Often the maximal memory loss occurs immediately after the injury with regaining of some memory function as time passes. Complete memory recovery for the event may not occur (U.S. National Library of Medicine, 2004).

TBI 1.01 Concussion with Academic Problem Impairments Associated with Traumatic Brain Injury

TBI 1.02 Concussion with Behavior or Mental Health Impairments Associated with Traumatic Brain Injury

TBI 1.03 Concussion with Cognition Impairments Associated with Traumatic Brain Injury

TBI 1.04 Concussion with Communication Impairments Associated with Traumatic Brain Injury

TBI 1.05 Concussion with Functional Impairments Associated with Traumatic Brain Injury

TBI 1.06 Concussion with Motor Impairments Associated with Traumatic Brain Injury

TBI 1.07 Concussion with Physical/Medical/Regulatory Impairments Associated with Traumatic Brain Injury

TBI 1.08 Concussion with Sensory Processing Impairments Associated with Traumatic Brain Injury

TBI 1.09 Concussion with Social Impairments Associated with Traumatic Brain Injury

TBI 2.00 Contrecoup

Definition Contrecoup is a contusion caused by the shaking of the brain back and forth within the confines of the skull (National Institute of Neurological Disorders and Stroke, 2005).

Diagnostic Symptoms The brain can be damaged at the point of impact and on the opposite side by striking the inside of the skull. Acceleration-deceleration injuries are sometimes called coup contrecoup (meaning hit-counterhit in French).

Contusions and lacerations may cause only minimal physical damage to the brain, with few symptoms. However, if swelling or bleeding is severe, these injuries can cause a severe headache, dizziness, and vomiting. One pupil may be larger than the other. Depending on which area of the brain is damaged, the ability to think, control emotions, move, feel, speak, see, hear, and remember may be impaired. The person may become irritable, restless, or agitated. One side of the body may become weak or feel numb. Confusion may develop. A more severe injury causes swelling within the brain, damaging brain tissue further. Herniation of the brain may result, sometimes leading to coma. A brain herniation is the displacement of brain tissue, cerebrospinal fluid, and blood vessels outside the compartments in the head where they usually are located. Severe brain damage is often accompanied by other injuries, especially scalp injuries, skull fractures, and injuries of the chest and spine (Merck, 2005).

Further Key Points Contrecoup occurs when the force hitting the head is not only great enough to cause a contusion at the site of impact, but also is able to move the brain and cause it to slam into the opposite side of the skull, which causes the additional contusion (Brain Injury Association of America, 2006). It often occurs in car accidents after high-speed stops and in shaken baby syndrome, a severe form of head injury that occurs when a baby is shaken forcibly enough to cause the brain to bounce against the skull. In addition, contrecoup can cause diffuse axonal injury, also called shearing, which involves damage to individual nerve cells (neurons) and loss of connections among neurons. This can lead to a breakdown of overall communication among neurons in the brain.

TBI 2.01 Contrecoup with Academic Problem Impairments Associated with Traumatic Brain Injury

TBI 2.02 Contrecoup with Behavior or Mental Health Impairments associated with Traumatic Brain Injury

TBI 2.03 Contrecoup with Cognition Impairments Associated with Traumatic Brain Injury

TBI 2.04 Contrecoup with Communication Impairments Associated with Traumatic Brain Injury

TBI 2.05 Contrecoup with Functional Impairments Associated with Traumatic Brain Injury

TBI 2.06 Contrecoup with Motor Impairments Associated with Traumatic Brain Injury

TBI 2.07 Contrecoup with Physical/Medical/Regulatory Impairments Associated with Traumatic Brain Injury

TBI 2.08 Contrecoup with Sensory Processing Impairments Associated with Traumatic Brain Injury

TBI 2.09 Contrecoup with Social Impairments Associated with Traumatic Brain Injury

TBI 3.00 Contusion

Definition Skull fractures can cause bruising of brain tissue, which is called a contusion. A contusion is a distinct area of swollen brain tissue mixed with blood released from broken blood vessels (National Institute of Neurological Disorders and Stroke, 2005).

Diagnostic Symptoms The signs and symptoms of a contusion include severe headache, dizziness, vomiting, increased size of one pupil, or sudden weakness in an arm or leg. The person may seem restless, agitated, or irritable. Often the person may have memory loss or seem forgetful. These symptoms may last for several hours to weeks, depending on the seriousness of the injury (University of Missouri Health Care, 2006).

Further Key Points Cerebral contusions are bruises on the brain, usually caused by a direct, strong blow to the head. Cerebral lacerations are tears in brain tissue, which often accompany visible head wounds and skull fractures (Merck, 2005). Depending on which area of the brain is damaged, the ability to think, control emotions, move, feel, speak, see, hear, and remember may be impaired. The person may become irritable, restless, or agitated.

TBI 3.01 Contusion with Academic Problem Impairments Associated with Traumatic Brain Injury.

TBI 3.02 Contusion with Behavior or Mental Health Impairments Associated with Traumatic Brain Injury

TBI 3.03 Contusion with Cognition Impairments Associated with Traumatic Brain Injury

TBI 3.04 Contusion with Communication Impairments Associated with Traumatic Brain Injury

TBI

TBI 3.05 Contusion with Functional Impairments Associated with Traumatic Brain Injury

TBI 3.06 Contusion with Motor Impairments Associated with Traumatic Brain Injury

TBI 3.07 Contusion with Physical/Medical/Regulatory Impairments Associated with Traumatic Brain Injury

TBI 3.08 Contusion with Sensory Processing Impairments Associated with Traumatic Brain Injury

TBI 3.09 Contusion with Social Impairments Associated with Traumatic Brain Injury

TBI 4.00 Depressed Skull Fracture

Definition Skull fractures may occur with head injuries. Although the skull is tough and resilient and provides excellent protection for the brain, a severe impact or blow can result in fracture of the skull. It may be accompanied by injury to the brain. A depressed skull fracture is a break in a cranial bone (or "crushed" portion of skull) with depression of the bone in toward the brain (National Institute of Neuroloical Disorders and Stroke, 2005).

Diagnostic Symptoms Diagnostic symptoms of a depressed skull fracture include:

- Bleeding from the wound, ears, nose, or around eyes
- Bruising behind the ears or under the eyes
- Changes in pupils (sizes unequal, not reactive to light)
- Confusion
- Convulsions
- Difficulties with balance
- Drainage of clear or bloody fluid from ears or nose
- Drowsiness
- Headache
- Loss of consciousness
- Nausea
- Restlessness, irritability
- Slurred speech
- Stiff neck
- Swelling
- Visual disturbances
- Vomiting (U.S. National Library of Medicine, 2006)

Further Key Points Depressed skull fractures are common after forceful impact by blunt objects—most commonly, hammers, rocks, or other heavy but fairly small objects. These injuries cause "dents" in the skull bone. If the depth of a depressed fracture is at least equal to the thickness of the surrounding skull bone (about one-quarter to one-half inch), surgery is often required to elevate the bony pieces and inspect the brain for evidence of injury. Minimally depressed fractures are less than the thickness of the bone. Other fractures are not depressed at all. They usually do not require surgical treatment unless other injuries are noted (National Institute of Neurological Disorders and Stroke, 2005).

TBI 4.01 Depressed Skull Fracture with Academic Problem Impairments Associated with Traumatic Brain Injury

TBI 4.02 Depressed Skull Fracture with Behavior or Mental Health Impairments Associated with Traumatic Brain Injury

TBI 4.03 Depressed Skull Fracture with Cognition Impairments Associated with Traumatic Brain Injury

TBI 4.04 Depressed Skull Fracture with Communication Impairments Associated with Traumatic Brain Injury

TBI 4.05 Depressed Skull Fracture with Functional Impairments Associated with Traumatic Brain Injury

TBI 4.06 Depressed Skull Fracture with Motor Impairments Associated with Traumatic Brain Injury

TBI 4.07 Depressed Skull Fracture with Physical/Medical/Regulatory Impairments Associated with Traumatic Brain Injury

TBI 4.08 Depressed Skull Fracture with Sensory Processing Impairments Associated with Traumatic Brain Injury

TBI 4.09 Depressed Skull Fracture with Social Impairments Associated with Traumatic Brain Injury

TBI 5.00 Diffuse Axonal Injury (Shearing)

Definition Diffuse axonal injury (shearing) is damage to individual neurons resulting in disruption of neural networks and the breakdown of overall communication among neurons in the brain (National Institute of Neurological Disorders and Stroke, 2005).

Diagnostic Symptoms Diffuse axonal injury can be caused by shaking or strong rotation of the head, as with shaken baby syndrome, or by rotational forces, such as with a car accident. Injury occurs because the unmoving brain lags behind the movement of the skull, causing brain structures to tear. There is extensive tearing of nerve tissue throughout the brain. This can cause brain chemicals to be released, causing additional injury. The tearing of the nerve tissue disrupts the brain's regular communication and chemical processes. This disturbance can produce temporary or permanent widespread brain damage, coma, or death. A person with a diffuse axonal injury could present a variety of functional impairments depending on where the shearing (tears) occurred in the brain.

Further Key Points The skull is hard and inflexible while the brain is soft, with the consistency of gelatin. The brain is encased inside the skull. The movement of the skull through space (acceleration) and the rapid discontinuation of this action when the skull meets a stationary object (deceleration) causes the brain to move inside the skull. The brain moves at a different rate from the skull because it is soft. Different parts of the brain move at different speeds because of their relative lightness or heaviness. The differential movement of the skull and the brain when the head is struck results in direct brain injury due to diffuse axonal shearing, contusion, and brain swelling (Brain Injury Association of America, 1996).

Diffuse axonal injury can occur without any direct impact on the head, as it requires only the condition of rapid acceleration and deceleration such as takes place in whiplash injuries due to acceleration and deceleration resulting in the rapid flexion-extension movement of the neck. The likelihood of significant diffuse axonal injury increases when the head hits something, such as a windshield, as the change in momentum is greater because of the sudden stopping of the head. But in a shearing mechanism, it is not the contact phenomenon that causes the injury but the change in momentum (Johnson, 2004).

TBI 5.01 Diffuse Axonal Injury with Academic Problem Impairments Associated with Traumatic Brain Injury

TBI 5.02 Diffuse Axonal Injury with Behavior or Mental Health Impairments Associated with Traumatic Brain Injury

TBI 5.03 Diffuse Axonal Injury with Cognition Impairments Associated with Traumatic Brain Injury

TBI 5.04 Diffuse Axonal Injury with Communication Impairments Associated with Traumatic Brain Injury

TBI 5.05 Diffuse Axonal Injury with Functional Impairments Associated with Traumatic Brain Injury

TBI 5.06 Diffuse Axonal Injury with Motor Impairments Associated with Traumatic Brain Injury

TBI 5.07 Diffuse Axonal Injury with Physical/Medical/Regulatory Impairments Associated with Traumatic Brain Injury

TBI 5.08 Diffuse Axonal Injury with Sensory Processing Impairments Associated with Traumatic Brain Injury

TBI 5.09 Diffuse Axonal Injury with Social Impairments Associated with Traumatic Brain Injury

TBI 6.00 Locked-In Syndrome Resulting from TBI

Definition This syndrome is due to stroke, tumor, or trauma to the ventral part of the rostral (meaning toward the front) pons (a part of the brain involved in motor control and sensory analysis). Lesions there render the individual quadriplegic, unable to speak and incapable of facial movement. One would think these individuals were in a coma except that they are able to move their eyes and can communicate with an eye communicating device (University of Idaho Medical Education Program, 2006).

Diagnostic Symptoms Locked-in syndrome is a condition in which a patient is aware and awake but cannot move or communicate due to complete paralysis of the body. Individuals with locked-in syndrome are conscious and can think and reason, but are unable to speak or move. The disorder leaves individuals completely mute and paralyzed. Communication may be possible with blinking eye movements (National Institute of Neurological Disorders and Stroke, 2005).

Further Key Points Locked-in syndrome resulting from TBI is a rare neurological disorder characterized by complete paralysis of voluntary muscles in all parts of the body except for those that control eye movement. It may result from traumatic brain injury, diseases of the circulatory system, diseases that destroy the myelin sheath surrounding nerve cells, or medication overdose. Individuals with locked-in syndrome are conscious and can think and reason, but are unable to speak or move. The disorder leaves individuals completely mute and paralyzed (National Institute of Neurological Disorders and Stroke, 2005).

Patients with complete paralysis, or locked-in syndrome, spend life mute. Often these conscious individuals are unable to relay even their most basic wishes because they have lost all muscle control. Research is now leading to the development of imaginative communication strategies for these patients. Several techniques that bypass the muscles and gain power directly from the brain are under investigation (Society for Neuroscience, 2006).

TBI 6.01 Locked-In Syndrome with Academic Problem Impairments Associated with Traumatic Brain Injury

TBI 6.02 Locked-In Syndrome with Behavior or Mental Health Impairments Associated with Traumatic Brain Injury

TBI 6.03 Locked-In Syndrome with Cognition Impairments Associated with Traumatic Brain Injury

TBI 6.04 Locked-In Syndrome with Communication Impairments Associated with Traumatic Brain Injury

TBI 6.05 Locked-In Syndrome with Functional Impairments Associated with Traumatic Brain Injury

TBI 6.06 Locked-In Syndrome with Motor Impairments Associated with Traumatic Brain Injury

TBI 6.07 Locked-In Syndrome with Physical/Medical/Regulatory Impairments Associated with Traumatic Brain Injury

TBI 6.08 Locked-In Syndrome with Sensory Processing Impairments Associated with Traumatic Brain Injury

TBI 6.09 Locked-In Syndrome with Social Impairments Associated with Traumatic Brain Injury

TBI 7.00 Penetrating Skull Fracture (Open Head Injuries)

Definition Open head injuries, also referred to as penetrating injuries, occur when both the skin and the dura (the tough fibrous membrane covering the brain and the spinal cord) are penetrated by either a foreign object such as a bullet or rod or a bone fragment of a fractured skull (Hyman-Newman Institute for Neurology and Neurosurgery, n.d.).

Diagnostic Symptoms Due to the fact that the various conditions differ in diagnostic symptoms, no generalization about symptoms should be made. However, according to Cornell University's Weill Medical College (2006), some common symptoms include:

- Behavior changes, including irritability
- Blood or clear fluid draining from the ears or nose
- Blurred vision
- Confusion
- Deep cut or laceration in the scalp

- Difficult walking
- Dizziness
- Foreign object penetrating the head
- Loss of consciousness
- Loss of short-term memory, such as difficulty remembering the events that led up to and through the traumatic event
- One pupil (dark area in the center of the eye) larger than the other eye
- Open wound in the head
- Pale skin color
- Seizures
- Severe headache
- Slurred speech
- Sweating
- Vomiting
- Weakness in one side or area of the body

Further Key Points Analysis of the trauma literature has shown that 50 percent of all trauma deaths are secondary to TBI, and gunshot wounds to the head caused 35 percent of these. The current increase in firearm-related violence and subsequent increase in penetrating head injury remains of concern to neurosurgeons in particular and to the community as a whole (Vinas & Pilitsis, 2004).

The extent of the person's recovery depends on the type of brain injury and other medical problems that may be present. It is important to focus on maximizing the person's capabilities at home and in the community. Positive reinforcement will encourage the patient to strengthen his or her self-esteem and promote independence (Cornell University Weill Medical College, 2003).

TBI 7.01 Penetrating Skull Fracture with Academic Problem Impairments Associated with Traumatic Brain Injury

TBI 7.02 Penetrating Skull Fracture with Behavior or Mental Health Impairments Associated with Traumatic Brain Injury

TBI 7.03 Penetrating Skull Fracture with Cognition Impairments Associated with Traumatic Brain Injury

TBI 7.04 Penetrating Skull Fracture with Communication Impairments Associated with Traumatic Brain Injury

TBI 7.05 Penetrating Skull Fracture with Functional Impairments Associated with Traumatic Brain Injury

TBI 7.06 Penetrating Skull Fracture with Motor Impairments Associated with Traumatic Brain Injury

TBI 7.07 Penetrating Skull Fracture with Physical/Medical/Regulatory Impairments Associated with Traumatic Brain Injury

TBI 7.08 Penetrating Skull Fracture with Sensory Processing Impairments Associated with Traumatic Brain Injury

TBI 7.09 Penetrating Skull Fracture with Social Impairments Associated with Traumatic Brain Injury

TBI 8.00 Shaken Baby Syndrome

Definition Shaken baby syndrome (SBS) is the collection of signs and symptoms resulting from the violent shaking of an infant or small child. It is a form of child abuse (National Center on Shaken Baby Syndrome, 2005).

Diagnostic Symptoms Diagnostic symptoms of shaken baby syndrome according to the National Center on Shaken Baby Syndrome (2005) include:

Less Serious Injury

- Lethargy, decreased muscle tone
- Extreme irritability
- Decreased appetite, poor feeding, or vomiting for no apparent reason
- Grab-type bruises on arms or chest (though these are rare)
- No smiling or vocalization
- Poor sucking or swallowing
- Rigidity or posturing

Serious Brain Injury

- Difficulty breathing
- Seizures
- Head or forehead appears larger than usual or soft spot on head appears to be bulging
- Inability to suck or swallow
- Inability to lift head
- Inability of eyes to focus or track movement or unequal size of pupils

Further Key Points In the United States in 2005, approximately twelve hundred to fourteen hundred children were shaken for whom treatment was sought. Of these tiny victims, 25 to 30 percent died as a result of their injuries. The rest will have lifelong complications. It is likely that many more babies suffered from the effects of SBS and no one knows, because SBS victims rarely have any external evidence of trauma (National Center on Shaken Baby Syndrome, 2005).

TBI 8.01 Shaken Baby Syndrome with Academic Problem Impairments Associated with Traumatic Brain Injury

TBI 8.02 Shaken Baby Syndrome with Behavior or Mental Health Impairments Associated with Traumatic Brain Injury

TBI 8.03 Shaken Baby Syndrome with Cognition Impairments Associated with Traumatic Brain Injury

TBI 8.04 Shaken Baby Syndrome with Communication Impairments Associated with Traumatic Brain Injury

TBI 8.05 Shaken Baby Syndrome with Functional Impairments Associated with Traumatic Brain Injury

TBI 8.06 Shaken Baby Syndrome with Motor Impairments Associated with Traumatic Brain Injury

TBI 8.07 Shaken Baby Syndrome with Physical/Medical/Regulatory Impairments Associated with Traumatic Brain Injury

TBI 8.08 Shaken Baby Syndrome with Sensory Processing Impairments Associated with Traumatic Brain Injury

TBI 8.09 Shaken Baby Syndrome with Social Impairments Associated with Traumatic Brain Injury

TBI 9.00 Other Types of TBI Not Otherwise Listed-Be Specific

References

Brain Injury Association of America. (2004). *Causes of brain injury.* McLean, VA: Author. Retrieved March 13, 2005, from http://www.biausa.org/Pages/causes_of_braininjury.html.

Brain Injury Association of America. (2006). *Types of brain injury.* Retrieved April 1, 2006, from http://www.biausa.org/Pages/types_of_brain_injury.html#coupe.

Clark, E., Russman, S., & Orme, S. (1999). Traumatic brain injury: Effects on school functioning and intervention strategies [electronic version]. *School Psychology Review, 28,* 242–250.

Colarusso, R., & O'Rourke, C. (2004). *Special education for all teachers.* Dubuque, IA: Kendall Hunt.

Cornell University Weill Medical College. (2003). *Head injury.* Retrieved January 17, 2006, from http://wo-pub2.med.cornell.edu/cgi-bin/WebObjects/PublicA.woa/9/wa/viewHContent?website=wmc+physicians&contentID=785&wosid=qtEo2TowYSYYdQaMzM6Nu0.

DePompei, R., Blosser, J., Savage, R., & Lash, M. (1998). *Special education: IEP checklist for a student with a brain injury.* Wolfeboro, NH: L&A Publishing/Training.

Gargiulio, R. (2004). *Special education in contemporary society: An introduction to exceptionality.* Belmont, CA: Thompson Learning.

Hallahan, D. P., & Kauffman, J. M. (2006). *Exceptional learners: An introduction to special education* (10th ed.). Needham Heights, MA: Allyn & Bacon.

Hibbard, M., Gordon, W., Martin, T., Rashkin, B., & Brown, M. (2001). *Students with traumatic brain injury: Identification, assessment, and classroom accommodations.* New York: Research and Training Center on Community Integration of Individuals with Traumatic Brain Injury.

Hyman-Newman Institute for Neurology and Neurosurgery. (n.d.). *Head injury.* Retrieved April 14, 2005, from http://neurosurgery.org/inside.html.

Keyser-Marcus, L., Briel, L., Sherron-Targett, P., Yasuda, S., Lohnson, S., & Wehman, P. (2002). Enhancing the schooling of students with traumatic brain injury. *Teaching Exceptional Children, 34*(4), 62–67.

Johnson, G. S. (2004). *Axonal brain injury without a blow to the head.* Retrieved February 8, 2006, from http://subtlebraininjury.com/shear1.html.

Merck. (2005). *Cerebral contusions and lacerations.* Retrieved April 7, 2005, from http://www.merck.com/mmhe/sec06/ch087/ch087d.html.

Michaud, L. J., Semel-Concepcion, J., Duhaime, A. C., & Lazar, M. F. (2002). Traumatic brain injury. In M. L. Batshaw (Ed.), *Children with disabilities* (5th ed., pp. 525–548). Baltimore, MD: Paul H. Brookes.

National Center for Injury Prevention and Control. (2006). *Facts about concussion and brain injury and where to get help.* Retrieved March 10, 2006, http://www.cdc.gov/ncipc/tbi/.

National Center on Shaken Baby Syndrome. (2005). *Shaken baby syndrome.* Retrieved April 23, 2005, from http://www.dontshake.com/Audience.aspx?CategoryID=7.

National Dissemination Center for Children with Disabilities. (2004). *Traumatic brain injury—Fact sheet #18.* Retrieved April 4, 2005, from http://www.nichcy.org/pubs/factshe/fs18txt.htm.

National Institute of Neurological Disorders and Stroke. (2005). *NINDS traumatic brain injury information page.* http://www.ninds.nih.gov/disorders/tbi/tbi.htm.

Society for Neuroscience. (2006). *Locked in syndrome.* Retrieved March 10, 2006, from http://web.sfn.org/index.cfm?pagename=brainBriefings_unlockingLockedIn Syndrome.

Turnbull, A., Turnbull, R., & Wehmeyer, M. L. (2007). *Exceptional lives: Special education in today's schools.* Upper Saddle River, NJ: Prentice Hall.

University of Idaho Medical Education Program. (2006). *Locked in syndrome.* Retrieved March 10, 2006, from http://www.sci.uidaho.edu/med532/Locked_in.htm.

University of Missouri Health Care. (2006). *Cerebral contusion.* Retrieved October 31, 2006, from http://www.muhealth.org/~neuromed/contusion.shtml.

U.S. Department of Education. (2004). *Twenty-Sixth Annual Report to Congress on the Implementation of the Individuals with Disabilities Education Act* (IDEA). Washington, DC: Author.

U.S. National Library of Medicine. (2004). *Concussion.* Retrieved March 10, 2006, http://www.nlm.nih.gov/medlineplus/ency/article/000799.htm.

U.S. National Library of Medicine. (2006). *Skull fracture.* Retrieved March 3, 2006, from http://www.nlm.nih.gov/medlineplus/ency/article/000060.htm#Alternative%20Names.

Vinas, C., & Pilitsis, J. (2004). *Penetrating skull fracture.* Retrieved September 6, 2005, from http://www. eMedicine.com.

Youse, K. M., Le, K. N., Cannizzaro, M. S., & Coelho, C. A. (2002, June 28). Traumatic brain injury: A primer for professionals. *ASHA Leader,* 4–7.

CHAPTER 12

DEAF–BLINDNESS

EDM CODE: DB

DB 1.00 Total Deafness and Total Blindness
- DB 1.01 Congenital Total Deafness and Congenital Total Blindness
- DB 1.02 Acquired Total Deafness and Acquired Total Blindness
- DB 1.03 Congenital Total Deafness and Acquired Total Blindness
- DB 1.04 Acquired Total Deafness and Congenital Total Blindness

DB 2.00 Total Deafness and Visually Impairment
- DB 2.01 Congenital Total Deafness and Congenital Visual Impairment
- DB 2.02 Acquired Total Deafness and Acquired Visual Impairment
- DB 2.03 Congenital Total Deafness and Acquired Visual Impairment
- DB 2.04 Acquired Total Deafness and Congenital Visual Impairment

DB 3.00 Hearing Impairment and Total Blindness
- DB 3.01 Congenital Hearing Impairment and Congenital Total Blindness
- DB 3.02 Acquired Hearing Impairment and Acquired Total Blindness
- DB 3.03 Congenital Hearing Impairment and Acquired Total Blindness
- DB 3.04 Acquired Hearing Impairment and Congenital Total Blindness

DB 4.00 Hearing Impairment and Visual Impairment
- DB 4.01 Congenital Hearing Impairment and Congenital Visual Impairment
- DB 4.02 Acquired Hearing Impairment and Acquired Visual Impairment
- DB 4.03 Congenital Hearing Impairment and Acquired Visual Impairment
- DB 4.04 Acquired Hearing Impairment and Congenital Visual Impairment

IDEA 2004 Definition of Deaf-Blindness

Deaf-blindness refers to concomitant hearing and visual impairments, the combination of which causes such severe communication and other developmental and educational needs that they cannot be accommodated in special education programs solely for children with deafness or children with blindness (34 CFR 300.7(c)(2)).

Overview of Deaf-Blindness

As used by most special educators, the term *severe disabilities* "generally encompasses students with significant disabilities in intellectual, physical, and or social functioning" (Heward, 2006, p. 469). Deaf-blindness is considered a severe disability and is a combination of vision and hearing loss, not necessarily complete deafness and complete blindness. There is a wide range of thinking and developmental ability among deaf-blind individuals, from gifted to profoundly multiply handicapped. Deaf-blindness creates problems in the areas of mobility and communication as well (Turnbull, Turnbull, & Wehmeyer, 2007; California Deaf-Blind Services, 1996).

The majority of children who have both visual and hearing impairments at birth experience major difficulties in acquiring communication and motor skills, mobility, and appropriate social skills. Because these individuals do not receive clear and consistent information from either sensory modality, a tendency exists to turn inward to obtain the desired level of stimulation. The individual therefore may appear passive, nonresponsive, or noncompliant.

Students with deaf-blindness (also referred to as dual sensory impairments) may not respond to or initiate appropriate interactions with others and often exhibit behavior that is considered socially inappropriate.

Individuals who are deaf-blind need early intervention and personal attention to stimulate their understanding and interest in the world around them. The information that most children pick up naturally must be deliberately introduced to children with dual sensory impairments. Effective programs for infants and toddlers with deaf-blindness are child and family centered. Child-centered approaches focus on meeting the child's individual needs, while a family-centered approach focuses on the child as a member of the family unit. The needs, structure, and preferences of the family often drive the delivery of the early intervention services (Ramey & Ramey, 1999).

Communication and mobility are often the most affected areas of life for a person with deaf-blindness, causing feelings of isolation and loneliness. Development of compensatory skills can help bridge this gap. Training and instructional strategies are available to parents and educators relative to communication and mobility (California Deaf-Blind Services, 1996).

Causes-Etiology of Deaf-Blindness

According to Friend (2005), there are three ways in which to categorize the causes of deaf-blindness:

- Prenatal conditions (before birth)—Chromosomal abnormalities, viral infections, drug and alcohol intake, malnutrition, physical trauma to mother
- Perinatal conditions (during birth)—Lack of oxygen supply to the baby's brain, physical injury to the brain during birth, contracted infections during birth
- Postnatal conditions (after birth)—Infections, traumatic brain injury, lead poisoning, reactions to medications, environmental conditions)

There are numerous genetic and chromosomal syndromes, prenatal conditions, and postnatal conditions that can cause deaf-blindness (SENSE, 2005). These include:

- Aicardi syndrome
- Alport syndrome
- Alström syndrome
- Apert syndrome
- Asphyxia
- Bardet-Biedl syndrome
- Batten-Mayou disease
- CHARGE association
- Chromosome 18
- Cockayne syndrome
- Cogan syndrome
- Congenital rubella
- Cornelia de Lange syndrome
- Cri-du-chat syndrome
- Crigler-Najjar syndrome
- Crouzon syndrome
- Cytomegalovirus
- Dandy-Walker syndrome
- Direct trauma to the eye and ear
- Down syndrome
- Encephalitis
- Fetal alcohol syndrome
- Goldenhar syndrome
- Herpes zoster
- Histiocytosis
- Hunter syndrome
- Hurler syndrome
- Hydrocephaly, hydrocephalus
- Infectious diseases

- Kearns-Sayre syndrome
- Klippel Feil/Wildervanck syndrome
- Klippel-Trenaunay-Weber syndrome
- Kniest dysplasia
- Leber's congenital amaurosis
- Leigh's disease
- Marfan syndrome
- Marshall syndrome
- Maroteaux-Lamy syndrome
- Maternal drug use
- Meningitis
- Microcephaly
- Möbius syndrome
- Monosomy 10p
- Morquio syndrome
- Neonatal herpes simplex
- NF1—Neurofibromatosis Type 1
- NF1—Neurofibromatosis Type 2
- Neurofibromatosis
- Norrie disease
- Pfeiffer syndrome
- Prader-Willi syndrome
- Pierre-Robin syndrome
- Refsum syndrome
- Scheie syndrome (MPS I-S)
- Severe head/brain injury
- Smith-Lemli-Opitz syndrome
- Stickler syndrome
- Stroke
- Sturge-Weber syndrome
- Congenital syphilis
- Toxoplasmosis
- Treacher Collins syndrome

- Trisomy 13
- Trisomy 18 (Edwards' syndrome)
- Turner syndrome
- Usher's syndrome
- Vogt-Koyanagi-Harada syndrome
- Waardenburg syndrome

Prevalence of Deaf-Blindness

The population of students having deaf-blindness represents a low incidence category. The U.S. Department of Education (2004) reports that during the 2003–2004 school year, 1,603 students aged six to twenty-one received special education services under the category of deaf-blindness. This makes up less than 0.1 percent of all school-age children receiving special education services. Although relatively few students have this classification, their needs are significant, and they may require substantial support and services to benefit from their special education programs (Friend, 2005).

Age of Onset of Deaf-Blindness

Due to the various causes of deaf-blindness, no specific age of onset can be generalized to the entire school-age population that receives special education services. Some students classified with deaf-blindness have had this condition since birth (congenital), and other students with deaf-blindness attained this diagnosis during their development (acquired) as a result of accident, illness, or unknown cause.

Gender Features of Deaf-Blindness

Information on this topic is not available.

Cultural Features of Deaf-Blindness

Information on this topic is not available.

Familial Pattern of Deaf-Blindness

Information on this topic is not available.

Characteristics of Deaf-Blindness

According to the Deaf Blind Services Division, Utah Schools for the Deaf and the Blind (n.d.), the child with deaf-blindness may develop particular characteristics that affect learning.

Depending on the age of onset, deaf-blindness can affect learning in the areas of cognition, communication, social interaction, motor skills, and motivation.

The child may have difficulty with communication. The child may have distorted perceptions. It is difficult for the child to see the whole picture or relate one element to the whole. The child may have difficulty anticipating what is going to happen. Clues from the environment or from the faces/actions of others may be difficult to read. The child-may be somewhat unmotivated. Things may not be seen or heard enough to be desirable. The child needs to learn mainly through first-hand experiences. The lack of vision and hearing make it hard to learn through incidental or group learning experiences. The child might have problems in communicating and navigating the environment.

Educational Implications of Deaf-Blindness

Deaf-blindness presents a unique challenge to special educators. It requires educational approaches that are well planned and draw on many techniques, technologies, and supportive services in order to ensure these children have the opportunity to reach their academic, social, and vocational potential.

The services offered by schools to children with deaf-blindness need to focus on the individual needs created by each disability. In the case of deaf or hard of hearing, services may include:

- Regular speech, language, and auditory training from a specialist
- Amplification systems
- Services of an interpreter for students who use manual communication
- Favorable seating in the class to facilitate speech reading
- Captioned films and videos
- Assistance of a note taker who takes notes for the student with a hearing loss so that the student can fully attend to instruction
- Instruction for the teacher and peers in alternate communication methods, such as sign language; and counseling (NEC Foundation of America, 2001)

The visual impairments should be assessed early so the child can benefit from early intervention programs. There is a crucial need, as with deaf and hard of hearing, to include assistive technology in the form of computers and low-vision optical and video aids. The introduction and use of these advanced technologies enable many partially sighted, low-vision, and blind children to participate in mainstream activities. Further assistance can result from the use of large-print materials, books on tape, braille books, frequency modulation (FM) trainers, and other augmentative communication devices.

The student with deaf-blindness needs additional help with special equipment and classroom and test modifications in the regular curriculum to emphasize listening skills, communication, orientation and mobility, vocation and career options, and daily living skills. These students have a great need for an interdisciplinary approach and may require greater emphasis on self-care and daily living skills.

Permissions and Authorization to Use Proprietary and Nonproprietary Sources

Due to the scientific and detailed nature of certain Level II and Level III disorders described in this chapter, we thought that some were best explained by national institutes and centers that conduct comprehensive scientific research in respective fields of study. The sources obtained were all written with explicit permission that the scientific and diagnostic information they prepared was in the public domain and can be used without restriction.

We thank the following national research offices for the opportunity to freely disseminate their scientific research and writing in this chapter:

- California Deaf-Blind Services
- U.S. Department of Education

EDM Codes, Definitions, and Explanations of Deaf-Blindness

DB 1.00 Total Deafness and Total Blindness

Total blindness means the individual has no light perception, and *total deafness* means that the individual cannot hear sounds over 80 dB.

DB 1.01 Congenital Total Deafness and Congenital Total Blindness

DB 1.02 Acquired Total Deafness and Acquired Total Blindness

DB 1.03 Congenital Total Deafness and Acquired Total Blindness

DB 1.04 Acquired Total Deafness and Congenital Total Blindness

DB 2.00 Total Deafness and Visual Impairment

Total deafness means that the individual cannot hear sounds over 80 dB, and *visual impairment* means that the individual has residual vision (useful sight).

DB 2.01 Congenital Total Deafness and Congenital Visual Impairment

DB 2.02 Acquired Total Deafness and Acquired Visual Impairment

DB 2.03 Congenital Total Deafness and Acquired Visual Impairment

DB 2.04 Acquired Total Deafness and Congenital Visual impairment

DB 3.00 Hearing Impairment and Total Blindness

Hearing impairment means that the individual has residual hearing, and *total blindness* means the individual has no light perception.

DB 3.01 Congenital Hearing Impairment and Congenital Total Blindness

DB 3.02 Acquired Hearing Impairment and Acquired Total Blindness

DB 3.03 Congenital Hearing Impairment and Acquired Total Blindness

DB 3.04 Acquired Hearing Impairment and Congenital Total Blindness

DB 4.00 Hearing Impairment and Visual Impairment

Hearing impairment means that the individual has residual hearing, and *visual impairment* means that the individual has residual vision (useful sight).

DB 4.01 Congenital Hearing Impairment and Congenital Visual Impairment

DB 4.02 Acquired Hearing Impairment and Acquired Visual Impairment

DB 4.03 Congenital Hearing Impairment and Acquired Visual Impairment

DB 4.04 Acquired Hearing Impairment and Congenital Visual Impairment

---

References

California Deaf-Blind Services. (1996). *Deaf-blindness.* Retrieved August 10, 2005, from http://www.sfsu.edu/~cadbs/Eng016.html.

Deaf Blind Services Division, Utah Schools for the Deaf and the Blind. (n.d.). *Deaf-blindness.* Retrieved April 2, 2006, from http://www.dblink.org/lib/dish/general_learning_char.pdf.

Friend, M. (2005). *Special education: Contemporary perspectives for school professionals.* Needham Heights, MA: Allyn & Bacon.

Heward, W. L. (2006). *Exceptional children: An introduction to special education* (8th ed.). Upper Saddle River, NJ: Pearson.

NEC Foundation of America. (2001). *Educational implications of visual impairments.* Retrieved March 7, 2006, from http://www.teachersandfamilies.com/sped/prof/visual/education.html.

Ramey, C. T., & Ramey, S. L. (1999). *Right from birth.* New York: Goddard Press.

SENSE. (2005). *About deaf-blindness.* Retrieved March 5, 2006, from http://www.sense.org.uk/deafblindness/.

Turnbull, A., Turnbull, R., & Wehmeyer, M. L. (2007). *Exceptional lives: Special education in today's school.* Upper Saddle River, NJ: Pearson.

U.S. Department of Education. (2004). *The Twenty-Sixth Annual Report to Congress on the Implementation of IDEA.* Washington, DC: U.S. Department of Education.

CHAPTER 13

INFANTS, TODDLERS, AND PRESCHOOLERS WITH DISABILITIES

EDM CODES: EI, PS

- EI 1.00 Developmental Delays in Infants and Toddlers
  - EI 1.01 Adaptive Developmental Delay in Infants and Toddlers
  - EI 1.02 Cognitive Developmental Delay in Infants and Toddlers
  - EI 1.03 Communication Developmental Delay in Infants and Toddlers
  - EI 1.03a Expressive Skills Delay in Infants and Toddlers
  - EI 1.03b Receptive Skills Delay in Infants and Toddlers
  - EI 1.04 Physical Developmental Delay in Infants and Toddlers
  - EI 1.05 Social and Emotional Developmental Delay in Infants and Toddlers
- EI 2.00 Conditions of Estab lished Risk
  - EI 2.01 Achondrogenesis I (Parenti-Fraccaro)
  - EI 2.02 Achondrogenesis II (Langer-Saldino)
  - EI 2.03 Achondroplasia
  - EI 2.04 Acrodysostosis
  - EI 2.05 Adrenoleukodystrophy
  - EI 2.06 Agenesis of the Corpus Callosum
  - EI 2.07 Alpers Disease
  - EI 2.08 Amelia
  - EI 2.09 Amniotic Band (Affecting Fetus or Newborn)
  - EI 2.10 Anencephaly
  - EI 2.11 Angelman's Syndrome
  - EI 2.12 Anoxic Insult to Brain
  - EI 2.13 Alpert Syndrome (Acrocephalosyndactyly)
  - EI 2.14 Aphasia
  - EI 2.15 Argininosuccinic Aciduria
  - EI 2.16 Arthrogryposis
  - EI 2.17 Ataxia-Telangiectasia
  - EI 2.18 Autism Spectrum Disorders
  - EI 2.19 Bartter's Syndrome
  - EI 2.20 Beals' Syndrome (Beals-Ilecht Syndrome
  - EI 2.21 Beckwith-Wiedemann Syndrome
  - EI 2.22 Biedl-Bardet Syndrome
  - EI 2.23 Brachial Plexus Injury, Perinantal Origin (Erb's Palsy)
  - EI 2.24 Brachial Plexus Injury, Post Perinatal Origin
  - EI 2.25 Camptomelic Dysplasia (CMD I, Camptomelic Dwarfism)
  - EI 2.26 Canavan Disease
  - EI 2.27 Carpenter Syndrome (Acrocephalopolysyndactyly)
  - EI 2.28 Caudal Regression Syndrome
  - EI 2.29 Cerebral Astrocytoma
  - EI 2.30 Cerebral Ataxia, Congenital
  - EI 2.31 Cerebral Cysts, Congenital
  - EI 2.32 Cerebral Dysplasia
  - EI 2.33 Cerebral Gigantism
  - EI 2.34 Cerebral Palsy
  - EI 2.35 Cerebrocostomandibular Syndrome
  - EI 2.36 Cerebrohepatorenal Syndrome
  - EI 2.37 CHARGE Syndrome

EI 2.38 Chondrodysplasia Punctata Syndromes
EI 2.39 Chromosomal Anomalies—Be Specific
EI 2.40 Cleft Hand, Congenital
EI 2.41 Cloverleaf Skull (Kleeb lattschädel)
EI 2.42 Clubfoot, Congenital
EI 2.43 Cockayne Syndrome
EI 2.44 Coffin-Lowry Syndrome
EI 2.45 Coffin-Siris Syndrome
EI 2.46 Convulsions in Newborn (Newborn Seizures)
EI 2.47 Crouzon's Disease (Craniofacial Dysostosis)
EI 2.48 Cryptophthalmos Syndrome
EI 2.49 Cutis Laxa Syndromes—Recessive Form
EI 2.50 Cytomegalic Inclusion Disease, Congenital
EI 2.51 Dandy-Walker Syndrome
EI 2.52 De Lange Syndrome
EI 2.53 Diaphragmatic Hernia
EI 2.54 Diastematomyelia
EI 2.55 Diastrophic Dysplasia
EI 2.56 DiGeorge Syndrome
EI 2.57 Down Syndrome
EI 2.58 Drug Addiction
EI 2.59 Drug Withdrawal Syndrome
EI 2.60 Dubowitz Syndrome
EI 2.61 Duchenne Muscular Dystrophy
EI 2.62 Dyggve-Melchoir-Clausen Syndrome
EI 2.63 Dystonia Musculorum Deformans—Torsion
EI 2.64 Dystonia
EI 2.65 Ehlers-Danlos Syndromes
EI 2.66 Encephalocele
EI 2.67 Encephalopathy, Congenital
EI 2.68 Encephalopathy, Hypoxic Ischemic
EI 2.69 Encephalopathy, Static
EI 2.70 Epilepsy
EI 2.71 Facial Clefts, Usual and Unusual
EI 2.72 Failure to Thrive
EI 2.73 Familial Dysautonomia
EI 2.74 Fanconi Syndrome
EI 2.75 Farber Disease
EI 2.76 Fetal Alcohol Syndrome
EI 2.77 Fracture of Vertebral Column with Spinal Cord Injury
EI 2.78 Fragile X Syndrome
EI 2.79 Fucosidosis
EI 2.80 Galactosemia
EI 2.81 Gastroschisis, Congenital
EI 2.82 Gaucher's Disease
EI 2.83 Glycinemia
EI 2.84 Gm1 Gangliosidosis
EI 2.85 Gm2 Gangliosidosis
EI 2.86 Goldenhar's Syndrome
EI 2.87 Hallervorden-Spatz Disease
EI 2.88 Hemiplegia
EI 2.89 Heterotopia
EI 2.90 HIV Positive After Fifteen Months of Age
EI 2.91 Holoprosencephaly
EI 2.92 Holt-Oram (Cardiac-Limb) Syndrome
EI 2.93 Homocystinuria
EI 2.94 Hydrancephaly
EI 2.95 Hydrocephalus
EI 2.96 Hypertrophic Interstitial Neuritis
EI 2.97 Hypoglossia-Hypodactylia Spectrum
EI 2.98 Hypothyroidism (Untreated), Congenital
EI 2.99 Hypotonia, Congenital, Nonbenign Form
EI 2.100 Ichthyosis Congenita
EI 2.101 Infantile Spasms, Epilepsy
EI 2.102 Intracerebral Hemorrhage
EI 2.103 Intraventricular Hemorrhage–Grade IV
EI 2.104 Isovaleric Acidemia
EI 2.105 Johnson-Blizzard Syndrome
EI 2.106 Juvenile Rheumatoid Arthritis
EI 2.107 Klinefelter's syndrome
EI 2.108 Klippel-Trenaunay-Weber Syndrome
EI 2.109 Kniest's Syndrome
EI 2.110 Krab be Disease
EI 2.111 Langer-Giedion Syndrome
EI 2.112 Larsen's Syndrome
EI 2.113 Leigh Disease
EI 2.114 Lennox-Gastaut Syndrome
EI 2.115 Leprechaunism
EI 2.116 Lesch-Nyan Syndrome
EI 2.117 Linear Sebaceous Nevus Syndrome
EI 2.118 Lissencephaly
EI 2.119 Lumbosacral Agenesis
EI 2.120 Mandibulofacial Dysostosis
EI 2.121 Mannosidosis
EI 2.122 Maple Syrup Urine Disease
EI 2.123 Marfan's Syndrome
EI 2.124 Meckel Disease
EI 2.125 Menkes Syndrome)
EI 2.126 Metachromatic Leukodystrophy
EI 2.127 Methylmalonic Aciduria with Glycinemia, Groups 1, 2, 3, 4
EI 2.128 Methylmalonic Aciduria without Glycinemia, Group 5

EI 2.129 Microcephaly
EI 2.130 Möbius (Poland) Syndrome
EI 2.131 Mucolipidosis
EI 2.132 Mucopolysaccharidosis
EI 2.133 Muscular Dystrophy, Congenital
EI 2.134 Myasthenia Gravis
EI 2.135 Myoclonic Encephalopathy of Childhood
EI 2.136 Myositis Ossificans Progressiva
EI 2.137 Myotonia Congenita—Thomsen Disease
EI 2.138 Myotonic Dystrophy
EI 2.139 Nemaline Rod Myopathy
EI 2.140 Neurofibromatosis
EI 2.141 Neuronal Ceroid-Lipofuscinoses-Amaurotic Familial Idiocy, Batten Disease, Jansky-Bielschowsky Syndrome, Spielmeyer-Vogt Disease, Kufs Disease, Niemann-Pick Disease
EI 2.142 Noonan Syndrome
EI 2.143 Norrie's Syndrome (Andersen-Warburg's Syndrome)
EI 2.144 Oculocerebrorenal Syndrome
EI 2.145 Oral-Facial-Digital Syndrome
EI 2.146 Orotic Aciduria
EI 2.147 Osteodystrophy, Congenital
EI 2.148 Osteogenesis Imperfecta Syndromes
EI 2.149 Otopalatodigital Syndrome
EI 2.150 Paralytic Syndromes
EI 2.151 Periventricular Leukomalacia
EI 2.152 Persistent Hyperplastic Primary Vitreous
EI 2.153 Pervasive Development Disorder, Unspecified
EI 2.154 Phenylketonuria
EI 2.155 Phocomelia
EI 2.156 Plagiocephaly
EI 2.157 Poland's Syndrome
EI 2.158 Polymicrogyria
EI 2.159 Pompe's Disease-Glycogen Storage Disease
EI 2.160 Porencephaly
EI 2.161 Prader-Willi Syndrome
EI 2.162 Prune Belly Syndrome
EI 2.163 Reduction Deformity of Brain
EI 2.164 Reduction Deformities of Limbs
EI 2.165 Roberts Syndrome
EI 2.166 Robin's Syndrome
EI 2.167 Rubinstein—Taybi Syndrome (Russell-Silver Syndrome)
EI 2.168 Saethre-Chotzen Syndrome
EI 2.169 Scimitar Syndrome
EI 2.170 Seizure Disorders
EI 2.171 Short Bowel Syndrome
EI 2.172 Sialidosis
EI 2.173 Sjögren-Larssen Syndrome
EI 2.174 Smith-Lemli-Opitz Syndrome
EI 2.175 Spastic Paraplegia, Hereditary
EI 2.176 Spina Bifida with Meningomyelocele
EI 2.177 Spinal Cord Injury
EI 2.178 Spondyloepiphyseal Dysplasia
EI 2.179 Sturge-Weber Syndrome
EI 2.180 Subacute Sclerosing Panencephalitis
EI 2.181 Symptomatic Torsion Dystonia
EI 2.182 Syringomyelia
EI 2.183 TAR Syndrome
EI 2.184 Thanatophoric Dysplasia
EI 2.185 Tuberous Sclerosis
EI 2.186 Tyrosinemia Type I (Tyrosinosis) and Type II
EI 2.187 VATER Syndrome
EI 2.188 Waardenburg's Syndrome, Type 1
EI 2.189 Werdnig-Hoffmann Disease
EI 2.190 Williams Syndrome
EI 2.191 Wilson Disease
EI 2.192 Wolman Disease and Cholesteryl Ester
EI 2.193 Xeroderma Pigmentosum

EI 3.00 "At Risk" Factors for a Developmental Delay in Infants and Toddlers

PS-DD 1.00 Developmental Delay in Preschool Children
- PS-DD 1.01 Adaptive Developmental Delay in Preschool Children
- PS-DD 1.02 Cognitive Developmental Delay in Preschool Children
- PS-DD 1.03 Communication Developmental Delay in Preschool Children
  - PS-DD 1.03a Expressive Skills Delay
  - PS-DD1.03b Receptive Skills Delay
- PS-DD 1.04 Physical Developmental Delay in Preschool Children
- PS-DD 1.05 Social and Emotional Developmental Delay in Preschool Children

IDEA 2004 Part C Definition of Early Intervention

Under Part C of IDEA, states must provide services to any child "under 3 years of age who needs early intervention services" (20 USC sec. 1432(5)(A)) because the child:

(i) is experiencing developmental delays, as measured by appropriate diagnostic instruments and procedures in one or more of the areas of cognitive development, physical development, communication development, social or emotional development, and adaptive development; or

(ii) has a diagnosed physical or mental condition which has a high probability of resulting in developmental delay]20 USC sec. 1432(5)(A)].

A state also may provide services, at its discretion, to at-risk infants and toddlers. An at-risk infant or toddler is defined under Part C as "an individual under 3 years of age who would be at risk of experiencing a substantial developmental delay if early intervention services were not provided to the individual" (20 USC sec. 1432(1)).

Overview of Early Intervention Services

In 1986, Congress created a nationwide incentive for states to implement coordinated systems of early intervention services for infants and toddlers with disabilities and their families by adding Part C to the Individuals with Disabilities Education Act (IDEA).

IDEA, Part C, is a federal law that provides financial assistance to states for the purpose of offering services to infants and toddlers (age birth through two) with disabilities. The purpose of these services is to enhance the development of infants and toddlers with disabilities and minimize their potential for developmental delay (Maryland State Department of Education, 2003).

Each year since 1987, the state lead agency has received federal funds by submitting an application to the U.S. Department of Education, which ensures that the state will implement the early intervention system in compliance with statutory and regulatory requirements.

Part C policies are based on the principles of family-centered and community-based service delivery and require that services to infants and toddlers with disabilities and their families be provided through a coordinated interagency system rather than a single agency (Maryland State Department of Education, 2003).

Research shows that participation in family-centered early intervention services during the first years of life has substantial positive effects on the cognitive development, social adjustment, and overall development of children with developmental disabilities. These services to eligible children are federally mandated under Part C of IDEA. On referral to an early intervention program, providers work with families to develop an Individualized Family Service Plan (IFSP), and each family is provided a service coordinator to advocate at their request.

In addition, the American Academy of Pediatrics has strongly advocated for a medical home for children with disabilities in which regular and specialized medical services are family centered and well coordinated with other early intervention services. Coordinated care should attempt to maximize appropriate services and avoid duplication and gaps in services. The relationship between the child, parents, and primary care physician is very important in promoting the long-term health and development of the child and should take the form of a partnership as much as possible. The family's culture, values, resources, priorities, and expectations may bear on family-centered services (Developmental Disabilities Digest, 2006).

Definition of Infant or Toddler

Under IDEA, infants and toddlers with disabilities are defined as children from birth through age two who need early intervention services because they. . .

> are experiencing developmental delays, as measured by appropriate diagnostic instruments and procedures, in one or more of the following areas:
>
> - Cognitive development;
> - Physical development, including vision and hearing;
> - Communication development;
> - Social or emotional development;
> - Adaptive development; or
> - Have a diagnosed physical or mental condition that has a high probability of resulting in developmental delay.
>
> The term may also include, if a state chooses, children from birth through age two who are at risk of having substantial developmental delays if early intervention services are not provided" (34 Code of Federal Regulations sec. 303.16).

Eligibility Criteria for Early Intervention Services

Referral to early intervention services can be based on objective criteria, screening tests, or clinical suspicion. Under IDEA (Part C), individual states retain the right to determine eligibility criteria for early intervention services, and some require referral within a certain time period.

The following two eligibility criteria are typical of most states: birth to three years of age and developmental delay or deficit in one or more of these areas (Alabama State Department of Education, 2002):

- Cognitive development (for example, limited interest in environment, play, and learning)
- Physical and motor development, including vision and hearing (for example, hypertonia, dystonia, asymmetry)

- Communication development (for example, limited sound use, limited response to speech)
- Emotional-social development (for example, impaired attachment, self-injurious behavior)
- Adaptive development (for example, feeding difficulties)

While most states require children to demonstrate one or more of these types of deficits, some states permit children to be enrolled who are at risk for delays or disabilities due to environmental factors (Developmental Disabilities Digest, 2006).

Evaluation of Infants and Toddlers for Early Intervention Services

IDEA requires that a child receive a timely, comprehensive, multidisciplinary evaluation and assessment. The purposes of the evaluation and assessment are to find out the nature of the child's strengths, delays, or difficulties; whether the child is eligible for early intervention services; and how the child functions in five areas of development: cognitive development, physical development, communication, social-emotional development, and adaptive development (Alabama State Department of Education, 2002).

When a child's needs are assessed and the child is found eligible for services, a service coordinator is assigned to the family. This person should have a background in early childhood development and methods for helping young children who may have developmental delays. The service coordinator should know the policies for early intervention programs and services in the state. This person can help parents locate other services in the community, such as recreation, child care, or family support groups. The service coordinator works with the family as long as the baby is receiving early intervention services; after the child is two years old, the service coordinator helps the family move on to programs for children ages three through five (National Dissemination Center for Children and Youth with Disabilities, 2005).

EDM Codes, Definitions, and Explanations of Early Intervention Services

Early intervention services help meet the developmental needs of the infant or toddler and the family. Needed services are identified during evaluation and assessment and agreed on at the IFSP meeting. The service coordinator helps the family coordinate the services from all agencies and providers of services and assists the family through transition.

Early intervention services include:

- Assistive technology
- Audiology

- Family training, counseling, and home visits
- Health services
- Medical services (for diagnostic or evaluation purposes only)
- Nursing
- Nutrition
- Occupational therapy
- Physical therapy
- Psychological services
- Service coordination
- Social work services
- Special instruction
- Speech and language pathology
- Transportation and related costs
- Vision services (California Department of Developmental Services, 2006)

Determination of Services for Infants and Toddlers

The decision is made at a meeting of an IFSP team. Required team members are the parents and anyone else the parents invite; the service coordinator; a person who was involved with the evaluation of the child; and, as appropriate, persons who will be involved in providing services to the child or family. The team develops an IFSP for the child and family.

The Individualized Family Service Plan (IFSP)

An IFSP documents and guides the early intervention process for children with disabilities and their families. This written plan is developed with the family. The information gathered during the evaluation process is used to identify all of the services the child needs and services the family needs to enhance the development of their child. The IFSP identifies and describes the services that are going to be provided and who will provide the services. The IFSP also identifies the service coordinator who will assist families throughout the child's eligibility (Alabama State Department of Education, 2002).

According to IDEA 2004, the IFSP shall be in writing and contain statements of:

- The child's levels of physical development, cognitive development, communication development, social or emotional development, and adaptive development
- The family's resources, priorities, and concerns relating to enhancing the development of the child with a disability

- The major outcomes to be achieved for the child and the family; the criteria, procedures, and time lines used to determine progress; and whether modifications or revisions of the outcomes or services are necessary
- Specific early intervention services necessary to meet the unique needs of the child and the family, including the frequency, intensity, and method of delivery
- The natural environments in which services will be provided, including justification of the extent, if any, to which the services will not be provided in a natural environment
- The projected dates for initiation of services and their anticipated duration
- The name of the service provider who will be responsible for implementing the plan and coordinating with other agencies and persons
- Steps to support the child's transition to preschool or other appropriate services

An IFSP is written within forty-five days after the referral. In an emergency and with the parent's permission, services can begin before the full evaluation is completed (Alabama State Department of Education, 2002).

Payment for Services for Infants and Toddlers

Part C of IDEA does not require that all services be provided at no cost to families. Several early intervention services, however, must be provided at no cost to the family. These include evaluations or assessments, the development of the IFSP, and service coordination for eligible children and their families. Some early intervention programs provide services at no charge to families. Other programs charge families on a sliding-fee scale. The law says that no family shall be denied needed services because they cannot afford them.

Transition Services for Infants and Toddlers

Transition can occur at any time there is a change from one service delivery system to another. The purpose of transition services is to ensure that children continue to receive services and support as they move within and between service delivery systems.

The federal law for early intervention and special education, IDEA Parts B and Part C, support a seamless system of services for children from birth through age five. The law requires that this should be a smooth activity, that services should continue throughout the transition period, and that there should be no interruption in services for the child (Alabama State Department of Education, 2002).

Two types of transition can be addressed by the IFSP. First are transitions within the early intervention program. These can include transitions between service providers or service settings. For example, support and planning would be required to move smoothly from a program designed for infants to a program for toddlers. The physical environment in the toddler setting will differ significantly to support the developmental goals of toddlers who are more mobile and expected to explore their environment.

The other type of transition takes place when the child moves from early intervention services to a variety of preschool settings. When the child with disabilities nears the age of three, he or she must be considered for services beyond early intervention services. These services include special education preschool programs (under Part B of the IDEA), Head Start programs, and public and private preschool programs.

Special education preschool programs are available to children with disabilities who are three to five years old. If the child is eligible for preschool special education services, he or she must have an Individualized Education Program (IEP) in place by age three. All services provided under the IEP must be free to the parents. If a child is not eligible for special education preschool, Head Start or public or private preschool programs should be considered (National Dissemination Center for Children and Youth with Disabilities, 2005).

Permissions and Authorization to Use Proprietary and Nonproprietary Sources

Due to the scientific and detailed nature of certain Level II disorders and level III types of disorders described in this chapter, we thought that some were best explained by national centers and state departments of education that conduct comprehensive scientific research in respective fields of study. The sources obtained were all written with explicit permissions that the scientific and diagnostic information they prepared was in the public domain and can be used without restriction. We thank the following national professional sources for the opportunity to freely disseminate certain parts of their publication materials in this chapter:

- Alabama State Department of Education
- California State Department of Education
- Maryland State Department of Education
- National Dissemination Center for Children with Disabilities

EDM Diagnosis for the Eligibility of Infants and Toddlers for Early Intervention Services: Birth Through Two Years of Age—EI

Under Part C, participating states and jurisdictions must provide services to two groups of children: those who are experiencing developmental delays and those who have a diagnosed mental or physical condition that has a high probability of resulting in developmental delay. In addition, states may choose to serve children who are at risk of having substantial developmental delays if early intervention services are not provided (California Department of Developmental Services, 2006).

Eligibility for Early Intervention Services

EI 1.00 Developmental Delays in Infants and Toddlers

Definition A developmental delay exists if there is a significant discrepancy between the child's current level of functioning and the expected level of development for his or her age in one or more area (National Dissemination Center for Children and Youth with Disabilities, 2005).

State criteria for delay are indicated in different ways. Those measured by assessment instruments are expressed in standard deviation, percentage delay, and delay in months, or developmental quotient. Other determinants include informed clinical opinion or the judgment of a multidisciplinary team (MDT). Areas refer to the five developmental areas cited in the law: "cognitive development, physical development, communication development, social or emotional development, and adaptive development" (20 USC §sec. 1432(5)(A)(i)), cited in Shackelford, 2005).

Diagnostic Symptoms Under Part C of IDEA, states must provide services to any child "under 3 years of age who needs early intervention services" (20 USC sec. 1432(5)(A)) because the child

> (i) is experiencing developmental delays, as measured by appropriate diagnostic instruments and procedures in one or more of the areas of:

- Cognitive development
  - Physical development
  - Communication development
  - Social or emotional development
- Adaptive development

Further Key Points The entire concept of developmental delay refers to a maturational lag or an abnormal or slower rate of development in which a child demonstrates a functioning level below that of an average child of the same age. Research has found that developmental delay is associated with other disabilities such as mental retardation, learning disabilities, and attention deficit disorders.

EI 1.01 Adaptive Developmental Delay in Infants and Toddlers

Definition A type of developmental delay characterized by a significant discrepancy between the child's current level of functioning and the expected level of development for his or her age in self-care or daily living skills (National Dissemination Center for Children and Youth with Disabilities, 2005).

Explanation Adaptive skills delays include but are not limited to daily living skills relating to feeding, dressing, hygiene, grooming, and toilet training.

EI 1.02 Cognitive Developmental Delay in Infants and Toddlers

Definition A type of developmental delay characterized by a significant discrepancy between the child's current level of functioning and the expected level of development for his or her age in the development of the functions of the brain and mental processes. These mental processes include functions such as learning, perception, memory, imagination, and use of language (National Dissemination Center for Children and Youth with Disabilities, 2005).

Explanation Types of delays in cognitive development include the ability to acquire, use, and retrieve information as demonstrated by the level of imitation, discrimination, representation, classification, sequencing, and problem-solving skills often observed in a child's play.

EI 1.03 Communication Developmental Delay in Infants and Toddlers

Definition A type of developmental delay characterized by a significant discrepancy between the child's current level of functioning and the expected level of development for his or her age in the ability to pass information to and receive information from, another person (National Dissemination Center for Children and Youth with Disabilities, 2005).

Explanation Types of delays in the development of communication skills include speech and language development, which encompasses expressive and receptive skills and nonverbal communication, including spoken sounds and words, repeating of sounds, as well as the child's ability to understand language.

EI 1.03a Expressive Skills Delay in Infants and Toddlers With respect to expressive language, delays are evident in such areas as the production of age-appropriate content, form, and use of language.

EI 1.03b Receptive Skills Delay in Infants and Toddlers With respect to receptive language, delays are evident in such areas as listening, receiving, and understanding language.

EI 1.04 Physical Developmental Delay in Infants and Toddlers

Definition A type of developmental delay characterized by a significant discrepancy between the child's current level of functioning and the expected level of development for his or her age in the use of large body movements (gross motor skills) and those that require small movements (fine motor skills; National Dissemination Center for Children and Youth with Disabilities, 2005).

Explanation Types of delays in physical development include gross motor skills used for postural control and movement and fine motor skills requiring precise coordinated use of the small muscles; sensory processing as well as tactile, vestibular, and kinesthetic input (sensory integration); motor development and body movements, such as sitting, crawling, standing, walking and running, and hand control; the ability to move around and interact with the environment with appropriate coordination, balance, and strength; or fine motor skills, such as manually controlling and manipulating toys, drawing utensils, and other useful objects in the environment.

EI 1.05 Social and Emotional Developmental Delay in Infants and Toddlers

Definition Emotional developmental delay is a type of developmental delay characterized by a significant discrepancy between the child's current level of functioning and the expected level of development for his or her age in understanding, expressing, and learning to regulate their emotions (emotional development).

Social development is a type of developmental delay characterized by a significant discrepancy between the child's current level of functioning and the expected level of development for his or her age in learning the skills, rules, and values that will enable the child to form connections and function among family members, peers, and members of society, that is, social development (National Dissemination Center for Children and Youth with Disabilities, 2005).

Explanation Social and emotional developmental delay includes attachment, interpersonal relationships, and interactions; playing with peers; the ability to feel and express emotions and develop a positive sense of oneself; and social activity, such as interacting with people, developing friendships with peers, and sustaining bonds with family.

EI 2.00 Conditions of Established Risk (Physical or Medical Condition That Has a High Probability of Resulting in a Developmental Delay)

Definition A condition of established risk is defined as a "diagnosed physical or mental condition which has a high probability of resulting in developmental delay" (20 USC sec. 1432(5)(A)(ii)).

Explanation In order to be eligible in this category, the child must have a diagnosed physical or mental condition that has a high probability of resulting in developmental delay. Specific diagnoses and conditions of eligibility are defined in state law. These diagnoses and conditions must be supported by a physician or psychologist indicating what the physical or mental condition is and a multidisciplinary evaluation report that early intervention services are needed (Sandall, McLean, and Smith, 2000). The categories are:

- Chromosomal abnormalities/genetic disorder
- Neurological disorder
- Congenital disorder
- Sensory impairment including vision and hearing
- Severe toxic exposure
- Severe infectious disease
- Atypical development disorder (34 CFR. sec. 303.16, Note 1)

Further Key Points It is very important to recognize that each state sets its own criteria for what is considered a "condition of established risk" for a developmental disability. Accordingly, it is imperative to follow state guidelines when making a determination of whether a child meets the criteria for diagnosis.

Types of Conditions of Established Risk

Following are the EDM diagnosis codes for infants and toddlers (birth to thirty-six months of age) with established conditions of risk for a developmental delay (physical or medical condition which has a high probability of resulting in a developmental delay).

EI 2.01 Achondrogenesis I (Parenti-Fraccaro)

EI 2.02 Achondrogenesis II (Langer-Saldino)

EI 2.03 Achondroplasia

EI 2.04 Acrodysostosis

EI 2.05 Adrenoleukodystrophy

EI 2.06 Agenesis of the Corpus Callosum

EI 2.07 Alpers Disease (Poliodystrophy)

EI 2.08 Amelia

EI 2.09 Amniotic Band (Affecting Fetus or Newborn)

EI 2.10 Anencephaly

EI 2.11 Angelman's Syndrome

EI 2.12 Anoxic Insult to Brain

EI 2.13 Alpert Syndrome (Acrocephalosyndactyly)

EI 2.14 Aphasia

EI 2.15 Argininosuccinic Aciduria

EI 2.16 Arthrogryposis

EI 2.17 Ataxia-Telangiectasia

EI 2.18 Autism Spectrum Disorders

EI 2.19 Bartter's Syndrome

EI 2.20 Beals' Syndrome (Beals-Hecht Syndrome)

EI 2.21 Beckwith-Wiedemann Syndrome

EI 2.22 Biedl-Bardet Syndrome

EI 2.23 Brachial Plexus Injury, Perinatal Origin (Erb's Palsy)

EI 2.24 Brachial Plexus Injury, Post Perinatal Origin

EI 2.25 Camptomelic Dysplasia (CMD I, Camptomelic Dwarfism)

EI 2.26 Canavan Disease

EI 2.27 Carpenter Syndrome (Acrocephalopolysyndactyly)

EI 2.28 Caudal Regression Syndrome

EI 2.29 Cerebral Astrocytoma

EI 2.30 Cerebral Ataxia, Congenital

EI 2.31 Cerebral Cysts, Congenital

EI 2.32 Cerebral Dysplasia

EI 2.33 Cerebral Gigantism

EI 2.34 Cerebral Palsy

EI 2.35 Cerebrocostomandibular Syndrome

EI 2.36 Cerebrohepatorenal Syndrome

EI 2.37 CHARGE Syndrome

EI 2.38 Chondrodysplasia Punctata Syndromes

EI 2.39 Chromosomal Anomalies—Be Specific

EI 2.40 Cleft Hand, Congenital

EI 2.41 Cloverleaf Skull (Kleeblattschädel)

EI 2.42 Clubfoot, Congenital

EI 2.43 Cockayne Syndrome

EI 2.44 Coffin-Lowry Syndrome

EI 2.45 Coffin-Siris Syndrome

EI 2.46 Convulsions in Newborn (Newborn Seizures)

EI 2.47 Crouzon's Disease (Craniofacial Dysostosis)

EI 2.48 Cryptophthalmos Syndrome

EI 2.49 Cutis Laxa Syndromes—Recessive Form

EI 2.50 Cytomegalic Inclusion Disease, Congenital

EI 2.51 Dandy-Walker Syndrome

EI 2.52 De Lange Syndrome

EI 2.53 **Diaphragmatic Hernia**

EI 2.54 **Diastematomyelia**

EI 2.55 **Diastrophic Dysplasia**

EI 2.56 **DiGeorge Syndrome**

EI 2.57 **Down Syndrome**

EI 2.58 **Drug Addiction**

EI 2.59 **Drug Withdrawal Syndrome**

EI 2.60 **Dubowitz Syndrome**

EI 2.61 **Duchenne Muscular Dystrophy**

EI 2.62 **Dyggve-Melchior-Clausen Syndrome**

EI 2.63 **Dystonia Musculorum Deformans—Torsion**

EI 2.64 **Dystonia**

EI 2.65 **Ehlers-Danlos Syndrome**

EI 2.66 **Encephalocele**

EI 2.67 **Encephalopathy, Congenital**

EI 2.68 **Encephalopathy, Hypoxic Ischemic**

EI 2.69 **Encephalopathy, Static**

EI 2.70 **Epilepsy**

EI 2.71 **Facial Clefts, Usual and Unusual**

EI 2.72 **Failure to Thrive**

EI 2.73 **Familial Dysautonomia (Riley-Day Syndrome)**

EI 2.74 Fanconi Syndrome

EI 2.75 Farber Disease

EI 2.76 Fetal Alcohol Syndrome

EI 2.77 Fracture of Vertebral Column with Spinal Cord Injury

EI 2.78 Fragile X Syndrome

EI 2.79 Fucosidosis

EI 2.80 Galactosemia

EI 2.81 Gastroschisis, Congenital

EI 2.82 Gaucher's Disease

EI 2.83 Glycinemia

EI 2.84 Gm1 Gangliosidosis

EI 2.85 Gm2 Gangliosidosis (Tay-Sachs or Sandhoff Disease)

EI 2.86 Goldenhar's Syndrome (Oculoauriculovertebral Dysplasia)

EI 2.87 Hallervorden-Spatz Disease

EI 2.88 Hemiplegia

EI 2.89 Heterotopia

EI 2.90 HIV Positive After Fifteen Months of Age

EI 2.91 Holoprosencephaly

EI 2.92 Holt-Oram (Cardiac-Limb) Syndrome (Atriodigital Dysplasia)

EI 2.93 Homocystinuria

EI 2.94 Hydrancephaly

EI 2.95	**Hydrocephalus**
EI 2.96	**Hypertrophic Interstitial Neuritis (Dejerine-Sottas Disease)**
EI 2.97	**Hypoglossia-Hypodactylia Spectrum**
EI 2.98	**Hypothyroidism (Untreated), Congenital**
EI 2.99	**Hypotonia, Congenital, Nonbenign Form**
EI 2.100	**Ichthyosis Congenita**
EI 2.101	**Infantile Spasms, Epilepsy (Infantile Myoclonic Seizures)**
EI 2.102	**Intracerebral Hemorrhage**
EI 2.103	**Intraventricular Hemorrhage–Grade IV**
EI 2.104	**Isovaleric Acidemia**
EI 2.105	**Johnson-Blizzard Syndrome**
EI 2.106	**Juvenile Rheumatoid Arthritis**
EI 2.107	**Klinefelter's syndrome**
EI 2.108	**Klippel-Trenaunay-Weber Syndrome**
EI 2.109	**Kniest's Syndrome (Metatrophic Dwarfism II)**
EI 2.110	**Krabbe Disease**
EI 2.111	**Langer-Giedion Syndrome**
EI 2.112	**Larsen's Syndrome**
EI 2.113	**Leigh Disease**
EI 2.114	**Lennox-Gastaut Syndrome**
EI 2.115	**Leprechaunism**

EI 2.116 Lesch-Nyan Syndrome

EI 2.117 Linear Sebaceous Nevus Syndrome

EI 2.118 Lissencephaly

EI 2.119 Lumbosacral Agenesis

EI 2.120 Mandibulofacial Dysostosis

EI 2.121 Mannosidosis

EI 2.122 Maple Syrup Urine Disease

EI 2.123 Marfan's Syndrome

EI 2.124 Meckel Disease

EI 2.125 Menkes Syndrome (Kinky Hair Disease)

EI 2.126 Metachromatic Leukodystrophy

EI 2.127 Methylmalonic Aciduria with Glycinemia, Groups 1, 2, 3, 4

EI 2.128 Methylmalonic Aciduria Without Glycinemia, Group 5

EI 2.129 Microcephaly

EI 2.130 Möbius (Poland) Syndrome (Congenital Facial Diplegia, Möbius II)

EI 2.131 Mucolipidosis

EI 2.132 Mucopolysaccharidosis

EI 2.133 Muscular Dystrophy, Congenital

EI 2.134 Myasthenia Gravis

EI 2.135 Myoclonic Encephalopathy of Childhood (Kinsbourne Syndrome)

EI 2.136 Myositis Ossificans Progressiva

EI 2.137 Myotonia Congenita—Thomsen Disease

EI 2.138 Myotonic Dystrophy

EI 2.139 Nemaline Rod Myopathy

EI 2.140 Neurofibromatosis

EI 2.141 Neuronal Ceroid-Lipofuscinoses-Amaurotic Familial Idiocy, Batten Disease, Jansky-Bielschowsky Syndrome, Spielmeyer-Vogt Disease, Kufs Disease, Niemann-Pick Disease (Classic Infantile and Juvenile)

EI 2.142 Noonan Syndrome

EI 2.143 Norrie's Syndrome (Andersen-Warburg's Syndrome)

EI 2.144 Oculocerebrorenal Syndrome

EI 2.145 Oral-Facial-Digital Syndrome

EI 2.146 Orotic Aciduria

EI 2.147 Osteodystrophy, Congenital

EI 2.148 Osteogenesis Imperfecta Syndromes

EI 2.149 Otopalatodigital Syndrome

EI 2.150 Paralytic Syndromes

EI 2.151 Periventricular Leukomalacia

EI 2.152 Persistent Hyperplastic Primary Vitreous

EI 2.153 Pervasive Development Disorder, Unspecified

EI 2.154 Phenylketonuria

EI 2.155 Phocomelia

EI 2.156 Plagiocephaly

EI 2.157 Poland's Syndrome

EI 2.158 Polymicrogyria

EI 2.159 Pompe's Disease-Glycogen Storage Disease

EI 2.160 Porencephaly

EI 2.161 Prader-Willi Syndrome

EI 2.162 Prune Belly Syndrome

EI 2.163 Reduction Deformity of Brain

EI 2.164 Reduction Deformities of Limbs

EI 2.165 Roberts Syndrome

EI 2.166 Robin's Syndrome

EI 2.167 Rubinstein-Taybi Syndrome (Russell [Silver] Syndrome)

EI 2.168 Saethre-Chotzen Syndrome

EI 2.169 Scimitar Syndrome

EI 2.170 Seizure Disorders

EI 2.171 Short Bowel Syndrome

EI 2.172 Sialidosis

EI 2.173 Sjögren-Larssen Syndrome

EI 2.174 Smith-Lemli-Opitz Syndrome

EI 2.175 Spastic Paraplegia, Hereditary

EI 2.176 Spina Bifida with Meningomyelocele

EI 2.177 Spinal Cord Injury

EI 2.178 Spondyloepiphyseal Dysplasia

EI 2.179 Sturge-Weber Syndrome

EI 2.180 Subacute Sclerosing Panencephalitis

EI 2.181 Symptomatic Torsion Dystonia

EI 2.182 Syringomyelia

EI 2.183 TAR Syndrome

EI 2.184 Thanatophoric Dysplasia

EI 2.185 Tuberous Sclerosis

EI 2.186 Tyrosinemia Type I (Tyrosinosis) and Type II

EI 2.187 VATER Syndrome

EI 2.188 Waardenburg's Syndrome, Type 1

EI 2.189 Werdnig-Hoffmann Disease

EI 2.190 Williams Syndrome

EI 2.191 Wilson Disease

EI 2.192 Wolman Disease and Cholesteryl Ester

EI 2.193 Xeroderma Pigmentosum

EI 3.00 "At Risk" Factors for a Developmental Delay in Infants and Toddlers

Definition Under Part C of IDEA, a state may provide services, at its discretion, to at-risk infants and toddlers. An at-risk infant or toddler is defined under Part C as "an individual under 3 years of age who would be at risk of experiencing a substantial developmental delay if early intervention services were not provided to the individual" (20 USC sec. 1432(1)).

Other risk factors associated with early intervention are normally categorized into two types:

- Biological/medical risk for a developmental delay (early medical conditions that are known to produce developmental delays in some children)
- Environmental risk (due to exposure to harmful agents either before or after birth

Currently, only eight states (and Guam) include at-risk children in their eligible population: California, Hawaii, Indiana, Massachusetts, New Hampshire, New Mexico, North Carolina, and West Virginia (Shackelford, 2006).

Diagnostic Symptoms Examples of biological and medical risk conditions that states have listed include low birth weight, intraventricular hemorrhage at birth, chronic lung disease, and failure to thrive. Other biological at risk factors include:

- Limited prenatal care
- Maternal prenatal substance abuse
- Severe prenatal complications
- Severe perinatal complications
- Asphyxia
- Very low birth weight
- Small for gestational age
- Severe postnatal complications (Shackelford, 2006)

Diagnostic symptoms of environmental risk include poor maternal nutrition, exposure to toxins (such as lead or drugs), and infections that are passed from a mother to her baby during pregnancy (such as measles or HIV).

Environmental risk also includes a child's life experiences. For example, children who are born prematurely, face severe poverty, mother's depression, poor nutrition, or lack of care are at increased risk for developmental delays (Sandall et al., 2000). Children at environmental risk include those whose caregiving circumstances and current family situation place them at greater risk for delay than the general population.

Further Key Points According to Shackelford (2006), "Because children with a history of significant biological or medical conditions or events have a greater chance of developing a delay or a disability than children in the general population, states may include them under the optional eligibility category of at risk" (p. 3).

Early Childhood Special Education (Preschoolers with Disabilities): Ages Three Through Five Years of Age

Special education and related services is a state and federally mandated program for children (ages three to five) who meet state eligibility criteria because they are experiencing developmental delays. Eligibility for children is determined by criteria that have been established by federal and state rules and regulations.

School districts and other public agencies are responsible for locating, identifying and evaluating eligible children and offering a free and appropriate public education (FAPE). Special education and related services for preschool age is referred to as early childhood special education (ECSE). It is important to remember that special education is not a place but a system of services and supports for children with disabilities. ECSE services are provided through federal funding under the IDEA and state general revenue funds.

Preschool children are eligible to receive services on their third birthday if they meet the eligibility requirements for any of the following:

- Developmental delay (the most common category of disability used with preschool children; Alabama State Department of Education, 2002)
- Emotional disturbance
- Hearing impairment
- Speech/language impairment
- Deaf/blindness
- Visual impairment
- Mental retardation
- Specific learning disabilities
- Multiple disabilities
- Autism
- Orthopedic impairment
- Traumatic brain injury
- Other health impairment

Under IDEA 2004, "children aged 3 through 9 experiencing developmental delays . . . may, at the discretion of the State and LEA [local education agency]. . . , include a child–

(1) . . . experiencing developmental delays, as defined by the State and as measured by appropriate diagnostic instruments and procedures, in one or more of the following areas:

- physical development
- cognitive development,
- communication development,
- social or emotional development, or
- adaptive development and

(2) who, by reason thereof, needs special education and related services [20 USC 1401(3)(A) and (B) sec. 300.7].

During the reauthorization process of IDEA, comments indicated a need to clarify the use of the term. The main questions and concerns addressed under the "Analysis of Comments and Changes" section of the Federal Register (1999) were related to the following:

> the application of the term DD and the respective roles of the state and local education agencies (SEA and LEA) in implementing the provision; the need for defining the term consistently under both Part B and the early intervention program under Part C of the Act; and the impact that the term would have for children with sensory disabilities or significant cognitive disabilities [Federal Register, 1999, p. 12540].

The conditions for using DD and specified disability categories were clarified in response to public comments. The regulations specify that:

(1) A State that adopts the term developmental delay . . . determines whether it applies to children aged 3 through 9, or to a subset of that age range (e.g., ages 3 through 5).

(2) A State may not require an LEA to adopt and use the term. . . .

(3) If an LEA uses the term . . . , the LEA must conform to both the State's definition of that term and to the age range that has been adopted by the State. [ages 3 through 9, or a subset of that range]

(4) If a State does not adopt the term . . . , an LEA may not independently use that term as the basis for establishing a child's eligibility . . . . [20 USC 1401 (3)(A), (B) sec. 300.313].

If a specific disability is diagnosed, the revisions clarified that it is still appropriate to use the more descriptive category for those children (sec. 300.7(b) and 300.313). A state may also choose to adopt a common definition of the term DD under both Parts B and C of IDEA.

In sum, IDEA allows states and local education agencies to apply the term *developmental delay* for children ages three to eight. Previously, this definition applied to children ages three to five.

EDM Diagnosis of Preschool Children: Ages Three Through Five Years of Age: PS-DD

To show that the child is a preschooler with a Developmental Delay, put PS- next to the actual developmental delay diagnosis (represented by DD). The PS represents that the child is a preschool child. The DD represents that the individual has been classified with a developmental delay. For example, a preschool child with a cognitive developmental delay receives the EDM code of PS-DD 1.02, Cognitive Developmental Delay. PS shows that the individual is a preschool child and DD that the child has a developmental delay; 1.02 is the EDM code for Cognitive Developmental Delay.

PS-DD 1.00 Developmental Delay in Preschool Children

Definition Children aged three through nine experiencing developmental delays. The term *child with a disability* for this age group may, at the discretion of the state and LEA and in accordance with Section 300.313, include a child

(1) Who is experiencing developmental delays, as defined by the State and as measured by appropriate diagnostic instruments and procedures, in one or more of the following areas: physical development, cognitive development, communication development, social or emotional development, or adaptive development; and

(2) Who, by reason thereof, needs special education and related services.

Diagnostic Symptoms Individuals experiencing developmental delay experience a delay in their development in one or more of the following areas: (1) cognitive development; (2) physical development, which includes hearing and vision; (3) communication development; (4) social and emotional development; or (5) adaptive development.

Further Key Points The concept of developmental delay refers to a maturational lag or an abnormal or slower rate of development in which a child demonstrates a functioning level below that of an average child of the same age. Research has found that developmental delay is associated with other disabilities such as mental retardation, learning disabilities, and attention deficit disorders.

PS-DD 1.01 Adaptive Developmental Delay in Preschool Children

Definition A type of developmental delay characterized by a significant discrepancy between the child's current level of functioning and the expected level of development for his or her age in self-care or daily living skills (National Dissemination Center for Children and Youth with Disabilities, 2005).

Explanation Adaptive skills delays include but are not limited to daily living skills relating to feeding, dressing, hygiene, grooming, and toilet training.

PS-DD 1.02 Cognitive Developmental Delay in Preschool Children

Definition A type of developmental delay characterized by a significant discrepancy between the child's current level of functioning and the expected level of development for his or her age in the development of the functions of the brain and mental processes. These mental processes include functions such as learning, perception, memory, imagination, and use of language (National Dissemination Center for Children and Youth with Disabilities, 2005).

Explanation Types of delays in cognitive development include the ability to acquire, use and retrieve information as demonstrated by the level of imitation, discrimination, representation, classification, sequencing, and problem-solving skills often observed in a child's play.

PS-DD 1.03 Communication Developmental Delay in Preschool Children

Definition A type of developmental delay characterized by a significant discrepancy between the child's current level of functioning and the expected level of development for his or her age in the ability to pass information to and receive information from another person (National Dissemination Center for Children and Youth with Disabilities, 2005).

Explanation Types of delays in the development of communication skills include speech and language development: expressive and receptive skills and nonverbal communication, including spoken sounds and words, repeating of sounds, and the child's ability to understand language.

PS-DD 1.03a **Expressive Skills Delay** With respect to expressive language, delays are evident in such areas as the production of age–appropriate content, form, and use of language.

PS-DD 1.03b **Receptive Skills Delay** With respect to receptive language, delays are evident in such areas as listening, receiving, and understanding language.

PS-DD 1.04 Physical Developmental Delay in Preschool Children

Definition A type of developmental delay characterized by a significant discrepancy between the child's current level of functioning and the expected level of development for his or her age in the use of large body movements (gross motor skills) and those that require small movements (fine motor skills (National Dissemination Center for Children and Youth with Disabilities, 2005).

Explanation Types of delays in physical development include gross motor skills used for postural control and movement and fine motor skills requiring precise, coordinated use of the small muscles; sensory processing as well as tactile, vestibular, and kinesthetic input (sensory integration); motor development and body movements such as sitting, crawling, standing, walking and running, and hand control; the ability to move around and interact with the environment with appropriate coordination, balance, and strength; or fine motor skills, such as manually controlling and manipulating toys, drawing utensils, and other useful objects in the environment.

PS-DD 1.05 Social and Emotional Developmental Delay in Preschool Children

Definition Emotional developmental delay is a type of developmental delay characterized by a significant discrepancy between the child's current level of functioning and the expected level of development for his or her age in understanding, expressing, and learning to regulate his or her emotions (emotional development). Social development delay is a type of developmental delay characterized by a significant discrepancy between the child's current level of functioning and the expected level of development for his or her age in learning the skills, rules, and values that will enable the child to form connections and function among family members, peers, and members of society (social development) (National Dissemination Center for Children and Youth with Disabilities, 2005).

Explanation Social and emotional developmental delay includes attachment, interpersonal relationships, and interactions; playing with peers; the ability to feel and express emotions, and develop a positive sense of oneself; and social activity, such as interacting with people, developing friendships with peers, and sustaining bonds with family.

EDM Diagnosis of a Preschool Child with a Disability Other Than a Developmental Delay as Defined Under IDEA

For EDM coding purposes, all preschool children who do not receive a classification of developmental delay (PS-DD) will receive a classification under IDEA.

IDEA Classification	IDEA Classification for Preschoolers
Autism (AU)	PS-AU
Emotional Disturbance (ED)	PS-ED
Multiple Disabilities (MD)	PS-MD
Other Health Impairment (OHI)	PS-OHI
Speech/Language Impairment (SL)	PS-SL
Visual Impairment (VI)	PS-VI
Deaf-Blindness (DB)	PS-DB
Hearing Impairment (HI)	PS-HI
Mental Retardation (MR)	PS-MR
Orthopedic Impairment (OI)	PS-OI
Specific Learning Disability (LD)	PS-LD
Traumatic Brain Injury (TBI)	PS-TBI

To show that the child is a preschooler with a disability (not a developmental delay), put PS- next to the EDM diagnosis code. For example, a preschool child diagnosed with a mixed hearing loss would be coded PS-HI 3.00. The PS- represents that the individual is a preschooler. HI 3.00 is the EDM code for mixed hearing loss. Therefore, the EDM code is PS-HI 3.00.

A preschool child diagnosed with epilepsy with partial seizures would get the code PS-OHI 17.07, Epilepsy with Partial Seizures. The PS- represents that the individual is a preschooler.

Developmental Delay Classification for Elementary School Students: Ages Six Through Nine Years of Age

If on entrance to elementary school, it is determined that the child's classification in special education will remain developmental delay, the PS- is removed from the diagnosis code, leaving only the DD. For example, a preschool child with a cognitive developmental delay receives the EDM code of PS-DD 1.02, Cognitive Developmental Delay. When the child enters elementary school, the diagnosis code changes to DD 1.02, Cognitive Developmental Delay (the PS is removed).

References

Alabama State Department of Education. (2002). *Services for Alabama's children with dis abilities: Ages birth through* 5. Montgomery: Alabama Department of Rehabilitation Services-Division of Early Intervention.

California Department of Developmental Services. (2006). *What is early start?* Retrieved April 29, 2006, from http://www.dds.ca.gov/EarlyStart/ESQuestionAnswers.cfm.

Developmental Disabilities Digest. (2006). *Early intervention of delays and disabilities.* Retrieved November 7, 2006, from http://www.ddhealthinfo.org/ggrc/doc2.asp?ParentID=4134.

Federal Register. (1999, March 12). Vol. 64, No. 48, p. 12540.

Maryland State Department of Education. (2003). *Program overview.* Retrieved May 15, 2005, from http://www.marylandpublicschools.org/MSDE/programs/esea/.

National Dissemination Center for Children and Youth with Disabilities. (2005). *Finding help for young children with disabilities (Birth-5).* Retrieved May 15, 2005, from http://www.nichcy.org/pubs/parent/pa2txt.htm.

Sandall, S., McLean, M., & Smith, B. (2000). *DEC recommended practices in early intervention/ early childhood special education.* Longmont, CO: Sopris West.

Shackelford, J. (2006). *State and jurisdictional eligibility definitions for infants and toddlers with disabilities under IDEA.* Chapel Hill: University of North Carolina, FPG Child Development Institute, National Early Childhood Technical Assistance Center.

CHAPTER 14

USING THE EDM IN IEP DEVELOPMENT

The goals of *The Educator's Diagnostic Manual of Disabilities and Disorders* (EDM) are to provide:

- A standard of IDEA diagnosis for children in special education throughout the country
- A comprehensive and descriptive diagnosis of a child's disabilities
- An indication of how the specific disabilities and disorders adversely affect a child's educational performance
- A thorough, comprehensive, and specific diagnostic profile
- A better understanding among teachers of the areas in need of remediation or attention
- A better understanding for parents of their child's disabilities
- Specific and helpful information for students, schools, committees, and parents to allow for a more comprehensive, practical, and realistic Individual Education Program (IEP)

Up to this point, all children under IDEA are classified on one level. This general level, which reflects one of the thirteen IDEA classifications, tells the reader of the IEP very little about the specific conditions that resulted in this classification.

What we have found over the years is that when parents are asked what type of disability their child has, most can repeat only this one level. For example, if questioned about the specific type of learning disability or speech and language impairment, the same parents will have no idea that the child has dyslexia or dyscalculia or cluttering, or something else. With an EDM diagnosis included on their child's IEP, there will be no problem in knowing the disorders, specific types of disorders, and subtypes of disorders. They will also have a greater awareness of how it adversely affects their child's educational performance.

We believe that examples of IEPs with the EDM diagnoses will provide a clearer idea of the tremendous advantages of the EDM coding system over the form currently used in schools for children with disabilities. However, we are presenting only the portion of an IEP that would pertain to the EDM diagnosis. The remaining sections of an IEP are not the subject of this book.

The format that an EDM-coded IEP can take is up to the discretion of the district, agency, or school.

The rest of this chapter provides five examples of students whose IEPs have been coded using the EDM coding system. We have also provided two different EDM IEP formats for each of the five examples to show the flexibility and comprehensive nature of this coding system.

EDM IEP Format Without Explanations of the EDM Codes—Learning Disabilities Individualized Education Program

INDIVIDUALIZED EDUCATIONAL PROGRAM

School District/Agency: Barlow School District
Name and Address: Edison Township, Va.

Section I: Background Information

Student Name: *Julian Danna*

Date of Birth: *2/5/92* Age: *14*

Street: *13 Benson Ave.*

City: *Edison* Zip: *19876*

Date of Referral for Committee Review: *March 17, 2006*

Telephone: *675–8976* County of Residence: *Edison Township*

Male _X_ Female ___ Student ID#: *3467H* Current Grade: *9*

Dominant Language of Student: *English* Interpreter Needed: Yes ___ No _X_

Medical Alerts: *none*

Mother's Name/Guardian's Name: *Leona*

Street Address: *same*

City: *same* Zip: *same*

Telephone: *same* County of Residence: *same*

Dominant Language of Parent/Guardian: *English* Interpreter Needed: Yes __ No _X_

Father's Name/Guardian's Name: *Malcolm*
Street Address: *same*
City: *same* Zip: same
Telephone: *same* County of Residence: *same*
Dominant Language of Parent/Guardian: *English* Interpreter Needed: Yes __ No _X_

Section II: Type of Meeting

A: Initial Evaluation

1. Date of Initial Evaluation Meeting: *March 2, 2006*
2. Area of Suspected Disability *(EDM Level I Diagnosis): Learning Disabilities*
3. Origin of Evaluation Used in Determining Classification:
   - In-school __X__ Nonschool Personnel Evaluation ____
4. Components of Present Evaluation:
   - Individual Standardized Testing __X__
   - Informal Assessment Measures __X__ (Portfolio Assessment) Observation __X__
   - Social History __X__
   - Teacher Reports __X__
   - Interviews with Child __X__
   - Review of Medical Records __X__
5. Specific Areas Covered in Evaluation:
   - Intelligence Testing __X__
   - Academic Testing __X__
   - Medical Evaluation __X__
   - Speech Language Evaluation _____
   - Occupational Evaluation __X__
   - Other (Be Specific) _____
   - Audiometric Evaluation _____
   - Psychiatric Evaluation _____
   - Psychological Evaluation __X__

- Portfolio Assessment __X__
- Curriculum-Based Assessment _____
- Authentic Assessment __X__
- Task Analysis __X__
- Outcome-Based Assessment _____
- Learning Styles Assessment __X__

6. Committee Recommendations:

   Classification (EDM Coding)

   Level I: Learning Disabilities, LD
   Level II: Dyslexia, LD 4.00
   Level III: Dysphonetic Dyslexia, LD 4.07
   Level IV: Not Applicable
   Level V: Mild

   Level I: Learning Disabilities, LD
   Level II: Dyscalculia, LD 2.00
   Level III: Temporal Dyscalculia, LD 2.12
   Level IV: Not Applicable
   Level V: Moderate

   Level I: Learning Disabilities, LD
   Level II: Organizational Disorder, LD 9.00
   Level III: External Disorganization Disorder, LD 9.04
   Level IV: Not Applicable
   Level V: Moderate

   Level I: Learning Disabilities, LD
   Level II: Visual Processing Disorder, LD 12.00
   Level III: Visual Motor Processing Disorder, LD 12.09
   Level IV: Not Applicable
   Level V: Mild

EDM IEP Format with Explanations of the EDM Codes

INDIVIDUALIZED EDUCATIONAL PROGRAM

School District/Agency: Barlow School District
Name and Address: Edison Township, Va.

Section I: Background Information

Student Name: *Julian Danna*
Date of Birth: *2/5/90* Age: *16*
Street: *13 Benson Ave.*
City: *Edison* Zip: *19876*
Date of Referral for Committee Review: *March 17, 2006*
Telephone: *675–8976* County of Residence: *Edison Township*
Male _X_ Female ___ Student ID#: *3467H* Current Grade: *11*
Dominant Language of Student: *English* Interpreter Needed: Yes ___ No _X_
Medical Alerts: *none*
Mother's Name/Guardian's Name: *Leona*
Street Address: *same*
City: *same* Zip: same
Telephone: *same* County of Residence: *same*
Dominant Language of Parent/Guardian: *English* Interpreter Needed: Yes ___ No _X_
Father's Name/Guardian's Name: *Malcolm*
Street Address: *same*
City: *same* Zip: same
Telephone: *same* County of Residence: *same*
Dominant Language of Parent/Guardian: *English* Interpreter Needed: Yes ___ No _X_

Section II: Type of Meeting

A: Initial Evaluation

1. Date of Initial Evaluation Meeting: *March l2, 2006*
2. Area of Suspected Disability *(EDM Level I Diagnosis)-Learning Disabilities*
3. Origin of Evaluation Used in Determining Classification:
    - In-school _X_ Nonschool Personnel Evaluation _____

4. Components of Present Evaluation:
   - Individual Standardized Testing __X__
   - Informal Assessment Measures __X__
     (Portfolio Assessment) Observation __X__
   - Social History __X__
   - Teacher Reports __X__
   - Interviews with Child __X__
   - Review of Medical Records __X__
5. Specific Areas Covered in Evaluation:
   - Intelligence Testing __X__
   - Academic Testing __X__
   - Medical Evaluation __X__
   - Speech Language Evaluation _____
   - Occupational Evaluation __X__
   - Other (Be Specific)_______________
   - Audiometric Evaluation _____
   - Psychiatric Evaluation _____
   - Psychological Evaluation __X__
   - Portfolio Assessment __X__
   - Curriculum-Based Assessment _____
   - Authentic Assessment __X__
   - Task Analysis __X__
   - Outcome-Based Assessment _____
   - Learning Styles Assessment __X__
6. Committee Recommendations:
   Classification (EDM Coding)

   Level I: Learning Disabilities, LD

   Level II: Dyslexia, LD 4.00.

   Dyslexia is one of several distinct learning disabilities. It is a specific language-based disorder of constitutional origin characterized by difficulties in single-word decoding, usually reflecting insufficient phonological processing abilities. These difficulties in single-word decoding are often unexpected in relation to age and other cognitive and academic abilities; they are not the result of generalized developmental disability or sensory impairment. Dyslexia is manifest by variable difficulty with different forms of language, often including, in addition to problems reading, a conspicuous problem with acquiring proficiency in writing and spelling.

Level III: Dysphonetic Dyslexia, LD 4.07.

Specifically, Julian has Dysphonesia Dyslexia. Dysphonic readers have difficulty relating letters to sounds, so their spelling is totally chaotic. They are able to recognize words they have memorized but cannot sound out new ones to figure out what they are. They may be able to read near the appropriate grade level but are poor spellers. This is the largest of the three divisions. This is viewed as a disability in associating symbols with sounds. The misspellings typical of this disorder are phonetically inaccurate. The misreadings are substitutions based on small clues, and are also semantic.

Level IV: Not Applicable

Level V: Moderate.

Moderate adverse effect implies a significant difference between the needs of the student with a disability when compared to the reasonable expectations of nondisabled peers of the same age and or grade level.

Level I: Learning Disabilities, LD

Level II: Dyscalculia, LD 2.00.

Arithmetic involves recognizing numbers and symbols, memorizing facts, aligning numbers, and understanding abstract concepts like place value and fractions. Any of these may be difficult for children with developmental arithmetic disorders, also called dyscalculia. Problems with number or basic concepts are likely to show up early. Disabilities that appear in the later grades are more often tied to problems in reasoning.

Level III: Temporal Dyscalculia, LD 2.12.

Specifically, Julian has a Temporal Dyscalculia. By definition, Temporal Dyscalculia is a type of dyscalculia specifically associated with difficulties in relating to time, telling time, keeping track of time, and estimating time.

Individuals with Temporal Dyscalculia have numerous difficulties understanding basic principles of time. These students often:

- Over- or underestimate how long a period of time is (e.g., tell them "10 more minutes" and they will either be back in 2 minutes or come back 30 minutes later)

- State the incorrect time due to position on the clock (e.g., saying "it's 3:00" instead of the correct time of 9:00; saying "it's 12:00" instead of the correct time of 6:00)
- Lose track of time
- Estimating the amount of time it will take to complete an assignment, homework, or exam.

Level IV: Not Applicable

Level V: Moderate.

Moderate adverse effect implies a significant difference between the needs of the student with a disability when compared to the reasonable expectations of nondisabled peers of the same age and or grade level.

Level I: Learning Disabilities, LD

Level II: Organizational Disorder, LD 9.00.

Developing good organizational skills is a key ingredient for success in school and in life. Children with this disorder have a very difficult time with routines and systems which provide for appropriate organization.

Level III: External Disorganization Disorder, LD 9.04.

Specifically, Julian has a problem with external disorganization. Children with this type of problem may have desks that are always cluttered and disorganized, notebooks and looseleafs with papers falling out, ripped pages, no awareness of order or neatness, absent-minded, and unable to incorporate suggestions dealing with organizational skills. Children with this disorder may have difficulty with organizing their room, clothing, and homework assignments. They very often forget things, misplace things, and seem confused with the reactions of frustration on the part of those around them.

Level IV: Not Applicable

Level V: Moderate.

Moderate adverse effect implies a significant difference between the needs of the student with a disability when compared to the reasonable expectations of nondisabled peers of the same age and or grade level.

Level I: Learning Disabilities, LD

Level II: Visual Processing Disorder LD 12.00.

A visual processing, or perceptual, disorder refers to a hindered ability to make sense of information taken in through the eyes. This is different from problems involving sight or sharpness of vision. Difficulties with visual processing affect how visual information is interpreted or processed by the brain.

Level III: Visual Motor Processing Disorder, LD 12.09.

Julian has a problem with a type of visual processing disorder specifically associated with difficulties in using feedback from the eyes to coordinate the movement of other parts of the body. An individual with visual motor processing disorder will be unable to relate visual stimuli to motor responses in an appropriate way. There is more to eye-hand coordination than coloring, cutting, writing, and catching a ball. This coordination demands more than a normal eye and a normal hand. The difficulties observed include writing within lines or margins of a piece of paper, copying from a board or book, moving around without bumping into things, and participating in sports that require well-timed and precise movements in space.

Level IV: Not Applicable

Level V: Mild.

Mild adverse effect implies a minimal difference between the needs of the student with a disability when compared to the reasonable expectations of nondisabled peers of the same age and or grade level.

Emotional Disturbance Individualized Education Program

INDIVIDUALIZED EDUCATIONAL PROGRAM

School District/Agency: Newtown School District
Name and Address: Newtown Province, IL

Section I: Background Information

Student Name: *David Morris*
Date of Birth: *2/5/95* Age: *11*
Street: *14 River Rd.*
City: *Newtown* Zip: *16753*
Date of Referral for Committee Review: *March 17, 2006*
Telephone: *768–0943* County of Residence: *Newtown*
Male _X_ Female ___ Student ID#: *8786Y* Current Grade: *5*

Dominant Language of Student: *English* Interpreter Needed: Yes ___ No _X_
Medical Alerts: *none*
Mother's Name/Guardian's Name: *Mary*
Street Address: *same*
City: *same* Zip: *same*
Telephone: *same* County of Residence: *same*
Dominant Language of Parent/Guardian: *English*
Interpreter Needed: Yes ___ No _X_ Father's Name/Guardian's Name: *Paul*
Street Address: *same*
City: *same* Zip: *same*
Telephone: *same* County of Residence: same
Dominant Language of Parent/Guardian: *English*
Interpreter Needed: Yes ___ No _X_

Section II: Type of Meeting

A: Initial Evaluation

1. Date of Initial Evaluation Meeting: *March 8, 2006*
2. Area of Suspected Disability *(EDM Level I Diagnosis)-Emotional Disturbance*
3. Origin of Evaluation Used in Determining Classification:
   - In-school __X__ Nonschool Personnel Evaluation __X__
4. Components of Present Evaluation:
   - Individual Standardized Testing __X__
   - Informal Assessment Measures __X__
     (Portfolio Assessment) Observation __X__
   - Social History __X__
   - Teacher Reports __X__
   - Interviews with Child __X__
   - Review of Medical Records __X__
5. Specific Areas Covered in Evaluation:
   - Intelligence Testing __X__
   - Academic Testing __X__

- Medical Evaluation __X__
- Speech Language Evaluation _____
- Occupational Evaluation _____
- Other (Be Specific) _______________
- Audiometric Evaluation _____
- Psychiatric Evaluation __X__
- Psychological Evaluation __X__
- Portfolio Assessment __X__
- Curriculum-Based Assessment _____
- Authentic Assessment __X__
- Task Analysis __X__
- Outcome-Based Assessment _____
- Learning Styles Assessment __X__

6. Committee Recommendations:

Classification (EDM Coding)

Level I: Emotional Disturbance, ED
Level II: Anxiety Reactive Disorder, ED 6.00
Level III: School Avoidance Anxiety Reactive Disorder, ED 6.02
Level IV: Not Applicable
Level V: Moderate

Level I: Emotional Disturbance, ED
Level II: Anxiety Reactive Disorder, ED 6.00
Level III: Panic Reaction Type, ED 6.01
Level IV: Not Applicable
Level V: Moderate

Level I: Emotional Disturbance, ED
Level II: Inappropriate Behavior or Feelings, ED 3.00
Level III: Disruptive Behavior Type, ED 3.02
Level IV: Not Applicable
Level V: Moderate

Level I: Emotional Disturbance, ED

Level II: Relationship Problems Disorder, ED 2.00

Level III: Not Applicable

Level IV: Not Applicable

Level V: Moderate

Level I: Emotional Disturbance ED

Level II: Somatic Complaints Disorder, ED 5.00

Level III: Not Applicable

Level IV: Not Applicable

Level V: Moderate

Note that in this case, the school district chose to use the five levels of the coding system. Because the system is flexible, the district can use as many levels as appropriate.

IEP Format with Explanations of the EDM codes

School District/Agency: Newtown School District

Name and Address: Newtown Province, IL

Section I: Background Information

Student Name: *David Morris*

Date of Birth: *2/5/95* Age: *11*

Street: *14 River Rd.*

City: *Newtown* Zip: *16753*

Date of Referral for Committee Review: *March 17, 2006* Telephone: *768–0943*

County of Residence: *Newtown*

Male _X_ Female ___ Student ID#: *8786Y* Current Grade: *5*

Dominant Language of Student: *English* Interpreter Needed: Yes ___ No _X_

Medical Alerts: *none*

Mother's Name/Guardian's Name: *Mary*

Street Address: *same*

City: *same* Zip: *same*

Telephone: *same* County of Residence: *same*

Dominant Language of Parent/Guardian: *English* Interpreter Needed: Yes ___ No _X_

Father's Name/Guardian's Name: *Paul*
Street Address: *same*
City: *same* Zip: *same*
Telephone: *same* County of Residence: *same*
Dominant Language of Parent/Guardian: *English* Interpreter Needed: Yes ___ No _X_

Section II: Type of Meeting

A: Initial Evaluation

7. Date of Initial Evaluation Meeting: *March 8, 2006*
8. Area of Suspected Disability *(EDM Level I Diagnosis)-Emotional* Disturbance
9. Origin of Evaluation Used in Determining Classification:
   - In-school _X_ Nonschool Personnel Evaluation _X_
10. Components of Present Evaluation:
    - Individual Standardized Testing _X_
    - Informal Assessment Measures _X_
      (Portfolio Assessment) Observation _X_
    - Social History _X_
    - Teacher Reports _X_
    - Interviews with Child _X_
    - Review of Medical Records _X_
11. Specific Areas Covered in Evaluation:
    - Intelligence Testing _X_
    - Academic Testing _X_
    - Medical Evaluation _X_
    - Speech Language Evaluation _____
    - Occupational Evaluation _____
    - Other (Be Specific) ________________
    - Audiometric Evaluation _____
    - Psychiatric Evaluation _X_
    - Psychological Evaluation _X_
    - Portfolio Assessment _X_

- Curriculum-Based Assessment _____
- Authentic Assessment __X__
- Task Analysis __X__
- Outcome-Based Assessment _____
- Learning Styles Assessment __X__

12. Committee Recommendations:
Classification (EDM Coding)

Level I: Emotional Disturbance, ED

Level II: Anxiety Reactive Disorder, ED 6.00.
Individuals with this disorder have a tendency to develop fears associated with personal or school problems.

Level III: School Avoidance Anxiety Reactive Disorder, ED 6.02.
Specifically, David has a type of Anxiety Reactive Disorder characterized by extreme anxiety manifested in an avoidance of school.

Individuals with this disorder may become very upset or ill when forced to go to school. They may stay in close contact with their parents or caregivers and are frequently (although not always) anxious and fearful. Truants may be distinguished from this group by their antisocial or delinquent behaviors, their lack of anxiety about missing school, and the fact that they are not in contact with parents or caregivers when they are avoiding school.

Level IV: Not Applicable

Level V: Moderate.
Moderate adverse effect implies a significant difference between the needs of the student with a disability when compared to the reasonable expectations of nondisabled peers of the same age and or grade level.

Level I: Emotional Disturbance, ED

Level II: Anxiety Reactive Disorder, ED 6.00.
Individuals with this disorder have a tendency to develop fears associated with personal or school problems.

Level III: Panic Reactive Disorder, ED 6.01.
David suffers from panic reactions. Individuals with this disorder may tend to exhibit in school high anxiety that is very sudden, appears unprovoked, and is often disabling.

Level IV: Not Applicable

Level V: Moderate.

Moderate adverse effect implies a significant difference between the needs of the student with a disability when compared to the reasonable expectations of nondisabled peers of the same age and or grade level.

Level I: Emotional Disturbance, ED

Level II: Inappropriate Behavior or Feelings, ED 3.00.

Individuals with this disorder exhibit inappropriate types of behavior or feelings under normal circumstances.

Level III: Disruptive Behavior Disorder ED 3.02.

David suffers from inappropriate behavior feelings that exhibit themselves in the form of disruptive behavior. This disorder may be characterized by defiance, hyperactivity, overactivity, making noises in class, calling out, touching other people or other people's property, and showing a complete disregard for the rights and property of others.

Level IV: Not Applicable

Level V: Moderate.

Moderate adverse effect implies a significant difference between the needs of the student with a disability when compared to the reasonable expectations of nondisabled peers of the same age and or grade level.

Level I: Emotional Disturbance, ED

Level II: Relationship Problems Disorder, ED 2.00.

Relationship problem disorder is characterized by an individual's inability to build or maintain satisfactory interpersonal relationships with peers and teachers. Furthermore, the individual exhibits inappropriate types of behavior or feelings under normal circumstances.

Level III: Not Applicable.

Level IV: Not Applicable

Level V: Moderate.

Moderate adverse effect implies a significant difference between the needs of the student with a disability when compared to the reasonable expectations of nondisabled peers of the same age and or grade level.

Level I: Emotional Disturbance, ED

Level II: Physical Complaints Disorder, ED 5.00.

David has a Physical Complaints Disorder. Individuals with this disorder have a tendency to develop physical symptoms associated with personal or school problems that significantly affect the child's ability to function in school. These physical systems are not connected to any medical problems but are considered psychological in nature. This disorder may be characterized by frequent headaches, stomachaches, somatic complaints, nausea, vomiting, diarrhea, or preoccupation with one's health.

Level III: Not Applicable

Level IV: Not Applicable

Level V: Moderate.

Moderate adverse effect implies a significant difference between the needs of the student with a disability when compared to the reasonable expectations of nondisabled peers of the same age and or grade level.

EDM IEP Format Without Explanations of the EDM Codes—Orthopedic Impairment Individualized Education Program

INDIVIDUALIZED EDUCATIONAL PROGRAM

School District/Agency: Lancaster School District
Name and Address: Lancaster, PA

Section I: Background Information

Student Name: *Lester Downs*

Date of Birth: *2/5/99* Age: *7*

Street: *45 Lake Rd.*

City: *Lancaster* Zip: *17685*

Date of Referral for Committee Review: *March 17, 2006*

Telephone: *768–0943* County of Residence: *Lancaster*

Male _X_ Female ___ Student ID#: *3786T* Current Grade: *2* Dominant Language of Student: *English* Interpreter Needed: Yes ___ No _X_

Medical Alerts: *none*

Mother's Name/Guardian's Name: *Mary*

Street Address: *same*

City: *same* Zip: *same*
Telephone: *same* County of Residence: *same*
Dominant Language of Parent/Guardian: *English* Interpreter Needed: Yes ___ No _X_
Father's Name/Guardian's Name: *Paul*
Street Address: *same*
City: *same* Zip: *same*
Telephone: *same* County of Residence: *same*
Dominant Language of Parent/Guardian: *English* Interpreter Needed: Yes ___ No _X_

Section II: Type of Meeting

A: Initial Evaluation

13. Date of Initial Evaluation Meeting: *March 8, 2006*
14. Area of Suspected Disability *(EDM Level I Diagnosis)-Orthopedic Impairment*
15. Origin of Evaluation Used in Determining Classification:
    - In-school __X__ Nonschool Personnel Evaluation __X__
16. Components of Present Evaluation:
    - Individual Standardized Testing __X__
    - Informal Assessment Measures __X__ (Portfolio Assessment) Observation __X__
    - Social History __X__
    - Teacher Reports __X__
    - Interviews with Child __X__
    - Review of Medical Records __X__
17. Specific Areas Covered in Evaluation:
    - Intelligence Testing __X__
    - Academic Testing __X__
    - Medical Evaluation __X__
    - Speech Language Evaluation _____
    - Occupational Evaluation __X__
    - Other (Be Specific)________________
    - Audiometric Evaluation _____

- Psychiatric Evaluation _____
- Psychological Evaluation __X__
- Portfolio Assessment __X__
- Curriculum-Based Assessment __X__
- Authentic Assessment __X__
- Task Analysis __X__
- Outcome-Based Assessment _____
- Learning Styles Assessment __X__

18. Committee Recommendations:
    Classification (EDM Coding)

    Level I: Orthopedic Impairment, OI

    Level II: Cerebral Palsy OI 2.00

    Level III: Spastic Cerebral Palsy, OI 2.04

    Level IV: Not Applicable

    Level V: Severe

IEP Format with Explanations of the EDM Codes

INDIVIDUALIZED EDUCATIONAL PROGRAM

School District/Agency: Lancaster School District

Name and Address: Lancaster, PA

Section I: Background Information

Student Name: *Lester Downs*

Date of Birth: *2/5/99* Age: *7*

Street: *45 Lake Rd.*

City: *Lancaster* Zip: *17685*

Date of Referral for Committee Review: *March 17, 2004*

Telephone: *768–0943* County of Residence: *Lancaster*

Male __X__ Female ___ Student ID#: *3786T* Current Grade: *2*

Dominant Language of Student: *English* Interpreter Needed: Yes ___ No _X_
Medical Alerts: *none*
Mother's Name/Guardian's Name: *Mary*
Street Address: *same*
City: *same* Zip: *same*
Telephone: *same* County of Residence: *same*
Dominant Language of Parent/Guardian: *English* Interpreter Needed: Yes ___ No _X_
Father's Name/Guardian's Name: *Paul*
Street Address: *same*
City: *same* Zip: *same*
Telephone: *same* County of Residence: *same*
Dominant Language of Parent/Guardian: *English* Interpreter Needed: Yes ___ No _X_

Section II: Type of Meeting

A: Initial Evaluation

19. Date of Initial Evaluation Meeting: *March 8, 2006*
20. Area of Suspected Disability *(EDM Level I Diagnosis)-Orthopedic Impairment*
21. Origin of Evaluation Used in Determining Classification:
    - In-school __X__ Nonschool Personnel Evaluation __X__
22. Components of Present Evaluation:
    - Individual Standardized Testing __X__
    - Informal Assessment Measures __X__ (Portfolio Assessment) Observation __X__
    - Social History __X__
    - Teacher Reports_ __X__
    - Interviews with Child __X__
    - Review of Medical Records __X__
23. Specific Areas Covered in Evaluation:
    - Intelligence Testing __X__
    - Academic Testing __X__
    - Medical Evaluation __X__
    - Speech Language Evaluation _____

- Occupational Evaluation __X__
- Other (Be Specific)________________
- Audiometric Evaluation _____
- Psychiatric Evaluation _____
- Psychological Evaluation __X__
- Portfolio Assessment __X__
- Curriculum-Based Assessment __X__
- Authentic Assessment __X__
- Task Analysis __X__
- Outcome-Based Assessment _____
- Learning Styles Assessment __X__

24. Committee Recommendations:
Classification (EDM Coding)

Level I: Orthopedic Impairment, OI

Level II: Cerebral Palsy, OI 2.0.

Lester has cerebral palsy, an umbrella term used to describe a group of chronic disorders impairing control of movement that appear in the first few years of life and generally do not worsen over time. The disorders are due to the effects of faulty development of or damage to motor areas in the brain that disrupts the brain's ability to control movement and posture. Symptoms of cerebral palsy include difficulty with fine motor tasks (such as writing or using scissors), difficulty maintaining balance or walking, and involuntary movements. The symptoms differ from person to person and may change over time.

Level III: Spastic Cerebral Palsy, OI 2.04.

Specifically, Lester has a type of cerebral palsy called spastic cerebral palsy, which occurs when the muscles are too tight. Patients have stiff and jerky movement and often have difficulty letting go of something in their hand. Approximately half of all those with cerebral palsy have spastic cerebral palsy Spastic cerebral palsy is divided into subcategories.

Level IV: Not Applicable

Level V: Severe.

Severe adverse effect implies a pervasive difference between the needs of the student with a disability when compared to the reasonable expectations of nondisabled peers of the same age and or grade level.

Conclusion

The EDM coding system allows for standardization, flexibility, depth of diagnosis, and practicality regardless of the IEP form chosen. When this coding system is used, students who move from their district or state can maintain the same level of services based on a standardized diagnosis.

Appendix A
Index of EDM Codes by Category

Specific Learning Disabilities (LD)

Speech and Language Impairments (SL)

Mental Retardation (MR)

Emotional Disturbance (ED)

Other Health Impairments (OHI)

Autism (AU)

Orthopedic Impairments (OI)

Hearing Impairments (HI)

Visual Impairments (VI)

Traumatic Brain Injury (TBI)

Deaf-Blindness (DB)

Early Intervention (EI)

Developmental Delay in Preschool Children (PS-DD)

Appendix B
Alphabetical Index of EDM Codes

Appendix C
Disability Clearinghouses and Organizations

Clearinghouses

Autism Information Center, Centers for Disease Control and Prevention, 1600 Clifton Rd., Atlanta, GA 30333; (800)CDC-INFO (232–4636); e-mail: bddi@cdc.gov; Web: www.cdc.gov/ncbddd/dd/aic/about/default.htm.

Cancer Information Service, National Cancer Institute, Room 3036A, 6116 Executive Blvd., MSC8322, Bethesda, MD 20892–8322; (800)422–6237 (voice), (800)332–8615 (TTY); e-mail: cancergovstaff@mail.nih.gov; Web: http://cancer.gov. Materials available in Spanish. Spanish speaker on staff.

Center on Positive Behavioral Interventions and Supports, 1761 Alder St., 1235 Univer-sity of Oregon, Eugene, OR 97403–5262; (541)346–2505, e-mail: pbis@uoregon.edu; Web: www.pbis.org. Materials available in Spanish.

Clearinghouse on Disability Information, Office of Special Education and Rehabilitative Services, Communication and Media Services, Room 3132, Switzer Building, 330 C St., S.W., Washington, DC 20202–2524; (202)205–8241 (voice), (202)205–0136 (TTY).

DB-LINK, National Information Clearinghouse on Children, Who Are Deaf-Blind, 345 N. Monmouth Avenue, Monmouth, OR 97361; (800)438–9376 (Voice), (800)854–7013 (TTY), e-mail: dblink@tr.wou.edu, Web: www.dblink.org. Materials available in Spanish.

ERIC Clearinghouse on Disabilities and Gifted Education, Council for Exceptional Children. This project is no longer in operation, but a substantial Web site of disability-related materials is still available: Web: http://ericec.org.

Fetal Alcohol Spectrum Disorders Center for Excellence, Center for Substance Abuse Prevention, Substance Abuse and Mental Health Services Administration, 2101 Gaither Rd., Suite 600, Rockville, MD 20850; (866)786–7327; e-mail via the Web: www.fascenter.samhsa.gov/about/contactUs/index.cfm, Web: http://www.fascenter.samhsa.gov/index.cfm.

Genetic and Rare Diseases Information Center, P.O. Box 8126, Gaithersburg, MD 20898–8126; (888)205–2311 (voice), (888)205–3223 (TTY); e-mail: gardinfo@nig.gov; Web: http://rarediseases.info.nih.gov/index.html. Spanish speaker on staff.

HEATH Resource Center, National Clearinghouse on Postsecondary Education for Individuals with Disabilities, George Washington University, 2121 K St., N.W., Suite 220, Washington, DC 20037; (800)544–3284 (V/TTY), (202)973–0904; e-mail: askheath@heath.gwu.edu; Web: www.heath.gwu.edu.

HRSA Information Center Health, Resources and Services Administration, U.S. Department of Health and Human Services, Parklawn Building, 5600 Fishers Lane, Rockville, MD 20857; (888)275–4772; e-mail: ask@hrsa.gov; Web: www.ask.hrsa.gov. For publications and resources on health care services for low-income, uninsured individuals and those with special health care needs. Publications available in Spanish. Spanish speaker on staff.

Laurent Clerc National Deaf Education Center and Clearinghouse, KDES PAS-6, 800 Florida Ave., N.E., Washington, DC 20002–3695; (202)651–5051 (voice), (202)651–5052 (TTY); e-mail: Clearinghouse.InfoToGo@gallaudet.edu; Web: http://clerccenter.gallaudet.edu/InfoToGo.

National Center on Birth Defects and Developmental Disabilities, Department of Health and Human Services, Centers for Disease Control and Prevention, 1600 Clifton Rd., Atlanta, GA 30333; (404)639–3534, (800)311–3435; e-mail: bddi@cdc.gov; Web: www.cdc.gov/ncbddd/.

National Center for Infectious Diseases, Centers for Disease Control and Prevention, Mailstop C-14, 1600 Clifton Rd., Atlanta, GA 30333; (404)639–3534, (800)311–3435; e-mail: use form at www.cdc.gov/ncidod/feedback1.htm; Web: www.cdc.gov/ncidod.

National Center on Secondary Education and Transition, University of Minnesota, 6 Pattee Hall, 150 Pillsbury Dr., S.E., Minneapolis, MN 55455; (612)624–2097; e-mail: ncset@umn.edu,; Web: www.ncset.org.

National Clearinghouse for Alcohol and Drug Information, P.O. Box 2345, Rockville, MD 20847–2345; (800)729–6686, (877)767–8432 (Spanish), (301)468–2600, (800)487–4899 (TTY); e-mail: info@health.org; Web: www.health.org. Materials available in Spanish. Spanish speaker on staff.

National Diabetes Information Clearinghouse, One Information Way, Bethesda, MD 20892; (800)860–8747, (301)654–3327; e-mail: ndic@info.niddk.nih.gov or via the Web at http://diabetes.niddk.nih.gov/about/contact.htm; Web: http://diabetes.niddk.nih.gov/about/index.htm. Materials available in Spanish.

National Digestive Diseases Information Clearinghouse, Two Information Way, Bethesda, MD 20892; (800)891–5389, (301)654–3810; e-mail: nddic@info.niddk.nih.gov or via the Web at http://digestive.niddk.nih.gov/about/contact.htm; Web: http://digestive.niddk.nih.gov/about/index.htm. Materials available in Spanish.

National Health Information Center, P.O. Box 1133, Washington, D.C. 20013–1133; (800) 336–4797, (301)565–4167; e-mail: info@nhic.org; Web: www.health.gov/nhic/. Materials available in Spanish. Spanish speaker on staff.

National Heart, Lung, and Blood Institute Information Center, P.O. Box 30105, Bethesda, MD 20824–0105; (800)575–9355, (301)592–8573, (240)629–3255 (TTY); e-mail: NHLBIinfo@rover.nhlbi.nih.gov; Web: www.nhlbi.nih.gov. Spanish speaker on staff.

National Institute of Allergy and Infectious Diseases, 31 Center Dr., MSC 2520, Building 31, Room 7A-50, Bethesda, MD 20892–2520; (301)496–2263; Web: www.niaid.nih.gov.

National Institute of Arthritis and Musculoskeletal, and Skin Diseases, Information Clearinghouse, 1 AMS Circle, Bethesda, MD 20892–3675; (877)226–4267, (301)495–4484 (voice), (301)565–2966 (TTY); e-mail: NIAMSinfo@mail.nih.gov; Web: www.niams.nih.gov. Materials available in Spanish. Spanish speaker on staff.

National Institute of Neurological Disorders and Stroke, NIH Neurological Institute, P.O. Box 5801, Bethesda, MD 20824; (800)352–9424, (301)496–5751, (301)468–5981(TTY); e-mail via the Web: http://www.ninds.nih.gov/contact_us.htm; Web: www.ninds.nih.gov. Materials available in Spanish. Spanish speaker on staff.

National Institute on Deafness and Other Communication Disorders Clearinghouse, 31 Center Drive, MCS 2320, Bethesda, MD 20892–3456; (800)241–1044 (voice), (800)241–1055 (TTY); e-mail: nidcdinfo@nidcd.nih.gov; Web: www.nidcd.nih.gov. Materials available in Spanish. Spanish speaker on staff.

National Institute on Mental Health, Public Inquiries, 6001 Executive Blvd., Room 8184, MSC 9663, Bethesda, MD 20892–9663; (866)615–6464, (301)443–4513 (voice), (301)443–8431 (TTY), e-mail: nimhinfo@nih.gov; Web: www.nimh.nih.gov/publicat/index.cfm. Materials available in Spanish. Spanish speaker on staff.

National Kidney and Urologic Diseases Information Clearinghouse, Three Information Way, Bethesda, MD 20892; (800)891–5390, (301)654–3327; e-mail: nkudic@info.niddk.nih.gov or via the Web at http://kidney.niddk.nih.gov/about/contact.htm; Web: http://kidney.niddk.nih.gov/about/index.htm. Materials available in Spanish.

National Lead Information Center, 422 South Clinton Avenue, Rochester, NY 14620; (800)424–5323; e-mail via the Web site; Web: www.epa.gov/lead/nlic.htm. Materials available in Spanish. Spanish speaker on staff.

National Organization for Rare Disorders, P.O. Box 1968, Danbury, CT 06813–1968; (800)999–6673, (203)744–0100 (voice), (203) 797–9590 (TTY); e-mail: orphan@rarediseases.org; Web: www.rarediseases.org.

National Rehabilitation Information Center, 4200 Forbes Boulevard, Suite 202, Lanham, MD 20706; (800)346–2742, (301)459–5900, (301) 59–5984 (TTY); e-mail: naricinfo@heitechservices.com; Web: www.naric.com.

Research and Training Center on Family Support and Children's Mental Health, Portland State University, P.O. Box 751, Portland, OR 97207–0751; (503)725–4040 (voice), (503)725–4165 (TTY); e-mail: gordon1@pdx.edu; Web: www.rtc.pdx.edu/. Materials available in Spanish. Spanish speaker on staff.

Research and Training Center on Independent Living, University of Kansas, 4089 Dole Building, 1000 Sunnyside Ave., Lawrence, KS 66045–7555; (785)864–4095 (voice), (785)864–0706 (TTY); e-mail: rtcil@ku.edu; Web: www.rtcil.org. Materials available in Spanish.

Weight-Control Information Network, 1 WIN Way, Bethesda, MD 20892–3665; (202)828–1025, (877)946–4627; e-mail: win@info.niddk.nih.gov; Web: http://win.niddk.nih.gov/index.htm.

Organizations

Alexander Graham Bell Association for the Deaf and Hard of Hearing, 3417 Volta Pl., N.W., Washington, DC 20007; (866)337–5220, (202)337–5220 (voice), (202) 337–5221 (TTY); e-mail: parents@agbell.org; Web: www.agbell.org. Materials available in Spanish. Spanish speaker on staff.

Alliance for Technology Access, 1304 Southpoint Blvd., Suite 240, Petaluma, CA 94954; (707)778–3011, (707)778–3015 (TTY); e-mail: atainfo@ataccess.org; Web: www.ataccess.org.

American Academy of Special Education Professionals, Metro Center, 700 12th Street, N.W., Suite 700, Washington DC 20005; (800)754-4421.

American Association of Kidney Patients, 3505 Frontage Rd., Suite 315, Tampa, FL 33607; (800)749–2257, (813)636–8100; e-mail: info@aakp.org; Web: www.aakp.org. Materials available in Spanish. Spanish speaker on staff.

American Association of Suicidology, 5221 Wisconsin Avenue, N.W., Washington, DC 20015; (800)273–8255, (202)237–2280, e-mail: info@suicidology.org; Web: www.suicidology.org.

American Brain Tumor Association, 2720 River Rd., Des Moines, IA 60018; (847)827–9910, (800)886–2282 (Patient Services); e-mail: info@abta.org; Web: www.abta.org/. One publication in Spanish.

American Council of the Blind, 1155 15th St., N.W., Suite 1004, Washington, DC 20005; (800)424–8666, (202)467–5081; e-mail: info@acb.org; Web: www.acb.org.

American Diabetes Association, 1701 North Beauregard St., Alexandria, VA 22311; (800)342–2383, (703)549–1500; e-mail: AskADA@diabetes.org; Web: www.diabetes.org. Materials available in Spanish. Spanish speaker on staff.

American Foundation for the Blind, 11 Penn Plaza, Suite 300, New York, NY 10001; (800)232–5463, (212)502–7662 (TTY); e-mail: afbinfo@afb.net; Web: www.afb.org. Materials available in Spanish, Spanish speaker on staff.

American Heart Association-National Center, 7272 Greenville Avenue, Dallas, TX 75231; (800)242–8721, (214)373–6300; e-mail: inquire@amhrt.org; Web: www.americanheart.org. Materials available in Spanish.

American Liver Foundation, 75 Maiden Lane, Suite 603, New York, NY 10038; (800)465–4872, (888)443–7872, (212)668–1000; e-mail: info@liverfoundation.org; Web: www.liverfoundation.org. Materials available in Spanish.

American Lung Association, 61 Broadway, 6th Floor, New York, NY 10006; (800)586–4872, (212)315–8700; e-mail via Web site; Web: www.lungusa.org/. Materials available in Spanish. Spanish speaker on staff.

American Occupational Therapy Association, 4720 Montgomery Lane, P.O. Box 31220, Bethesda, MD 20824–1220; (301)652–2682 (voice), (800)377–8555 (TTY); Web: www.aota.org.

American Physical Therapy Association, 1111 North Fairfax St., Alexandria, VA 22314; (800)999–2782, (703)684–2782 (voice), (703)683–6748 (TTY); e-mail: practice@apta.org; Web: www.apta.org. Materials available in Spanish. Spanish speaker on staff.

American Society for Deaf Children, P.O. Box 3355, Gettysburg, PA 17325; (800)942–2732, (717)334–7922 (V/TTY); e-mail: asdc@deafchildren.org; Web: www.deafchildren.org.

American Speech-Language-Hearing Association, 10801 Rockville Pike, Rockville, MD 20852; (800)638–8255, (301)897–5700 (TTY); e-mail: actioncenter@asha.org; Web: www.asha.org. Materials available in Spanish. Spanish speaker on staff.

American Syringomyelia Alliance Project, P.O. Box 1586, Longview, TX 75606–1586; (800)272–7282, (903)236–7079; e-mail: info@asap.org; Web: www.asap.org.

American Therapeutic Recreation Association, 1414 Prince St., Suite 204, Alexandria, VA 22314; (703)683–9420; e-mail: atra@atra-tr.org; Web: www.atra-tr.org.

Angelman Syndrome Foundation, 3015 East New York St., Suite A2265, Aurora, IL 60504; (805)432–6435, (630)978–4245; e-mail: info@angelman.org; Web: www.angelman.org. Materials available in Spanish.

Anxiety Disorders Association of America, 8730 Georgia Ave., Suite 600, Silver Spring, MD 20910; (240)485–1001; e-mail: AnxDis@adaa.org; Web: www.adaa.org.

Aplastic Anemia and MDS International Foundation, P.O. Box 613, Annapolis, MD 21404–0613; (800)747–2820, (410)867–0242; e-mail: help@aamds.org; Web: www.aamds.org. Materials available in Spanish. Spanish speaker on staff.

The Arc (formerly the Association for Retarded Citizens of the U.S.), 1010 Wayne Ave., Suite 650, Silver Spring, MD 20910; (301)565–3842; e-mail: Info@thearc.org; Web: www.thearc.org.

ARCH National Respite Network and Resource Center, Chapel Hill Training-Outreach Project, 800 Eastowne Dr., Suite 105, Chapel Hill, NC 27514; (800)773–5433 (National Respite Locator Service); (919)490–5577; Web: www.archrespite.org.

Arthritis Foundation, P.O. Box 7669, Atlanta, GA 30357; (800)568–4045, (404)872–7100; e-mail: help@arthritis.org; Web: www.arthritis.org. Materials available in Spanish. Spanish speaker on staff.

Asthma and Allergy Foundation of America; 1233 20th St., N.W., Suite 402, Washington, DC 20036; (800)727–8462, (202)466–7643; e-mail: info@aafa.org; Web: www.aafa.org/. Materials available in Spanish.

Autism Society of America, 7910 Woodmont Ave., Suite 300, Bethesda, MD 20814–3015; (800)328–8476, (301)657–0881;, e-mail: info@autism-society.org; Web: www.autism-society.org. Materials available in Spanish.

Beach Center on Disability, University of Kansas, Haworth Hall, Room 3136, 1200 Sunnyside Ave., Lawrence, KS 66045–7534; (785)864–7600, (785)864–3434 (TTY); e-mail: beachcenter@ku.edu; Web: www.beachcenter.org.

Best Buddies International, 100 S.E. Second St., Suite 1990, Miami, FL 33131; (800)892–8339, (305)374–2233, e-mail: info@bestbuddies.org; Web: www.bestbuddies.org.

Blind Childrens Center, 4120 Marathon St., Los Angeles, CA 90029–0159; (323)664–2153, (800)222–3566; e-mail: info@blindchildrenscenter.org; Web: www.blindchildrenscenter.org. Materials available in Spanish. Spanish speaker on staff.

Brain Injury Association of America, 8201 Greensboro Dr., Suite 611, McLean, VA 22102; (703)761–0750, (800)444–6443, e-mail: FamilyHelpline@biausa.org; Web: www.biausa.org. Materials available in Spanish. Spanish speaker on staff.

CADRE (Consortium for Appropriate Dispute Resolution in Special Education), Direction Service, P.O. Box 51360, Eugene, OR 97405–0906; (541)686–5060, (541)284–4740 (TTY), (800)695–0285 (NICHCY); e-mail: cadre@directionservice.org; Web: www.directionservice.org/cadre. Materials available in Spanish. Spanish speaker on staff.

Center for Effective Collaboration and Practice (Improving Services for Children and Youth with Emotional and Behavioral Problems), 1000 Thomas Jefferson St., N.W., Suite 400, Washington, DC 20007; (888)457–1551, (202)944–5300, (877)334–3499 (TTY); e-mail: center@air.org; Web: http://cecp.air.org.

Center for Evidence Based Practice: Young Children with Challenging Behavior, Louis de la Parte Florida Mental Health Institute, University of South Florida, 13301 Bruce B. Downs Blvd., Tampa, FL 33612–3807; (813)974–6111, e-mail: dunlap@fmhi.usf.edu; Web: http://challengingbehavior.fmhi.usf.edu.

Center for Universal Design, North Carolina State University, College of Design, Campus Box 8613, Raleigh, NC 27695–8613; (800)647–6777, (919)515–3082 (V/TTY); e-mail: cud@ncsu.edu; Web: www.design.ncsu.edu/cud.

Child and Adolescent Bipolar Foundation, 1000 Skokie Blvd., Suite 425, Wilmette, IL 60091; (847)256–8525, e-mail: cabf@bpkids.org; Web: www.bpkids.org. Materials available in Spanish. Spanish speaker on staff.

Childhood Apraxia of Speech Association of North America, 123 Eisele Rd., Cheswick, PA 15024; (412)767–6589, (412)343–7102; e-mail: helpdesk@apraxia-kids.org; Web: www.apraxia-kids.org.

Children and Adults with Attention-Deficit/Hyperactivity Disorder, 8181 Professional Place, Suite 150, Landover, MD 20785; (301)306–7070, (800)233–4050 (to request information packet); Web: www.chadd.org. Materials available in Spanish. Spanish speaker on staff.

Children's Craniofacial Association, 13140 Coit Rd., Suite 307, Dallas, TX 75240; (800)535–3643, (214)570–9099; e-mail: contactCCA@ccakids.com; Web: www.ccakids.com.

Children's Liver Alliance; e-mail: mail@liverkids.org.au, Web: http://www.liverkids.org.au. Web site only.

Children's Tumor Foundation (formerly National Neurofibromatosis Foundation), 95 Pine St., 16th Floor, New York, NY 10005; (800)323–7938, (212)344–6633; e-mail: info@ctf.org; Web: www.ctf.org. Materials available in Spanish. Spanish speaker on staff.

Chronic Fatigue and Immune Dysfunction Syndrome Association, P.O. Box 220398, Charlotte, NC 28222–0398; (800)442–3437, (704)365–2343; e-mail: cfids@cfids.org; Web: www.cfids.org.

Closing the Gap, P.O. Box 68, 526 Main St., Henderson, MN 56044; (507)248–3294; Web: www.closingthegap.com. For information on computer technology in special education and rehabilitation.

Consortium for Appropriate Dispute Resolution in Special Education. See CADRE.

Council for Exceptional Children, 1110 N. Glebe Rd., Suite 300, Arlington, VA 22201–5704; (888)232–7733, (866)915–5000 (TTY); (703)620–3660, e-mail: service@cec.sped.org; Web: www.cec.sped.org/.

Craniofacial Foundation of America, 975 East Third St., Box 269, Chattanooga, TN 37403; (800)418–3223, (423)778–9192; e-mail: farmertm@erlanger.org; Web: www.erlanger.org/craniofacial/found1.html. Materials available in Spanish. Spanish speaker on staff.

Crohn's and Colitis Foundation of America, 386 Park Ave. South, 17th Floor, New York, NY 10016; (800)932–2423, (212)685–3440; e-mail: info@ccfa.org; Web: www.ccfa.org, Materials available online only in Spanish. Spanish speaker on staff.

Cystic Fibrosis Foundation, 6931 Arlington Rd., Bethesda, MD 20814; (800)344–4823, (301)951–4422; e-mail: info@cff.org, Web: www.cff.org. Materials available in Spanish. Spanish speaker on staff.

Depression and Bipolar Support Alliance, 730 N. Franklin St., Suite 501, Chicago, IL 60610; (800)326–3632, (312)642–0049; e-mail: questions@dbsalliance.org, Web: www.dbsalliance.org. Materials available in Spanish. Spanish speaker on staff.

Disability Statistics Rehabilitation, Research and Training Center, 3333 California St., Room 340, University of California at San Francisco, San Francisco, CA 94118l (415)502–5210 (voice), (415)502–5216 (TTY)l e-mail: distats@itsa.ucsf.edu; Web: www.dsc.ucsf.edu.

Disabled Sports USA, 451 Hungerford Drive, Suite 100, Rockville, MD 20850; (301)217–0960 (voice), (301)217–0963 (TTY); e-mail: Information@dsusa.org; Web: www.dsusa.org.

Easter Seals—National Office, 230 West Monroe St., Suite 1800, Chicago, IL 60606l (800)221–6827, (312)726–6200 (voice), (312)726–4258 (TTY); e-mail: info@easter-seals.org; Web: www.easter-seals.org. Materials available in Spanish. Spanish speaker on staff.

Epilepsy Foundation—National Office, 4351 Garden City Dr., 5th Floor, Landover, MD 20785–4941; (800)332–1000, (301)459–3700; e-mail via the Web site; Web: www.epilepsyfoundation.org. Materials available in Spanish. Spanish speaker on staff.

FACES: The National Craniofacial Association, P.O. Box 11082, Chattanooga, TN 37401, (800)332–2373, (423)266–1632, e-mail: faces@faces-cranio.org, Web: www.faces-cranio.org

Family Center for Technology and Disabilities, Academy for Educational Development, 1825 Connecticut Ave., N.W., 7th Floor, Washington, DC; 20009–5721; (202)884–8068; e-mail: fctd@aed.org; Web: www.fctd.info.

Family Empowerment Network: Support for Families Affected by FAS/E, 772 S. Mills St., Madison, WI 53715; (800)462–5254, (608)262–6590; e-mail: fen@fammed.wisc.edu; Web: www.fammed.wisc.edu/fen.

Family Resource Center on Disabilities, 20 East Jackson Boulevard, Room 300, Chicago, IL 60604; (800)952–4199 (voice/TTY, toll free in Illinois only); (312)939–3513 (voice), (312)939–3519 (TTY); Web: www.frcd.org/. Materials available in Spanish. Spanish speaker on staff.

Family Village, Waisman Center, University of Wisconsin-Madison, 1500 Highland Ave., Madison, WI 53705–2280; (608)263–5776 (voice), (608)263–0802 (TTY); e-mail: familyvillage@waisman.wisc.edu; Web: www.familyvillage.wisc.edu/. A global community of disability-related resources.

Family Voices, 2340 Alamo SE, Suite 102, Albuquerque, NM 87106; (888)835–5669, (505)872–4774; e-mail: kidshealth@familyvoices.org; Web: www.familyvoices.org, Materials available in Spanish. A national coalition speaking for children with special health care needs.

Federation of Families for Children's Mental Health, 1101 King St., Suite 420, Alexandria, VA 22314; (703)684–7710; e-mail: ffcmh@ffcmh.com; Web: www.ffcmh.org, Materials available in Spanish.

First Signs, P.O. Box 358, Merrimac, MA 01860; (978)346–4380; e-mail: info@firstsigns.org; Web: www.firstsigns.org.

Forward Face, 317 East 34th St., Suite 901A, New York, NY 10016; (212)684–5860; e-mail: info@forwardface.org; Web: www.forwardface.org. An organization for children with craniofacial conditions.

Foundation for Ichthyosis and Related Skin Types, 1601 Valley Forge Rd., Lansdale, PA 19446; (800)545–3286, (215)631–1411; e-mail: info@scalyskin.org; Web: www.scalyskin.org. Materials available in Spanish.

Genetic Alliance, 4301 Connecticut, N.W., Suite 404, Washington, DC 20008; (800)336–4363, (202)966–5557; e-mail: info@geneticalliance.org; Web: www.geneticalliance.org. Materials available in Spanish.

Head Start Bureau, Administration on Children, Youth and Families, U.S. Department of Health and Human Services, P.O. Box 1182, Washington, DC 20013; Web: www.acf.dhhs.gov/programs/hsb/.

Human Growth Foundation, 997 Glen Cove Ave., Suite 5, Glen Head, NY 11545; (800)451–6434; e-mail: hgf1@hgfound.org; Web: www.hgfound.org, Materials available in Spanish.

Huntington's Disease Society of America, 158 West 29th St., 7th Floor, New York, NY 10001–5300; (800)345–4372, (212)242–1968; e-mail: hdsainfo@hdsa.org; Web: www.hdsa.org. Materials available in Spanish.

Hydrocephalus Association, 870 Market St. #705, San Francisco, CA 94102; (888)598–3789, (415)732–7040;, e-mail: info@hydroassoc.org; Web: www.hydroassoc.org. Materials available in Spanish.

IBM Accessibility Center, 11400 Burnet Rd., Austin, TX 78758; (800)426–4832 (voice), (800)426–4833 (TTY); e-mail via the Web site; Web: www-3.ibm.com/able/index.html.

Immune Deficiency Foundation, 40 W. Chesapeake Ave., Suite 308, Towson, MD 21204; (800)296–4433; e-mail: idf@primaryimmune.org; Web: www.primaryimmune.org. Materials available in Spanish.

Independent Living Research Utilization Project, Institute for Rehabilitation and Research, 2323 South Sheppard, Suite 1000, Houston, TX 77019; (713)520–0232 (voice/TTY); e-mail: ilru@ilru.org. Web: www.ilru.org, Spanish speaker on staff.

International Dyslexia Association (formerly the Orton Dyslexia Society), Chester Building #382, 8600 LaSalle Rd., Baltimore, MD 21286–2044; (800)222–3123, (410)296–0232; e-mail: info@interdys.org; Web: www.interdys.org. Materials available in Spanish.

International Resource Center for Down Syndrome, Keith Building, 1621 Euclid Ave., Suite 802, Cleveland, OH 44115; (216)621–5858, (800)899–3039 (toll free in Ohio only).

International Rett Syndrome Association, 9121 Piscataway Rd., Clinton, MD 20735–2561; (800)818–7388, (301)856–3334; e-mail: irsa@rettsyndrome.org; Web: www.rettsyndrome.org. Materials available in Spanish.

Internet Mental Health; e-mail: internetmentalhealth@telus.net; Web: www.mentalhealth.com. Web site only.

Job Accommodation Network, West Virginia University, P.O. Box 6080, Morgantown, WV 26506–6080; (800)526–7234 (voice/TTY), (800)232–9675 (voice/TTY; information on the Americans with Disabilities Act); e-mail: jan@jan.wvu.edu; Web: www.jan.wvu.edu. Materials available in Spanish. Spanish speaker on staff.

Kristin Brooks Hope Center, 2001 N. Beauregard St., 12th floor, Alexandria, VA 22311; (800)784–2433 (National Hopeline Network), (703)837–3364; e-mail: info@hopeline.com; Web: www.livewithdepression.org.

LDOnline; Web: www.ldonline.org. Spanish site: www.ldonline.org/ccldinfo/spanish index.html. Web site on learning disabilities.

Learning Disabilities Association of America, 4156 Library Rd., Pittsburgh, PA 15234; (412)341–1515, e-mail: info@ldaamerica.org; Web: www.ldaamerica.org.

Let's Face It USA, P.O. Box 29972, Bellingham, WA 98228–1972; (360)676–7325; e-mail: letsfaceit@faceit.org; Web: www.faceit.org. For information and support on facial differences.

Leukemia and Lymphoma Society (formerly Leukemia Society of America), 1311 Mamaronack Ave., White Plains, NY 10605, (800)955–4572; (914)949–5213; e-mail: infocenter@leukemia-lymphoma.org; Web: www.leukemia-lymphoma.org, or www.leukemia.org. Materials available in Spanish. Spanish speaker on staff.

Little People of America—National Headquarters, 5289 N.E. Elam Young Parkway, Suite F-100, Hillsboro, OR 97124, (888)572–2001; e-mail: info@lpaonline.org; Web: www.lpaonline.org. Spanish speaker on staff.

Lupus Foundation of America, 2000 L St., N.W., Suite 710, Washington, DC 20036; (800)558–0121, (800)558–0231 (Spanish), (202)349–1155; e-mail: info@lupus.org; Web: www.lupus.org. Materials available in Spanish. Spanish speaker on staff.

MAAP Services for the Autism Spectrum, P.O. Box 524, Crown Point, IN 46308; (219)662–1311; e-mail: chart@netnitco.net; Web: www.maapservices.org.

MAGIC Foundation (Major Aspects of Growth Disorders in Children), 6645 W. North Ave., Oak Park, IL 60302; (708)383–0808; e-mail: mary@magicfoundation.org; Web: www.magicfoundation.org.

March of Dimes Birth Defects Foundation, 1275 Mamaroneck Ave., White Plains, NY 10605; (914)428–7100, (888)663–4637; e-mail: askus@marchofdimes.com; Web: www.marchofdimes.com, Spanish site: www.nacersano.org. Materials available in Spanish. Spanish speaker on staff.

Mental Help Net; Web: http://mentalhelp.net. Web site only.

MUMS, National Parent-to-Parent Network, 150 Custer Ct., Green Bay, WI 54301–1243; (920)336–5333, (877)336–5333 (parents only); e-mail: mums@netnet.net; Web: www.netnet.net/mums/.

Muscular Dystrophy Association, 3300 East Sunrise Dr., Tucson, AZ 85718; (800)572–1717, (520)529–2000; e-mail: mda@mdausa.org; Web: www.mdausa.org. Web site in Spanish: www.mdaenespanol.org. Materials available in Spanish. Spanish speaker on staff.

National Alliance for the Mentally Ill, Colonial Place Three, 2107 Wilson Blvd., Suite 300, Arlington, VA 22201–3042; (800)950–6264, (703)524–7600, (703)516–7227 (TTY); e-mail: info@nami.org; Web: www.nami.org. Materials available in Spanish.

National Association for the Dually Diagnosed, 132 Fair St., Kingston, NY 12401; (800)331–5362, (845)331–4336; e-mail: info@thenadd.org; Web: www.thenadd.org. For mental illness and mental retardation.

National Association of the Deaf, 814 Thayer Ave., Suite 250, Silver Spring, MD 20910; (301)587–1788, (301)587–1789 (TTY); e-mail: nadinfo@nad.org; Web: www.nad.org.

National Association of Hospital Hospitality Houses, P.O. Box 18087, Asheville, NC 28814–0087; (800)542–9730, (828)253–1188; Web: helpinghomes@nahhh.org .

National Association of Parents with Children in Special Education, 1201 Pennsylvania Avenue N.W., Suite 300, Washington DC 20004; (800) 754-4421 e-mail: contact@napcse.org

National Association of Private Special Education Centers, 1522 K St. N.W., Suite 1032, Washington, DC 20005; (202)408–3338; e-mail: napsec@aol.com; Web: www.napsec.com.

National Association of Protection and Advocacy Systems, 900 Second St., N.E., Suite 211, Washington, DC 20002; (202)408–9514 (voice), (202)408–9521 (TTY); e-mail: info@napas.org; Web: .

National Association of Special Education Teachers, 1201 Pennsylvania Avenue N.W., Suite 300, Washington DC 20004; (800) 754–4421 e-mail: contactus@naset.org.

National Ataxia Foundation, 2600 Fernbrook Lane, Suite 119, Minneapolis, MN 55447; (763)553–0020; e-mail: naf@ataxia.org; Web: www.ataxia.org. Materials available in Spanish.

National Attention Deficit Disorder Association, P.O. Box 543, Pottstown, PA 19464; (484)944–2101; e-mail: mail@add.org; Web: www.add.org.

National Brain Tumor Foundation, 22 Battery St., Suite 612, San Francisco, CA 94111; (800)934–2873, (415)834–9970; e-mail: nbtf@braintumor.org; Web: www.braintumor.org. Materials available in Spanish. Spanish speaker on staff.

National Center for Learning Disabilities, 381 Park Ave. South, Suite 1401, New York, NY 10016; (212)545–7510, (888)575–7373; e-mail: help@getreadytoread.org; Web: www.ld.org, www.getreadytoread.org. Materials available in Spanish.

National Center for PTSD (Post-Traumatic Stress Disorder), VA Medical Center (116D), 215 North Main St., White River Junction, VT 05009; (802)296–6300; e-mail: ncptsd@ncptsd.org; Web: www.ncptsd.org.

National Center for Special Education Personnel and Related Service Providers, 1800 Diagonal Rd., Suite 320, Alexandria, VA 22314; (866)232–6631, (703)519–3800 Ext. 333, (703)519–7008 (TTY); e-mail: use form at www.personnelcenter.org/contactus.cfm; Web: www.personnelcenter.org.

National Center on Physical Activity and Disability, 1640 W. Roosevelt Rd., Chicago, IL 60608–6904; (800)900–8086 (V/TTY); e-mail: ncpad@uic.edu; Web: www.ncpad.org. Materials available in Spanish. Spanish speaker on staff.

National Chronic Fatigue Syndrome and Fibromyalgia Association, P.O. Box 18426, Kansas City, MO 64133; (816)313–2000; e-mail: information@ncfsfa.org; Web: www.ncfsfa.org.

National Council on Independent Living, 1916 Wilson Blvd., Suite 209, Arlington, VA 22201; (877)525–3400 (V/TTY), (703)525–3406, (703)525–4153 (TTY); e-mail: ncil@ncil.org; Web: www.ncil.org. Spanish speaker on staff.

National Down Syndrome Congress, 1370 Center Drive, Suite 102, Atlanta, GA 30338; (800)232–6372, (770)604–9500; e-mail: info@ndsccenter.org; Web: www.ndsccenter.org. Parent packet available in Spanish.

National Down Syndrome Society, 666 Broadway, 8th Floor, New York, NY 10012–2317; (800)221–4602, (212)460–9330; e-mail: info@ndss.org; Web: http://ndss.org; Materials available in Spanish. Spanish speaker on staff.

National Eating Disorders Association (formerly Eating Disorders Awareness and Prevention), 603 Stewart St., Suite 803, Seattle, WA 98101; (800)931–2237, (206)382–3587,; e-mail: info@NationalEatingDisorders.org; Web: www.nationaleatingdisorders.org. Materials available in Spanish.

National Federation for the Blind, 1800 Johnson St., Baltimore, MD 21230; (410)659–9314; e-mail: nfb@nfb.org, Web: www.nfb.org. Materials available in Spanish. Spanish speaker on staff.

National Fragile X Foundation, P.O. Box 190488, San Francisco, CA 94119–0488; (800)688–8765, (925)938–9315; e-mail: NATLFX@FragileX.org; Web: www.fragilex.org. Materials available in Spanish.

National Gaucher Foundation, 5410 Edson Lane, Suite 260, Rockville, MD 20852–3130; (800)428–2437, (301)816–1515; e-mail: ngf@gaucherdisease.org; Web: www.gaucherdisease.org.

National Kidney Foundation, 30 East 33rd St., New York, NY 10016; (800)622–9010, (212)889–2210; e-mail: info@kidney.org; Web: www.kidney.org. Materials available in Spanish.

National Library Service for the Blind and Physically Handicapped, Library of Congress, 1291 Taylor St. N.W., Washington, DC 20011; (800)424–8567, (202)707–5100 (voice), (202)707–0744 (TTY); e-mail: nls@loc.gov; Web: www.loc.gov/nls. Materials available in Spanish. Spanish speaker on staff.

National Limb Loss Information Center, Amputee Coalition of America, 900 East Hill Ave., Suite 285, Knoxville, TN 37915–2568; (888)267–5669; e-mail: nllicinfo@amputee-coalition.org; Web: www.amputee-coalition.org/nllic_about.html. Materials available in Spanish.

National Lymphedema Network, 1611 Telegraph Ave., Suite 1111, Oakland, CA 94612; (800)541–3259, (510)208–3200; e-mail: nln@lymphnet.org; Web: www.lymphnet.org.

National Mental Health Association, 2001 N. Beauregard, 12th Floor, Alexandria, VA 22311; (800)969–6642, (703)684–7722, (800)433–5959 (TTY); e-mail via the Web site; Web: www.nmha.org. Materials available in Spanish. Spanish speaker on staff.

National Mental Health Information Center (formerly Knowledge Exchange Network), P.O. Box 42557, Washington, DC 20015; (800)789–2647, (866)889–2647 (TTY); Web: www.mentalhealth.org. Materials available in Spanish. Spanish speaker on staff.

National Multiple Sclerosis Society, 733 Third Ave., New York, NY 10017; (800)344–4867; e-mail via the Web site; Web: www.nationalmssociety.org. Materials available in Spanish. Spanish speaker on staff.

National Organization for Albinism and Hypopigmentation; P.O. Box 959, East Hampstead, NH 03826–0959; (800)473–2310, (603)887–2310; e-mail: webmaster@albinism.org; Web: www.albinism.org. Materials available in Spanish.

National Organization on Disability, 910 16th St., N.W., Suite 600, Washington, DC 20006; (202)293–5960 (voice), (202)293–5968 (TTY); e-mail: ability@nod.org; Web: www.nod.org. Spanish speaker on staff.

National Organization on Fetal Alcohol Syndrome, 900 17th St., N.W., Suite 910, Washington, DC 20006; (800)666–6327, (202)785–4585; e-mail: information@nofas.org; Web: www.nofas.org. Materials available in Spanish. Spanish speaker on staff.

National Patient Air Transport Hotline, c/o Mercy Medical Airlift, 4620 Haygood Rd., Suite 1, Virginia Beach, VA 23445; (800)296–1217, (757)318–9174; e-mail: mercymedical@erols.com; Web: www.patienttravel.org.

National Resource Center for Family Centered Practice, University of Iowa, 100 Oakdale Hall, W206 OH, Iowa City, IA 52242–5000; (319)335–4965; Web: www.uiowa.edu/~nrcfcp. Materials available in Spanish. Spanish speaker on staff.

National Resource Center for Paraprofessionals in Education and Related Services, 6526 Old Main Hill, Utah State University, Logan, UT 84322–6526; (435)797–7272; e-mail: twallace@nrcpara.org; Web: www.nrcpara.org.

National Resource Center on Supported Living and Choice, Syracuse University, Center on Human Policy, 805 S. Crouse Ave., Syracuse, NY 13244–2280; (800)894–0826, (315)443–3851, (315)443–4355 (TTY); e-mail: thechp@sued.syr.edu; Web: http://thechp.syr.edu/nrc.html.

National Reye's Syndrome Foundation, P.O. Box 829, Bryan, OH 43506; (800)233–7393, (419)636–2679; e-mail: nrsf@reyessyndrome.org; Web: www.reyessyndrome.org. Materials available in Spanish.

National Scoliosis Foundation, 5 Cabot Place, Stoughton, MA 02072; (800)673–6922, (781)341–6333; e-mail: NSF@scoliosis.org; Web: www.scoliosis.org. Materials available in Spanish.

National Sleep Foundation, 1522 K St., N.W., Suite 500, Washington, DC 20005; (202)347–3471; e-mail: nsf@sleepfoundation.org; Web: www.sleepfoundation.org. Materials available in Spanish.

National Spinal Cord Injury Association, 6701 Democracy Blvd., Suite 300–9, Bethesda, MD 20817; (800)962–9629, (301)214–4006; e-mail: info@spinalcord.org; Web: www.spinalcord.org. Spanish speaker on staff.

National Stuttering Association, 119 W. 40th St., 14th Floor, New York, NY 10018; (800)937–8888; e-mail: info@westutter.org; Web: www.westutter.org.

National Tay-Sachs and Allied Diseases Association, 2001 Beacon St., Suite 204, Brighton, MA 02135; (800)906–8723; e-mail: info@ntsad.org; Web: www.ntsad.org. Materials available in Spanish.

Neurofibromatosis, 9320 Annapolis Rd., Suite 300, Lanham, MD 20706–3123; (800)942–6825, (301)918–4600; e-mail: nfinfo@nfinc.org, Web: www.nfinc.org. Materials available in Spanish.

NLD (Nonverbal Learning Disorder); Web: www.NLDontheweb.org. Web site only.

Nonverbal Learning Disorders Association, 2446 Albany Ave., West Hartford, CT 06117; (800)570–0217; e-mail: NLDA@nlda.org; Web: www.nlda.org.

Obsessive Compulsive Foundation, 676 State St., New Haven, CT 06511; (203)401–2070, e-mail: info@ocfoundation.org; Web: www.ocfoundation.org. Materials available in Spanish. Spanish speaker on staff.

Online Asperger Syndrome Information and Support; www.udel.edu/bkirby/asperger/frame1.html. Web site only.

Osteogenesis Imperfecta Foundation, 804 Diamond Ave., Suite 210, Gaithersburg, MD 20878; (800)981–2663, (301)947–0083; e-mail: bonelink@oif.org; Web: www.oif.org. Materials available in Spanish.

Parents Helping Parents: The Parent-Directed Family Resource Center for Children with Special Needs, 3041 Olcott St., Santa Clara, CA 95054; (408)727–5775, e-mail: info@php.com; Web: www.php.com. Materials available in Spanish. Spanish speaker on staff.

Parents of Galactosemic Children, 1519 Magnolia Bluff Dr., Gautier, MS 39553; e-mail: president@galactosemia.org;, Web: www.galactosemia.org.

Parent to Parent of the United States; Web: www.p2pusa.org/index.html. Web site only.

Pathways Awareness Foundation, 150 N. Michigan Ave., Suite 2100, Chicago, IL 60601; (800)955–2445; e-mail: friends@pathwaysawareness.org; Web: www.pathwaysawareness.org. Brochure and video available in Spanish.

Prader-Willi Syndrome Association, 5700 Midnight Pass Rd., Suite 6, Sarasota, FL 34242;, (800)926–4797, (941)312–0400; e-mail: national@pwsausa.org; Web: www.pwsausa.org. Materials available in Spanish.

Recording for the Blind and Dyslexic, Anne T. Macdonald Center, 20 Roszel Rd., Princeton, NJ 08540; (800)221–4792, (866)732–3585; e-mail: custserv@rfbd.org; Web: www.rfbd.org.

Registry of Interpreters for the Deaf, 333 Commerce St., Alexandria, VA 22314; (703)838–0030, (703)838–0459 (TTY); e-mail: info@rid.org; Web: www.rid.org.

RESNA (Rehabilitation Engineering and Assistive Technology Society of North America), 1700 N. Moore St., Suite 1540, Arlington, VA 22209–1903; (703)524–6686 (voice), (703)524–6639 (TTY); e-mail: info@resna.org; Web: www.resna.org.

Schwab Learning, 1650 S. Amphlett Blvd., Suite 300, San Mateo, CA 94402; (800)230–0988, (650)655–2410; e-mail: webmaster@schwablearning.org. Web: www.schwablearning.org. Portion of Web site in Spanish.

Scleroderma Foundation, 12 Kent Way, Suite 101, Byfield, MA 01922; (800)722–4673; (978)463–5843; e-mail: sfinfo@scleroderma.org; Web: www.scleroderma.org. Materials available in Spanish. Can refer to Spanish speaker.

Self Help for Hard of Hearing People, 7910 Woodmont Ave., Suite 1200, Bethesda, MD 20814; (301)657–2248, (301)657–2249 (TTY); e-mail: information@hearingloss.org; Web: www.hearingloss.org.

Special Needs Advocate for Parents, 11835 W. Olympic Blvd, Suite 465, Los Angeles, CA 90069; (888)310–9889, (310)479–3755; e-mail: info@snapinfo.org; Web: www.snapinfo.org.

Special Olympics International, 1133 19th St., N.W., Washington, DC 20036; (800)700–8585, (202)628–3630; e-mail: info@specialolympics.org; Web: www.specialolympics.org/. Materials available in Spanish and French. Spanish and French speaker on staff.

Spina Bifida Association of America, 4590 MacArthur Boulevard, N.W., Suite 250, Washington, DC 20007–4226; (800)621–3141, (202)944–3285; e-mail: sbaa@sbaa.org; Web: www.sbaa.org. Materials available in Spanish. Spanish speaker on staff.

Stuttering Foundation, 3100 Walnut Grove Rd. #603, P.O. Box 11749, Memphis, TN 38111; (800)992–9392; (901)452–7343, e-mail: stutter@stutteringhelp.org; Web: www.stutteringhelp.org. Materials available in Spanish.

TASH (formerly the Association for Persons with Severe Handicaps), 29 W. Susquehanna Ave., Suite 210, Baltimore, MD 21204; (410)828–8274 (voice), (410)828–1306 (TTY); e-mail: info@tash.org; Web: www.tash.org.

Technical Assistance Alliance for Parent Centers, PACER Center, 8161 Normandale Blvd., Minneapolis, MN 55437–1044; (888)248–0822, (952)838–9000, (952)838–0190 (TTY); e-mail: alliance@taalliance.org; Web: www.taalliance.org. Materials available in Spanish. Spanish speaker on staff.

Tourette Syndrome Association, 42–40 Bell Boulevard, Bayside, NY 11361; (718)224–2999; e-mail: ts@tsa-usa.org; Web: www.tsa-usa.org. Materials available in Spanish.

Trace R&D Center, 1550 Engineering Drive, 2107 Engineering Hall, Madison, WI 53706; (608)262–6966, (608)263–5408 (TTY); e-mail: info@trace.wisc.edu; Web: www.trace.wisc.edu/.

Tuberous Sclerosis Alliance, 801 Roeder Rd., Suite 750, Silver Spring, MD 20910; (800)225–6872, (301)562–9890; e-mail: info@tsalliance.org; Web: www.tsalliance.org.

United Cerebral Palsy Association, 1660 L St., N.W., Suite 700, Washington, DC 20036; (202)776–0406, (800)872–5827, (202)973–7197 (TTY); e-mail: national@ucp.org or Webmaster@ucp.org, Web: www.ucp.org. Materials available in Spanish.

United Leukodystrophy Foundation, 2304 Highland Drive, Sycamore, IL 60178; (800)728–5483;, e-mail: ulf@tbcnet.com, Web: www.ulf.org. Materials available in Spanish.

U.S. Society of Augmentative and Alternative Communication, P.O. Box 21418, Sarasota, FL 34276; (941)925–8875; e-mail: USSAAC@msn.com; Web: www.ussaac.org.

Vestibular Disorders Association, P.O. Box 13305, Portland, OR 97213, Portland OR 97208–4467; (800)837–8428, (503)229–7705; e-mail: veda@vestibular.org; Web: www.vestibular.org.

Williams Syndrome Association, P.O. Box 297, Clawson, MI 48017–0297; (800)806–1871, (248)244–2229; e-mail: info@williams-syndrome.org; Web: www.williams-syndrome.org. Materials available in Spanish.

World Association of Persons with Disabilities, 4503 Sunnyview Drive, Suite 1121, P.O. Box 14111, Oklahoma City, OK 73135; (405)672–4440; e-mail: thehub@wapd.org, Web: www.wapd.org.

Zero to Three (National Center for Infants, Toddlers, and Families), 2000 M St., N.W., Suite 200, Washington, DC 20036; (800)899–4301 (for publications); (202)638–1144, Web: www.zerotothree.org. Materials available in Spanish.

Ch. 2 excerpts from American Speech-Language-Hearing Association, 1996, 2002, 2005: Reprinted by permission from "Communication facts: Incidence and prevalence of communication disorders and hearing loss in children." Retrieved on September 27, 2006 from www.asha.org/members/research/reports/children. Copyright © 2005 by the American Speech-Language-Hearing Association. All rights reserved.

Ch. 2: Reprinted with permission from "Pediatric speech pathology-apraxia" from www.stronghealth.com, Golisano's Children's Hospital, University of Rochester Medical Center.

Ch. 2 excerpts from Penn State-Milton Hershey Medical Center College of Medicine, 2005: Reprinted by permission of Penn State Milton S. Hershey Medical Center.

Ch. 2 excerpts from American Speech-Language-Hearing Association, 1996, 2002, 2005: Reprinted by permission from "Central auditory processing: Current status of research and implications for clinical practice," *American Journal of Audiology, 5*(2), pp. 41–54, July, 1996. Copyright © 1996 by the American Speech-Language-Hearing Association. All rights reserved.

Ch. 2 excerpts from Turnbull, Turnbull, & Wehmeyer, 2007: Turnbull, A., Turnbull, H. R., & Wehmeyer, M. L. *Exceptional lives: Special education in today's schools* (5th ed.). © 2007. Electronically reproduced by permission of Pearson Education Inc., Upper Saddle River, New Jersey.

Ch. 3 excerpts from Beirne-Smith, Patton, & Kim, 2006: Beirne-Smith, M., Patton, J. R., & Kim, S. H. *Mental retardation: An introduction to intellectual disabilities* (7th ed.). © 2006. Electronically reproduced by permission of Pearson Education Inc., Upper Saddle River, New Jersey.

Ch. 4 excerpts from Kauffman, 2005: Kauffman, J. M. *Characteristics of emotional and behavioral disorders of children and youth* (8th ed.). © 2005. Electronically reproduced by permission of Pearson Education Inc., Upper Saddle River, New Jersey.

Ch. 5 excerpts from Lupus Foundation of America, 2004: Reprinted by permission of the Lupus Foundation of America, www.lupus.org.

Ch. 5 excerpts from Epilepsy Foundation, 2005a, b, c: Copyright © 2006 Epilepsy Foundation of America, Inc. Reprinted with permission.

Ch. 5 excerpts from Epilepsy Ontario, 2005: Reprinted with permission from the Web site of Epilepsy Ontario, www.epilepsyontario.org.

Ch. 5 excerpts from National Society for Epilepsy, 2002: Excerpts from "Epilepsy: Information on seizures" was kindly provided by the National Society for Epilepsy.

Ch. 7 excerpts from Yale Developmental Disabilities Clinic, 2005: Excerpts reprinted with permission from "Multiplex Developmental Disorder," http://info.med.yale.edu/chldstdy/autism/mdd.html.

Ch. 8 excerpt from Milton S. Hershey Medical Center College of Medicine at Penn State, 2006: Reprinted by permission of Penn State Milton S. Hershey Medical Center.

Ch. 8 excerpts from Muscular Dystrophy Association, 2003a, 2003b, 2004: Copyright © Muscular Dystrophy Australia. Reprinted with permission.

Ch. 8 excerpts from Families of Spinal Muscular Atrophy, 2004: Excerpts from "Understanding SMA" are reprinted courtesy of Families of Spinal Muscular Atrophy, www.fsma.org.

Ch. 11 excerpts from Merck, 2005: Reprinted with permission from *The Merck Manual of Medical Information,* Second Home Edition, p. 517, edited by Mark H. Beers. Copyright © 2003 by Merck & Co., Inc., Whitehouse Station, NJ.

Ch. 11 excerpts from National Center on Shaken Baby Syndrome, 2005: Excerpts from "Shaken Baby Syndrome" are reprinted by permission of the National Center on Shaken Baby Syndrome.

Ch. 12 excerpts from SENSE, 2005: Excerpts from "About Deaf-blindness" are reprinted by permission of SENSE, www.sense.org.uk.